The World Transformed

1945 TO THE PRESENT

A Documentary Reader

Michael H. Hunt

The University of North Carolina at Chapel Hill

Bedford / St. Martin's   Boston ◆ New York

For Bedford/St. Martin's

Publisher for History: Patricia A. Rossi
Director of Development for History: Jane Knetzger
Developmental Editor: Louise Townsend
Production Editor: Bridget Leahy
Production Associate: Christie Gross
Marketing Manager: Jenna Bookin Barry
Editorial Assistants: Molly Minturn, Elizabeth Wallace
Copyeditor: Alison Greene
Cover Design: Donna Lee Dennison
Cover Art: A Chinese woman makes a phone call between barbed wires and para-military officers in Beijing, China. AP/Wide World Photos.
Composition: Karla Goethe, Orchard Wind Graphics
Printing and Binding: R.R. Donnelley & Sons Company

President: Joan E. Feinberg
Editorial Director: Denise B. Wydra
Director of Marketing: Karen Melton Soeltz
Director of Editing, Design, and Production: Marcia Cohen
Managing Editor: Elizabeth M. Schaaf

Library of Congress Control Number: 2003112720

Manufactured in the United States of America.

8   7   6
f   e   d   c   b

For information, write: Bedford/St. Martin's, 75 Arlington Street, Boston, MA 02116 (617-399-4000)

ISBN: 0–312–40296–1

Acknowledgments

Bina Agarwal. Excerpts from *A Field of One's Own: Gender and Land Rights in South Asia.* Copyright © Bina Agarwal. Reprinted by permission of the University of Cambridge Press.

Acknowledgments and copyrights are continued at the back of the book on pages 443–46, which constitute an extension of the copyright page. It is a violation of the law to reproduce these selections by any means whatsoever without the written permission of the copyright holder.

PREFACE

The World Transformed, 1945 to the Present: A Documentary Reader has its origins in a survey that I teach along with other faculty at the University of North Carolina. From the beginning of my involvement in that course in the late 1980s, I gave prominence to primary sources of one sort or another. Students, especially those new to college-level history, find them engaging, while I for my part regard primary sources as excellent vehicles for teaching historical skills. Whereas students encountering a work by a historian tend to lapse into passivity, primary materials encourage them not only to read more actively and imaginatively but also to interpret, evaluate, and judge, even to learn to construct their own stories and analytic perspectives. They thus gain an idea of how historians come to write what they do. Even more important, students going through this process of reading, digesting, and interpreting gain broadly applicable skills.

My aim for this reader was to provide an introduction to historical sources that would invite students to exercise those skills. It does so by presenting over 120 documents organized into 36 topical sections ranging over the last sixty years and virtually the entire globe. It stands as a companion volume to my survey text, *A World Transformed: 1945 to the Present,* but it can also serve as a stand-alone reader in a variety of courses in history, international relations, and global studies.

FEATURES

Documents that capture the richness of contemporary history. The primary sources collected here cover a wide array of themes—from decolonization to land issues to superpower competition to consumer culture to global integration. They explore a diversity of perspectives—from ordinary people as well as elites, women as well as men, the poor as well as the affluent, peasants as well as city folk, and detached observers as well as committed activists. Finally, they focus on a representative sample of developing and developed countries from all the world's major regions.

A wide variety of source material. This collection gives students a sense of the diverse kinds of materials that are the historian's stock-in-trade. Some are public, others private. Some are fictional creations, others are careful reportage. Verse is included along with prose; images and vital statistics appear together with the written word. Thus alongside official government documents and speeches, students will find oral histories by Vietnamese peasants and a Guatemalan torturer, European public opinion polls, graffiti from the 1968 student uprising in Paris, an illustrated Cold War pamphlet explaining nuclear fallout, a short story from a Soviet prison, data on global inequality, and an excerpt from Sony founder Morita Akio's autobiography.

Pedagogical flexibility. While its ten chapters cover times and topics corresponding with the material in parallel chapters in the text version of *The World Transformed,* the reader should mesh nicely with other readings and survey textbooks. The wide range of topics and document types included here should give instructors considerable flexibility in constructing their own syllabi and devising assignments.

An introduction for students. A two-part introduction provides students with an overview of the post-1945 period, pointing to some of the major themes and issues that emerge from the collection. The introduction goes on to offer guidance on how to read primary sources, encouraging students to ask questions about background, audience, and intent and thus to realize that evidence is eminently debatable and thus requires interpretation.

Useful chapter apparatus. Each chapter begins with a general introduction, followed by three or four topical sections each with its own introduction and each posing broad questions for students to consider while reading the material. Each document has its own headnote providing background and context on the source, its author, and its audience, plus a set of specific questions to stimulate interpretation of the document.

Documents that strike a balance between brevity and richness. Two competing concerns guided the editing of these documents: to make them short enough so that students can easily digest them but to keep them long enough so that they offer ample grist for interpretation.

This volume carries with it my hope that other instructors will find this set of materials as effective a tool and as much fun to use as it has been for me. I have an additional hope: that this collection encourages students to become more engaged readers and that the process of reading and analyzing primary sources will not only open insights onto the past but perhaps more importantly help them develop broadly applicable skills for the future. In this latter sense the reader works like an exercise machine to tone minds for the challenges of life ahead.

ACKNOWLEDGMENTS

I benefited greatly from the discerning comments of the readers solicited by Bedford/St. Martin's: Henry W. Berger (Washington University in St. Louis), Brian Bonhomme (University of Central Arkansas), Charles Bright (University of Michigan), Mark C. Carnes (Barnard College), Gary Darden (Rutgers University), Charles T. Evans (Northern Virginia Community College), Carol Fink (The Ohio State University), Kenneth Orosz (University of Maine at Farmington), Donald Reid (University of North Carolina at Chapel Hill), and David S. Trask (Guilford Technical Community College).

As with the main text, the Bedford/St. Martin's staff performed with exemplary professionalism. In particular, I want to acknowledge the fine work of production editor, Bridget Leahy. Editorial assistants Elizabeth Wallace and Molly Minturn helped out with numerous tasks, Donna Dennison and Billy Boardman produced a terrific cover, while Sandy Schechter and Diane Kraut worked hard on the permissions. Throughout this project, I have appreciated the steady encouragement of Patricia Rossi and the ongoing support of Jane Knetzger, Joan Feinberg, and Denise Wydra. My development editor Louise Townsend was once again my expert guide, pointing the way with enthusiasm and good sense.

A small army of folks closer to home played a role in this project, often without knowing it. Those at the University of North Carolina teaching our post-1945 world survey have been generous over the years in sharing ideas that have helped to shape this collection. An able and interested set of graduate students (most now professional colleagues) have been the most directly involved as they assisted in assembling as well as teaching the documents on which this reader is in substantial measure based. In particular I am grateful to Peter Coogan, Christopher Endy, Anthony Fins, John Hepp, Matthew Jacobs, Alan McPherson, Howard Odell, Leah Potter, Nathaniel Smith, and Odd Arne Westad. Nathaniel Smith was generally helpful in assembling the reader and especially helpful with the material on the Columbian drug trade (alas, lost in the permissions process) and the Seattle WTO protest. Heather Hunt lent an able hand and a quick mind to the sections on HIV/AIDS and on human rights. The following responded to incidental requests for expert guidance: Chad Bryant, David Carlson, John Chasteen, Arturo Escobar, Shuhua Fan, Miles Fletcher, Michaela Hoenicke Moore, Yokiko Koshiro, Madeline Levine, Lisa Lindsay, Jongnam Na, Louis Pérez, and Don Reid. Paula Hunt brought to this round of bookmaking her usual interest, good cheer, and support. To all, my thanks!

I bear responsibility for whatever problems remain in the pages that follow despite the effort of so many to save me from error and confusion.

CONTENTS

INTRODUCTION:
THE REWARDS AND CHALLENGES
OF READING PRIMARY SOURCES

PEOPLE AROUND THE WORLD have over the last half-century experienced an extraordinary transformation. A new era beginning in 1945 encompassed changes so profound and wide ranging that they make this time unique in human history. While much about those changes seems in retrospect worrisome, there are also grounds for celebrating the dramatic improvement in human life and prospects that they effected.

A young person coming into maturity in the late 1940s, in the wake of a massively destructive world war, would have faced a gloomy scene. Cities were in ruins, economies barely functioning, families scattered, and populations decimated by wartime losses. Hard-pinched by hunger and exposure and inured to sacrifice, ordinary people had little reason to expect a significant turnaround in their living conditions anytime soon. Most of these people had powerful foreigners — troops, administrators, diplomats, and settlers — exercising direct rule or significant informal control over them. Despite stirrings among the subjugated, few would have predicted dramatic progress toward liberation anytime soon — nor for that matter the emergence of a vigorous, even militant third-world movement marked by shared aspirations to catch up with the living standards of former foreign masters and achieve real political and economic independence. Finally, postwar observers saw the rise of a rivalry between the United States and the Soviet Union. Their Cold War — so called for the global tensions it generated and for the major, hot confrontation that never came — was more than just a military contest between two superpowers and their allies. It was also a collision between divergent worldviews and models of social, political, and economic development that had global repercussions. This rivalry mocked a world desperate for peace and compounded the insult by spawning regional wars and weapons of unprecedented destructiveness, indeed the potential to wipe out human life.

Imagine that same person surveying the world some fifty years later, near the turn of the new century. It was by then a world made over — in many ways much for the better. The leading economies had recovered, creating a level of material wealth beyond the dreams of previous generations. Those economies had become integrated through trade and investment but also immigration and cultural exchange. Though oriented toward the free market, the leading economies retained a distinct sense of identity that resisted homogenization in economic not to mention cultural matters. People almost everywhere lived longer and richer lives, although along with this progress came widening gaps between the rich and the poor and widespread environmental damage inflicted by ever-greater production and consumption. The colonial world was no more, having disappeared in what had by the 1960s turned into a stampede toward independence. The record of these new nations was distinctly mixed by century's end. Some had made great strides, while others were no better off than they had been on independence day. The cumulative effect was to dissolve the commonalities that had made the third world a reality during the early postwar decades. Finally, the Cold War with its repression and nuclear fear had ended. In its place emerged an unusual and perhaps unstable international order, defined by U.S. dominance as a military, economic, and cultural force, by rising resentment, even anger over that dominance, and by problems of instability and inequality spawned by the rising forces of globalization.

The stunning transformation over the last half century is the subject of this reader. Its aim is to provide a sense of how gloom turned into hope and how change had consequences that were bad as well as good. Above all, the reader makes available the voices of people who lived through this time of change and themselves sought to influence and understand it. Thus we hear from eager revolutionaries, impatient student protestors, anxious environmentalists, hard-pressed peasants, and confident nationalists as they each render their own accounts.

DOCUMENTING THE RECENT PAST

Historians are trained to reconstruct the past through primary sources, those pieces of evidence of some earlier time that provide insight into how people then lived and thought. How deeply, and broadly, the historian can explore any problem depends heavily on the availability of these sources. If they are few and scattered, then even tentative conclusions may require much hard spade work and careful surmise. Blessed is the historian with an abundance of diverse sources.

Students of the recent past are blessed. They have at hand an amazing range of materials opening exciting investigative vistas. Great libraries, vast government archives, the files of innumerable private organizations, caches of personal papers (some still in private hands and some already open to the public), and an abundance of personal recollections offer an inexhaustible source. This evidence takes a variety of forms (as the selections in this reader will show): private letters, intimate diaries, taped telephone conversations, reflective oral histories, carefully groomed published memoirs, searching schol-arly debates, lively cartoons, and stirring public speeches. (Moving images, available on an unprecedented scale, deserve a prominent place on this list, but alas they are not compatible with older book technology.)

Even so, studying the recent past carries challenges beyond the simple and pleasant task of sorting through this rich array of material. Above all, events so close and still so important to the living are inevitably controversial. The past is hardly "dead," and the temptation for those directly involved in one issue or another to engage in special pleading — to see that their version of the past survives and prevails — is great. The historian is not immune to this partisan impulse — to favor one side over another — even if training in the discipline aims to bring bias into the open where it can be controlled and corrected. Compounding this problem is the unevenness of documentation, especially where governments and powerful individuals want to monopolize the docu-ments so that their version of the past overshadows alternative ones. Even in the most open societies the constraints imposed by those who run the ar-chives or place their papers there impose significant limits on public knowl-edge and the free investigation of historians and journalists.

There is a second, more mundane set of challenges posed by current docu-mentation that is familiar to historians of any age: the need to be sensitive to strengths and weaknesses of different types of records and the varying tech-niques that the interpreter needs to apply to them. Each kind of evidence has something special to reveal, while also posing special traps for the unwary. Usually the issue is not the truth or falsity of information and impressions conveyed by the particular kind of historical record but rather more subtle problems such as bias, wishful thinking, omission, or defective memory. It is important to remain alert to the ways a document can be a window on the past but one that may also distort or color what the historian sees.

Some examples should clarify these points. American and Soviet leaders framed the birth of the atomic age in terms of their mutual struggle, while atomic physicists quickly spotted the worrisome potential of their creation to unleash a costly arms race and even terrible destruction on the world. To the residents of Hiroshima and Nagasaki, neither grand strategic visions nor sci-entific insight mattered a whit as they stood amidst the rubble and radiation in August 1945. To U.S. soldiers assembled for an invasion of Japan, the atomic bomb was a god-send that spared the lives of many. All perspectives are in some sense true and all are inevitably partial. The danger lies in letting one perspective obscure the others. Each in its own way is revealing, and taken together, they provide a fuller, richer sense of the past.

Guarding against overreliance on one point of view is just the beginning. We also need to ask tough questions about the way those perspectives reach us. For example, how accurately can a resident of Hiroshima recall the nuclear trauma some thirty years later? How much has subsequent personal reflec-tion, the repression of painful memories, or public controversy reshaped that recollection?

THE HOW AND WHY OF USING PRIMARY SOURCES

Finally, it is useful to reflect on the how and why of reading documents. There are striking similarities between historical and detective work.[1] Both involve getting at "the facts"; both are based on the assumption that witness testimony and forensic evidence will be incomplete, possibly unreliable, and perhaps contradictory. Circumstantial evidence must be weighed and context supplied. A sense of psychology and culture helps in the attempt to understand the parties involved. All this effort is harnessed to one ultimate goal — to figure out what happened and what it means.

The human impulse to order experience — whether mundane or extraordinary — is what makes us turn to history as both a vehicle for popular entertainment and a means of understanding our world. Only by imposing some kind of order can our mind begin to find a flow in history, to appreciate its dramatic moments and personalities, and to develop an understanding of the past that would otherwise seem a collection of random events. Historians do this ordering by reconstructing the past (creating narratives) and by making sense of that past (subjecting what we know to analysis). At the heart of this process is grappling with evidence — first gathering it, then putting it in some coherent pattern, and finally developing a sense of its meaning. In terms of method, history is then really about the discipline of evidence. This discipline differs significantly from the widespread conception of history as little more than a collection of names and dates. The documents here offer an opportunity to know history as something complex, intricate, and intellectually challenging.

This collection of primary sources is intended to give you a chance to discover that challenge and to learn how to make sense of the past. A word of caution on learning the historian's craft: No one learns to walk, ride a bike, or use a computer on the first try. It takes time and practice, and the more practice, the easier and more internalized the process becomes. The same is true with handling evidence. In approaching evidence, it is best to start with the most basic questions and work toward deeper and more difficult ones. Again, it is useful to think of the parallel with detective work, which involves careful examination of the crime scene, wide-ranging interviews, and close interrogation of suspects before finally a credible sense of what happened begins to emerge.

The first stage is essentially one of gathering information, beginning not with the documents but with filling in the broad background needed to read the documents. It is impossible to make meaningful sense of a problem with little or no context, and conversely the more you know, the more revealing individual documents will be. This background will likely come from lectures, a textbook, or other assigned reading.

---

[1]Mark H. Lytle and James W. Davidson, *After the Fact: The Art of Historical Detection,* 3rd ed. (New York: McGraw-Hill, 1992), develops this point through an engaging set of case studies drawn from U.S. history.

Once you have established context for the source, you can more confidently approach the task of reading and interpreting it. The actual reading of a document is an art in itself. By giving you direct access to a particular mindset or moment, the document invites you to use your imagination and build a picture in your mind from the evidence at hand. What might have been the concerns or even the emotional state of the author of a document at the time it was created? For whom was the document intended? What impact was the document (the words or an image in the case of a cartoon or film) supposed to have had on that audience? How did the author attempt to create that impact? Fundamentally, these questions involve looking closely at the content of the document so that we grasp its story or argument and become aware of the assumptions from which the author works.

It is worth stressing that finding answers to these questions requires a careful reading — and persistent, patient inquiry. Documents are sometimes dense, sometimes unclear, sometimes recalcitrant. They are not going to tell you what to think. You must do that work yourself. As you read, it is helpful to keep a record of your encounter by scribbling questions or insights in the margin of the text, underlining key phrases, and noting at the end of each document what you think it is saying. You have to talk to the document if you want it to talk back to you.

Let's imagine ourselves about to plunge into Mao Zedong's autobiography. Its significance derives from the outsized impact that Mao had as the leader of the Chinese revolution. So knowing not only about Mao but also about the course of that revolution will make for a much richer reading of his personal account and in turn prompt revealing questions about how his early years might have prepared him for his later role. What experiences seem formative? How does his thinking and behavior evolve? What threads seem to hold the disparate elements of his account together? What sorts of language does he use in recalling his youth? Where are the areas that seem to challenge the assumptions common in our own culture about growing up and becoming politically engaged? And of course, how much can we trust this self-portrait by an ambitious political leader bent on elbowing his way to national power?

This example highlights the importance of asking some basic questions about our evidence. Is the document credible? Is it consistent with other kinds of evidence? What does its language tell us about the particular culture, institution, social stratum, or period from which it comes? What does the document mean to you? What response does it provoke from you and why are you responding that way? This last may seem an odd question, but the study of history requires that we be conscious of our own values and outlook and of the ways they may influence our interpretations.

Once you have considered these questions, you are ready to try out your understanding against that of others looking at the same evidence. Because history is ultimately about interpreting evidence, different interpreters will come to different conclusions. Historians differ in their command of the relevant information, in the personal background, biases, and assumptions that they will bring to their reading of that information, and in their skill as compelling storytellers and searching analysts. Invariably we benefit by seeing how others have interpreted the past, perhaps by having pointed to something we left out or by having proposed a strikingly different version of our story or argument.

As you compare interpretations, you will discover that it is not enough for the story to simply match the evidence. A chronicle of names and dates may tell a story but it will reveal little of significance. Imagine the detective reporting that the crime occurred to such a person at such a place on such a date but failing to identify the cause of the crime (who did it and why?). Similarly, with history, a good story is one that moves beyond simple description and offers both broader and deeper insights.

The documents from this period of transformation, from 1945 to the beginning of the twenty-first century, can tell us much about how individual leaders make a difference, how prevailing visions create a sense of possibilities and a readiness for sacrifice by individuals and entire groups, and how an expanding market economy changes peoples' lives profoundly and often in subtle ways. Important in themselves, these kinds of historical insights can contribute to a firmer, more secure sense of personal identity. Those without a past not only are condemned to repeat mistakes (as the old saying goes) but worse still are doomed to drift uncertain of where they are going because they have no idea of where they have come from.

This history of the recent past is especially critical for Americans. As citizens of a wealthy and mighty republic, they are ultimately responsible for their country's conduct on the world's stage and for the well being of their own experiment in democracy. Thomas Jefferson put the case for an educated citizenry well. He wanted Americans educated "so much as may enable them to read and understand what is going on in the world, and to keep their part of it going on right: for nothing can keep it right but their own vigilant and distrustful superintendence."[2]

Finally, a historical sense is essential for the intelligent exercise of moral agency, which requires an understanding of the point of view of others, of the limits of change, and of the likelihood of unintended consequences bedeviling even the best intentioned. History can help banish both a pessimism that leaves us feeling powerless and a mindless optimism that promotes the illusion that no problem or situation is beyond our control. The basis for these several claims should become evident as the daily news becomes more personally engaging, intellectually accessible, and even emotionally compelling. The documents in this collection thus offer real, enduring, practical rewards to go along with the intellectual challenges that they pose.

---

[2] Thomas Jefferson to Mann Page, August 30, 1795, in *The Writings of Thomas Jefferson,* ed. Andrew A. Lipscomb and Albert Ellery Bergh (Washington, D.C.: Thomas Jefferson Memorial Association, 1903–04), 9:306.

CHAPTER 1

THE COLD WAR: TOWARD SOVIET-AMERICAN CONFRONTATION

IN 1945 MOST PEOPLE AROUND THE WORLD looked to a period of peace during which they could dig out from the rubble of war, grieve for and memorialize the dead, and rebuild their lives. In less than two years those hopes sagged beneath the tensions rising between the two leading powers on the victorious allied side, the United States and the Soviet Union under the leadership of President Harry S. Truman and Premier Joseph Stalin. The mutual suspicions of the two powers erupted into public denunciation in 1947, and each began raising their military spending, looking for allies, mobilizing their publics, and developing nuclear weapons. The climax came in June 1950 when war broke out on the divided Korean peninsula. The Soviets and the United States maneuvered to avoid a direct collision, but even so the Cold War was well on its way to becoming global in its reach. It would continue for another forty years with varying degrees of intensity and danger not just for Americans and Soviets but for people all around the world.

The documents in this chapter highlight the major characteristics defining the Cold War at its origins. The conflict was above all ideological in nature. American and Soviet leaders carried into the postwar period thoroughly internalized notions about the nature of their countries and their proper place in the world. These notions were far-reaching in scope and mutually incompatible in substance. The conflict was at the start also influenced by the vastly different styles and personalities of the Soviet and American leaders; their handling of the difficult transition from war to peace in 1945 and 1946 is one important element in explaining the origins of the Cold War. Yet a third feature relates to the broad ramifications that the superpower contest had right from the start. Cold War mobilization on both sides rapidly chilled political and intellectual life at home (as we'll see here) just as it led Moscow and Washington to make overseas commitments. In examining this critical moment in the early postwar period, we would do well to think about the reasons for the onset of the conflict. Were the causes so potent that they made the collision virtually inevitable? Might the rivalry have taken a different form?

THE UNITED STATES AS THE CHAMPION OF LIBERTY

Nationalism was one of the most powerful forces of the twentieth century. Although often denounced as the source of hatred and regional strife, nationalism retains an enormous appeal for the way it gives peoples a sense of solidarity and governments a means to create loyalty and mobilize support. The American version of nationalism took shape in the late eighteenth century as part of the struggle for independence from Britain. Then and later Americans differed over whether the national mission of the United States was to perfect its democratic experiment at home or to play a larger role in the world as the leading democratic power.

The following two documents are classic expressions of American nationalism. They give us an opportunity to reflect on how Americans thought they should relate to the world and how their nationalist notions might have influenced post–World War II policymakers.

1.1

President Woodrow Wilson on Creating a Free and Democratic World

Challenged by war in Europe, President Woodrow Wilson in 1917 articulated a powerful statement of the activist version of American nationalism. He himself sought principles to guide his response to the European war, and he was looking for a position that would win broad popular support. In his speech, Wilson professed a profound faith that it was the duty of Americans to make the world safe for democracy. On the basis of this faith, Wilson would lead the country the following April into a war that he described as a crusade, and in 1918 he would lay down a fourteen-point program for fundamentally revising relations among nations. Wilson's vision proved controversial. It collapsed under the weight of opposition at home and abroad. But in time praise and blame would give way to a wide acceptance of his definition of America's role in the world. By 1945 Wilson was a hero to American leaders and his ideas a compass by which many postwar policymakers claimed to set their course.

This speech deserves close attention because of all Wilson's writings, it best embodies what has come to be called Wilsonianism. What was Wilson's vision of his country's fundamental values? How were those values to define the U.S. international role? What aspects of his position have a familiar ring today? This item gives us a chance to think about how to assess public statements. Should we write this speech off as mere rhetoric, of little evidentiary value, or perhaps even worse — a clever play to obscure the real intentions of its author?

Address to the Senate
January 22, 1917

In every discussion of the peace that must end this war it is taken for granted that that peace must be followed by some definite concert of power which will make it virtually impossible that any such catastrophe should ever over-whelm us again. Every lover of mankind, every sane and thoughtful man must take that for granted. . . .

It is inconceivable that the people of the United States should play no part in that great enterprise. To take part in such a service will be the opportunity for which they have sought to prepare themselves . . . ever since the days when they set up a new nation in the high and honourable hope that it might . . . show mankind the way to liberty. . . . But they owe it to themselves and to the other nations of the world to state the conditions under which they will feel free to render it. . . .

. . . It will be absolutely necessary that a force be created as a guarantor of the permanency of the settlement so much greater than the force of any nation now engaged or any alliance hitherto formed or projected that no nation, no probable combination of nations could face or withstand it. If the peace presently to be made is to endure, it must be a peace made secure by the organized major force of mankind. . . .

The equality of nations upon which peace must be founded if it is to last must be an equality of rights; the guarantees exchanged must neither recog-nize nor imply a difference between big nations and small, between those that are powerful and those that are weak. Right must be based upon the common strength, not upon the individual strength, of the nations upon whose con-cert peace will depend. . . . Mankind is looking now for freedom of life, not for equipoises of power.

. . . No peace can last, or ought to last, which does not recognize and accept the principle that governments derive all their just powers from the consent of the governed, and that no right anywhere exists to hand peoples about from sovereignty to sovereignty as if they were property. . . .

So far as practicable, moreover, every great people now struggling towards a full development of its resources and of its powers should be assured a direct outlet to the great highways of the sea. . . .

And the paths of the sea must alike in law and in fact be free. The freedom of the seas is the *sine qua non* of peace, equality, and cooperation. . . .

. . . There can be no sense of safety and equality among the nations if great preponderating armaments are henceforth to continue here and there to be built up and maintained. The statesmen of the world must plan for peace and nations must adjust and accommodate their policy to it as they have planned for war and made ready for pitiless contest and rivalry. . . .

Arthur S. Link, ed., *The Papers of Woodrow Wilson* (Princeton, N.J.: Princeton University Press, 1966–94), 40:534–39.

I am proposing, as it were, that the nations should with one accord adopt the doctrine of President Monroe[1] as the doctrine of the world: that no nation should seek to extend its polity over any other nation or people, but that every people should be left free to determine its own polity, its own way of development, unhindered, unthreatened, unafraid, the little along with the great and powerful.

I am proposing that all nations henceforth avoid entangling alliances[2] which would draw them into competitions of power, catch them in a net of intrigue and selfish rivalry, and disturb their own affairs with influences intruded from without. There is no entangling alliance in a concert of power. When all unite to act in the same sense and with the same purpose all act in the common interest and are free to live their own lives under a common protection.

I am proposing government by the consent of the governed; that freedom of the seas which in international conference after conference representatives of the United States have urged with the eloquence of those who are the convinced disciples of liberty; and that moderation of armaments which makes of armies and navies a power for order merely, not an instrument of aggression or of selfish violence.

These are American principles, American policies. We could stand for no others. And they are also the principles and policies of forward looking men and women everywhere, of every modern nation, of every enlightened community. They are the principles of mankind and must prevail.

1.2

"The American Century"

The resurgence of danger in Europe in the late 1930s together with Japanese aggression in Asia seemed to vindicate the need for a bold American vision of the sort Wilson had promoted. No one articulated that renewed sense of mission better than Henry Luce. He was the creator and publisher of the influential *Time* and *Life* mass-circulation magazines. Not only were they great commercial successes but they also served as Luce's vehicle for promoting, often not so subtly, his own views. Those views derived in large measure from growing up as the child of missionaries in China. Concerned about divisions in the United States over intervention in a Europe once more at war, Luce put his "American Century" essay before his readers.

---

[1]In 1823 James Monroe pronounced a fundamental political division between the new world and the old and indicated that on the basis of that principle the United States would oppose European intervention to restore control over former colonies in the Americas. In 1904 Theodore Roosevelt extended the Monroe Doctrine to include the right of the United States to intervene to maintain order in the hemisphere. Wilson was thinking of the original, more modest 1823 version of the doctrine, not the more assertive version that had emerged in his own lifetime.

[2]By using the phrase "entangling alliances" Wilson is drawing from George Washington, whose advice against such alliances became the watchword of nineteenth-century U.S. policymakers. Here Wilson turns this American principle into one for all states to observe.

Luce's essay is best known for its title. What does he mean by "the American Century"? How does Luce define American national identity? In what direction did he want to point postwar U.S. policy? How much does Luce build on Wilson's ideas and how much does he go beyond them?

Henry R. Luce
Life *Magazine Article*
February 17, 1941

[T]he fundamental trouble with America has been, and is, that whereas their nation became in the 20th Century the most powerful and the most vital nation in the world, nevertheless Americans were unable to accommodate themselves spiritually and practically to that fact. Hence they have failed to play their part as a world power — a failure which has had disastrous consequences for themselves and for all mankind. And the cure is this: to accept wholeheartedly our duty and our opportunity as the most powerful and vital nation in the world and in consequence to exert upon the world the full impact of our influence, for such purposes as we see fit and by such means as we see fit. . . .

. . . [T]he world of the 20th Century, if it is to come to life in any nobility of health and vigor, must be to a significant degree an American Century. . . .

. . . [T]here is already an immense American internationalism. American jazz, Hollywood movies, American slang, American machines and patented products, are in fact the only things that every community in the world, from Zanzibar to Hamburg, recognizes in common. Blindly, unintentionally, accidentally and really in spite of ourselves, we are already a world power in all the trivial ways — in very human ways. But there is a great deal more than that. America is already the intellectual, scientific, and artistic capital of the world. Americans — Midwestern Americans — are today the least provincial people in the world. They have traveled the most and they know more about the world than the people of any other country. America's worldwide experience in commerce is also far greater than most of us realize.

Most important of all, we have that indefinable, unmistakable sign of leadership: prestige. And unlike the prestige of Rome or Genghis Khan or 19th Century England, American prestige throughout the world is faith in the good intentions as well as in the ultimate intelligence and ultimate strength of the whole American people. . . .

Consider four areas of life and thought in which we may seek to realize such a vision:

First, the economic. It is for America and for America alone to determine whether a system of free economic enterprise — an economic order compatible with freedom and progress — shall or shall not prevail in this century. . . . The vision of America as the principal guarantor of the freedom of

Henry R. Luce, "The American Century," *Life* 10 (February 17, 1941): 63–65.

the seas, the vision of Americas [sic] as the dynamic leader of world trade, has within it the possibilities of such enormous human progress as to stagger the imagination. . . .

Closely akin to the purely economic area and yet quite different from it, there is the picture of an America which will send out through the world its technical and artistic skills. Engineers, scientists, doctors, movie men, makers of entertainment, developers of airlines, builders of roads, teachers, educators. Throughout the world, these skills, this training, this leadership is needed and will be eagerly welcomed, if only we have the imagination to see it and the sincerity and good will to create the world of the 20th Century.

But now there is a third thing which our vision must immediately be concerned with. We must undertake now to be the Good Samaritan of the entire world. It is the manifest duty of this country to undertake to feed all the people of the world who as a result of this worldwide collapse of civilization are hungry and destitute — all of them, that is, whom we can from time to time reach consistently with a very tough attitude toward all hostile governments. . . .

But all this is not enough. All this will fail and none of it will happen unless our vision of America as a world power includes a passionate devotion to great American ideals. We have some things in this country which are infinitely precious and especially American — a love of freedom, a feeling for the equality of opportunity, a tradition of self-reliance and independence and also of co-operation. In addition to ideals and notions which are especially American, we are the inheritors of all the great principles of Western Civilization — above all Justice, the love of Truth, the ideal of Charity. . . . It now becomes our time to be the powerhouse from which the ideals spread throughout the world and do their mysterious work of lifting the life of mankind from the level of the beasts to what the Psalmist[1] called a little lower than the angels.

America as the dynamic center of ever-widening spheres of enterprise, America as the training center of the skillful servants of mankind, America as the Good Samaritan, really believing again that it is more blessed to give than to receive, and America as the powerhouse of the ideals of Freedom and Justice — out of these elements surely can be fashioned a vision of the 20th Century to which we can and will devote ourselves in joy and gladness and vigor and enthusiasm.

Other nations can survive simply because they have endured so long — sometimes with more and sometimes with less significance. But this nation, conceived in adventure and dedicated to the progress of man — this nation cannot truly endure unless there courses strongly through its veins from Maine to California the blood of purposes and enterprise and high resolve.

---

[1]Luce is referring here to the Bible's Book of Psalms.

SOVIET COMMUNISM ON THE MARCH

For the Soviet Union no less than for the United States, 1917 was a critical time. Vladimir Lenin's Bolsheviks seized power late in the year and pressed ahead on a revolutionary course guided by a vision derived from Karl Marx, reshaped by Lenin himself, and explicitly at odds with the plans promoted by Wilson. To many outsiders Soviet ideology has been difficult to take seriously, and the collapse of the Soviet Union and its client regimes to the west between 1989 and 1991 has compounded the difficulty. To recreate the prism through which Stalin and his successors saw the world, it remains important to take that ideology seriously — to understand it as a living faith that influenced but did not determine behavior, that provoked debate, and that underwent change.

Understanding a set of basic propositions on which Marxism in general depends will facilitate reading the selections that follow. First, material needs, not ideas, shape human life and history. The economy (or means of production) is the determining force for all societies. Consciousness is a reflection of economic forces. Second, societies develop through distinct historical stages corresponding to their level of economic development (in modern times from feudalism to capitalism to socialism and then to the final stage, communism). Third, the advancement of societies from one stage to the other depends on class conflict. Each system has an elite that controls the means of production and that exploits the mass of people doing the work. As one kind of economy matures, the successor economy begins to take form within it. The class associated with that new economy clashes with those controlling the old economy and eventually overwhelms it. The best known of these clashes is between capitalists and a growing, discontented working class (the proponents of an emergent socialist economy and society). Because class position rather than national identity is fundamental, a Marxist would argue that whether states cooperate or compete depends on the class identity of those wielding state power and that classes within a state will have more in common with others of the same class in other states than with their fellow citizens. Thus while workers around the world have a fundamentally shared interest that leads them toward cooperation, their capitalist leaders face a hostile population at home, rival capitalists in power in other countries, independence movements in their colonies and dependencies, and an ever more powerful grouping of socialist states led by the Soviet Union. Isolated and embattled on every front, the capitalist powers are doomed to defeat, according to this class-defined view of how the world works. Finally, Communist (or Leninist) parties are an important agent of change. While historical development from one stage to the other is inevitable, humans can intervene to accelerate the process. Communist parties serve to organize and heighten the consciousness of the working class (proletariat), to lead the overthrow of capitalism and consolidate the control of the working class in a system of socialism, and to then guide socialist societies to communism (the withering away of the state, the emergence of economic abundance, and the end of class conflict).

1.3

Joseph Stalin on the Essentials of Soviet Ideology

Joseph Stalin (1879–1953) has many claims to historical fame. He was first of all the sponsor of a brutal, determined drive to modernize a largely rural, agricultural country and to catch up with Europe. Stalin was also the architect of a revived Russian empire in the course of World War II, regaining by force the territory and influence along the Russian periphery lost in a time of weakness earlier in the twentieth century. These achievements, linked to the victory over Germany, made Stalin's Russia after World War II one of the world's two great powers. Most to the point here, Stalin was the codifier of a formal state ideology beginning with his 1924 lectures on "The Foundations of Leninism." Following Lenin's death in January of 1924, Stalin made his bid for leadership of the Soviet Communist Party. These lectures were meant to bolster that bid by establishing his standing as an authority on party ideology. They were delivered at Sverdlov University, a college run by the Central Committee to train party leaders, and were then published in the party paper *Pravda* in April–May 1924.

As a systematic treatment of Lenin's ideas, "The Foundations of Leninism" became a party primer that circulated widely in the Soviet Union as well as abroad in translation. Imagine yourself a young worker in a tractor factory in the provinces engaged in political education or a Chinese revolutionary struggling to learn the secret to the success of the Soviet model. As an eager student, what would you identify as the key tenets of party orthodoxy? What points would leave you confused, doubtful, or hopeful? Looking back from our current perspective, how would you describe Stalin's worldview and his hopes and fears for the Soviet system?

Lectures on "The Foundations of Leninism"
April–May, 1924

[THREE CONTRADICTIONS ENFEEBLING MATURE CAPITALISM]

Lenin called imperialism "moribund capitalism." Why? Because imperialism carries the contradictions of capitalism to their last bounds, to the extreme limit, beyond which revolution begins. Of these contradictions, there are three which must be regarded as the most important.

The *first contradiction* is the contradiction between labour and capital. Imperialism is the omnipotence of the monopolist trusts and syndicates, of the banks and the financial oligarchy, in the industrial countries. . . . Either place yourself at the mercy of capital, eke out a wretched existence as of old and sink lower and lower, or adopt a new weapon — this is the alternative imperialism puts before the vast masses of the proletariat. Imperialism brings the working class to revolution.

J. V. Stalin, *Works,* ed. Marx-Engels-Lenin Institute of the Central Committee of the Communist Party of the Soviet Union (Bolshevik), vol. 6 (Moscow: Foreign Languages Publishing House, 1953), 74–76, 99–101, 110–12, 116–19, 189. Bracketed headings added to indicate major themes.

The *second contradiction* is the contradiction among the various financial groups and imperialist Powers in their struggle for sources of raw materials, for foreign territory. . . . This frenzied struggle among the various groups of capitalists is notable in that it includes as an inevitable element imperialist wars, wars for the annexation of foreign territories. This circumstance, in its turn, is notable in that it leads to the mutual weakening of the imperialists, to the weakening of the position of capitalism in general, to the acceleration of the advent of the proletarian revolution and to the practical necessity of this revolution.

The *third contradiction* is the contradiction between the handful of ruling, "civilized" nations and the hundreds of millions of the colonial and dependent peoples of the world. Imperialism is the most barefaced exploitation and the most inhuman oppression of hundreds of millions of people inhabiting vast colonies and dependent countries. . . . But in exploiting these countries imperialism is compelled to build there railways, factories and mills, industrial and commercial centres. The appearance of a class of proletarians, the emergence of a native intelligentsia, the awakening of national consciousness, the growth of the liberation movement — such are the inevitable results of this "policy." The growth of the revolutionary movement in all colonies and dependent countries . . . . saps radically the position of capitalism by converting the colonies and dependent countries from reserves of imperialism into reserves of the proletarian revolution. . . .

[IMPROVED PROSPECTS FOR WORLD REVOLUTION]

. . . Now we must speak of the world proletarian revolution; for the separate national fronts of capital have become links in a single chain called the world front of imperialism, which must be opposed by a common front of the revolutionary movement in all countries.

. . . Now the proletarian revolution must be regarded primarily as the result of the development of the contradictions within the world system of imperialism, as the result of the breaking of the chain of the world imperialist front in one country or another.

Where will the revolution begin? Where, in what country, can the front of capital be pierced first?

Where industry is more developed, where the proletariat constitutes the majority, where there is more culture, where there is more democracy — that was the reply usually given formerly.

No, objects the Leninist theory of revolution, *not necessarily where industry is more developed,* and so forth. The front of capital will be pierced where the chain of imperialism is weakest, for the proletarian revolution is the result of the breaking of the chain of the world imperialist front at its weakest link; and it may turn out that the country which has started the revolution, which has made a breach in the front of capital, is less developed in a capitalist sense than other, more developed, countries, which have, however, remained within the framework of capitalism.

In 1917 the chain of the imperialist world front proved to be weaker in Russia than in the other countries. It was there that the chain broke and provided an outlet for the proletarian revolution. Why? Because in Russia a great popular revolution was unfolding, and at its head marched the revolutionary proletariat, which had such an important ally as the vast mass of the peasantry, which was oppressed and exploited by the landlords. Because the revolution there was opposed by such a hideous representative of imperialism as tsarism, which lacked all moral prestige and was deservedly hated by the whole population. The chain proved to be weaker in Russia, although Russia was less developed in a capitalist sense than, say, France or Germany, Britain or America.

Where will the chain break in the near future? Again, where it is weakest. It is not precluded that the chain may break, say, in India. . . .

But the overthrow of the power of the bourgeoisie and establishment of the power of the proletariat in one country does not yet mean that the complete victory of socialism has been ensured. . . . For this the victory of the revolution in at least several countries is needed. Therefore, the development and support of revolution in other countries is an essential task of the victorious revolution. . . .

[FEATURES OF THE DICTATORSHIP OF THE PROLETARIAT]

1) *The dictatorship of the proletariat as the instrument of the proletarian revolution.* The question of the proletarian dictatorship is above all a question of the main content of the proletarian revolution. The proletarian revolution, its movement, its sweep and its achievements acquire flesh and blood only through the dictatorship of the proletariat. The dictatorship of the proletariat is the instrument of the proletarian revolution, its organ, its most important mainstay, brought into being for the purpose of, firstly, crushing the resistance of the overthrown exploiters and consolidating the achievements of the proletarian revolution, and, secondly, carrying the proletarian revolution to its completion, carrying the revolution to the complete victory of socialism. . . .

2) The dictatorship of the proletariat as the rule of the proletariat over the bourgeoisie. . . . The dictatorship of the proletariat is not a change of government, but a new state, with new organs of power, both central and local; it is the state of the proletariat, which has arisen on the ruins of the old state, the state of the bourgeoisie.

The dictatorship of the proletariat arises not on the basis of the bourgeois order, but in the process of the breaking up of this order, after the overthrow of the bourgeoisie, in the process of the expropriation of the landlords and capitalists, in the process of the socialisation of the principal instruments and means of production, in the process of violent proletarian revolution. The dictatorship of the proletariat is a revolutionary power based on the use of force against the bourgeoisie.

The state is a machine in the hands of the ruling class for suppressing the resistance of its class enemies. *In this respect* the dictatorship of the proletariat does not differ essentially from the dictatorship of any other class, for the proletarian state is a machine for the suppression of the bourgeoisie. But there is one *substantial* difference. This difference consists in the fact that all hitherto existing class states have been dictatorships of an exploiting minority over the exploited majority, whereas the dictatorship of the proletariat is the dictatorship of the exploited majority over the exploiting minority....

... Only under the proletarian dictatorship are real liberties for the exploited and real participation of the proletarians and peasants in governing the country possible. Under the dictatorship of the proletariat, democracy is *proletarian* democracy, the democracy of the exploited majority, based on the restriction of the rights of the exploiting minority and directed against this minority....

[A DISCIPLINED COMMUNIST PARTY AS THE INSTRUMENT
OF THE DICTATORSHIP OF THE PROLETARIAT]

... The achievement and maintenance of the dictatorship of the proletariat is impossible without a party which is strong by reason of its solidarity and iron discipline. But iron discipline in the Party is inconceivable without unity of will, without complete and absolute unity of action on the part of all members of the Party.... [I]ron discipline does not preclude but presupposes criticism and conflict of opinion within the Party.... But after a conflict of opinion has been closed, after criticism has been exhausted and a decision has been arrived at, unity of will and unity of action of all Party members are the necessary conditions without which neither Party unity nor iron discipline in the Party is conceivable.

1.4

Polish Communist Jakub Berman on Communism's Postwar Appeal

The campaign by the Soviet Communist Party to win converts abroad, set in motion during the first years after the revolution, paid off richly in regions all around the world — but above all in eastern Europe. When the Soviet army swept through the neighboring lands on their way to Germany in the final phase of the war in Europe, Moscow's hand-picked cadre of true believers marched right behind, ready to assume control. Jakub Berman was one of these Soviet allies. He was a leading figure in the Polish Communist Party from the late 1940s well into the 1950s. Fluent in Russian and trained in the Soviet Union, he and a handful of other Polish Communists took up the daunting task of ruling a country with a large peasantry resolutely opposed to collective farms, a long history of anti-Russian feeling, a strong Catholic church, and a proud and independent intellectual class.

The following excerpt offers insight into the thinking of those who cast their lot with the Soviets. These interviews were conducted between April 1982 and April 1984, a time of cultural thaw within Poland. They were conducted by Teresa Torańska, a sympathizer with the anti-Communist Solidarity labor movement that would eventually topple Poland's Communist Party. How does Berman justify embracing communism and aligning with the Soviet Union? How convincing a case does he make for the course that he followed? Though the questions in this interview are often abrasive and the responses heated, why does neither party break off the conversation? What purposes might these interviews serve? To what extent is Berman's worldview shaped by the principles sketched out in Stalin's 1924 lectures (Document 1.3) and to what extent by his country's location between two powerful states, Germany and the USSR?

Teresa Torańska
Interview with Jakub Berman
1982–1984

[Y]ou brought yet another disaster upon this nation.
That's not true. We brought it liberation.
Did you?
Yes, we did. We didn't come to this country as its occupiers and we never even imagined ourselves in that role. After all the disasters that had befallen this country, we brought it its ultimate liberation, because we finally got rid of those Germans, and that counts for something. I know these things aren't simple. We wanted to get this country moving, to breathe life into it; all our hopes were tied up with the new model of Poland, which was without historical precedent and was the only chance it had had throughout its thousand years of history; we wanted to use that chance 100 per cent. And we succeeded. In any case we were bound to succeed, because we were right; not in some irrational, dreamed-up way we'd plucked out of the air, but historically—history was on our side.
More specifically, the Red Army and the NKVD [Soviet secret police].
Naturally, you can claim now that the Red Army sympathized with the communists—yes, it did. And you can also accuse us of having been in the minority, and yes, we were. And so what? Nothing! That doesn't mean anything! Because what does the development of mankind teach us? It teaches us first of all that it was always the minority, the avant-garde, that rescued the majority, often against the will of that majority. It was spat at and misunderstood, or it lost and perished. Let's admit it honestly: who organized the uprisings in Poland? A handful of people. That's simply the way history is made. You only have to look at how other countries in Europe or Asia were liberated. In China the communist party didn't have any support either, I'm sure. . . .
Certainly, this sovereignty of ours became stronger, greater and more independent after Stalin's death — that's why I introduced the division into the years before his death and the years after — but even then, during his lifetime, we tried to ensure the greatest possible autonomy and independence for

Teresa Torańska, *"Them": Stalin's Polish Puppets,* trans. Agnieszka Kolakowska (New York: Harper & Row, 1987), 256–57, 298–300, 302–303.

Poland. That was what the Polish road to socialism was about; that was how we understood it.

But you didn't ensure it!

That's not true. There were indeed attempts, after 1949, to check our independence to some extent, and our efforts to retain it in full were stifled by the extraordinary pressure of the Cold War atmosphere and by a genuine threat from America, but even then we tried not to allow Polish affairs to suffer. For what was happening was that America had decided to appropriate the whole of Europe for herself. She wanted to invest in Europe (hence the Marshall Plan[1]) in order to make it dependent on her. Her aim was for us and the other countries of the Eastern bloc to break away from the Soviet Union. Such were her intentions, and neither the Soviet Union nor we — we all the less — could agree to this, because for us it would probably have ended in disaster from the point of view of the state, quite apart from the ideological point of view. For us to break away from the Soviet Union would have meant losing the Recovered Territories,[2] and Poland would have become the Duchy of Warsaw.[3] Yes, that's right, the Duchy of Warsaw. There's no other possibility that I can see.

And who was supposed to take these western territories away from us? America?

The Germans, naturally. Because America immediately placed her bets on Germany and made efforts to unite it, and if she had succeeded, a victorious Germany would have been created, and thus an aggressive and greedy Germany, ten times worse than it is now, just as Hitler's Germany turned out to be worse than Wilhelmian Germany. It would have posed a complicated problem for us, and maybe even a new threat, for a united Germany would have become a pro-American Germany, and thus hostile to the Soviet Union and to us. And the existence of a pro-American centre bordering on the Soviet Union would lead to an inevitable clash, because the whole of Europe would be in danger of being subordinated to America. In such a situation we would immediately be the first to foot the bill, since we would be the first to be exposed to the dangers of such a clash. We're in the middle, after all; we'd be crushed to bits, and then the Recovered Territories would be taken away from us. The whole Adenauer[4] strategy was directed towards taking the Recovered Territories away from us at the appropriate moment, and that's what would have happened, I've no doubt at all about that. Because, look: it's been so many years since the war, and yet the issue of Vilnius and Lvov is still alive

---

[1]A U.S. initiative, inaugurated in 1947, to help European economies recover from wartime destruction.

[2]German lands gained by Poland in the west in compensation for Polish territory in the east absorbed into the Soviet Union.

[3]A Polish state created by Napoleon in 1807 and partitioned on his fall.

[4]Konrad Adenauer, political leader of the West German state that emerged after World War II.

in Polish society,[5] so how alive must the issue of our western territories be in Germany. Germans lived en masse on those territories; millions, millions of Germans were born and raised there. I'm convinced that if circumstances were favourable they would claim that land back, without, of course, giving anything in return. Which would be only logical, after all, because they could hardly be expected to start waging a struggle with the Soviet Union over Vilnius and Lvov, which in the meantime have undergone a complete transformation as regards nationality. And then what would be left of Poland? Well, what? The Duchy of Warsaw! Of course, one might even reconcile oneself to a Duchy of Warsaw, but would it be the fulfillment of those pretentions to be a great power which are so deeply rooted in the mentality of the Polish nation? Historical opportunity is something you either seize or you lose; we, the communists, seized it and made it a reality. We based ourselves on the status quo, and we were able to polonize the western territories, to manage, incorporate and homogenize them. The new shape of Poland became our trump card. I don't know when the Poles will get that into their heads. I don't mean the uneducated, backward ones, but those enlightened, rational, thinking members of the Polish intelligentsia. I'm waiting for the time when it finally gets through to them that Poland will always be a lost cause in any other constellation than the one we succeeded in winning as its only historical chance. I don't know when another one will come along — perhaps in a few decades; I can't predict, I'm not a prophet, and beside, playing at prophecies would be risky. We're in a state of development, of flux; everything will still go on changing, modify, evolving. At this point there's only one thing I can say: we, the communists, rescued Poland from the worst fate; if it weren't for us, it would be a Duchy of Warsaw, a truncated scrap, a mean, pathetic little Central European state with very limited possibilities of development, or it wouldn't be there at all. . . . .

At what price?

Of course we paid a high price, in coal for one thing.

I mean the moral cost.

Certainly, but what was there to do? Stalin would have regarded any opposition to his politics as a sign of disloyalty on our part, which would have led him to reject responsibility for the future shape of Poland. So we had a choice: either we put ourselves in a position where the Soviet Union does what it wants, with us in the middle, and whatever happens to Poland depends on the Soviet Union, or we try to find some sort of compromise which would give us the possibility of waiting it out until better days. A web of complexity. In the final analysis Poland never had any alternative, either then or now, other than to endure in the shape it's in and at all costs to maintain the shape it's in, because it's our only chance. And for the sake of that chance, for the sake of those borders, it was worth making many concessions and

---

[5] Cities lost to Polish control, now part of Lithuania and Ukraine respectively.

agreeing to many sacrifices. Because sacrifices are a transitory thing, painful only for single individuals, whereas the shape of Poland and its greatness are a basis for the development of future generations.

No. The basis is the nation, with its tradition and its culture, both reactionary and progressive, in your terminology, because they, and not its borders, shape the nation's spirit and identity. But you chose the third and most frightful, option: the sovietization of the nation.

No, that's not true! Even if we did to a large extent model ourselves on the forms of the Soviet system or make use of Soviet experiences (which is after all understandable, since the Soviet Union was the only country that was trying to build socialism, so we could transfer various experiences to Poland, there's no sin in that), still we never copied them automatically; we always, I repeat, always, tried to secure, as far as we could, the greatest possible measure of autonomy for Poland, and resisted suggestions and even moral pressure to shape Poland to the Soviet mould and make even more use of their experiences. We always tried to defend Polish autonomy, both in its cultural aspects and in its economic development. We retained economic autonomy in matters in which we thought it had to be retained. One example is the Catholic Church, towards which we took the attitude that we would absolutely not hinder the carrying out of Church functions, which was entirely contrary to what was going on in Russia on a huge scale.

THE COLD WAR TAKES SHAPE

The moment real wars begin is easy to identify by the first shot fired or the first armed violation of national boundaries. The Cold War is another matter. Some trace its origins to the Bolshevik revolution of 1917 and the denunciations and fear it inspired in Europe and the United States. Others believe that strains between Soviet and American allies during World War II over strategic and territorial issues planted the seeds of mistrust. The victory over Germany and Japan and the urgent need to settle a host of postwar issues allowed those strains to develop rapidly and come more fully into the open.

The following sample of key American and Soviet documents from the late 1940s and early 1950s provide an opportunity to trace the emergence of the Cold War and to gauge the influences (from the atomic bomb to personality and ideology) that gave rise to hostility. Of all the questions to consider, perhaps most fundamental is: When did the Soviet-American tensions become so serious that we are justified in saying that the Cold War had begun? Was it when leaders harbored serious private enmity, or was that enmity significant only when it was put before the public, thus entrenching leaders in their position? Or was it when political elites on both sides began to take action, for example mobilizing their publics, raising their military budgets, or creating alliances? Once that date is determined, it becomes easier to identify the main forces at work.

1.5
American and Soviet Leaders Move
from War to Peace, 1943–1946

World War II drew to a close in a dizzying rush of events. In early 1943 Soviet forces turned the tide against the German invaders and began their march into the heart of Europe. In June 1944 American and British forces made a lodgment on the European continent. With Hitler's Germany in a tightening vise, the leaders of the United States, the Soviet Union, and Britain met in early 1945 at Yalta on the Soviet shores of the Black Sea to shape postwar Europe as well as to coordinate the final assault on Japan. President Franklin D. Roosevelt's death in April thrust an inexperienced Harry S. Truman into the presidency — on the eve of German surrender in May. The following July the American, Soviet, and British leaders met in Potsdam outside a devastated Berlin. Japan's surrender followed the next month, hastened by the dropping of two atomic bombs and the Soviet declaration of war against Japan.

This batch of short documents provides a rapid-fire review of these developments through the eyes of leaders trying to control them. What concerns defined Roosevelt's, Truman's, and Stalin's approaches to U.S.–Soviet relations? Is there a moment evident here when the cooperation that defined the wartime alliance turned to doubt and then enmity? What issue seems to have been most corrosive of trust? How much importance would you assign to personality and personal style — especially the paranoia that some have seen in Stalin and the differences between Roosevelt and Truman?

The diversity of forms the evidence takes adds another layer of questions. Do we assign the same interpretive weight to letters, officially recorded conversations, diary entries, and public pronouncements? How might the context have influenced what the leaders said and how they expressed themselves? Should we trust speeches? But on the other hand, can we trust the records of private meetings and rapid-fire telephone conversations to capture the parry and thrust of the exchanges and the tone of the comments not to mention the exact phrasing? How sound a basis does the evidence given here provide for a judgment on Cold War origins?

President Franklin D. Roosevelt
Letter on Postwar Great-Power Relations
to George W. Norris[1]
September 21, 1943

[W]e should have a trial or transition period after the fighting stops — we might call it even a period of trial and error.

Peoples all over the world are shell shocked — and they will require a period of recuperation before final terms are laid down in regard to bound-

---

[1]George W. Norris was a Liberal Republican from Nebraska who had just retired from the Senate.

Elliott Roosevelt, ed., *F.D.R.: His Personal Letters,* (New York: Duell, Sloan and Pearce, 1947–50), 4:1446–47.

aries, transfers of population, free intercourse, the lowering of economic barriers, planning for mutual reconstruction, etc. It has long been my thought
that the world cannot successfully take up all these things if fear of war hangs
over the world.

Therefore, I have been visualizing a superimposed — or if you like it,
superassumed — obligation by Russia, China, Britain, and ourselves that we
will act as sheriffs for the maintenance of order during the transition period.
Such a period might last two or even three or four years. And, in the meantime, through the holding of many special conferences the broad ideals which
you and I have in mind might be cleared up.

Premier Joseph Stalin
Speech on Postwar Great-Power Relations
November 6, 1944

[T]he alliance between the U.S.S.R., Great Britain, and the United States is
founded not on casual, short-lived considerations but on vital and lasting
interests. There need be no doubt that having stood the strain of over three
years of war and being sealed with the blood of nations risen in defense of
their liberty and honor, the fighting alliance of the democratic powers will all
the more certainly stand the strain of the concluding phase of the war. . . .

. . . But winning the war is not in itself synonymous with insuring for the
nations lasting peace and guaranteed security in the future. The thing is not
only to win the war but also to render new aggression and new war impossible, if not forever then at least for a long time to come.

After her defeat Germany will of course be disarmed both in the economic and the military-political sense. It would however be naive to think
that she will not attempt to restore her might and launch new aggression. . . .

Well, what means are there to preclude fresh aggression on Germany's
part . . . ?

There is only one means to this end, in addition to the complete disarmament of the aggressive nations: that is, to establish a special organization made
up of representatives of the peace-loving nations to uphold peace and safeguard security; to put the necessary minimum of armed forces required for
the averting of aggression at the disposal of the directing body of this organization, and to obligate this organization to employ these armed forces without delay if it becomes necessary to avert or stop aggression and punish the
culprits. . . .

Can we expect the actions of this world organization to be sufficiently
effective? They will be effective if the great powers which have borne the
brunt of the war against Hitler['s] Germany continue to act in a spirit of
unanimity and accord. They will not be effective if this essential condition is
violated.

Joseph Stalin, *The Great Patriotic War of the Soviet Union* (New York: International Publishers,
1945), 139–42.

Roosevelt, Stalin, and British Prime Minister Winston Churchill
Yalta Conference Discussion of Poland
February 6, 1945

[Roosevelt said that] he wished to see the creation of a representative government which could have the support of all the great powers and which could be composed of representatives of the principal parties of Poland. . . . [and] that Poland should maintain the most friendly and cooperative relations with the Soviet Union. . . .

[Stalin said that] . . . for the Russians [the Polish situation] was a question . . . of honor because Russia had many past grievances against Poland and desired to see them eliminated. It was [also] a question of strategic security not only because Poland was a bordering country but because throughout history Poland had been the corridor for attack on Russia. . . . Since it was impossible by the force of Russian armies alone to close from the outside this corridor, it could be done only by Poland's own forces. It was very important, therefore, to have Poland independent, strong and democratic. . . .

[Regarding the make-up of the Polish government Stalin said:] As a military man I demand from a country liberated by the Red Army that there be no civil war in the rear. The men in the Red Army are indifferent to the type of government as long as it will maintain order and they will not be shot in the back. The [Moscow-backed] Warsaw, or Lublin, government has not badly fulfilled this task. There are, however, agents of the London government [of Polish conservatives in exile] who claim to be agents of the underground forces of resistance. I must say that no good and much evil comes from these forces. . . .

. . . [Churchill expressed doubts] that the Lublin government represents more than one third of the people and would not be maintained in power if the people were free to express their opinion. . . . [T]he British Government could not agree to recognizing the Lublin government of Poland.

Meeting minutes by Charles E. Bohlen (assistant to the secretary of state), in U.S. Department of State, *Foreign Relations of the United States* [hereafter *FRUS*]: *The Conferences at Malta and Yalta, 1945* (Washington, D.C.: U.S. Government Printing Office, 1955), 667, 669–71.

President Harry S. Truman
Conversation with Ambassador to the Soviet Union W. Averell Harriman
April 20, 1945

The President [said] that he intended to be firm with the Russians and make no concessions from American principles or traditions for the fact of winning their favor. He said he felt that only on a give and take basis could any relations be established.

Ambassador Harriman said that in effect what we were faced with was a "barbarian invasion of Europe", that Soviet control over any foreign country did not mean merely influence on their foreign relations but the extension of the Soviet system with secret police, extinction of freedom of speech, etc., and that we had to decide what should be our attitude in the face of these unpleasant facts. . . . He said that obviously certain concessions in the give and take of negotiation would have to be made. The President said that he thoroughly understood this and said that we could not, of course, expect to get 100 percent of what we wanted but that on important matters he felt that we should be able to get 85 percent.

Memo of conversation by Bohlen, in *FRUS, 1945,* vol. 5 (Washington, D.C.: U.S. Government Printing Office, 1967), 232–33.

President Truman
Record of Meeting with Chief Foreign Policy Advisors
April 23, 1945

The President said that he had told Mr. [Vyacheslav] Molotov [visiting Soviet Foreign Minister] last night that he intended fully to carry out all the agreements reached by President Roosevelt at the Crimea [Yalta]. He added that he felt our agreements with the Soviet Union so far had been a one-way street and that could not continue; it was now or never. He intended to go on with the plans for San Francisco [the meeting to organize the United Nations] and if the Russians did not wish to join us they could go to hell. The President then asked in rotation the officials present for their view.

. . . [Secretary of War Henry L. Stimson] said in the big military matters the Soviet Government had kept their word and that the military authorities of the United States had come to count on it. In fact he said that they had often been better than their promise. He said it was important to find out what motives they had in mind in regard to these border countries and that their ideas of independence and democracy in areas that they regarded as vital to the Soviet Union are different from ours. . . . In this case he said that without fully understanding how seriously the Russians took this Polish question we might be heading into very dangerous water. He remarked that 25 years ago virtually all of Poland had been Russian.

[Secretary of Navy James V. Forrestal] said that he felt that this difficulty over Poland could not be treated as an isolated incident, that there had been many evidences of the Soviet desire to dominate adjacent countries and to disregard the wishes of her allies. He said he had felt that for some time the Russians had considered that we would not object if they took over all of

---

Memo of conversation discussing alternative approaches to the Soviet Union by Bohlen, in *FRUS, 1945,* 5:253–55.

Eastern Europe into their power. He said it was his profound conviction that if the Russians were to be rigid in their attitude we had better have a show down with them now than later.

Ambassador Harriman . . . remarked that the real issue was whether we were to be a party to a program of Soviet domination of Poland. He said obviously we were faced with a possibility of a real break with the Russians but he felt that if properly handled it might be avoided. . . .

Mr. Stimson observed that he would like to know how far the Russian reaction to a strong position on Poland would go. He said he thought that the Russians perhaps were being more realistic than we were in regard to their own security.

Admiral [William] Leahy [Chief of Staff to the President] said that he had left Yalta with the impression that the Soviet Government had no intention of permitting a free government to operate in Poland. . . . In his opinion the Yalta agreement was susceptible to two interpretations. He added that he felt that it was a serious matter to break with the Russians but that we should tell them that we stood for a free and independent Poland.

The Secretary of State [Edward R. Stettinius] . . . said he felt that [the Yalta decision on Poland] was susceptible of only one interpretation.

[Army Chief of Staff General George C. Marshall] said from the military point of view the situation in Europe was secure but that they hoped for Soviet participation in the war against Japan at a time when it would be useful to us. The Russians had it within their power to delay their entry into the Far Eastern war until we had done all the dirty work. He said the difficulties with the Russians . . . usually straightened out. He was inclined to agree with Mr. Stimson that possibility of a break with Russia was very serious.

Mr. Stimson observed that he agreed with General Marshall and that he felt that the Russians would not yield on the Polish question. He said we must understand that outside the United States with the exception of Great Britain there was no country that understood free elections; that the party in power always ran the election. . . .

. . . The President [said that the] issue was the execution of agreements entered into between this Government and the Soviet Union. He said he intended to tell Mr. Molotov that we expected Russia to carry out the Yalta decision. . . .

The President [added] that he was satisfied that from a military point of view there was no reason why we should fail to stand up to our understanding of the Crimean [Yalta] agreements.

President Truman
Diary Entry on the First Successful Atomic Bomb
July 25, 1945

We have discovered the most terrible bomb in the history of the world. It may be the fire destruction prophesied in the Euphrates Valley Era, after Noah and his fabulous Ark. . . .

. . . It is certainly a good thing for the world that Hitler's crowd or Stalin's did not discover this atomic bomb. It seems to be the most terrible thing ever discovered, but it can be made the most useful.

Diary entry, July 25, 1945 in "Ross" folder, Box 322, President's Secretary's Files, Papers of Harry S. Truman, Truman Library, Independence, Missouri. Also in Eduard Mark, "'Today Has Been A Historical One': Harry S. Truman's Diary of the Potsdam Conference," *Diplomatic History* 4 (Summer 1980): 323–24. For the handwritten version of the diary, see the Truman Library website: <http://www.trumanlibrary.org/whistlestop/study_collections/bomb/large/truman_diaries/bma 3-5.htm and bma 3-6.htm>.

Premier Stalin
Telephone Comments to Lavrenti Beria[1] about U.S. Pressure
Probably Late July 1945

Truman is trying to exert pressure, to dominate . . . His attitude is particularly aggressive toward the Soviet Union. Of course, the factor of the atom bomb was working for Truman. We understand that. But a policy of blackmail and intimidation is unacceptable to us. We therefore gave no grounds for thinking that anything could intimidate us. Lavrentiy, we should not allow any other country to have a decisive superiority over us. Tell Comrade [Igor] Kurchatov that he has to hurry with his parcel [the Soviet bomb project]. And ask him what our scientists need to accelerate work.[2]

[1] Lavrenti Beria was the leader assigned to oversee the Soviet atomic project.

[2] Well before Potsdam Stalin had known about the secret U.S. atomic project and had launched his own bomb-building program. Truman's announcement of the successful U.S. test gave a new sense of urgency to the Soviet effort. Stalin is supposed to have prodded Kurchatov, "If a child does not cry, the mother does not understand what he needs." Stalin added, "Ask for anything you like. You will not be turned down." Zaloga, *Target America,* 27.

Steven J. Zaloga, *Target America: The Soviet Union and the Strategic Arms Race, 1945–1964* (Novato, Calif.: Presidio Press, 1993), 27.

Premier Stalin
Radio Address on World War II and Its Aftermath
February 9, 1946

[The Second World War] was the inevitable result of the development of world economic and political forces on the basis of modern monopoly capitalism.

House Committee on Foreign Affairs, *The Strategy and Tactics of World Communism,* Supplement I: *One Hundred Years of Communism, 1848–1948,* 80th Cong., 2d Sess., 1948, H. Doc. 619, 168–71, 176–77.

Marxists have declared more than once that the capitalist system of world economy harbors elements of general crises and armed conflicts and that, hence, the development of world capitalism in our time proceeds not in the form of smooth and even progress but through crises and military catastrophes.

The fact is, that the unevenness of development of the capitalist countries usually leads in time to violent disturbance of equilibrium in the world system of capitalism, that group of capitalist countries which considers itself worse provided than others with raw materials and markets usually making attempts to alter the situation and repartition the "spheres of influence" in its favor by armed force. The result is a splitting of the capitalist world into two hostile camps and war between them. . . .

That does not mean of course that the Second World War is a copy of the first. . . .

. . . [U]nlike the First World War, the Second World War against the Axis states from the very outset assumed the character of an anti-fascist war, a war of liberation, one the aim of which was also the restoration of democratic liberties. The entry of the Soviet Union into the war against the Axis states could only enhance, and indeed did enhance, the anti-fascist and liberation character of the Second World War.

It was on this basis that the anti-fascist coalition of the Soviet Union, the United States of America, Great Britain, and other freedom-loving states came into being. . . .

And so, what are the results of the war? . . .

Our victory means, first of all, that our Soviet social order . . . has successfully passed the ordeal in the fire of war and has proved its unquestionable vitality. . . .

Second, our victory means . . . that our multinational Soviet State has stood all the trials of war and has proved its vitality. . . .

Third, our victory means . . . that the Red Army bore up heroically under all the trials of war, utterly routed the armies of our enemies and came out of the war as a victor. . . .

Now a few words about the Communist Party's plans of work for the immediate future. As is known these plans are set forth in the new Five-Year Plan which is shortly to be endorsed. The principal aims of the new Five-Year Plan are to rehabilitate the ravaged areas of the country, to restore the prewar level in industry and agriculture, and then to surpass this level in more or less substantial measure. . . .

As regards the plans for a longer period ahead, the Party means to organize a new mighty upsurge in the national economy, which would allow us to increase our industrial production, for example, three times over as compared with the prewar period. . . . Only under such conditions can we consider that our homeland will be guaranteed against all possible accidents.[1] (*Stormy ap-*

---

[1]This phrase was also translated at the time as "our country will be insured against any eventuality." *Vital Speeches of the Day* 12 (March 1, 1946): 303.

plause.) That will take three more Five-Year Plans, I should think, if not more. But it can be done and we must do it. (*Stormy applause.*)

1.6
Two Diplomats Assess the International Situation, 1946

High-level diplomats do not make their country's policy, but they do their best to influence it. While the leaders of the Soviet Union and the United States tried to size up the international situation, experts offered their own assessments. George Kennan, the second in command in the Moscow embassy and leading government specialist on the Soviet Union, prepared a "long telegram" on Soviet foreign policy that was avidly read in the Truman administration. His Soviet counterpart was Nikolai Novikov, the Soviet ambassador in the United States. He was in Paris working with Soviet Foreign Minister Vyacheslav Molotov, who pressed for an analysis of U.S. policy. Handed the report at the end of the month, Molotov went over it carefully (as his underlinings in the text of the report indicate).

These two reports are interesting in their own right. First step, look closely at the insights this pair of seasoned observers were offering their superiors. What were their respective positions and how fundamental were the differences in their interpretations? How good were their analyses? Specifically, how well did Kennan seem to grasp Stalin's approach, and how well did Novikov grasp the U.S. policy as it had evolved from Roosevelt to Truman? These two documents also provide an opportunity to gauge the lines of influence between each of these men and their respective national policies. Were they themselves constrained by or at odds with positions already taken by their leaders? Did they agree with long-standing notions about their countries' role in the world? Is there any evidence in the documents (1.7 to 1.9) that follow that they had a significant impact on the evolution of Cold War policy?

George F. Kennan
"Long Telegram" Analyzing Soviet Policy
February 22, 1946

At bottom of Kremlin's neurotic view of world affairs is traditional and instinctive Russian sense of insecurity. . . . [Russian rulers] have always feared foreign penetration, feared direct contact between Western world and their own, feared what would happen if Russians learned truth about world without or if foreigners learned truth about world within. And they have learned to seek security only in patient but deadly struggle for total destruction of rival power, never in compacts and compromises with it. . . .

. . . After establishment of Bolshevist regime, Marxist dogma . . . became a perfect vehicle for sense of insecurity with which Bolsheviks, even more than previous Russian rulers, were afflicted. In this dogma, with its basic altruism

FRUS, 1946, vol. 6 (Washington, D.C.: U.S. Government Printing Office, 1969): 699–700, 706–707.

of purpose, they found justification for their instinctive fear of outside world, for the dictatorship without which they did not know how to rule, for cruelties they did not dare not to inflict, for sacrifices they felt bound to demand. In the name of Marxism they sacrificed every single ethical value in their methods and tactics. Today they cannot dispense with it. It is fig leaf of their moral and intellectual respectability. Without it they would stand before history, at best, as only the last of that long succession of cruel and wasteful Russian rulers who have relentlessly forced country on to ever new heights of military power in order to guarantee external security of their internally weak regimes. . . . [Their dogma depicts the] outside world as evil, hostile and menacing, but as bearing within itself germs of creeping disease and destined to be wracked with growing internal convulsions until it is given final *coup de grace* by rising power of socialism and yields to new and better world. This thesis provides justification for that increase of military and police power of Russian state, for that isolation of Russian population from outside world, and for that fluid and constant pressure to extend limits of Russian police power which are together the natural and instinctive urges of Russian rulers. Basically this is only the steady advance of uneasy Russian nationalism. . . . But in new guise of international Marxism, with its honeyed promises to a desperate and war torn outside world, it is more dangerous and insidious than ever before. . . .

. . . [W]e have here a political force committed fanatically to the belief that with US there can be no permanent *modus vivendi*, that it is desirable and necessary that the internal harmony of our society be disrupted, our traditional way of life be destroyed, the international authority of our state be broken, if Soviet power is to be secure. This political force has complete power of disposition over energies of one of world's greatest peoples and resources of world's richest national territory, and is borne along by deep and powerful currents of Russian nationalism. In addition, it has an elaborate and far flung apparatus for exertion of its influence in other countries, an apparatus of amazing flexibility and versatility, managed by people whose experience and skill in underground methods are presumably without parallel in history. Finally, it is seemingly inaccessible to considerations of reality in its basic reactions. . . . Problem of how to cope with this force . . . [*is*] undoubtedly greatest task our diplomacy has ever faced and probably greatest it will ever have to face.

Nikolai Novikov

Report to Foreign Minister Molotov
Analyzing U.S. Policy

September 27, 1946

The foreign policy of the United States, which reflects the imperialist tendencies of American monopolistic capital, is characterized in the postwar period by a striving for world supremacy.[1] This is the real meaning of the many statements by President Truman and other representatives of American ruling circles: that the United States has the right to lead the world. . . .

The foreign policy of the United States is not determined at present by the circles in the Democratic party that (as was the case during Roosevelt's lifetime) strive to strengthen the cooperation of the three great powers that constituted the basis of the anti–Hitler coalition during the war. The ascendance to power of President Truman, a politically unstable person but with certain conservative tendencies, and the subsequent appointment of [James] Byrnes as Secretary of State meant a strengthening of the influence on U.S. foreign policy of the most reactionary circles of the Democratic party. The constantly increasing reactionary nature of the foreign policy course of the United States . . . laid the groundwork for close cooperation in this field between the far right wing of the Democratic party and the Republican party. This cooperation of the two parties . . . took shape in both houses of Congress in the form of an unofficial bloc of reactionary Southern Democrats and the old guard of the Republicans. . . .

Obvious indications of the U.S. effort to establish world dominance are also to be found in the increase in military potential in peacetime and in the establishment of a large number of naval and air bases both in the United States and beyond its borders. . . .

One of the stages in the achievement of dominance over the world by the United States is its understanding with England concerning the partial division of the world on the basis of mutual concessions. [Those two countries have agreed to include] Japan and China in the sphere of influence of the United States in the Far East, while the United States, for its part, has agreed not to hinder England either in resolving the Indian [demands for independence] or in strengthening its influence in Siam [Thailand] and Indonesia. . . .

In recent years American capital has penetrated very intensively into the economy of the Near Eastern countries, in particular into the oil industry. . . .

In expanding in the Near East, American capital has English capital as its greatest and most stubborn competitor. The fierce competition between them is the chief factor preventing England and the United States from reaching an understanding on the division of spheres of influence in the Near East. . . .

Relations between the United States and England are determined by two basic circumstances. On the one hand, the United States regards England as its greatest potential competitor; on the other hand, England constitutes a possible

[1]Molotov marginal query: "A difference from [the] prewar [period]?"

Underlining here indicates sections Molotov marked for attention. This telegram comes from the Soviet Foreign Ministry archives. It was supplied by Vladimir Shustov and translated by John Glad. Kenneth M. Jensen, ed., *Origins of the Cold War: The Novikov, Kennan, and Roberts "Long Telegrams" of 1946* (Washington, D.C.: United States Institute of Peace, 1991), 3, 5–6, 8, 10–11, 14–16. Also available on the Cold War International History Project website at <http://wwics.si.edu/index.cfm?fuseaction-library.document&topic_id-1409&id-67>.

ally for the United States. Division of certain regions of the globe into spheres of influence of the United States and England would create the opportunity, if not for preventing competition between them, which is impossible, then at least of reducing it. At the same time, such a division facilitates the achievement of economic and political cooperation between them. . . .

The present policy of the American government with regard to the USSR is also directed at limiting or dislodging the influence of the Soviet Union from neighboring countries. In implementing this policy in former enemy or Allied countries adjacent to the USSR, the United States attempts . . . to support reactionary forces with the purpose of creating obstacles to the process of de-mocratization of these countries. In so doing, it also attempts to secure posi-tions for the penetration of American capital into their economies. Such a policy is intended to weaken and overthrow the democratic governments in power there, which are friendly toward the USSR, and replace them in the future with new governments that would obediently carry out a policy dictated from the United States. . . .

. . . [T]he United States is considering the possibility of terminating the Allied occupation of German territory before the main tasks of the occupa-tion — the demilitarization and democratization of Germany — have been implemented. This would create the prerequisites for the revival of an im-perialist Germany, which the United States plans to use in a future war on its side. One cannot help seeing that such a policy has a clearly outlined anti-Soviet edge and constitutes a serious danger to the cause of peace.

The numerous and extremely hostile statements by American government, political, and military figures with regard to the Soviet Union and its foreign policy. . . . are echoed in an even more unrestrained tone by the overwhelm-ing majority of the American press organs. Talk about a "third war," meaning a war against the Soviet Union, and even a direct call for this war — with the threat of using the atomic bomb — such is the content of the statements on relations with the Soviet Union by reactionaries at public meetings and in the press. . . .

The basic goal of this anti-Soviet campaign of American "public opinion" is to exert political pressure on the Soviet Union and compel it to make concessions. Another, no less important goal of the campaign is the attempt to create an atmosphere of war psychosis among the masses, who are weary of war, thus making it easier for the U.S. government to carry out measures for the maintenance of high military potential.

1.7

The Truman Doctrine

In the course of 1947 measured public comment and stifled anger gave way to public expressions of hostility. Truman's speech in March was one watershed. Oc-casioned by a communist guerrilla threat to Greece and Soviet pressure on Turkey, the president decided to take a dramatic stand.

The words leaders use matter: How does Truman represent the contest with the Soviet Union? What values does he invoke in his appeal for public support? Is his language here consistent with his earlier private comments? On what basis did he see the world dividing? Moreover, how those words work in a particular context also matters: Why would Truman have selected the particular language that he did to convince the public? Finally, words acquire meaning over time: To what extent do Truman's comments derive from the views of Wilson and Luce examined earlier (Documents 1.1 and 1.2)?

President Truman
Address to Congress
March 12, 1947

At the present moment in world history nearly every nation must choose between alternative ways of life. The choice is too often not a free one.

One way of life is based upon the will of the majority, and is distinguished by free institutions, representative government, free elections, guarantees of individual liberty, freedom of speech and religion, and freedom from political oppression.

The second way of life is based upon the will of a minority forcibly imposed upon the majority. It relies upon terror and oppression, a controlled press and radio, fixed elections, and the suppression of personal freedoms.

I believe that it must be the policy of the United States to support free peoples who are resisting attempted subjugation by armed minorities or by outside pressures.

I believe that we must assist free peoples to work out their own destinies in their own way.

I believe that our help should be primarily through economic and financial aid which is essential to economic stability and orderly political processes. . . .

Should we fail to aid Greece and Turkey in this fateful hour, the effect will be far reaching to the West as well as to the East.

We must take immediate and resolute action.

I therefore ask the Congress to provide authority for assistance to Greece and Turkey [in the form of a $400 million grant, the dispatch of civilian and military advisers, and the training of Greek and Turkish personnel]. . . .

The seeds of totalitarian regimes are nurtured by misery and want. They spread and grow in the evil soil of poverty and strife. They reach their full growth when the hope of a people for a better life has died.

We must keep that hope alive.

The free peoples of the world look to us for support in maintaining their freedoms.

If we falter in our leadership, we may endanger the peace of the world — and we shall surely endanger the welfare of this Nation.

Public Papers of the Presidents of the United States: Harry S. Truman, 1947 (Washington, D.C.: U.S. Government Printing Office, 1963), 178–80.

1.8
Stalin Responds to U.S. Plans for Europe

Stalin seems at first to have shrugged off the Truman Doctrine in March 1947, but alarm bells went off following the announcement in June of the Marshall Plan (Document 2.9), an ambitious American offer to help rebuild European econo-mies. In September Stalin sent two lieutenants, Molotov and Andrei Zhdanov, to meet in western Poland with the leading European Communist parties (Poland, Hungary, Czechoslovakia, Romania, Bulgaria, Yugoslavia, Italy, and France) for the purposes of countering the U.S. initiatives. The meeting created the Communist Information Bureau (or Cominform) as a means of coordinating the actions of the member parties. Zhdanov spoke to the meeting with Stalin's full authority behind him.

Think about this document as we did the Truman doctrine speech. What kind of language does Zhdanov use to indict U.S. policy and characterize the division of the world? How might his audience have influenced his presentation? And how does he draw on a Marxist worldview previously articulated in Stalin's primer on Leninism and his 1946 election speech (Documents 1.3 and 1.5) to explain U.S. behavior and the likely constraints on U.S. action?

Politburo Member Andrei Zhdanov
Speech at the Inauguration of the Cominform
Late September 1947

A new alignment of political forces has arisen. The more the war recedes into the past, the more distinct become two major trends in post-war interna-tional policy, corresponding to the division of the political forces operating on the international arena into two major camps[:] the imperialist and anti-democratic camp, on the one hand, and the anti-imperialist and democratic camp, on the other. The principal driving force of the imperialist camp is the U.S.A. Allied with it are Great Britain and France. . . . The imperialist camp is also supported by colony-owning countries, such as Belgium and Holland, by countries with reactionary anti-democratic regimes, such as Turkey and Greece, and by countries politically and economically dependent on the United States, such as the Near-Eastern and South-American countries and China.

The cardinal purpose of the imperialist camp is to strengthen imperialism, to hatch a new imperialist war, to combat Socialism and democracy, and to sup-port reactionary and anti-democratic pro-fascist regimes and movements every-where. . . .

The anti-fascist forces comprise the second camp. This camp is based on the U.S.S.R. and the new democracies [of eastern Europe]. It also includes countries that have broken with imperialism and have firmly set foot on the path of democratic development, such as Rumania, Hungary and Finland.

House Committee on Foreign Affairs, *The Strategy and Tactics of World Communism*, 216–17, 223–24, 229.

Indonesia and Viet Nam are associated with it; it has the sympathy of India, Egypt and Syria. The anti-imperialist camp is backed by the labour and democratic movement and by the fraternal Communist parties in all countries, by the fighters for national liberation in the colonies and dependencies, by all progressive and democratic forces in every country. The purpose of this camp is to resist the threat of new wars and imperialist expansion, to strengthen democracy and to extirpate the vestiges of fascism....

... [T]he expansionist ambitions of the United States find concrete expression in the Truman doctrine and the Marshall Plan....

The main features of the Truman doctrine as applied to Europe are as follows:

1. Creation of American bases in the Eastern Mediterranean with the purpose of establishing American supremacy in that area.

2. Demonstrative support of the reactionary regimes in Greece and Turkey as bastions of American imperialism against the new democracies in the Balkans....

3. Unintermitting pressure on the countries of the new democracy, as expressed in false accusations of totalitarianism and expansionist ambitions, in attacks on the foundations of the new democratic regime[s], in constant interference in their domestic affairs, in support of all anti-national, anti-democratic elements within these countries, and in the demonstrative breaking off of economic relations with these countries with the idea of creating economic difficulties, retarding their economic development, preventing their industrialization, and so on.

The Truman doctrine, which provides for the rendering of American assistance to all reactionary regimes which actively oppose the democratic peoples, bears a frankly aggressive character.... Progressive public elements in the USA and other countries vigorously protested against the provocative and frankly imperialistic character of Truman's announcement.

The unfavorable reception which the Truman doctrine was met with accounts for the necessity of the appearance of the Marshall Plan[,] which is a more carefully veiled attempt to carry through the same expansionist policy.

The vague and deliberately guarded formulations of the Marshall Plan amount in essence to a scheme to create a bloc of states bound by obligations to the United States, and to grant American credits to European countries as a recompense for their renunciation of economic, and then of political, independence. Moreover, the cornerstone of the Marshall Plan is the restoration of the industrial areas of Western Germany controlled by the American monopolies.

It is the design of the Marshall Plan ... to render aid in the first place, not to the impoverished victor countries, America's allies in the fight against Germany, but to the German capitalists, with the idea of bringing under American sway the major sources of coal and iron needed by Europe and by Germany, and of making the countries which are in need of coal and iron dependent on the restored economic might of Germany....

... The need for mutual consultation and voluntary coordination of action between individual [European Communist] parties has become particularly urgent at the present juncture. ...

... [T]here has devolved upon the Communists the special historical task of leading the resistance to the American plan for the enthrallment of Europe, and of boldly denouncing all coadjutors of American imperialism in their own countries. ... The Communists must be the leaders in enlisting all anti-fascist and freedom-loving elements in the struggle against the new American expansionist plans for the enslavement of Europe.

1.9

Responses to the Enemy Threat

The momentum toward rivalry that gathered during 1947 continued in the years that followed. Stalin tightened his grip on eastern Europe, while the Truman administration settled on a policy of containing any Soviet expansionist impulse. Washington began by building alliances, first in Latin America and western Europe. In 1949 the Soviet Union tested its first atomic bomb, thus breaking the American monopoly, and Communist forces took power in China.

Following this series of events, both sides had good reason to step back and take stock. The major U.S. assessment was a top-secret report drafted in early 1950 by Paul Nitze, head of the State Department's Policy Planning Staff, for the National Security Council. On April 12, 1950 President Truman gave his approval to the general analysis developed in this report (known as NSC 68) but not to its specific recommendations for a dramatic boost in military spending. After the outbreak of the Korean War in June, Truman put those spending recommendations into effect. The most revealing Soviet assessment dates from 1952 when an elderly and ailing Stalin intervened in a theoretical debate over whether leading capitalist countries faced the major economic crisis predicted by Marxist theory to mark the beginning of the end of the capitalist system. How Stalin decided to resolve this theoretical issue reveals a great deal about his picture of the postwar world and the relative strengths of capitalism and socialism.

On the basis of these two documents, how intractable would you judge the conflict between the United States and the Soviet Union by the early 1950s? What was at the heart of the contest? Are the positions taken here consistent with earlier ones or a break from them? Which side appears to have felt the most confident in its position?

National Security Council Report 68 (NSC 68)

April 7, 1950

Within the past thirty-five years the world has experienced two global wars of tremendous violence. It has witnessed two revolutions — the Russian and the Chinese — of extreme scope and intensity. It has also seen the collapse of five empires — the Ottoman, the Austro-Hungarian, German, Italian, and Japanese — and the drastic decline of two major imperial systems, the British and the French. During the span of one generation, the international distribution of power has been fundamentally altered. For several centuries it had proved impossible for any one nation to gain such preponderant strength that a coalition of other nations could not in time face it with greater strength. The international scene was marked by recurring periods of violence and war, but a system of sovereign and independent states was maintained, over which no state was able to achieve hegemony.

. . . [T]he Soviet Union, unlike previous aspirants to hegemony, is animated by a new fanatic faith, antithetical to our own, and seeks to impose its absolute authority over the rest of the world. Conflict has, therefore, become endemic and is waged, on the part of the Soviet Union, by violent or non-violent methods in accordance with the dictates of expediency. With the development of increasingly terrifying weapons of mass destruction, every individual faces the ever-present possibility of annihilation should the conflict enter the phase of total war.

. . . It is in this context that this Republic and its citizens in the ascendancy of their strength stand in their deepest peril.

The issues that face us are momentous, involving the fulfillment or destruction not only of this republic but of civilization itself. . . .

. . . Soviet efforts are now directed toward the domination of the Eurasian land mass. The United States, as the principal center of power in the non-Soviet world and the bulwark of opposition to Soviet expansion, is the principal enemy whose integrity and vitality must be subverted or destroyed by one means or another if the Kremlin is to achieve its fundamental design.

The Kremlin regards the United States as the only major threat to the achievement of its fundamental design. There is a basic conflict between the idea of freedom under a government of laws, and the idea of slavery under the grim oligarchy of the Kremlin. . . . The idea of freedom, moreover, is peculiarly and intolerably subversive of the idea of slavery. . . .

The free society values the individual as an end in himself, requiring of him only that measure of self-discipline and self-restraint which make the rights of each individual compatible with the rights of every other individual. . . .

. . . The free society attempts to create and maintain an environment in which every individual has the opportunity to realize his creative powers. It also explains why the free society tolerates those within it who would use their freedom to destroy it. By the same token, in relations between nations, the prime reliance of the free society is on the strength and appeal of its idea, and it feels no compulsion sooner or later to bring all societies into conformity with it.

For the free society does not fear, it welcomes, diversity. It derives its strength from its hospitality even to antipathetic ideas. It is a market for free trade in

"United States Objectives and Programs for National Security," in *FRUS, 1950,* vol. 1 (Washington, D.C.: U.S. Government Printing Office, 1977), 237–42, 252, 255, 265–67, 285.

ideas, secure in its faith that free men will take the best wares, and grow to a fuller and better realization of their powers in exercising their choice.

The idea of freedom is the most contagious idea in history, more contagious than the idea of submission to authority. For the breadth of freedom cannot be tolerated in a society which has come under the domination of an individual or group of individuals with a will to absolute power. . . .

The assault on free institutions is world-wide now, and in the context of the present polarization of power a defeat of free institutions anywhere is a defeat everywhere. . . .

Thus unwillingly our free society finds itself mortally challenged by the Soviet system. No other value system is so wholly irreconcilable with ours, so implacable in its purpose to destroy ours, so capable of turning to its own uses the most dangerous and divisive trends in our own society, no other so skillfully and powerfully evokes the elements of irrationality in human nature everywhere, and no other has the support of a great and growing center of military power. . . .

In a shrinking world, which now faces the threat of atomic warfare, it is not an adequate objective merely to seek to check the Kremlin design, for the absence of order among nations is becoming less and less tolerable. This fact imposes on us, in our own interests, the responsibility of world leadership. It demands that we make the attempt, and accept the risks inherent in it, to bring about order and justice by means consistent with the principles of freedom and democracy. . . .

. . . It is only by developing the moral and material strength of the free world that the Soviet regime will become convinced of the falsity of its assumptions and that the pre-conditions for workable agreements can be created. . . .

. . . [T]he policy of "containment" . . . seeks by all means short of war to (1) block further expansion of Soviet power, (2) expose the falsities of Soviet pretensions, (3) induce a retraction of the Kremlin's control and influence, and (4) in general, so foster the seeds of destruction within the Soviet system that the Kremlin is brought at least to the point of modifying its behavior to conform to generally accepted international standards. . . .

As we ourselves demonstrate power, confidence, and a sense of moral and political direction, so those same qualities will be evoked in Western Europe. In such a situation, we may also anticipate a general improvement in the political tone in Latin America, Asia, and Africa and the real beginnings of awakening among the Soviet totalitariat.

In the absence of affirmative decision on our part, the rest of the free world is almost certain to become demoralized. Our friends will become more than a liability to us; they can eventually become a positive increment to Soviet power. . . .

. . . [T]here are risks in making ourselves strong. A large measure of sacrifice and discipline will be demanded of the American people. They will be asked to give up some of the benefits which they have come to associate with their freedoms. . . .

It is estimated that, within the next four years, the U.S.S.R. will attain the [atomic] capability of seriously damaging vital centers of the United States, provided it strikes a surprise blow and provided further that the blow is opposed by no more effective opposition than we now have programmed. Such a blow could so seriously damage the United States as to greatly reduce its superiority in economic potential. . . .

A further increase in the number and power of our atomic weapons is necessary in order to assure the effectiveness of any U.S. retaliatory blow . . . . Greatly increased general air, ground and sea strength, and increased air defense and civilian defense programs would also be necessary to provide reasonable assurance that the free world could survive an initial surprise atomic attack of the weight which it is estimated the U.S.S.R. will be capable of delivering by 1954 and still permit the free world to go on to the eventual attainment of its objectives. Furthermore, such a build-up of strength could safeguard and increase our retaliatory power, and thus might put off for some time the date when the Soviet Union could calculate that a surprise blow would be advantageous. This would provide additional time for the effects of our policies to produce a modification of the Soviet system. . . .

A program for rapidly building up strength and improving political and economic conditions will place heavy demands on our courage and intelligence; it will be costly; it will be dangerous. But half-measures will be more costly and more dangerous, for they will be inadequate to prevent and may actually invite war. Budgetary considerations will need to be subordinated to the stark fact that our very independence as a nation may be at stake.

Joseph Stalin
Remarks on the Destructive Contradictions within Capitalism
February 1, 1952

[As a result of World War II] Germany and Japan were put out of action as competitors of the three major capitalist countries: the U.S.A., Great Britain and France. But at the same time China and the European people's democracies broke away from the capitalist system and, together with the Soviet Union, formed a united and powerful socialist camp confronting the camp of capitalism. The economic consequences of the existence of two opposite camps was that the single all-embracing world market disintegrated, so that now we have two parallel world markets also confronting one another. . . .

. . . [I]t follows from this that the sphere of exploitation of the world's resources by the major capitalist countries (U.S.A., Britain, France) will not

"Remarks on Economic Questions Connected with the November Discussion," in Joseph Stalin, *Economic Problems of Socialism in the U.S.S.R.* (New York: International Publishers, 1952), 26–30.

expand, but contract; that their opportunities for sale in the world market will deteriorate, and their industries will be operating more and more below capacity. . . .

. . . They are trying to offset these difficulties with the "Marshall Plan," the war in Korea, frantic rearmament, and industrial militarization. But that is very much like a drowning man clutching at a straw. . . .

Some comrades hold that, owing to the development of new international conditions since the Second World War, wars between capitalist countries have ceased to be inevitable. They consider that the contradictions between the socialist camp and the capitalist camp are more acute than the contradictions among the capitalist countries; that the U.S.A. has brought the other capitalist countries sufficiently under its sway to be able to prevent them going to war among themselves and weakening one another; that the foremost capitalist minds have been sufficiently taught by the two world wars and the severe damage they caused to the whole capitalist world not to venture to involve the capitalist countries in war with one another again — and that, because of all this, wars between capitalist countries are no longer inevitable.

These comrades are mistaken. . . .

Outwardly, everything would seem to be "going well": the U.S.A. has put Western Europe, Japan and other capitalist countries on rations; Germany (Western), Britain, France, Italy and Japan have fallen into the clutches of the U.S.A. and are meekly obeying its commands. But it would be mistaken to think . . . that these countries will tolerate the domination and oppression of the United States endlessly, that they will not endeavor to tear loose from American bondage and take the path of independent development. . . .

. . . Would it not be truer to say that capitalist Britain, and, after her, capitalist France, will be compelled in the end to break from the embrace of the U.S.A. and enter into conflict with it in order to secure an independent position and, of course, high profits? . . .

It is said that the contradictions between capitalism and socialism are stronger than the contradictions among the capitalist countries. Theoretically, of course, that is true. . . . Yet the Second World War began not as a war with the U.S.S.R., but as a war between capitalist countries. Why? Firstly, because war with the U.S.S.R., as a socialist land, is more dangerous to capitalism than war between capitalist countries; for whereas war between capitalist countries puts in question only the supremacy of certain capitalist countries over others, war with the U.S.S.R. must certainly put in question the existence of capitalism itself. Secondly, because the capitalists, although they clamor, for "propaganda" purposes, about the aggressiveness of the Soviet Union, do not themselves believe that it is aggressive, because they are aware of the Soviet Union's peaceful policy and know that it will not itself attack capitalist countries. . . .

Consequently, the struggle of the capitalist countries for markets and their desire to crush their competitors proved in practice to be stronger than the contradictions between the capitalist camp and the socialist camp. . . .

. . . [I]t follows from this that the inevitability of wars between the capitalist countries remains in force.

THE COLD WAR AT HOME

Wars, cold no less than hot, have pervasive repercussions. Leaders and diplomats may be the first to sense the rivalry, but almost inevitably modern states seek to mobilize their citizens. Official propaganda popularizes the terms of the conflict as leaders see it and asks for popular support and sacrifices. As some beliefs become heretical and some citizens fall under suspicion, the chill spreads from the rarified realm of policy to everyday life.

In considering these documents, it is worth comparing the justification for mobilization and repression in a time of trial with the experience of ordinary people caught up in the repression. It is also worth comparing the justifications both sides used for bringing the Cold War home, the scope of those placed under suspicion, and the actual treatment they received.

1.10
Soviet Society Feels the Chill

The widespread hope for a postwar thaw in the Soviet Union — less political repression, more cultural openness, and more consumer goods — suffered the first of a series of blows in September 1946. Zhdanov, the Soviet leader in charge of cultural affairs, fired the first shot in what would prove intensifying pressure for orthodoxy and mobilization. As Cold War tensions rose, the hunt for spies and skeptics intensified. Where are the sources of the domestic weakness that Zhdanov points to? Why are these weak points worrying to him?

One of the victims of this new wave of repression was Dmitry Mironovich Stonov (1892–1962). He had joined the Bolsheviks as a young man in the first years of the Soviet regime, but left the party in disillusionment and began life anew in Moscow as a newspaper correspondent and the author of fiction. Late one evening in March 1949, as Stalin's suspicions began to focus on Jewish intellectuals, came the knock at the door. Arrested on charges of anti-Soviet activity, he gave a forced confession and received a ten-year sentence. While in prison he recorded his stories on cigarette paper, which was then smuggled out for safekeeping. "Seven Slashes" is the first that Stonov wrote, describing his seven days of isolation in a cramped, cold "cabinet." In this fictional rendering Stonov names his protagonist Mironov after his own middle name, and makes him an architect who has already undergone five months of interrogation in the infamous Lubyanka detention center in the middle of Moscow. Only the portion of the story dealing with the first and last day of the Stonov/Mironov encounter with the cabinet made it out of the prison. Stonov was released in August 1954 as the first of a tide of revoked sentences following Stalin's death, but he was never able to bring himself to reconstruct the lost portion of this story.

Fiction as a historical source is appealing because of its power to capture the feel of a time and place. In this case it allows us to put ourselves in the shoes of the victims of Stalinist repression and to consider what our reactions would have been in the circumstances. But fiction also raises the potential problem of the author's imagination carrying the story out of the realm of the real. We are thus left to wonder why Stonov chose to portray his ordeal through the medium of fiction rather than a memoir, and where he may have exaggerated for artistic effect.

Andrei Zhdanov
Speech Published in Pravda
September 21, 1946

Some of our writers began to look upon themselves not as teachers but as pupils of bourgeois-philistine writers, began to adopt a tone of obsequiousness and worship before philistine foreign literature. Is such obsequiousness becoming to us, Soviet patriots, to us, who have built the Soviet social order, which is a hundred times higher and better than any bourgeois social order? Does it become our advanced Soviet literature, the most revolutionary literature in the world, to bow low before the narrow philistine-bourgeois literature of the West? . . .

The bourgeois world is not pleased by our success both within our country and in the international arena. As a result of World War II the positions of socialism have been fortified. The question of socialism has been placed on the order of the day in many European countries. This displeases imperialists of all hues; they are afraid of socialism, afraid of our socialist country, which is a model for the whole of advanced humanity. The imperialists and their ideological henchmen, their writers and journalists, their politicians and diplomats strive in every way to slander our country, to present it in a false light, to slander socialism. In these conditions the task of Soviet literature is not only to reply, blow for blow, to all this base slander and the attacks on our Soviet culture, on socialism, but also boldly to lash and attack bourgeois culture, which is in a state of marasmus [wasting away] and corruption.

However outwardly beautiful the form that clothes the creations of the fashionable modern bourgeois western European and American writers, and also film and theatrical producers, they still cannot rescue or raise up their bourgeois culture, for its moral foundation is rotten and baneful, for this culture has been put at the service of private capitalist property, at the service of the egoistic, selfish interests of the bourgeois upper layers of society. The whole host of bourgeois writers, film and theatrical producers is striving to distract the attention of the advanced strata of society from the acute questions of the political and social struggle and to divert their attention into the channel of vulgar, ideologically empty literature and art, replete with gangsters, chorus girls, eulogies of adultery, and of the doings of all sorts of adventurers and rogues. . . .

. . . [T]he writer must educate the people and arm them ideologically. While selecting the best feelings and qualities of the Soviet man and revealing his tomorrow, we must at the same time show our people what they must not be, we must castigate the remnants of yesterday, remnants that hinder the Soviet people in their forward march. Soviet writers must help the people, the state, and the party to educate our youth to be cheerful and confident of their own strength, unafraid of any difficulties.

Andrei Zhdanov, *Essays on Literature, Philosophy, and Music* (New York: International Publishers, 1950), 27, 41–43.

Dmitry Stonov
"Seven Slashes"

The charges on the paper were brief. The stoop-shouldered lieutenant read them perfunctorily: "For provocative behavior during investigation, seven days in the cabinet."

"What behavior? What provocation?" asked Mironov desperately.

"You know better than I do," answered the officer and hurried out. The guards hurried as well. Lifting Mironov by both elbows, they swept him down the steps, down and down past several floors and then, on the last — the lowest — they stopped. The corridor was half-dark. At the end, under a dim bulb, they searched Mironov and told him to take off his clothes. Bewildered, Mironov took off his jacket. "Faster," ordered the guards, "take off everything." His fingers wouldn't obey and opened the buttons awkwardly. "Everything, everything," they hurried him, "leave only your socks and your underwear."

They pushed Mironov thus clad into the cabinet, and then they locked the door.

Mironov took a shuddering breath. "So . . ." he whispered thoughtfully. Looking around, he saw that the box was a rectangle — very high, without windows, and just three feet in every direction. On the ceiling, caught in a metal net, blazed a bright bulb. Into the wall opposite the door a bench had been built.

Perspiring, yet chilled to the bone, Mironov sat. He sensed he was doing something he had never done before; his hands were tucked beneath his buttocks and he was sitting on them for warmth. . . .

Mironov listened to the steady stream of words tattooing in his head. Underneath them he sensed a layer of poison, but still he was touched to tears. Breathing heavily, he stood. Since it was impossible to walk in any direction, he shifted from one foot to the other. Another click sounded in the eye of the door. Mironov sat, and again, though he blocked his ears and shook his head, the words continued to resound.

"Lev Vasilyevich Mironov didn't become an artist. He became an architect, greatly respected and admired. In the whole city there might be only a few who failed to know it was he who had designed and built the theater, the post office, and the magnificent railway depot. Then swiftly and suddenly, in one dark disastrous moment, all that melted away forever. Forever! Vile people roared at him in vile, repellent voices. Who was this miserable puffy man in his blue underwear and striped socks? Lev Vasilyevich Mironov? Nonsense. Nonsense. Lev Vasilyevich Mironov had vanished from the face of the earth forever. In his place, with his hands beneath his buttocks, sat a good-for-nothing convict — no longer called person but prostitute.["]

Dmitry Stonov, *In the Past Night: The Siberian Stories,* trans. Natasha Stonov and Kathryn Darrell (Lubbock, Texas: Texas Tech University Press, 1995), 175–77, 179–81, 183, 185, 189–90.

Agonized, Mironov cried out, "Stop! No more, no more!" The peeping eye opened sharply. The guard shouted in a loud voice that flattened against the wall, "It is forbidden to speak!" The words with which he answered would be the last Mironov would utter while he was in the cage. Like a little boy caught in mischief, Mironov flushed and said, "I didn't know." Hearing himself, he wondered from where this weak, whining sound of a supplicant had suddenly come — the voice of a slave. Maybe Lev Vasilyevich had not just vanished a moment ago. Maybe he had been lost for a long time. "I won't do it again," he whispered and wanted to weep. . . .

. . . Mironov asked to be taken to the toilet. Stepping out in the corridor, he felt unfettered, and it was much easier for him to breathe. But how good it was in the foul-smelling toilet! To him the air seemed full and clean. The sun was rising beyond the open window. Behind the bars there was a lilac sky. . . . Even more, he reveled in the sounds. It had to be about six in the morning, no less. "After all," he thought, "after all, twelve hours have passed. How many more remain? When I go to the cabinet, I can count there."

But when he returned, the small space gripped him like a vise. Deafened by the silence, his mouth open and gasping for stale air, he stood in the middle of his tomb. Stretching his arms, he tried to extend them to their fullest. It was not possible; the distance was too small. Rage enveloped him and he wanted to stamp his feet against the floor. "No! It's not to be borne. What monster devised this obscenity?" He thought of all the ordinary people who happily made their homes adjacent to this seemingly innocuous place of horror. "All of you decent citizens, raising your children and prattling about truth and justice. How do you dare live without guilt, right next door to this building?" Rage had exhausted him and, still sweating, he lowered himself onto the bench. Rocking from side to side — because sitting had already become awkward — he realized that, until quite recently, he himself had belonged to those good people babbling about honesty and respect for humankind. Huge monoliths like this in the middle of the city had never deterred him from living quietly and immersing himself in his work. . . .

But what about the jail physicians? The whole staff of doctors, nurses, and aides? Mironov turned his thoughts toward them. For two months, an epileptic student had been sitting in the cell. With every day his health deteriorated. His seizures came more often, his falls to the floor bruised his whole body, for long hours he lay in a coma. How many times did the convicts beg that the student be taken to the infirmary? But the doctor, that gray old man, had never considered it necessary even to answer them. And the student had not been alone. There had been the artist who was consumptive. After every interrogation, blood would rush from his throat. The doctor would check his temperature then casually move away. At night, this same clean, perfumed doctor would sit in the circle of his family, and his three-year-old grandson would come to him, babbling words that touched his heart. Filled with love, the old doctor would toss him up in the air. . . .

And what could be said about the rest of them — the vast staff of investigators, detectives, secret agents, stenographers, typists, rude and ignorant guards? . . .

...He had understood nothing. Nothing! He was trapped inside an animal's den, where every second was equal to an hour; where all day and all night the eternal bulb would burn with unnatural brilliance — itself trapped in a wire cage. No. He was doomed never to leave this coffin; the stuffiness would suffocate him and, dying, he would still be blinded by the deadly, dazzling light. "Lost!" he moaned. . . . "Lost. Forever lost. Forever lost." . . .

. . . [T]he eye [in the door] slid open and the guard pushed through half the usual ration of bread and one cup of boiled water.

Mironov wasn't hungry that day, nor would he be on those that followed; still — without knowing why — he was overjoyed by the sight of the bread. For several long seconds he lifted it in the palm of one hand, then shifted it to the other. Now he had to divide it into three parts — breakfast, dinner, and supper. Taking his time, he scored it evenly then tore it into three equal pieces. Unwillingly, he forced himself to let them go, placing each on the bench with an equal distance between them.

What had happened? Absolutely nothing. He, Mironov, had been given his earned ration of bread, that was all. So why was he so excited, so overjoyed?

Suddenly, it swept over him. He was sentenced to the box for seven days and nights. During these seven days and nights, he would receive seven daily rations. Bread. The bread could be the measure of his time! One portion had already been received — therefore one day no longer existed. Now it was truly possible to subtract it from the total number — and now he had a new number — not seven but six.

Mironov looked quickly at the eye. It was closed. Decisively, with a burst of speed that was no longer characteristic of him, he rushed to the wall near the bench. There, with his thumbnail, he scratched a line no longer than a match — one slash. "Done!" he exclaimed with exuberance. Incredibly, he was happy. The slash was visible from three feet away. He sat on the bench. By turning his head, he could even see the slash while he was seated. Upon awakening, he would be able to see it instantly. . . .

He sat with his head drooping down, practically between his spread legs. His arms hung lifelessly at his side. On the wall, toward his left, were the seven slashes. It was possible to make them out again, to try to check them again, but he sat as if paralyzed, without moving or even turning his head. The slashes no longer interested him. How could anything possibly interest him now? In his youth he had never been able to face the fact of his death; it had maddened him. Never, even in the years that followed, could he think quietly about his end. But in prison, among strange people on strange beds with straw-filled pillows, the thought of death was never far away. The postmortem, the protocol, the legal papers and finally — in the late night — the body with the nameplate on the ankle rolling inexorably toward the crematorium. While the surrounding city slept, a truck with a crate was rushing down the road. Inside the crate — growing cold, growing stiff — would be his body. The flame, the all-consuming flame, then the ashes — cast into some unknown pit or just tossed into the wind. With great difficulty, struggling against an immobilizing lassitude, he lifted his shirt and looked at his chest.

It was about to become a handful of ashes.

He listened to his thought but was completely unmoved by it. It melted as quickly as it materialized. There was a family he loved, who lived less than a kilometer away from where he was entombed. It was an unattainable place, and he would never see them again. Never. But even that failed to arouse any emotion. Even that failed to terrify him. He wanted only to sit motionless and never move again.

The guards appeared in the cabinet. In the glaring light he saw their polished boots, inhaled the scent of their shoe polish. They could shoot him or hang him; it was all the same. They had brought his clothing. Dimly, he wondered why. They ordered him to put it on. The harsh voices hurt his ears. How difficult it was to dress, to force himself to act. How exhausting to pull on the prison pants, to pull the boots over his bloated legs.

Looking as if he had aged twenty years, hardly shifting his swollen feet, he shuffled over the threshold of his cell.

1.11
The "Red Menace" in the United States

Two weeks after the Truman doctrine speech, the head of the Federal Bureau of Investigation, J. Edgar Hoover, made a rare appearance before a congressional committee. His testimony to the revealingly named House Un-American Activities Committee (better known as HUAC) addressed the Soviet menace from a domestic direction. The concrete consequences of this fear of subversion at home become evident in the case of a postal worker investigated for past associations and activities under the internal security laws aimed at federal employees. Doubting his loyalty, the reviewing commission deprived him of his job.

Wars, even cold ones, are marked by fear of the enemy that leads to the use of language that almost always appears in retrospect astonishing. What expressions does Hoover use to characterize the communist enemy? Where does he see the points of American vulnerability? Set Hoover's abstract fear alongside the practical application of security measures in the case of the postal worker. How might Hoover and the postal worker have differed in their understanding of the Cold War and of freedom? To what extent do we get an insight on U.S. and Soviet popular views through examining the cases of the postal worker and of Stonov?

FBI Director J. Edgar Hoover
Testimony before HUAC on the Communist Threat
March 26, 1947

The Communist movement in the United States . . . . stands for the destruction of our American form of government; it stands for the destruction of American democracy; it stands for the destruction of free enterprise; and it

---

Ellen Schrecker, *The Age of McCarthyism: A Brief History with Documents* (Boston: Bedford Books, 1994), 114, 119–20.

stands for the creation of a "Soviet of the United States" and ultimate world revolution. . . .

. . . The best antidote to communism is vigorous, intelligent, old-fashioned Americanism with eternal vigilance. I do not favor any course of action which would give the Communists cause to portray and pity themselves as martyrs. I do favor unrelenting prosecution wherever they are found to be violating our country's laws.

As Americans, our most effective defense is a workable democracy that guarantees and preserves our cherished freedoms.

I would have no fears if more Americans possessed the zeal, the fervor, the persistence, and the industry to learn about this menace of Red fascism. I do fear for the liberal and progressive who has been hoodwinked and duped into joining hands with the Communists. I confess to a real apprehension so long as Communists are able to secure ministers of the gospel to promote their evil work and espouse a cause that is alien to the religion of Christ and Judaism. I do fear so long as school boards and parents tolerate conditions whereby Communists and fellow travelers, under the guise of academic freedom, can teach our youth a way of life that eventually will destroy the sanctity of the home, that undermine[s] faith in God, that causes them to scorn respect for constituted authority and sabotage our revered Constitution.

I do fear so long as American labor groups are infiltrated, dominated, or saturated with the virus of communism. I do fear the palliation and weasel-worded gestures against communism indulged in by some of our labor leaders who should know better but who have become pawns in the hands of sinister but astute manipulations for the Communist cause.

I fear for ignorance on the part of all our people who may take the poisonous pills of Communist propaganda. . . .

The Communists have been, still are, and always will be a menace to freedom, to democratic ideals, to the worship of God, and to America's way of life.

I feel that once public opinion is thoroughly aroused as it is today, the fight against communism is well on its way. Victory will be assured once Communists are identified and exposed, because the public will take the first step of quarantining them so they can do no harm. Communism, in reality, is not a political party. It is a way of life — an evil and malignant way of life. It reveals a condition akin to disease that spreads like an epidemic and like an epidemic a quarantine is necessary to keep it from infecting the Nation.

Report of an Investigation of a Postal Worker under the Federal Loyalty-Security Program
1954

In late February 1954, the employee was working in a clerical capacity as a substitute postal employee. He performed no supervisory duties. His tasks were routine in nature.

One year prior to the initiation of proceedings, the employee had resigned from his position as an executive officer of a local union whose parent union had been expelled from the CIO[1] in 1949 as Communist dominated. The employee had served as an officer for one year prior to the expulsion, had helped to lead his local out of the expelled parent and back into the CIO, and had thereafter remained in an executive capacity until his resignation in 1953. He resigned from that position upon being appointed a substitute clerk with the United States Post Office in early 1953. . . .

In the last week of February 1954, the employee received notice, by mail, that he was under investigation by the Regional Office of the United States Civil Service Commission. . . .

[The employee immediately answered the first set of charges against him only to be suspended without pay at the end of March on the following charges:]

"3. In January 1948, your name appeared on a general mailing list of the Spanish Refugee Appeal of the Joint Anti-Fascist Refugee Committee.[2] . . .

"5. Your wife . . . was a member of the . . . Club of the Young Communist League.[3]

"6. In 1950, Communist literature was observed in the bookshelves and Communist art was seen on the walls of your residence in ———.

"7. Your signature appeared on a Communist Party nominating petition in the November 1941 Municipal Elections in ———.

"8. You falsely replied 'No' on your Standard Form 60, 'Application for Federal Employment,' in answer to question 16, which is as follows: 'Are you now, or have you ever been, a member of the Communist Party, USA, or any Communist or Fascist organization?'" . . .

The employee had a hearing four months later, in July 1954. The members of the board were three (3) civilian employees of military installations.

---

[1]Congress of Industrial Organizations, a labor initiative aimed at unskilled workers. — M.H.

[2]The Joint Anti-Fascist Refugee Committee was a so-called front group that had been organized to help antifascist refugees from the Spanish Civil War. It was on the attorney general's list.

[3]The Young Communist League was the Communist party's youth organization from the 1920s to the 1940s. It was on the attorney general's list.

Schrecker, *The Age of McCarthyism*, 156–60. Information in the footnotes and in brackets in the text supplied by Schrecker unless otherwise noted.

None of them were attorneys. The Post Office establishment was represented by an Inspector, who administered the oath to the employee and his witnesses, but did not otherwise participate in the proceedings. There was no attorney-adviser to the Board. There was no testimony by witnesses hostile to the employee, nor was any evidence introduced against him. . . .

. . . Before the employee testified, he submitted a nine-page autobiography to the Hearing Board. . . .

. . . The autobiography set forth in some detail the employee's activities as an officer of his local union, and discussed particularly his role therein as an anti-Communist. . . . The employee's autobiography recited . . . that the victory of the employee and his supporters represented a victory over Communist adherents in the local, and that the employee was the frequent target of threats and slander by the pro-Communist faction of his local. . . .

With respect to the third charge against the employee (that his name had been on a general mailing list of the Spanish Refugee Appeal of the Joint Anti-Fascist Refugee Committee), the employee reiterated his denial of any knowledge concerning it, and his counsel reminded the Board that no Attorney General's list existed in January 1948 — the date contained in the charge. The employee testified, further, that he had no recollection of ever having received any mail from the organization involved. . . .

With respect to charge No. 5 against the employee (that his wife had been a member of the Young Communist League), the Chairman of the Hearing Board advised the employee that the date involved was March 1944. The employee testified that he and his wife were married in February 1944, and that the charge was ridiculous. He testified, further, that he had no independent recollection that his wife was ever a member of the said organization. In addition, the employee testified that he had never lived in the neighborhood in which the organization was alleged to have existed, and that he had never heard of said organization. . . .

The Chairman then read charge No. 6 in which it was alleged that Communist literature was observed in the employee's bookshelves at home and Communist art was seen on the walls of his residence in 1950. Immediately following his reading of the charge, the Chairman stated that:

"The Board is at a loss just to what Communist literature they are referring to."

Counsel for the employee then questioned him concerning his courses in college, and the books which he was there required to read for those courses. In this connection, counsel for the employee asked whether books had been recommended as part of study courses by instructors, and whether one of these books had been *Das Kapital* by Karl Marx, and whether the employee had bought *Das Kapital*, following such a recommendation. The employee responded that certain books had been recommended by his instructors, that *Das Kapital* was one. . . .

Counsel then asked the employee whether, in 1950, he had reproductions of paintings by great painters hanging on the walls of his home, and following the employee's answer in the affirmative, counsel asked him to name some of the artists whose reproductions were hanging upon the walls of the employee's home. The employee named Picasso, Matisse, Renoir, and Moddigliotti [Modigliani?].

Counsel then asked the employee whether pictures by those artists were hanging in museums, including the largest museum in the city in which the employee resides, and following the employee's answer in the affirmative, counsel asked whether there was "any relationship between the art and the Communist Party." The employee responded that he had "no idea of what any relationship there might be that exists there at all."

Thereafter, in response to counsel's question, the employee testified that he had not read *Das Kapital* in its entirety, that he had been required to read "a chapter or two for classwork," and that "he had found it a little dull and tedious." . . .

The Chairman read charge No. 7, in which it was alleged that the employee's signature appeared on a Communist Party nominating petition in 1941 municipal elections in the employee's home city.

The employee had answered this charge by stating that he had signed such a petition; that in 1941, the Communist Party appeared on the initial ballot; that his recollection was that on the cover page of the petition it stated that the signers were not members of the Communist Party, and that prior to 1941 and at all times thereafter, the employee had been registered as a member of one of the two major political parties, and that he had no recollection of voting for any political party other than one of the two major political parties. . . .

Thereafter, counsel for the employee objected to the charge on the ground that the signing of a petition for a party which had a legal place on the ballot in 1941 had no relationship to present security. The Chairman then asked the employee to recall the circumstances in which his signature had been solicited in 1941. The employee responded by stating that, so far as he could recall, someone came down the street and seeing him working on the premises asked him to sign the petition, after explaining the petition to him. In response to a question by a member of the Board, the employee stated that he did not know the person who had solicited his signature, and that he had never seen or heard from him thereafter, nor had he thereafter heard from the Communist Party.

[At the hearing, the employee and his attorney sought unsuccessfully to find out the basis for the final charge against him that he had been in the Communist party or other Communist or fascist organization. In September 1954, the employee was dismissed from his job. He then appealed to the regional director of the Civil Service Commission, who reaffirmed his dismissal. The case then went to the Civil Service Commission in Washington, whose chair upheld the regional director's ruling in February 1955 with the following explanation:]

"A careful study of the facts in Mr. ———'s case has been completed. It has been established and he has admitted that he signed a petition in November 1941 that the Communist party be placed on the ballot in the ———— municipal elections. . . . His name was reported as being on the general mailing list of the Joint Anti-Fascist Refugee Committee. . . . Mrs. ———— is reported as having been at one time a member of the ———— Club of Young Communist League.

"Mr. ———— was an officer of Local ———— of the [parent union] at the time this organization was expelled from the CIO because of Communist domination. Consideration has been given to information that he was reputed to be one of the leaders of the anti-Communist group which brought Local ———— back into the CIO as the ————. However, it is not felt that this information sufficiently outweighs his reported connections with organizations and individuals whose interests and aims are inimical to those of the United States. . . ."

CHAPTER 2

THE INTERNATIONAL ECONOMY: REFORM AND REVIVAL

THE LATTER HALF OF THE 1940s was a transitional moment in the world economy. The flourishing system of global trade and investment that arose in the course of the nineteenth century suffered a series of reversals early in the twentieth century — two world wars, a sustained and worldwide depression, and a marked trend toward sealing off national economies. As World War II ended, the future was by no means clear. One possibility was that the world's economy would continue to fragment into a collection of inward-oriented national units. A second possibility was that reconstruction of war-devastated societies would stumble, giving rise to pervasive impoverishment and political discontent. Yet a third possibility was that a concerted and successful effort would revitalize and reintegrate the advanced sectors of the world economy.

As it turned out, the last of these proved the dominant trend. The documents in this chapter provide insight not only on the wartime destruction but also on people's dogged determination to reconstruct their lives. Like damaged tissue, societies showed impressive powers of healing. But the sort of economic system that should emerge from this healing process was a matter of notable contention. In the wide-ranging discussions over this issue, the problem of reconciling free-market principles with aspirations for democracy and freedom was at the forefront. In both the process of recovery and the debate over economic principles, the United States assumed an influential position as a source of capital, a major market for foreign exporters, a model of mass consumption, and an exporter in its own right of cultural products and influences seductive to some and deeply disturbing to others.

In reading the material to follow, perhaps the single most important issue is how far did Americans go toward creating a world of trade and investment that worked on their terms and how much did the outcome reflect the diverse interests and outlooks of Europeans and Japanese. Underlying this question is the long-term problem of how much the international economy tends toward uniformity and how much toward a plurality of practices.

THE JAPANESE COPE WITH THE DEVASTATION OF WAR

The political and economic miracle that western Europe and Japan would enjoy in the early postwar decades is hard to fully grasp without a sense of the damage that battles and bombs had done. In no other place was that damage greater than in Japan, whose economy and people had been stretched to the breaking point as its leaders created a colonial empire and then confronted the far more powerful United States. As the war turned against Japan, it lost the merchant fleet that was its economic lifeline, and Japanese cities became the target of an increasingly heavy bombing campaign. Japanese individually and collectively were fast spending down the resources accumulated through several generations of hard work. Homes were gone; unemployment was rampant; and rations sank below subsistence levels. An observer who arrived with the U.S. military occupation following the surrender of this exhausted country could not have imagined how rapid the recovery would be. By the early 1950s the Japanese had, like the Europeans, regained prewar levels of production, and by the 1960s were enjoying levels of prosperity not previously known.

The depths to which the war had pulled Japan are evident in the sources that follow. They put us in the shoes of someone caught amidst the chaos of war's end and help us imagine the material problems survivors were contending with and the state of mind adversity created. These accounts also provide clues to the political democratization and economic recovery that would follow so rapidly. Finally, the two distinctly different kinds of evidence about everyday life at the end of the war offered here — oral history looking back and letters capturing the concerns of a particular moment — each have strengths and weaknesses that are worth thinking about.

2.1

Hiroshima Residents Remember Death and Destruction, August 6, 1945

While U.S. bombers flattened many Japanese cities, Hiroshima seemed to live a charmed life — until luck ran out on the morning of August 6 and the American bomber *Enola Gay* passed overhead. Its cargo, a single atomic bomb, engulfed those below in a maelstrom of searing heat, devastating blast, and deadly radiation. One hundred thousand died at once and another thirty to fifty thousand would soon follow. Nagasaki underwent a similar ordeal three days later — a city destroyed and thousands upon thousands charred, crushed, and maimed.

Japanese recollections of that day invite us to think about the growing destructiveness of military technology during World War II and its diminished discrimination between combatants and civilians. It is also worth considering how the passage of time may have shaped or altered memories. The first item by Mr. Katsutani (his first name as well as his background is lost to us) was recorded just after the bombing. The second one dates from 1951 when a fifth grader, Wakasa Ikuko, struggled to put on paper her reaction to the blast six years earlier when she was five years old. The third recollection is by Ryōso Fujie in 1981, thirty-six years after she witnessed the bombing while living with her family in the village of Kuchita outside Hiroshima. How do the images created by these accounts extend or clash with the reaction of Truman and Stalin to the dawn of the nuclear age (in Documents 1.5)?

Mr. Katsutani
Account Rendered Just After the Bombing

I had just finished breakfast . . . and was getting ready to light a cigarette, when all of a sudden I saw a white flash. In a moment there was a tremendous blast. Not stopping to think, I let out a yell and jumped into an air-raid dugout. In a moment there was such a blast as I have never heard before. It was terrific! I jumped out of the dugout and pushed my wife into it. Realizing something terrible must have happened in Hiroshima, I climbed up onto the roof of my storehouse to have a look.

. . . Towards Hiroshima, I saw a big black cloud go billowing up, like a puffy summer cloud. Knowing for sure then that something terrible had happened in the city, I jumped down from my storehouse and ran as fast as I could to the military post. . . . I ran up to the officer in charge and told him what I had seen and begged him to send somebody to help in Hiroshima. But he didn't even take me seriously. . . .

. . . I looked all around to find someone to help me make a rescue squad, but I couldn't find anybody. While I was still looking for help, wounded people began to stream into the village. I asked them what had happened, but all they could tell me was that Hiroshima had been destroyed and everybody was leaving the city. With that I got on my bicycle. . . . [T]he road was jammed with people, and so was every path and byway.

. . . The nearer I got to Hiroshima the more I saw until by the time I had reached Koi [the western limits of the city], they were all so badly injured, I could not bear to look into their faces. They smelled like burning hair.

. . . The area around Koi station was not burned, but the station and the houses nearby were badly damaged. Every square inch of the station platform was packed with wounded people. Some were standing; others lying down. They were all pleading for water. Now and then you could hear a child calling for its mother. It was a living hell, I tell you. It was a living hell!

. . . I left Koi station and went over to the Koi primary school. By then, the school had been turned into an emergency hospital and was already crowded with desperately injured people. Even the playground was packed with the dead and dying. They looked like so many cod fish spread out for drying. What a pitiful sight it was to see them lying there in the hot sun. Even I could tell they were all going to die.

This account, rearranged here to follow chronologically, was recorded in Michihiko Hachiya, *Hiroshima Diary: The Journal of a Japanese Physician, August 6–September 30, 1945,* trans. and ed. Warner Lee Wells (originally published 1955; Chapel Hill: University of North Carolina Press, 1995), 15–17.

[Today (7 August) in walking along the railroad tracks I saw that] even they were littered with electric wires and broken railway cars, and the dead and wounded lay everywhere. When I reached the bridge, I saw a dreadful thing. It was unbelievable. There was a man, stone dead, sitting on his bicycle as it leaned against the bridge railing. It is hard to believe that such a thing could happen! [He repeated himself two or three times.]

. . . It seems that most of the dead people were either on the bridge or beneath it. You could tell that many had gone down to the river to get a drink of water and had died where they lay. I saw a few live people still in the water, knocking against the dead as they floated down the river. There must have been hundreds and thousands who fled to the river to escape the fire and then drowned.

The sight of the soldiers, though, was more dreadful than the dead people floating down the river. I came onto I don't know how many, burned from the hips up; and where the skin had peeled, their flesh was wet and mushy. They must have been wearing their military caps because the black hair on top of their heads was not burned. It made them look like they were wearing black lacquer bowls.

And they had no faces! Their eyes, noses and mouths had been burned away, and it looked like their ears had melted off. It was hard to tell front from back. One soldier, whose features had been destroyed and was left with his white teeth sticking out, asked me for some water, but I didn't have any. I clasped my hands and prayed for him. He didn't say anything more. His plea for water must have been his last words. . . .

Wakasa Ikuko
Impressions the Bombing Left on a Five-Year-Old

I completely hate thinking about the day the atom bomb was dropped, and remembering things about the war. Even when I read a book, I skip anything about war. At the movies, I shudder during the newsreels when there are scenes of the Korean War. It is part of my homework to write about the bomb and I am writing what I can, though I don't want to and it makes me tremble.

On the morning of the sixth of August, my brother's friends were waiting for him. They were supposed to go to their temporary classroom together. They were in second grade. I was five years old and my little sister was two. We were playing house in the garden. Father usually got to work by eight, but that day he said, "Today, I'm going in at half past eight." He was sitting at his desk, facing a window looking north, and was practicing calligraphy. My mother was by a south-facing window clearing the breakfast table. From the kitchen came the sound of the cups and bowls clinking as she put them down.

Children of Hiroshima, ed. Arata Osada (originally published 1951; New York: Harper & Row, 1982), 9–11.

Suddenly, the humming sound of an airplane echoed high above in the sky. Taking it for a Japanese plane, I cried out loudly, "An airplane!" The moment I looked up into the sky, a white light flashed and the green trees in the garden looked brown like dead trees. I rushed into the house, shouting, "Daddy!" At the same moment, there was a terrific boom and the bookcases and the chest of drawers in the room fell down. Broken pieces of window-pane went flying over my head. I ran back to the garden. Mother called, "Come here, Ikuko!" Automatically, I ran toward my mother's voice and jumped into the air-raid shelter. Pretty soon, my ears started to bleed and wouldn't stop. There was a lot of blood, and even when I pressed cotton on them, the blood still kept oozing between my fingers. Daddy and Mummy were worried about my bleeding and put a bandage over my ears. Daddy's little finger was cut so badly it seemed it might fall off. He had another big cut below his eye. Mummy was practically covered with blood from the waist down. I guess she was injured by pieces of glass from the north window. . . .

After they bandaged me, my ears began to throb so I lay down. When I woke up, I was lying in a funny shack. I tried to lift my head but couldn't, because the blood had soaked through the bandages and my head was stuck to the sheet. Daddy carried me on his back to an Army hospital in the neighborhood, because he was afraid I might get worse. The hospital was crowded with people. Some were almost naked and others were groaning with pain. I was so frightened that I asked Daddy to take me back home. At last, Daddy said, "There are so many people here that we'll have to wait forever before your turn comes. And most of them are worse off than you." Then he took me home on his back.

Ryōso Fujie
Recollections of Her Husband's Disappearance in the Blast

My husband was a kind-hearted man and we used to work really hard.

On the day when the atom bomb fell, we had breakfast just after 6 o'clock. . . .

For the last three days, my husband had been going off with his horse and cart to work on dismantling buildings in Hiroshima. He'd planned to bring home a load of old timber. . . .

I was tending the crops, doing things like weeding, when I made out a B29 flying in from over beyond Hiroshima. B29s would often fly over and I was wondering whether this was another one when, as I looked, it left a trail of smoke behind it. At that very moment, I heard a loud noise from the direction of Hiroshima. A moment later, it was as though the earth shook and a fierce wind sprang up. When I looked over towards Hiroshima, a great cloud

Widows of Hiroshima: The Life Stories of Nineteen Peasant Wives, ed. Mikio Kanda and trans. Taeko Midorikawa (New York: St. Martin's Press, 1989), 37–42, 45.

of smoke billowed up. That was what afterwards people called the mushroom cloud. Thinking to myself that something terrible must have happened, I rushed back to the house almost on all fours. Inside the house, doors had crashed down and everything was in an awful state. Grandma (mother-in-law) had been looking after two of my kids, but when I got back to the house, she was crouched in a corner of the back room, clutching the kids to her, and saying: "Oh, my god! Oh, my god!" My youngest (Miyoko) was 8 months old and my other girl, Kazuko, was 2. Our second boy, Takeo, was in the fourth year of elementary school.

I couldn't do anything with myself, what with worrying if my husband and [son] Masaru were safe. I couldn't help fearing the worst.

Close to noon, word started to get around that something terrible had happened to Hiroshima. People were saying that Hiroshima was a sea of fire and that it looked as though many people had been killed. I was like a cat on hot bricks, but there wasn't a thing I could do.

It was turned 4 o'clock when our eldest boy, Masaru, came into the house, calling out: "Mum, I'm back!" All I could say was: "You've done well to get back! You've done well to get back!" His hands and face, and his legs too, were caked with dirt, and his clothes were in tatters.

... From about the time when Masaru got back home, burnt and blistered people came streaming along the road from Hiroshima. I kept wondering if Dad was all right. I kept going out into the yard to take a look, but he didn't come back. ...

I stayed up all night, but my husband didn't come back. I said:

"Grandma, I'm going to search for Dad, so please look after the kids." ...

Even so, I couldn't go and leave behind the baby. She was only 8 months old and I was still feeding her. I strapped her to my back and set off. It was dawn and I walked as fast as I could for 2 *ri* (about 8 kilometres) along the road to Yokokawa. At the roadside, there were people who were charred all over or had their skin hanging off. They were squatting down, groaning and asking for water.

As I got close to Hiroshima, the air-raid warning sounded again and again. Every time, I'd look for an air-raid shelter and take cover. The shelters were full of charred people. They were pressed up against each other and groaning. It was like something out of hell. I remembered that my husband had said that he'd be dismantling houses round Nakajima Shinmachi (the present-day Peace Memorial Park). Picking my way across the scorched earth, where everything looked like a picture of hell, I finally made it to the River Motoyasu. At the riverside there were lots of dead bodies piled up. In the river, charred bodies were floating about, bobbing up and down. It was just like hell again.

Among the burnt ruins, there were people who were still alive. In their agony, you could hear them calling out over and over again: "Mum! . . . Mum! . . ." Thinking that my husband might have tried to get away from Hiroshima in the direction of the Koi Hills, I walked along the railway line. When I crossed the railway bridge at Koi, I was trembling with fear; it was like taking my life in my hands. But there was no other way to cross the river because all the other bridges had burnt down.

My husband wasn't in Koi either. There was nothing more I could do, so I gave up and went home. All day long, the baby just stayed quietly on my back and didn't cry at all.

The next day I set out to search for my husband again. . . .

Day after day, I kept at it, searching through the piles of bodies which they'd pulled out of the River Motoyasu. With my baby strapped on my back, I must have picked over those bodies for about six days in all. I wonder how many tens of thousands of bodies I checked as I walked about? Strange to say, I wanted to find my husband so much that at the time, I didn't feel scared at all. After about seven days had gone by, they said there weren't any more bodies in the River Motoyasu, so I walked about in the Yoshijima District. I checked all the charred bodies in the trams, but my husband wasn't there.

. . . I still live in hope that my husband will come back. I'm turned 70 now, but even so, if I hear a noise outside in the middle of the night, my heart starts pounding, thinking that he's come back. People say, "You should forget your husband now", but I can't forget him. It's unfeeling of them to ask me to forget a husband who disappeared without trace on the day that the atom bomb was dropped. Even now I remember him as though it were yesterday. The older I get, the clearer become my memories. You can laugh at me for being a silly woman, if you like.

When my grandchildren come at the *Bon* Festival or New Year, I always tell them how cruel the atom bomb was and how frightening war is. They don't really listen . . . but all the same, I tell them the same thing over and over again. "War is really cruel; it's really cruel. Never make war!" I say to them.

2.2

The Japanese Write from out of the Ruins: Letters to General MacArthur, 1945–1947

In the course of the U.S. occupation of Japan (1945–1952), Japanese citizens frequently wrote to the American general who exercised ultimate power over the islands, Douglas MacArthur. Their letters, petitions, and postcards usually began respectfully "Dear General MacArthur" but some were considerably more effusive. They dealt with a host of topics, personal as well as public. Some half million of these missives survive. The Japanese scholar, Sodei Rinjirō, made a selection for publication from some ten thousand letters that he read. From his culling come the seven items that appear below — all dealing with personal matters and all dating from the first two grim years of the occupation when no one could be certain about the official U.S. promise of a new era of democracy, peace, and prosperity. These selections are arranged chronologically so that they can be read in the sequence that MacArthur might have seen them. What he read, of course, was not the original but a translation, usually a summary prepared by his staff.

Imagine yourself MacArthur, living in godlike isolation but curious about the world you controlled and about your reputation among the Japanese you ruled. What would these letters have told you about public opinion, problems the occupation was encountering, and the progress of the occupation-sponsored reforms in promoting democracy and eliminating militarism? But also imagine the authors of these letters. What kind of people might be more likely to write and how might that bias the picture of conditions in Japan and the attitude of Japanese conveyed here? How might addressing a foreigner of MacArthur's power and stature have influenced the appeals? Why might the correspondents have thought that MacArthur could or would help them? How did these Japanese look back on the war, especially the role played by their own leaders and soldiers? How did they view the United States in general and the American occupation in particular? What social values do these letters reveal?

From H. K.

Tokyo, October 20, 1945

Not only I, but anyone who has a heart would abhor those in power right now. During the war and even now after the war, some high police officials and military officers live in my neighborhood, and police officials come home in cars and have their subordinates carry in case upon case of beer and sake[1], and the officers too get cases of food and drink brought to their homes.

The municipal government ordered us to evacuate our home, and the house we finally found was bombed within ten days. We lost our home and all our belongings in one night. My eighty-year-old mother was sick, we had no shelter and no food, we even contemplated suicide. Just at that time, my younger sister's home was burned during the bombing of May 25, and her husband was killed. The stress she went through must have affected her, for she fell ill while mourning her husband, and she is still sick. No one even feels sorry for our poor family of women; the local community leaders are that in name only and do not have any feeling for their fellow Japanese. . . .

It is inevitable in a war that one country must win. We women knew that your country would win. It was obvious you would win. I lost my home during the war, but I am not bitter or sad about that. What bothers me is that those in high positions use their power and money to have mistresses and buy expensive things on the black market and lead extravagant lives. . . .

I think we are better off having been defeated. How sad to have been born in Japan. If I knew your country's language, at least I could work as your wife's maid, but unfortunately I cannot speak your language and it saddens me that I cannot be of use. . . . For my rudeness, I apologize over and over. The weather in Japan is not the same as what you are accustomed to, how incon-

---

[1]Fermented rice wine that stands along with tea as Japan's national ceremonial drink.

Sodei Rinjirō, *Dear General MacArthur: Letters from the Japanese during the American Occupation,* ed. John Junkerman and trans. Shizue Matsuda (Lanham, Md.: Rowman & Littlefield, 2001), 22, 52–53, 108–19, 213–15, 269, 273–74, 279. The spelling and grammar here follow the published versions of these communications.

venient it must be for you to live here. I pray to God that you will please, please, please take care of yourself.

From "the Child of Buddha"
Tokyo, October 20, 1945

Congratulations on Your Excellency's bountiful happiness.

Ordinarily I am one who breaks down the barriers of nationality, and I even smiled at reports of Your Excellency's high praise for American soldiers. But on the night of October 17 at 7 P.M., I was in the women's side of a public bath on Asakusa Dōri [avenue] in Mukō Yanagihara 2-chōme — a person bombed out by the war, washing away the day's toil from my tired body — when a commotion began: "An American soldier is peeping." I could not believe that an American soldier with any intellectual pride would do this, but I happened to see your country's soldiers taking turns laughing and peeping from a small window by the side of the bath. If Your Excellency were to hear about this incident, I knew you would be deeply aggrieved, and I secretly felt sorry for you. You have said that Japanese soldiers may have done so and so, and I do not wish to negate your words, but not all of the young Japanese men sent to the front were uncivilized. There were many who were capable of human reflection and cherished refined aesthetics. Your Excellency, please bear in mind that there are some among your soldiers who have the lowest tastes. Women of your country and my country too are all God's children. I pray the best of health to you.

From "a Mother"
Kure City, November 18, 1945

The autumn coolness increases by the day, and you must be extremely busy. . . .

My son is still with the Manchurian corps (along the Soviet border), but we do not know what unit he belongs to, and besides, we do not know whether he is alive or dead, so I worry about him day and night. Recently a few soldiers, including the son of a friend, escaped and returned home. According to him, Russia is using Japanese soldiers as laborers to expand military installations, but once the construction is complete the soldiers will be shot because repatriating them would mean revealing classified information. . . . They have struggled a great deal in Manchuria for food, clothing, and fuel, but on top of that, to be treated like slaves and then to be shot . . . there is no suffering worse than this for a mother.

If my son was killed in battle, fighting bravely, at least it would be some comfort and allow me to face society. But for a parent to hear that he may be treated like an animal and face an undignified death makes me feel that I would go through anything to save him. . . .

. . . Please save the soldiers in Manchuria. Whether I am awake or asleep my heart aches with this problem. Please forgive me for my many difficult requests. I wait eagerly for the general's early action.

As the cold season is approaching, I pray to God that you will take care of yourself.

From Shiomi Kitarō

Okayama City, February 18, 1946

During the war, the leaders deceived the people by telling them that Americans are terrible. American soldiers are kind. . . .

. . . If I were young, I would like to go to the United States, but I am sixty-two so this is not possible. My eldest son, Tarō, twenty-three, is a former army doctor and second lieutenant who was reported missing two years ago as a member of the Mori 1353d Squadron in Burma. If he is so lucky as to return alive, I will bring him to see you. I want him to go to America, and I beg you to assist in making this happen. In March of last year, the newspaper reported that the whole army in Burma had been annihilated. An army doctor is a noncombatant, so if he was taken as a prisoner of war by Britain, he may still be alive. I am worried because he was taught by the Japanese state to fight to the death.

If the Japanese were kind, they could contribute to the world, even with their small stature, but whoever forms a government will not think about the Japanese people, they will only think about themselves. For the sake of all Japanese and our descendants, I believe that the future of Japan will be brighter under American control.

From Tachibana Mitsuko

Kōchi Prefecture, April 6, 1946

Please forgive my impoliteness in sending you a poorly written letter without warning. . . .

. . . I am the wife of Tachibana Masao, who is in Prison Camp One on Luzon in the Philippines, waiting to be executed, and my request concerns nothing else. I want to get word to him before he leaves this earth, because he still does not know whether his child is a boy or a girl. He has not heard that his son was born on January 1 last year. I wrote to him shortly after New Year's Day this year; but it seems the letter has not reached him. The baby has been named Norio, and I wish more than anything I could show him our child, but there is nothing I can do, so I request at least that:

Your Excellency, Commander MacArthur, by your mercy, please inform him before he is executed that Norio was born and will be raised as his heir.

Please consider this as a gift to Tachibana Masao, who will fall like a cherry blossom. No matter how much I have thought about it, nothing can be done, so I have decided to appeal to you.[2]

From Mitsuji Yoshiko (A Young Girl Using a Pseudonym)
Kyoto, April 1, 1947

We learned from our teacher that Japan was defeated and the people have the obligation of paying reparations through taxes, so I am thinking that when I grow up I too will work hard. Recently the tax bill came, and it is so very high that the grownups are all crying. I thought that Japan had become a democratic country, but in the same line of work, those who do more business pay lower taxes and those who eke out a meager living pay higher taxes. In my family, my mother was often sick, and she was staying with relatives in the country during the war when she was killed in a bomb attack. My father is also frail, but he works as a plasterer and supports my older sister, my brother, and me. The recent tax bill was so high that even if he sold some tools and kimono it would not cover the taxes, so he went to the tax office for a consultation. They told him that once set, the tax bill cannot be changed.

My father says that unless he sells my older sister to pay the taxes, the tax office will confiscate his tools, and he is also worried about next year's taxes. These days he is saying strange things.

I overheard my father and many other people saying that they should set fire to the tax office.

Dear General MacArthur, the people really resent those former military leaders who forced us into war and still make us suffer.

I request fairer taxes before my father and others burn down the tax office. . . .

From Okumura Kazunori
Probably from Kagawa Prefecture, July 4, 1947

Please forgive me for this poor paper and the impolite form I am using.

I have been active as a cell member of the Japan Communist Party from April of last year to the present, but I have been reading Your Excellency's clear and appropriate directives and statements issued from time to time, and I was so moved that I could not help but have a change of heart.

---

[2] The condemned husband, Tachibana Masao, had served as warrant officer in the military police in Manila, the Philippines. After the war an Allied military tribunal had convicted him of murder and other crimes. He was hanged on April 11, less than a week after this appeal and nearly a month before MacArthur saw it.

One also learns the meaning of liberty by viewing movies like *Boys Town* and *Going My Way*.[3]

...I love Japan. I thought, we should make Japan into a country of liberty, Fuji, and cherry blossoms....

Japan has little land, a growing population, and few raw materials. I thought that to build a new Japan, we had to adopt socialism, so I joined the Communist Party. But what do you think I learned there? Behind the principle of gaining fundamental human rights, I found the trampling of human rights. Under the beautiful name of liberation there was oppression, and while saying it was for the people's sake, it was for the benefit of a foreign country. What the Communist Party called "liberty" was actually destruction, sacrifice, and tyranny....

By the time this letter reaches the general, I probably will have left the Communist Party.

In closing, I pray for the General's health and praise forever his distinguished service of bringing good tidings to East Asia.

EUROPE: HERE COME THE AMERICANS!

The importance of the United States hit peoples around the world with a jolt in the latter half of the 1940s. American troops arrived as liberators and conquerors in both Europe and Asia. They stayed on in Japan, Korea, Germany, and Austria. And in Korea they were once more engaged in combat as points along the Cold War skirmish line turned hot. American cultural influence, already on the rise in the decades before the war, became even more important. However, the United States meant different things to different people suddenly drawn within the U.S. orbit, depending on their country's wartime experience and their personal background (class, education, and age to name only the most obvious). Thus for a young person whose side had just lost the war and who felt socially constrained, Hollywood films and GI's chewing gum had a potent appeal. For others with a longer memory and a keener sense of economic and political vulnerability, this postwar colossus was a troubling presence. The two selections that follow capture these two distinctly different kinds of reactions to the United States.

---

[3] Popular Hollywood films (released in 1938 and 1944 respectively) which were both about Catholic priests and both part of the return of U.S. cinema to markets closed off during the war.

2.3
An Austrian Youth Welcomes the Occupation

Reinhold Wagnleitner, a specialist on U.S. influence in Europe, looked back in the early 1990s on his youth growing up in the U.S.-occupied section of Austria right after the war and on his own encounter with American culture. His recollections highlight an enduring appeal that the United States has exercised over several generations of European youth.

Wagnleitner poses for us a set of basic questions about the process known as Americanization: Why were he and his brother so susceptible to U.S. cultural imports? What do you suspect might be the limits of their admiration for the United States? His highly public reconstruction of his encounters with things American some forty years after the fact deserve scrutiny: How might those recollections be "tainted" by intervening events, for example his professional absorption in the study of Americanization?

Historian Reinhold Wagnleitner
From *Coca-Colonization and the Cold War*

When I was born in Upper Austria in 1949, Mauerkirchen was a small, sleepy market town — but it was also situated in the American occupation zone of Austria. Although during the period of occupation, 1945–55, the U.S. Army was barely visible in our part of the woods, we children religiously waited for the best action of the year: the annual U.S. Army maneuvers and our rations of chewing gum.

For us, the horrors of the Second World War were in the distant past, but still they were everywhere. Our everyday experience included quite a few mutilated men, and for the nicer ones we picked up cigarette butts from the streets. It seemed absolutely normal that most men and many women looked old and tired — and not only because we were children and they wore dark clothes. But what a contrast when we saw pictures of GIs or, even better, met "the real thing." Somehow, they clashed with our images of soldiers. They looked young and healthy. Contrasted to our poverty, they seemed incredibly rich, and many were generous to us kids. Of course, their casualness and loudness were proverbial — but we admired them precisely for that.

Although most families with a Nazi past repressed and hid this past from the children, the war remained everywhere — and we did not need a war memorial to be reminded of the many ghosts roaming our streets. Unspoken Nazi-past or not, it was clear that most adults objected to those crass boys from across the Atlantic. "We" had indeed lost the war, but look at those uncultured American guys who chewed gum and put their feet on the table. (This, it seemed, was the utmost crime!) How could an army manned by such unmilitaristic, childish, and undisciplined boys (even blacks!) win a war, espe-

Reinhold Wagnleitner, *Coca-Colonization and the Cold War: The Cultural Mission of the United States in Austria after the Second World War* (Chapel Hill, University of North Carolina Press, 1994), ix–xi.

cially one against Germany! A few of us children, however, secretly suspected that an army advancing to the rhythm of swing music *deserved* to win the war. It did not help our elders to warn us that if we chewed gum we would look like Americans: that was exactly what we wanted to look like!

In my family, I was spared this routine of Austrian cultural superiority versus American cultural inferiority mostly for two reasons. First, my parents and grandparents had not been Nazis, and my mother loved American music, while my father enjoyed American action movies, which had returned to Mauerkirchen's little cinema in the wake of the U.S. Army. Second, a traumatic incident in my father's childhood — he had lost one foot in a car accident at age thirteen — spared him the fate of having to fight in the Second World War. It was rather rare, indeed, to grow up in Austria during the 1950s with parents like that. (Of course, for most of my teenage friends, American pop culture became *the* major vehicle of protest against their parents.)

While our household was uncharacteristically open to what parents of my friends despised as "American trash," I was far from being the vanguard of American popular culture in our family. It is my only brother, Günter, born in 1940, who has to take the main responsibility for my un-Austrian behavior. Günter is extremely musical. He started to take piano lessons at age four and passed the entrance exam to the Vienna Boys Choir at age six — we still possess a 78 shellac recording of Günter's voice, which my father had ordered for this occasion. But in the end, my parents decided against sending him to Vienna. They did not want to hand over their six-year-old boy to a boarding school, especially to a boarding school in Vienna, which was surrounded by the Soviet occupation zone. . . .

Yet, my parents had no idea that they built the perfect stage for American music for their still-unborn second child. Günter, who had a voracious appetite for any kind of good music, did more than simply improve his playing of Mozart and Beethoven, Bach and Brahms, Schubert and Strauss; he also discovered Frank Sinatra and Ray Charles, Dizzy Gillespie and Miles Davis. And when he discovered rock 'n' roll in the middle of the 1950s, nothing remained the same. While he worked the piano and made our living room rock like a jailhouse, I would work the matchboxes and pretend I was something like a rock 'n' roll drum machine. Many were the sighs of my poor parents — not because we played American music, but because we didn't do *anything else*. And then one day Günter really became the King. A friend of my mother gave him the absolutely most yearned for article of clothing imaginable: the first and only pair of Levi's in Mauerkirchen, which she had received as a present from an American officer.

2.4

A British Intellectual Looks across the Atlantic

Bertrand Russell (1872–1970) is best known as one of the leading British philosophers of the twentieth century. Born into the aristocracy, he quickly gained prominence as a Cambridge academic in the decade before the outbreak of World War

I and as the proponent of controversial positions on such social issues as sex and marriage. His political radicalism took the form of pacifism during World War I, a position he abandoned during the next world war only to take it up again in reaction to the Cold War and its prospect of nuclear disaster. He was a leading figure in the European "ban the bomb" movement and in the opposition during the 1960s to the U.S. war in Vietnam. Russell's writings won him the Nobel Prize for literature the year before this essay appeared.

Russell's age (almost eighty when he wrote this) and intellectual makeup help explain his reaction to the suddenly prominent United States. What sort of images of the United States does Russell conjure up? How do they differ from those expressed above — by Wagnleitner and by the Japanese under U.S. occupation (Documents 2.2 and 2.3)? How do we account for that difference? Are there points about the United States on which they agree?

Bertrand Russell
From *The Impact of America on European Culture*
1951

What America stood for in the minds of Europeans of the early nineteenth century was, in many ways, the exact opposite of what America stands for at the present day. From 1776 to the death of Lincoln, America was the Mecca of Radicals, the only large country where democracy was successfully practiced. Now America has become the bulwark of capitalism, the main hope of those who dread the advancing tide of socialism and communism, and the chief promise of stability amid the kaleidoscopic transformations that bewilder the puzzled inhabitants of Europe and Asia. I once lectured in New York in a building called the "Hall of Liberty," erected by German Radicals who fled from their native country after the failure of the Revolution of 1848. Their portraits hung on the walls, and among them was the father of Heinz of the 57 varieties [of ketchup]. The contrast between what the father hoped of America and what the son made of it (and out of it) typifies the change of which I am speaking. . . .

The change in the attitude to America of European left-wing opinion is more due to a change in Europe than to a change in America. America in the time of Jefferson believed in democracy and free enterprise, and America believes in them still. . . . [L]eft-wing Europeans, nowadays, are Socialists or Communists, and find in America the chief obstacle to the realization of their hopes. There is also another reason for the change of sentiment: people of a rebellious disposition are temperamentally compelled to be against the rich and powerful, and America is more rich and powerful than any other nation. If you praise Sweden to a Communist, he may think you misguided, but will

---

Bertrand Russell, "The Political and Cultural Influence," in Russell et al., *The Impact of America on European Culture* (Boston: Beacon Press, 1951), 3–7, 12–19.

not call you a lackey of capitalism, because Sweden is not great and strong; but if you praise America, there is no limit to the subservience and moral obliquity of which he will suspect you. . . .

Although America is opposed to socialism, it would be a mistake to think of the country as unprogressive. Since 1933 immense strides have been taken in social legislation. And in industrial technique — which most Americans think more important than politics — the United States remains the least wedded to tradition and the most receptive to innovations of all the industrial countries with the possible exception of Russia. . . . In the world of ideas, also, there is a readiness for novelty which is usually absent in Europe. Anyone who has attempted to present a new philosophy to Oxford and the Sorbonne and the universities of America will have been struck by the greater readiness of the Americans to think along unfamiliar lines. And if one could present a new philosophy to Moscow without being liquidated, one would find Russians less open to new ideas than even the most hide-bound old dons in our older universities. All these are facts which left-wing opponents of America fail to recognize.

In international affairs the record of America compares very favorably with that of other Great Powers. There have been, it is true, two short periods of imperialism, one connected with the Mexican War of 1846, the other with the Spanish-American War of 1898, but in each case a change of policy came very soon. In China, where the record of Britain, France, Germany, and Russia is shameful, that of the United States used to be generous and liberal. . . . Since 1945, American policy, both as regards control of atomic power and as regards the Marshall Plan, has been generous and farsighted. Western Union, economic and political, which America urges, is obviously to the interest of Western Europe; in fact, American authorities have shown more awareness of what Western Europe needs than Western Europe itself has shown. . . .

I believe almost every European would agree that the English, the French, the Germans, and the Russians of some twenty years ago, all produced artistically better movies than those emanating from Hollywood. When we see an American film we know beforehand that virtue will be rewarded, that crime will be shown not to pay, and that the heroine, always faultlessly dressed in spite of incredible tribulations, will emerge happily to life-long bliss with the hero. If you object, "But this is a sugary fairy tale only fit for children," producers and American public alike will be simply puzzled, since the object is not to produce something that corresponds to fact, but something that makes you happy by corresponding to daydreams. . . .

The American outlook is the result of inhabiting a large country, not yet over-populated, with immense natural resources, and with greater wealth and less poverty than any of the old countries of Europe and Asia. A young American can be adventurous without folly; he does not need, to nearly the same extent as a European, to force himself into acquiescence with a narrow groove and a career that can be foreseen with dreary accuracy. . . .

A great deal of nonsense is talked about American so-called "materialism" and what its detractors call "bathroom civilization." I do not think Americans are in any degree more "materialistic," in the popular sense of that word, than people of other nations. We think they worship the "almighty dollar" because they succeed in getting it. But a needy aristocrat or a French peasant will do things for the sake of money that shock every decent American. Very few Americans marry from mercenary motives. A willingness to sacrifice income for idealistic reasons is at least as common in America as in England. I think the belief that Americans are fonder of money than we are is mainly inspired by envy. . . .

As for "bathroom civilization," it is altogether to the good, unless it is thought to be all-sufficient. Every traveler owes a debt of gratitude to American tourists for the improvement in hotels that has been brought about by their grumbling. The love of "gadgets," for which we are inclined to make fun of Americans, ought not to be decried. An American middle-class housewife, compelled, like an English housewife, to do her own cooking, does it with far less labor than is required in most English kitchens. The habit of keeping food in the refrigerator is wholly to be commended from the point of view of health. The more we copy America in these respects, the better. . . .

There is one aspect of American life which I have not yet touched on, and which I think wholly undesirable — I mean, the tyranny of the herd. Eccentricity is frowned upon, and unusual opinions bring social penalties upon those who hold them. At the present day, people suspected of even the slightest sympathy with communism are exposed to a kind of ostracism which would be absurd if it were not tragic. . . . The guilt lies with the general public, which is intolerant to a degree that must astonish any Englishman. It has nothing to do with industrialism; indeed, it is worst in purely rural communities. . . . It is, I think, the worst feature of America. I earnestly hope that fear of Russia will not cause us to imitate it.

. . . From the sixteenth century onward, Europe increasingly dominated the world, from a cultural no less than a military point of view. Now that domination is lost; the inheritance is divided between Russia and America. The culture of America is closely akin to our own, and adaptation can be easy and painless. The culture of Russia, on the other hand, is profoundly alien: partly Byzantine, partly Mongol, only quite superficially European. Only appalling suffering could force us into the Russian mold. It is therefore the part of wisdom to facilitate co-operation with America, cultural as well as political and economic.

In some respects, it must be admitted, adoption of American standards, in so far as it occurs, is likely to be harmful. Aesthetic standards, except in architecture, will probably be lowered. There will be less respect for art and learning, and more for the forceful "executive." The movement towards socialism will be retarded — but whether that is to be regarded as a gain or a loss is a controversial question.

On the other side, however, are to be set gains which far outweigh possible losses. Our continued existence as free nations is only capable of being maintained by co-operation with America. . . . Above all things, European culture, if it is to remain vital, needs hope and imaginative vision. These things are common in America, as they were in Victorian England. If we can recover them by contact with Americans, there is every possibility of a future no less glorious and no less happy than our past.

THE STATE AND THE FREE MARKET

During the 1930s and early 1940s some of the great minds of western Europe turned to the troubled problem of the relationship between the state and the economy. The political and economic turmoil of the 1930s helped thrust this issue to the top of the intellectual agenda. The Great Depression had brought widespread misery and thrown into doubt the idea of the free market as a self-righting mechanism. Rather than bouncing back after the initial crisis, production continued to stagnate and unemployment remained high. The resulting populist discontents made national socialism possible in Germany and Italy. In both places the state stepped in to soften the hard edges of suffering. Though bound for defeat by 1944–1945, Germany and Italy remained a reminder that economic hardship could drive hard-pressed populations to embrace authoritarian regimes. An additional consideration was the apparent success of the socialist experiment in the Soviet Union. Central planning and control had catapulted the USSR to the front ranks of the economic powers, and the socialist emphasis on state planning and ownership of industry enjoyed high prestige. Finally, the prospect of rebuilding Europe's economies from the ground up after World War II fueled debate about the practical as well as the moral and political advantages of various economic models.

In the following documents, the term laissez-faire figures in a central way. Whatever their attitude toward it, those involved in this great economic debate understood the term to mean an economic system in which the free market should function with only the most minimal state intervention. For them laissez-faire and liberal were roughly equivalent terms, in stark contrast to the more recent association of liberal with big government managing a wide range of social programs and taxing heavily to pay for those programs. In this older sense the liberal was the defender of individual economic and political rights, while in the more recent meaning liberals seek to address social needs and values that transcend the individual.

2.5

John Maynard Keynes on State Intervention in the Economy

John Maynard Keynes was the best-known proponent of state intervention to make the free market function more efficiently. He was also a prolific author, trusted government adviser, and devotee of the arts, good food, and stimulating conversation. Born in 1883 and educated at Cambridge, he made that British university town and London his home during an intensely engaged professional career. During the Great Depression, his chief concern was why markets did not spring back as classic economic theory said they were supposed to do as part of a natural self-correcting mechanism. Keynes's findings on this point made him one of the most influential economists of the mid-twentieth century. His death came in 1946 just as his ideas were becoming orthodoxy worldwide.

Keynes, as the first to speak in this debate over the postwar economy, can help us grasp what the main issues were. What weaknesses did he find in the free-market or *laissez-faire* ideal? How in turn do those weaknesses justify state intervention in the economy? What in Keynes's thinking were the limits of state intervention? How did the Soviet, German, and Italian record of state intervention in the economy during the 1930s influence his thinking?

From *The Collected Writings of John Maynard Keynes*
1924 and 1932

ON THE INADEQUACY OF *LAISSEZ-FAIRE* ECONOMIC PRINCIPLES (1924)

[I]t was the economists who gave the notion [*of laissez-faire* or governmental non-interference in the economy] a good scientific basis. Suppose that by the working of natural laws individuals pursuing their own interests with enlightenment in conditions of freedom always tend to promote the general interest at the same time! Our philosophical difficulties are resolved — at least for the practical man, who can then concentrate his efforts on securing the necessary conditions of freedom. To the philosophical doctrine that government has no right to interfere, and the divine that it has no need to interfere, there is added a scientific proof [offered by the economists] that its interference is inexpedient. This is the third current of thought, just discoverable in Adam Smith,[1] who was ready in the main to allow the public good to rest on "the natural effort of every individual to better his own condition" . . . .

. . . [*Laissez-faire*] is a method of bringing the most successful profit-makers to the top by a ruthless struggle for survival, which selects the most efficient by the bankruptcy of the less efficient. It does not count the cost of the struggle, but looks only to the benefits of the final result which are assumed to be permanent. . . .

Let us clear from the ground the metaphysical or general principles upon which, from time to time, *laissez-faire* has been founded. It is *not* true that individuals possess a prescriptive 'natural liberty' in their economic activities. There is *no* 'compact' conferring perpetual rights on those who Have or on those who Acquire. The world is *not* so governed from above that private and social interest always coincide. It is *not* so managed here below that in practice they coincide. It is *not* a correct deduction from the principles of economics that enlightened self-interest always operates in the public interest. Nor is it

---

[1]Eighteenth-century Scottish economist whose influential *An Inquiry into the Nature and Causes of the Wealth of Nations* (1776) staked out the *laissez-faire* position.

"The End of Laissez-Faire," published as a pamphlet in 1926 and reproduced in *The Collected Writings of John Maynard Keynes,* ed. Elizabeth Johnson et al., vol. 9: *Essays in Persuasion* (London: Macmillan, 1972), 274–75, 282–83, 287-88.

true that self-interest generally *is* enlightened; more often individuals acting separately to promote their own ends are too ignorant or too weak to attain even these. Experience does *not* show that individuals, when they make up a social unit, are always less clear-sighted than when they act separately....

ON THE VIRTUES OF STATE PLANNING (1932)

There is a new conception in the air today — a new conception of the possible functions of government....

It is called planning — state planning.... We can accept the desirability and even the necessity of *planning* without being a Communist, a Socialist or a Fascist. But whether it is going to prove possible to carry out *planning* in actual practice without a great change in the traditions and in the machinery of democratic government — that is the big question mark....

The forces which are driving the notion of planning into our heads are drawn from two distinct sources. The first is the force of example. The Russian Five-Year Plan has assaulted and captured the imagination of the world. This dream is not yet a realised success — it is much too soon to say that — but it is not the preposterous failure which many wise and experienced people expected it to be. We are now — as a reaction from our mistake — much more inclined, I think, to exaggerate its success than to underestimate it.... We had been taught to think of Communism as involving so complete a destruction of human organisation, that when we learned that, after enormous sufferings and an incredible national effort of self-denial and the exercise of will, a Russian peasant can positively build a tractor of which the wheels go round and that there is a large electric power station at Leningrad, we gape with wonder and rush to the opposite conclusion that Communism is a roaring success.

And there is a second force of example — Italian Fascism which — attacking the same problem with an opposite mentality — seems to have saved Italy from chaos and to have established a modest level of material prosperity within a poor and over-populated country. Here again, when an Englishman learns that an Italian train has run to time, he gapes with wonder and is ready to accept the conclusion that Fascism is a roaring success....

Nevertheless let us not belittle these magnificent experiments or refuse to learn from them. For it is a remarkable and a significant thing that the two most extraordinary political movements of the modern age, approaching their task from opposite moral and emotional poles, should agree in this vital particular — that state planning, that intelligence and deliberation at the centre must supersede the admired disorder of the 19th century.

... There is also the failure of the unplanned economic systems of the world, of those where intelligent deliberation at the centre is minimised or rejected. Not indeed a relative failure; for England or the United States with

From a radio talk of March 14, 1932 (part of a series on state and industry), in *The Collected Writings of John Maynard Keynes*, vol. 21: *Activities, 1931–1939: World Crises and Policies in Britain and America* (London: Macmillan, 1982), 84–92.

a quarter of the population and a third of the productive plant at a standstill can nevertheless support a standard of life at least twice as high, I should suppose, as any existing Bolshevist or even Fascist state. But an absolute failure in relation to their own potentialities. That is what demands our attention. . . .

For what are the economic events of the modern world which must most strike the apprehension of the dullest observer? The extraordinary capacity for the production of material wealth — though it were for the purposes of subsequent destruction — which we developed during [World War I]; and the opposite picture today of starvation amidst plenty, our incredible inability to carry to our mouths the nourishment which we have produced with our hands. For the War was the nearest thing we have ever had in this country to a planned regime. The environment was unfavourable, the haste was excessive and hurried improvisations were inevitable. Yet it showed us the potentialities of modern technique to produce. On the other hand today it is in the United States, where the national tradition is most antagonistic to the notion of planning and the forms of government least adapted to improvised planning, that the failure of the economic system, relatively to its opportunity, is most obvious. . . .

To remedy this failure is the problem of planning. . . .

. . . [T]he essence of state planning [is] to do those things which in the nature of the case lie outside the scope of the individual. It differs from Socialism and from Communism in that it does not seek to aggrandise the province of the state for its own sake. It does not aim at superseding the individual within the field of operations appropriate to the individual, or of transforming the wage system, or of abolishing the profit motive. Its object is to take hold of the central controls and to govern them with deliberate foresight and thus modify and condition the environment within which the individual freely operates with and against other individuals. . . .

The distribution of the burden of taxation with a view to its effect on industry and on the divisions of incomes and of wealth is an example of state planning. . . . Tariffs can be a signal and outstanding example of planning. . . . So is the regulation of transport by road and by rail. . . .

But at such a time as the present the most outstanding opportunity for state planning throughout the world is to be found in the avoidance, or in the mitigation of industrial slumps during which there is so vast a loss of the world's potentialities for the creation of wealth. Here again we have a problem which lies completely outside the scope of the individual. . . . There is virtually nothing that he can do, however ardent his desire and however pressing his personal interest. He is swept along, together with all his fellows, on a flood which he cannot control or direct. And nothing can be of the least avail which does not come from concerted action at the centre. . . .

. . . [State planning] will lead us I believe to far more deliberate and far-reaching policies of credit control, to a great preoccupation with the appropriate level of the rate of interest, and in general to an attempt to control the rate at which new investment is encouraged and facilitated to take place.

It used to be believed that the level of interest and the rate of investment were self-regulatory, and needed no management and no planning; and that all would be for the best if natural forces were left to discover and establish the inner harmonies. But such a view does not square with the facts of experience. As I began by saying, it is the failure of the unplanned industrial world of Western Europe and America to regulate itself to the best advantage, or to reap the fruits of the genius of its scientists and its engineers and its business organisers, which is predisposing many persons to consider without prejudice those far-reaching experimental projects of the most constructive minds of the post-war world which go, conveniently, by the name of planning.

. . . But is it practicable in a democratic community? May it not be a necessary price to pay for the benefits of state planning, that we also suffer those other affronts to the individual which seem to be inseparable from a Bolshevist or a Fascist state? For myself, I do not see why this need be so. At least I should like to try whether it be not possible to enjoy the advantages of both worlds. . . .

Moreover it should prove compatible with democratic and parliamentary government to introduce modern improvements and new organs of administration. . . . State planning, as I conceive it, would not be administered or supervised in detail by democratically elected bodies. The latter would be judges, not of first, but of final instance, reserve forces to effect a change when grave mistakes had been made. The day-to-day tasks of state planning would be carried out in the same sort of way and with the same kind of instruments of administration under a democratic government, as they would be under an autocratic government. . . .

2.6

Friedrich Hayek on State Economic Control as a Threat to Political Freedom

Friedrich Hayek was born and raised in Vienna in the years preceding World War I, a time of enormous intellectual and cultural vitality in that city. After the war he earned his doctorate in political science, converted to free-market principles, and in 1931 settled in London. He loved the manners of the British upper class, and spoke English fluently. There he taught and wrote the best known of his works, *The Road to Serfdom*, which made him the darling of conservatives intent on turning back the tide of socialist and New Deal measures building since the 1930s. Hayek moved to the United States to teach at the University of Chicago where he stayed until 1962. He would close out his teaching career in West Germany. Throughout his career, Hayek was overshadowed by Keynes with whom he had locked horns on economic issues but with whom he was on a friendly basis. Hayek's time would come later in the twentieth century as the free-market idea gained fresh popularity thanks in part to the advocacy of Hayek's disciples.

The excerpts from *The Road to Serfdom* that follow come from the nineteen-page condensed version featured in the April 1945 edition of the popular *Reader's Digest*. Although Hayek did not participate in the condensation prepared by Max

Eastman (a radical turned anti-communist), he heartily approved of the results. And indeed he should have since the condensation saw wide circulation, probably winning more readers than the original work did during its first few years in print. How do you think those readers would have understood the meaning of a "road to serfdom"? On which points does Hayek appear to disagree with Keynes and on which do they seem to agree?

The Reader's Digest *Synopsis of* The Road to Serfdom
April 1945

[THE RISING THREAT TO FREEDOM]

In the democracies at present, many who sincerely hate all of Nazism's manifestations are working for ideals whose realization would lead straight to the abhorred tyranny. Most of the people whose views influence developments are in some measure socialists. They believe that our economic life should be "consciously directed," that we should substitute "economic planning" for the competitive system. Yet is there a greater tragedy imaginable than that, in our endeavor consciously to shape our future in accordance with high ideals, we should in fact unwittingly produce the very opposite of what we have been striving for? . . .

Many socialists have the tragic illusion that by depriving private individuals of the power they possess in an individualist system, and transferring this power to society, they thereby extinguish power. What they overlook is that, by concentrating power so that it can be used in the service of a single plan, it is not merely transformed but infinitely heightened. By uniting in the hands of some single body power formerly exercised independently by many, an amount of power is created infinitely greater than any that existed before, so much more far-reaching as almost to be different in kind. . . .

[INDIVIDUALISM AND THE FREE MARKET]

In every real sense a badly paid unskilled workman in this country has more freedom to shape his life than many an employer in Germany or a much better paid engineer or manager in Russia. If he wants to change his job or the place where he lives, if he wants to profess certain views or spend his leisure in a particular way, he faces no absolute impediments. There are no dangers to bodily security and freedom that confine him by brute force to the task and environment to which a superior has assigned him.

Our generation has forgotten that the system of private property is the most important guaranty of freedom. It is only because the control of the

The Reader's Digest 46 (April 1945): 2–20. The Book-of-the-Month Club offered reprints of the condensation. The article also appeared in London in booklet form. The University of Chicago Press had published the original of *The Road to Serfdom* in 1944. Bracketed headings added to indicate major themes in the selection that follows.

means of production is divided among many people acting independently that we as individuals can decide what to do with ourselves. When all the means of production are vested in a single hand, whether it be nominally that of "society" as a whole or that of a dictator, whoever exercises this control has complete power over us. In the hands of private individuals, what is called economic power can be an instrument of coercion, but it is never control over the whole life of a person. But when economic power is centralized as an instrument of political power it creates a degree of dependence scarcely distinguishable from slavery. It has been well said that, in a country where the sole employer is the state, opposition means death by slow starvation.

Individualism, in contrast to socialism and all other forms of totalitarianism, is based on the respect of Christianity for the individual man and the belief that it is desirable that men should be free to develop their own individual gifts and bents. This philosophy, first fully developed during the Renaissance, grew and spread into what we know as Western civilization. The general direction of social development was one of freeing the individual from the ties which bound him in feudal society.

. . . Wherever the barriers to the free exercise of human ingenuity were removed, man became rapidly able to satisfy ever-widening ranges of desire. By the beginning of the 20th century the workingman in the Western world had reached a degree of material comfort, security and personal independence which 100 years before had hardly seemed possible.

[THE DANGERS OF SOCIALISM AND PLANNING]

The effect of this success was to create among men a new sense of power over their own fate, the belief in the unbounded possibilities of improving their own lot. What had been achieved came to be regarded as a secure and imperishable possession, acquired once and for all; and the rate of progress began to seem too slow. Moreover, the principles which had made this progress came to be regarded as obstacles to speedier progress, impatiently to be brushed away. It might be said that the very success of liberalism became the cause of its decline. . . .

. . . [I]n the democracies the majority of people still believe that socialism and freedom can be combined. They do not realize that democratic socialism, the great utopia of the last few generations, is not only unachievable but that to strive for it produces something utterly different — the very destruction of freedom itself. . . .

The successful use of competition does not preclude some types of government interference. For instance, to limit working hours, to require certain sanitary arrangements, to provide an extensive system of social services is fully compatible with the preservation of competition. There are, too, certain fields where the system of competition is impracticable. For example, the harmful effects of deforestation or of the smoke of factories cannot be confined to the owner of the property in question. But the fact that we have to resort to direct regulation by authority where the conditions for the proper working of competition cannot be created does not prove that we should suppress competition where it can be made to function. To create conditions in which competition will be as effective as possible, to prevent fraud and deception, to break up monopolies — these tasks provide a wide and unquestioned field for state activity.

This does not mean that it is possible to find some "middle way" between competition and central direction, though nothing seems at first more plausible, or is more likely to appeal to reasonable people. . . .

Planning and competition can be combined only by planning *for* competition, not by planning *against* competition. The planning against which all our criticism is directed is solely the planning against competition. . . .

What is promised to us as the Road to Freedom is in fact the Highroad to Servitude. For it is not difficult to see what must be the consequences when democracy embarks upon a course of planning. The goal of the planning will be described by some such vague term as "the general welfare." There will be no real agreement as to the ends to be attained, and the effect of the people's agreeing that there must be central planning, without agreeing on the ends, will be rather as if a group of people were to commit themselves to take a journey together without agreeing where they want to go: with the result that they may all have to make a journey which most of them do not want at all. . . .

Once you admit that the individual is merely a means to serve the ends of the higher entity called society or the nation, most of those features of totalitarianism which horrify us follow of necessity. From the collectivist standpoint intolerance and brutal suppression of dissent, deception and spying, the complete disregard of the life and happiness of the individual are essential, and unavoidable. Acts which revolt all our feelings, such as the shooting of hostages or the killing of the old or sick, are treated as mere matters of expediency; the compulsory uprooting and transportation of hundreds of thousands becomes an instrument of policy approved by almost everybody except the victims. . . .

[ANGLO–AMERICAN VALUES IN PERIL]

. . . [T]he virtues which are held less and less in esteem in Britain and America are precisely those on which Anglo-Saxons justly prided themselves and in which they were generally recognized to excel. These virtues were independence and self-reliance, individual initiative and local responsibility, the successful reliance on voluntary activity, noninterference with one's neighbor and tolerance of the different, and a healthy suspicion of power and authority.

Almost all the traditions and institutions which have molded the national character and the whole moral climate of England and America are those which the progress of collectivism and its centralistic tendencies are progressively destroying. . . .

[THE SUPERIORITY OF THE FREE MARKET]

One argument frequently heard is that the complexity of modern civilization creates new problems with which we cannot hope to deal effectively except by central planning. This argument is based upon a complete misapprehension of the working of competition. The very complexity of modern conditions makes competition the *only* method by which a coordination of affairs can be adequately achieved.

There would be no difficulty about efficient control or planning were conditions so simple that a single person or board could effectively survey all the facts. But as the factors which have to be taken into account become numerous and complex; no one center can keep track of them. The constantly changing conditions of demand and supply of different commodities can never be fully known, or quickly enough disseminated by any one center.

Under competition — and under no other economic order — the price system automatically records all the relevant data. Entrepreneurs, by watching the movement of comparatively few prices, as an engineer watches a few dials, can adjust their activities to those of their fellows.

Compared with this method of solving the economic problem — by decentralization plus automatic coordination through the price system — the method of central direction is incredibly clumsy, primitive, and limited in scope. . . . Any further growth in economic complexity, far from making central direction more necessary, makes it more important than ever that we should use the technique of competition and not depend on conscious control. . . .

[MORE ON THE DANGERS OF ECONOMIC PLANNING]

Most planners who have seriously considered the practical aspects of their task have little doubt that a directed economy must be run on dictatorial lines, that the complex system of interrelated activities must be directed by staffs of experts, with ultimate power in the hands of a commander-in-chief whose actions must not be fettered by democratic procedure. The consolation our planners offer us is that this authoritarian direction will apply "only" to economic matters. This assurance is usually accompanied by the suggestion that, by giving up freedom in the less important aspects of our lives, we shall obtain freedom in the pursuit of higher values. On this ground people who abhor the idea of a political dictatorship often clamor for a dictator in the economic field. . . .

The so-called economic freedom which the planners promise us means precisely that we are to be relieved of the necessity of solving our own economic problems and that the bitter choices which this often involves are to be made for us. Since under modern conditions we are for almost everything dependent on means which our fellow men provide, economic planning would involve direction of almost the whole of our life. There is hardly an aspect of it, from our primary needs to our relations with our family and friends, from the nature of our work to the use of our leisure, over which the planner would not exercise his "conscious control."

[STRIKING A BALANCE ON SECURITY]

[T]here are two kinds of security: the certainty of a given minimum of sustenance for all and the security of a given standard of life, of the relative position which one person or group enjoys compared with others.

There is no reason why, in a society which has reached the general level of wealth ours has, the first kind of security should not be guaranteed to all without endangering general freedom; that is: some minimum of food, shelter and clothing, sufficient to preserve health. Nor is there any reason why the state should not help to organize a comprehensive system of social insurance in providing for those common hazards of life against which few can make adequate provision.

It is planning for security of the second kind which has such an insidious effect on liberty. It is planning designed to protect individuals or groups against diminutions of their incomes. . . .

If we are not to destroy individual freedom, competition must be left to function unobstructed. Let a uniform minimum be secured to everybody by all means; but let us admit at the same time that all claims for a privileged security of particular classes must lapse, that all excuses disappear for allowing particular groups to exclude newcomers from sharing their relative prosperity in order to maintain a special standard of their own. . . .

[Conclusion]

We must regain the conviction on which liberty in the Anglo-Saxon countries has been based and which Benjamin Franklin expressed in phrase applicable to us as individuals no less than as nations:

"Those who would give up essential liberty to purchase a little temporary safety deserve neither liberty nor safety." . . .

. . . It is, indeed, those who cry loudest for a planned economy who are most completely under the sway of the ideas which have created this war and most of the evils from which we suffer.

The guiding principle in any attempt to create a world of free men must be this: A policy of freedom for the individual is the only truly progressive policy.

2.7

Karl Polanyi on the State as the Creator of the Free Market and the Savior of Societies

If Keynes was the darling of economic planners in the early decades after World War II and Hayek was the prophet of economic trends to dominate the last third of the century, then what Karl Polanyi had to say in *The Great Transformation* could make him the man of the future. Like Hayek, Polanyi had roots in central Europe. He grew up in Budapest, Hungary, and worked in Vienna in the 1920s. He too had left the continent (in his case anti-Semitism drove him away) to pursue an academic career in Britain and the United States. Like Hayek, Polanyi was especially influenced by his stay in England, which offered him an ideal place for examining the industrial revolution as the defining force in the making of the modern world. Though neglected when it appeared in 1944, *The Great Transformation* is a challenging masterwork of historical sociology that has attracted increasing numbers of admirers in recent decades. They have been struck by how Polanyi's analysis of the market's advance in the nineteenth century offers cautions about the revival of free-market ideology in the late twentieth century.

Listen to Polanyi as the third voice in this debate over the operation of the free market. What does Polanyi mean by his core concept of the "double movement"? With whom does he seem to agree more — Keynes or Hayek — in his assessment of state intervention? How does he stand on the relationship between economic principles on the one side and individual freedom and political democracy on the other?

From *The Great Transformation*
1944

[SELF-REGULATING MARKETS EXERT CONTROL OVER SOCIETY]

[M]an's economy, as a rule, is submerged in his social relationships. He does not act so as to safeguard his individual interest in the possession of material goods; he acts so as to safeguard his social standing, his social claims, his social assets. He values material goods only in so far as they serve this end. . . .

A market economy is an economic system controlled, regulated, and directed by markets alone; order in the production and distribution of goods is entrusted to this self-regulating mechanism. An economy of this kind derives from the expectation that human beings behave in such a way as to achieve maximum money gains. . . .

A further group of assumptions follows in respect to the state and its policy. Nothing must be allowed to inhibit the formation of markets, nor must incomes be permitted to be formed otherwise than through sales. Neither must there be any interference with the adjustment of prices to changed market conditions. . . . Neither price, nor supply, nor demand must be fixed or regulated; only such policies and measures are in order which help to ensure the self-regulation of the market by creating conditions which make the market the only organizing power in the economic sphere. . . .

. . . A market economy can exist only in a market society. . . . A market economy must comprise all elements of industry, including labor, land, and money. . . . But labor and land are no other than the human beings themselves of which every society consists and the natural surroundings in which it exists. To include them in the market mechanism means to subordinate the substance of society itself to the laws of the market. . . .

[HOW STATES MADE THE FREE MARKET POSSIBLE]

There was nothing natural about *laissez-faire;* free markets could never have come into being [during the nineteenth century] merely by allowing things

---

Karl Polanyi, *The Great Transformation: The Political and Economic Origins of Our Times* (Boston: Beacon Press, 1957), 46, 68–69, 71, 73, 76, 132–33, 139–41, 144, 156, 159–60, 214, 250, 256–57. I have rearranged sections of this work in order to improve the flow of the argument. Bracketed headings added to indicate major themes.

to take their course. Just as cotton manufactures — the leading free trade industry [in Britain] — were created by the help of protective tariffs, export bounties, and indirect wage subsidies, *laissez-faire* itself was enforced by the state. The [eighteen] thirties and forties saw not only an outburst of legislation repealing restrictive regulations, but also an enormous increase in the administrative functions of the state, which was now being endowed with a central bureaucracy able to fulfill the tasks set by the adherents of liberalism. . . . It was the task of the executive to collect statistics and information, to foster science and experiment, as well as to supply the innumerable instruments of final realization in the field of government. . . .

The road to the free market was opened and kept open by an enormous increase in continuous, centrally organized and controlled [state] interventionism. . . . [T]he introduction of free markets, far from doing away with the need for control, regulation, and intervention, enormously increased their range. Administrators had to be constantly on the watch to ensure the free working of the system. . . .

[THE MARKET'S DESTRUCTIVE SOCIAL EFFECTS IN ENGLAND AND INDIA]

. . . To allow the market mechanism to be sole director of the fate of human beings and their natural environment, indeed, even of the amount and use of purchasing power, would result in the demolition of society. For the alleged commodity "labor power" cannot be shoved about, used indiscriminately, or even left unused, without affecting also the human individual who happens to be the bearer of this peculiar commodity. In disposing of a man's labor power the system would, incidentally, dispose of the physical, psychological, and moral entity "man" attached to that tag. Robbed of the protective covering of cultural institutions, human beings would perish from the effects of social exposure; they would die as the victims of acute social dislocation through vice, perversion, crime, and starvation. Nature would be reduced to its elements, neighborhoods and landscapes defiled, rivers polluted, military safety jeopardized, the power to produce food and raw materials destroyed. Finally, the market administration of purchasing power would periodically liquidate business enterprise, for shortages and surfeits of money would prove as disastrous to business as floods and droughts in primitive society. Undoubtedly, labor, land, and money markets *are* essential to a market economy. But no society could stand the effects of such a system of crude fictions even for the shortest stretch of time unless its human and natural substance as well as its business organization was protected against the ravages of this satanic mill. . . .

. . . Improvements . . . are, as a rule, bought at the price of social dislocation. If the rate of dislocation is too great, the community must succumb in the process. . . . [N]othing saved the common people of England from the impact of the Industrial Revolution. A blind faith in spontaneous progress had taken hold of people's minds, and with the fanaticism of sectarians the most enlightened pressed forward for boundless and unregulated change in society. The effects on the lives of the people were awful beyond description. . . .

. . . For some seventy years, scholars and Royal Commissions alike had denounced the horrors of the Industrial Revolution [in England], and a galaxy of poets, thinkers, and writers had branded its cruelties. It was deemed an established fact that the masses were being sweated and starved by the callous exploiters of their helplessness. . . .

. . . Indian masses in the second half of the nineteenth century . . . perished in large numbers because the Indian village community had been demolished. . . . The actual source of famines in the last fifty years was the free marketing of grain combined with local failure of incomes. Failure of crops was, of course, part of the picture, but despatch of grain by rail made it possible to send relief to the threatened areas; the trouble was that the people were unable to buy the corn at rocketing prices, which on a free but incompletely organized market were bound to be the reaction to a shortage. In former times small local stores had been held against harvest failure, but these had been now discontinued or swept away into the big market. . . . While under the regime of feudalism and of the village community, *noblesse oblige,*[1] clan solidarity, and regulation of the corn market checked famines, under the rule of the market the people could not be prevented from starving according to the rules of the game. . . .

[THE "DOUBLE MOVEMENT" PITTING THE MARKET SYSTEM AGAINST SOCIETY]

Social history in the nineteenth century was thus the result of a double movement. . . . While on the one hand markets spread all over the face of the globe and the amount of goods involved grew to unbelievable proportions, on the other hand . . . a deep-seated movement sprang into being to resist the pernicious effects of a market-controlled economy. Society protected itself against the perils inherent in a self-regulating market system — this was the one comprehensive feature in the history of the age. . . .

. . . [On one side of the double movement] was the principle of economic liberalism, aiming at the establishment of a self-regulating market, relying on the support of the trading classes, and using largely *laissez-faire* and free trade as its methods; the other was the principle of social protection aiming at the conservation of man and nature as well as productive organization, relying on the varying support of those most immediately affected by the deleterious action of the market — primarily, but not exclusively, the working and the landed classes — and using protective legislation, restrictive associations, and other instruments of intervention as its methods.

. . . [T]he trading classes had no organ to sense the dangers involved in the exploitation of the physical strength of the worker, the destruction of family life, the devastation of neighborhoods, the denudation of forests, the pollu-

---

[1]The obligations of those privileged by birth or accomplishment to serve society in some way.

tion of rivers, the deterioration of craft standards, the disruption of folkways, and the general degradation of existence including housing and arts, as well as the innumerable forms of private and public life that do not affect profits. The middle class fulfilled their function by developing an all but sacramental belief in the universal beneficence of profits.... Roughly, to the landed aristocracy and the peasantry fell the task of safeguarding the martial qualities of the nation which continued to depend largely on men and soil, while the laboring people, to a smaller or greater extent, became representatives of the common human interests that had become homeless....

...While *laissez-faire* economy was the product of deliberate state action, subsequent restrictions on *laissez-faire* started in a spontaneous way. *Laissez-faire* was planned; planning was not....The legislative spearhead of the countermovement against a self-regulating market as it developed in the half century following 1860 turned out to be spontaneous, undirected by opinion, and actuated by a purely pragmatic spirit....

...The agrarian crisis and the Great Depression of 1873-86 had shaken confidence in economic self-healing. From now onward the typical institutions of market economy could usually be introduced only if accompanied by protectionist measures, all the more so because since the late 1870's and early 1880's nations were forming themselves into organized units which were apt to suffer grievously from the dislocations involved in any sudden adjustment to the needs of foreign trade or foreign exchanges....

Much of the massive suffering inseparable from a period of transition is already behind us. In the social and economic dislocation of our age, in the tragic vicissitudes of the depression, fluctuations of currency, mass unemployment, shiftings of social status, spectacular destruction of historical states, we have experienced the worst. Unwittingly we have been paying the price of the change....

[THE CONFLICT BETWEEN THE FREE MARKET AND FREEDOM]

...The root of all evil, the liberal insists, was precisely this interference with the freedom of employment, trade and currencies practiced by the various schools of social, national, and monopolistic protectionism since the third quarter of the nineteenth century; but for the unholy alliance of trade unions and labor parties with monopolistic manufacturers and agrarian interests, which in their shortsighted greed joined forces to frustrate economic liberty, the world would be enjoying today the fruits of an almost automatic system of creating material welfare. Liberal leaders never weary of repeating that the tragedy of the nineteenth century sprang from the incapacity of man to remain faithful to the inspiration of the early liberals; that the generous initiative of our ancestors was frustrated by the passions of nationalism and class war, vested interests, and monopolists, and above all, by the blindness of the working people to the ultimate beneficence of unrestricted economic freedom to all human interests, including their own. A great intellectual and moral advance was thus, it is claimed, frustrated by the intellectual and moral weaknesses of the mass of the people; what the spirit of Enlightenment had achieved was put to nought by the forces of selfishness[.] In a nutshell, this is the economic liberal's defense. Unless it is refuted, he will continue to hold the floor in the contest of arguments. . . .

. . . Planning and control are being attacked as a denial of freedom. Free enterprise and private ownership are declared to be essentials of freedom. No society built on other foundations is said to deserve to be called free. The freedom that regulation creates is denounced as unfreedom; the justice, liberty and welfare it offers are decried as a camouflage of slavery. In vain did socialists promise a realm of freedom, for means determine ends: the U.S.S.R., which used planning, regulation and control as its instruments, has not yet put the liberties promised in her Constitution into practice, and, probably, the critics add, never will. . . . But to turn against regulation means to turn against reform. With the liberal the idea of freedom thus degenerates into a mere advocacy of free enterprise — which is today reduced to a fiction by the hard reality of giant trusts and princely monopolies. This means the fullness of freedom for those whose income, leisure and security need no enhancing, and a mere pittance of liberty for the people, who may in vain attempt to make use of their democratic rights to gain shelter from the power of the owners of property. Nor is that all. Nowhere did the liberals in fact succeed in re-establishing free enterprise, which was doomed to fail for intrinsic reasons. It was as a result of their efforts that big business was installed in several European countries and, incidentally, also various brands of fascism, as in Austria. Planning, regulation and control, which they wanted to see banned as dangers to freedom, were then employed by the confessed enemies of freedom to abolish it altogether. Yet the victory of fascism was made practically unavoidable by the liberals' obstruction of any reform involving planning, regulation, or control. . . .

The passing of market-economy can become the beginning of an era of unprecedented freedom. Juridical and actual freedom can be made wider and more general than ever before; regulation and control can achieve freedom not only for the few, but for all. Freedom not as an appurtenance of privilege, tainted at the source, but as a prescriptive right extending far beyond the narrow confines of the political sphere into the intimate organization of society itself. Thus will old freedoms and civic rights be added to the fund of new freedom generated by the leisure and security that industrial society offers to all. Such a society can afford to be both just and free.

RECONSTRUCTING THE JAPANESE
AND EUROPEAN ECONOMIES

American, British, and other delegations meeting at Bretton Woods in New Hampshire in 1944 laid down important principles that would come to shape the postwar economy. But more urgent than working out global rules for trade and investment was reviving individual national economies and creating functioning internal economic systems that delivered goods to desperate populations. Stalin quickly made clear that in the Soviet Union and eastern Europe, reconstruction would follow well-worn lines of five-year plans tied to the build up of heavy industry (see his February 1946 speech in Document 1.5). There was much less certainty about the way out of the ruins in Japan and western Europe, as advocates ranging from Communist parties to strict *laissez-faire* proponents jumped into the fray. The ad hoc decisions that each country made, usually for short-term reasons, began to cumulate into a variety of national economic approaches that would in time ensure diversity within a system framed by the rules and institutions created at Bretton Woods. The first document that follows highlights the prevailing Japanese approach that looked to the leadership of the state. In the second document, we see the first steps that would carry Europe toward unprecedented levels of international cooperation both within the region and between the regional economies and the United States.

2.8

Japan's Blueprint for Recovery

Hardly had the Pacific War with the United States and its allies begun than young Japanese technocrats with access to inside information realized the likelihood of defeat was high and the need for postwar planning urgent. In June 1945 with the end near, like-minded officials began discussing post-surrender economic policy under what they anticipated would be a U.S. occupation. The economists involved were a new breed, eclectic in their approach, statistical in their methods, and averse to the strongly philosophical approaches that had dominated the field of economics. The consensus among them, building on war as well as prewar experience, was that the state would have to guide a resource-poor and war-devastated country back to prosperity. In September 1946 the Ministry of Foreign Affairs, which had served as the host for the planners, published their handiwork.

What are the goals that this plan sets and how does it suggest realizing them? How does it assess Japan's economic strengths and weaknesses, and what recommendations does it make to maximize one and minimize the other? How does it define the international context in which the postwar economy will have to operate? How would Keynes, Hayek, and Polanyi have reacted to this Japanese blueprint for recovery?

Foreign Ministry Special Survey Committee
Plans for the Postwar Economy
September 1946

In the present time, when unexplored markets no longer exist anywhere and the scale of production has expanded phenomenally, free competition motivated by pursuit of profits would only lead to confusion and stagnation of an economy's progress and thus usher in an age when planned adjustment be-

---

Saburo Okita, comp., *Postwar Reconstruction of the Japanese Economy* (Tokyo: University of Tokyo Press, 1992), 12–14, 77, 88–89, 91, 94, 98.

tween production and consumption would be required. The period of a growing capitalism based on the principle of laissez-faire is already past. The world
economy has passed even the stage of private monopolistic capital which was
initiated in the late nineteenth century, and has at last entered an era of State
capitalism or of controlled, organized capitalism.

During the war, various nations moved to highly controlled economic
systems under the supreme imperative to increase military production, with
the result that State power penetrated deep into the structures of economic
communities. Even after the war, with the pressure of war removed, such
trends will be promoted as a natural stage of social evolution. . . . In the
United States–Britain bloc[,] capitalistic free competition will undoubtedly
continue to be waged in the future. In particular, after the postwar emergency
conditions have run their course, a return to economies as free as possible will
be contemplated. But even if "freedom" is attained, it will be a "freedom"
restricted by planning.

For the maintenance of world peace, too, planned management of the
world economy is desirable because the world will again be led into a devastating war if economic competition is left to be waged among the nations as
in the past. . . .

Attention should also be drawn to the growing trends toward the socialization of economies resulting from the rise of laboring classes in various
countries after the late world war. The nationalization of coal mines and of
the Bank of England in Britain are outstanding examples. Moves in the same
direction are under way in France, Czechoslovakia, and other European countries and in neighboring China as well. Such trends toward socialization are
aimed at liberalizing [liberating?] major industries from the object of profit-
making and placing them under an operation that will serve the betterment
of people's lives. The trends originate in the tendency of the times calling for
the guarantee of people's livelihoods by states and organizations. . . .

Japan has emerged from the war with the foundation of its economy markedly reduced and the national economy completely impoverished. If things
continue as they are, the Japanese economy will return to the stage in which
the majority of people consume almost 90% of their energies in acquiring
food, as if they were Eskimos; this situation will in the end merely bring
about a substantial reduction of the population.

In order to check such a reversal and ensure future progress, the nation has
to endure scarcities and strive for the accumulation and restoration of economic power on the one hand and, on the other, to take the first step toward
actual reconstruction as early as possible by preparing an economic timetable
based on a new foundation and by laying down annual reconstruction programs in accordance with the timetable. . . .

Among the industrial goods Japan should export, priority will be given
first to light industrial manufactures, such as textiles, rubber products, and
sundry goods. When the prospective rapid growth of light industries in various parts of Asia is taken into account, however, it is clear that Japan will need
to depend to a fairly high degree on the export of machinery and chemical

goods. When it is taken into consideration that the nation has an abundance of labor but lacks raw material resources, it is appropriate from the viewpoint of international specialization that Japan should choose industries that require as much labor as possible and in which the production process is difficult to automate. Such industries, for example, include those manufacturing such machinery as electrical equipment, communications apparatus, precision instruments, tools, meters and gauges, scientific equipment, bicycles, and motor vehicles, and industries that produced such chemicals as medical supplies, agricultural and industrial medicines, dyestuffs, and seasonings. In agriculture, too, more sophistication will become necessary in such forms as the production and exportation of fruit trees, raw materials for the manufacture of paper, and other industrial crops in addition to raw silk. . . .

Viewed from such a standpoint, Japan should pursue, in principle, a low-tariff policy in the future. While on the one hand this may inflict great damage on domestic industries, particularly agriculture and certain other industries that are disadvantaged by geographic conditions, on the other hand the prosperity of the economy as a whole will have to be maintained by fostering those industries that are suited by location for exporting their products to world markets. In this case, however, Japan will need to depend on foreign trade to a greater degree and to develop export-oriented industries on a larger scale.

In reality, however, the Japanese economy suffered great damage in the war. . . . It is also anticipated that Japan will lag far behind the United States, Great Britain, and the Soviet Union, the winners of the war, in economic reconstruction and become markedly inferior in productive power and technology. As a result Japan will experience great difficulties in importing even its minimum requirements of food and other commodities, due to shortages of the means of payment, for a considerably long period to come. While aiming at positively participating in the system of international division of labor, as mentioned earlier, Japan will at the same time need to enhance to the maximum its self-sufficiency in food, industrial manufactures, and other necessities for the time being.

. . . The trend of the postwar world economy is toward the realization of full employment and better living standards all over the globe by the breaking down of autarchic tendencies in various countries, the removal of world trade barriers, and the promotion of international trade to the maximum under the leadership of the United States. . . .

A comprehensive and specific year-to-year reconstruction program will have to be formulated in order to revive the Japanese economy from the extreme destitution in which it finds itself now. The waste of economic power that would result from allowing laissez-faire play to market forces will not be permitted in order that all the meager economic power remaining may be concentrated in a direction toward reproduction on an enlarged scale and that the process of reconstruction may be expedited.

The specific process of devising a plan for economic reconstruction would be, first, to fix a target living standard to be attained and the time period during which this target should be reached; then, taking as a starting point a demand and supply plan for essential materials and also a national land reconstruction plan formulated on the basis of the target and time period, to work out in a coordinated manner programs regarding production, exports and imports, funds, public finance, employment, and so on. It might be a good idea, for instance, in formulating the plan, to make the target the restoration within the next ten years of that standard of consumer life per capita of the mainland population in about 1929–30. . . . Such a plan should not be drawn in the bureaucratic and coercive way as was done in the past but would need to be formulated in a democratic manner that would fully reflect views in private business or at the labor site.

2.9

Secretary of State George C. Marshall Makes the Case for Assisting Europe

By mid-1947, Europe faced severe economic problems, with serious political and social implications. Reconstruction, especially in the industrial sector, required investments that cash-short European businessmen and government officials could not afford to make. Lagging recovery was sure to create popular discontent, enhance the appeal of Communist parties tied to the Soviet Union, and weaken anti-communist parties aligned with the United States. Complicating the situation was strong sentiment for ending the system of rival nation-states that had repeatedly plunged Europe into conflict. Anti-fascist groups during the war had made a forceful case for a European federation as the surest way to transcend the old nationalist order and create a new Europe on a fresh, cooperative foundation. An alternative position proposed state-to-state agreements to gradually build up areas of common interest and cooperation such as joint measures to promote region-wide economic recovery.

At this critical moment of flux in European affairs, U.S. Secretary of State George Marshall intervened with a hastily constructed offer of help and a plea for collaborative efforts. Whatever it lacked in eloquence, this proposal — soon to be known as the "Marshall Plan" — had a dramatic impact. It buoyed the pro–U.S. ruling parties in the western portion of Europe, put regional Communist parties on the defensive, alarmed the Soviet Union, and gave a decisive push to advocates of step-by-step, state-to-state cooperation. In this light, Marshall's speech stands alongside the Truman doctrine (Document 1.7) as a major moment in the timeline of the Cold War. But it also figures as a major impetus to European integration — the rise of the European Community and its transformation into the European Union (treated below in Documents 5.5 and 8.6–8.9).

To what extent does Marshall make the case for assistance in terms of Cold War fears, humanitarian obligations, or abstract notions of trans-Atlantic cooperation? What is it about this speech that makes it less rhetorically powerful than the Truman Doctrine speech? How do the fundamental ideas guiding this approach to European recovery differ from those expressed above in Japan's economic plan? Are there any hints of which broad economic approach Marshall hoped the Europeans would follow?

Speech at Harvard University
June 4, 1947

I need not tell you that the world situation is very serious. . . .

In considering the requirements for the rehabilitation of Europe, the physi-cal loss of life, the visible destruction of cities, factories, mines, and railroads was correctly estimated, but it has become obvious during recent months that this visible destruction was probably less serious than the dislocation of the entire fabric of European economy. For the past ten years conditions have been abnormal. The feverish preparation for war and the more feverish main-tenance of the war effort engulfed all aspects of national economies. Machin-ery has fallen into disrepair or is entirely obsolete. Under the arbitrary and destructive Nazi rule, virtually every possible enterprise was geared into the German war machine. Long-standing commercial ties, private institutions, banks, insurance companies, and shipping companies disappeared through loss of capital, absorption through nationalization, or by simple destruction. In many countries, confidence in the local currency has been severely shaken. The breakdown of the business structure of Europe during the war was com-plete. Recovery has been seriously retarded by the fact that two years after the close of hostilities a peace settlement with Germany and Austria has not been agreed upon. But even given a more prompt solution of these difficult problems, the rehabilitation of the economic structure of Europe quite evi-dently will require a much longer time and greater effort than has been fore-seen.

There is a phase of this matter which is both interesting and serious. The farmer has always produced the foodstuffs to exchange with the city dweller for the other necessities of life. This division of labor is the basis of modern civilization. At the present time it is threatened with breakdown. The town and city industries are not producing adequate goods to exchange with the food-producing farmer. Raw materials and fuel are in short supply. Machin-ery is lacking or worn out. The farmer or the peasant cannot find the goods for sale which he desires to purchase. So the sale of his farm produce for money which he cannot use seems to him an unprofitable transaction. He, therefore, has withdrawn many fields from crop cultivation and is using them for grazing. He feeds more grain to stock and finds for himself and his family an ample supply of food, however short he may be on clothing and the other ordinary gadgets of civilization. Meanwhile, people in the cities are short of

---

This is a verbatim version of the speech taken from a tape recording in the George C. Marshall Foundation archives. Transcript available from the George C. Marshall International Center website: <http://www.georgecmarshall.org/lt/speeches/marshall_plan.cfm> (January 1, 2003). It differs from the published versions mainly in additions Marshall made to the opening and closing paragraphs. Published versions can be found in *The Department of State Bulletin* 16 (June 15, 1947): 1159–60 and on the website for the U.S. State Department's International Information Programs at <http://usinfo.state.gov/usa/infousa/facts/democrac/57.htm> (Janu-ary 1, 2003).

food and fuel, and in some places approaching the starvation levels. So the governments are forced to use their foreign money and credits to procure these necessities abroad. This process exhausts funds which are urgently needed for reconstruction. Thus a very serious situation is rapidly developing which bodes no good for the world. The modern system of the division of labor upon which the exchange of products is based is in danger of breaking down.

The truth of the matter is that Europe's requirements for the next three or four years of foreign food and other essential products — principally from America — are so much greater than her present ability to pay that she must have substantial additional help or face economic, social, and political deterioration of a very grave character.

The remedy lies in breaking the vicious circle and restoring the confidence of the European people in the economic future of their own countries and of Europe as a whole. . . . Our policy is directed not against any country or doctrine but against hunger, poverty, desperation, and chaos. Its purpose should be the revival of a working economy in the world so as to permit the emergence of political and social conditions in which free institutions can exist. Such assistance, I am convinced, must not be on a piecemeal basis as various crises develop. Any assistance that this Government may render in the future should provide a cure rather than a mere palliative. Any government that is willing to assist in the task of recovery will find full cooperation, I am sure, on the part of the United States Government. Any government which maneuvers to block the recovery of other countries cannot expect help from us. Furthermore, governments, political parties or groups which seek to perpetuate human misery in order to profit therefrom politically or otherwise will encounter the opposition of the United States.

It is already evident that, before the United States Government can proceed much further in its efforts to alleviate the situation and help start the European world on its way to recovery, there must be some agreement among the countries of Europe as to the requirements of the situation and the part those countries themselves will take in order to give proper effect to whatever action might be undertaken by this Government. It would be neither fitting nor efficacious for this Government to undertake to draw up unilaterally a program designed to place Europe on its feet economically. This is the business of the Europeans. The initiative, I think, must come from Europe. The role of this country should consist of friendly aid in the drafting of a European program and of later support of such a program so far as it may be practical for us to do so. The program should be a joint one, agreed to by a number, if not all, European nations. . . .

. . . [W]e are remote from the scene of these troubles. It is virtually impossible at this distance merely by reading, or listening, or even seeing photographs or motion pictures, to grasp at all the real significance of the situation. And yet the whole world of the future hangs on a proper judgment.

CHAPTER 3

THE THIRD WORLD: FIRST TREMORS IN ASIA

THE THIRD WORLD — the large sweep of the globe that was in 1945 under direct or indirect foreign control — was the stage for one of the great transformations of the postwar era. Rising demands for national independence and unfettered sovereignty threw foreigners on the defensive and sent colonialism into eclipse. In mounting this resistance Asia took the lead. Well before World War II, Chinese, Vietnamese, Indian, and other nationalists in the region were demanding an end to empire. The war added impetus to their cause by undermining the strength and will of colonial powers.

The postwar bids for liberation within China, Vietnam, and India each revealed two fundamental lines of cleavage that would become commonplace as third-world resistance spread to other regions. One was the difference in priorities between political elites heading their countries' liberation projects and the vast majority of their fellows living in the countryside. Elites embraced grand national visions inspired by ideas derived from the West, while those in the countryside focused with a ferocious intensity on the everyday concerns critical to survival. The second basic line of cleavage was defined by the divergent goals pursued by political elites in different countries. Some sought nothing less than a fundamental remaking of the entire society, a task usually conceived in Marxist terms. Others were determined in pursuit of political independence, but hesitant in the face of such social ills as poverty, illiteracy, and discrimination.

The material in this chapter explores these two patterns as they evolved in China, Vietnam, and India. How revolutionary was the outlook of these countries' leaders? Were their goals limited to political independence, or did they imagine broader changes (social and economic as well as political)? How well did their concerns mesh with those of the vast majority of their people living in the countryside?

CHINA'S TRIUMPHANT REVOLUTION

China's twentieth-century revolution is inextricably linked with the history of the Chinese Communist Party (CCP). It is also tied up with the dreams of national revival that had gripped Chinese elites watching their country's decline through the nineteenth century and into the early twentieth. Those who founded the party in 1921 were searching for a solution to China's prolonged crisis, and thought they had found it in Marxism, an ideology thrust to international prominence by the Bolshevik revolution. At the time of the party's founding, however, its leaders were but one, hardly audible voice in the debate over China's way forward.

It would have taken a bold observer to predict the CCP's ultimate success. There were no more than fifty members, and the party's young and inexperienced leaders, schooled in Soviet orthodoxy, operated under the thumb of Soviet advisers and were heavily dependent on Soviet funding. After a period of slow growth, the Communists fell victim in 1927 to a purge by their chief political rival and sometime ally, the Nationalist Party headed by Chiang Kai-shek. The survivors took refuge in the remote, northwestern part of China. The "Long March" that led to the northwest in the mid-1930s marked the emergence of Mao Zedong as party leader and a turn in party fortunes. Mao had pursued his revolutionary career apart from the emissaries from Moscow, and had taken increasing interest in rural areas as a base from which the party might build its strength with peasant support. Mao's strategy paid off. The CCP's wartime alliance with the Nationalists, a patriotic marriage of convenience, degenerated into civil war in 1946. Communist forces, at first outmanned and outgunned, rallied and in 1949 claimed victory and embarked on a fundamental transformation of China. The international implications were as great as the domestic ones. Mao's Soviet backers had gained a major ally, while the Americans, who had picked the losing side, fumed over this major setback.

3.1

Mao Zedong Recounts His Path to Socialism

In mid-1936 an American journalist, Edgar Snow, traveled to the remote operations center of the Communist Party in China's northwest and coaxed from the party's emerging leader an account of his early years. Putting aside the reticence usually so marked a feature of Chinese autobiography, Mao Zedong highlighted his own moment of Marxist illumination and his strong revolutionary commitment. Mao devoted over ten evenings to telling his story. Snow listened to a translator and took notes, which were translated back into Chinese for Mao to review. Many of Mao's colleagues were hearing his life story for the first time. But Mao had a broader audience in mind. He wanted to win support for the party among Chinese and foreigners. Inviting Snow, a reliably progressive American, to see Chinese Communism in action was thus part of a publicity campaign. Snow's *Red Star over China* appeared in 1938 to acclaim as a sympathetic portrait of the

Chinese Communist movement. The first Chinese version of Mao's story had appeared the year before. That Chinese edition and others would circulate within Nationalist- as well as CCP-controlled areas.

In this authorized version of Mao's formative years, what themes did Mao seek to highlight regarding his own personality and road to communism? Would American and Chinese readers have carried away the same impression from this life story? How much should the historian rely on this account for insight into the intellectual influences and personality of the young Mao? To ask an even more fundamental question, is the old adage about the child being the father of the man really so reliable that we should attempt to apply it here?

Edgar Snow
From *Red Star over China*
1938

I was born in the village of Shao Shan, in Hsiang T'an *hsien* [county], Hunan province, in 1893. . . .

My father was a poor peasant and while still young was obliged to join the army because of heavy debts. He was a soldier for many years. Later on he returned to the village where I was born, and by saving carefully and gathering together a little money through small trading and other enterprise he managed to buy back his land.

As middle peasants then my family owned fifteen *mou*[1] of land. On this they could raise sixty *tan* of rice a year. The five members of the family consumed a total of thirty-five *tan* — that is, about seven each — which left an annual surplus of twenty-five *tan*[2]. Using this surplus, my father accumulated a little capital and in time purchased seven more *mou*, which gave the family the status of "rich" peasants. We could then raise eighty-four *tan* of rice a year. . . .

I began studying in a local primary school when I was eight and remained there until I was thirteen years old. In the early morning and at night I worked on the farm. During the day I read the Confucian Analects and the Four Classics. My Chinese teacher belonged to the stern-treatment school. He was harsh and severe, frequently beating his students. Because of that I ran away from the school when I was ten. I was afraid to return home for fear of receiving a beating there, and set out in the general direction of the city, which I believed to be in a valley somewhere. I wandered for three days before I was finally found by my family. . . .

After my return to the family, however, to my surprise conditions somewhat improved. My father was slightly more considerate and the teacher was

---

[1]One *mou* (also romanized *mu*) equals a sixth of an acre. Thus fifteen *mou* equal about two and a half acres. — M.H.

[2]One *tan* equals 133.5 lbs. So the total yearly rice production was roughly 8,000 lbs, of which over 3,000 lbs was not consumed but sold for cash. — M.H.

Edgar Snow, *Red Star over China* (New York: Bantam Books, 1978), chaps. 1–3. The editorial notes that follow are Snow's unless otherwise indicated.

more inclined to moderation. The result of my act of protest impressed me very much. It was a successful "strike." . . .

My mother was a kind woman, generous and sympathetic, and ever ready to share what she had. She pitied the poor and often gave them rice when they came to ask for it during famines. But she could not do so when my father was present. He disapproved of charity. We had many quarrels in my home over this question.

There were two "parties" in the family. One was my father, the Ruling Power. The Opposition was made up of myself, my mother, my brother, and sometimes even the laborer. In the "united front" of the Opposition, however, there was a difference of opinion. My mother advocated a policy of indirect attack. She criticized any overt display of emotion and attempts at open rebellion against the Ruling Power. She said it was not the Chinese way. . . .

My father had had two years of schooling and he could read enough to keep books. My mother was wholly illiterate. Both were from peasant families. I was the family "scholar." I knew the Classics, but disliked them. What I enjoyed were the romances of Old China, and especially stories of rebellions. . . . I used to read them in school, covering them up with a Classic when the teacher walked past. So also did most of my schoolmates. We learned many of the stories almost by heart, and discussed and rediscussed them many times. We knew more of them than the old men of the village, who also loved them and used to exchange stories with us. I believe that perhaps I was much influenced by such books, read at an impressionable age.

I finally left the primary school when I was thirteen and began to work long hours on the farm, helping the hired laborer, doing the full labor of a man during the day and at night keeping books for my father. Nevertheless, I succeeded in continuing my reading, devouring everything I could find except the Classics. . . . I read a book called *Sheng-shih Wei-yen* [*Words of Warning*],[3] which I liked very much. The author, one of a number of old reformist scholars, thought that the weakness of China lay in her lack of Western appliances — railways, telephones, telegraphs, and steamships — and wanted to have them introduced into the country. . . .

I continued to read the old romances and tales of Chinese literature. It occurred to me one day that there was one thing peculiar about such stories, and that was the absence of peasants who tilled the land. All the characters were warriors, officials, or scholars; there was never a peasant hero. I wondered about this for two years, and then I analyzed the content of the stories. I found that they all glorified men of arms, rulers of the people, who did not have to work the land, because they owned and controlled it and evidently made the peasants work it for them. . . .

Sheng-shih Wei-yen [*Words of Warning*] stimulated in me a desire to resume my studies. I had also become disgusted with my labor on the farm. My father

---

[3] By Chung Kuang-ying, who advocated many democratic reforms, including parliamentary government and modern methods of education and communications. His book had a wide influence when published in 1898. . . .

naturally opposed me. We quarreled about it, and finally I ran away from home. I went to the home of an unemployed law student, and there I studied for half a year. After that I studied more of the Classics under an old Chinese scholar, and also read many contemporary articles and a few books.

At this time an incident occurred in Hunan which influenced my whole life. . . .

There had been a severe famine that year, and in Changsha [the provincial capital] thousands were without food. The starving sent a delegation to the civil governor to beg for relief, but he replied to them haughtily, "Why haven't you food? There is plenty in the city. I always have enough." When the people were told the governor's reply, they became very angry. They held mass meetings and organized a demonstration. . . . A new governor arrived, and at once ordered the arrest of the leaders of the uprising. Many of them were beheaded and their heads displayed on poles as a warning to future "rebels."

. . . I felt that there with the rebels were ordinary people like my own family and I deeply resented the injustice of the treatment given to them. . . .

Another influence on me at this time was the presence in a local primary school of a "radical" teacher. He was "radical" because he was opposed to Buddhism and wanted to get rid of the gods. He urged people to convert their temples into schools. He was a widely discussed personality. I admired him and agreed with his views.

. . . I began to have a certain amount of political consciousness, especially after I read a pamphlet telling of the dismemberment of China. I remember even now that this pamphlet opened with the sentence: "Alas, China will be subjugated!" It told of Japan's occupation of Korea [a Chinese dependent] and Taiwan [Chinese territory], of the loss of [China's] suzerainty in Indochina, Burma, and elsewhere. After I read this I felt depressed about the future of my country and began to realize that it was the duty of all the people to help save it.

. . . [A]bout this time I heard of an unusual new school and made up my mind to go there, despite my father's opposition. . . .

In the new school I could study natural science and new subjects of Western learning. . . .

. . . I was more poorly dressed than the others. I owned only one decent coat-and-trousers suit. . . . Many of the richer students despised me because usually I was wearing my ragged coat and trousers. . . .

I made good progress at this school. The teachers liked me, especially those who taught the Classics, because I wrote good essays in the Classical manner. But my mind was not on the Classics. I was reading two books sent to me by my cousin, telling of the reform movement [to revitalize the imperial system under the control of the Manchu dynasty]. . . .

. . . I was fascinated by accounts of the rulers of ancient China. . . . I also learned something of foreign history at this time, and of geography. I had first heard of America in an article which told of the American Revolution and contained a sentence like this: "After eight years of difficult war, Washington won victory and built up his nation." In a book called *Great Heroes of the World,* I read also of Napoleon, Catherine of Russia, Peter the Great, Wellington, Gladstone, Rousseau, Montesquieu, and Lincoln. . . .

In Changsha [while attending middle school] I read my first newspaper . . . a nationalist revolutionary journal which told of the [armed uprising] against the Manchu Dynasty. . . . The country was on the eve of the First Revolution [of 1911 that would make China a republic]. I was so agitated that I wrote an article, which I posted on the school wall. It was my first expression of a political opinion, and it was somewhat muddled. . . .

. . . [During the fall of 1911] I decided to join the regular army . . . and help complete the revolution. The Ch'ing Emperor had not yet abdicated, and there was a period of struggle. . . .

My next scholastic adventure was in the First Provincial Middle School. I registered for a dollar, took the entrance examination, and passed at the head of the list of candidates. It was a big school, with many students, and its graduates were numerous. . . .

. . . After six months I left the school and arranged a schedule of education of my own, which consisted of reading every day in the Hunan Provincial Library. I was very regular and conscientious about it, and the half-year I spent in this way I consider to have been extremely valuable to me. I went to the library in the morning when it opened. At noon I paused only long enough to buy and eat two rice cakes, which were my daily lunch. I stayed in the library every day reading until it closed.

During this period of self-education I read many books, studied world geography and world history. There for the first time I saw and studied with great interest a map of the world. I read Adam Smith's *The Wealth of Nations,* and Darwin's *Origin of Species,* and a book on ethics by John Stuart Mill. I read the works of Rousseau, Spencer's *Logic,* and a book on law written by Montesquieu. I mixed poetry and romances, and the tales of ancient Greece, with serious study of history and geography of Russia, America, England, France, and other countries. . . .

I was a student in the normal school for five years.[4] . . . Finally I actually got my degree. . . . [D]uring this period my political ideas began to take shape. Here also I acquired my first experiences in social action. . . .

[Mao and a circle of friends formed] a serious-minded little group of men and they had no time to discuss trivialities. Everything they did or said must have a purpose. They had no time for love or "romance" and considered the times too critical and the need for knowledge too urgent to discuss women or personal matters. I was not interested in women. My parents had married me when I was fourteen to a girl of twenty, but I had never lived with her — and never subsequently did. I did not consider her my wife and at this time gave little thought to her. . . . My friends and I preferred to talk only of large matters — the nature of men, of human society, of China, the world, and the universe!

We also became ardent physical culturists. In the winter holidays we tramped through the fields, up and down mountains, along city walls, and across the

---

[4]Mao was nineteen when he enrolled in this school to prepare primary-school teachers. — M.H.

streams and rivers. If it rained we took off our shirts and called it a rain bath. When the sun was hot we also doffed shirts and called it a sun bath. In the spring winds we shouted that this was a new sport called "wind bathing." We slept in the open when frost was already falling and even in November swam in the cold rivers. All this went on under the title of "body training." Perhaps it helped much to build the physique which I was to need so badly later on in my many marches back and forth across South China, and on the Long March from Kiangsi to the Northwest....

At this time my mind was a curious mixture of ideas of liberalism, democratic reformism, and utopian socialism. I had somewhat vague passions about "nineteenth-century democracy," utopianism, and old-fashioned liberalism, and I was definitely antimilitarist and anti-imperialist....

[In mid-1918 Mao traveled to Beijing where he worked for seven months as an assistant librarian at Peking National University and met Li Ta-chao, an early leader of the Communist Party.]

My interest in politics continued to increase, and my mind turned more and more radical. I have told you of the background for this. But just now I was still confused, looking for a road, as we say. I read some pamphlets on anarchy, and was much influenced by them....

When I returned to Changsha I took a more direct role in politics. After the May Fourth Movement[5] I had devoted most of my time to student political activities, and I was editor of the *Hsiang River Review,* the Hunan students' paper, which had a great influence on the student movement in South China. In Changsha I helped found the Wen-hua Shu-hui [Cultural Book Society], an association for study of modern cultural and political tendencies....

... Our group had demanded equal rights for men and women, and representative government, and in general approval of a platform for a bourgeois democracy.... We led an attack on the provincial parliament, the majority of whose members were landlords and gentry appointed by the militarists....

... From this time on I became more and more convinced that only mass political power, secured through mass action, could guarantee the realization of dynamic reforms.[6]

In the winter of 1920 I organized workers politically for the first time, and began to be guided in this by the influence of Marxist theory and the history of the Russian Revolution.... I had read much about the events in Russia and had eagerly sought out what little Communist literature was then available in Chinese. Three books especially deeply carved my mind, and built up in me a faith in Marxism, from which, once I had accepted it as the correct interpretation of history, I did not afterwards waver. These books were the *Communist Manifesto* ... ; *Class Struggle,* by Kautsky; and a *History of Socialism,* by Kirkup. By the summer of 1920 I had become, in theory and to some

---

[5]Considered the beginning of the "Second Revolution," and of modern Chinese nationalism.

[6]In October, 1920, Mao organized a Socialist Youth Corps branch in Changsha, in which he worked with Lin Tsu-han to set up craft unions in Hunan.

extent in action, a Marxist, and from this time on I considered myself a Marxist. In the same year I married Yang K'ai-hui.[7]

---

[7]Mao made no further reference to his life with Yang K'ai-hui, except to mention her execution. She was a student at Peking National University and later became a youth leader during the Great Revolution, and one of the most active women Communists. Their marriage had been celebrated as an "ideal romance" among radical youths in Hunan.

3.2
Mao Proclaims "The Chinese People Have Stood Up!"

Though a founding member of the CCP, Mao served fifteen years as a journeyman revolutionary. During that time he tried his hand at organizing and reflected on the sources of the party's repeated failures. When he assumed the leadership role in the mid-1930s, this earlier time of personal and ideological testing gave him confidence and insight critical to the innovations that would help bring the party victory. Among Mao's innovations, two stand out: a strong emphasis on winning peasant support and an embrace of the popular cause of resistance to Japan's attempted conquest of China. Together they helped the CCP to overcome the Nationalist government. This second Mao document captures the moment of triumph in 1949 on the eve of the creation of the Communist-controlled People's Republic of China.

In this speech before representatives of a wide range of left-wing and independent groups that had supported the Communists, how did Mao characterize China's situation domestically and internationally? What did China's revolution mean to him? To what extent do the language and outlook here echo the young Mao captured above in his autobiography (Document 3.1)?

Address to the Chinese People's Political Consultative Conference
September 21, 1949

[O]ur work will go down in the history of mankind, demonstrating that the Chinese people, comprising one quarter of humanity, have now stood up. The Chinese have always been a great, courageous and industrious nation; it is only in modern times that they have fallen behind. And that was due entirely to oppression and exploitation by foreign imperialism and domestic reactionary governments. For over a century our forefathers never stopped waging unyielding struggles against domestic and foreign oppressors. . . . [N]ow we are proclaiming the founding of the People's Republic of China. From now on our nation will belong to the community of the peace-loving and freedom-loving nations of the world and work courageously and industriously to

---

Selected Works of Mao Tse-tung, vol. 5 (Beijing: Foreign Languages Press, 1977), 16–18.

foster its own civilization and well-being and at the same time to promote world peace and freedom. Ours will no longer be a nation subject to insult and humiliation. We have stood up. Our revolution has won the sympathy and acclaim of the people of all countries. We have friends all over the world. . . .

Our state system, the people's democratic dictatorship,[1] is a powerful weapon for safeguarding the fruits of victory of the people's revolution and for thwarting the plots of domestic and foreign enemies for restoration, and this weapon we must firmly grasp. Internationally, we must unite with all peace-loving and freedom-loving countries and peoples, and first of all with the Soviet Union and the New Democracies, so that we shall not stand alone in our struggle to safeguard these fruits of victory and to thwart the plots of domestic and foreign enemies for restoration. As long as we persist in the people's democratic dictatorship and unite with our foreign friends, we shall always be victorious.

The people's democratic dictatorship and solidarity with our foreign friends will enable us to accomplish our work of construction rapidly. We are already confronted with the task of nation-wide economic construction. We have very favourable conditions: a population of 475 million people and a territory of 9,600,000 square kilometres. There are indeed difficulties ahead, and a great many too. But we firmly believe that by heroic struggle the people of the country will surmount them all. The Chinese people have rich experience in overcoming difficulties. If our forefathers, and we also, could weather long years of extreme difficulty and defeat powerful domestic and foreign reactionaries, why can't we now, after victory, build a prosperous and flourishing country? As long as we keep to our style of plain living and hard struggle, as long as we stand united and as long as we persist in the people's democratic dictatorship and unite with our foreign friends, we shall be able to win speedy victory on the economic front.

An upsurge in economic construction is bound to be followed by an upsurge of construction in the cultural sphere. The era in which the Chinese people were regarded as uncivilized is now ended. We shall emerge in the world as a nation with an advanced culture.

Our national defence will be consolidated and no imperialists will ever again be allowed to invade our land. Our people's armed forces must be maintained and developed with the heroic and steeled People's Liberation Army as the foundation. We will have not only a powerful army but also a powerful air force and a powerful navy.

---

[1] By this term Mao meant control by an alliance making up the bulk of China's population, notably workers and peasants but also most of the bourgeoisie (middle class). Those supportive of the revolution would operate within a democratic framework of cooperation and persuasion over which the CCP party-state would preside, while exercising dictatorial control and compulsion over the small hostile minority of class enemies. Since the 1920s Mao had insisted on thinking about China's revolution as a process that united virtually all patriotic Chinese.

Let the domestic and foreign reactionaries tremble before us! Let them say we are no good at this and no good at that. By our own indomitable efforts we the Chinese people will unswervingly reach our goal. . . .

Hail the founding of the People's Republic of China!

3.3
Peasant Perspectives on Poverty and Village Politics

The peasants that Mao sought to rally to his cause were a diverse lot. Peasants in the north, especially in remote, inland areas, lived under harsh conditions that made them ready recruits for Communist forces. The village reforms sponsored by the Communists helped mobilize support, well before the triumph of Communist forces in 1949. In the south by contrast, conditions were on the whole less grim. The party did not become a force in most southern villages until after 1949, when work teams arrived to implement the reforms already effected in the north.

The document that follows takes us into a remote area in the north and offers a perspective on developments at a key time in the Chinese revolution — on the road to power and the consolidation of that power — as ordinary Chinese experienced it. This oral history is based on extended conversations recorded by historian Peter Seybolt in Houhua village, in the northern part of Henan province, during the late 1980s and early 1990s. The leading figure is Wang Fucheng, a Communist Party secretary from 1954 to 1984. Despite his illiteracy and limited knowledge of the world beyond his locale, he proved an effective leader with a reputation for integrity. His recollections are supplemented by comments from a friend and from his wife. What are the most striking features in the picture of village life and politics that emerges here? How did the party recruit supporters, and in what ways did peasants respond? How close are village concerns to those Mao articulated?

Peter Seybolt
Oral Histories Collected in Houhua Village
Late 1980s and Early 1990s

WANG FUCHENG RECALLING CONDITIONS IN RURAL NORTH CHINA
AND THE GROWING CHINESE COMMUNIST PRESENCE

I was born in this village [of Houhua] sixty-seven years ago [1923]. My father was a farmer and salt maker. We were very poor. I was the youngest of four children, two boys and two girls. First sister was twelve or thirteen years older than I, second sister was seven or eight years older, and my brother was three years older.

When I was six years old, my father died. At that time, he smoked a white powder [opium or morphine] that had been brought to China by foreigners.

Peter Seybolt, *Throwing the Emperor from His Horse: Portrait of a Village Leader in China, 1923–1995* (Boulder, Colo.: Westview, 1996), 20–30, 33–37.

Five or six people in this village smoked it. My father was very poor and had to steal to buy it. He stole from one of my uncles and was killed by him. I think he was buried without a coffin in the family grave plot. I don't remember. He was only in his thirties.

Before my father started smoking opium, our family was fairly well-off compared to many others. . . . The house was made of mud bricks, but it had a tile roof, which was fairly unusual here. Most houses had roofs made of sorghum stalks. Only a few comparatively rich families had houses made from kiln-fired bricks and with tile roofs. The farmland my father inherited was of poor quality, but it was enough to support us. Then, because of his drug addi[c]tion, my father gradually sold all of the land except the two *mu*[1] where the family grave plots were. He also sold the house with the tile roof and built a two-room mud house with stalks on the roof. Eventually he no longer worked, and my mother, sisters, and brother and I had to beg from our relatives to survive.

After my father was killed, my mother took me to live with my grandfather and grandmother in Jiang Village, six *li* [two miles] from here. I lived there until 1946, when I was twenty-three. When I returned to Houhua, I knew no one.

The family broke up after my father died. My brother went to Shanxi Province as a long-term laborer and later was conscripted as a soldier. . . . He was killed by the Japanese during the War of Resistance [1937–1945]. My two sisters were married and went to other villages. They were introduced to their husband's families by relatives. There was no special marriage ceremony. We were too poor. They just went to live with a man's family and were considered married. . . .

Both of my sisters had bound feet, as did most of the women around here, some until the late 1940s. There was an old saying: "big feet, loss of face." I remember the ribbons binding my sisters' feet. My sisters mostly stayed at home. If they went out on the street, the village people would laugh at them and look down on them for being out. Because women with bound feet could do no farm work, those in the poorest families didn't bind their daughters' feet. The first concern was survival. But, I would say that about 80 percent of the women here had bound feet even though Houhua was a very poor village. It was difficult for my sisters to walk. It took my older sister over an hour to walk three *li* [a mile] to Taiping Village. . . . It is a twenty minute walk for me. . . .

After my mother took me to live in Jiang Village with her parents, our life was very difficult. My grandfather had lost his sight because he was old and had overworked. He had the white eye disease [cataracts]. My mother was deaf. She had been ill when she was young and couldn't hear after that. We had about six *mu* of poor land, enough to feed us for only about half a year. We had no meat and rarely ate vegetables. Every year we ate sorghum porridge twice a day until it ran out, then we ate tree leaves, grasses, roots, and

---

[1]As noted earlier, one *mu* (or *mou*) is a sixth of an acre.

wild vegetables. . . . I was always hungry. I never went to school. Having nothing to eat, how could I study? To this day I cannot read or write. Later, when I was Communist Party secretary of Houhua Village for thirty years, I did everything by memory. I kept everything in my head. In Jiang Village my mother helped support us by weaving cotton cloth. Someone would take it to market and buy more raw cotton for her to weave. Our clothes were made from the cloth she wove, as were our cotton shoes, which were dyed with red soil. We never had much to wear. We couldn't even afford a long overcoat for winter, so I wore a short cotton-filled jacket with a belt around the waist. Even when I was twenty years old my mother and I had to share a single quilt when we slept. . . .

I sometimes worked as a short-term laborer for the more prosperous households in the village. I was used only for a few days at harvest time to cut corn and sorghum. I received no pay but was given my food for the day. I remember well that when I was about eighteen I was working for a rich peasant and was given five steamed wheat buns at noon and four more in the evening. They were the best thing I had ever eaten, and that was the first time I had ever had enough to eat. The next day there was no work, and I was hungry again. . . .

Because of my poor diet I was always sick. That is why I am so short. I often had diarrhea, but I never saw a doctor. How could I? I had no money. There were no doctors in our village. When rich people got sick they called in a doctor from 10 to 20 *li* [four to seven miles] away. Doctors wouldn't treat sick people until they had been given a banquet. . . .

In those days, of one hundred children who were born, eighty wouldn't grow up. . . . In those days few people lived to be sixty. Today many are in their seventies and eighties. . . .

When I was a child I did kowtow [bow] to gods in the temples, but I never believed in it. I just followed others. We had pictures of gods in our house, and we kowtowed and burned incense in a bowl when unusual things happened or when we ran short of something. We had pictures of the grandfather god, the god of wealth, and the stove god. I seldom bowed to them, but the old women of the house did. When I was older, after the war with Japan, I helped smash the temples and the statues. The temple bricks were then given to retired soldiers for building houses. . . . I don't know much about that religion. None of the gods were useful for solving real problems.

The worst time I can remember was the great famine of 1942. It rained some in the spring of that year, but then it was completely dry for three planting seasons. The crops all died. During the summer of 1942, 80 percent of the people of Jiang Village and Houhua left home to beg. . . . Many never returned. One or two hundred people from Houhua either never returned or starved to death. More starved in Houhua than in Jiang Village. Many young children, especially girls, were sold at that time. A girl cousin of mine who was twelve years old was sold to a stranger for seven or eight *dou* [about two bushels] of grain. Another uncle sold both his daughters. Some people gave away their children just to save them from starving. . . . It makes me very sad to discuss those times. It was a sorrowful period of our history. We had to sell my grandfather's house. . . . We then built a very simple mud house with sorghum stalks on the roof. When it rained, water poured through the roof, making mud of the floor. We also had to sell our six *mu* of land, all we had. From then on we had to rely on relatives. . . .

The [Nationalist] government didn't help at all during the famine. It was a time of great confusion. Before the Japanese came [in 1938] the villages here were administered by a village head, also called a guarantor head, who was responsible for all village affairs, especially tax collection. . . .

Taxes were paid in silver and copper money based on the amount and value of your land. We got the money by selling our products at the market. If a family could not or would not pay, the family head might be taken to jail by the armed county police and beaten badly. . . . Actually, often there was no fixed tax standard and no fixed time for collection. They just called for taxes when they wanted them, usually after the harvest. Sometimes bandits also came and made us pay. . . .

. . . There was no formal Guomindang [Nationalist] government in this area from 1938 to 1945 [after Japanese forces had moved in]. Many bandits came out then, and many more secret religious societies with superstitious beliefs were formed. They burned incense, kowtowed, and chanted, thinking that knives and bullets would not then hurt them. I don't know all the details, but their purpose was to get power. They got recruits by giving food and clothing and protecting families. They were out to control several hundred villages; then they could be like kings and collect crops and money from the people. . . . Both types of bandits killed a lot of people and stole crops. They were very cruel. . . .

Most of the area north of here was controlled during the war by . . . Chinese traitors who collaborated with the Japanese. We called them "Japanese running dogs." Many were former Nationalist troops. . . . [T]he situation was very chaotic nevertheless. There were many armed forces that came any time they wanted, and we were left impoverished. . . .

[Communist Party activities] first began here [in the late 1920s]. My uncle Wang Congwu and my cousin Wang Zhuoru were among the first people in this area to join the Communist Party. . . .

Congwu was intelligent and clever. He had many friends and was a natural leader. . . . He joined the Communist Party in 1927 when he was only sixteen years old. He and Wang Zhuoru, who joined when he was fifteen, began to mobilize the masses to struggle against the landlords. My friend Wang Changmin, who was here at the time, can tell you more about it.

Wang Changmin

They organized a peasant association, which most of the poor peasants joined, and started a peasants' night school in Houhua. It had over fifty students. . . . The Communist Party was a secret organization at that time. There were about eight members here in Houhua, including three women. They did a lot of propaganda work, urging the poor to form peasant associations and to rise up and settle accounts with landlords. They organized the hired laborers to demand more money from the landlords and threatened to go on strike if they didn't get satisfaction. They wanted the landlords to tell publicly how much interest they made on loans and how much land they took. This was happening in many villages. In early 1928 there was a peasant uprising in Houhua, Qiankou, and about ten other villages in this area. Over a thousand peasant association members went to Wenxinggu Village to settle accounts with Cai Hongbin, a big, evil landlord and the head of the landlords' united village militia. They were successful, and the struggle spread. . . .

WANG FUCHENG CONTINUES

. . . [T]here was not much Communist activity in this village [again] until 1937, when the war with Japan began. . . . One Party member, Wang Debin, later became a traitor to the Japanese. Party members at that time did mostly underground work, such as organizing peasants to oppose giving grain to the landlords after the harvest. They had successes and failures. The landlords had guns. . . .

When the Japanese troops got to Houhua Village there was a great massacre. . . . The Japanese killed about three hundred people, about eighty of them from Houhua. All of them were men between eighteen and fifty years old. They didn't kill women, old people, or children. Many of the men who died were first stripped naked and forced into two houses which were then soaked with gasoline and set on fire. Everyone in them died. . . .

. . . No one else from here was killed until April 12, 1941, when there was a big "mop-up" campaign. . . .

Life was very hard in this area after the mop-up. The Japanese and traitors continued to come twice a year for grain, but gradually the Communist-led guerrillas got stronger and stronger. . . . By 1945, Communist guerrillas were the principal force in Houhua and about thirty other villages nearby. . . .

I did not join the guerrillas at that time. . . . [B]ut I started to go to meetings at the house of someone named Peng. We discussed how the poor should get organized and how the land of poor people was grabbed by the rich households. If we owed them money and couldn't pay, we had to sell land to them bit by bit. They had all the wealth and gave us nothing. This kind of talk made a deep impression on me. They asked me to join the peasant association, and one evening, at a meeting in a grain mill, I did. . . .

[Wang Fucheng then left Jiang Village to return to Houhua Village.]

We got a house when a relative of ours, an old woman, died. . . . The family then gave my mother and me eight *mu* of land and the shell of an abandoned house that had no roof because it had been burned by the Japanese. Our relatives helped us build a roof with the logs we brought from Jiang Village. We lived in that house until after liberation [1949]. We were able to have a relatively peaceful life then, but we still didn't have enough to eat.

I remember that shortly after we returned to Houhua Village there was a locust plague. That was in 1947 or 1948. One morning I saw the locusts in the air. The sky was black with them, like a big cloud. You couldn't see the sun, they were so thick. The large locusts with wings came first. I could catch three or four at once in my hand. Then smaller insects came. The plague lasted a long time, probably two months. Insects ate the crops completely — corn, sweet potatoes, even reeds. They ate everything. We dug ditches to catch them, then we dried them for food. . . .

After the war, when I returned, there was a campaign led by the Communist Party to reduce interest rates and the rent paid to landlords and to return confiscated land to peasant ownership. The situation was very complex. Many bandits and secret religious societies were still active. The Communist Party was still a secret organization. . . . Some people didn't dare take land. They feared that if [the forces of the Nationalist leader] Jiang Kaishek [Chiang Kai-shek] came back they would be punished. . . .

In late 1946 the Guomindang did return. Its New Fifth Army came through chasing the [Communist] Eighth Route Army from south to north. The whole region fell under their control for about two months. . . . They killed a number of Communist Party members and cadres. No one was killed in Houhua, but thirteen new Communist Party members capitulated to the enemy and renounced their Communist affiliation. . . . I didn't dare to speak at that time. I was not a cadre, but I was an activist in the land reform movement, so I kept quiet for two months until the bad people left. . . .

[Wang Fucheng then described how the Communists consolidated their local control by eliminating other armed groups and trying their leaders.]

Land reform began again after the Guomindang New Fifth Army left. A work team of two or three people from the district came to promote it. Some were Communist Party members and some were not, but all represented the Party. They reorganized a peasant association and held meetings where people were told about the landlords' crimes and taught how to criticize them.

There were two rich peasant households in the village . . . and two landlord households. . . . There were about 40 middle peasant households, 100 poor peasant households, and 10 hired laborers. . . . The landlords and rich peasants owned almost two-thirds of the crop land, about 1,600 *mu*. Middle peasant families owned between 5 and 20 *mu* each, and poor peasants owned almost none — 3.5 *mu* per family at most. Most earned their livelihood by making salt; 100 *jin* [110 lb] of salt was worth about 6 *jin* [almost 7 lb] of grain. Some poor peasants and hired laborers worked long-term for rich peasants, and some worked only at harvest time; some begged. . . .

During land reform I was not a Party member, but I was an activist working for the Party. I would do anything I was asked to do. I shouted slogans and went from house to house to collect people for meetings. I criticized the landlords, telling them to confess that their property came from us. I led people to their houses and brought their furniture to our office to be distributed to poor peasants. Sometimes we would go to the landlords' houses at night and beat them.

Wang Zengduo (Wu Loada) was the only person from this village who was killed during land reform. He had left the village and come back with the Guomindang. He wasn't really even a landlord. He had about 100 *mu* of land that he farmed himself as well as hiring others to help him, so he was really just a rich peasant. We called him a landlord because people hated him. So, you see, we had two criteria for landlord status — one was based on land and labor, and the other was based on the attitude of the masses. Wang Zengduo was the kind of person commonly referred to as *eba* (evil tyrant). If the poor went to his fields to scavenge after harvest, he beat them, especially women and children. Once he stripped naked a woman who was gleaning his field. This enraged the people. When the poor wanted to borrow anything, he would beat and curse them. His crimes were very serious. The poor peasants themselves decided he should be killed. . . .

There were other sharp struggles in the village. We struggled against Wang Zengduo's widow in the east of the village. We hung her from a big tree with a rope tied to her hands behind her body. I was the director of the meeting. Most people taking part were women and children. They beat her to find out where she had hidden family property. . . .

Wang Yingchun's wife was also hung from a tree and beaten. I shouted "Down with the landlords. If you don't confess, we'll hang you higher."

Redistribution of land was based on the number of people in each household. In this village each person was to get 1.5 *mu* of crop land. The amount differed according to the quality of the land. There were many arguments and much bitterness over the division of property. One rich peasant family didn't talk to their neighbors for several decades after land reform.

I got half an ox [shared with another family], five hundred bricks from rich people's houses that the poor peasants had destroyed, a wooden spade, and a manure fork. I didn't get any additional land because I already had eight *mu* from the relative who died. There were three in our household then. I had recently gotten married. . . .

My wife's uncle acted as go-between. My future wife and I didn't even know each other before we were married. That was feudalism. I went to her house with empty hands to talk to her mother. I went several times and each time talked to her mother, never to her. . . .

Wang Xianghua, Wang Fucheng's Wife, Continues the Story

My mother listened to Wang Zhuoru's wife [the wife of Wang Fucheng's cousin] because they often worked together. They were both Communist Party members. . . . As a Party member her duties were to go to meetings and struggle against the landlords. She mostly worked with women. My mother did what the Party told her to do. She told the women that they were equal to men and should leave their gates to go out and farm and help build socialist villages. Men were also educated by the Party and told not to bully women. A woman's organization was established, and the men became afraid to treat their wives badly. . . . There were about thirty Party members in the village then, and ten of them were women. Today there are few women Party members, and none of those is active.

My mother never asked my opinion about the marriage. I had no opinion of my own. I didn't know Wang Fucheng. . . . My mother arranged everything. . . .

There was no marriage ceremony at all. An old village woman came and asked me to go with her. I went to Wang Fucheng's house, where he and his mother lived in three rooms. We were too poor to ask any relatives to come.

The first meal we ate was boiled cucumber. There was no meat at all. . . .

After the marriage I mostly stayed at home, weaving cotton cloth and selling it for more cotton. When necessary I did farm work in the fields, especially at harvest time when I cut crops. Our life gradually got better. We raised a donkey and a pig. Sometimes we even ate meat.

VIETNAM AND THE PATH TO NATIONAL LIBERATION

The Vietnamese struggle against French colonialism was almost a century old at the end of World War II. Incursions by missionaries, gunboats, and diplomats in the course of the nineteenth century had set off repeated bouts of resistance inspired by a loyalty to the Vietnamese monarchy and Confucian values. The turn of the century was a time of transition with the Vietnamese resentful but also filled with self-doubts and with French enterprise and culture making a major imprint on the major cities and in the countryside. Out of this period of change emerged a resistance of a new sort — self-consciously nationalist and increasingly radical. World War II brought a Japanese occupation that not only disrupted French rule but also punctured French prestige. The war thus provided an opening that the resistance seized, preparing the way for a declaration of independence shortly after Japanese surrender and the beginning of an anti-colonial war in 1946 when Paris insisted on restoring full control.

3.4

Ho Chi Minh Discovers Communist Anti-Colonialism

Ho Chi Minh, the founder of Vietnam's Communist Party and its leader through almost four tumultuous decades of nearly incessant struggle for national liberation and unity, never found an Edgar Snow to record his life. From the available fragments we know that he was born in 1890 in the northern and markedly anti-French Nghe An province to a well-to-do, anti-French family. Ho's father, trained in the Confucian classics, refused to work in the French administration, while Ho and his siblings all engaged in anti-colonial activities. Ho himself was schooled in both the classics and the new Western subjects introduced by the French. In 1915 he left Vietnam to explore the sources of the West's power, settling in Paris. There as an activist in the nascent Vietnamese independence movement, he appealed to the victors of World War I to honor the principle of self-determination promoted by U.S. President Woodrow Wilson. Their indifference led him in turn to involvement in the French Socialist Party and then in the founding of the French Communist Party.

In the process of searching for external support for the Vietnamese cause, Ho chanced upon the writings of Lenin. His description of that moment of illumination in 1920 did not take shape until forty years later when he prepared a piece on the occasion of Lenin's ninetieth birthday that appeared in a Soviet journal. Reading this recollection, a cynic might wonder if Ho did not exaggerate his enthusiasm for Lenin to impress his senior and more powerful allies whose support Vietnam still needed. An even more subversive voice says that Ho could not have clearly remembered an event some forty years earlier. Taking his account at face value, what seems to have led Ho to Marxism and the Soviet model? How do his early preoccupations compare to those of the young Mao? What alternative paths had they considered and found wanting?

"The Path Which Led Me to Leninism"
1960

After World War One, I made my living in Paris, at one time as an employee at a photographer's, at another as painter of "Chinese antiques" (turned out by a French shop). I often distributed leaflets denouncing the crimes committed by the French colonialists in Viet Nam.

At that time, I supported the October Revolution[1] only spontaneously. I did not yet grasp all its historic importance. I loved and respected Lenin because he was a great patriot who had liberated his fellow-countrymen; until then, I had read none of his books. . . .

Heated discussions were then taking place in the cells of the Socialist Party, about whether one should remain in the [Socialist] Second International, found a "Second-and-a-half" International or join Lenin's Third [Moscow-based Communist] International[.] I attended the meetings regularly, two or three times a week, and attentively listened to the speakers. . . .

What I wanted most to know — and what was not debated in the meetings — was: which International sided with the peoples of the colonial countries?

I raised this question — the most important for me — at a meeting. Some comrades answered: it was the Third, not the Second International. One gave me to read Lenin's "Theses on the national and colonial questions" [1920]. . . .

In those Theses, there were political terms that were difficult to understand. But by reading them again and again finally I was able to grasp the essential part. What emotion, enthusiasm, enlightenment and confidence they communicated to me! I wept for joy. Sitting by myself in my room, I would shout as if I were addressing large crowds: "Dear martyr compatriots! This is what we need, this is our path to liberation!" . . .

. . . [F]rom then on, I . . . plunged into the debates and participated with fervour in the discussions. Though my French was still too weak to express all my thoughts, I hit hard at the allegations attacking Lenin and the Third International. My only argument was: "If you do not condemn colonialism, if you do not side with the colonial peoples, what kind of revolution are you then waging?"

---

[1]The 1917 seizure of power by the Bolsheviks in Russia.

Ho Chi Minh, "The Path Which Led Me to Leninism," April 1960, in Ho, *Selected Writings (1920–1969)* (Hanoi: Foreign Languages Publishing House, 1973), 250–51.

3.5

Ho Declares Vietnamese Independence

After his Leninist revelation in 1920, Ho went to work for the Communist International in Moscow, laboring as an itinerant political organizer among Vietnamese living overseas, especially in China and Thailand. He paid special attention to recruiting young Vietnamese radicals in the mid-1920s and to bringing together rival communist groups in 1930 into what was called the Indochina Communist Party. The outbreak of war in the Pacific created an opportunity for him as it did for Mao. In 1941 Ho proclaimed the founding of the Viet Minh, a broad-based organization which quickly established itself as the leading anti-Japanese and anti-French resistance force. The sudden surrender of the Japanese in August 1945 gave him the chance to occupy Hanoi and declare Vietnam an independent state. He was aware, however, of French military strength and sought to negotiate a transitional arrangement with the French to avoid conflict, all the while appealing to President Truman to make good on the promise of self-determination that the Americans had once again made central to their publicly stated war aims.

Ho's declaration of independence on September 2 was a dramatic moment attended by an enormous crowd in central Hanoi. On what grounds did Ho base his claim? Who was his audience — perhaps overseas as well as at home — and how did he seek to win support from different groups? How well does this document mesh with the Leninist values that Ho claims to have espoused during his residence in Paris?

Statement Read in Hanoi
September 2, 1945

"All men are created equal. They are endowed by their Creator with certain unalienable Rights; among these are Life, Liberty and the pursuit of Happiness." . . .

Those are undeniable truths.

Nevertheless, for more than eighty years, the French imperialists, abusing the standard of Liberty, Equality and Fraternity, have violated our Fatherland and oppressed our fellow-citizens. They have acted contrary to the ideals of humanity and justice.

Politically, they have deprived our people of every democratic liberty.

They have enforced inhuman laws; they have set up three different political regimes in the North, the Centre and the South of Viet Nam in order to wreck our country's oneness and prevent our people from being united.

They have built more prisons than schools. They have mercilessly massacred our patriots. They have drowned our uprisings in seas of blood.

They have fettered public opinion and practised obscurantism.

They have weakened our race with opium and alcohol.

In the field of economics, they have sucked us dry, driven our people to destitution, and devastated our land. . . .

Ho, *Selected Writings,* 53–56.

We, the Provisional Government of the new Viet Nam, representing the entire Vietnamese people, hereby declare that from now on we break off all relations of a colonial character with France; cancel all treaties signed by France on Viet Nam, and abolish all privileges held by France in our country.

The entire Vietnamese people are of one mind in their determination to oppose all wicked schemes by the French colonialists.

We are convinced that the Allies . . . cannot fail to recognize the right of the Vietnamese people to independence.

A people who have courageously opposed French enslavement for more than eighty years, a people who have resolutely sided with the Allies against the fascists during these last years, such a people must be free, such a people must be independent.

3.6
Vietnamese Peasants Reflect on the Communist Appeal

Like China, Vietnam's population at mid-century was overwhelmingly rural. It was also, like China's, geographically diverse. Peasants in the north had responded earliest to Communist appeals, beginning with a rebellion in 1930–1931 in Ho's home region. While ultimately crushed by the French, it convinced the party of the depth of peasant anger over the injustices and deprivation they faced on a daily basis. The Viet Minh actively recruited peasants during wartime and demonstrated that village support could sustain a guerrilla campaign over a long period of time, a lesson applied in struggles against French and later American forces.

The accounts that follow capture peasant perspectives at different times, one in the south and the other in the north. The first is from Nguyen Thi Dinh, born into a peasant family in Ben Tre province in the Mekong Delta in 1920, telling of her joining the resistance in her teens. Known for its revolutionary tradition, Ben Tre was the site of repeated uprisings from the 1860s onward. Vietnam's Communist Party had a presence there from the 1930s and weathered repeated rounds of French repression. Dinh was eventually imprisoned for her political activity but released in 1943 in time to participate in the Viet Minh seizure of power in Ben Tre and to play a prominent role in the southern anti-French resistance and later in the effort to expel the Americans and unify the southern part of the country with the socialist north.

Following the Dinh account are a pair of interviews from the Red River Delta in the north. Two political activists in Hung Yen province near Hanoi recall difficult rural conditions and the appearance of anti-French resistance forces at the end of World War II. The setting for their stories is a long and densely settled landscape in which Vietnamese culture had originated and resistance to invaders had flourished for a thousand years. In contrast to the south, villages in the north were compact, with homes closely built together and carefully shielded from the outside world.

The fundamental question here is similar to the China case: What led people in the countryside to embrace the Communist cause? How important was nationalism? Once more, some skepticism is needed in arriving at an answer. Dinh's recollections were recorded in November 1965 and published in Hanoi in 1968 — in other words, at a time when the Vietnamese Communist Party was fighting a desperate war with the United States and was seeking to do everything possible to rally support. How might Dinh have altered her account to fit events or how might events have reconfigured her memory? Is there reason to give this recollection any credibility? The two oral histories from Hung Yen are equally problematic. They too were gathered in the midst of the American war (in October–November 1967). The interviews were conducted by Gérard Chaliand, a French academic sympathetic to the Vietnamese cause, carrying out his investigations under the watchful eyes of Vietnamese officials among peasants known for their suspicion of outsiders and especially foreigners. Do these accounts ring true? Where might bias have intruded? Finally, does a comparison of the personal stories from the two parts of Vietnam reveal any commonalities or differences? If we step back and look at the Chinese and Vietnamese peasant perspectives together, what common themes emerge?

Nguyen Thi Dinh
1965 Memoir Recalling Her Road to
Revolutionary Politics in the 1930s

By the time I was 10 years old, my father no longer had to work day and night rowing a sampan for hire, and my family was no longer in a situation in which my mother would have to force herself, a few days after giving birth, to sit up and sew [to earn a little extra income]. We now had enough to eat and were not as hard-pressed economically as before, because we children — "the flock of ten blackbirds" — had grown strong enough to work in the ricefields, tend the vegetable garden and catch fish. I was the youngest in the family and could not as yet perform heavy manual labor, so I usually rowed the sampan and went to sell fish with my sister-in-law. We got up at 2:00 or 3:00 A.M. every day, rowed all night and arrived at the My Long market in the morning. After selling the fish, we hurriedly turned around and went home. . . .

. . . My parents wanted to send me to school, but the school was located in My Long market, more than 10 kilometers [6 miles] away. It would be too far for me to go there and come back every day, and if I boarded there it would be too expensive. I had to study at home, and Ba Chan, my older brother, taught me. . . . Whenever we had nothing to do at night, we would gather around the oil lamp — my mother lying in the hammock, cradling her grandchild, my father sitting silent in front of a small teapot, my sisters sitting around mending clothes. We all kept quiet and listened to my brother read [Luc Van Tien[1]]. . . . Sometimes . . . I wept and the neighbors also wept. Once in a while my father nodded his head in approval and commented:

---

[1]This classic novel in verse tells of the triumph of a young couple over wicked people and in the process affirms both Confucian ideas of virtue and the Buddhist faith in the ultimate victory of good over evil. The author was Nguyen Dinh Chieu, a prominent nineteenth-century southern scholar and foe of the French.

Nguyen Thi Dinh, *No Other Road to Take: Memoir of Mrs. Nguyen Thi Dinh,* trans. Mai V. Elliott (Ithaca, N.Y.: Cornell University Southeast Asia Program and Department of Asian Studies, 1976), 24–33.

"This story teaches people all the virtues they must have in life: humanity, kindness, filial piety, courage, determination and loyalty."

. . . I hated those in the old days who abused their power, position and wealth to harm honest people. . . . But I did not know enough as yet to understand that I should also hate the wicked people who were bringing miseries and poverty to my family and other families at the time. On one occasion, the landlord in the village came to my house and demanded paddy [unmilled rice] in a threatening manner. My parents had to hastily prepare food and wine to regale him. We were out of chickens then, so they had to catch the hen about to lay eggs which I had been raising, and slaughter it for him to eat. When he finally left, his face crimson with all the drinking, I broke down and cried in anger, and demanded that my mother compensate me for the hen. In that period (1930) I noticed that my brother Ba Chan came and went at odd hours. Sometimes men came to the house, sat and whispered for a while and then disappeared. One day, I heard whispers in the room, I looked in and saw my brother hand to my father a piece of red cloth embroidered with something yellow inside. Seeing me, he ran out and pulled me inside, signaled to me to keep quiet and said:

"Don't breathe a word or our heads will be loped off."

My father quietly went into the garden, climbed to the top of the coconut tree and hid the package there. Threatened by my brother, I hastily nodded my head in assent, but felt very annoyed and wondered what the fuss was all about. A few days later, as I was walking toward the market carrying the fish basket on my head, I suddenly heard many people whisper to each other:

"There's a hammer and sickle flag at the three-way confluence of the Huong Diem river."

"The Communists in Ben Tre Province will soon rise up like those in Phu Rieng."

All at once many things rose in my mind: hammer and sickle flag, Communism, Phu Rieng. On the way back from the market, I went all the way to the three-way confluence of the Huong Diem river to take a look. I had the vague feeling that the flag was exactly the red piece of cloth that I had seen in my house a few days before. The yellow lines I could not make out now appeared clearly as the crossed hammer and sickle. I did not understand anything, but felt very happy about what my brother had done.

A few days later, my older brother Ba Chan was suddenly arrested by the puppet village officials who took him and jailed him. . . . My mother and whole family worried and cried a lot. This happened at the end of 1930. I often went to visit him in jail because I was small and would not arouse the suspicion of the enemy. Every day I had to row a sampan for more than 4 kilometers to bring him food. It was there in the prison that I witnessed for the first time scenes of brutal torture. It was Muon, the same Canton Chief — the tyrannical landlord who had come to my house to collect rent, drink and swallow my hen which was about to lay eggs — who now angrily hit the prisoners with a walking stick while drinking and shouting. . . .

. . . My brother was not the only one who was tortured, many other old and young people were also tortured. Many men were beaten until they passed out, blood trickling from their mouths, heads and feet, and dyeing the cement floor a greyish and purplish color. I loved my brother and I hated the soldiers so intensely that I wanted to run out to hold them back and defend my brother, but I was too frightened so I just stood there, frozen, and wept in anger. . . .

. . . My brother was not released until half a year later. We wept with joy. He loved me even more than before because I was the only one in the family who had taken care of him during his imprisonment. I asked him:

"You didn't do anything to them, then why did they beat you up so brutally?"

He smiled and said:

"Of course I did something, why not?"

"You mean you were a subversive?"

"Don't be silly! I make revolution to overthrow the landlords who are oppressing and exploiting us, like Canton Chief Muon, and also to overthrow the French who have stolen our country from us."

He explained to me at great length, but I did not understand anything more than that the Communists loved the poor and opposed the officials in the village. My love for my brother and the men who had been jailed blossomed and deepened with such new and significant events. When I remembered the villagers' comment that the Communists would soon rise up in Ben Tre province, I immediately thought that the time was coming when Canton Chief Muon . . . would perish. I was very happy and eagerly looked forward for that day to arrive. . . .

In 1936, I was 16 years old. . . . I grew very tall, much taller than before, and I was less skinny, though I had not put on much weight. . . . Suddenly my hair became curly and wavy near the temples. My girl friends used to tease me:

"Dinh, did you wave your hair because you're about to get married?"

I only smiled because in my head I was entertaining ideas very different from those of my friends. At that time the movement was on the rise. People from many areas frequently came to hold meetings in my house. My brother Ba Chan persuaded me to help and cook for them. I agreed at once. They all treated me with affection like my brother Ba. They were all good people and my parents were very fond of them. . . .

. . . [B]esides cooking when they came to hold meetings I was given the job of delivering letters, propagandizing people in the hamlets and village to join mutual aid associations and rice transplanting and hoeing teams, encouraging people to buy the "Dan Chung" (People) newspaper, and mobilizing women. . . . Whatever task I was given I performed with a lot of zeal.

One day my brother Chan called me into the room — the same room where he had whispered to my father and handed him a package of documents years ago. He took down a large package from the ceiling and asked me:

"Would you dare to disseminate these leaflets?"

I was both happy and worried, and said:

"Alright, but unless you tell me how to do it, I won't know what to do."
He smiled and gave me detailed instructions. Finally, he reminded me:

"If the enemy catch you red-handed, just tell them over and over again that these papers were given to you by a man who said that they were publicity pamphlets for drugs. You are illiterate so you don't know what the papers say. The man told you to disseminate the papers, gave you some money, and then disappeared you don't know where."

After accepting this honorable task which was assigned to me for the first time, I felt agitated and restless. In the afternoon, I crawled inside the mosquito net and pulled out one leaflet to read in secret. Not knowing how to read very well, I had to spell each word slowly, and it took me a long time to read the leaflet. It was an appeal to the peasants to oppose the cruel rich people and village officials. That night, I could not sleep in peace and got up at midnight. At 3:00 A.M. I pretended to leave to sell fish as I had been doing every day. I gradually let the leaflets, which I had tucked under my pants at the waistline, fall down to the ground at my feet. When it was almost daylight and I was at the market I had gotten rid of all the leaflets. The sky began to brighten. At around 8:00 A.M., the people started whispering to each other, and rumor was thick that the Communists had spread a lot of leaflets. Policemen hurriedly grabbed their weapons and ran off in a panic. . . .

. . . After succeeding in a few tasks, I became very eager to operate and wanted to leave because if I stayed home a lot of chores, such as cooking, working in the ricefields and tending the vegetable garden, would get in the way of my work. I began to move around more [going on mission]. Some nights I stayed out and came home very late. My parents were afraid I would become "bad" and said, "State affairs are not for girls to take care of. And even if women can do it, they must be very capable. What can our daughter Dinh do? If she's caught, she'll confess everything and harm others." At that time, I had reached the puberty period and caught the attention of many youths in the village. Several sent matchmakers to my house to ask for my hand. My parents wanted to accept and give me away in marriage to put an end to their worries, but I absolutely refused to go along. I often confided to my brother Ba:

"I only want to work for the revolution, I don't want to get married yet. . . ."

. . . [M]y brother Chan . . . told me in private that Bich [a well-known intellectual from the provincial capital who had attended political meetings in Dinh's home] wanted to marry me, and asked me what I thought of it. When I heard the news, I was both happy and embarrassed, and my face burned as though I had had a sunstroke. But I still had my doubts and wondered whether Bich really loved me.

My parents who had always been fond of Bich agreed immediately. From then on, Bich frequently came to the house. He loved to stay in the garden, so we often went and sat for hours under the tangerine trees to confide in each other. We got married at the end of 1938. . . .

After spending a few days together, Bich again left to travel and operate. As for me, I continued working in the mutual aid associations and the rice transplanting teams of the women. Once in a while, the brothers brought back "Dan Chung" newspapers and gave them to us to sell within the organization. It was much later that I discovered that Bich was a member of the Ben Tre Province Party Committee and belonged to the group that operated openly under legal cover. . . . At that time Bich was busy with many things, so he only came home once every month or two, and then left immediately. The third time we saw each other he knew I was expecting. He was overjoyed. The next day, he made me go and see a doctor, and then bought all sorts of supplies for the baby — clothes and diapers — before leaving. He wanted to have a child very much, and especially a son. . . .

. . . In 1939 when my confinement period drew near, Bich came home and stayed a week with me. That was the longest time we spent together since our wedding. He took great care of me. . . .

Our life was so happy and lovely when suddenly security police agents came to the house, surrounded it and arrested Bich. The baby had been born only three days before. . . .

After they took Bich away, it seemed as though the earth and sky had suddenly turned black. I looked around the room, and looked at my baby and felt I was dying a thousand deaths. I was overcome with worry and grief, and had the feeling I would be separated from Bich forever. We had been married for one year, but had spent less than two months together. We had not even had time to choose a name for our baby when he was arrested. I remembered the time when my brother Ba Chan was beaten in jail, and felt full of pity and worry for my husband. . . .

On 18 July, I took my baby with me and went to see my husband. At the prison, it took me a long time to obtain all the necessary papers, and in the end I was only allowed to see him for fifteen minutes. But at that point, to be able to see him for even one minute, for us to be able to look at each other's face and for him to see the baby was good enough. . . . [W]hen I saw him standing behind the iron bars, looking out and smiling at me, my eyes suddenly became blurred, I felt dizzy and swayed on my feet. I noticed that he was emaciated, had lost a lot of weight, and looked haggard. I thought of scenes of enemy torture and felt full of pity for him. He stretched out his arms, took the baby, and kissed him for a long time. As we were passing the baby back and forth, I asked him about my leaving the baby behind and going off to operate. . . . He loved his son very much, so he thought about it for a long time and then encouraged me:

"It's right for you to do that, I approve of it wholeheartedly."

I asked him:

"Is there anything else you want to tell me?"

He looked at me with affection:

"I've been sentenced to five years of imprisonment and five years of deportation. I'm resigned to my arrest, but I feel very sorry for you and the baby. It's because of me that you two are suffering. Try to bring up the baby, go with the brothers to operate, and wait for my return. I'm very confident that you will overcome all challenges, as you told me before we got married."

Before I had time to add anything further, the guard came in to announce the end of the visit and to throw me out. I suddenly remembered and asked Bich hurriedly:

"What name shall we give to the baby?"

"[Let's call him] On."

"On" was our first born. The guard shoved me outside. I did not leave at once, and kept walking back and forth in front of the prison gate with the baby in my arms, so my husband could see us a while longer.[2]

On 19 July 1940, I returned home with the baby in my arms. Before the 21st arrived, the day on which [a prominent party leader] was coming to fetch me as had been pre-arranged, I was arrested by the security police. They took me to the prison in Ben Tre [province town] and kept me there for three weeks. They interrogated me about Bich's activities and then about my own. ...When I thought of our situation — my husband in jail in one place, me in exile in another, and the baby separated from both his parents — my heart broke to pieces. The day I handed the baby to my mother to take home, seeing his innocent face and his steady breathing as he lay sleeping, I bent down to kiss him but tears filled my eyes. The moment my mother turned around to leave, I broke out sobbing. My mother also wept pitifully. . . .

. . . [W]e learned that they had deported us to Ba Ra. This was one of the highest mountain peaks in South Vietnam, near the border with Cambodia. This region was infamous because of its insalubrious environment, and people used to say that those who went there never came back alive. . . .

---

[2]This was the last Dinh saw of her husband. He would die in prison.

Tuan Doanh[1]
1967 Interview

The province was so poor that it used to be known as Beggars' Province. . . .

Historically, our province has been a battlefield ever since . . . the second and third centuries. The marshes and reeds provided an excellent terrain for guerrilla warfare in the lowlands, and the dense vegetation stopped the enemy from advancing. There were also major battles against the Mongols in the thirteenth century. It is fair to say that the peasants of Hung Yen have had

---

[1]Tuan Doanh was a member of the Communist Party Provincial Committee for Hung Yen. Gérard Chaliand, *The Peasants of North Vietnam,* trans. Peter Wiles (Baltimore: Penguin, 1969), 71–75.

to withstand continual attempts at invasion throughout their history, in addition to long periods of drought and flooding. They've had the French to contend with, too! It was the Scholars who organized a resistance movement in the villages. There is not a single village in these parts which did not play a part in the resistance. That was in my grandfather's day, and he did his share. It was a peasant uprising on a really large scale, and even the women fought.

...All in all, the resistance against the French was kept up for over twenty years ....

The first [Communist] Party cell in the province was set up in 1930. ... Between 1933 and 1940 they established contact with the general population and began to build up a mass following. ... By 1940, repression or no repression, we were able to get on with our propaganda work and agitation. Each militant was required to establish contact with several villages ... and do his best to establish nests of sympathizers. This went on from 1940 until 1944. There were very few professional revolutionaries in the area — no more than four or five in the entire province; the rest did ordinary jobs as well as working for the Party. And then, round about 1943 or 44, we started making military preparations. On a very small scale, mind: we had no arms and ammunition as yet. ...

On 9 March 1945 came the Japanese coup toppling the colonial administration. ... The French were in such disarray that they could do nothing to stop us. Side by side with the armed conflict, the masses were incited to lay hands on the stocks of rice held by the Japanese. ... The communal rice-stocks in the possession of the village elders ... were shared out, together with the supplies appropriated by the Japanese. In addition, all taxes were withheld. As a result of these steps, starvation was averted in the province. ... This seizure of rice for public use finally removed the peasants' uncertainties about the revolution. ...

In August 1945, we took over every district in the land. ... Suddenly we found ourselves enjoying independence and freedom. The mood of the country was unbelievable: people were burning with enthusiasm. I shall never forget those times.

And then, in December, the French invaded us again. ...

After 1949 the people living in the delta became [the target of French forces]. ... [O]ur army and cadres could not be dislodged; the peasants continued to hide them. A complete network of underground shelters and communication trenches was established, stretching for tens of miles, with exits in or on the outskirts of villages. As the war dragged on, it became possible to conceal and accommodate whole regiments and, eventually, whole divisions.

The French set up puppet municipal councils, staffed with collaborators. It was our task to smash these councils. So we turned the villages into military strongholds, barricading them and digging underground passages. Sometimes a guerrilla platoon was able to withstand a siege by an enemy regiment. After dark, parties of our men would go and harass enemy posts defended by entire battalions. ...

Pham Van Ha[1]
1967 Interview

My own family were landless peasants: all they had was a house and a small yard. They were hired labourers, working for landowners. . . .

I was eleven when my father died, after an illness, at the age of fifty-four. My mother died of starvation during the great famine of 1945. I was fourteen at the time. We were a family of six. . . . My little sister and I took jobs, looking after landowners' children. . . . At that time, I ate one meal a day: rice with fig-leaves, and usually a soup made from rice and bran. There were no vegetables: all we had was rice and salt. One of my sisters died of starvation in 1945; another was killed during a bombardment in 1948. And one of my brothers was killed in the army in 1953. That leaves the three of us. . . .

. . . The landowners used to hold huge feasts and make the villagers con-tribute. Some of them had three wives. They ate meat or chicken every day. When you were working for them, you got a few sweet potatoes in the morning and some rice at midday. That was for heavy labour. . . . If they wanted to grab a peasant's land, they would plant some liquor in his home (the colonial ad-ministration had exclusive rights to liquor) and tip off the authorities. The peasant was duly prosecuted and had to sell his plot. That is how my uncle was dispossessed. And another thing: peasants would run into debt whenever the taxes fell due. The interest rate was 50 per cent for a period of six months. They would just manage to pay off the interest. The debt itself was never disposed of. . . . The poorer a family was, the greater the attempts to make it sell its land, fall into debt and move to another part of the country. . . . In 1943 the village notables decided to put pressure on my family. At their bidding a man came to my uncle's house, feigned insanity and set fire to the place. . . . [M]y two uncles were arrested for laying hands on the notables. There was pandemonium at the district court. In the end, my uncles had to sell all they owned to pay for the trial and were sentenced to three months' imprison-ment. We had already lost three *saos* [a third of an acre] as a result of the liquor incident, and now the last four *saos* had to be sold. We had nothing left. In 1945, the young uncle to whom all this had happened was the first person in Quoc Tri to join the self-defence forces; afterwards, the whole family served in the Resistance.

INDIA ON THE EVE OF INDEPENDENCE

By 1945 Indians had done the hard work of convincing the British to aban-don their colonial position in South Asia, the centerpiece of one of the world's major empires. At the head of the independence movement was the Indian

---

[1] Pham Van Ha was a local Party secretary in Hung Yen.
Chaliand, *Peasants of North Vietnam,* 93–95.

National Congress, organized in 1885. Its leaders were British-educated members of the upper classes who had enjoyed opportunities for advancement under the colonial regime. They formulated their demands for independence with care. Their wish was to take over, not destroy, the institutions created by the British. Nor did they wish to upset the caste, class, or gender systems on which their privileged position depended. Their dream was to make India modern by building steel mills and to make it internationally respected.

Mohandas Gandhi emerged as the charismatic leader of the Congress party's drive for independence. Trained in London in law, he returned home in 1915 and pressed his demands on the British following a strategy of nonviolence and observing in his daily life a simplicity and a spirituality that gave him broad popular appeal unique among the independence leadership. Frustrated by the British during the 1920s and 1930s, Gandhi seized on wartime to demand immediate independence. By the end of World War II it was clear that colonial control was no longer tenable. The prospect of Britain's departure precipitated communal clashes. Hindus and Muslims turned on each other, leading to calls for separation of the colony into two states. Much against Gandhi's wishes, the division did occur, with Pakistan overwhelmingly Muslim and India preponderantly Hindu. In 1947 Britain handed India its formal political independence. Shortly thereafter, Gandhi, aging and ill, died from a bullet fired by a Hindu extremist. The baton of national leadership passed to his chief lieutenant, Jawaharlal Nehru.

3.7

Jawaharlal Nehru Recounts the Influences That Shaped His Social Outlook and Politics

Nehru figures prominently in twentieth century Indian history — as one of the leading figures during the independence movement, as the prime minister and commanding personality during his country's first decades of independence, and as the founder of a political dynasty whose influence would extend into the 1990s. His reflections on his early years and India's anti-colonial struggle, *Toward Freedom*, is a product of prison life to which the British repeatedly subjected Nehru as well as Gandhi and their colleagues in the Indian National Congress from the 1920s through World War II. Nehru enjoyed preferential treatment at the hands of his jailors including relatively comfortable accommodations and special leaves to visit acutely ill family members. After hectic rounds of public speaking and organizing on the outside, prison gave him time for reading, reflecting, and finally in 1934–1935 penning this personal account. It was published in 1936, and in 1940 during another prison stint, Nehru updated his story.

The autobiography tells us a lot about Nehru's family background (upper class), his cultural orientation (including a preference for writing in English), and his political loyalties (nationalist and socialist). What are the major problems that he admits to grappling with? How do his experiences and aspirations compare with those recounted by Mao and Ho? Why did all three find it important to chronicle the origins of their political activism?

From *Toward Freedom*
1941

My childhood was . . . a sheltered and uneventful one. I listened to the grown-up talk of my cousins without always understanding all of it. Often this talk related to the overbearing character and insulting manners of the English people, as well as Eurasians, toward Indians, and how it was the duty of every Indian to stand up to this and not to tolerate it. Instances of conflicts between the rulers and the ruled were common and were fully discussed. It was a notorious fact that whenever an Englishman killed an Indian he was acquitted by a jury of his own countrymen. In railway trains compartments were reserved for Europeans, and, however crowded the train might be — and they used to be terribly crowded — no Indian was allowed to travel in them, even though they were empty. . . . Benches and chairs were also reserved for Europeans in public parks and other places. I was filled with resentment against the alien rulers of my country who misbehaved in this manner; and, whenever an Indian hit back, I was glad. . . .

Much as I began to resent the presence and behavior of the alien rulers, I had no feeling whatever, so far as I can remember, against individual Englishmen. I had had English governesses, and occasionally I saw English friends of my father's visiting him. In my heart I rather admired the English. . . .

[Sometime in 1920 Nehru and some colleagues visited a remote area where peasants were protesting their dire conditions.] That visit was a revelation to me. We found the whole countryside afire with enthusiasm and full of a strange excitement. Enormous gatherings would take place at the briefest notice by word of mouth. One village would communicate with another, and the second with the third, and so on; and presently whole villages would empty out, and all over the fields there would be men and women and children on the march to the meeting place. . . . They were in miserable rags, men and women, but their faces were full of excitement and their eyes glistened and seemed to expect strange happenings which would, as if by a miracle, put an end to their long misery.

They showered their affection on us and looked on us with loving and hopeful eyes, as if we were the bearers of good tidings, the guides who were to lead them to the promised land. Looking at them and their misery and overflowing gratitude, I was filled with shame and sorrow — shame at my own easygoing and comfortable life and our petty politics of the city which ignored this vast multitude of semi-naked sons and daughters of India, sorrow at the degradation and overwhelming poverty of India. A new picture of India seemed to rise before me, naked, starving, crushed, and utterly miserable. And their faith in us, casual visitors from the distant city, embarrassed me and filled me with a new responsibility that frightened me.

Jawaharlal Nehru, *Toward Freedom: The Autobiography of Jawaharlal Nehru,* rev. ed. (New York: John Day, 1941), 20–21, 56–57, 73, 189–92, 229–30, 232, 234, 266.

I listened to their innumerable tales of sorrow, their crushing and ever-growing burden of rent, illegal exactions, ejectments from land and mud hut, beatings; surrounded on all sides by vultures who preyed on them — zamindar's agents,[1] moneylenders, police; toiling all day to find what they produced was not theirs and their reward was kicks and curses and a hungry stomach. Many of those who were present were landless people who had been ejected by the landlords and had no land or hut to fall back upon. The land was rich, but the burden on it was very heavy, the holdings were small, and there were too many people after them. Taking advantage of this land hunger, the landlords . . . charged huge illegal premiums. The tenant, knowing of no other alternative, borrowed money from the moneylender and paid the premium, and then, unable to pay his debt or even the rent, was ejected and lost all he had. . . .

[The force beginning to drive the independence movement forward in the early 1920s] was a strange mixture of nationalism and politics and religion and mysticism and fanaticism. Behind all this was agrarian trouble and, in the big cities, a rising working-class movement. Nationalism and a vague but intense countrywide idealism sought to bring together all these various, and sometimes mutually contradictory, discontents, and succeeded to a remarkable degree. And yet this nationalism itself was a composite force, and behind it could be distinguished a Hindu nationalism, a Moslem nationalism partly looking beyond the frontiers of India, and, what was more in consonance with the spirit of the times, an Indian nationalism. For the time being they overlapped and all pulled together. . . . It was remarkable how Gandhiji[2] seemed to cast a spell on all classes and groups of people and drew them into one motley crowd struggling in one direction. He became, indeed (to use a phrase which has been applied to another leader), "a symbolic expression of the confused desires of the people." . . .

Whether Gandhiji is a democrat or not, he does represent the peasant masses of India; he is the quintessence of the conscious and subconscious will of those millions. . . . A man of the keenest intellect, of fine feeling and good taste, wide vision; very human, and yet essentially the ascetic who has suppressed his passions and emotions, sublimated them and directed them in spiritual channels; a tremendous personality, drawing people to himself like a magnet, and calling out fierce loyalties and attachments — all this so utterly unlike and beyond a peasant. And yet withal he is the greatest peasant, with a peasant's outlook on affairs, and with a peasant's blindness to some aspects of life. But India is peasant India, and so he knows his India well, reacts to her slightest tremors, gauges a situation accurately and almost instinctively, and has a knack of acting at the psychological moment. . . .

Many of us had cut adrift from this peasant outlook, and the old ways of thought and custom and religion had become alien to us. We called ourselves

---

[1]Zamindars were landholders who carried out grass-roots government functions such as tax collection under the British colonial system.

[2]The "ji" added to Gandhi's name is a widely used term of respect.

moderns and thought in terms of "progress," and industrialization and a higher standard of living and collectivization. We considered the peasant's viewpoint reactionary; and some, a growing number, looked with favor toward socialism and communism. . . .

To me, personally, Gandhiji had always shown extraordinary kindness and consideration, and my father's death had brought him particularly near to me. He had always listened patiently to whatever I had to say and had made every effort to meet my wishes. This had, indeed, led me to think that perhaps some colleagues and I could influence him continuously in a socialist direction, and he had himself said that he was prepared to go step by step as he saw his way to do so. It seemed to me almost inevitable then that he would accept the fundamental socialist position, as I saw no other way out from the violence and injustice and waste and misery of the existing order. He might disagree about the methods but not about the ideal. So I thought then, but I realize now that there are basic differences between Gandhiji's ideals and the socialist objective. . . .

I had long been drawn to socialism and communism, and Russia had appealed to me. Much in Soviet Russia I dislike — the ruthless suppression of all contrary opinion, the wholesale regimentation, the unnecessary violence (as I thought) in carrying out various policies. But there was no lack of violence and suppression in the capitalist world, and I realized more and more how the very basis and foundation of our acquisitive society and property was violence. Without violence it could not continue for many days. A measure of political liberty meant little indeed when the fear of starvation was always compelling the vast majority of people everywhere to submit to the will of the few, to the greater glory and advantage of the latter.

. . . With all her blunders, Soviet Russia had triumphed over enormous difficulties and taken great strides toward this new order. While the rest of the world was in the grip of the depression and going backward in some ways, in the Soviet country a great new world was being built up before our eyes. Russia, following the great Lenin, looked into the future and thought only of what was to be, while other countries lay numbed under the dead hand of the past and spent their energy in preserving the useless relics of a bygone age. . . . [T]he presence and example of the Soviets was a bright and heartening phenomenon in a dark and dismal world. . . .

Russia apart, the theory and philosophy of Marxism lightened up many a dark corner of my mind. History came to have a new meaning for me. The Marxist interpretation threw a flood of light on it, and it became an unfolding drama with some order and purpose, howsoever unconscious, behind it. In spite of the appalling waste and misery of the past and the present, the future was bright with hope, though many dangers intervened. It was the essential freedom from dogma and the scientific outlook of Marxism that appealed to me. . . .

It seemed clear to me that nationalism would remain the outstanding urge, till some measure of political freedom was attained. Because of this the Congress had been, and was still (apart from certain labor circles), the most advanced organization in India, as it was far the most powerful. During the past thirteen years, under Gandhiji's leadership, it had produced a wonderful awakening of the masses, and, in spite of its vague bourgeois ideology, it had served a revolutionary purpose. It had not exhausted its utility yet and was not likely to do so till the nationalist urge gave place to a social one. . . .

. . . [I]t is absurd to say that the leaders [of the Indian national movement] betray the masses because they do not try to upset the land system or the capitalist system. They never claimed to do so. Some people in the Congress, and they are a growing number, want to change the land system and the capitalist system, but they cannot speak in the name of the Congress. . . .

. . . I write this sitting in a British prison. . . . I dislike British imperialism, and I resent its imposition on India; I dislike the capitalist system; I dislike exceedingly and resent the way India is exploited by the ruling classes of Britain. But I do not hold England or the English people as a whole responsible for this. . . .

Personally, I owe too much to England in my mental make-up ever to feel wholly alien to her. And, do what I will, I cannot get rid of the habits of mind, and the standards and ways of judging other countries as well as life generally, which I acquired at school and college in England. My predilections (apart from the political ones) are in favor of England and the English people, and, if I have become what is called an uncompromising opponent of British rule in India, it is, almost in spite of these.

3.8
Gandhi and Nehru Exchange Ideas
on Development Strategy

By fall 1945, all understood that the end of British colonial rule was only a matter of time. Gandhi was ready to face the question of what to do with the independence that his Congress party had won. The discussions within the leadership of the party worried him and prompted him to turn for clarification (or was it reassurance?) from Nehru. The subject preoccupying Gandhi was the fate of the countryside, which he saw as the hope for holding at bay the values of the modern world — materialism, violence, and quarrelsomeness — that he had long opposed. The way in which the government chose to develop India would have a strong bearing on which values prevailed and, in turn, on India's national identity and its role in the world community.

The stakes were high but the tone of the exchange was cordial, even deeply affectionate between two men who had worked together almost as father and son to secure India's freedom. What is the vision for India's future that each champions? What is the critical point of difference between them and how deep is it? How might Mao have reacted to the issues raised by this exchange?

Personal Letters
October 1945

GANDHI TO NEHRU, OCTOBER 5, 1945

I am convinced that if India is to attain true freedom and through India the world also, then sooner or later the fact must be recognised that people will have to live in villages, not in towns, in huts, not in palaces. Crores [literally ten of millions] of people will never be able to live at peace with each other in towns and palaces. They will then have no recourse but to resort to both violence and untruth. I hold that without truth and non-violence there can be nothing but destruction for humanity. We can realise truth and non-violence only in the simplicity of village life and this simplicity can best be found in the Charkha [spinning wheel] and all that the Charkha connotes. I must not fear if the world today is going the wrong way. It may be that India too will go that way and like the proverbial moth burn itself eventually in the flame round which it dances more and more furiously. But it is my bounden duty up to my last breath to try to protect India and through India the entire world from such a doom. The essence of what I have said is that man should rest content with what are his real needs and become self-sufficient. If he does not have this control he cannot save himself. . . .

 . . . You must not imagine that I am envisaging our village life as it is today. . . . My ideal village will contain intelligent human beings. They will not live in dirt and darkness as animals. Men and women will be free and able to hold their own against anyone in the world. There will be neither plague, nor cholera nor smallpox; no one will be idle, no one will wallow in luxury. Everyone will have to contribute his quota of manual labour. . . . It is possible to envisage railways, post and telegraph offices etc. . . .

 . . . We both live for the cause of India's freedom and we would both gladly die for it. We are not in need of the world's praise. Whether we get praise or blame is immaterial to us. There is no room for praise in service. I want to live to 125 for the service of India but I must admit that I am now an old man. You are much younger in comparison and I have therefore named you as my heir. I must, however, understand my heir and my heir should understand me. Then alone shall I be content.

NEHRU'S REPLY TO GANDHI, OCTOBER 9, 1945

Briefly put, my view is that the question before us is not one of truth versus untruth or non-violence versus violence. One assumes as one must that true cooperation and peaceful methods must be aimed at, and a society which encourages these must be our objective. The whole question is how to achieve this society and what its content should be. I do not understand why a village should necessarily embody truth and non-violence. A village, normally speak-

---

Jawaharlal Nehru, *A Bunch of Old Letters* (London: Asia Publishing House, 1958), 506–509.

ing, is backward intellectually and culturally and no progress can be made from a backward environment. Narrow-minded people are much more likely to be untruthful and violent.

Then again we have to put down certain objectives like a sufficiency of food, clothing, housing, education, sanitation etc. which should be the minimum requirements for the country and for everyone. It is with these objectives in view that we must find out specifically how to attain them speedily. Again it seems to me inevitable that modern means of transport as well as many other modern developments must continue and be developed. There is no way out of it except to have them. If that is so, inevitably a measure of heavy industry exists. How far will that fit in with a purely village society? Personally I hope that heavy or light industries should all be decentralised as far as possible and this is feasible now because of the development of electric power. If two types of economy exist in the country[,] there should be either conflict between the two or one will overwhelm the other.

The question of independence and protection from foreign aggression, both political and economic, has also to be considered in this context. I do not think it is possible for India to be really independent unless she is a technically advanced country. I am not thinking for the moment in terms of just armies but rather of scientific growth. In the present context of the world we cannot even advance culturally without a strong background of scientific research in every department. There is today in the world a tremendous acquisitive tendency both in individuals and groups and nations, which leads to conflicts and wars. Our entire society is based on this more or less. That basis must go and be transformed into one of cooperation, not of isolation which is impossible. If this is admitted and is found feasible[,] then attempts should be made to realise it not in terms of an economy, which is cut off from the rest of the world, but rather one which cooperates. From the economic or political point of view an isolated India may well be a kind of vacuum which increases the acquisitive tendencies of others and thus creates conflicts.

There is no question of palaces for millions of people. But there seems to be no reason why millions should not have comfortable up-to-date homes where they can lead a cultured existence. Many of the present overgrown cities have developed evils which are deplorable. Probably we have to discourage this overgrowth and at the same time encourage the village to approximate more to the culture of the town.

3.9

Nehru Reacts to Communal Violence

As the British promising independence headed out one door, the horror of communal violence — pitting Hindus and Sikhs against Muslims — came in the other. Nehru directly confronted this gathering hatred in the fall of 1946 when an incendiary call by the party representing the Muslim perspective, the Muslim League, led to the killing of some four thousand Hindus in Calcutta. Retaliation against Muslims living in Bihar province soon followed. Nehru rushed to the scene to quiet passions and restore order. His efforts were in the long term unavailing. The violence spread as the day of independence approached, sharpening concern over who would control which territory. In the end, partition was achieved at the cost of as many as a million dead and some fourteen million more displaced. The trauma of those days became part of the national memory for Pakistanis and Indians alike.

For Nehru as well as Gandhi the ferocity of feeling that erupted in 1946 and 1947 was a shock as the following letter to a close associate in the Congress party leadership makes clear. What clues appear in Nehru's letter and his autobiography above to explain his surprise and shock? How does he hope to resolve the clashes?

Letter to Vallabhbhai Patel
November 5, 1946

These two days here have been so full of horror for me that I find it difficult to believe in the reality of things I must believe in. . . . In the affected areas, that is Patna district, in a part of Monghyr district and in Gaya, there has been a definite attempt on the part of Hindu mobs to exterminate the Muslims. They have killed, indiscriminately, men, women and children *en masse*. Some stories are incredibly brutal and inhuman. Indeed one can only explain all this by saying that a madness had seized the people. I have addressed some large crowds in the rural areas and I have no doubt that many of them had participated in this bad business. They were the ordinary peasant folk of Bihar, very simple, unsophisticated, and rather likeable. . . . [W]hen I spoke sternly to them they seemed full of shame of what they had done. Almost everywhere after my speech I asked them to pledge themselves to behave in future and they seemed to do so with some conviction, raising their hands all together. . . .

It is obvious that this big uprising could not come out of nothing. I could not make out who were the leaders of this business. Probably they are mostly local village leaders but they have received their inspiration from others. . . .

It is impossible to say what the total number of deaths is. But it must be a very large number. I doubt if it is under 2000 and it may be double that number. Some small Muslim villages have been completely wiped out. . . .

The number of Muslim refugees is very large. I do not know what it is but it may well go up to fifteen thousand in various places and the problem of looking after them, feeding them, clothing them and finding accommodation for them as well as guarding them is a difficult one.

The military are coming into the scene with fairly adequate forces now, or they will begin to function in a big way in about two days time. As I told you, there is news of their firing on a mob today, inflicting 400 deaths. We have not got correct figures yet. In a couple of days time all the affected areas will be

---

S. Gopal, ed., *Selected Works of Jawaharlal Nehru,* second series, vol. 1 (New Delhi: Jawaharlal Nehru Memorial Fund, 1984), 63–64.

sufficiently held by the military which will reach even the villages in the interior of these areas.

My own rough guess is that the next three days will see the end, more or less, of the active part of the disturbances. . . . Of course the ill will that has been generated and the terrible effects of this horror will last a long time.

3.10
Rural Life: Land and Gender

The Indian countryside at midcentury may have been no less filled with hardship than China's, but it was distinctly more complex. As well as the predictable regional variations resulting from different climates, soil, economic activity, and class differences was an important cultural overlay that deeply divided communities. The fundamental division was religious — between Hindus and Muslims — and among Hindus a further division in which each person inherited a place within an intricate, rigid caste system that governed social contact, marriage, educational opportunities, and work. Yet too much can be made of these uniquely Indian features. As the documents here suggest, the struggle to gain and hold land was no less fundamental than in China or Vietnam. In addition, gender roles constraining women did much to shape life in the countryside.

Documenting these and other facets of rural life is notoriously difficult. Gathering oral histories is one possibility, though the examples earlier in this chapter reveal some of the difficulties. Another is fiction written by knowledgeable outsider observers. The first document is from the novel *Nectar in a Sieve*. Published in 1954 and set in the years right after independence, the novel celebrates the stoic determination of its peasant characters, above all the heroine Rukmani. The fourth daughter of a village headman whose fortunes are going downhill, she is married to a poor tenant farmer, Nathan. This harmonious couple face the familiar plagues of the peasant — too much rain, too little rain, and debt. To these problems is added a new threat in the form of a tannery that disrupts village life, offering work for a wage, eating up village land, and driving up prices. The excerpt that follows captures the moment when the couple, having persevered through one trial after another to hold onto their land, learn that it is about to be sold out from under them to the tannery. Later in the novel, the stoic Rukmani and Nathan move to the city where they hope to find a way to survive. Nathan dies there, and Rukmani returns penniless to the village and the care of her surviving children. The author, Kamala Markandaya, was herself the daughter of a railway employee who attended university and pursued a career in journalism. The travel afforded by her family's access to the railway was most likely the way she gained insight into rural life. She wrote this novel in England to which she had moved in 1948.

Yet a third kind of revealing evidence is verse that survives as part of the local oral tradition. Below are five such verses. Though they total only twenty-six lines, they are surprisingly rich in their evocation of sentiment and their insights into such topics as family, marriage, and property.

Novels and oral tradition, like other forms of evidence, have to be used with care. For example, we cannot be sure how well Markandaya knew rural life if she saw it only through a train window or whether a bit of village verse is a recent invention, eons old, a variant on a sentiment widely shared, or one person's unique point of view. But these additional types of evidence should be welcome for the ways that they can help us better understand rural conditions distant to most of us in time, space, and culture. What are the main concerns expressed by the women in these documents? Imagine how Rukmani or someone reciting the short verses would respond to the Gandhi-Nehru exchange of views. How well do concerns of ordinary women expressed here correspond with those of the two elite men? Do the novel excerpt and the verses lend support to either man's position, or do they open a fresh perspective on the debate over development? More broadly, how do the concerns with land and the views of women compare with the material above on Chinese and Vietnamese rural life?

Kamala Markandaya
From *Nectar in a Sieve*
1954

I was out gathering cow dung [for fuel], I did not see Sivaji [the landowner] come, and he left quickly as soon as he had delivered his message. I came with my basket half-laden and saw my husband sitting on the floor staring out before him, a dazed expression on his face and his lips trembling loosely. . . . I sent the child out and went to Nathan, thinking he had had another of his attacks, but he seemed to wake up when he heard my voice and waved me away.

"I am all right."

"Here — drink this. You will feel better." I tipped the mud pot and filling his bowl handed it to him. He drank obediently as if to please me, spilling a little in the process. He was still shaking. I sat beside him waiting.

"The land is to be sold," he said. "We are to move. Sivaji came this morning. He says there is nothing to be done."

I could not take it in. I gaped at him unbelieving. He nodded as if to emphasize that what he had said was so.

"The tannery owners are buying the land. They pay good prices."

The tannery! That word brought instant understanding. Realisation came like a rocket, swift and fiery.

"They can't," I remember saying helplessly. "It is our land; we have been here thirty years."

Nathan opened his hands, trembling, impotent.

"Sivaji tells me there is a profit to be made. The landlord has completed the deal, papers have been signed. We must leave."

Where can we go? I wanted to ask; but that was a question at present without an answer, and I refrained. Instead he put the question. "Where are we to go? What shall we do?"

"How much time have we got?" I asked, preparing for the worst.

Kamala Markandaya, *Nectar in a Sieve* (New York: John Day, 1954), 178–82.

"He does not expect us to leave at once. He has given us two weeks' time in which to go, which is lenient."

A dozen lines of thought began and continued in my brain without ending; crossing, tangling, like threads on some meaningless warp. My head was whirling. I must sit down and think, I said to myself, but not now, later. Follow each thought to its conclusion, decide what we are to do for ourselves and our children. This present chaos is madness.

"I do not know why they need this bit of land," I said, in the manner of people who must say something for the sake of the sanity which speech can bring.

"Certainly they cannot build on it; it is a swamp, meant only for rice-growing."

Nathan shrugged. "Who knows. Perhaps they can drain it, tighten the soil; they have resources beyond our imagining. Or perhaps they wish to grow rice for their own men."

He too was speaking like me, automatically, for the sake of speaking. I made another effort, a pitiful one, for the words I said were the last to bring comfort.

"At least we shall not have much to carry. The granary is almost empty."

He nodded in dull agreement. Then once again we relapsed into silence, sunk in our own thoughts.

Somehow I had always felt the tannery would eventually be our undoing. I had known it since the day the carts had come with their loads of bricks and noisy dusty men, staining the clear soft greens that had once coloured our village and cleaving its cool silences with clamour. Since then it had spread like weeds in an untended garden, strangling whatever life grew in its way. It had changed the face of our village beyond recognition and altered the lives of its inhabitants in a myriad ways. Some — a few — had been raised up; many others cast down, lost in its clutches. And because it grew and flourished it got the power that money brings, so that to attempt to withstand it was like trying to stop the onward rush of the great juggernaut. Well, I suppose there were some families who saw in it hope for their sons: indeed, many still depended on such earnings, and if my sons had still been there my thoughts might have been different; but for us as we were now, and others like us, there could be only resignation and resentment. There had been a time when we, too, had benefited — those days seemed very remote now, almost belonging to another life — but we had lost more than we had gained or could ever regain. Ira [Rakmani's daughter] had ruined herself at the hands of the throngs that the tannery attracted. None but these would have laid hands on her, even at her bidding. My sons had left because it frowned on them; one of them had been destroyed by its ruthlessness. And there were others its touch had scathed. . . .

Yet I must be honest, as my husband and sons have always been: the tannery cannot be blamed for every misfortune we suffered. Tannery or not, the land might have been taken from us. It had never belonged to us, we had never prospered to the extent where we could buy, and Nathan, himself the son of a landless man, had inherited nothing. And whatever extraneous influence the tannery may have exercised, the calamities of the land belong to it alone, born of wind and rain and weather, immensities not to be tempered by man or his creations. To those who live by the land there must always come times of hardship, of fear and of hunger, even as there are years of plenty. This is one of the truths of our existence as those who live by the land know: that sometimes we eat and sometimes we starve. We live by our labours from one harvest to the next, there is no certain telling whether we shall be able to feed ourselves and our children, and if bad times are prolonged we know we must see the weak surrender their lives and this fact, too, is within our experience. In our lives there is no margin for misfortune.

Still, while there was land there was hope. Nothing, now, nothing whatever. My being was full of the husks of despair, dry, lifeless. I went into the hut and looked about me. Brown mud walls that had crumbled many a time and been rebuilt many a time. Coconut thatching, some of it still part of the old palm lightning had destroyed, as I could tell from the colour. Bare, beaten floor of baked mud, hardened with dung-wash. This home my husband had built for me with his own hands in the time he was waiting for me; brought me to it with a pride which I, used to better living, had so very nearly crushed. In it we had lain together, and our children had been born. This hut with all its memories was to be taken from us, for it stood on land that belonged to another. And the land itself by which we lived. It is a cruel thing, I thought. They do not know what they do to us.

Women's Verses on Subordination and Dependence

1. A SONG POPULAR IN NORTHERN INDIA, WHERE A COMPANION OF THE BRIDE SINGS IT ON THE BRIDE'S BEHALF AS SHE LEAVES HER FATHER'S HOME

To my brother belonged the storied palaces;
But, alas, for me, the foreign land . . .
O my father.

2. A SONG FROM HINDU WOMEN IN NORTHERN INDIA

To my brother belong your green fields
O father, while I am banished afar . . .
This year when the monsoon arrives, dear father,
send my brother to fetch me home.
When my childhood companions return O my father
send me a message, O.

Bina Agarwal, *A Field of One's Own: Gender and Land Rights in South Asia* (Cambridge, Eng.: Cambridge University Press, 1994), 249, 263, 428, 466.

3–4. Two Fragments on the Theme of Mothers-in-Law from Songs That Come from a Village in Uttar Pradesh in Northern India

O my friend! My in-laws' house is a wretched place.
My mother-in-law is a very bad woman.
She always struts about full of anger.

O mother-in-law! Why do you strut about
And pretend that you love me so much?
I will not get down from my palanquin
Unless you give me a separate fireplace.
O Father-in-law! Why do you jingle your moneybag?
I will not get down from my palanquin
Unless you build a separate big house for me.

5. A Compressed Story in Verse about Which Little Is Known

For my father's house I worked hard.
So I should get half of the property.
But father says,
"If I give you land, we will not have enough;
Perhaps I could give you unirrigated land."
But my brother says,
"No, I will not even give you dry land."

CHAPTER 4

THE COLD WAR:
A TENUOUS ACCOMMODATION

IN THE 1950S AND 1960S, the Cold War took a significant turn. The costs and risks of confrontation between the superpowers increasingly concerned leaders in Moscow and Washington, leading them to search for ways to stabilize their rivalry and avoid a direct, possibly nuclear, collision. Nuclear fear was perhaps the single most effective brake on superpower rivalry. But a close second could be found on the home front. Post-Stalin Soviet leaders were having difficulty maintaining a large military budget while also providing the better life demanded by their citizens. In the United States the popular fear of communism was beginning to fade by the 1960s, and youth began to challenge the domestic and international status quo. Despite the general pressures toward moderation and caution, leaders did blunder twice into dangerous adventures. The first was in Cuba in 1962, a nuclear confrontation whose rapid and peaceful resolution reinforced the resolve to bring the arms race under better control. The second was in Vietnam, a war prompted by U.S. Cold War commitments that would drag on and on and would feed the mounting discontent at home.

This chapter draws attention to the complicated constituents of the Cold War at mid-course. The national values and international perceptions of leaders played a part (as we saw in chapter 1). But the leaders' actions were profoundly shaped by the growing destructiveness and cost of military technology and by changes in public opinion. In highlighting the links between foreign policy and domestic developments, we are reminded that leaders do not act in isolation and that they do not have a free hand in international affairs. The Vietnam decision is a reminder of how strong Cold War currents remained into the 1960s; they could be controlled but not ignored. While reading these materials it might be useful to consider which facets of the Cold War were stabilizing and which were still dynamic and hard to control.

REFORMING THE SOVIET SYSTEM

By the time of Stalin's death in March 1953, he had created a system rife with tensions and discontents. His successors moved at once to reform policy both at home and abroad. Nikita Khrushchev emerged as the dominant figure in the Kremlin and during his decade of leadership pressed for policies that would improve the economy and also relations with the United States and western Europe. But at the heart of Khrushchev's reforms was his critical appraisal of Stalin's rule. Khrushchev was himself a product of the Stalinist system in a double sense. He had absorbed its values but he had also suffered through its insecurities. No one knew its flaws better than he. In trying to bring a degree of reform to the Soviet Union, Khrushchev had to deal with this very personal past.

4.1

Nikita Khrushchev Recalls Life with the Elderly Stalin

The personal impulse behind Khrushchev's de-Stalinization is amply evident in his recollections of Stalin's last years. After his forced retirement in 1964, Khrushchev started dictating his memoirs into a tape recorder; the tapes were smuggled out of the country and published in three volumes. Doubts about the authenticity of the tapes were finally resolved by comparing voiceprints from the tapes with recorded speeches that he had given.

As with any memoir, you should be aware that the author might be seeking to burnish his reputation and settle scores with old antagonists. What biases might be at work in Khrushchev's account of the dictator who was his boss and patron? What kind of person emerges from this sketch of the elderly Stalin and what kind of relationship does he have to those around him? What does this source add to our picture of Stalin the ideologue and cold warrior (treated in chapter 1)?

From *Khrushchev Remembers*

1970

Stalin would get up from an afternoon nap around seven or eight o'clock in the evening and drive to the Kremlin. We would meet him there. He used to select the movies himself. The films were usually what you might call captured trophies; we got them from the West. Many of them were American pictures. He liked cowboy movies especially. He used to curse them and give them the proper ideological evaluation but then immediately order new ones. . . .

As a rule, when a movie ended, Stalin would suggest, "Well, let's go get something to eat, why don't we?" The rest of us weren't hungry. By now it was usually one or two o'clock in the morning. It was time to go to bed, and

Nikita Khruschev, *Khrushchev Remembers,* trans. and ed. Strobe Talbott (Boston: Little, Brown, 1970), 297–301, 303, 307–308.

the next day we had to go to work. But Stalin didn't have to work in the morning, and he didn't think about us. Everyone would say, yes, he was hungry, too. This lie about being hungry was like a reflex. We would all get into our cars and drive out to the nearby Dacha [country house]. . . .

When we got to the dacha, "the session" continued, if you can call it a session. This system of work, if you can call it work, continued from after the war until Stalin's death. Neither the Central Committee, nor the Politbureau, nor the Presidium Bureau worked regularly.[1] But Stalin's regular sessions with his inner circle went along like clockwork. If he didn't summon us for two or three days, we would think something had happened to him, that he'd gotten sick.

He suffered terribly from loneliness. He needed people around him all the time. When he woke up in the morning, he would immediately summon us, either inviting us to the movies or starting some conversation which could have been finished in two minutes but was stretched out so that we would stay with him longer. This was an empty pastime for us. It's true that sometimes State and Party questions were decided, but we spent only a fraction of our time on those. The main thing was to occupy Stalin's time so he wouldn't suffer from loneliness. He was depressed by loneliness and he feared it.

He had a deep fear of more than just loneliness and being ambushed by his enemies on the road to the dacha. Whenever we had dinner with him, Stalin wouldn't touch a single dish or hors d'oeuvre or bottle until someone else had tested it. This shows that he had gone off the deep end. He didn't even trust the people serving him, people who had served him for years and who were undoubtedly loyal to him. . . .

These dinners were frightful. We would get home from them early in the morning, just in time for breakfast, and then we'd have to go to work. During the day I usually tried to take a nap in my lunch hour because there was always a risk that if you didn't take a nap and Stalin invited you for dinner, you might get sleepy at the table; and those who got sleepy at Stalin's table could come to a bad end. There were often serious drinking bouts, too. . . .

. . . I'd say that Stalin found it entertaining to watch the people around him get themselves into embarrassing and even disgraceful situations. For some reason he found the humiliation of others very amusing. I remember once Stalin made me dance the "Gopak" [a Ukrainian folk dance] before some top Party officials. I had to squat down on my haunches and kick out my heels, which frankly wasn't very easy for me. But I did it and I tried to keep a pleasant expression on my face. As I later told Anastas Ivanovich Mikoyan,[2] "When Stalin says dance, a wise man dances." . . .

. . . [Stalin] once picked up a gun when we were having dinner at the Nearby Dacha and went outside to drive away some sparrows. All he succeeded in doing was wounding one of [those serving] in his bodyguard. An-

---

[1] Khrushchev refers here to the highest levels of the Soviet Community Party.

[2] A leading figure in the Communist Party who continued in political service into the 1970s.

other time he was fiddling with a gun, and it went off and just barely missed killing Mikoyan. Stalin was sitting next to Mikoyan. The shot ripped into the ground and spewed gravel all over the table and all over Mikoyan. No one said a word, but we were all horrified. . . .

All of us around Stalin were temporary people. As long as he trusted us to a certain degree, we were allowed to go on living and working. But the moment he stopped trusting you, Stalin would start to scrutinize you until the cup of his distrust overflowed. Then it would be your turn to follow those who were no longer among the living. That's what it was like for all the people who worked with him and struggled beside him in the ranks of the Party for the Party's sake. Many of these people, Stalin's most dedicated comrades-in-arms, were eliminated. . . .

In the last days before his death, we usually met with Stalin in a group — [Lavrenti] Beria, [Georgi] Malenkov, [Nikolai] Bulganin, and myself. Bulganin wasn't always present at these dinner sessions of the inner circle. Every year it became more and more obvious that Stalin was weakening mentally as well as physically. This was particularly evident from his eclipses of mind and losses of memory. When he was well and sober, he was still a formidable leader, but he was declining fast. I recall once he turned to Bulganin and started to say something but couldn't remember his name. Stalin looked at him intently and said, "You there, what's your name?"

"Bulganin."

"Of course, Bulganin! That's what I was going to say." Stalin became very unnerved when this kind of thing happened. He didn't want others to notice. But these slips of memory occurred more and more frequently, and they used to drive him crazy.

4.2

Khrushchev Denounces Stalin's Crimes

In 1956 Khrushchev electrified leading members of the Soviet Communist Party gathered for a secret session of their twentieth congress. To their shock, he delivered a detailed indictment of the deceased dictator. Khrushchev intended this secret report to legitimize the new direction he planned for the Soviet Union. But the report could not serve its purpose if it remained secret. Copies were circulated among trusted circles at home and within the international communist movement in such numbers that they fell into the hands of the CIA, thence quickly into the pages of the *New York Times*. Khrushchev's revelations caused a stir among foreign Communist parties and confirmed what anti-communists had been claiming all along.

The indictment of Stalin is also an indictment of Lavrenti P. Beria, a Stalin's loyalist who had jumped to prominence in 1938 as head of the security forces, the chief instrument of Stalinist repression. Right after Stalin's death, Beria had moved quickly to consolidate his position and set changes in motion both at home and abroad that were in some ways more far-reaching than Khrushchev's reforms three years later. Khrushchev and his allies feared that Beria was on his way to succeeding Stalin and so had him arrested in June 1953 and executed the following December. Why might Khrushchev have decided to make Beria part of his indictment? What charges did Khrushchev make against Stalin and Beria? How radical was his attack on Stalin and the Soviet system? What aspects of Stalinism did Khrushchev continue to accept? Why? How well do the Stalin of the memoir and the secret speech fit together? Does one help illuminate the other?

Secret Speech to the Twentieth Party Congress
February 25, 1956

[Stalin's Cult of Personality]

After Stalin's death the Central Committee of the party began to implement a policy of explaining concisely and consistently that it is impermissible and foreign to the spirit of Marxism-Leninism to elevate one person, to transform him into [a] superman possessing supernatural characteristics akin to those of a god. Such a man supposedly knows everything, sees everything, thinks for everyone, can do anything, is infallible in his behavior.

Such a belief about a man, and specifically about Stalin, was cultivated among us for many years. . . .

[Lenin's Doubts about Stalin]

During Lenin's life the central committee of the party was a real expression of collective leadership of the party and of the Nation. . . . Lenin never imposed by force his views upon his coworkers. He tried to convince; he patiently explained his opinions to others. . . .

. . . [Lenin] detected in Stalin in time those negative characteristics which resulted later in grave consequences. Fearing the future fate of the party and of the Soviet nation, V. I. Lenin made a completely correct characterization of Stalin, pointing out that it was necessary to consider the question of transferring Stalin from the position of Secretary General because of the fact that Stalin is excessively rude, that he does not have a proper attitude toward his comrades, that he is capricious and abuses his power.

In December 1922, in a letter to the party congress Vladimir Ilyich [Lenin] wrote: "After taking over the position of Secretary General, Comrade Stalin accumulated in his hands immeasurable power and I am not certain whether he will be always able to use this power with the required care." . . .

[Stalin's Repressive Policies]

The negative characteristics of Stalin, which, in Lenin's time, were only incipient, transformed themselves during the last years into a grave abuse of power by Stalin, which caused untold harm to our party.

We have to consider seriously and analyze correctly this matter in order that we may preclude any possibility of a repetition in any form whatever of

U.S. Senate, *Congressional Record,* 84th Cong., 2nd Sess., 1956, 102, pt. 7:9389–95, 9397–9402.

what took place during the life of Stalin, who absolutely did not tolerate collegiality in leadership and in work, and who practiced brutal violence, not only toward everything which opposed him, but also toward that which seemed to his capricious and despotic character, contrary to his concepts.

Stalin acted not through persuasion, explanation, and patient cooperation with people, but by imposing his concepts and demanding absolute submission to his opinion. Whoever opposed this concept or tried to prove his viewpoint, and the correctness of his position — was doomed to removal from the leading collective and to subsequent moral and physical annihilation. This was especially true during the period following the 17th party congress [1934], when many prominent party leaders and rank-and-file party workers, honest and dedicated to the cause of communism, fell victim to Stalin's despotism. . . .

Stalin originated the concept ["]enemy of the people.["] This term automatically rendered it unnecessary that the ideological errors of a man or men engaged in a controversy be proven; this term made possible the usage of the most cruel repression, violating all norms of revolutionary legality, against anyone who in any way disagreed with Stalin, against those who were only suspected of hostile intent, against those who had bad reputations. . . . In the main, and in actuality, the only proof of guilt used, against all norms of current legal science, was the confession of the accused himself, and, as subsequent probing proved, confessions were acquired through physical pressures against the accused. . . .

. . . [Stalin] discarded the Leninist method of convincing and educating; he abandoned the method of ideological struggle for that of administrative violence, mass repressions, and terror. He acted on an increasingly larger scale and more stubbornly through punitive organs, at the same time often violating all existing norms of morality and of Soviet laws.

Arbitrary behavior by one person encouraged and permitted arbitrariness in others. Mass arrests and deportations of many thousands of people, execution without trial and without normal investigation created conditions of insecurity, fear, and even desperation. . . .

[STALIN'S VIOLATION OF COLLECTIVE LEADERSHIP]

In the most difficult period for our party and our country, Lenin considered it necessary regularly to convoke congresses, party conferences, and plenary sessions of the Central Committee at which all the most important questions were discussed and where resolutions, carefully worked out by the collective of leaders, were approved. . . .

. . . [W]hen Stalin began increasingly to abuse his power, these principles were brutally violated. This was especially evident during the last 15 years of his life. Was it a normal situation when 13 years elapsed between the 18th and 19th Party congresses [1939–1952], years during which our party and our country had experienced so many important events? . . .

Central committee plenums were hardly ever called. It should be sufficient to mention that during all the years of the patriotic war not a single central committee plenum took place. . . .

In practice Stalin ignored the norms of party life and trampled on the Leninist principle of collective party leadership. . . .

[LEGAL INJUSTICES INFLICTED BY STALIN'S POLICIES]

[M]any party, Soviet, and economic activists, who were branded in 1937–38 as enemies, were actually never enemies, spies, wreckers, etc., but were always honest Communists; they were only so stigmatized, and often no longer able to bear barbaric tortures, they charged themselves (at the order of the investigative judges — falsifiers) with all kinds of grave and unlikely crimes. . . .

It was determined that of the 139 members and candidates of the party's Central Committee who were elected at the 17th congress, 98 persons, that is, 70 percent were arrested and shot (mostly in 1937-38). [Indignation in the hall.] . . .

The same fate met not only the central committee members but also the majority of the delegates to the 17th party congress. Of 1,966 delegates with either voting or advisory rights, 1,108 persons were arrested on charges of antirevolutionary crimes, i.e., decidedly more than a majority. This very fact shows how absurd, wild, and contrary to commonsense were the charges of counter-revolutionary crimes made out, as we now see, against a majority of participants at the 17th party congress. [Indignation in the hall.]

. . . Delegates to the congress were active participants in the building of our Socialist state; many of them suffered and fought for party interests during the prerevolutionary years in the conspiracy and at the civil war fronts; they fought their enemies valiantly and often nervelessly looked into the face of death. How then can we believe that such people could prove to be two-faced and had joined the camps of the enemies of socialism . . . ? . . .

An example of vile provocation[,] of odious falsification[,] and of criminal violation of revolutionary legality is the case of the former candidate for the central committee political bureau, one of the most eminent workers of the party and of the Soviet Government, Comrade Eikhe, who was a party member since 1905.[1] [Commotion in the hall.]

Comrade Eikhe was arrested on April 29, 1938, on the basis of slanderous materials. . . .

Eikhe was forced under torture to sign ahead of time a protocol of his confession prepared by the investigative judges. . . .

On February 4 [1940] Eikhe was shot. [Indignation in the hall.] It has been definitely established now that Eikhe's case was fabricated; he has been posthumously rehabilitated. . . .

This is the kind of vile things which were then practiced. [Movement in the hall.]

---

[1]R. I. Eikhe, an old Bolshevik, rose to the position of party secretary in Siberia. He may have joined other influential delegates to the 1934 party congress in discussing ways to reduce Stalin's power and thus planted the seeds of suspicion in the dictator's mind.

Even more widely was the falsification of cases practiced in the provinces. . . .

A large part of these cases are being reviewed now and a great part of them are being voided because they were baseless and falsified. Suffice it to say that from 1954 to the present time the military collegium of the supreme court has rehabilitated 7,679 persons, many of whom were rehabilitated posthumously.

Mass arrests of party, Soviet, economic, and military workers caused tremendous harm to our country and to the cause of Socialist advancement.

Mass repressions had a negative influence on the moral-political condition of the party, created a situation of uncertainty, contributed to the spreading of unhealthy suspicion, and sowed distrust among Communists. All sorts of slanderers and careerists were active. . . .

[STALIN'S PERSONAL FLAWS]

Stalin was a very distrustful man, sickly suspicious; we knew this from our work with him. He could look at a man and say: "Why are your eyes so shifty today," or "Why are you turning so much today and avoiding to look me directly in the eyes?" The sickly suspicion created in him a general distrust even toward eminent party workers whom he had known for years. Everywhere and in everything he saw enemies, "two-facers" and spies.

Possessing unlimited power he indulged in great willfulness and choked a person morally and physically. A situation was created where one could not express one's own will.

When Stalin said that one or another should be arrested, it was necessary to accept on faith that he was an "enemy of the people." Meanwhile, Beriya's [Beria's] gang, which ran the organs of state security, outdid itself in proving the guilt of the arrested and the truth of materials which it falsified. And what proofs were offered? The confessions of the arrested, and the investigative judges accepted these confessions. And how is it possible that a person confesses to crimes which he has not committed? Only in one way, because of application of physical methods of pressuring him, tortures, bringing him to a state of unconsciousness, deprivation of his judgment, taking away of his human dignity. In this manner were confessions acquired. . . .

. . . Stalin very energetically popularized himself as a great leader; in various ways he tried to inculcate in the people the version that all victories gained by the Soviet nation during the great patriotic war [World War II] were due to the courage, daring, and genius of Stalin and of no one else. . . .

[Not] Stalin, but the party as a whole, the Soviet Government, our heroic army, its talented leaders and brave soldiers, the whole Soviet nation — these are the ones who assured the victory in the great patriotic war. [Tempestuous and prolonged applause.] . . .

[INJUSTICES DONE TO NATIONAL GROUPS WITHIN THE SOVIET UNION]

The Soviet Union is justly considered as a model of a multinational state because we have in practice assured the equality and friendship of all nations which live in our great fatherland.

All the more monstrous are the acts whose initiator was Stalin and which are rude violations of the basic Leninist principles of the nationality policy of the Soviet state. We refer to the mass deportations from their native places of whole nations . . . ; this deportation action was not dictated by any military considerations.

Thus, already at the end of 1943, when there occurred a permanent breakthrough at the fronts of the Great Patriotic War benefiting the Soviet Union, a decision was taken and executed concerning the deportation of all the Karachai from the lands on which they lived.[2] In the same period, at the end of December 1943, the same lot befell the whole population of the Autonomous Kalmyk Republic. In March 1944 all the Chechen and Ingush peoples were deported and the Chechen-Ingush Autonomous Republic was liquidated. In April 1944, all Balkars were deported to faraway places from the territory of the Kabardyno-Balkar Autonomous Republic and the Republic itself was renamed the Autonomous Kabardnian Republic. The Ukrainians avoided meeting this fate only because there were too many of them and there was no place to which to deport them. Otherwise, he would have deported them also. [Laughter and animation in the hall.] . . .

[STALIN'S POSTWAR PARANOIA]

[A]fter the war the situation became even more complicated. Stalin became even more capricious, irritable, and brutal; in particular his suspicion grew. His persecution mania reached unbelievable dimensions. Many workers were becoming enemies before his very eyes. After the war Stalin separated himself from the collective [leadership] even more. Everything was decided by him alone without any consideration for anyone or anything.

This unbelievable suspicion was cleverly taken advantage of by the abject provocateur and vile enemy, Beriya. . . .

Let us . . . recall the affair of the doctor plotters. [Animation in the hall.] Actually there was no affair outside of the declaration of the woman doctor Timashuk, who was probably influenced or ordered by someone (after all, she was an unofficial collaborator of the organs of state security) to write Stalin a letter in which she declared that doctors were applying supposedly improper methods of medical treatment.

Such a letter was sufficient for Stalin to reach an immediate conclusion that there are doctor plotters in the Soviet Union. He issued orders to arrest a group of eminent Soviet medical specialists. He personally issued advice on the conduct of the investigation and the method of interrogation of the arrested persons. He said that the academician Vinogradov should be put in chains, another one should be beaten. Present at this Congress as a delegate is the former Minister of State Security Comrade Ignatiev. Stalin told him curtly,

---

[2]The Karachai as well as the various people and territories referred to later in this paragraph are located in the Caucasus region of southern Soviet Union. Russia brought this area with its rich array of peoples under formal control during the nineteenth century.

"If you do not obtain confessions from the doctors we will shorten you by a head." [Tumult in the hall.]

Stalin personally called the investigative judge, gave him instructions, advised him on which investigative methods should be used; these methods were simple — beat, beat and, once again, beat.

Shortly after the doctors were arrested we members of the Political Bureau received protocols with the doctors['] confessions of guilt. After distributing these protocols Stalin told us, "You are blind like young kittens; what will happen without me? The country will perish because you do not know how to recognize enemies."

The case was so presented that no one could verify the facts on which the investigation was based. There was no possibility of trying to verify facts by contacting those who had made the confessions of guilt.

We felt, however, that the case of the arrested doctors was questionable. We knew some of these people personally because they had once treated us. When we examined this case after Stalin's death, we found it to be fabricated from beginning to end.

This ignominious case was set up by Stalin; he did not, however, have the time in which to bring it to an end (as he conceived that end), and for this reason the doctors are still alive. . . .

[BERIA'S COMPLICITY IN STALIN'S CRIMES]

The indictment in the Beriya case contains a discussion of his crimes. . . . I wish to recall Beriya's bestial disposition of the cases of Kedrov, Golubiev, and Golubiev's adopted mother, Baturina — persons who wished to inform the Central Committee concerning Beryia's treacherous activity. They were shot without any trial and the sentence was passed ex post facto, after the execution.

Here is what the old Communist, Comrade Kedrov, wrote to the Central Committee through Comrade Andreyev (Comrade Andreyev was then a Central Committee secretary):

"I am calling to you for help from a gloomy cell of the Lefortorsky prison. Let my cry of horror reach your ears; do not remain deaf; take me under your protection; please, help remove the nightmare of interrogations and show that this is all a mistake.

"I suffer innocently. Please believe me. Time will testify to the truth. I am not an agent-provocateur of the Tsarish Okhrana [secret police]; I am not a spy; I am not a member of an anti-Soviet organization of which I am being accused on the basis of denunciations. I am also not guilty of any other crimes against the party and the Government. I am an old Bolshevik, free of any stain; I have honestly fought for almost 40 years in the ranks of the party for the good and the prosperity of the nation. . . .

"Today I a 62-year-old man, am being threatened by the investigative judges with more severe, cruel, and degrading methods of physical pressure. They [the judges] are no longer capable of becoming aware of their error and of recognizing that their handling of my case is illegal and impermissible. They try to justify their actions by picturing me as a hardened and raving enemy and are demanding increased repressions. But let the party know that I am innocent and that there is nothing which can turn a loyal son of the party into an enemy, even right up to his last dying breath.

"But I have no way out. I cannot divert from myself the hastily approaching new and powerful blows.

"Everything, however, has its limits. My torture has reached the extreme. My health is broken, my strength and my energy are waning, the end is drawing near. To die in a Soviet prison, branded as a vile traitor to the fatherland — what can be more monstrous for an honest man. And how monstrous all this is. Unsurpassed bitterness and pain grips my heart. No. No. This will not happen; this cannot be, I cry. Neither the party, nor the Soviet government, nor the people's commissar, L. P. Beriya, will permit this cruel irreparable injustice. I am firmly certain that given a quiet, objective examination, without any foul rantings, without any anger and without the fearful tortures, it would be easy to prove the baselessness of the charges. I believe deeply that truth and justice will triumph. I believe. I believe."

The old Bolshevik, Comrade Kedrov, was found innocent by the military collegium. But despite this, he was shot at Beriya's order. [Indignation in the hall.] . . .

Beriya was unmasked by the party's central committee shortly after Stalin's death. As a result of the particularly detailed legal proceedings it was established that Beriya had committed monstrous crimes and Beriya was shot.

The question arises why Beriya, who had liquidated tens of thousands of party and Soviet workers, was not unmasked during Stalin's life. He was not unmasked earlier because he had utilized very skillfully Stalin's weaknesses; feeding him with suspicions, he assisted Stalin in everything and acted with his support. . . .

[The Harm Done the Soviet System by Repression]

[D]ue to the numerous arrests of party, Soviet and economic leaders, many workers began to work uncertainly, showed overcautiousness, feared all which was new, feared their own shadows and began to show less initiative in their work.

Take, for instance, party and Soviet resolutions. They were prepared in a routine manner often without considering the concrete situation. . . .

Stalin's reluctance to consider life's realities and the fact that he was not aware of the real state of affairs in the provinces can be illustrated by his direction of agriculture.

All those who interested themselves even a little in the national situation saw the difficult situation in agriculture, but Stalin never even noted it. Did we tell Stalin about this? Yes, we told him, but he did not support us. Why? Because Stalin never traveled anywhere, did not meet city and Kolkhoz [collective farm] workers; he did not know the actual situation in the provinces.

He knew the country and agriculture only from films. And these films had dressed up and beautified the existing situation in agriculture.

Many films so pictured Kolkhoz life that the tables were bending from the weight of turkeys and geese. Evidently Stalin thought that it was actually so. . . .

If we are to consider this matter [as] Marxists and as Leninists, then we have to state unequivocally that the leadership practice which came into being during the last years of Stalin's life became a serious obstacle in the path of Soviet social development.

Stalin often failed for months to take up some unusually important problems concerning the life of the party and of the state whose solution could not be postponed. . . .

Some comrades may ask us: Where were the members of the Political Bureau of the Central Committee? Why did they not assert themselves against the cult of the individual in time? And why is this being done only now? . . .

. . . Initially, many of them backed Stalin actively because Stalin was one of the strongest Marxists and his logic, his strength, and his will greatly influenced the cadres and party work.

. . . Later, however, abusing his power more and more, [Stalin] began to fight eminent party and government leaders and to use terroristic methods against honest Soviet people. . . .

In the situation which then prevailed I have talked often with Nikolai Aleksandrovich Bulganin [a Khrushchev colleague in the Political Bureau]; once when we two were traveling in a car, he said, "It has happened sometimes that a man goes to Stalin on his invitation as a friend. And when he sits with Stalin he does not know where he will be sent next — home or to jail."

It is clear that such conditions put every member of the Political Bureau in a very difficult situation. . . .

[ASSESSING STALIN'S LEGACY]

Comrades, in order not to repeat errors of the past, the central committee has declared itself resolutely against the cult of the individual. We consider that Stalin was excessively extolled. However, in the past Stalin doubtlessly performed great services to the party, to the working class, and to the international workers' movement.

This question is complicated by the fact that all this which we have just discussed was done during Stalin's life under his leadership and with his concurrence; here Stalin was convinced that this was necessary for the defense of the interests of the working classes against the plotting of the enemies and against the attack of the imperialist camp. He saw this from the position of the interest of the working class, of the interest of the laboring people, of the interest of the victory of socialism and communism[.] We cannot say that these were the deeds of a giddy despot. He considered that this should be done in the interest of the party; of the working masses, in the name of the defense of the revolution's gains. In this lies the whole tragedy.

4.3
Milovan Djilas Indicts the Stalinist System

Milovan Djilas was a prominent member of the Yugoslav Communist Party after World War II. His criticism of the privileges of party members and his call for political pluralism reflected the widespread ferment among East-bloc intellectuals following Stalin's death. But so stinging were his criticisms of socialist regimes that they got him expelled from the party in 1954. He responded in 1956 with a book, *The New Class*. There he charged that Communist parties had not created class-less societies but rather that their leaders had become a new elite controlling the means of production and benefiting personally from that control. This affront got him a term in jail.

What themes does Djilas develop in his critique? How does Djilas's analysis reflect his Marxist background and outlook? Is he repudiating socialism? Djilas is best read alongside Khrushchev's Twentieth Party Congress speech, delivered the same year that *The New Class* was published. In what way does Djilas go beyond the indictment handed down in the Khrushchev speech? What does Djilas see as the prospects for reform of the regimes controlled by Communist parties?

From *The New Class*
1956

Everything happened differently in the U.S.S.R. and other communist countries from what the leaders — even such prominent ones as Lenin, Stalin, Trotsky, and Bukharin — anticipated. They expected that the state would rapidly wither away, that democracy would be strengthened. The reverse happened. They expected a rapid improvement in the standard of living — there has been scarcely any change in this respect, and in the subjugated East European countries, the standard has even declined. In every instance, the standard of living has failed to rise in proportion to the rate of industrialization, which was much more rapid. It was believed that the differences between cities and villages, between intellectual and physical labor, would slowly disappear; instead these differences have increased. . . .

The greatest illusion was that industrialization and collectivization in the U.S.S.R., and destruction of capitalist ownership, would result in a classless society. In 1936, when the new [Soviet] constitution was promulgated, Stalin announced that the "exploiting class" had ceased to exist. The capitalist and other classes of ancient origin had in fact been destroyed, but a new class, previously unknown to history, had been formed. . . .

. . . The new class may be said to be made up of those who have special privileges and economic preference because of the administrative monopoly they hold. . . .

Milovan Djilas, *The New Class* (New York: Praeger, 1957), 37–39, 44–47, 59, 65, 68–69.

If we assume that membership in this bureaucracy or new owning class is predicated on the use of privileges inherent in ownership — in this instance nationalized material goods — then membership in the new party class, or political bureaucracy, is reflected in a larger income in material goods and privileges than society should normally grant for such functions. . . .

. . . The new class obtains its power, privileges, ideology, and its customs from one specific form of ownership — collective ownership — which the class administers and distributes in the name of the nation and society. . . .

To divest communists of their ownership rights would be to abolish them as a class. To compel them to relinquish their other social powers, so that workers may participate in sharing the profits of their work — which capitalists have had to permit as a result of strikes and parliamentary action — would mean that communists were being deprived of their monopoly over property, ideology, and government. This would be the beginning of democracy and freedom in communism, the end of communist monopolism and totalitarianism. Until this happens, there can be no indication that important, fundamental changes are taking place in communist systems, at least not in the eyes of men who think seriously about social progress.

. . . Discrepancies between the pay of workers and party functionaries are extreme; this could not be hidden from persons visiting the U.S.S.R. or other communist countries in the past few years. . . .

. . . The emergence of the new class has been concealed under socialist phraseology and, more important, under the new collective forms of property ownership. The so-called socialist ownership is a disguise for the real ownership by the political bureaucracy. . . .

. . . No other class in history has been as cohesive and singleminded in defending itself and in controlling that which it holds — collective and monopolistic ownership and totalitarian authority.

On the other hand, the new class is also the most deluded and least conscious of itself. Every private capitalist or feudal lord was conscious of the fact that he belonged to a special discernible social category. He usually believed that this category was destined to make the human race happy and that without this category chaos and general ruin would ensue. A communist member of the new class also believes that without his party, society would regress and founder. But he is not conscious of the fact that he belongs to a new ownership class, for he does not consider himself an owner and does not take into account the special privileges he enjoys. He thinks that he belongs to a group with prescribed ideas, aims, attitudes, and roles. That is all he sees. He cannot see that at the same time he belongs to a special social category: the *ownership* class. . . .

The new class instinctively feels that national goods are, in fact, its property, and that even the terms "socialist," "social," and "state" property denote a general legal fiction. The new class also thinks that any breach of its totalitarian authority might imperil its ownership. Consequently, the new class opposes *any* type of freedom, ostensibly for the purpose of preserving "socialist" ownership. Criticism of the new class's monopolistic administration of property generates the fear of a possible loss of power. . . .

In defending its authority, the ruling class must execute reforms every time it becomes obvious to the people that the class is treating national property as its own. Such reforms are not proclaimed as being what they really are but, rather, as part of the "further development of socialism" and "socialist democracy." The groundwork for reforms is laid when the discrepancy mentioned above becomes public. From the historical point of view the new class is forced to fortify its authority and ownership constantly, even though it is running away from the truth. It must constantly demonstrate how it is successfully creating a society of happy people, all of whom enjoy equal rights and have been freed of every type of exploitation. The new class cannot avoid falling continuously into profound internal contradictions; for in spite of its historical origin it is not able to make its ownership lawful, and it cannot renounce ownership without undermining itself. Consequently, it is forced to try to justify its increasing authority, invoking abstract and unreal purposes.

This is a class whose power over men is the most complete known to history. For this reason it is a class with very limited views, views which are false and unsafe. Closely ingrown, and in complete authority, the new class must unrealistically evaluate its own role and that of the people around it. . . .

When the new class leaves the historical scene — and this must happen — there will be less sorrow over its passing than there was for any other class before it. Smothering everything except what suited its ego, it has condemned itself to failure and shameful ruin.

SPREADING NUCLEAR FEAR

By the 1950s both Moscow and Washington were rushing to expand their nuclear arsenals. Between 1950 and 1956 the United States had increased its warheads from nearly four hundred to well over four thousand; the Soviet Union had stockpiled slightly more than four hundred warheads; and Britain had broken into the nuclear club, to be followed in 1964 by France and China. At the same time bombs were getting more powerful, and delivery systems were becoming more elaborate and accurate — first, longer range bombers, then missiles, and finally missile-carrying submarines.

Even before the first nuclear test, some American and Soviet scientists had an inkling of the dangers ahead. Early tests confirmed their fears. As the arsenals of destruction grew at a frightening pace, as fallout from nuclear tests threatened human health, and as preparation for nuclear war became part of daily life and cultural imagination, the sense of alarm spread to policymakers, intellectuals, and even the broader public.

4.4

The U.S. Perspective

Even under the Truman administration there was a growing awareness among policymakers that nuclear war posed profound moral issues and practical problems, especially after the USSR broke into the nuclear club in 1949. However, publicly U.S. leaders maintained a brave front well into the 1950s. The gap between the public stance and the private is strikingly evident in the two documents to follow. The 1955 civil defense pamphlet was part of a publicity campaign to reassure the public. The entry from the Eisenhower diary a year later directly and clinically confronts the grim implications of relying on nuclear weapons in waging the Cold War.

What strategies does the pamphlet use to minimize fear about nuclear war? On what points does the pamphlet collide with the information available to President Eisenhower?

U.S. Civil Defense Pamphlet, "Facts about Fallout"
1955

Fallout is nothing more than particles of matter in the air, made radioactive by nuclear or thermonuclear explosions. When an atomic or hydrogen bomb is exploded close to the ground, thousands of tons of atomized earth, building materials, rocks, and gases are sucked upward, sometimes to a height of 80,000 feet or more. They help form the mushroom cloud which is always seen with one of these explosions.

Some of these radioactive particles spill out in the immediate area of the explosion soon after it occurs, but others may be carried by the upper winds for many miles. Sooner or later, however, they settle to earth. This is called fallout.

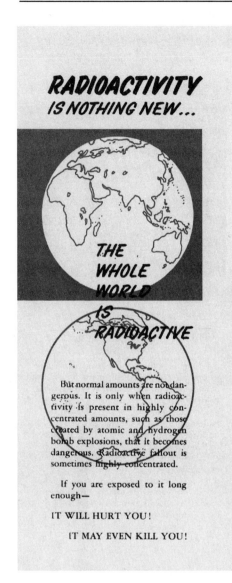

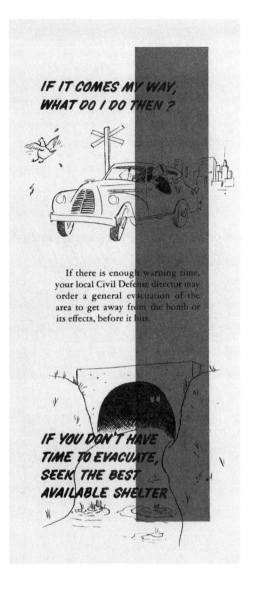

RADIOACTIVITY IS NOTHING NEW...

THE WHOLE WORLD IS RADIOACTIVE

But normal amounts are not dangerous. It is only when radioactivity is present in highly concentrated amounts, such as those created by atomic and hydrogen bomb explosions, that it becomes dangerous. Radioactive fallout is sometimes highly concentrated.

If you are exposed to it long enough—

IT WILL HURT YOU!

IT MAY EVEN KILL YOU!

IF IT COMES MY WAY, WHAT DO I DO THEN?

If there is enough warning time, your local Civil Defense director may order a general evacuation of the area to get away from the bomb or its effects, before it hits.

IF YOU DON'T HAVE TIME TO EVACUATE, SEEK THE BEST AVAILABLE SHELTER

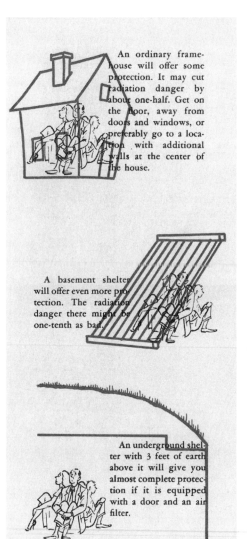

An ordinary frame-house will offer some protection. It may cut radiation danger by about one-half. Get on the floor, away from doors and windows, or preferably go to a location with additional walls at the center of the house.

A basement shelter will offer even more protection. The radiation danger there might be one-tenth as bad.

An underground shelter with 3 feet of earth above it will give you almost complete protection if it is equipped with a door and an air filter.

An old-fashioned storm cave or root cellar is ideal. Stock it with food staples as Grandmother did. Add water supplies, first-aid kits, blankets, a lantern, fuel . . .

EVERYTHING YOU NEED TO LIVE IN IT FOR A FEW DAYS

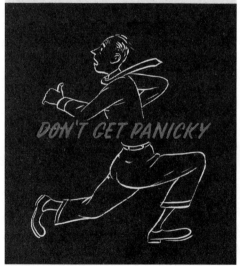

FOLLOW
THESE
SIMPLE
RULES

Prepare a shelter area in your home or backyard, whether you live in a city or in the country.

Stock your shelter with a 7-day supply of emergency food and water.

Get a radio, preferably battery-operated, and keep it in a safe place. Mark the Conelrad frequencies. Civil Defense news and instructions will be provided at these frequencies.

If you think you have been in a serious fallout area, remove your outer clothing and wash the exposed parts of your body thoroughly. Unless you have been subjected to serious contamination, it may not be necessary to destroy or discard the clothing, since it can be made safe by laundering or by simply waiting for the radioactivity to decay.

Dwight D. Eisenhower
Diary Entry
January 23, 1956

General George (retired from the air force), assisted by a staff group, made a presentation on net evaluation of the damage that would be anticipated in the initial stages of nuclear war between Russia and the United States [in mid-1956]. . . .

Under the first case [virtually no warning of Soviet attack], the United States experienced practically total economic collapse, which could not be restored to any kind of operative conditions under six months to a year. Members of the federal government were wiped out and a new government had to be improvised by the states. Casualties were enormous. It was calculated that something on the order of 65 percent of the population would require some kind of medical care and, in most instances, no opportunity whatsoever to get it.

The limiting factor on the damage inflicted was not so much our own defensive arrangements as the limitations on the Soviet stockpile of atomic weapons. . . .

While these things were going on, the damage inflicted by us against the Soviets was roughly three times greater. The picture of total destruction of the areas of lethal fallout, of serious fallout, and of at least some damage from fallout, was appalling. Under such an attack, it would be completely impossible for Russia to carry a war on further. . . .

Under the second case [one month advance warning], it was concluded that the major effort of the Soviets would be made against our airbases rather than against the United States alone. Nevertheless, there was no significant difference in the losses we would take.

It was concluded that there was little we could do during the month of warning in the way of dispersal of populations, of industries, or of perfecting defenses that would cut down losses. The only possible way of reducing these losses would be for us to take the initiative sometime during the assumed month in which we had the warning of an attack and launch a surprise attack against the Soviets. This would be not only against our traditions, but it would appear to be impossible unless the Congress would meet in a highly secret session and vote a declaration of war which would be implemented before the session was terminated. It would appear to be impossible that any such thing would occur.

Robert H. Ferrell, ed., *The Eisenhower Diaries* (New York: W. W. Norton, 1981), 311–12.

4.5

The Soviet Perspective

The Soviet Union lagged behind the United States in getting the bomb and in grasping the dangerous implications of nuclear warfare. But by the mid-1950s the Soviets had caught up thanks to Igor Kurchatov, the father of the Soviet atomic bomb project. His team successfully tested the first Soviet bomb in 1949, breaking the U.S. monopoly, and then moved quickly to match the United States in the creation of far more powerful hydrogen bombs. He was also the sober voice of caution. Already in the early 1950s, Kurchatov began raising with Soviet leaders the horrible implications of nuclear war. In late March 1954 he and three colleagues submitted a draft article to the leaders in the Kremlin. Khrushchev was not persuaded. But after consolidating his control, Khrushchev changed his stance as became evident in 1956 at the historic Twentieth Party Congress. There he delivered alongside his attack on Stalin a speech advocating "peaceful coexistence." While an understanding of the destructiveness of nuclear war in part prompted the speech, Khrushchev also wanted to appeal to peace advocates in western Europe, Japan, and the third world and to advance the cause of arms control, which he badly needed in order to shift limited Soviet economic resources to domestic priorities, especially the demands of Soviet consumers.

The logic in the Kurchatov and Khrushchev pieces are worth following with care. What kind of case are they each making? How in their views do nuclear weapons change the nature of war? How closely does Kurchatov's draft article correspond to the report received by Eisenhower (just above)? How much does Khrushchev borrow from Kurchatov and how much does he put his own spin on the nuclear problem?

Igor V. Kurchatov et al.
Draft Article for Soviet Leaders
1954

Today the H-bomb's destructive power can be compared to the most destructive natural forces such as large-scale earthquakes, volcanic eruptions, large meteorites falling on earth. . . .

While a normal atomic bomb releases energy equivalent to tens of thousands of tons of TNT an H-bomb produces many million of tons of energy. One bomb can destroy all residential buildings and structures within a radius of 10 to 15 km, i.e., to eliminate all above-ground constructions in a city with a population of many millions. The power of one or two modern hydrogen bombs translated into an equivalent quantity of TNT is comparable to the total amount of explosives used by the fighting sides in the last world war.

Contemporary military hardware allows the side possessing nuclear weapons to reach targets several thousand of kilometers from the frontier. Obvi-

From the "Race for the Superbomb," in the PBS "American Experience" series, available at <http://www.pbs.org/wgbh/amex/bomb/filmmore/reference/primary/igoratomic.html> (January 11, 2003).

ously, defense against such weapons is practically impossible — it is clear that the use of atomic weapons on a mass scale will lead to devastation in the warring countries. Aside from the destructive impact of atomic and hydrogen bombs there is another threat for mankind involved in atomic war — poisoning the atmosphere and the surface of the globe with radioactive substances originating from nuclear explosions. In the form of minuscule particles and gases, these are lifted by the force of the blast together with dust particles to comparatively high altitudes. Wind spreads them all over the earth's atmosphere. Later these radioactive substances fall onto the surface of the earth with rain, snow, and dust, thus poisoning it.

. . . Today, after only several scores of atomic and hydrogen bomb tests, radioactivity in the upper layers of the earth has grown considerably. Bodies of water are also being contaminated.

. . . The rate of growth of atomic explosives is such that in just a few years the stockpile will be large enough to create conditions under which the existence of life on the whole globe will be impossible. The explosion of around one hundred hydrogen bombs could lead to this result.

Nikita S. Khrushchev
Report to the Twentieth Party Congress
on Peaceful Coexistence
February 14, 1956

Soon after the Second World War ended, the influence of reactionary and militarist groups began to be increasingly evident in the policy of the United States of America, Britain and France. Their desire to enforce their will on other countries by economic and political pressure, threats and military provocation became dominant. This became known as the "positions of strength" policy. . . .

The international atmosphere was poisoned by war hysteria. The arms race began to assume more and more monstrous dimensions. Many big U.S. military bases aimed against the U.S.S.R. and the People's Democracies were built in countries thousands of miles from the borders of the United States. "Cold war" was begun against the socialist camp. . . .

Can peace be promoted by an arms race? It would seem that it is simply absurd to pose such a question. Yet the adherents of the "positions of strength" policy offer the arms race as their main recipe for the preservation of peace! It is perfectly obvious that when nations compete to increase their military might, the danger of war becomes greater, not lesser. . . .

We will continue to work to end the arms drive and ban atomic and hydrogen weapons. Prior to agreement on important aspects of disarmament we are willing to take certain partial steps, for example, to discontinue ther-

Nikita S. Khrushchev, *Report of the Central Committee of the Communist Party of the Soviet Union to the 20th Party Congress* (Moscow: Foreign Languages Publishing House, 1956), 21–22, 34–35, 39–40.

monuclear [hydrogen] weapon tests, to see that the troops stationed in Germany should have no atomic weapons, and to cut military budgets. Implementation of such measures by the nations could pave the way to understanding on other, more intricate aspects of disarmament. . . .

We want to be friends with the United States and to co-operate with it for peace and international security and also in the economic and cultural spheres. We propose this with good intentions, without holding a knife behind our back. . . .

If good relations between the Soviet Union and the United States are not established and mutual distrust continues, it will lead to an arms race on a still bigger scale and to a still more dangerous build-up of strength on both sides. Is this what the peoples of the Soviet Union and the United States want? Of course not. . . .

To this day the enemies of peace allege that the Soviet Union is out to overthrow capitalism in other countries by "exporting" revolution. It goes without saying that among us Communists there are no supporters of capitalism. But this does not mean that we have interfered or plan to interfere in the internal affairs of countries where capitalism still exists. . . . It is ridiculous to think that revolutions are made to order. . . .

When we say that the socialist system will win in the competition between the two systems — the capitalist and the socialist — this by no means signifies that its victory will be achieved through armed interference by the socialist countries in the internal affairs of the capitalist countries. Our certainty of the victory of communism is based on the fact that the socialist mode of production possesses decisive advantages over the capitalist mode of production. . . . We have always held and continue to hold that the establishment of a new social system in one or another country is the internal affair of the peoples of the countries concerned. . . .

The principle of peaceful co-existence is gaining ever wider international recognition. . . . Indeed there are only two ways: either peaceful co-existence or the most destructive war in history. There is no third way.

4.6

The Western European Perspective

A nuclear war that would incinerate most of Europe understandably concerned many in the region, especially the Germans on the frontline and the British as hosts to U.S. bases for nuclear bombers. Western Europeans were wary Cold War partners to the United States and notably restive when Moscow or Washington seemed passive or indifferent in the face of the nuclear danger, or indeed expanded their arsenals heedless of the possible consequences. The late 1950s was one of those moments.

The first document, a manifesto, had the backing of eighteen German physicists, including four winners of the Nobel Prize. The second is by J. B. Priestley, a World War I veteran, a prolific author, and an outspoken member of the Labour Party. This article drew broad support and led to the creation of the Campaign for Nuclear Disarmament, the major vehicle for anti-nuclear activists then and again in the early 1980s. To what extent do the views here echo points made from the American and Soviet perspectives, and to what extent do they reflect peculiarly European concerns? What action do the authors of these items propose? Do they share the superpowers' conception of the Cold War?

The Göttingen Manifesto on the Nuclear Threat
April 13, 1957

Today a tactical atomic bomb can destroy a small city; a hydrogen bomb can make uninhabitable a region the size of the industrial district of the Ruhr. The whole population of the German Federal Republic [West Germany] could be exterminated today by means of the spreading radioactivity of hydrogen bombs. We do not know any practical possibility to protect large populations from this danger.

. . . We support wholeheartedly the idea of freedom as represented today by the Western world against the ideas of communism. We do not deny that the mutual fear of the hydrogen bombs represents today an essential contribution to the maintenance of peace in the whole world and of freedom in a part of the world. However, we consider, in the long run, this way to maintain peace and freedom as completely unreliable and the danger in the case of its failure as deadly.

We do not feel competent to make concrete propositions for the policies of the great powers. We think that today a small country such as the Federal Republic can protect itself best and promote world peace by renouncing explicitly and voluntarily the possession of atomic weapons of any kind. Be that as it may, none of the undersigned would be ready in any way to take part in the production, the tests, or the application of atomic weapons.

Bulletin of the Atomic Scientists 13 (June 1957): 228.

J. B. Priestley
"Britain and the Nuclear Bombs"
November 2, 1957

One "ultimate weapon," the final deterrent, succeeds another. After the bombs, the intercontinental rockets; and after the rockets, according to the First Lord of the Admiralty, the guided-missile submarine . . . . And we have arrived at an insane regress of ultimate weapons that are not ultimate.

But all this is to the good; and we cannot have too much of it, we are told, because no men in their right minds would let loose such powers of destruc-

J. B. Priestley, "Britain and the Nuclear Bombs," *New Statesman* (November 2, 1957), 254, 555–56.

tion. Here is the realistic view. Any criticism of it is presumed to be based on wild idealism. But surely it is the wildest idealism, at the furthest remove from a sober realism, to assume that men will always behave reasonably and in line with their best interests? Yet this is precisely what we are asked to believe, and to stake our all on it.

For that matter, why should it be assumed that the men who create and control such monstrous devices *are* in their right minds? They live in an unhealthy mental climate, an atmosphere dangerous to sanity. They are responsible to no large body of ordinary sensible men and women, who pay for these weapons without ever having ordered them, who have never been asked anywhere yet if they wanted them. When and where have these preparations for nuclear warfare ever been put to the test of public opinion? . . .

The more elaborately involved and hair-triggered the machinery of destruction, the more likely it is that this machinery will be set in motion, if only by accident. Three glasses too many of vodka or bourbon-on-the-rocks, and the wrong button may be pushed. Combine this stock-piling of nuclear weapons with a crazy competitiveness, boastful confidence in public and a mounting fear in private, and what was unthinkable a few years ago now at the best only seems unlikely and very soon may seem inevitable. Then western impatience cries "Let's get the damned thing over!" and eastern fatalism mutters "If this has to be, then we must accept it.". . .

. . . But what will happen . . . will not be anything recognisable as a war, an affair of victories and defeats, something that one side can win or that you can call off when you have had enough. It will be universal catastrophe and apocalypse, the crack of doom into which Communism, western democracy, their way of life and our way of life, may disappear for ever. . . .

Britain runs the greatest risk by just mumbling and muddling along, never speaking out, avoiding any decisive creative act. . . . The catastrophic antics of our time have behind them men hag-ridden by fear, which explains the neurotic irrationality of it all, the crazy disproportion between means and ends. If we openly challenge this fear, then we might break the wicked spell that all but a few uncertified lunatics desperately wish to see broken, we could begin to restore the world to sanity and lift this nation from its recent ignominy to its former grandeur. Alone, we defied Hitler; and alone we can defy this nuclear madness into which the spirit of Hitler seems to have passed, to poison the world. There may be other chain-reactions besides those leading to destruction; and we might start one[:] . . . a declaration to the world that after a certain date one power [Britain] able to engage in nuclear warfare will reject the evil thing for ever.

LYNDON JOHNSON GOES TO WAR IN VIETNAM, 1965

While the Cold War was subsiding, extensive Cold War commitments and pervasive Cold War attitudes still guided Washington and Moscow and sustained the environment of suspicion and worst-case thinking. No better example of the difficulties of moving beyond the Cold War can be found than in the rising U.S. involvement in Vietnam. There were many good reasons to stop that involvement short of war, yet the Johnson administration pressed on.

Lyndon Johnson sharply increased U.S. forces in South Vietnam in mid-1965 in response to the alarming success by the Communist-supported National Liberation Front. Its forces were extending control across the countryside, while the U.S.-backed government in Saigon was demoralized and wracked by internal divisions. In making his decision Johnson leaned heavily on advisers inherited from the Kennedy administration who were well versed in the details of Vietnam policy. He also had to consider how a war in Vietnam would fit with his own Great Society programs intended to advance social justice at home. How reluctantly the president made his decision and how much it was influenced by his advisers, by his awareness of earlier U.S. commitments to Vietnam, and by the grip of well-worn and widely accepted Cold War thinking are issues that historians continue to debate.

4.7
President Johnson Justifies the U.S. Commitment to South Vietnam

Johnson carried to Johns Hopkins University in early April 1965 a carefully crafted speech in which he had been personally involved. By then he had already made some critical decisions on Vietnam. In August 1964, he had struck back with U.S. airpower after North Vietnamese ships had seemingly attacked U.S. navy vessels in the Tonkin Gulf, and he had secured from Congress authorization to use U.S. military power in the region. The following March (just before this speech) he had begun sustained bombing of North Vietnam and dispatched U.S. marines to safeguard an airbase at Da Nang from which U.S. aircraft operated. But these were small incremental decisions, not a major commitment of U.S. forces.

Does the speech give hints of what specific policies or general concerns would guide Johnson in future Vietnam decisions? How did he justify the U.S. stake in Vietnam? How did his interest in popular welfare, so prominent a part of his domestic agenda, intrude into this speech and perhaps influence his view of the U.S. options in Vietnam? Did Johnson believe what he was saying in this speech? If so, why did he not make a quick decision on increasing the U.S. troop commitment in Vietnam? If not, what purpose did the speech serve? Imagine the response of the audience of bright (and draft-eligible) undergraduates at Johns Hopkins University listening to their president.

Speech at Johns Hopkins University
April 7, 1965

Why must this Nation hazard its ease, and its interest, and its power for the sake of a people so far away?

We fight because we must fight if we are to live in a world where every country can shape its own destiny. And only in such a world will our own freedom be finally secure. . . .

The world as it is in Asia is not a serene or peaceful place.

The first reality is that North Viet-Nam has attacked the independent nation of South Viet-Nam. Its object is total conquest.

Of course, some of the people of South Viet-Nam are participating in attack[s] on their own government. But trained men and supplies, orders and arms, flow in a constant stream from north to south.

This support is the heartbeat of the war.

And it is a war of unparalleled brutality. Simple farmers are the targets of assassination and kidnapping. Women and children are strangled in the night because their men are loyal to their government. And helpless villages are ravaged by sneak attacks. Large-scale raids are conducted on towns, and terror strikes in the heart of cities. . . .

Over this war — and all Asia — is another reality: the deepening shadow of Communist China. The rulers in Hanoi are urged on by Peking. This is a regime which has destroyed freedom in Tibet, which has attacked India, and has been condemned by the United Nations for aggression in Korea. It is a nation which is helping the forces of violence in almost every continent. The contest in Viet-Nam is part of a wider pattern of aggressive purposes.

Why are these realities our concern? Why are we in South Viet-Nam?

We are there because we have a promise to keep. Since 1954 every American President has offered support to the people of South Viet-Nam. . . .

We are also there to strengthen world order. Around the globe, from Berlin to Thailand, are people whose well-being rests, in part, on the belief that they can count on us if they are attacked. To leave Viet-Nam to its fate would shake the confidence of all these people in the value of an American commitment and in the value of America's word. The result would be increased unrest and instability, and even wider war.

We are also there because there are great stakes in the balance. Let no one think for a moment that retreat from Viet-Nam would bring an end to conflict. The battle would be renewed in one country and then another. The central lesson of our time is that the appetite of aggression is never satisfied. To withdraw from one battlefield means only to prepare for the next. . . .

In recent months attacks on South Viet-Nam were stepped up. Thus, it became necessary for us to increase our response and to make attacks by air. This is not a change of purpose. It is a change in what we believe that purpose requires.

We do this in order to slow down aggression.

We do this to increase the confidence of the brave people of South Viet-Nam who have bravely borne this brutal battle for many years with so many casualties.

And we do this to convince the leaders of North Viet-Nam — and all who seek to share their conquest — of a very simple fact:

We will not be defeated.

Public Papers of the Presidents of the United States: Lyndon B. Johnson, 1965 (Washington, D.C.: U.S. Government Printing Office, 1966), 1:394–99.

We will not grow tired.

We will not withdraw, either openly or under the cloak of a meaningless agreement. . . .

. . . We have no desire to see thousands die in battle — Asians or Americans. We have no desire to devastate that which the people of North Viet-Nam have built with toil and sacrifice. We will use our power with restraint and with all the wisdom that we can command.

But we will use it. . . .

. . . [O]ur generation has a dream. It is a very old dream. But we have the power, and now we have the opportunity to make that dream come true.

For centuries nations have struggled among each other. But we dream of a world where disputes are settled by law and reason. And we will try to make it so.

For most of history men have hated and killed one another in battle. But we dream of an end to war. And we will try to make it so.

For all existence most men have lived in poverty, threatened by hunger. But we dream of a world where all are fed and charged with hope. And we will help to make it so. . . .

This generation of the world must choose: destroy or build, kill or aid, hate or understand.

We can do all these things on a scale never dreamed of before.

Well, we will choose life. In so doing we will prevail over the enemies within man, and over the natural enemies of all mankind.

4.8

The Debate within the Johnson Administration

Reports from the U.S. military commander in South Vietnam several weeks after the Hopkins speech forced on Washington a difficult decision: either introduce U.S. forces or risk defeat by the Hanoi-backed National Liberation Front (also known as the Viet Cong). Johnson did not rush into this decision. He relied on the experienced men that he had inherited from Kennedy: Secretary of State Dean Rusk, Secretary of Defense Robert McNamara, White House adviser McGeorge Bundy, and Undersecretary of State George Ball. Ball emerged as the chief skeptic, who drew on his knowledge of the difficulties the French had encountered in Vietnam. The strongest voice on the other side of the debate was McNamara's.

The documents that follow show the debate through two different media. Thanks to Johnson's system of secretly recording telephone conversations, we have the candid comments that the president made to McNamara. Ball's and McNamara's positions appear in formal memoranda written for the president but circulated among the inner-circle of senior military and civilian advisers that Johnson involved in the final decision. What insights does an informal telephone conversation yield that do not emerge from a formal memo? What does a memo provide that is missing in a conversation over the telephone?

In thinking about the substance of this debate, it would be helpful at the outset to identify the two or three concerns that dominate the cases for and against a massive American commitment of force. How to reconcile Johnson's private doubts expressed over the phone with the confidence and determination that mark his Hopkins speech? What were Johnson's and Ball's reservations about a greater commitment in Vietnam? How perceptive were they? And why did Johnson, despite a long list of reasons for caution, finally go ahead? Does the Hopkins speech suggest that he had already made up his mind and thus his "debate" was in fact a charade?

President Johnson
Telephone Remarks to Robert McNamara
June 21, 1965

I think that in time it's going to be like the Yale professor[1] said — that it's going to be difficult for us to very long prosecute effectively a war that far away from home with the divisions that we have here, particularly the potential divisions. And it's really had me concerned for a month, and I'm very depressed about it 'cause I see no program from either [Department of] Defense or State that gives me much hope of doing anything except just prayin' and gasping to hold on during the monsoon [season] and hope they'll quit. I don't believe they ever goin' to quit. I don't see how, that we have any way of either a plan for victory militarily or diplomatically. And I think that's something that you and Dean [Rusk, the Secretary of State] got to sit down and try to see if there's any people that we have in those departments that can give us any program or plan or hope; or, if not, we got to see if we have you go out there or somebody else go out there and take one good look at it and say to these new people, "Now, you've changed your government about the last time and this is it." Call the Buddhists and the Catholics and the generals and everybody together and say, "We're going to do our best." And be sure they're willing to let new troops come in and be sure they're not gonna resent us. "If not, why ya'll can run over us and have a government of your own choosing. But we just can't take these changes all [the] time." That's the Russell plan. Russell[2] thinks we ought to take one of these changes [in the government in Saigon] to get out of there. I don't think we can get out of there with our treaty like it is and with what all we've said. And I think it would just lose us face in the world, and I shudder to think what all of 'em would say.

Transcript from an audio tape, declassified in April 1995 by the Lyndon B. Johnson Library, Austin, Texas. Excerpts in Robert S. McNamara's memoirs, prepared with Brian VanDeMark, *In Retrospect: The Tragedy and Lessons of Vietnam* (New York: Times Books, 1995), 190–91.

[1] Staughton Lynd, a historian at Yale University.

[2] Richard Russell, Democratic senator from Georgia, influential conservative chair of the armed services committee, and former Johnson mentor in the Senate. He counseled Johnson against committing U.S. forces to a ground war in Vietnam.

George Ball
Memorandum on "A Compromise Solution in Vietnam"
July 1, 1965

The South Vietnamese are losing the war to the Viet Cong. No one can assure you that we can beat the Viet Cong or even force them to the conference table on our terms, no matter how many hundred thousand *white, foreign* (U.S.) troops we deploy.

No one has demonstrated that a white ground force of whatever size can win a guerrilla war — which is at the same time a civil war between Asians — in jungle terrain in the midst of a population that refuses cooperation to the white forces (and the South Vietnamese) and thus provides a great intelligence advantage to the other side. Three recent incidents vividly illustrate this point: (a) the sneak attack on the Da Nang Air Base which involved penetration of a defense perimeter guarded by 9,000 Marines. This raid was possible only because of the cooperation of the local inhabitants; (b) the B-52 raid that failed to hit the Viet Cong who had obviously been tipped off; (c) the search and destroy mission of the 173rd Air Borne Brigade which spent three days looking for the Viet Cong, suffered 23 casualties, and never made contact with the enemy who had obviously gotten advance word of their assignment. . . .

. . . So long as our forces are restricted to advising and assisting the South Vietnamese, the struggle will remain a civil war between Asian peoples. Once we deploy substantial numbers of troops in combat it will become a war between the U.S. and a large part of the population of South Vietnam, organized and directed from North Vietnam and backed by the resources of both Moscow and Peiping.

The decision you face now, therefore, is crucial. Once large numbers of U.S. troops are committed to direct combat, they will begin to take heavy casualties in a war they are ill-equipped to fight in a non-cooperative if not downright hostile countryside.

Once we suffer large casualties, we will have started a well-nigh irreversible process. Our involvement will be so great that we cannot — without national humiliation — stop short of achieving our complete objectives. *Of the two possibilities I think humiliation would be more likely than the achievement of our objectives — even after we have paid terrible costs.*

. . . Should we commit U.S. manpower and prestige to a terrain so unfavorable as to give a very large advantage to the enemy — or should we seek a compromise settlement which achieves less than our stated objectives and thus cut our losses while we still have the freedom of maneuver to do so?

The Senator Gravel Edition, *The Pentagon Papers: The Defense Department History of United States Decisionmaking on Vietnam* (Boston: Beacon Press, 1971–72), 4:615–16.

. . . In my judgment, if we can act before we commit a substantial U.S. truce [troop force] to combat in South Vietnam we can, by accepting some short-term costs, avoid what may well be a long-term catastrophe. . . .

Robert McNamara
Memorandum to President Johnson
July 20, 1965

The situation in South Vietnam is worse than a year ago (when it was worse than a year before that). After a few-months of stalemate, the tempo of the war has quickened. A hard VC [Viet Cong] push is now on to dismember the nation and to maul the army. The VC main and local forces, reinforced by militia and guerrillas, have the initiative and, with large attacks (some in regimental strength), are hurting ARVN [Army of the Republic of Vietnam] badly. . . . The central highlands could well be lost to the National Liberation Front during this monsoon season. Since June 1, the GVN [Government of Vietnam] has been forced to abandon six district capitals; only one has been retaken. US combat troop deployments and US/VNAF [Vietnamese Air Force] strikes against the North have put to rest most South Vietnamese fears that the United States will forsake them, and US/VNAF air strikes in-country have probably shaken VC morale somewhat. Yet the government is able to provide security to fewer and fewer people in less and less territory as terrorism increases. . . .

. . . Nor have our air attacks in North Vietnam produced tangible evidence of willingness on the part of Hanoi to come to the conference table in a reasonable mood. The DRV/VC [Democratic Republic of Vietnam/Viet Cong] seem to believe that South Vietnam is on the run and near collapse; they show no signs of settling for less than a complete take-over. . . .

. . . There are now 15 US (and 1 Australian) combat battalions in Vietnam; they, together with other combat personnel and non-combat personnel, bring the total US personnel in Vietnam to approximately 75,000.

I recommend that the deployment of US ground troops in Vietnam be increased by October to 34 maneuver battalions. . . . The battalions — together with increases in helicopter lift, air squadrons, naval units, air defense, combat support and miscellaneous log[istical] support and advisory personnel which I also recommend — would bring the total US personnel in Vietnam to approximately 175,000. . . . It should be understood that the deployment of more men (perhaps 100,000) may be necessary in early 1966, and that the deployment of additional forces thereafter is possible but will depend on developments. . . .

National Security Council History, Deployment of Major Forces to Vietnam, July 1945, box 43, National Security File, Lyndon B. Johnson Papers, Johnson Library. Senator Gravel Edition, *Pentagon Papers,* 4:619–22, contains a draft version of this memorandum.

...The DRV, on the other hand, may well send up to several divisions of regular forces in South Vietnam to assist the VC if they see the tide turning and victory, once so near, being snatched away. This possible DRV action is the most ominous one, since it would lead to increased pressures on us to "counter-invade" North Vietnam and to extend air strikes to population targets in the North; acceding to these pressures could bring the Soviets and the Chinese in. The Viet Cong, especially if they continue to take high losses, can be expected to depend increasingly upon the PAVN [People's Army of (North) Vietnam] forces as the war moves into a more conventional phase; but they may find ways to continue almost indefinitely their present intensive military, guerrilla and terror activities, particularly if reinforced by some regular PAVN units. . . .

4.9
Lyndon Johnson Makes His Decision Public

After several major meetings with his advisers and with leading members of Congress, Johnson made his decision public. But he kept his announcement low key: a press conference scheduled for noon when it would attract the least attention rather than a dramatic, live address during evening hours when television could have reached into every home around the country.

The language of this statement deserves as close attention as its form and timing. Why does Johnson invoke what "we learned from Hitler at Munich"? Why does he place emphasis on the war's likely impact on ordinary people? Why does he link the war effort to his Great Society programs? Finally, with this document, we can consider Johnson as a political leader (was he honest?) and the function of political rhetoric (merely obfuscation or the expression of his real concerns?). Does a comparison of this statement with the April speech delivered at Johns Hopkins suggest that Johnson's thinking had changed little in the interval?

Statement at White House Press Conference
July 28, 1965

We did not choose to be the guardians at the gate, but there is no one else.

Nor would surrender in Viet-Nam bring peace, because we learned from Hitler at Munich that success only feeds the appetite of aggression. The battle would be renewed in one country and then another country, bringing with it perhaps even larger and crueler conflict, as we have learned from the lessons of history.

Moreover, we are in Viet-Nam to fulfill one of the most solemn pledges of the American Nation. Three Presidents — President Eisenhower, President Kennedy, and your present President — over 11 years have committed themselves and have promised to help defend this small and valiant nation.

Strengthened by that promise, the people of South Viet-Nam have fought for many long years. Thousands of them have died. Thousands more have been crippled and scarred by war. We just cannot now dishonor our word, or abandon our commitment, or leave those who believed us and who trusted us to the terror and repression and murder that would follow. . . .

Let me also add now a personal note. I do not find it easy to send the flower of our youth, our finest young men, into battle. . . . I have seen them in a thousand streets, of a hundred towns, in every State in this Union — working and laughing and building, and filled with hope and life. I think I know, too, how their mothers weep, and how their families sorrow.

This is the most agonizing and the most painful duty of your President.

There is something else, too. When I was young, poverty was so common that we didn't know it had a name. An education was something that you had to fight for, and water was really life itself. I have now been in public life 35 years, more than three decades, and in each of those 35 years I have seen good men, and wise leaders, struggle to bring the blessings of this land to all of our people.

And now I am the President. It is now my opportunity to help every child get an education, to help every Negro and every American citizen have an equal opportunity, to have every family get a decent home, and to help bring healing to the sick and dignity to the old.

As I have said before, that is what I have lived for, that is what I have wanted all my life since I was a little boy, and I do not want to see all those hopes and all those dreams of so many people for so many years now drowned in the wasteful ravages of cruel wars. I am going to do all I can to see that that never happens.

But I also know, as a realistic public servant, that as long as there are men who hate and destroy, we must have the courage to resist, or we will see it all, all that we have built, all that we hope to build, all of our dreams for freedom — all, *all* will be swept away on the flood of conquest.

So, too, this shall not happen. We will stand in Viet-Nam.

4.10

A Marine Recoils from His Vietnam War

Philip Caputo, a U.S. marine officer, was one of the first to experience the new U.S.-led war. He landed at Da Nang in March 1965 to guard the U.S. air base there. But his unit became more actively involved in patrolling into the countryside, a role that would become routine for American troops. From the very start, they would find these operations a strain as they struggled to distinguish civilians from combatants, friend from foe. They grew angry and frustrated over the daily loss of comrades to mines and snipers and the lack of progress in pacifying the countryside. One of Caputo's patrols went wrong when he killed two Vietnamese; he was then called before a court-martial. Exonerated and honorably discharged, he became active in the anti-war movement. This account, one of the first published by a U.S. soldier, gives a sense of what a guerrilla war looked like from the ground and how that kind of conflict would demoralize U.S. forces. This excerpt draws from the time of Caputo's trial in Vietnam and his departure for home.

Once more we have a memoir that poses fascinating questions about how the author gets his message across and how much of that message is self-justification. How does Caputo convey his sense of disillusionment with the war? How might we judge the reliability of his treatment? How might he have weighed in on the debate within the Johnson administration?

Philip Caputo
A Rumor of War
1977

I already regarded myself as a casualty of the war, a moral casualty, and like all serious casualties, I felt detached from everything. I felt very much like a man who has lost a leg or an arm, and, knowing he will never have to fight again, loses all interest in the war that has wounded him. As his physical energies are bodily injuries, so were all of my emotional energies spent on maintaining my mental balance. I had not broken during the five-month ordeal. I would not break. No matter what they did to me, they could not make me break. All my inner reserves had been committed to that battle for emotional and mental survival. I had nothing left for other struggles. The war simply wasn't my show any longer; I had declared a truce between me and the Viet Cong, signed a personal armistice, and all I asked for now was a chance to live for myself on my terms. I had no argument with the Viet Cong. It wasn't the VC who were threatening to rob me of my liberty, but the United States government, in whose service I had enlisted. Well, I was through with that. I was finished with governments and their abstract causes, and I would never again allow myself to fall under the charms and spells of political witch doctors like John F. Kennedy. . . .

We stood waiting in the sun at the edge of the runway. There were about a hundred and fifty of us, and we watched as a replacement draft filed off the big transport plane. They fell into formation and tried to ignore the dusty, tanned, ragged-looking men who jeered them. The replacements looked strangely young, far younger than we, and awkward and bewildered by this scorched land to which an indifferent government had sent them. I did not join in the mockery. I felt sorry for these children, knowing that they would all grow old in this land of endless dying. I pitied them, knowing that out of every ten, one would die, two more would be maimed for life, another two would be less seriously wounded and sent out to fight again, and all the rest would be wounded in other, more hidden ways.

Philip Caputo, *A Rumor of War* (New York: Ballantine Books, 1977), 314–15, 319–20.

The replacements were marched off toward the convoy that waited to carry them to their assigned units and their assigned fates. None of them looked at us. They marched away. Shouldering our seabags, we climbed up the ramp into the plane, the plane we had all dreamed about, the grand, mythological Freedom Bird. A joyous shout went up as the transport lurched off the runway and climbed into the placid sky. Below lay the rice paddies and the green, folded hills where we had lost our friends and our youth.

The plane banked and headed out over the China Sea, toward Okinawa, toward freedom from death's embrace. None of us was a hero. We would not return to cheering crowds, parades, and the pealing of great cathedral bells. We had done nothing more than endure. We had survived, and that was our only victory.

YOUTH ERUPTS, 1968

Waves of discontent among young people swept across much of the world during the 1960s and the early 1970s disrupting the Cold War status quo. In prosperous countries such as the United States and France and in third world countries such as Mexico, youth protest unsettled national life. In broad terms the pattern was similar. Youth felt a sense of identity, solidarity, and efficacy as they confronted the authority of their government. They first became active in the name of relatively moderate demands regarding university policy and educational practice. But these would give way to more sweeping critiques of political authority, economic opportunity, and international violence (especially in Vietnam) as the protest movements flexed their muscles and encountered government resistance. By 1968 it was beginning to seem that "everything is possible" — or at least that fundamental changes in institutions and values were imperative. But in all three cases considered here governments struck back, using the police and the army. Paris exploded in May; Chicago witnessed riots in August; and Mexico City experienced a traumatic repression in October. The authorities regained control of the streets, put the leading protestors in jail (to face at best long trials and at worst torture), and shattered the protest movement, sending a few protestors underground to experiment with counterviolence (assassination and other acts of terrorism) and turning most toward bitter resentment.

In examining the U.S., French, and Mexican perspectives, consider the concerns or issues that animated young people and that might justify labeling them all "new left" (to distinguish them from the old, doctrinaire, communist left of their parents' generation). Are there significant differences in substance or style in the three national cases treated here? How do the views of young people relate to well-established Cold War preoccupations? How do these expressions of youth protest resonate a third of a century later?

4.11
Stirrings in the United States

Colleges and universities were the focal point of youth discontent from the outset of the 1960s. Not surprisingly in a racially divided country, that discontent had a white and a black face. The Students for a Democratic Society (SDS), organized at the University of Michigan in 1960, was a loose national network that attracted well-to-do, young whites from the suburbs. The "Port Huron Statement" — so named for the place in Michigan where the SDS met in 1962 — was the work primarily of one of its leaders, Tom Hayden. Young African Americans attending college and drawn to issues of civil rights in the South had created their own organization in 1960, the Student Nonviolent Coordinating Committee (SNCC), after growing impatience with their elders at the head of the civil rights cause. In 1966 Stokely Carmichael, then a twenty-five-year-old graduate of Howard University, became its president — and quickly a household name when he proclaimed the notion of "black power."

These two statements, separated by four years, highlight the shift in tone and substance as youth protest turned more radical in the face of resistance to social change at home and the commitment to war in Vietnam. They also reveal the underlying themes in the protest movement. How do Hayden and Carmichael define the problems confronting the United States, the nature of the changes needed, and the role of young people in effecting those changes? What does democracy mean to Hayden and black power to Carmichael? Put in the same room, what would Hayden and Carmichael have said to each other?

Tom Hayden
"Port Huron Statement"
June 1962

We are people of this generation, bred in at least modest comfort, housed now in universities, looking uncomfortably to the world we inherit. . . .

. . . The declaration "all men are created equal . . ." rang hollow before the facts of Negro life in the South and the big cities of the North. The proclaimed peaceful intentions of the United States contradicted its economic and military investments in the Cold War status quo.

We witnessed, and continue to witness, other paradoxes. With nuclear energy whole cities can easily be powered, yet the dominant nation-states seem more likely to unleash destruction greater than that incurred in all wars of human history. Although our own technology is destroying old and creating new forms of social organization, men still tolerate meaningless work and idleness. While two-thirds of mankind suffers under nourishment, our own upper classes revel amidst superfluous abundance. Although world population is expected to double in forty years, the nations still tolerate anarchy as a major principle of international conduct and uncontrolled exploitation governs the sapping of the earth's physical resources. Although mankind desperately needs revolutionary leadership, America rests in national stalemate, its goals ambiguous and tradition-bound instead of informed and clear, its democratic system apathetic and manipulated rather than "of, by, and for the people." . . .

Some would have us believe that Americans feel contentment amidst prosperity — but might it not better be called a glaze above deeply felt anxieties about their role in the new world? And if these anxieties produce a developed indifference to human affairs, do they not as well produce a yearning to believe that there *is* an alternative to the present, that something *can* be done to change circumstances in the school, the workplaces, the bureaucracies, the government? It is to this latter yearning, at once the spark and engine of change, that we direct our present appeal. The search for truly democratic alternatives to the present, and a commitment to social experimentation with them, is a worthy and fulfilling human enterprise, one which moves us and, we hope, others today. . . .

Men have unrealized potential for self-cultivation, self-direction, self-understanding, and creativity. It is this potential that we regard as crucial and to which we appeal, not to the human potentiality for violence, unreason, and submission to authority. The goal of man and society should be human independence: a concern not with image of popularity but with finding a meaning in life that is personally authentic . . . .

We would replace power rooted in possession, privilege, or circumstance by power and uniqueness rooted in love, reflectiveness, reason, and creativity. As a social system we seek the establishment of a democracy of individual participation, governed by two central aims: that the individual share in those social decisions determining the quality and direction of his life; that society be organized to encourage independence in men and provide the media for their common participation. . . .

In the last few years, thousands of American students demonstrated that they at least felt the urgency of the times. They moved actively and directly against racial injustices, the threat of war, violations of individual rights of conscience, and, less frequently, against economic manipulation. They succeeded in restoring a small measure of controversy to the campuses after the stillness of the McCarthy period [of repressive anti-communism]. They succeeded, too, in gaining some concessions from the people and institutions they opposed, especially in the fight against racial bigotry.

. . . [S]tudents are breaking the crust of apathy and overcoming the inner alienation that remain the defining characteristics of American college life. . . .

But we need not indulge in illusions: the university system cannot complete a movement of ordinary people making demands for a better life. From its schools and colleges across the nation, a militant left might [must?] awaken its allies, and by beginning the process towards peace, civil rights, and labor struggles, reinsert theory and idealism where too often reign confusion and political barter. The power of students and faculty united is not only potential; it has shown its actuality in the South, and in the reform movements of the North. . . .

[The next step] will involve national efforts at university reform by an alliance of students and faculty. They must wrest control of the educational process from the administrative bureaucracy. They must make fraternal and functional contact with allies in labor, civil rights, and other liberal forces outside the campus. They must import major public issues into the curriculum — research and teaching on problems of war and peace is an outstanding example. They must make debate and controversy, not dull pedantic cant, the common style for educational life. They must consciously build a base for their assault upon the loci of power.

As students for a democratic society, we are committed to stimulating this kind of social movement, this kind of vision and program in campus and community across the country. If we appear to seek the unattainable, as it has been said, then let it be known that we do so to avoid the unimaginable.

Stokely Carmichael
Speech at the University of California at Berkeley
October 1966

People ought to understand that we were never fighting for the right to integrate, *we were fighting against white supremacy.* In order to understand white supremacy we must dismiss the fallacious notion that white people can give anybody his freedom. A man is born free. You may enslave a man after he is born free, and that is in fact what this country does. It enslaves blacks after they're born. The only thing white people can do is *stop denying black people their freedom.* . . .

The white supremacist attitude, which you have either consciously or subconsciously, is running rampant through society today. For example, missionaries were sent to Africa with the attitude that blacks were automatically inferior. . . . [N]ow we have "modern-day missionaries," and they come into

Stokely Carmichael, "Berkeley Speech," in *Contemporary American Voices,* ed. James R. Andrews and David Zarefsky (White Plains, N.Y.: Longman, 1992), 102–107. Available online at <http://www.svdltd.com/sells/cpa/speeches/carmichaeltxt.htm> (January 3, 2003).

our ghettos — they Head Start, Upward Lift, Bootstrap, and Upward Bound us into white society. They don't want to face the real problem. A man is poor for one reason and one reason only — he does not have money. If you want to get rid of poverty, you give people money. . . .

We are now engaged in a psychological struggle in this country about whether or not black people have the right to use the words they want to use without white people giving their sanction. We maintain the use of the words Black Power . . . . A man was picked as a slave for one reason — the color of his skin. Black was automatically inferior, inhuman, and therefore fit for slavery. . . . We are oppressed as a group because we are black, not because we are lazy or apathetic, not because we're stupid or we stink, not because we eat watermelon or have good rhythm. We are oppressed because we are black. . . .

. . . We must begin to start building those institutions and to fight to articulate our position, to fight to be able to control our universities (we need to be able to do that), to fight to control the basic institutions that perpetuate racism by destroying them and building new ones. That's the real question that faces us today . . . .

. . . We cannot have white people working in the black community — on psychological grounds. The fact is that all black people question whether or not they are equal to whites, since every time they start to do something, white people are around showing them how to do it. If we are going to eliminate that for the generation that comes after us, then black people must be in positions of power, doing and articulating for themselves. . . .

. . . We not only say we are against the war in Vietnam; we are against the draft. . . . Any time a black man leaves the country where he can't vote to supposedly deliver the vote to somebody else, he's a black mercenary. Any time a black man leaves this country, gets shot in Vietnam on foreign ground, and returns home and you won't give him a burial place in his own homeland, he's a black mercenary. . . .

We have found all the myths of the country to be nothing but downright lies. We were told that if we worked hard we would succeed, and if that were true we would own this country lock, stock, and barrel. We have picked the cotton for nothing; we are the maids in the kitchens of liberal white people; we are the janitors, the porters, the elevator men; we sweep up your college floors. We are the hardest workers and the lowest paid. It is nonsensical for people to talk about human relationships until they are willing to build new institutions. Black people are economically insecure. White liberals are economically secure. Can you begin to build an economic coalition? Are the liberals willing to share their salaries with the economically insecure black people they so much love? Then if you're not, are you willing to start building new institutions that will provide economic security for black people? That's the question *we* want to deal with! . . .

We must question the values of this society, and I maintain that black people are the best people to do that since we have been excluded from that society. . . . I do not want to be a part of the American pie. The American pie means raping South Africa, beating Vietnam, beating South America, raping the Philippines, raping every country you've been in. I don't want any of your blood money. I don't want to be part of that system. We are the generation who has found this country to be a world power and the wealthiest country in the world. We must question whether or not we want this country to continue being the wealthiest country in the world at the price of raping everybody else. And because black people are saying we do not now want to become a part of you, we are called reverse racists. Ain't that a gas?

. . . We won't get caught up in questions about power. This country knows what power is. It knows what Black Power is because it deprived black people of it for over four hundred years. White people associate Black Power with violence because of their own inability to deal with blackness. If we had said "Negro power" nobody would get scared. Everybody would support it. If we said power for colored people, everybody'd be for that, but it is the word "black" that bothers people in this country, and that's their problem, not mine. That's the lie that says anything black is bad. . . .

We are on the move for our liberation. We're tired of trying to prove things to white people. We are tired of trying to explain to white people that we're not going to hurt them. We are concerned with getting the things we want, the things we have to have to be able to function. The question is, Will white people overcome their racism and allow for that to happen in this country? If not, we have no choice but to say very clearly, "Move on over, or we're going to move over you."

4.12

Paris in Upheaval, 1968

With a power not seen in either the United States or Mexico, the French protest movement convulsed the nation for several months, drew wide support outside the university, threw the government into confusion, and nearly toppled it. The immediate impulse came out of Nanterre, a new campus just outside Paris and part of the national education system. Students there — primarily in the social sciences — began to protest a traditional and unresponsive curriculum of instruction. Students in Paris took up the cause in a series of demonstrations that turned violent on May 10 in what was known as the "night of the barricades." The brutality of the security forces drew widespread condemnation. Industrial workers, themselves unhappy with factory regimentation and out-of-touch union leaders, went on strike to show their support. Strikes and continued demonstrations paralyzed the country. Dreams of sweeping changes in French life seemed within grasp until the government rallied, the public grew uneasy with disruption of daily life, and labor leaders regained control of the rank and file. As rapidly as it developed, youth protest collapsed.

A leaflet distributed at Nanterre in March captures students' initial concern with university-related issues. The second document, a collection of graffiti that appeared on walls during the protest, provides a sense of the spirit of the times. Put together, what do these two documents tell us about the values that animated French youth? How do their concerns compare with those expressed by their American counterparts in SDS and SNCC?

"How to Train Stuffed Geese"
Mid-March 1968

Lethargy, disappointment, and disgust compose the daily atmosphere of all lecture halls, nor is this peculiar to the first year. Collapse of any real vocation, dearth of professional openings and esteem, a specialty that boils down to making children count red balls and blue balls, these are the ultimate results for psychologists and sociologists of years of "study," during which all real value, all intellectual dynamism has been nibbled away little by little by the requirements of a type of teaching which is more or less brilliant on the surface, but illusory and rigid in its substratum. Actually, what the *faculté* offers us, when what we are looking for are possibilities of extending our mental horizons, is a crude paternalism which, by promoting the breeding of "stuffed geese"[1] . . . maintains us in a state of intellectual sterility.

The problem appears to us to be clearly rooted, on the one hand, in the structure of the kind of instruction given us and, on the other, in the way examinations are held and marked.

TEACHING METHODS

Existing

To begin with, this type of teaching bores us even before we become disgusted by its mechanical, deadly aspects, as also by the banality and extremely insipid way it is presented. The student, being unconcerned by its insipidness, and maintained in a state of mental passivity, becomes a mere scribe who copies the teacher's lifeless words; later, these copies will be useful to him, since he will reproduce them, without omitting a comma, on his examination paper, as he is required to do by the teacher.

Demanded

We demand an end to illusory, rigid teaching methods, an end to the *faculté* for "stuffed geese." We demand the introduction of genuine dialogue, of real student-professor cooperation. We demand that the insipidness and lethargy of the lecture halls be replaced by an atmosphere of life, enthusiasm, research, and real work in common. . . .

EXAMINATIONS

Existing

Copying: obviously, any eighth grader would exult in such tests as these, which would recall his easiest written interrogations. He would excel in these exams because he would lend himself perfectly to these checkups merely of the student's faculty of memory. . . .

---

[1]Geese fed to excess to produce oversized livers appropriate for making paté de foie gras.
Alain Schnapp and Pierre Vidal-Naquet, eds., *The French Student Uprising, November 1967–June 1968: An Analytical Record,* trans. Maria Jolas (Boston: Beacon Press, 1971), 108–110.

Demanded

Open books, justice: we demand that examinations be held with our books open, and should take into consideration, above all, the student's capacity for intellectual initiative and his powers of analysis and in-depth reflection and not, as now, merely the sterile feat of memory. . . .

Graffiti
1968

Commute, work, commute, sleep . . .

Meanwhile everyone wants to breathe and nobody can
and many say, "We will breathe later."
And most of them don't die because they are already dead.

Boredom is counterrevolutionary.

We don't want a world where the guarantee of not dying
of starvation brings the risk of dying of boredom.

Don't beg for the right to live — take it.

In a society that has abolished every kind of adventure
the only adventure that remains is to abolish the society.

The revolution is incredible because it's really happening.

Live in the moment.

We will ask nothing. We will demand nothing. We will take, occupy.

Down with the state.

Don't liberate me — I'll take care of that.

Abolish class society.

Nature created neither servants nor masters.
I want neither to rule nor to be ruled.

We will have good masters as soon as everyone is their own.

We want structures that serve people, not people serving structures.

Translated by Ken Knabb drawing primarily from Julien Besançon's *Les murs ont la parole* (Tchou, 1968), Walter Lewino's *L'imagination au pouvoir* (Losfeld, 1968), Marc Rohan's *Paris '68* (Impact, 1968), René Viénet's *Enragés et situationnistes dans le mouvement des occupations* (Gallimard, 1968), and Gérard Lambert's *Mai 1968: brûlante nostalgie* (Pied de nez, 1988). Knabb's translations are available at <http://www.slip.net/~knabb/CF/graffiti.htm> (August 6, 2002) along with original French texts. Knabb's address: Bureau of Public Secrets, PO Box 1044, Berkeley, CA 94701, USA; <http://www.bopsecrets.org>; knabb@slip.net.

Politics is in the streets.

A proletarian is someone who has no power over his life and knows it.

Workers of all countries, enjoy!

Humanity won't be happy till the last capitalist is hung
with the guts of the last bureaucrat.

We refuse to be highrised, diplomaed, licensed,
inventoried, registered, indoctrinated, suburbanized,
sermonized, beaten, telemanipulated, gassed, booked.

Poetry is in the streets.

The most beautiful sculpture is a paving stone thrown at a cop's head.

I'm a Groucho Marxist.

I take my desires for reality because I believe
in the reality of my desires.

Practice wishful thinking.

Be realistic, demand the impossible.

Power to the imagination.

Those who lack imagination cannot imagine what is lacking.

Alcohol kills. Take LSD.

Unbutton your mind as often as your fly.

Forget everything you've been taught. Start by dreaming.

Professors, you make us grow old.

We don't want to be the watchdogs or servants of capitalism.

Exams = servility, social promotion, hierarchical society.

When examined, answer with questions.

Insolence is the new revolutionary weapon.

Take revolution seriously, but don't take yourself seriously.

Making revolution also means breaking our internal chains.

A cop sleeps inside each one of us. We must kill him.

Religion is the ultimate con.

If God existed it would be necessary to abolish him.

We want a place to piss, not a place to pray.

I suspect God of being a leftist intellectual.

The bourgeoisie has no other pleasure than to degrade all pleasures.

Going through the motions kills the emotions.

The more I make love, the more I want to make revolution.
The more I make revolution, the more I want to make love.

Revolutionary women are more beautiful.

Make love, not war.

Down with consumer society.

You can't buy happiness. Steal it.

How sad to love money.

First, disobey; then write on the walls.
(Law of 10 May 1968)

Only the truth is revolutionary.

No freedom for the enemies of freedom.

4.13
Massacre in Mexico City, 1968

If the American protest was slow building and long-lasting and the French a sudden burst of enthusiasm quickly punctured, the Mexican case has a claim to distinction as the most brutal and traumatic. Protests began in July 1968 over police intervention on school grounds to stop feuding among student groups and quickly broadened to an attack on the autocratic and long-governing Institutional Revolutionary Party (PRI). Demands for democratization and civil rights moved to the forefront, directly challenging the party-state. The potential embarrassment to the government of having the Olympics, scheduled to be held in the city in the fall, disrupted by protest added to the pressure for action. On the evening of October 2, troops surrounded some five thousand protestors and set about arresting, beating, and shooting them. Several hundred died in this massacre and others were subjected to torture and long prison terms. The government finished what it had begun by waging a dirty war against its critics in the years following. Only recently, following the PRI's loss of national power, has public discussion of the repression and an accounting from those responsible become possible.

The recollections that follow were gathered by Elena Poniatowska, a Mexican journalist sympathetic to the students' cause. They provide the perspective of students from different backgrounds and shed light on key facets of the protest movement — from initial appeal to growing momentum to repression and arrest. What concerns motivated these young people? How does the retrospective nature of these documents make them both stronger and weaker than documents from the time?

Pablo Gómez[1]
*Prison Interview Reflecting on the Antecedents
of the 1968 Protest*

The 1968 Student Movement was not suddenly born that same year; it did not come about by spontaneous generation. Countless revolutionary political organizations and important student groups had previously made the same demands. In Mexico freedom for political prisoners is a demand that goes back as far as political imprisonment itself. The same is true of the fight to do away with Article 145, which establishes penalties for "social dissolution," and the fight to do away with the *granaderos* [riot police known for their brutality]. The 1968 Movement took up all of these demands and not only pressed for [additional reforms] but also became the spokesman for the reforms most urgently sought by Mexican students, workers, and intellectuals.

In many parts of the country, students had previously led the entire nation in protest movements whose general tenor was very much like that of the 1968 Movement. The most important movements of this sort were those in Puebla in 1964, Morelia in 1966, and Sonora and Tabasco in 1967. Moreover, the demonstrations in support of Cuba, Vietnam, and the Dominican Republic mobilized large groups of students, particularly in Mexico City, and the awareness of the oppression of other peoples greatly raised their level of political consciousness and their awareness of their own strength. This was quite evident in the student protests in Morelia during 1962 and 1963; the movement for university reform in Puebla in 1962; the UNAM strike in 1966; the frequent student strikes for economic and academic reforms in various parts of the country (in particular in the rural normal schools); the student movement in the School of Agronomy in Ciudad Juárez, Chihuahua, which was supported by the other schools of agronomy and by the students of IPN [the National Polytechnic Institute], and many other student protests.

I do not believe that these protests are isolated incidents. On the contrary, I believe that after the national strike in April 1956 there was a sharp escalation of student protest movements. The Teachers' Movement in 1958, the Railway Workers' Movement in 1958–1959, and the demonstrations in support of the Cuban revolution all contributed to this process, which reached its peak in 1968. Doubtless the Student Movement has hopes that workers and peasants will carry on the struggle. . . .

During the entire Student Movement there was never a more representative organization, never one that the students felt belonged to them as much as this one did. The kids didn't just sit back and applaud one or two big shots;

---

[1]Gómez was an economics student and activist at the National School of Economics, Autonomous National University of Mexico (UNAM), and member of the Communist Youth.
Elena Poniatowska, Massacre in Mexico, trans. Helen R. Lane (New York: Viking Press, 1975), 9–10, 64–65.

they felt they were really participating; they were not objects but subjects. They were the ones who decided and they were very much aware of this, because the most important decisions were all left to them. When the Army occupied University City, for example, the students from UNAM were scattered. Nonetheless the brigades that had been active in the CU [University City or student quarter] continued working outside the University. They got out handbills and manifestos that established a clear-cut policy, and the rank and file went on fighting.

Carolina Pérez Cicero[1]
Interview Blaming Government Repression for Energizing Students

I think that repression was responsible for the effectiveness and the importance of the Student Movement. More than any political speech, the very fact of repression politicized people and led the great majority to participate actively in the meetings. It was decided that classes would be suspended in each school, and that was what got us to thinking about forming brigades and action committees in each department. The members of the brigades were students who engaged in all sorts of activities, from collecting money to organizing "lightning meetings" in the streets, in the most isolated working-class districts. Mass demonstrations were one of the most effective political weapons of the Movement.

---

[1]Pérez Cicero was a student at the Faculty of Philosophy and Letters, UNAM. Poniatowska, *Massacre in Mexico,* 7.

Daniel Esparza Lepe[1]
Interview Articulating the Economic Issues That Energized Him

I'm from a peasant family in the country. I'm twenty-five years old and I've seen friends my age die the same way they were born: fucked by the system. My family moved to the Federal District [greater Mexico City] because they were starving to death. At first we stayed with some aunts of ours out near Atzcapotzalco. My father was a bricklayer. When I was still in grade school, I began working in an oxygen-bottling factory; later I made up my mind I'd go to secondary school. I wanted very much to get into Poli [National Polytechnic Institute], but since I had no inside contacts and no money,

---

[1]Esparza Lepe was a student from a peasant background at the School of Mechanical and Electrical Engineering (ESIME), the National Polytechnic Institute (IPN) in Mexico City. Poniatowska, *Massacre in Mexico,* 74–75.

how could I? I didn't know anybody. When you're an outsider, that's the way it is: you hardly ever even talk to anyone. I was the sort of person who had no interest in political discussions. What I wanted most was to get ahead so my family wouldn't have to suffer any more, to endure things I'll never forget: the way they treated my mother in houses where she worked as a laundress and all that. There were places where instead of paying her money they'd say, "Here, take this food home with you" — and I could plainly see that it was table scraps. When you're starving you have to put up with things like that, but it made me mad. I finally got into Poli. I worked nights and studied in the afternoon; that's how I got into engineering school. I didn't join any organizations at Poli, and I looked down on anybody who started any sort of organization. I slaved like a robot at my job in the factory and at school I was a grind; nothing interested me but my work. I hadn't been back to the part of the country I came from for a long time, and when I finally did go back I saw that my relatives' living conditions hadn't changed at all, and I was very discouraged. I'd been discouraged, in fact, ever since I was twelve, when I began working in the oxygen factory. The representative of the do-nothing, government-approved union, the CTM [Confederation of Mexican Workers], dropped around every once in a while to collect dues and all he ever said was, "Everything's going fine, men." Any worker who pressed for his rights was kicked out. All this got me to thinking, and when I saw that the Student Movement was really making headway, I said to myself, This time I'm going to take part. I felt very grown up, and said to myself, I hope we get somewhere. The Movement didn't seem political to me; it was something more than that. First of all, all of the members were young, they were all pissed off, and ready to fight for what they wanted. . . . And secondly, their ideas were different: they were making concrete demands, and it seemed to me they weren't pulling the wool over anybody's eyes. . . . I never felt that I was being lied to or that it was all play-acting, the way the relations between the CTM and the workers had been in the factory!

Félix Sánchez Hernández[1]
Prison Interview Talking about Support for Protests outside the Universities

I'm a worker. I used to package candy in the Sanborn chocolate factory. My name is Félix Sánchez Hernández, and I'm twenty-nine years old. I was in favor of the Movement from the very beginning — or at any rate interested in it. I knew [Luis Tomás Cervantes] Cabeza de Vaca [a leader of the National Strike Committee] and several others and they urged me to go to the demonstrations, so I went to most of them. I also helped hand out leafleats, both in

---

[1]Sánchez Hernández was a working-class participant.
Poniatowska, *Massacre in Mexico,* 34–36.

the chocolate factory and in the streets. The workers went to some of the demonstrations, but on an individual basis — on their own, so to speak. There were around five hundred of us who attended. We went to the Silent Demonstration and to the one before that, on the twenty-seventh; we went from Tacubaya — because the factory is at Benjamín Hill — to Chapultepec, and from there we marched in a group all the way down the Reforma to the Zócalo. In the demonstration on the twenty-seventh, I happened by chance to be with the group of electricians; there were about six hundred of us, plus the friends that joined us along the line of march. Many workers sympathized with the Movement but lots of them didn't dare show it for fear of reprisals, or because they were lazy or indifferent, since all of us were very tired when we got off work, but it was mostly because they were afraid of losing their jobs. We have a company union at the Sanborn chocolate factory. Movement propaganda was delivered to the factory and the workers themselves would pass the handbills out.

I don't know what I'm going to do when I get out of jail. I can't go back to the factory. They fired my sister-in-law because they said the three of us — my wife, my sister-in-law, and I — were in cahoots, agitating for better wages and making trouble for the management. I was earning thirty-two pesos a day [about $2.60 in 1968] — I arrived at work at five-thirty in the morning and got out at two in the afternoon.

I don't know why they put me in Lecumberri [Prison]. I'm a worker, so the only connection I had with the Student Movement was the fact that I'd shown my support by attending public student functions as a spectator, the demonstration on August 27, and the Silent Demonstration on September 13. Or maybe they threw me in jail because I visited a pal of mine who's from the state of Oaxaca, the same as me, a prisoner in cell block N of Lecumberri Prison, Señor Justino Juárez. When I read in the paper that he was in prison, I went to see him because he's a friend of mine. I found out later that the prison authorities gave a copy of the lists of names of people who visited political prisoners to the judicial and federal security police, who have been using these lists to threaten the families of prisoners, and as happened in my case, to arbitrarily arrest people and accuse them of some sort of crime.

On the first of October, 1968, I came to work, the same as any other day. At twelve-forty-five that day four men dressed in civvies entered the factory with pistols in their hands and immediately started roughing me up. Then they grabbed me and hauled me out of the building. I asked them who they were and where they were taking me, and the only answer I got was more punches while one of them held my hands behind my back. They shoved me into a car, and once they got me inside they blindfolded me with a rag and gagged me with another one. This outrage was witnessed by my pals at work — several of them are willing to testify. At the headquarters of the Federal Judicial Police I was stripped naked, beaten, given electric shocks, and robbed of all my personal belongings. The police officers accused me of having gone to see Justino Juárez to "get orders from him." They subjected me to all sorts of tortures, and made threats so as to try and get me to sign a confession:

"Listen, you jackass, we've got you right where we want you, so you have to confess, even though you haven't done anything. You have to say you're guilty because everybody we haul in here gets sent to the jug, whether he's done anything or not. Either you sign or we'll kill you."

I don't know what it said in the statement I signed. On October 9, 1968, I was sent to Lecumberri Prison and I've been here ever since.

Gilberto Guevara Niebla[1]
Interview Recalling the Night of the Massacre (October 2, 1968)

The Army units approached from all directions and encircled the crowd in a pincers movement, and in just a few moments all the exits were blocked off. From up there on the fourth floor of the Chihuahua building, where the speakers' platform had been set up, we couldn't see what the Army was up to and we couldn't understand why the crowd was panicking. The two helicopters that had been hovering over the Plaza almost from the very beginning of the meeting had suddenly started making very hostile maneuvers, flying lower and lower in tighter and tighter circles just above the heads of the crowd, and then they had launched two flares, a green one first and then a red one; when the second one went off the panic started, and we members of the Committee did our best to stop it: none of us there on the speakers' stand could see that the Army troops below us were advancing across the Plaza. When they found themselves confronted by a wall of bayonets, the crowd halted and immediately drew back; then we saw a great wave of people start running toward the other side of the Plaza; but there were Army troops on the other side of the Plaza too; and as we stood watching from up there on the speakers' stand, we saw the whole crowd head in another direction. That was the last thing we saw down below, for at that moment the fourth floor was taken over by the Olimpia Battalion. Even though we had no idea why the crowd had panicked and was running first in one direction and then in the other, those of us who had remained there at the microphone till the very last found ourselves looking down the barrels of machine guns when we turned around. The balcony had been occupied by the Olimpia Battalion and we were ordered to put our hands up and face the wall, and given strict orders not to turn around in the direction of the Plaza; if we so much as moved a muscle, they hit us over the head or in the ribs with their rifle butts. Once the trap they had set snapped shut, the collective murder began.

---

[1]Guevara Niebla was a member of the National Strike Committee.
Poniatowska, *Massacre in Mexico,* 213–14.

CHAPTER 5

ABUNDANCE AND DISCONTENT IN THE DEVELOPED WORLD

ECONOMIES IN THE DEVELOPED WORLD had not only recovered from war by the early 1950s but prospered — no mean achievement given the damage done industry and commerce by global depression followed by global warfare. For Americans, Japanese, and Europeans, the economic growth of the 1950s and 1960s stands as a golden age unprecedented and since unmatched.

High rates of growth along with rising levels of trade suggest dry statistics. But these economic trends influenced ordinary people's lives in profound ways. Boom times hastened the spread of consumerism, which had already progressed in the United States in the 1920s. They gave Japanese and Europeans the resources and confidence to change the course of their nations, in ways both similar to and different from the course Americans were taking. Finally and paradoxically, abundance created discontents. Some worried about the damage that material abundance was doing to the environment. Women began to ask about their social, political, and economic role in the emerging postwar society, in effect reviving questions posed by nineteenth- and early twentieth-century feminists.

THE FLOWERING OF CONSUMER SOCIETY

Consumerism — the outlook and practices that define a society preoccupied with the acquisition of nonessential products and services — was not the creation of the postwar period. It grew out of the late nineteenth-century development of mass production of low-cost, standardized goods and all that went with it economically — the need for a mass market of consumers with discretionary income (a surplus after covering the costs of basic housing and food), distribution systems to reach them, advertising to persuade them, and sales on credit to draw them to big-ticket items. But no economic changes as significant as these unfold without profound cultural changes, including the emergence of a personal and social identity defined in terms of participation within this system — of knowing and acquiring the latest products and services, of the multiplication of needs, of judging personal and national success in terms of the ability to acquire, and of the growing divorce between burdensome public obligations and connections and private pleasures afforded by the consumer culture.

Consumerism was a new expression of an old phenomenon. The consumption of prestige goods had long been a preoccupation of small, privileged segments of societies. But in its modern popular guise, consumerism reached virtually the entire population. The United States was the leader in this trend. By the 1920s the middle class and even some of the working class commanded the discretionary income essential to a consumer lifestyle, and the postwar period would see a preoccupation with consumption become society wide. Consumerism was also international. The United States got a head start. But in the 1950s and 1960s Europeans and Japanese would begin to catch up. And behind them stood peoples in the developing world eager to have their own version of the consumer society.

5.1
The United States Leads the Way

The enthusiasm with which Americans took to consumerism can be traced in the personal debt they accumulated to acquire goods. At the end of World War II they owed $6 billion. By 1958 that debt had jumped to $45 billion, and by 1965 to $95 billion. And it continued to climb to the end of the century and beyond.[1] Going into debt to buy cars, homes, kitchen appliances, electronic goods, and vacations had emerged in the early postwar years as a defining feature of American life. Rising consumer debt was based on high levels of discretionary income, which most Americans could expect to increase as they grew older and climbed the economic ladder.

Two types of evidence — an advertisement for consumer debt (published in 1928 by the chain of Julian Goldman Stores) and the cover of a popular, mainstream magazine from the 1950s — suggest the pervasiveness and power of consumerism. What appeal is the advertisement making? What kind of prudential responses might a wary consumer make? What are the broad implications of accepting the logic of this appeal? How should we "read" the more subtle message of the magazine cover — as a pleasant fantasy, a bit of commercial propaganda, or a social reality?

---

[1]Data from Lendol Calder, *Financing the American Dream: A Cultural History of Consumer Credit* (Princeton: Princeton University Press, 1999), 9–10, 291.

Advertisement for Consumer Loans
Circa 1930

He makes only $3,000 a year . . . *but is worth* $112,290!

At least that's what the insurance companies say, and they ought to know.

Jim Jones is twenty-seven years old. According to the insurance companies' tables, he can expect to live for another thirty-seven years and one hundred and fifty-six days. As long as he keeps his health, he'll keep his job. Even if he never gets a raise, Jim's future is worth $112, 290!

Wouldn't it be nice, said somebody, if Jim could use some of that money now?

Well, it would be. *And it is.* Because Jim is actually using some of it now!

He bought a car last year, bought it on his future — from General Motors. He paid one-third of its cost at first, and the balance within a year. (Three out of every four cars in this country are bought that way.)

Jim Jones has bought furniture that way, too. (Nine out of every ten families in America buy furniture on credit, and pay for it with installments.) Jim is buying a bond with installment payments, too.

And he buys his clothes the same way. Jim likes good clothes, and like most people he often hasn't enough cash on hand for a new suit. So he pays for the suit easily and conveniently.

Reproduced in Julian Goldman, *Prosperity and Consumer Credit* (New York: Harper & Brothers, 1930), 169; and in Calder, *Financing the American Dream,* 205.

Saturday Evening Post *Cover*
August 15, 1959

5.2
An Anthropologist Traces Changing Rural Life in France

Laurence Wylie, an American anthropologist, was an acute witness to the French countryside as it passed through several decades of dramatic changes. His classic of rural anthropology, *Village in the Vaucluse,* provided snapshots of rapidly evolving country life in the village of Roubillon (thinly disguised here as Peyrane). Wylie and his family spent a year in the village in the early 1950s when it was still a viable community and almost half of the population of France was still rural. This visit served as the basis for the first edition in 1957. In subsequent visits (the bases for new editions in 1964 and 1974), Wylie watched the population dwindle at the same time that the village established ever more extensive connections with the outside world. Demographics changed as the young left and city dwellers sought vacation homes and retirees sought quiet. Values and the sense of community also changed as consumerism encroached into the countryside.

This account draws attention to the international dimensions of the consumer trends evident so early and emphatically in the United States. What are the changing features of village life chronicled by Wylie? How do they relate to consumerism? In what ways are these changes American in style or influence? How might Wylie's training as an anthropologist, his background as an American, and his attachment to his village neighbors have influenced his account?

Laurence Wylie
From *Village in the Vaucluse*
1957, 1964, 1974

PEYRANE TODAY [1957 EDITION]

Peyrane is profoundly conservative. . . . [T]hey want to be left alone so they will not have to change. Not that the state of things is good as it is. It is neither good nor bad; it is tolerable. Or rather it would be tolerable if it were not for the malevolence of human beings organized into groups. For organization means power, and power means the oppression of the individual.

. . . People say they do not want to belong to an organization because they do not want to put themselves in a position where other people will spy on them, boss them, criticize them, burden them with responsibilities, make them the butt of gossip and ridicule, commit them to action against their will. . . .

. . . [T]here has never been a time since the beginning of Peyrane's history, when contact with organized humanity has meant anything but the exploitation and manipulation of the individual. The wandering hordes, the Romans, the feudal lords — including the neighboring papal rulers, the agents of Provençal counts and French kings, the nineteenth-century régimes set up by Paris, the twentieth-century bureaucracy centralized in Paris — all these form an unbroken past in the vague memory of the village. They all mean domina-

Laurence Wylie, *Village in the Vaucluse,* 3rd ed. (Cambridge, Mass.: Harvard University Press, 1974), 330, 332, 337–38, 340, 342–43, 345, 347–48, 369–71, 377–83.

tion by a human power beyond the control of the individual. At best the domination has brought unsought modifications in living habits. At worst it has brought disaster. And so it has become conventional to think of human power as a plague to be classed with the plagues of nature. . . .

Peyrane is a place where a person can live with himself. He sees himself in the perspective of time and nature. . . . He has a clear conception of his roles in life, and he makes an effort to fulfill them without violating his inner needs. He enjoys being with himself. He can sit alone with no other entertainment than the contemplation of what goes on within him and around him. He listens to the radio occasionally and goes to the movies and to church now and then, but organized entertainment, comics, and pulp magazines do not interest him.

He also enjoys and is even stimulated by the company of other individuals. His relations with other people and his observation of their personal dramas bring warmth and excitement into his life. . . . Peyrane is a community where crime is almost unknown, a community with almost no homicide, suicide, theft, juvenile delinquency, or criminal assault. Consumption of alcohol is general, but there is almost no drunkenness.

Life in Peyrane is centered about the family, and the family is a strong, healthy organism. Children are wanted. They are treated with love, and they are carefully trained. There is little divorce. Old people are cared for. The most solemn occasion of the year is the celebration of All Souls' Day which unites the family about the family tomb. . . .

Peyrane is a hard-working, productive community. Though only one-third of the land is profitably arable, though it is inefficiently distributed, and though there are few other important natural resources in the commune, the people produce more than they consume. The wealth of the community is rather evenly divided: no one is extremely rich, and there is no misery. The health of the community is good. Housing is poor, but everyone is sheltered. Clothes may be patched, but everyone is clothed. Food is expensive, but everyone is fed. . . .

Peyrane Ten Years Later [1964 Edition]

As we drove into Peyrane for a return visit in the summer of 1959 we were surprised to find the way barred at the entry to the village. . . . In the center of the streets of the village there were deep trenches where Algerians and Spaniards, yellow with ochre dust, were shoveling earth into mounds. Trenches branched off into the houses on either side of the streets. . . .

Through the open doors of the houses one could see the reason for the upheaval. New porcelain sinks, water closets, and an occasional bathtub had recently been delivered and were being installed in each house by the masons of Peyrane. For years the Town Council had talked about having a sewage system in Peyrane, and at last it had come to pass. . . .

As the prices rose and as artists fled from the non-artists, other villages in the region became refuges. Eventually it was the turn of the beautiful ochre-colored town of Peyrane — and the invasion by city people began. Real estate prices rocketed. Today the $90 windmill is not for sale; the Notaire told me that the present owner had just turned down an offer of $3000! The $450

Charrin house belongs to a well-known American violinist who would undoubtedly not sell it for ten times that amount. The $500 Leporatti house was
sold for $3000. . . .

As Peyrane has developed its new function as a resort town the last vestiges of the former agricultural center have almost disappeared. . . . Monsieur
Prayal retired as blacksmith at the age of seventy [in 1953]. His son Roger,
who had worked with him and was to succeed him, moved to Apt to work as
a clerk in a hardware store. Since the farmers were selling their horses and
buying tractors there was little to keep him in Peyrane. The Prayal smithy is
boarded up.

Since all of the Prayals' nine children have left Peyrane to live elsewhere,
the Prayals are understandably lonely, increasingly lonely since their old friends
are fast disappearing. When we returned to Peyrane in 1961 we found the old
couple sitting with their friend Madame Lanval on a bench in the shade
outside the closed smithy. They found distraction in watching the tourists and
summer people drive in and out of the village . . . . The young women dress
more like city women, so there is little incongruity between the villagers and
the tourists and summer people who gather beneath the gay umbrellas in
front of the three cafés on the Place de la Mairie.

These umbrellas — along with the stainless steel *café espresso* machines —
are the symbols of the new function as a resort town, for as a result of the
changed economy the café business is booming. . . .

. . . Peyrane seems somehow to have attracted too many whose taste led
them to destroy the traditional simple architecture. In its place they have built
the gingerbread houses so characteristic of the Riviera and of so much of
French suburbia. . . .

Television came to Peyrane in the late fifties, when a transmitter was erected
on the Luberon Mountain in order to bring the Marseille programs to the
communities of the valley around Apt. Emile bought a set at once, or rather
he brought it home and paid for it on the installment plan over a period of
twelve months. This sort of transaction was new to him and contrary to his
family training and tradition, according to which one should never buy on
credit. Now, however, he is convinced that he has been foolish all these years
to stay out of debt. "The way prices keep going up," he said, "it's stupid not to
get what you want when you want it — within reason, of course." Since every year he has more business and there seems to be no end of it, the future
appears less insecure. His attitude is that of the younger people of Peyrane, an
attitude new to Peyrane since 1950 when the blacksmith Prayal had said to
me: "No one here will ask for credit if he can avoid it. No one wants to be
obligated to anyone." Most of the television sets operating in Peyrane were
bought on the installment plan. . . .

The effect of television on community life is noteworthy. The farmer
Paulin never used to miss a boules tournament.[1] Yet I met him on Sunday

---

[1] A French version of bowling, popular among men, often played in public spaces near cafés.

afternoon in the summer of 1959 walking toward home instead of to the café where a tournament was being organized. "I don't play much any more," he said when I asked him about this change in his habits. "Sometimes I watch, but not much because it's mostly just the resort people playing boules. I'd rather stay at home and watch a good program on the *télé*." . . .

Television seems to have atomized still further the social contacts of the people of Peyrane, which were already badly fragmented in 1950. However, the Peyranais who watch television instead of playing boules with their neighbors and gossiping about village affairs no doubt feel as though they have more in common with Frenchmen in general . . . .

Now that Emile Pian has a different attitude toward buying on credit and being in debt he has satisfied another long-standing desire: he travels. In 1959 his wife and he thought nothing of driving to a remote corner of the department on their new scooter to visit friends and relations, and by 1961 he had acquired a Citroën 2CV truck so that his son and parents-in-law could go along, too. . . .

So in Peyrane we have two aspects of France today — the glamorous side of change and prosperity, and the darker side of what it means for many of the human beings caught in this change. In the country, the brighter side is seen in the adoption of modern farming methods, in the growth of the coöperatives and especially in a new sense of participation in the commonweal that did not exist in 1950. In the village we find that Peyrane has a new function, symbolized by the remodeled houses, the modern sewage system, the gay umbrellas in front of the cafés. Peyrane is today a young community teeming with children who have a constantly improving opportunity to study in a modern, well-lighted, well-equipped communal school or to go to the city for more advanced and more technical education.

The darker side is symbolized by the *cadastre,* the huge tomes in the Town Hall where the records of property ownership are kept. There one sees the intricate patterns of land tenure, mirroring the perpetually complicating factors of marriage, birth, death, and the consequent sharing of the family heritage. Before the problem of regrouping the madly dispersed plots of land is solved — or drifts toward a solution, since it seems unlikely that a rational and acceptable solution may be found — many of the people of Peyrane will have lost their independence. . . .

Of course, when we speak of the threat to the independent farmers and shopkeepers, when we describe the modernization of France, it is often assumed that France as we knew it has disappeared. Modernization has always been equated with "Americanization," "mass culture," the "death of individuality" — the loss of those very ideals and values that seem to have characterized French culture and that have appeared to depend on the economic independence of the little men.

There are other forces, however, that hold back economic change or pattern it so that the traditional values are still expressed in new forms. Carette's son may have to give up farming and work for Shell Oil in Berre, but he cannot divest himself of the basic values he learned at home and at school in Peyrane. . . .

PEYRANE TWENTY-FIVE YEARS LATER [1974 EDITION]

[S]ince 1970 I became increasingly aware that Peyranais . . . no longer feel themselves defined, in any sense of the word, by the limits of their community. At first, on these returns to Peyrane, which I felt I knew so well, I planned to arrive just before noon so that I could greet my friends at the aperitif hour. . . . In the past the Town Secretary, the doctor, the postman, the *notaire,* the husband of the schoolteacher, the café owner had, as a group, been the town's vital nerve center. By spending an hour with these men I had always been sure that no important event, past or present, would escape me.

I found to my disappointment that there was no longer a regular group at the bar. On my first return visit in 1973 I met Rivet, but he told me at once that since retiring three years before as Town Secretary, he no longer "comes up" to the village regularly. . . .

I now realize why the noon aperitif group has disappeared: Peyrane has ceased to be a tight little community in which such a group plays an essential role. The Peyranais no longer feel themselves to be — in fact no longer are — a unit functioning as autonomously as possible in defense against the Outside World; they have become an integral part of the world they once staunchly resisted. . . .

. . . It used to be that only the well-to-do had a *résidence secondaire,* a country house, as well as a city dwelling. Now most middle-class people have a house in the country, and the upper classes seek a third and even a fourth residence, one for the sun in the Midi, one in the mountains for the snow, one in Brittany for the ocean. Now that the French working class has been largely replaced at the bottom of the social scale by foreign workers, the aspiration for a *résidence secondaire* is beginning to reach these French, too. . . .

Many of the *résidences secondaires* are acquired with retirement in mind. . . . Peyrane has once more become a town of older people. When we lived there, a quarter of the population was over 60. Then the increased birth rate following the war created a community dominated by the young. Now, with the increasing number of retired people, the atmosphere is not unlike that of a Florida retirement community. . . .

The economy of the village is geared to the needs of its new population. When we lived in Peyrane, there were five groceries; now there is one. The old groceries had the only refrigerators in the village. We shopped from meal to meal at Arène's, four yards from our front door. His grocery was our larder and our pantry. Now every house in the village has a refrigerator, and for most of their shopping people drive to a city supermarket. . . .

In the fifties we were surrounded by artisans. Across the street in Chanzeaux was the wooden-shoe maker. Our landlord was a harnessmaker. . . . Now there is scarcely a horse in either community; the smiths and the harnessmaker have retired. Wooden shoes and tin pails have been replaced by plastic ones bought in the city. . . .

Supplying energy to modern homes brings prosperity to some merchants. When we were in Peyrane, Monsieur Borel used to bring truckloads of oak logs and *petits bois* to our courtyard; our fireplace and the wood stove in the kitchen provided the only heat in the house all winter. Now Borel's sons carry on a prosperous business in bottled gas for the cooking and heating facilities of the whole village. . . . Farmers no longer spend long winter hours harvesting branches from the trees in the hedges that separated the fields.

In Peyrane, what little trash there was in the past was customarily dumped over the cliff into the surrounding valley. In 1950 every old bottle, every piece of paper, every piece of cast-off clothing was put to use. When we bought olives at Monsieur Reynard's grocery, he wrapped them in a neat square of newspaper taken from a pile he used only when necessary. We saved the oily paper because we learned it was helpful in starting a fire. Now newspapers seldom have a second use. Wood fires are not used for cooking and heating; for wrapping, everyone has a supply of plastic bags saved from trips to the supermarket; the coming of toilet paper eliminated another use for newspapers. The dump at the foot of the cliff is a growing pile of paper and plastic flapping in the mistral.[2]

In the fifties, there was a water shortage . . . . Peyrane's new supply comes from the Durance River. But water was plentiful only for a brief time. The supply was soon outrun by new demands — for irrigation, toilets, bathtubs, clothes- and dishwashers, even swimming pools.

When the French standard of living began its phenomenal rise during the nineteen-fifties, many French saw in it the corruption of French culture by "Americanization." They denounced the *civilisation du gadget* and the *Coca-colonisation* of France. These terms are not heard now. Everyone knows that the increase in the standard of living was simply the result of the modernization of a country that had so long remained economically backward. Today the French proudly repeat the prediction, made by the Hudson Institute in the U.S., that by the 1980's their country will be the first industrial power of Europe. They take it for granted that all French (though perhaps not the foreign immigrant laborers) should enjoy the comforts of a highly industrialized society. . . .

. . . In both teacher-child and parent-child relations, the traditional figures of authority are less sure in their exercise of power and have communicated their lack of conviction to the children.

Twenty years ago the five-year-old Dédou Favre might occasionally have talked back to his mother; he might even have been impudent to another adult, if he were verbally clever — and stayed out of reach of a punishing hand. Fundamentally, Dédou expected to obey his elders, however. . . . This year I saw Dédou's nephew, another Dédou Favre, having a tantrum in the street in front of his house; his mother seemed completely indifferent to what in the past would have been a neighborhood scandal. In school, children now speak more freely, just as at home they take part in adult conversations without being regularly silenced with the traditional "Mange et tais-toi!"

---

[2]A harsh, chilling north wind associated with winters in southern France.

The loss of control is even more obvious with older children, especially with adolescents who in increasing numbers go to the city every day, some to work, some to continue their education. A few parents try desperately — and unhappily — to enforce traditional patterns of authority and hierarchy, but in most families there is acceptance, though tinged perhaps with nostalgia, of the young people's new independence. Village parents may be shocked by their children's involvement with city schoolmates in the lycée revolts of recent years, but at the same time they rather wonderingly admire the daring of the young in confronting authority. . . .

Despite the evolution in human relations, the families I know in both the provinces and Paris seem more unified than before. The belief in hierarchy has given way to a concern for each individual's will, a mutual respect, a tolerance of differences that I would never have thought possible. The independence of the individual has grown, while the unity of the family is less tense and even more solid. I conclude with more conviction than I did in 1960 that the most basic and enduring element in French civilization is the individual's acceptance of his responsibilities in the family with his concomitant refusal to compromise his right to independence.

5.3
Growing Up in 1950s Britain: From Scarcity to Affluence

These recollections from 1950s Britain graphically convey how the transition from wartime scarcity to greater abundance affected the lives of ordinary people. In effect, within one lifetime consumerism would become a mass phenomenon. Born in 1947, both women writing here watched the explosion of income and acquisition in the course of their childhood and youth. But these recollections also reveal that consumerism did not entirely remake society. For example, class status remained an important social marker. Liz Heron grew up working class in Glasgow, Scotland. Ursula Huws's Welsh Catholic father was a draftsman who got a foothold in the middle class when he became a teacher, while her mother came from a family slipping out of the upper class. Both Heron and Huws went on to attend university, thus solidifying their own position in the middle class and testifying to the widening educational opportunities for women.

In the memory of these two women, what marked the transition from scarcity to consumerism? How did their awareness of class, family, and gender figure in? How might the passage of time have reshaped their memories of growing up and into greater affluence?

Liz Heron
Recollections of a Working Class Family

We lived in the tenement block that ran its whole length, in a top-storey "room and kitchen" with no bathroom and an outside toilet shared with several other families and reached by an open staircase. At night I slept in the big kitchen on the brown leatherette bed settee, and my parents slept in the box room.

This is a time of austerity, of playing with ration books, of knowing we are "overcrowded," of squabbles between the women over doing the stairs and cleaning the toilet. . . .

At home there were often rows about spending money. But the year I was seven something gave. The world spread out for me in a new map of associations and sensations. We went to Paris to see one of my father's sisters. . . . This was my father's first visit to her since the war; what made it possible was the free travel concession he now had, working for British Railways as a painter and decorator. . . .

. . . On Sunday nights at home we listen to Dan Dare on Radio Luxemburg and that week's episode is replayed and embellished, with Ann and her brother, who also read it in the *Eagle.* Television at home came later; for now we watch it in the Italian café, where the price of a penny ice lolly opens the dusty chenille curtain and we can join the other children huddled in the darkness in front of the flickering screen in the corner. . . .

For a while television was a rare and special thing; not many people had it and they were well off. Then not having it rapidly became a sign of poverty. We got ours in 1956, and the filmed reports of the Hungarian uprising and of its refugees arriving in Britain gave me my first image of dramatic world events. This was of a different order from my imaginings about the Chinese communists, arch villains whose evil doings were retailed to us in the classroom with the same ferocious didacticism that accompanies the telling of a lurid fairy tale and enhances its horrifying fascination. The imaginary and timeless cruelties of the Chinese are relished as they frighten us, while the drama of the Hungarians is a disturbing intrusion of someone else's reality that, glimpsed on the television screen, is not entirely unlike our own: worried-looking men in square-shouldered, belted coats; forlorn children.

Television came in the wake of other consumer durables: a vacuum cleaner and a boiler for the washing . . . .

In school this progressive acquisition of domestic technology was taken for granted, and we felt sorry for those children who lagged behind. These were the children some of the teachers looked down on because they came to school with unmended holes in their jumpers, or no proper shoes, only canvas sandshoes to see them through the winter. They were clearly destined for the junior secondary, with no hope of passing the "qualie." Most of us, children of tradesmen, miners and semi-skilled factory workers, were better off than that and had higher hopes, though there was a good scattering of nits and lice and dirty feet around the classroom when the nurse came to do her inspection. We'd been filled with school milk and cod-liver oil and orange juice, but only the few scheme-housing children had bathrooms.

Liz Heron, ed., *Truth, Dare or Promise: Girls Growing Up in the Fifties* (London: Virago, 1985), 154, 160–63.

Ursula Huws
On Breaking into the Middle Class

Until the autumn of 1953, when I was six, we lived in a tiny Anglesey village [in Wales] in a house which became more and more overcrowded as the family expanded. By the time my younger brother was born, in 1950, we numbered five children, with a gap of eighteen years between the two boys. My sisters, six and nine years older than me, and referred to as "the girls," had to share a room with us two little ones, known as "the children." The whole village lacked electricity, gas and water mains. Our drinking water came from a well, and washing water from two large corrugated-iron tanks, erected by my father, which collected rainwater at the back of the house. The lavatory was . . . in a stone outhouse next to the goatshed at the top of the garden. Lighting came from tilley lamps which made a ferocious panting noise as they were pumped up, and, in our bedrooms, diminutive paraffin lamps known as "moons." My parents had lived there for fourteen years, and we were, or so it felt to me, an accepted part of the community, despite our oddities.

Where everyone was known to everyone else, and all, to some extent, shared the same material hardships; where nobody had a car, or a television or a washing machine, the differences which were most apparent were those of individual character and behaviour rather than class. . . . By the age of three I was happily integrated into the one-classroom village school, parroting alphabets and tables in Welsh and English and rewarded with approving smiles for my precocity. The carless lanes were a safe playground, giving on to other homes many of which were welcoming. . . .

I suppose we must have been poor during this period. My father could rarely afford to come home to visit us, and was desperately homesick. . . . It was a tragedy when two fountain pens he had sent as presents for my sisters did not arrive. There was no way he could afford to replace them. I can remember too how one sister saved her pocket money for months on end to buy Mother a *blanket*. But some of the things that now seem evidence of poverty may well have been common experiences of post-war shortages and rationing. Mother saving every piece of paper with a picture on it, from old Christmas cards to *Picture Post* covers, to make scrapbooks for us. Clothes cut down from cast-offs which arrived in parcels from America, or lined with a brilliant yellow nylon known as parachute silk. Old ration books for drawing in. . . .

In straightforward class terms, our position was, however, improving. We owned a large, if dilapidated house. My father's status as a lecturer earned him the nickname "professor," locally. We began to acquire material possessions. A car (but no television), a hoover (but no fridge). Presents became more lavish. By the end of the decade I was the proud owner of a transistor radio, an alarm clock (not yet the watch I coveted), a hula hoop, and even a few new clothes

---

Heron, *Truth, Dare or Promise*, 173–75, 180–81.

(my first pair of jeans was purchased, against fierce opposition, out of saved-up pocket money). It is difficult to be sure to what extent this was the result of our own rise in the world and how much a product of the general surge in consumerism. However, it certainly left me with the feeling that I was lucky. I was constantly being reminded by my eldest sister that "when I was your age we never had . . ." . . .

In 1959, it was my turn to become the beneficiary of my aunt's generosity, and I was despatched to a boarding school on the coast, full of the daughters of minor diplomats posted overseas and Lancashire businessmen too snobbish to send their eleven-plus failures to a secondary modern.[1] There, I was made aware yet again of how my family deviated from the bourgeois norm. My mother possessed neither a fur coat nor a pair of high-heeled shoes. Her hair was long and unpermed. My father drove a second-hand Morris Traveller instead of a Jaguar and, most unforgiveable of all, sometimes wore a beret. When the other girls described their holidays it could have been life on another continent for all the relation it bore to my experience. There were the television programmes I had never watched, and expensive sports like horseriding or sailing. There was also a somewhat self-conscious suburban middle-class teenage lifestyle which seemed based on shared expectations and common values — tennis parties, tickets to Adam Faith concerts, "dates" with boys in cinemas. Some of this aped American teenage culture, as embodied in the lyrics of songs by Connie Francis or the Everley Brothers and in films. What was astonishing about it, to me, was the extent to which it appeared to be connived at and encouraged by their parents who, unlike mine, seemed positively to want their daughters paired off as quickly as possible.

---

[1]The less selective track of the postwar British school system. Tests given at age eleven sent the more academically able to "grammar schools," while others went to "secondary moderns."

5.4

Nixon and Khrushchev Spar over Satisfying the Consumer

That the personal can be public and political is amply demonstrated by this exchange between Vice President Richard M. Nixon and Premier Nikita S. Khrushchev. Nixon was in Moscow for the American National Exhibit in 1959 when this "Kitchen Debate" took place. While touring the exhibit, Khruschchev and Nixon plunged into a discussion over which country was superior. What makes this Cold War debate so interesting is that the standard of comparison was not nuclear weapons, political influence, or territorial control but technological innovation and provision of the good life for their citizens.

The public nature of this debate — playing out before reporters and workers at the exhibit and instantly retailed in the press in the United States — makes this an especially interesting document. How much are the two leaders in agreement about the nature of consumerism as well as gender roles and the Cold War? How much can we take the views publicly expressed here as genuinely theirs?

The "Kitchen Debate"
Moscow, July 24, 1959

Khrushchev: ". . . How long has America existed? Three hundred years?"

Nixon: "One hundred and fifty years."

Khrushchev: "One hundred and fifty years? Well, then, we will say America has been in existence for 150 years and this is the level she has reached. We have existed not quite forty-two years and in another seven years we will be on the same level as America.

"When we catch you up, in passing you by, we will wave to you. Then if you wish we can stop and say: Please follow up. Plainly speaking, if you want capitalism you can live that way. That is your own affair and doesn't concern us. We can still feel sorry for you but since you don't understand us — live as you do understand. . . .

. . . [Wrapping his arms about a Soviet workman] "Does this man look like a slave laborer? [Waving at others] With men with such spirit how can we lose?"

Nixon (pointing to American workmen): "With men like that we are strong. But these men, Soviet and American, work together well for peace, even as they have worked together in building this exhibition. This is the way it should be.

"[T]his color television is one of the most advanced developments in communication that we have.

"I can only say that if this competition in which you plan to outstrip us is to do the best for both of our peoples and for peoples everywhere, there must be a free exchange of ideas. After all, you don't know every-thing —"

Khrushchev: "If I don't know everything, you don't know anything about communism except fear of it."

Nixon: "There are some instances where you may be ahead of us, for ex-ample in the development of the thrust of your rockets for the investiga-tion of outer space; there may be some instances in which we are ahead of you — in color television, for instance."

Khrushchev: "No, we are up with you on this, too. We have bested you in one technique and also in the other." . . .

Nixon: "Wait till you see the picture. Let's have far more communication and exchange in this very area that we speak of. We should hear you more on our television. You should hear us more on yours."

Khrushchev: "That's a good idea. Let's do it like this. You appear before our people. We will appear before your people. People will see and appreciate this." . . .

Based on "The Two Worlds: a Day-Long Debate," an edited transcript in the *New York Times*, July 25, 1959, pp. 1, 3. Online at <http://www.cnn.com/SPECIALS/cold.war/episodes/14/documents/debate/> (January 4, 2003). Audio versions of the debate available at <http://www.webcorp.com/sounds/nixondebates.htm> and at <http://odin.himinbi.org/speeches/>.

Nixon (halting Khrushchev at model kitchen in model house): "You had a very nice house in your exhibition in New York. My wife and I saw and enjoyed it very much. I want to show you this kitchen. It is like those of our houses in California."

Khrushchev (after Nixon called attention to a built-in panel-controlled washing machine): "We have such things."

Nixon: "This is the newest model. This is the kind which is built in thousands of units for direct installation in the houses."

He added that Americans were interested in making life easier for their women. Mr. Khrushchev remarked that in the Soviet Union they did not have "the capitalist attitude toward women."

Nixon: "I think that this attitude toward women is universal. What we want to do is make easier the life of our housewives."

He explained that the house could be built for $14,000 and that most veterans had bought houses for between $10,000 and $15,000.

Nixon: "Let me give you an example you can appreciate. Our steel workers, as you know, are on strike. But any steel worker could buy this house. They earn $3 an hour. This house costs about $100 a month to buy on a contract running twenty-five to thirty years."

Khrushchev: "We have steel workers and we have peasants who also can afford to spend $14,000 for a house." He said American houses were built to last only twenty years, so builders could sell new houses at the end of that period. "We build firmly. We build for our children and grandchildren."

Mr. Nixon said he thought American houses would last more than twenty years, but even so, after twenty years many Americans want a new home or a new kitchen, which would be obsolete then. The American system is designed to take advantage of new inventions and new techniques, he said. . . .

Khrushchev: "Don't you have a machine that puts food into the mouth and pushes it down? Many things you've shown us are interesting but they are not needed in life. They have no useful purpose. They are merely gadgets. . . ."

Khrushchev (manifesting a lack of interest in a data-processing machine that answers questions about the United States): "I have heard of your engineers. I am well aware of what they can do. You know for launching our missiles we need lots of calculating machines."

Nixon (hearing jazz music): "I don't like jazz music."

Khrushchev: "I don't like it either."

Nixon: "But my girls like it." . . .

Khrushchev: "The Americans have created their own image of the Soviet man and think he is as you want him to be. But he is not as you think. You think the Russian people will be dumbfounded to see these things, but the fact is that newly built Russian houses have all this equipment right now. Moreover, all you have to do to get a house is to be born in the Soviet Union. You are entitled to housing. I was born in the Soviet Union.

So I have a right to a house. In America, if you don't have a dollar — you have the right to choose between sleeping in a house or on the pavement. Yet you say that we are slaves of communism." . . .

Nixon: ". . . To us, diversity, the right to choose, the fact that we have 1,000 builders building 1,000 different houses, is the most important thing. We don't have one decision made at the top by one government official. This is the difference."

Khrushchev: "On political problems we will never agree with you. For instance, Mikoyan[1] likes very peppery soup. I do not. But this does not mean that we do not get along."

Nixon: "You can learn from us and we can learn from you. There must be a free exchange. Let the people choose the kind of house, the kind of soup, the kind of ideas they want."

Mr. Khrushchev shifted the talk back to washing machines.

Nixon: "We have many different manufacturers and many different kinds of washing machines so that the housewives have a choice."

Khrushchev (noting Nixon gazing admiringly at young women modeling bathing suits and sports clothes): "You are for the girls too."

Nixon (indicating a floor sweeper that works by itself and other appliances): "[Y]ou don't need a wife."

Khrushchev chuckled.

Nixon: "We do not claim to astonish the Russian people. We hope to show our diversity and our right to choose. We do not wish to have decisions made at the top by government officials who say that all homes should be built in the same way. Would it not be better to compete in the relative merits of washing machines than in the strength of rockets[?] Is this the kind of competition you want?"

Khrushchev: "Yes that's the kind of competition we want. But your generals say: 'Let's compete in rockets. We are strong and we can beat you.' But in this respect we can also show you something."

Nixon: "To me you are strong and we are strong. In some ways, you are stronger than we are. In others, we are stronger. We are both strong not only from the standpoint of weapons but from the standpoint of will and spirit. Neither should use that strength to put the other in a position where he in effect has an ultimatum. In this day and age that misses the point. With modern weapons it does not make any difference if war comes. We both have had it."

---

[1]A leading figure in the Communist Party who continued in political service into the 1970s.

ECONOMIC CULTURE AND THE GOOD SOCIETY

Economics may be denigrated as the "dismal science," but in reality it raises issues of value and is tightly tied to something that might be called "economic culture." How we make our living shapes our outlook, and conversely our general outlook (especially the ideas that we prize) shapes the economy and informs the principles it runs by — or at least that we want it to run by. Does growth at any cost get priority? Should the economy promote social stability? Should all share more or less equally in the fruits of production and prosperity in the interest of group solidarity? The answers to these questions help create the ground rules for economies of individual countries as well as the international economy. Precisely because there is no settled answer to these questions within any one country or around the world, there will always be debate over the "proper" economic principles (as we have already seen in the chapter 2 debate among Hayek, Polanyi, and Keynes).

The material in this section highlights the degree to which western Europeans and Japanese pursued economic development in a way consistent with their values and experiences. The outcome was, not surprisingly, economies and societies that did not operate like each other or like those of the United States and that did not follow rigorously free-market rules. The European path was toward the integration of once proud, rival nations and the elaboration of long-established principles of social welfare. The emergent Japanese model was marked by a strong preoccupation with national and group welfare and a suspicion of the impatient individualism that was most often associated with the United States.

5.5
Robert Schuman Endorses European Cooperation

By the early 1950s the European impulse toward cooperation was gaining headway. The Marshall Plan (Document 2.9) had put a premium on regional economic cooperation, an idea already on the minds of forward-looking Europeans. The next benchmark toward a stable, prosperous, integrated new Europe was a declaration issued by French Foreign Minister Robert Schuman in mid-1950. The real author of the declaration was Jean Monnet (1888–1979), an influential figure in French finance and economic planning, now widely recognized as the father of European integration. In the immediate aftermath of World War II, he was put in charge of plans to revive and modernize his country's economy. His conviction that cooperation with Germany was in French economic and European security interests led him to draft the Schuman statement. The quickly realized product of this declaration was the European Coal and Steel Community, which proved in turn the practical working basis for the European Community and ultimately the European Union. Appropriately, when the European Coal and Steel Community started up in 1952, Monnet was at the head.

What are the major justifications offered here for greater cooperation? How important are political calculations, historical memory of war, and economic objectives in shaping the vision of a new Europe?

Declaration Presented at a Press Conference
May 9, 1950

Europe will not be made all at once, or according to a single plan. It will be built through concrete achievements which first create a de facto solidarity. The coming together of the nations of Europe requires the elimination of the age-old opposition of France and Germany. Any action taken must in the first place concern these two countries.

With this aim in view, the French Government proposes that action be taken immediately on one limited but decisive point:

The French Government proposes placing Franco-German production of coal and steel as a whole under a common High Authority, within the framework of an organization open to the participation of the other countries of Europe.

The pooling of coal and steel production should immediately provide for the setting up of common foundations for economic development as a first step in the federation of Europe, and will change the destinies of those regions which have long been devoted to the manufacture of munitions of war, of which they have been the most constant victims.

The solidarity in production thus established will make it plain that any war between France and Germany becomes not merely unthinkable, but materially impossible. The setting up of this powerful productive unit, open to all countries willing to take part and bound ultimately to provide all the member countries with the basic elements of industrial production on the same terms, will lay a true foundation for their economic unification. . . .

To promote the realization of the objectives defined, the French Government is ready to open negotiations on the following bases:

The task with which this common High Authority will be charged will be that of securing in the shortest possible time the modernization of production and the improvement of its quality; the supply of coal and steel on identical terms to the French and German markets, as well as to the markets of other member countries; the development in common of exports to other countries; the equalization and improvement of the living conditions of workers in these industries.

. . . The movement of coal and steel between member countries will immediately be freed from all customs duty. . . . Conditions will gradually be created which will spontaneously provide for the more national distribution of production at the highest level of productivity.

From the website of the European Union: <http://europa.eu.int/abc/symbols/9-may/decl_en.htm> (January 1, 2003), here modified on the basis of the original text available at <http://www.diplomatie.gouv.fr/archives/dossiers/schuman/pages/331a.html–331d.html> (June 28, 2003). A variant translation from *Le Monde,* May 11, 1950, can be found in David de Giustino, *Reader in European Integration* (London: Longman, 1996), 58–60.

In contrast to international cartels, which tend to impose restrictive practices on distribution and the exploitation of national markets, and to maintain high profits, the organization will ensure the fusion of markets and the expansion of production.

5.6
Pope John XXIII on a Socially Just Capitalism

Pope John XXIII was born Giuseppe Roncalli in 1881 in Italy. He served in the Vatican bureaucracy from the mid-1920s on. During his tenure as pope — from his election in 1958 to his death in 1963 — he proved a champion of interfaith dialogue, church reform, social justice, and world peace. These commitments together with his personal warmth made him an extremely popular figure. This papal encyclical (or formal statement on the faith from the pope to his bishops), issued in 1961, carries forward a line of critical Church commentary on capitalism from another encyclical, "Rerum Novarum," issued by Pope Leo XIII in 1891. That earlier encyclical indicted a materialistic, market-driven industrial system that allowed the strong to dominate and exploit the weak, that created class tensions and radicalized politics, and that disrupted family life and denied spiritual values.

This document is a powerful articulation of "welfare capitalism." What themes does John XXIII sound in this document? How would non-Catholics in Europe — for example, socialists and communists — have responded to this papal appeal? How antagonistic is it toward the rules of the free market? How does it fit with the approaches championed by Keynes, Hayek, and Polanyi (in chapter 2) and Khrushchev and Nixon (just above)?

"Mater et Magistra" ("Mother and Teacher")
May 15, 1961

[T]hough the Church's first care must be for souls . . . , she concerns herself too with the exigencies of man's daily life, with his livelihood and education, and his general, temporal welfare and prosperity. . . .

[The Church's basic economic and social principles] concern first of all the question of work, which must be regarded not merely as a commodity, but as a specifically human activity. In the majority of cases a man's work is his sole means of livelihood. Its remuneration, therefore, cannot be made to depend on the state of the market. It must be determined by the laws of justice and equity. . . .

Secondly, private ownership of property, including that of productive goods, is a natural right which the State cannot suppress. But it naturally entails a social obligation as well. It is a right which must be exercised not only for one's own personal benefit but also for the benefit of others.

This encyclical can be found in the archives for the Vatican website: <http://www.vatican.va/holy_father/john_xxiii/encyclicals/documents/hf_j-xxiii_enc_15051961_mater_en.html> (April 12, 2003).

As for the State, its whole raison d'être is the realization of the common good in the temporal order. It cannot, therefore, hold aloof from economic matters. On the contrary, it must do all in its power to promote the production of a sufficient supply of material goods .... It has also the duty to protect the rights of all its people, and particularly of its weaker members, the workers, women and children. It can never be right for the State to shirk its obligation of working actively for the betterment of the condition of the workingman.

It is furthermore the duty of the State to ensure that terms of employment are regulated in accordance with justice and equity, and to safeguard the human dignity of workers by making sure that they are not required to work in an environment which may prove harmful to their material and spiritual interests. . . .

[The Church has] defended the worker's natural right to enter into association with his fellows. Such associations may consist either of workers alone or of workers and employers, and should be structured in a way best calculated to safeguard the workers' legitimate professional interest. And it is the natural right of the workers to work without hindrance, freely, and on their own initiative within these associations for the achievement of these ends.

Finally, both workers and employers should regulate their mutual relations in accordance with the principle of human solidarity and Christian brotherhood. Unrestricted competition in the liberal sense, and the Marxist creed of class warfare, are clearly contrary to Christian teaching and the nature of man. . . .

[CONTEMPORARY CONDITIONS
IN DEVELOPED COUNTRIES]

The present advance in scientific knowledge and productive technology clearly puts it within the power of the public authority to a much greater degree than ever before to reduce imbalances which may exist between different branches of the economy or between different regions within the same country or even between the different peoples of the world. It also puts into the hands of public authority a greater means for limiting fluctuations in the economy and for providing effective measures to prevent the recurrence of mass unemployment. . . .

But however extensive and far-reaching the influence of the State on the economy may be, it must never be exerted to the extent of depriving the individual citizen of his freedom of action. It must rather augment his freedom while effectively guaranteeing the protection of his essential personal rights. Among these is a man's right and duty to be primarily responsible for his own upkeep and that of his family. . . .

Moreover, as history itself testifies with ever-increasing clarity, there can be no such thing as a well-ordered and prosperous society unless individual citizens and the State co-operate in the economy. Both sides must work together in harmony, and their respective efforts must be proportioned to the needs of the common good in the prevailing circumstances and conditions of human life. . . .

We are filled with an overwhelming sadness when We contemplate the sorry spectacle of millions of workers in many lands and entire continents condemned through the inadequacy of their wages to live with their families in utterly sub-human conditions. This is probably due to the fact that the process of industrialization in these countries is only in its initial stages, or is still not sufficiently developed.

Nevertheless, in some of these lands the enormous wealth, the unbridled luxury, of the privileged few stands in violent, offensive contrast to the utter poverty of the vast majority. In some parts of the world men are being subjected to inhuman privations so that the output of the national economy can be increased at a rate of acceleration beyond what would be possible if regard were had to social justice and equity. And in other countries a notable percentage of income is absorbed in building up an ill-conceived national prestige, and vast sums are spent on armaments.

In economically developed countries, relatively unimportant services, and services of doubtful value, frequently carry a disproportionately high rate of remuneration, while the diligent and profitable work of whole classes of honest, hard-working men gets scant reward. Their rate of pay is quite inadequate to meet the basic needs of life. It in no way corresponds to the contribution they make to the good of the community, to the profits of the company for which they work, and to the general national economy.

We therefore consider it Our duty to reaffirm that the remuneration of work is not something that can be left to the laws of the marketplace; nor should it be a decision left to the will of the more powerful. It must be determined in accordance with justice and equity; which means that workers must be paid a wage which allows them to live a truly human life and to fulfill their family obligations in a worthy manner. . . .

. . . [T]he economic prosperity of a nation is not so much its total assets in terms of wealth and property, as the equitable division and distribution of this wealth. . . .

But a further point needs emphasizing: Any adjustment between wages and profits must take into account the demands of the common good of the particular country and of the whole human family.

What are these demands? On the national level they include: employment of the greatest possible number of workers; care lest privileged classes arise, even among the workers; maintenance of equilibrium between wages and prices; the need to make goods and services accessible to the greatest number; elimination, or at least the restriction, of inequalities in the various branches of the economy — that is, between agriculture, industry and services; creation of a proper balance between economic expansion and the development of social services, especially through the activity of public authorities; the best possible adjustment of the means of production to the progress of science and technology; seeing to it that the benefits which make possible a more human way of life will be available not merely to the present generation but to the coming generations as well. . . .

State and public ownership of property is very much on the increase today. This is explained by the exigencies of the common good, which demand that public authority broaden its sphere of activity. . . . The State and other agencies of public law must not extend their ownership beyond what is clearly required by considerations of the common good properly understood, and even then there must be safeguards. Otherwise private ownership could be reduced beyond measure, or, even worse, completely destroyed.

It is important, too, not to overlook the fact that the economic enterprises of the State and other agencies of public law must be entrusted to men of good reputation who have the necessary experience and ability and a keen sense of responsibility towards their country. Furthermore, a strict check should constantly be kept upon their activity, so as to avoid any possibility of the concentration of undue economic power in the hands of a few State officials, to the detriment of the best interests of the community. . . .

[Relations between Rich and Poor Countries]

The solidarity which binds all men together as members of a common family makes it impossible for wealthy nations to look with indifference upon the hunger, misery and poverty of other nations whose citizens are unable to enjoy even elementary human rights. The nations of the world are becoming more and more dependent on one another and it will not be possible to preserve a lasting peace so long as glaring economic and social imbalances persist. . . .

Justice and humanity demand that those countries which produce consumer goods, especially farm products, in excess of their own needs should come to the assistance of those other countries where large sections of the population are suffering from want and hunger. It is nothing less than an outrage to justice and humanity to destroy or to squander goods that other people need for their very lives. . . .

Of itself, however, emergency aid will not go far in relieving want and famine when these are caused — as they so often are — by the primitive state of a nation's economy. The only permanent remedy for this is to make use of every possible means of providing these citizens with the scientific, technical and professional training they need, and to put at their disposal the necessary capital for speeding up their economic development with the help of modern methods. . . .

In helping these nations . . . , the more advanced communities must recognize and respect this individuality. They must beware of making the assistance they give an excuse for forcing these people into their own national mold.

There is also a further temptation which the economically developed nations must resist: that of giving technical and financial aid with a view to gaining control over the political situation in the poorer countries, and furthering their own plans for world domination.

Let us be quite clear on this point. A nation that acted from these motives would in fact be introducing a new form of colonialism — cleverly disguised, no doubt, but actually reflecting that older, outdated type from which many nations have recently emerged. Such action would, moreover, have [a] harmful impact on international relations, and constitute a menace to world peace. . . .

Scientific and technical progress, economic development and the betterment of living conditions, are certainly valuable elements in a civilization. But we must realize that they are essentially instrumental in character. They are not supreme values in themselves.

It pains Us, therefore, to observe the complete indifference to the true hierarchy of values shown by so many people in the economically developed countries. Spiritual values are ignored, forgotten or denied, while the progress of science, technology and economics is pursued for its own sake, as though material well-being were the be-all and end-all of life. This attitude is contagious, especially when it infects the work that is being done for the less developed countries, which have often preserved in their ancient traditions an acute and vital awareness of the more important human values, on which the moral order rests.

5.7

Morita Akio on the Collectivist Principles Guiding Sony

Morita Akio, long-time chairman of Sony Corporation, was born in 1921 into a business-oriented, Westernizing family just outside Nagoya, Japan. His interest in science led him to participate in the founding of Sony immediately after World War II. During the Morita years, Sony pioneered a long string of innovative and highly profitable consumer products such as the transistor radio, the Walkman, and the 3.5-inch computer floppy disk and emerged as one of the leading producers of consumer electronic goods and entertainment in the international economy.

Morita's memoir, *Made in Japan,* defines not only the approach of this successful corporation but also the impulse within a resurgent Japanese economy more generally toward cooperation among businesses and between business and government and business and labor. What specific principles guide Japanese corporate life (to judge from Morita's observations)? What distinctions does he see between Japanese and U.S. styles of doing business? What does Morita bring that is new to this economic debate over the role of the state that we first examined in chapter 2? (See Documents 2.5–2.7.)

From *Made in Japan*
1986

[The Firm as Family]

I have always made it a point to know our employees, to visit every facility of our company, and to try to meet and know every single employee. This became more and more difficult as we grew, and it is impossible to really know the more than forty thousand people who work for us today, but I try. I encourage all of our managers to know everybody and not to sit behind a

Akio Morita with Edwin M. Reingold and Mitsuko Shimomura, *Made in Japan: Akio Morita and Sony* (New York: E. P. Dutton, 1986), 148–49, 153–54, 178, 180–81, 199–201.

desk in the office all day. I enjoy showing up at a factory or a branch office and chatting with people when I can. Not long ago I found myself in downtown Tokyo with a few extra minutes in my schedule, and I noticed a small office of Sony Travel Service. I had never been there, and so I just walked in and introduced myself. "I came here to show my face," I said. "I am sure you know me by seeing me on TV or in the newspaper, so I thought you might be interested in seeing Morita in the flesh." Everybody laughed, and I went around the office chatting with the staff, and in those few minutes we all felt good about our sense of shared effort. On a visit to a small Sony lab near Palo Alto one day, our manager, an American, asked me if I would pose for some pictures and I said I would be happy to. Before the hour was over, I had posed with all thirty or forty employees and I said to the manager, "I appreciate your attitude. You understand the Sony family policy."

On the twenty-fifth anniversary of Sony America, Yoshiko [Morita's wife] and I flew to the U.S. where we had a picnic or a meal with all the employees. We arranged it so that we could have a picnic with our New York staff and could sit down to a meal with the three shifts at our Dothan, Alabama, tape plant and also at our San Diego factory. We dined and danced with employees in Chicago and Los Angeles. It was a very satisfying thing for me, and I think they were pleased to see me and my wife. It was not just part of my job; I like those people. They are family.

A company will get nowhere if all of the thinking is left to management. Everybody in the company must contribute, and for the lower-level employees their contribution must be more than just manual labor. We insist that all of our employees contribute their minds. Today we get an average of eight suggestions a year from each of our employees, and most of the suggestions have to do with making their own jobs easier or their work more reliable or a process more efficient. Some people in the West scoff at the suggestion process, saying that it forces people to repeat the obvious, or that it indicates a lack of leadership by management. This attitude shows a lack of understanding. We don't force suggestions, and we take them seriously and implement the best ones. And since the majority of them are directly concerned with a person's work, we find them relevant and useful. After all, who could tell us better how to structure the work than the people who are doing it? . . .

Not all businessmen were exploiters during the bad old days, but there is a difference between old-fashioned paternalism and the shared-fate and egalitarian system that exists today. I cannot understand why there is anything good in laying off people. If management takes the risk and responsibility of hiring personnel, then it is management's ongoing responsibility to keep them employed. The employee does not have the prime responsibility in this decision, so when a recession comes, why should the employee have to suffer for the management decision to hire him? Therefore, in times of boom we are very careful about increasing our personnel. Once we have hired people, we try to make them understand our concept of a fate-sharing body and how if a recession comes the company is willing to sacrifice profit to keep them in the company. Their wage increases or bonuses might also have to be sacrificed, because we all must share this difficulty. They know that management does not lavish bonuses on itself — only workers get bonuses under our system — and . . . there are no "golden parachutes" for managers except a simple lifetime parachute of guaranteed employment and a life of constructive work. And when a company is in trouble, it is the top managers who take salary cuts before the lower-level employees. . . .

[GOVERNMENT-BUSINESS COOPERATION]

Many Americans seem proud of the adversarial relationship between government and business, as though their aims are naturally antagonistic. In Japan we do not see it that way. To put it bluntly, whether we like it or not, the government is a partner in our business without owning a single share of Sony stock or running any risk. And the American government is a partner of American business, too, in the same way. The Japanese government takes away more than 50 percent of our profits, and that in a sense makes it a majority partner. So from our government's viewpoint, it wants its partner to work hard and make a profit. By doing so, business is able to keep people employed, enabling the company and its employees to pay taxes rather than to go on the public dole. This is done with a long-range viewpoint. So while we often have our disagreements with the government and its bureaucracy, which actually runs the government, and while I often criticize specific government programs or policies, I know the relationship is basically supportive.

[TAKING THE LONG VIEW]

The American system of management, in my opinion, also relies too much on outsiders to help make business decisions, and this is because of the insecurity that American decision makers feel in their job, as compared with most top Japanese corporate executives. The legal requirement for disclosure puts the manager's performance on show every quarter and the main evaluation of an executive too often is done in this shortsighted way. . . .

[WORKER-MANAGEMENT RELATIONS]

After the war, both the labor law reforms and the destruction of the family-controlled holding companies were major contributors to Japan's reconstruction. We also devised a union system in which the company family became the labor unit rather than the impersonal industry-wide kind of unions that finally developed in the United States. Of course, the Japanese company unions belong to associations of unions that set goals and generally attempt to coordinate the concerns and demands of the member unions. But we have labor peace in Japan mainly because management does not use labor as a tool and tries to be aware of the concerns of labor. Some companies are, of course, better at this than others.

In Paris not too long ago, someone said rather innocently to me that Japan is a capitalistic country. I said that it would appear so, but that actually, it would be more accurate to say Japan has a socialistic and egalitarian free

economic system. When the laws were changed after the war, it appeared to
many Americans as well as Japanese that the swing to the left could be dangerous. The labor laws that made it virtually impossible to fire people seemed
a terrible intrusion into the traditional discretionary powers of management,
especially to the older managers. But they were forced to accept these laws
and they turned them to everyone's advantage. Japanese managers thought
that if everybody could have a familial attitude — and after all, Japanese tend
to feel that way almost instinctively about their "Japanese-ness" — perhaps it
would be easier to pull Japan out of the hole in which it found itself. That was
the spirit that created what an American first called "Japan Inc."

Generally, in the United States, management's attitude toward the labor
force and even the lower-level executives is very hierarchical, much more so
than in Japan, an Oriental country where Westerners always expect to see
such hierarchies. When I visited the Illinois television assembly plant of
Motorola, one of the first things I noticed was that the offices were air-
conditioned, but out on the shop floor it was stifling, people were dripping
with sweat, and big noisy fans were blowing the hot air around. The workers
were plainly uncomfortable, and I thought, "How can you get quality work
from people laboring under such conditions? And what kind of loyalty can
they be expected to show to the big bosses in their cool offices!" In Japan
people often used to say that the shop floor where the goods were made was
always more comfortable than the workers' homes. . . .

[On the Nature of Business Leadership]

The group management system of Japan, where decisions often are made
based on proposals from younger management, can be an advantage for a
company. Young managers can be expected to remain with the same company for twenty or thirty years, and in ten years or so they will move into top
management jobs. Because of this the young managers are always looking
ahead to what they want the company to be when they take it over. If top
management looks down at middle and lower management and is always pressing them to show profits this year or next, as is common in the West, and fires
these managers for not producing profits, it is killing the company. If a middle
manager says his plan or program may not break even now, but will make big
profits ten years from now, nobody will listen to him, and he may even be
fired.

Our encouragement of long-range plans from up-and-coming employees
is a big advantage for our system, despite all the meetings and the time spent
in discussing and formulating plans. It enables us to create and maintain something that is rare in business in the West: a company philosophy. Since our
employees stay with us a long time, they can maintain a consistent outlook.
Company ideals do not change. When I leave the company, the Sony philosophy will continue to exist. In the United States it is rare for a company to
have its own philosophy, because whenever top management changes, the
new person imposes his own very strong views. In fact very often boards of
directors will go far out of the field of business of their company to bring in
a new top officer to "clean house" and change everything in the company.

Recently, one of these outsiders came into an American company, closed down several factories, laid off thousands of employees — and was hailed by other executives in articles in *The Wall Street Journal* as a great manager. In Japan such a performance would be considered a disgrace. Closing factories and firing employees and changing corporate direction in a business slump may be the expedient and convenient thing to do and may make the balance sheet look better at the end of the next quarter, but it destroys the company spirit. And when the business rebounds, where will the company go to get experienced workers who will produce quality goods and work hard and loyally for the company?

I think one of the main advantages of the Japanese system of management over the American or the Western system in general is this sense of corporate philosophy. Even if a new executive takes over he cannot change that. In Japan the long-range planning system and the junior management proposal system guarantee that the relationship between top management and junior management remains very close and that over the years they can formulate a specific program of action that will maintain the philosophy of the company. It also may explain why in the initial stages progress is very slow in a Japanese company. But once the company communicates its philosophy to all employees, the company has great strength and flexibility.

THE RISE OF AN ENVIRONMENTAL MOVEMENT

Postwar abundance spelled deepening trouble for the environment. The rise in living standards in the United States, western and eastern Europe, the Soviet Union, and Japan created industrial and consumer waste that fouled rivers, soil, and the atmosphere, while heedless use of chemicals and frequent nuclear testing became a threat to all forms of life. The first reaction against these worrisome trends appeared in the late 1950s, and gained impetus and energy through the 1960s.

Foes of environmental restrictions quickly rallied. They included devotees of the free market, industry unwilling to pay the costs of pollution, and a developing world that valued growth over conservation. By the early 1970s the battle lines had been drawn that would continue to define the environmental debate both nationally and internationally up to the present.

5.8

Rachel Carson Heralds a New Environmental Consciousness

Few books have had such a galvanizing impact as *Silent Spring*, and no champion of a cause has used the written word to better effect than its author, Rachel Carson. She brought to this indictment of the heedless use of chemicals a rare combination of gifts. She was a trained scientist, a best-selling author, and a knowledgeable social critic of industry, the government, and consumers and their pursuit of profit and convenience regardless of its consequences. While the problem was broad,

Carson took aim at a specific but telling part of it — the deleterious effects of DDT (dichlorodiphenyltrichloroethane), an insecticide that came into use during World War II and gained popularity after the war on farms and in suburbia as an easy way to control pests such as fire ants and mosquitos.

What are the main elements in the indictment that Carson develops here? What are the sources of the chief threats facing nature and humans? What kinds of solutions to the problem does she advance, and how radical are they? How much do the concerns that she raised in 1962 apply to conditions today? Beyond substance, consider Carson's prose style. What devices does Carson use to make her case so compelling?

From *Silent Spring*
1962

The history of life on earth has been a history of interaction between living things and their surroundings. To a large extent, the physical form and the habits of the earth's vegetation and its animal life have been molded by the environment. Considering the whole span of earthly time, the opposite effect, in which life actually modifies its surroundings, has been relatively slight. Only within the moment of time represented by the present century has one species — man — acquired significant power to alter the nature of his world.

During the past quarter century this power has not only increased to one of disturbing magnitude but it has changed in character. The most alarming of all man's assaults upon the environment is the contamination of air, earth, rivers, and sea with dangerous and even lethal materials. This pollution is for the most part irrecoverable; the chain of evil it initiates not only in the world that must support life but in living tissues is for the most part irreversible. In this now universal contamination of the environment, chemicals are the sinister and little-recognized partners of radiation in changing the very nature of the world — the very nature of its life. . . . [C]hemicals sprayed on croplands or forests or gardens lie long in soil, entering into living organisms, passing from one to another in a chain of poisoning and death. Or they pass mysteriously by underground streams until they emerge and, through the alchemy of air and sunlight, combine into new forms that kill vegetation, sicken cattle, and work unknown harm on those who drink from once pure wells. . . .

To adjust to these chemicals would require time on the scale that is nature's; it would require not merely the years of a man's life but the life of generations. And even this, were it by some miracle possible, would be futile, for the new chemicals come from our laboratories in an endless stream; almost five hundred annually find their way into actual use in the United States alone. The figure is staggering and its implications are not easily grasped — 500 new chemicals to which the bodies of men and animals are required some-

Rachel Carson, *Silent Spring* (Boston: Houghton Mifflin, 1962), 5–8, 12–13, 99–100, 278, 296–97.

how to adapt each year, chemicals totally outside the limits of biologic experience.

Among them are many that are used in man's war against nature. Since the mid-1940's over 200 basic chemicals have been created for use in killing insects, weeds, rodents, and other organisms described in the modern vernacular as "pests"; and they are sold under several thousand different brand names.

These sprays, dusts, and aerosols are now applied almost universally to farms, gardens, forests, and homes — nonselective chemicals that have the power to kill every insect, the "good" and the "bad," to still the song of birds and the leaping of fish in the streams, to coat the leaves with a deadly film, and to linger on in soil — all this though the intended target may be only a few weeds or insects. Can anyone believe it is possible to lay down such a barrage of poisons on the surface of the earth without making it unfit for all life? They should not be called "insecticides," but "biocides."

The whole process of spraying seems caught up in an endless spiral. Since DDT was released for civilian use, a process of escalation has been going on in which ever more toxic materials must be found. This has happened because insects, in a triumphant vindication of Darwin's principle of the survival of the fittest, have evolved super races immune to the particular insecticide used, hence a deadlier one has always to be developed — and then a deadlier one than that. . . . Thus the chemical war is never won, and all life is caught in its violent crossfire.

Along with the possibility of the extinction of mankind by nuclear war, the central problem of our age has therefore become the contamination of man's total environment with such substances of incredible potential for harm — substances that accumulate in the tissues of plants and animals and even penetrate the germ cells to shatter or alter the very material of heredity upon which the shape of the future depends. . . .

It is not my contention that chemical insecticides must never be used. I do contend that we have put poisonous and biologically potent chemicals indiscriminately into the hands of persons largely or wholly ignorant of their potentials for harm. We have subjected enormous numbers of people to contact with these poisons, without their consent and often without their knowledge. If the Bill of Rights contains no guarantee that citizen shall be secure against lethal poisons distributed either by private individuals or by public officials, it is surely only because our forefathers, despite their considerable wisdom and foresight, could conceive of no such problem. . . .

. . . Future generations are unlikely to condone our lack of prudent concern for the integrity of the natural world that supports all life.

There is still very limited awareness of the nature of the threat. This is an era of specialists, each of whom sees his own problem and is unaware of or intolerant of the larger frame into which it fits. It is also an era dominated by industry, in which the right to make a dollar at whatever cost is seldom challenged. When the public protests, confronted with some obvious evidence of damaging results of pesticide applications, it is fed little tranquilizing pills of half truth. We urgently need an end to these false assurances, to the sugar coating of unpalatable facts. It is the public that is being asked to assume the risks that the insect controllers calculate. The public must decide whether it wishes to continue on the present road, and it can do so only when in full possession of the facts. . . .

. . . The question is whether any civilization can wage relentless war on life without destroying itself, and without losing the right to be called civilized.

These insecticides are not selective poisons; they do not single out one species of which we desire to be rid. Each of them is used for the simple reason that it is a deadly poison. It therefore poisons all life with which it comes in contact: the cat beloved of some family, the farmer's cattle, the rabbit in the field, and the horned lark out of the sky. These creatures are innocent of any harm to man. Indeed, by their very existence they and their fellows make his life more pleasant. Yet he rewards them with a death that is not only sudden but horrible. Scientific observers . . . described the symptoms of a meadowlark found near death: "Although it lacked muscular coordination and could not fly or stand, it continued to beat its wings and clutch with its toes while lying on its side. Its beak was held open and breathing was labored." Even more pitiful was the mute testimony of the dead ground squirrels, which "exhibited a characteristic attitude in death. The back was bowed, and the forelegs with the toes of the feet tightly clenched were drawn close to the thorax . . . The head and neck were outstretched and the mouth often contained dirt, suggesting that the dying animal had been biting at the ground."

By acquiescing in an act that can cause such suffering to a living creature, who among us is not diminished as a human being? . . .

A truly extraordinary variety of alternatives to the chemical control of insects is available. Some are already in use and have achieved brilliant success. Others are in the stage of laboratory testing. Still others are little more than ideas in the minds of imaginative scientists, waiting for the opportunity to put them to the test. All have this in common: they are *biological* solutions, based on understanding of the living organisms they seek to control, and of the whole fabric of life to which these organisms belong. . . .

Through all these new, imaginative, and creative approaches to the problem of sharing our earth with other creatures there runs a constant theme, the awareness that we are dealing with life — with living populations and all their pressures and counter-pressures, their surges and recessions. Only by taking account of such life forces and by cautiously seeking to guide them into channels favorable to ourselves can we hope to achieve a reasonable accommodation between the insect hordes and ourselves.

The current vogue for poisons has failed utterly to take into account these most fundamental considerations. As crude a weapon as the cave man's club, the chemical barrage has been hurled against the fabric of life — a fabric on the one hand delicate and destructible, on the other miraculously tough and resilient, and capable of striking back in unexpected ways. These extraordinary capacities of life have been ignored by the practitioners of chemical control who have brought to their task no "high-minded orientation," no humility before the vast forces with which they tamper.

The "control of nature" is a phrase conceived in arrogance, born of the Neanderthal age of biology and philosophy, when it was supposed that nature exists for the convenience of man. The concepts and practices of applied entomology for the most part date from that Stone Age of science. It is our alarming misfortune that so primitive a science has armed itself with the most modern and terrible weapons, and that in turning them against the insects it has also turned them against the earth.

5.9
Club of Rome Report on the Looming Environmental Crisis

Public interest in environmental issues soared following the appearance of Carson's *Silent Spring*, but with interest also came a growing realization of the magnitude of the problem. Nothing seemed then more daunting than the world's rising population. More people meant more pressure on finite resources and thus an accentuation of the existing environmental strains. The Club of Rome report, published in 1972, was a scholarly effort to gauge the severity of the problem. The team of researchers concluded with one of the most alarming appraisals of the time and set off widespread debate over its findings, its methods, and its policy implications. If Carson defined the emergence of an environmental consciousness, the Club of Rome report signaled the maturing of environmentalism into an area of sharp contention.

What is the core of the report's argument? How does it build on and depart from Carson? In retrospect how compelling an analysis did the report offer?

Donella H. Meadows et al.
From *The Limits to Growth*
1972

Our world model was built specifically to investigate five major trends of global concern — accelerating industrialization, rapid population growth, widespread malnutrition, depletion of nonrenewable resources, and a deteriorating environment. . . .

The model we have constructed is, like every other model, imperfect, oversimplified, and unfinished. . . .

Our conclusions are:

1. If the present growth trends in world population, industrialization, pollution, food production, and resource depletion continue unchanged, the limits to growth on this planet will be reached sometime within the next one hun-

Donella H. Meadows, Dennis L. Meadows, Jørgen Randers, and William W. Behrens III, *The Limits to Growth: A Report for the Club of Rome's Project on the Predicament of Mankind* (New York: Universe Books, 1972), 21, 23–24, 125–28, 151, 153–54, 181–84. The treatment here follows in the main the abstract created by Eduard Pestel, available at <http://www.clubofrome.org/archive/reports.html> (August 12, 2002).

dred years. The most probable result will be a rather sudden and uncontrollable decline in both population and industrial capacity.

2. It is possible to alter these growth trends and to establish a condition of ecological and economic stability that is sustainable far into the future. The state of global equilibrium could be designed so that the basic material needs of each person on earth are satisfied and each person has an equal opportunity to realize his individual human potential.

3. If the world's people decide to strive for this second outcome rather than the first, the sooner they begin working to attain it, the greater will be their chances of success. . . .

[A model projecting rising population pressures on earth's resources indicates an outcome] of overshoot and collapse. In this run the collapse occurs because of nonrenewable resource depletion. The industrial capital stock grows to a level that requires an enormous input of resources. In the very process of that growth it depletes a large fraction of the resource reserves available. As resource prices rise and mines are depleted, more and more capital must be used for obtaining resources, leaving less to be invested for future growth. Finally investment cannot keep up with depreciation, and the industrial base collapses, taking with it the service and agricultural systems, which have become dependent on industrial inputs (such as fertilizers, pesticides, hospital laboratories, computers, and especially energy for mechanization). For a short time the situation is especially serious because population, with the delays inherent in the age structure and the process of social adjustment, keeps rising. Population finally decreases when the death rate is driven upward by lack of food and health services.

The exact timing of these events is not meaningful, given the great aggregation and many uncertainties in the model. It is significant, however, that growth is stopped well before the year 2100. We have tried in every doubtful case to make the most optimistic estimate of unknown quantities, and we have also ignored discontinuous events such as wars or epidemics, which might act to bring an end to growth even sooner than our model would indicate. In other words, the model is biased to allow growth to continue longer than it probably can continue in the real world. *We can thus say with some confidence that, under the assumption of no major change in the present system, population and industrial growth will certainly stop within the next century, at the latest. . . .*

Is the future of the world system bound to be growth and then collapse into a dismal, depleted existence? Only if we make the initial assumption that our present way of doing things will not change. We have ample evidence of mankind's ingenuity and social flexibility. There are, of course, many likely changes in the system, some of which are already taking place. The Green Revolution is raising agricultural yields in nonindustrialized countries. Knowledge about modern methods of birth control is spreading rapidly. . . .

. . . Is it better to try to live within that limit by accepting a self-imposed restriction on growth? Or is it preferable to go on growing until some other natural limit arises, in the hope that at that time another technological leap will allow growth to continue still

longer? For the last several hundred years human society has followed the second course so consistently and successfully that the first choice has been all but forgotten.

There may be much disagreement with the statement that population and capital growth must stop *soon*. But virtually no one will argue that material growth on this planet can go on forever. . . .

. . . We strongly believe that many of the technological developments mentioned here — recycling, pollution-control devices, contraceptives — will be absolutely vital to the future of human society *if they are combined with deliberate checks on growth.* We would deplore an unreasoned rejection of the benefits of technology as strongly as we argue here against an unreasoned acceptance of them. Perhaps the best summary of our position is the motto of the Sierra Club: "Not blind opposition to progress, but opposition to blind progress." . . .

The final, most elusive, and most important information we need deals with human values. As soon as society recognizes that it cannot maximize everything for everyone, it must begin to make choices. Should there be more people or more wealth, more wilderness or more automobiles, more food for the poor or more services for the rich? Establishing the societal answers to questions like these and translating those answers into policy is the essence of the political process. Yet few people in any society even realize that such choices are being made every day, much less ask themselves what their own choices would be. The equilibrium society will have to weigh the trade-offs engendered by a finite earth not only with consideration of present human values but also with consideration of future generations. . . . [L]ong-term goals must be specified and short-term goals made consistent with them. . . .

. . . Every day of continued exponential growth brings the world system closer to the ultimate limits to that growth. A decision to do nothing is a decision to increase the risk of collapse. We cannot say with certainty how much longer mankind can postpone initiating deliberate control of its growth before it will have lost the chance for control. We suspect on the basis of present knowledge of the physical constraints of the planet that the growth phase cannot continue for another one hundred years. Again, because of the delays in the system, if the global society waits until those constraints are unmistakably apparent, it will have waited too long.

If there is cause for deep concern, there is also cause for hope. Deliberately limiting growth would be difficult, but not impossible. The way to proceed is clear, and the necessary steps, although they are new ones for human society, are well within human capabilities. Man possesses, for a small moment in his history, the most powerful combination of knowledge, tools, and resources the world has ever known. He has all that is physically necessary to create a totally new form of human society — one that would be built to last for generations. The two missing ingredients are a realistic, long-term goal that can guide mankind to the equilibrium society and the human will to achieve that goal. Without such a goal and a commitment to it, short-term concerns will generate the exponential growth that drives the world system toward the limits of the earth and ultimate collapse. With that goal and that commitment, mankind would be ready now to begin a controlled, orderly transition from growth to global equilibrium.

5.10
Indira Gandhi Offers a Third-World Perspective

Responsibility to future generations, a theme of *Silent Spring* and *The Limits of Growth,* also appears prominently in an address by Indira Gandhi. The head of the Indian government and daughter of Jawaharlal Nehru spoke for a strongly held view in the third world: environmental constraints should not impede rapid growth essential to pulling the poor out of poverty. Despoiling the environment meant different things in different parts of the globe. This difference over how best to act responsibly toward the future created a major divide in the environmental movement.

How does Gandhi understand environmentalism? How does her position compare with that of *Silent Spring* and *The Limits of Growth?*

Address to the U.N. Environmental Conference
Stockholm, June 14, 1972

We are gathered here under the aegis of the United Nations. We are supposed to belong to the same family sharing common traits and impelled by the same basic desires, yet we inhabit a divided world.

. . . Many of the advanced countries of today have reached their present affluence by their domination over other races and countries, the exploitation of their own masses and their own natural resources. They got a head start through sheer ruthlessness, undisturbed by feelings of compassion or by abstract theories of freedom, equality or justice. The stirrings of demands for the political rights of citizens, and the economic rights of the toiler came after considerable advance had been made. The riches and the labour of the colonized countries played no small part in the industrialization and prosperity of the West. Now, as we struggle to create a better life for our people, it is in vastly different circumstances, for obviously in today's eagle-eyed watchfulness, we cannot indulge in such practices even for a worthwhile purpose. We are bound by our own ideals. We owe allegiance to the principles of the rights of workers and the norms enshrined in the charters of international

Indira Gandhi, *The Years of Endeavor: Selected Speeches of Indira Gandhi,* vol. 2, *August 1969–August 1972* (New Delhi: Government of India Ministry of Information and Broadcasting, 1975), 448–52.

organisations. Above all, we are answerable to the millions of politically awakened citizens in our countries. All these make progress costlier and more complicated.

On the one hand the rich look askance at our continuing poverty — on the other they warn us against their own methods. We do not wish to impoverish the environment any further and yet we cannot for a moment forget the grim poverty of [a] large number of people. Are not poverty and need the greatest polluters? . . . How can we speak to those who live in villages and in slums about keeping the oceans, the rivers and the air clean when their own lives are contaminated at the source? The environment cannot be improved in conditions of poverty. Nor can poverty be eradicated without the use of science and technology. . . .

It is an over-simplification to blame all the world's problems on increasing population. Countries with but a small fraction of the world population consume the bulk of the world's production of minerals, fossil fuels and so on. Thus we see that when it comes to the depletion of natural resources and environmental pollution the increase of one inhabitant in an affluent country, at his level of living, is equivalent to an increase of many Asians, Africans or Latin Americans at their current material levels of living.

The inherent conflict is not between conservation and development, but between environment and the reckless exploitation of man and earth in the name of efficiency. . . . The industrial civilisation has promoted the concept of the efficient man, he whose entire energies are concentrated on producing more in a given unit of time and from a given unit of man-power. Groups or individuals who are less competitive and, according to this test, less efficient are regarded as lesser breeds — for example the older civilizations, the black and brown peoples, women and certain professions. Obsolescence is built into production, and efficiency is based on the creation of goods which are not really needed and which cannot be disposed of, when discarded. What price such efficiency now, and is not reckless a more appropriate term for such behaviour?

All the "isms" of the modern age — even those which in theory disown the private profit principle — assume that man's cardinal interest is acquisition. The profit motive, individual or collective, seems to overshadow all else. This over-riding concern with self today is the basic cause of the ecological crisis. . . .

It is clear that the environmental crisis which is confronting the world will profoundly alter the future destiny of our planet. No one among us, whatever our status, strength or circumstance, can remain unaffected. The process of change challenges present international policies. Will the growing awareness of "one earth" and "one environment" guide us to the concept of "one humanity"? Will there be more equitable sharing of environment costs and greater international interest in the accelerated progress of the less developed world? Or will it remain confined to a narrow concern, based on exclusive self-sufficiency?

FEMINISM IN THE NORTH ATLANTIC WORLD

One of the major currents reshaping the United States and western Europe during the last third of the twentieth century was feminism, a critical examination by women of their identity and by extension their social and economic roles. Feminism was not a new outlook; women on both sides of the Atlantic had been calling for greater political equality, economic opportunity, and social support since the nineteenth century. During the late 1960s feminist sentiment flared among a new generation that had come of age within societies blessed with stability, awash in wealth, and preoccupied with human welfare. So striking were feminist achievements that young women today who might deny that they are feminists have available a rich array of opportunities and resources that simply did not exist half a century earlier.

But despite the common timing and sweeping achievements that characterize this phase of Western feminism, strong regional variations are evident in the way that women tackled feminist issues. In the United States and Britain, the language of legal rights tended to dominate discussions, while in continental Europe a more theoretical approach preoccupied with differences between women and men was prominent.

5.11

Simone de Beauvoir on "What is Woman? . . . She is the Other"

Simone de Beauvoir's *The Second Sex*, published in France in 1949, foreshadowed the rise of a new feminist movement in the 1960s and early 1970s and stands as a classic of feminist writings. De Beauvoir started to write an autobiography in 1946 but found herself more and more engrossed in the issues of gender that had shaped her life. The resulting book tackled those issues including oppression within marriage, women's control over their bodies, and the nature of domestic labor. But perhaps her most important single point was the constructed nature of gender identity. Women are in effect made, she stressed, not born. *The Second Sex* — two volumes totaling 1,200 pages — sold 22,000 copies in its first week on the shelves, was condemned by the Catholic Church, and provoked controversy and attacks on de Beauvoir for being too politically left and too "unwomanly" (she earned a Sorbonne doctorate, participated in the resistance movement during World War II, had an active writing career, was unmarried and childless, and was involved in a long-term relationship with philosopher and public intellectual Jean-Paul Sartre). Later French feminists were respectful of de Beauvoir's work but not always in agreement with her approach. She died in 1986, having not only witnessed but also participated in a feminist movement that her introspection had helped begin.

Given the standing of the book and the pioneering nature of its analysis, de Beauvoir's arguments deserve careful consideration. What claims is de Beauvoir making about gender and especially the sources of women's identity? Which elements seem compelling, even taken for granted today, and which elements seem debatable?

From *The Second Sex*
1949

All agree in recognizing the fact that females exist in the human species; today as always they make up about one half of humanity. And yet we are told that femininity is in danger; we are exhorted to be women, remain women, become women. It would appear, then, that every female human being is not necessarily a woman; to be so considered she must share in that mysterious and threatened reality known as femininity. Is this attribute something secreted by the ovaries? Or is it . . . a product of the philosophic imagination? Is a rustling petticoat enough to bring it down to earth? . . .

But . . . [t]he biological and social sciences no longer admit the existence of unchangeably fixed entities that determine given characteristics, such as those ascribed to woman, the Jew, or the Negro. Science regards any characteristic as a reaction dependent in part upon a *situation*. If today femininity no longer exists, then it never existed. But does the word *woman*, then, have no specific content? . . . In truth, to go for a walk with one's eyes open is enough to demonstrate that humanity is divided into two classes of individuals whose clothes, faces, bodies, smiles, gaits, interests, and occupations are manifestly different. Perhaps these differences are superficial, perhaps they are destined to disappear. What is certain is that right now they do most obviously exist.

If her functioning as a female is not enough to define woman, if we decline also to explain her through "the eternal feminine," and if nevertheless we admit, provisionally, that women do exist, then we must face the question: what is a woman?

To state the question is, to me, to suggest, at once, a preliminary answer. The fact that I ask it is in itself significant. A man would never get the notion of writing a book on the peculiar situation of the human male. But if I wish to define myself, I must first of all say: "I am a woman"; on this truth must be based all further discussion. A man never begins by presenting himself as an individual of a certain sex; it goes without saying that he is a man. The terms *masculine* and *feminine* are used symmetrically only as a matter of form, as on legal papers. In actuality the relation of the two sexes is not quite like that of two electrical poles, for man represents both the positive and the neutral, as is indicated by the common use of *man* to designate human beings in general; whereas woman represents only the negative, defined by limiting criteria, without reciprocity. . . . Woman has ovaries, a uterus; these peculiarities imprison her in her subjectivity, circumscribe her within the limits of her own nature. It is often said that she thinks with her glands. Man superbly ignores the fact that his anatomy also includes glands, such as the testicles, and that

Simone de Beauvoir, *The Second Sex,* trans. H. M. Parshley (New York: Knopf, 1953), xiii–xvi, xx–xxi, xxiii–xxvi. *The Second Sex* is also available in full at <http://www.marxists.org/reference/subject/philosophy/works/fr/debeauv.htm> (August 19, 2002).

they secrete hormones. He thinks of his body as a direct and normal connection with the world, which he believes he apprehends objectively, whereas he regards the body of woman as a hindrance, a prison, weighed down by everything peculiar to it. . . .

Thus humanity is male and man defines woman not in herself but as relative to him; she is not regarded as an autonomous being. . . . [S]he is simply what man decrees; thus she is called "the sex," by which is meant that she appears essentially to the male as a sexual being. For him she is sex — absolute sex, no less. She is defined and differentiated with reference to man and not he with reference to her; she is the incidental, the inessential as opposed to the essential. He is the Subject, he is the Absolute — she is the Other. . . .

. . . Here is to be found the basic trait of woman: she is the Other in a totality of which the two components are necessary to one another.

. . . In truth woman has not been socially emancipated through man's need — sexual desire and the desire for offspring — which makes the male dependent for satisfaction upon the female. . . .

. . . [T]he two sexes have never shared the world in equality. And even today woman is heavily handicapped, though her situation is beginning to change. Almost nowhere is her legal status the same as man's, and frequently it is much to her disadvantage. Even when her rights are legally recognized in the abstract, long-standing custom prevents their full expression in the mores. In the economic sphere men and women can almost be said to make up two castes; other things being equal, the former hold the better jobs, get higher wages, and have more opportunity for success than their new competitors. In industry and politics men have a great many more positions and they monopolise the most important posts. In addition to all this, they enjoy a traditional prestige that the education of children tends in every way to support, for the present enshrines the past — and in the past all history has been made by men. At the present time, when women are beginning to take part in the affairs of the world, it is still a world that belongs to men — they have no doubt of it at all and women have scarcely any. To decline to be the Other, to refuse to be a party to the deal — this would be for women to renounce all the advantages conferred upon them by their alliance with the superior caste. Man-the-sovereign will provide woman-the-liege with material protection and will undertake the moral justification of her existence; thus she can evade at once both economic risk and the metaphysical risk of a liberty in which ends and aims must be contrived without assistance. Indeed, along with the ethical urge of each individual to affirm his subjective existence, there is also the temptation to forgo liberty and become a thing. This is an inauspicious road, for he who takes it — passive, lost, ruined — becomes henceforth the creature of another's will, frustrated in his transcendence and deprived of every value. But it is an easy road; on it one avoids the strain involved in undertaking an authentic existence. . . .

. . . [T]here are deep similarities between the situation of woman and that of the Negro. Both are being emancipated today from a like paternalism, and the former master class wishes to "keep them in their place" — that is, the place chosen for them. In both cases the former masters lavish more or less sincere eulogies, either on the virtues of "the good Negro" with his dormant, childish, merry soul — the submissive Negro — or on the merits of the woman who is "truly feminine" — that is, frivolous, infantile, irresponsible — the submissive woman. In both cases the dominant class bases its argument on a state of affairs that it has itself created. . . . Yes, women on the whole *are* today inferior to men; that is, their situation affords them fewer possibilities. The question is: should that state of affairs continue?

Many men hope that it will continue; not all have given up the battle. The conservative bourgeoisie still see in the emancipation of women a menace to their morality and their interests. Some men dread feminine competition. . . . And economic interests are not the only ones concerned. One of the benefits that oppression confers upon the oppressors is that the most humble among them is made to *feel* superior; thus, a "poor white" in the South can console himself with the thought that he is not a "dirty nigger" — and the more prosperous whites cleverly exploit this pride.

Similarly, the most mediocre of males feels himself a demigod as compared with women. . . .

. . . Here is miraculous balm for those afflicted with an inferiority complex, and indeed no one is more arrogant towards women, more aggressive or scornful, than the man who is anxious about his virility. . . .

. . . It is, in point of fact, a difficult matter for man to realize the extreme importance of social discriminations which seem outwardly insignificant but which produce in woman moral and intellectual effects so profound that they appear to spring from her original nature. The most sympathetic of men never fully comprehend woman's concrete situation. And there is no reason to put much trust in the men when they rush to the defense of privileges whose full extent they can hardly measure. We shall not, then, permit ourselves to be intimidated by the number and violence of the attacks launched against women, nor to be entrapped by the self-seeking eulogies bestowed on the "true woman," nor to profit by the enthusiasm for woman's destiny manifested by men who would not for the world have any part of it. . . .

Now, what peculiarly signalizes the situation of woman is that she — a free and autonomous being like all human creatures — nevertheless finds herself living in a world where men compel her to assume the status of the Other. . . . How can a human being in woman's situation attain fulfillment? What roads are open to her? Which are blocked? How can independence be recovered in a state of dependency? What circumstances limit woman's liberty and how can they be overcome? These are the fundamental questions on which I would fain throw some light. This means that I am interested in the fortunes of the individual as defined not in terms of happiness but in terms of liberty. . . .

5.12
The U.S. Campaign for Women's Rights

In the United States a campaign for expanded opportunities for women got going in the early 1960s. Increasingly mobilized, activists issued a landmark statement in the fall of 1966 when the National Organization for Women (NOW) met for the first time in Washington, D.C. Betty Friedan, author of *The Feminine Mystique,* and Pauli Murray, an African-American Episcopal minister, drafted that statement, which would significantly define the direction for future feminist action in the United States.

Note the goals that this document sets, the rationale for pursuing those goals, and the language in which the goals are couched. How would you characterize NOW's overriding objectives? On what basis did NOW ground its demands for change? And what are the influences that shaped the tone and style of this formal statement? Given its importance, this statement deserves comparison with de Beauvoir's argument from seventeen years earlier. Did NOW draw from or offer an alternative to de Beauvoir? To what extent has the NOW program been realized?

NOW Statement of Purpose
October 29, 1966

We, men and women who hereby constitute ourselves as the National Organization for Women, believe that the time has come for a new movement toward true equality for all women in America, and toward a fully equal partnership of the sexes, as part of the world-wide revolution of human rights now taking place within and beyond our national borders.

The purpose of NOW is to take action to bring women into full participation in the mainstream of American society now, exercising all the privileges and responsibilities thereof in truly equal partnership with men.

We believe the time has come to move beyond the abstract argument, discussion, and symposia over the status and special nature of women which have raged in America in recent years; the time has come to confront, with concrete action, the conditions that now prevent women from enjoying the equality of opportunity and freedom of choice which is their right, as individual Americans, and as human beings.

NOW is dedicated to the proposition that women, first and foremost, are human beings, who, like all other people in our society, must have the chance to develop their fullest human potential. We believe that women can achieve such equality only by accepting to the full the challenges and responsibilities they share with all other people in our society, as part of the decision-making mainstream of American political, economic and social life.

We organize to initiate or support action, nationally, or in any part of this nation, by individuals or organizations, to break through the silken curtain of

Available at the National Organization for Women website: <http://www.now.org/history/purpos66.html> (April 14, 2003).

prejudice and discrimination against women in government, industry, the professions, the churches, the political parties, the judiciary, the labor unions, in education, science, medicine, law, religion and every other field of importance in American society.

Enormous changes taking place in our society make it both possible and urgently necessary to advance the unfinished revolution of women toward true equality, now. With a life span lengthened to nearly 75 years it is no longer either necessary or possible for women to devote the greater part of their lives to child-rearing; yet childbearing and rearing — which continue to be a most important part of most women's lives — still are used to justify barring women from equal professional and economic participation and advance.

Today's technology has reduced most of the productive chores which women once performed in the home and in mass-production industries based upon routine unskilled labor. This same technology has virtually eliminated the quality of muscular strength as a criterion for filling most jobs, while intensifying American industry's need for creative intelligence. In view of this new industrial revolution created by automation in the mid-twentieth century, women can and must participate in old and new fields of society in full equality — or become permanent outsiders.

Despite all the talk about the status of American women in recent years, the actual position of women in the United States has declined, and is declining, to an alarming degree throughout the 1950's and 60's. Although 46.4% of all American women between the ages of 18 and 65 now work outside the home, the overwhelming majority — 75% — are in routine clerical, sales, or factory jobs, or they are household workers, cleaning women, hospital attendants. About two-thirds of Negro women workers are in the lowest paid service occupations. Working women are becoming increasingly — not less — concentrated on the bottom of the job ladder. As a consequence, full-time women workers today earn on the average only 60% of what men earn, and that wage gap has been increasing over the past twenty-five years in every major industry group. . . .

Further, with higher education increasingly essential in today's society, too few women are entering and finishing college or going on to graduate or professional school. Today, women earn only one in three of the B.A.'s and M.A.'s granted, and one in ten of the Ph.D.'s.

In all the professions considered of importance to society, and in the executive ranks of industry and government, women are losing ground. Where they are present it is only a token handful. Women comprise less than 1% of federal judges; less than 4% of all lawyers; 7% of doctors. Yet women represent 51% of the U.S. population. And, increasingly, men are replacing women in the top positions in secondary and elementary schools, in social work, and in libraries — once thought to be women's fields.

Official pronouncements of the advance in the status of women hide not only the reality of this dangerous decline, but the fact that nothing is being done to stop it. . . . Discrimination in employment on the basis of sex is now prohibited by federal law, in Title VII of the Civil Rights Act of 1964. But although nearly one-third of the cases brought before the Equal Employment Opportunity Commission during the first year dealt with sex discrimination and the proportion is increasing dramatically, the Commission has not made clear its intention to enforce the law with the same seriousness on behalf of women as of other victims of discrimination. Many of these cases were Negro women, who are the victims of the double discrimination of race and sex. Until now, too few women's organizations and official spokesmen have been willing to speak out against these dangers facing women. Too many women have been restrained by the fear of being called "feminist." There is no civil rights movement to speak for women, as there has been for Negroes and other victims of discrimination. The National Organization for Women must therefore begin to speak.

WE BELIEVE that the power of American law, and the protection guaranteed by the U.S. Constitution to the civil rights of all individuals, must be effectively applied and enforced to isolate and remove patterns of sex discrimination, to ensure equality of opportunity in employment and education, and equality of civil and political rights and responsibilities on behalf of women, as well as for Negroes and other deprived groups.

We realize that women's problems are linked to many broader questions of social justice; their solution will require concerted action by many groups. Therefore, convinced that human rights for all are indivisible, we expect to give active support to the common cause of equal rights for all those who suffer discrimination and deprivation, and we call upon other organizations committed to such goals to support our efforts toward equality for women.

WE DO NOT ACCEPT the token appointment of a few women to high-level positions in government and industry as a substitute for a serious continuing effort to recruit and advance women according to their individual abilities. To this end, we urge American government and industry to mobilize the same resources of ingenuity and command with which they have solved problems of far greater difficulty than those now impeding the progress of women.

WE BELIEVE that this nation has a capacity at least as great as other nations, to innovate new social institutions which will enable women to enjoy the true equality of opportunity and responsibility in society, without conflict with their responsibilities as mothers and homemakers. In such innovations, America does not lead the Western world, but lags by decades behind many European countries. We do not accept the traditional assumption that a woman has to chose between marriage and motherhood, on the one hand, and serious participation in industry or the professions on the other. We question the present expectation that all normal women will retire from job or profession for 10 or 15 years, to devote their full time to raising children, only to reenter the job market at a relatively minor level. This, in itself, is a deterrent to the aspirations of women, to their acceptance into management or professional training courses, and to the very possibility of equality of opportunity or real choice, for all but a few women. Above all, we reject the assumption that these problems are the unique responsibility of each individual woman, rather than a basic social dilemma which society must solve. True equality of opportunity and freedom of choice for women requires such practical, and possible innovations as a nationwide network of child-care centers, which will make it unnecessary for women to retire completely from society until their children are grown, and national programs to provide retraining for women who have chosen to care for their own children full-time.

WE BELIEVE that it is as essential for every girl to be educated to her full potential of human ability as it is for every boy — with the knowledge that such education is the key to effective participation in today's economy and that, for a girl as for a boy, education can only be serious where there is expectation that it will be used in society. We believe that American educators are capable of devising means of imparting such expectations to girl students. Moreover, we consider the decline in the proportion of women receiving higher and professional education to be evidence of discrimination. This discrimination may take the form of quotas against the admission of women to colleges, and professional schools; lack of encouragement by parents, counselors and educators; denial of loans or fellowships; or the traditional or arbitrary procedures in graduate and professional training geared in terms of men, which inadvertently discriminate against women. We believe that the same serious attention must be given to high school dropouts who are girls as to boys.

WE REJECT the current assumptions that a man must carry the sole burden of supporting himself, his wife, and family, and that a woman is automatically entitled to lifelong support by a man upon her marriage, or that marriage, home and family are primarily woman's world and responsibility — hers, to dominate — his to support. We believe that a true partnership between the sexes demands a different concept of marriage, an equitable sharing of the responsibilities of home and children and of the economic burdens of their support. We believe that the proper recognitions should be given to the economic and social value of homemaking and child-care. To these ends, we will seek to open a reexamination of laws and mores governing marriage and divorce, for we believe that the current state of "half-equality" between the sexes discriminates against both men and women, and is the cause of much unnecessary hostility between the sexes.

WE BELIEVE that women must now exercise their political rights and responsibilities as American citizens. They must refuse to be segregated on the basis of sex into separate-and-not-equal ladies' auxiliaries in the political parties, and they must demand representation according to their numbers in the regularly constituted party committees — at local, state, and national levels — and in the information power structure, participating fully in the selection of candidates and political decision-making, and running for office themselves.

IN THE INTEREST OF THE HUMAN DIGNITY OF WOMEN, we will protest, and endeavor to change, the false image of women now prevalent in the mass media, and in the texts, ceremonies, laws, and practices of our major social institutions. Such images perpetuate contempt for women by society and by women for themselves. We are similarly opposed to all policies and practices — in church, state college, factory, or office — which, in the guise of protectiveness, not only deny opportunities but also foster in women self-denigration, dependence, and evasion of responsibility, undermine their confidence in their own abilities and foster contempt for women.

NOW WILL HOLD ITSELF INDEPENDENT OF ANY POLITICAL PARTY in order to mobilize the political power of all women and men intent on our goals. We will strive to ensure that no party, candidate, president, senator, governor, congressman, or any public official who betrays or ignores the principle of full equality between the sexes is elected or appointed to office. If it is necessary to mobilize the votes of men and women who believe in our cause, in order to win for women the final right to be fully free and equal human beings, we so commit ourselves.

WE BELIEVE THAT women will do most to create a new image of women by acting now, and by speaking out in behalf of their own equality, freedom, and human dignity — not in pleas for special privilege, not in enmity toward men, who are also victims of the current half-equality between the sexes — but in active, self-respecting partnership with men. By so doing, women will develop confidence in their own ability to determine actively, in partnership with men, the conditions of their life, their choices, their future, and their society.

5.13
The Awakening of the French Feminist Movement

The May 1968 explosion of student activism in Paris proved a critical spur to French feminism. Women found themselves marginalized within the protest movement, serving as secretaries, cooks, and cleaners. Demeaned by their male colleagues, they began asking questions following the collapse of the protest in June. Women had participated in all aspects of the protest movement, yet their voices were nowhere heard and their concerns nowhere articulated. It was time to recognize, as one statement posted in the Sorbonne asserted, that "change in relationships between men also implied change in relationships between men and women."[1] To explore this problem, small discussion groups sprang up, mostly in Paris and soon to exclude men. "Anne Tristan" (Annie Sugier adapting the name of Flora Tristan, 1803–1844, one of the first socialist feminists, famous for her flamboyant lifestyle) recalls the first hesitant steps following the May 1968 upheaval. Her account reveals the strong theoretical turn of the movement from the outset, the academic background of the handful of pioneering participants (she was herself an engineer working for the state nuclear power agency), and the contentious and highly self-conscious style of these young vanguard women. This account is especially valuable because it includes some of the leading figures in French femi-

---

[1] Alain Schnapp and Pierre Vidal-Naquet, eds., *The French Student Uprising, November 1967–June 1968: An Analytical Record,* trans. Maria Jolas (Boston: Beacon Press, 1971), 435.

nism without naming them explicitly. A knowledgeable reader would have easily guessed the surnames that went with the given names supplied here.

These outspoken women were soon not only debating fiercely among themselves but boldly challenging public attitudes. Their first dramatic announcement came in 1970 with a march to a sacred national site, the Tomb of the Unknown Soldier, to lay a wreath in memory of his wife. Feminists followed with public protests demanding legalized abortion and with publications that explored gender roles, using either the language of psychoanalysis or of exploitation (with gender substituting for class). Among the earliest of many publications from these articulate and impatient feminists was the *Torchon Brûle* (The Burning Rag). Reproduced on page 230 is one of a number of its eye-catching covers that begs interpretation. What does it say about the rule of women?

Comparisons across time and space are now possible. Looking back to de Beauvoir, how do Tristan's recollection and the cover drawing suggest that thinking of French feminists had evolved? How much is de Beauvoir's influence evident? Looking across the Atlantic, how closely related are the language and concerns of French feminists of the early 1970s with the women who launched NOW in the mid-1960s?

Anne Tristan
Recollections in "Tales from the Women's Movement"
1977

There is always somebody even more "unknown" than the soldier:
his wife. . .

Unbelievable. *Le Nouvel Observateur* [weekly news magazine] had actually published a letter from the FMA.[1] It earned us a few replies, including one from a group of women who called themselves the "Oreilles vertes."[2] They wanted to meet us.

---

[1]The FMA was a small group organized by Anne and some of her (male and female) friends towards the end of 1967. The initials stand for "Féminin–Masculin–Avenir" or "Female–Male–Future." The group was intended as a radical alternative to the only other active women's organization at the time, the "Mouvement démocratique féminin" ("The democratic movement of women"). In spite of the radical climate at the time, the FMA was struggling to recruit more than four or five members for the first two or three years of its existence.

[2]The name literally means the "green ears." It would seem to be a pun both on the idea of being "green" in the sense of presenting a new and fresh view of the world, and on the expression "*avoir une lange verte*" (literally: "to have a green tongue" — to use salacious language). The "green ears" would then be "ready to hear anything."

Anne Tristan and Annie de Pisan, "Tales from the Women's Movement," trans. Roisin Mallaghan, in *French Feminist Thought: A Reader,* ed. Toril Moi (Oxford, Eng.: Basil Blackwell, 1987), 33–37. This account originally appeared as Anne Tristan and Annie de Pisan, *Histoires du MLF* (Paris: Calmann-Lévy, 1977). The notes that accompany the following excerpt are supplied by Toril Moi unless otherwise indicated.

It was May 1970. Two years on already. The cover of *L'Idiot international*,[3] a leftist newspaper, featured a large woman's head, accompanied by the headline: "Women's Liberation." I snatched it from the news-stand. Great excitement in the FMA. It was essential to make contact immediately with these young women, authors of an article we could so easily have written ourselves. It was signed with four Christian names. I wrote at once. No reply. In contrast, we had already managed to arrange a meeting with the "Oreilles vertes."

It took place in a flat belonging to one of their number. We arrived, all six of us, the entire FMA. There were about a dozen women there. On the young side. Introductions were made in a relaxed atmosphere. The women, all academics and all married, had suddenly become acutely and painfully aware of their oppression during the previous Easter vacation. They had gone on holiday with their husbands: while the men talked incessantly amongst themselves, the women took care of the cooking. . . . And this in spite of the fact that they were all "on the left."

On their return, the women had decided to set up a women-only consciousness-raising group. Our letter had come just at the right moment. During the meeting, two other women showed up. They stood in the doorway. One was small, squat, with dishevelled hair, her eyes hidden behind dark specs. The other, large, solid, with the head of a sad lioness.

The former began to speak in a gruff voice, using an academic jargon I thought might come from psychoanalysis. Her name was Antoinette,[4] and she was one of the group who had written the article in *L'Idiot international*. The other, a sort of tight-lipped bodyguard, remained resolutely silent.

The conversation moved on to mixed groups. It was decided that for the time being they were out of the question. Christine[5] had been trying for ages to convince us of this at the FMA. We couldn't bring ourselves to agree with her, clinging to our falsely idealistic notions. Liberation was an issue which concerned men and women: why be divided in what was a battle to be united? Because we were divided. As a political group, women, exploited by another political group, men, had to set themselves apart from their objective oppressors in order better to analyse the nature of this exploitation, and to discover

---

[3]*L'Idiot international* was one of many extreme left-wing or Maoist newspapers which flourished after the uprising of May 1968. They were soon threatened by closure by the right-wing government in power after the May events. As the authorities could only close the papers down by prosecuting the responsible editor-in-chief, Jean-Paul Sartre and Simone de Beauvoir offered to help protect the freedom of the press by becoming the official editors of some of these papers. In 1970 Sartre became the editor of *La Cause du peuple,* and later also of *Tout* and *La Parole du peuple,* whereas Simone de Beauvoir accepted the same role in *L'Idiot international.*

[4]Antoinette Fouquet: a psychoanalyst and leading figure in the wing of French feminism championing a psychoanalytic approach to feminist issues. Fouquet's associates, all influential in their own right, were Julia Kristeva, Luce Irigaray, and Hélène Cixous. — M.H.

[5]Christine Delphy: proponent of a Marxist analysis of feminist issues. She completed her degree in sociology at the Sorbonne in 1962, and went on to study at Berkeley and participate in the U.S. civil rights movement before returning to France in 1966. — M.H.

for themselves the means to resist it, away from those who were responsible for it. In the short term, men had nothing to gain from our liberation, which was going to deprive them of their unearned privileges. It would only take a few men at the meetings for them to monopolize the discussion. That evening, we were persuaded once and for all, while in their corner our two male members huddled together. An emergency general meeting of the FMA determined their exclusion. It was a painful affair. Roger,[6] who couldn't accept being thrown out, took it very badly. He wasn't ready to accept that even well-intentioned oppressors were oppressors all the same. I learnt from Christine why we had no reply to our letter to *L'Idiot international*. There had been some kind of disagreement between the women who had written the article and the group to which they belonged: we will call it the Vincennes group. The crucial thing was to meet them. A large meeting was arranged between them, the "Oreilles vertes" and the FMA.

The evening came. The meeting was at 8 p.m., on the top floor of an old building on the Rue Descartes. Jacqueline and I were amongst the first to arrive, full of excitement at the idea of finding ourselves amongst all these feminists. The women came in. They were young, left-wing, student types, all rather surly looking. They didn't look at us, and didn't smile. I felt uncomfortable. I was slumped on the settee, with our manifesto in my hands. We were going to read it out by way of introduction. The room was soon full. Not since May 1968 had I seen so many women gathered together at once, at least 30 of us. The room was full of smoke. The time for the meeting to open had long since passed.

A woman squatting on the floor glanced curiously at us from time to time, and enquired on several occasions if there was an agenda. No one replied. The conversations continued. No one paid any attention to us. Their attitude upset me. The woman, who kept looking at us, asked again if there was an agenda. Shyly, Jacqueline informed her that we were present, we, the FMA. Amid the cacophony, the woman shouted out: "Our friends from the FMA are here. We might let them speak." She didn't seem too happy about the general indifference. Her name was Monique[7]; she was one of the ones who had written the article in *L'Idiot international*.

Silence gradually gained the room. People looked at us. I took the manifesto, and in a trembling voice began to read it. After some considerable confusion, the discussion got going. Two points in our manifesto were particularly fiercely contested. It was difficult, on the spot, to follow the discussion, and especially to see what the exact lines of the argument were. Those who shouted loudest and with most self-assurance got to speak. The whole pro-

---

[6]Roger is Anne's live-in boyfriend at the time. As her feminist involvement grows, they decide to live apart.

[7]Monique Wittig: a lesbian feminist who saw women as a distinct social class. She published her first cutting-edge and prize-winning novel in 1964 and studied at the Sorbonne in oriental studies. In 1976 she moved to the United States while remaining active in the French feminist scene. — M.H.

ceedings were a real shambles, the more so because there was no chairperson, nor any effort to speak one at a time. The first point of controversy was the term feminist, which we had claimed for ourselves. We saw ourselves as the direct spiritual descendants of the suffragettes, especially as far as the use of direct action was concerned. Up to now, unfortunately, the opportunity to take such action had not materialized.

"But the 'feminists' were nothing but women from the bourgeoisie. They merely fought for the same rights as men, and only wanted to be part of male society," asserted Antoinette.

And we, what were we? I only had to look at these women to see that they too belonged to the bourgeoisie. Their vocabulary, often intellectual and highly specialized, their appearance, their confidence, all made that plain.

"They fought against the most obvious injustice: the law. It was the nineteenth century, not the twentieth! They raised questions appropriate to their particular historical situation. I defy anyone to tell me that all feminists thought only of integration into male society. Who wrote their story, anyway?" replied Christine.

"That's true, it's always been blokes who have spoken about us. It isn't in their interest to portray us as we really are. . .," said one woman.

"It's clear that they had no sense of class issues," Antoinette went on, "that they were seeking the same privileges as the men of their own class. They didn't feel any real solidarity with other women, with the women of the working class. It's important not to confuse the issues. The feminists were not revolutionaries, feminism isn't a revolutionary movement. And the same is true to-day; any woman's movement which isn't joined in solidarity with the working-class movement is nothing more than a petty-bougeoisie group of no real consequence.". . .

This last remark was a deliberate allusion to the second contentious point in our manifesto. "We refuse to allow the search for a solution to the female 'problem' to be subordinated to the workers' or students' movements." This point was particularly important to us, as it was a conclusion we had reached after long discussions between ourselves and other left-wingers who had broken away from the FMA. Christine, who had personally developed this idea, spoke out.

"Solidarity doesn't have to mean subordination. All forms of oppression must be raised at the same time and with the same degree of commitment. History has shown that revolutions which subordinate the ending of exploitation to the changing of economic systems are doomed to failure. The deviations we have witnessed in the case of the revolution in Russia are to a large extent due to the failure of the revolution in the sexual and cultural sphere. The overthrow of capitalism does not solve the problem of oppression in general. Its roots are elsewhere, they go much deeper, buried in our patriarchal system, which has as its basis the exploitation of women by men."

There were indignant noises in the room. Only Monique seemed to be in agreement with Christine.

"Your analysis is interesting. How do you define women?"

"But honestly, Monique, that amounts to saying that women constitute a class!" exclaimed Antoinette. "Nothing divides Mme Dassault[8] from my cleaner! It's obvious that they have the same kind of life, the same problems.". . .

Laughter all around. Had I been able to speak, I would have said that I didn't find such cheap jibes funny. Mme Dassault and the cleaner weren't part of the "system" (how often that word was going to crop up), neither in bed, nor at the table. They both had husbands made of flesh and blood who acted in more or less identical ways. In the case of the cleaner, it was a question of: "Have you sent my suit to the cleaners?"; in the case of Mme Dassault it was: "I say, darling, have you reminded Noémie to collect my smoking jacket from the dry-cleaners?"

"Even so, you're not going to try and suggest that women form a homogeneous class?" Antoinette went on.

"Yes, I'm saying exactly that," replied Christine. "Above and beyond social classes, women form a category of oppressed individuals, with common characteristics and constitute a political group whose common enemy is 'man' in the social sense of the term. Our 'main enemy,' above and beyond capitalism, is male civilization, sustained entirely by our labour, labour which is neither acknowledged nor remunerated — our domestic services — and able to perpetuate itself thanks to the reproduction which we guarantee. This power of reproduction is not in our exclusive control, because we do not choose maternity. Men control our wombs — abortion and contraception are denied us for the benefit of their society.". . .

The discussion was concentrating increasingly in the hands of Antoinette, Monique and Christine. The room divided into those for, and those against the "FMA-Christine" thesis, with the majority following the line of Antoinette and her sympathisers, and the minority case being put by Monique. The future groupings of what was to become the MLF[9] were born that night. They would all in effect be variations of the same fundamental opposition between the "class struggle" tendency, and the "feminist" tendency.

I left the meeting exhausted, at once pleased and disappointed. Disappointed by the atmosphere. There was a singular lack of warmth, of goodwill. Hostility reigned supreme. No mercy was shown: certain words could not be uttered without their author being literally jeered. Each intervention was eagerly awaited, each remark scrutinized; people were not allowed to finish what they were saying, or to explain what they really meant. I was alienated by the dominant vocabulary, borrowed from Marxism and psychoanalysis. I had never had anything to do with any sort of political group, I hadn't read the *Selected Extracts*

---

[8]"Madame Dassault" signals the name of the wife of one of the richest and most powerful men in France, Marcel Dassault.

[9]The initials stand for the "*Mouvement de la libération des femmes,*" the French equivalent of the American "Women's Liberation Movement."

from Marx, I barely knew who Freud was. I'd rather have had my tongue cut out than speak in front of people who weren't prepared to listen. . . .

But I was nonetheless a feminist. And for that reason I felt that something very important had happened that night. Something was in the process of being born anew. And whether my companions liked it or not, that something was definitely feminism.

Cover of Le Torchon Brûle
1972

Photocopy from Claire Duchen, *Feminism in France: From May '68 to Mitterand* (London: Routledge & Kegan Paul, 1986), 48.

CHAPTER 6

THIRD-WORLD HOPES
AT HIGH TIDE

THE 1950S AND 1960S WERE HEADY DECADES in the third world. Decolonization gathered pace. The resulting multiplication of new states was reflected by the increase of UN members from 51 in 1945 to 127 by 1970. Brash and impatient, the leaders of these new states challenged the status quo in every corner of the globe. The emergence of the Nasser regime in Egypt and the outbreak of the Algerian liberation movement in the mid-1950s marked the beginning of a time of tumult in the Middle East. Ghana's independence in 1957 signaled the imminent collapse of colonialism in that region. Unrest in the U.S. sphere of influence in Latin America, anticipated by the reformist Arbenz regime in Guatemala in the early 1950s, reached its peak with the Castro revolution in Cuba and its support for revolutionary sentiment in the hemisphere. The victory of Ho Chi Minh's forces over France in 1954 and his bold decision to confront the Americans meant that the revolutionary impulse in Asia was spreading beyond Mao's China, itself still in the midst of radical experiments.

The hopes that gave identity and energy to the third world across these two decades invite close scrutiny. In this time of ferment, third-world elites felt a strong sense of solidarity born of their bitter experience with colonialism and capitalism and of their hope for true independence for their countries and prosperity for their peoples. To this shared sense of the past and hopes for the future was joined a common faith in socialism as the mechanism by which they could remake their particular worlds and create a more just international society. Containing the deleterious effects of the Cold War and pressing for state-directed economic development were practical concerns that began to bring leaders together in the mid-1950s in what would become a third-world non-aligned movement. The underlying values that sustained this movement were a complex mix of nationalism, Marxism, and such region-specific outlooks as pan-Arabism.

EGYPT UNDER NASSER

Gamal Abdul Nasser gave coherent expression to an anti–colonial sentiment that had been bubbling among Egyptian nationalists since early in the twentieth century. Born in 1919 into a lower-middle-class family, Nasser had become intensely nationalist in the 1930s and set off on a military career, one of the few paths of advancement open to a young man of modest means. He came to power in 1952 as part of the Young Officer Movement, impatient with the compromises of the king and the leading politicians. Nasser's first priority was ending subordination to Britain, which meant most urgently the removal of British bases and privileges and acquire greater control over the Suez Canal. He survived an Anglo–French–Israeli invasion in 1956, a triumph that emboldened him to try more radical measures at home and to exploit the influence that he had gained as a hero throughout the Arab world. His domestic policy moved toward large-scale industrialization and government planning of the economy. His foreign policy championed non–aligned and pan–Arab movements. The latter involvement led to a short-lived union between Egypt and Syria and a united front in opposition to Israel.

Nasser provides a fascinating exemplar of two prominent features of the third world in this period. He freely mixed various ideological currents to create an amalgam uniquely his own. And far from having some master plan, he improvised — but with a general tendency to implement ever-more ambitious programs. In both these respects — the complexity of his outlook and the rising tempo of his programs — Nasser was fully in step with other third-world leaders in this era.

6.1

"We Almost Lost Our Balance, But We Have Not Fallen"

In 1952 Nasser produced a work that was half autobiographical and half programmatic. It offers an account of how he and other officers who overthrew the monarchy on July 23 of that year came to a decision to seize power and how they planned to use their new-won power. The relative moderation of the document reflects the uncertainties and optimism that marked the early Nasser years.

How does Nasser account in personal and national terms for the revolution? What are the major goals or objectives of the revolution and what major threats or obstacles seem to stand in the way of revolutionary success? How does Nasser see developments in Egypt in broader regional and global context?

Gamal Abdul Nasser
"The Philosophy of the Revolution"
1952

I can now say that we are going through two revolutions, not one.

All people on earth go through two revolutions: a political revolution to recover their right to self-government from the hands of a despot who has imposed himself upon them, or to free themselves from the domination of alien armed forces which have installed themselves in the land against their will; and a social revolution — a class conflict that ultimately ends in realising social justice for all the inhabitants of the country. . . .

There was no alternative to carrying out the two revolutions together. In fact, the day we proceeded towards political revolution and dethroned [King] Farouk, we took a similar step towards social revolution and limited the ownership of land.

. . . One revolution demanded that we should stand united and forget the past. And another revolution demanded that we should restore the lost dignity of moral values, and not forget the past. . . .

At a certain phase of my life, enthusiasm represented "positive action." But I later came to realise that it is not enough to be alone in that enthusiasm. To be effective, it should be communicated to others. I was then a student at the Nahda School, leading many demonstrations in those days, shouting myself hoarse along with other fellow-students, in our importunate demand for complete independence. But it was to no avail; our cries died into faint echoes that moved no mountains and blasted no rocks.

Then I came to believe that "positive action" rested on the solidarity and agreement of all the leaders of the nation. So our rebellious roaring ranks went round visiting these leaders, in their own homes, calling on them in the name of Egypt's youth to agree on concerted action. They did actually agree, but it was on the calamitous decision which destroyed my conviction — they agreed to conclude the 1936 Treaty.[1]

Infuriated by World War II, and the tragic events which immediately preceded that conflagration, not only our youth but the whole generation began to tend towards violence. I confess — and may the Public Prosecutor not take me severely to task for making such a confession — that political assassination struck my then inflamed mind as the inevitable positive action to be taken, if we were to save the future of the homeland. . . .

. . . [I]t would have been grossly unjust to have had a reign of terror imposed on us, taking into account the historical circumstances through which our people had lived — circumstances which have left their mark on our souls and have made of us what we now are. . . .

If the Crusades marked the first dawnings of the Renaissance in Europe, they heralded the beginning of the ages of darkness in our country. Our people alone bore almost the whole brunt of those battles, which left them completely impoverished and utterly helpless. And at the very time when they were weakened by the shattering blows of battle, it was their lot to suffer further humiliation and misery under the heels of Circassian tyrants and the Mongol despots. . . .

---

[1]The treaty assured Britain military bases in Egypt and maintained British control in Sudan despite promises from London to turn that territory over to Egypt.

Gamal Abdul-Nasser, *Nasser Speaks: Basic Documents,* trans. E.S. Farag (London: The Morssett Press, 1972), 26, 28, 30, 34–38, 44–46, 50, 52–57.

My soul is torn with grief when I think . . . of that period in our history when a despotic feudalism was formed, a feudalism directed towards bleeding the people and depriving them of their last vestige of power and dignity. We shall have to fight hard and long before we can rid ourselves completely of the influences of that system.

What still remains latent in our souls from those influences has on many occasions provided me with an explanation of some aspects of our political life. Sometimes, for instance, it seems to me that many adopt towards the revolution the attitude of mere onlookers, interested simply in the result of a fight between two sides with whom they are in no way connected. . . .

It would also seem to me that we depend too much on our imagination to realise our aims and solve our problems, so that more often than not our indulgence in such flights of imagination hinders us from exerting real efforts to attain our aims. Many have still not discarded that attitude, nor have they realised that the country is theirs, and they are the masters. . . .

. . . Our contacts with Europe and the whole world began anew [over the course of the nineteenth century]. So also began our modern awakening, but it began with a new crisis. . . .

We were subjected to currents of ideas for which we were not ready at that stage of our development. Our minds were still under the influence of the 13th century when they were invaded by some aspects of the 19th and then the 20th century. We were trying to catch up with the advancing human caravan from which we had dropped out five centuries or more before. The race was terrible but decisive.

Undoubtedly this state of affairs is responsible for the lack of strong united public opinion in our country. The difference between one individual and another is vast; that between one generation and another is vaster still.

There was a time when I complained that the people did not know what they were about, that they never agreed on the same road. I later realised, however, that I was asking for the impossible, that I had not taken the society in which we live into account. Actually we live in a society which is not yet crystallised. It is still in a state of ferment and agitation. It is not yet stabilised in its gradual development compared with other people who have passed before on the same road.

I believe, without intending to flatter my countrymen by expressing such a belief, that our people have wrought a veritable miracle. Any other society subjected to the same severe trials as ours might possibly have succumbed. It would have been swept away by the powerful currents that overtook us. We have, however, weathered the tempest. It is true we almost lost our balance, but we have not fallen. . . .

I see all this and feel in my heart that I know the cause of the perplexity torturing our minds, and the confusion destroying our very existence. I then say to myself: "Surely our society will crystallise; surely it will be solidified; surely it will be welded into a strong homogeneous whole. But it is essential that we strain every nerve to hold our ground during this period of transition." . . .

. . . I often ask myself: 'What is our positive role in this troubled world, and in which region do we play that role?' I review our circumstances and find that we are in a group or circle which should be the theatre of our activity, and in which we try to move as much as possible. . . .

There is no doubt that the Arab Circle is the most important of all these circles and the circle most closely connected with us. Its history merges with ours. We suffered in common the same hardships, lived through the same crises, and when we were trampled under foot by the conquerors, it suffered with us the same fate. We are also bound by the ties of a common religion. The centres of religious radiation moved within the boundaries of its capitals from Mecca to Koufa and then to Cairo. Furthermore, neighbourliness has welded us all into a homogeneous whole, strengthened by all these spiritual, historic and material factors.

I remember, as far as I am personally concerned, that the first notions of Arab consciousness began to creep into my mind when I was still a secondary school student. I used to come out with my fellow-students on general strike every year on the 2nd December as a protest against the Balfour Declaration which favoured establishing a national home for the Jewish people in Palestine, despotically usurped from the legitimate owners of the land. When I asked myself at that time why I should be carried away with enthusiasm and why I should be furious for a country I had never seen, the only echoes that rang in my ears were those of sympathy.

I began to have a better understanding of the situation, however, when I joined the Military Academy and studied the history of that region in general, and the history of the Palestine campaigns in particular, and the conditions which made it in recent times an easy prey, torn to shreds and ravaged by a pack of wild beasts. The situation became still clearer when I joined the Staff College and began studying the details of the Palestine campaign and other Mediterranean problems. And when the Palestine crisis began, I became fully convinced that fighting in Palestine was neither a war in an alien country nor a matter of sympathy. It was a sacred duty of self-defence. . . .

It was clear that imperialism was the most prominent of all these forces. Even Israel itself was nothing but a manifestation of . . . imperialism. Indeed, had not Palestine fallen under the British Mandate, Zionism could never have found the support it needed to realise the national home project, which would have remained a fantastic idea never destined to see light. . . .

After all these facts had become firmly established in my mind, I began to believe in one common struggle. I said to myself that since the region is one, with the same conditions, the same problems, the same future and the same enemy, no matter how different the masks that enemy might wear to conceal his identity, why should our efforts be dissipated? . . .

. . . When I analyse the elements of our strength, I cannot help being struck by three sources standing in bold relief, which should be taken into account before everything else.

The first of these sources lies in the fact that we [in the first circle consisting of Arab countries] are a group of neighbouring nations welded into a homogeneous whole by every possible material and moral tie that would unite any group of nations. Moreover, our peoples possess characteristics, potentialities and a civilisation inspired by the spiritual principles of the three divine religions, which can never be overlooked in any attempt to build a new stable and peaceful world.

The second source is our land itself and the position it occupies on the map of the world — that important strategic position which makes it the crossroads of the world, the main route of its trade and the highway of its armies.

There remains the third source. This is oil, which is the backbone of material civilisation, and without which all the world's largest factories, all means of land, sea and air transport, all war weapons whether they be the fighters and bombers flying high above the clouds or the submarines diving deep into the unfathomable depths of the ocean, would become mere iron blocks, devoid of motive power. . . .

As for the Second Circle — the African Continent Circle — . . . we cannot under any condition, even if we wanted to, stand aloof from the terrible and terrifying battle now raging in the heart of that continent between five million whites and two hundred million Africans. We cannot stand aloof for one important and obvious reason — we ourselves are in Africa. Surely the people of Africa will continue to look to us as the people who are the guardians of the Continent's northern gate and who constitute the connecting link between the Continent and the outer world. We certainly cannot, under any conditions, relinquish our responsibility to help spread the light of knowledge and civilisation into the very depths of the virgin jungles of the Continent. . . .

There remains the Third Circle — the circle encompassing continents and oceans which, as I have said, is the circle of our brethren-in-Islam who, wherever their place under the sun, turn with us towards the Qibla,[2] their lips solemnly saying the same prayers. . . .

As I contemplate the eighty million Moslems in Indonesia, the fifty million in China, the several millions in Malaya, Thailand and Burma, the hundred million or so in Pakistan, the well nigh over a hundred million in the Middle East, the forty million in the Soviet Union, and the millions of others in the far-flung corners of the earth — as I think of these hundreds of millions of Moslems, all united by the same Faith, I become increasingly aware of the potential achievements which co-operation among all these millions could accomplish — co-operation naturally not going beyond their loyalty to their own countries, but which would ensure for them and their brethren-in-Islam unlimited power.

---

[2]The direction for prayer pointing to the holy Islamic site in Mecca, Saudi Arabia.

6.2
Nasser Proclaims Arab Socialism

In May 1962, Nasser presented to the national congress a National Charter that he had largely drafted and that Congress adopted the next month. The Charter reviews the origin and course of the 1952 revolution as well as the pan-Arab movement leading to union between Egypt and Syria (under strain by 1962). This history builds up to its most important policy innovation — the formal proclamation of an Arab socialism to be implemented in Egypt.

Socialism has been famous for the way it has accommodated national or regional conditions. In what ways does Nasser's conception of socialism reflect peculiarly Egyptian or Arab conditions or concerns? How specific is it as a guide to action? How does his socialism compare to other variants such as Stalin's, Mao's, and Ho's? What might explain the more strident tone of this document compared to his 1952 reflections on the military takeover (just above)?

"The National Charter"
May 21, 1962

The devotion of the Egyptian people to the cause of the Revolution, the clarity of their vision and their unremitting struggle against all challenges have enabled them to produce a wonderful example of the national revolution, which is the contemporary phase of the free man's struggle throughout history for a better life, free of the chains of exploitation and underdevelopment in all their material and moral forms. . . .

The Egyptian people's revolutionary will, appears in its great and proper perspective if we recall that these valiant people began their revolutionary march with no political organisation to face the problems of the battle. Moreover, this revolutionary march started without a complete theory of revolutionary change.

In those eventful circumstances, the famous six principles, carved out of the demands and needs of the people's struggle, formed the sole basis for work. The mere declaration of those principles, amid the difficulties, dangers and darkness, was proof of the strength and unshakable foundation of the will for the revolutionary change.

(1) In the face of the lurking British occupation troops in the Suez Canal zone, the first principle was: Elimination of imperialism and its traitorous Egyptian collaborators.

(2) In the face of the despotism of feudalism, which dominated the land and those on it, the second principle was: Ending of feudalism.

(3) In the face of the exploitation of wealth and resources to serve the interests of a group of capitalists, the third principle was: Ending of monopoly and the domination of capital over the Government.

Nasser, *Nasser Speaks,* 61–63, 103–106, 112.

(4) In the face of the exploitation and despotism which were the inevitable consequences of all that the fourth principle was: Establishment of social justice.

(5) In the face of conspiracies to weaken the army (which was eager for revolution) and use the reserve of its strength to threaten the internal front, the fifth aim was: Building of a powerful national army.

(6) In the face of political deceit, which tried to veil the landmarks of true nationalism, the sixth aim was: Establishment of a sound democratic system. . . .

Socialism is the way to social freedom.

Social freedom cannot be realised except through an equal opportunity for every citizen to obtain a fair share of the national wealth. This is not confined to the mere redistribution of the national wealth among the citizens but foremost and above all it requires an expansion of the base of this national wealth, to accede to the lawful rights of the working masses. This means that socialism with its two supports, sufficiency and justice, is the way to social freedom. . . .

Those who call for freedom of capital, imagining that to be the road to progress, are gravely mistaken. In the countries forced to remain underdeveloped, capital in its natural development is no longer able to lead the economic drive, whilst the great capitalist monopolies in the advanced countries have developed by relying on the exploitation of the sources of wealth in the colonies. . . .

. . . [T]he wide gap of underdevelopment which separates the advanced states and those trying to catch up no longer allows the method of progress to be left to desultory individual efforts motivated by mere selfish profit. . . .

. . . Work aimed at expanding the base of national wealth can never be left to the haphazard methods of exploiting private capital with its unruly tendencies. The redistribution of surplus national labor on the basis of justice can never be accomplished through voluntary efforts based on good intentions, however sincere they may be.

. . . This socialist solution is the only way towards achieving economic and social progress. It is the way to democracy in all its social and political forms.

The people's control over the machinery of production does not necessitate the nationalisation of all means of production, the abolition of private ownership, or encroachment on the legitimate right of inheritance following therefrom. . . .

Efficient socialist planning is the sole method which guarantees the use of all national resources, be they material, natural or human, in a practical, scientific and humane way, aimed at realising the common good of the masses and ensuring a life of prosperity for them. It is the guarantee for the sound exploitation of existing resources and those which are latent or potential. At the same time it is a guarantee for the continued distribution of fundamental services. It is also a guarantee for raising the standard of the services already offered. It is a guarantee for extending those services to the areas which have fallen victim to negligence and inefficiency as a result of long deprivation imposed by the selfishness of the ruling classes who looked down upon the struggling people. . . .

Progress through socialism is a consolidation of the bases of sound democracy, the democracy of the people. Progress in the political domain under capitalism — even if we imagined it possible in the present international conditions — can only mean a confirmation of the rule of the class possessing and monopolising all interests. In this event, the returns would go to a small minority of people who have so much money that they squander it on various forms of wasteful luxury defying the deprivation of the majority. This sharpens the edge of the class strife and wipes out every hope for democratic evolution. But the socialist path providing opportunities for a peaceful settlement of class strife and affording possibilities for dissolving the distinctions between classes leads to the distribution of the returns among all the people according to the principle of equality of opportunity for all. The socialist path thereby paves the way for an inevitably political development leading to liberation from the rule of the feudalist dictatorship allied with capitalism and the establishment of the rule of democracy representing the rights and aspirations of the working people.

The political liberation of man cannot be achieved unless an end is put to every shackle of exploitation limiting his freedom. And socialism and democracy form the wings of freedom with which socialism can soar to the distant horizons aspired to by the masses.

6.3
Feminist Voices of Discontent

The centralizing, activist state run by Nasser nationalized foreign property holdings, redistributed land, maintained pressure on Israel, launched great public works projects such as the Aswan High Dam, and promoted pan-Arab cooperation. But pressing for greater gender equality was generally off limits — much to the dismay of educated urban women, in the forefront of the feminist cause since early in the twentieth century. Amina Said (born 1914) was one of the strongest public voices of this feminism. She entered Cairo University in 1931 in the third class open to women and played an active role in the Egyptian Feminist Union as editor of its publication. The first woman to establish a full-time career in journalism, she founded the mass-circulation magazine for women, *Hawa*, in 1954 and penned editorials for the next twenty-seven years that reached a wide audience throughout the Arab world. She was also a novelist, an author of children's stories, and a translator.

The following editorial, written in 1973 on the fiftieth anniversary of the founding of the Egyptian Feminist Union, appraises the advances women had made. What verdict does Said deliver on the state of the feminist cause only three years after Nasser's death? What sort of women might have embraced her point of view, and how might conservative Islamic clerics, increasingly influential at the time, have reacted? Why does she link feminism to colonialism and national liberation? How does her notion of feminism compare with de Beauvoir, NOW, or the French feminists of the early 1970s? (See Documents 5.11–5.13.)

Amina Said
Editorial in Hawa
1973

[V]eiling is the greatest enemy of civilisation and advancement, and . . . nationalism cannot be worthy of mention nor respect if it does not exist in the form of courageous, constructive acts based on belief in values and morals. It is important that every good woman citizen should perform these acts if she feels it her duty to serve her country so that the Arabs would regain their former dignity that has unfortunately gone as a result of rigid thinking dominating the minds of the ignorant majority causing us to move backwards, from being at the forefront of the world, to being at the rear. It had made us who have the greatest and most civilised religion in the world be despised by our enemies and pitied by our friends.

I'm addressing my words in particular to the young women of the modern Arab feminist generation. While in Egypt we celebrate the golden anniversary of the liberation of women, I want them and us to ask themselves what they have added to the efforts of the feminist vanguards? Unveiling and education at various levels were achieved through the efforts of those generations who have gone before. Work (for women) at various levels was also realized through the efforts and struggle of the first vanguards. Even the political rights that women in some Arab countries enjoy have come about in later years as the fruit of the early feminist struggle and the great political roles played by Egyptian, Syrian and Lebanese women, in the battles of national liberation against foreign colonisation.

I believe that if the modern Arab woman is honest in examining herself on this magnificent, historical occasion, she will discover that she has not added anything new to the efforts of those who have gone before and that she has not been part of any effort worth mentioning in advancing the feminist liberation movement in spite of the wide horizons before the woman of today, the abundance of opportunities and the advancement of social thinking and the development of life outside our area.

The modern woman of today can make miracles with her own hands. She can make gains and achieve suitable status in the world of civilisation, knowledge, freedom and advancement but she chooses to stand still, content with the little that has been realized for her by others imagining that she has attained everything while, in spite of the early victories, she has not achieved more than the crumbs from the table. In all Arab countries she is veiled, underdeveloped, and unqualified to perform national roles to help reconstruct her society. Even in those countries where the veil has disappeared the great majority of women are still prey to illiteracy. We remain in the era of the

Translated from the Arabic by Ali Badran and Margot Badran, in *Opening the Gates: A Century of Arab Feminist Writing,* ed. Margot Badran and Miriam Cooke (Bloomington: Indiana University Press, 1990), 361–62.

midwife while other nations are living in the space age and walk on the surface of the moon.

This is our greatest tribulation. How long will it last?

NKRUMAH'S VISION FOR GHANA AND AFRICA

Kwame Nkrumah led the drive by a colonized sub-Saharan Africa to win independence and promote economic development. Better than anyone else he articulated the dreams of national and continental renewal. Nkrumah's background was typical of many leaders of the generation who were devoted to liberation: Born on Ghana's coast, he was educated in missionary schools and in 1935 went abroad (in his case the United States) for advanced education. He returned home in 1947 afire with nationalist and Marxist ideas and eager to plunge into politics. He proved an effective organizer, whose mass base intimidated British colonial authorities. In 1957 Ghana gained its independence — the first sub-Saharan country to shed colonialism — with Nkrumah its president. He would remain the dominant figure until his overthrow in a military coup in 1966.

During those nine years in power, Nkrumah had a chance to put into practice his ideas on the future of Ghana and its neighbors in black Africa. In directing his country's economic development, he followed a model that was both socialist and Western. He concentrated on cities and big industrial projects, but neglected the "backward" countryside, the home of most his people and the center of gravity of his national economy. He championed self-determination and democracy, but his Convention People's Party proved autocratic as well as corrupt — its members more preoccupied with personal gain than Nkrumah's ambitious agenda. Finally, he boldly championed decolonization elsewhere in Africa and wide-ranging cooperation among states gaining their independence. Here too his ambitions fell short, gaining the support of few other heads of state. Despite these setbacks and disappointments, Nkrumah continued to dream, even after his ouster from power. In exile in Guinea, he shifted his hopes from Ghana and Africa to the black diaspora (the communities of Africans planted overseas by the slave trade).

6.4

Independence on the Horizon

The war years were a critical seedtime for Nkrumah and many other third-world leaders. They had grown up with nationalist ideas and self-consciously readied themselves for their day of independence by studying in the West. They were galvanized by Allied propaganda promising that self-determination would be fundamental in shaping the postwar international system. Their time to lead was drawing close, prompting feverish private conversations and public conferences about the future.

Nkrumah's writings from this period capture some of the excitement, impatience, and even anxiety of the war years. How does Nkrumah evaluate the prospects for decolonization, especially the motives of colonialists and the likelihood that they will decamp? What is his vision for post-independence Ghana? How much does his analysis echo or transcend the thinking of an older generation of nationalists represented by Mao, Ho, and Nehru (treated in chapter 3)?

Kwame Nkrumah
Commentary on Colonialism
1942–1945

The aim of all colonial governments in Africa and elsewhere has been the struggle for raw materials; and not only this, but the colonies have become the dumping ground, and colonial peoples the false recipients, of manufactured goods of the industrialists and capitalists of Great Britain, France, Belgium and other colonial powers who turn to the dependent territories which feed their industrial plants. This is colonialism in a nutshell.

The basis of colonial territorial dependence is economic, but the basis of the solution of the problem is political. Hence political independence is an indispensable step towards securing economic emancipation. This point of view irrevocably calls for an alliance of all colonial territories and dependencies. All provincial and tribal differences should be broken down completely. By operating on tribal differences and colonial provincialism, the colonial powers' age-long policy of "divide and rule" has been enhanced, while the colonial national independence movement has been obstructed and bamboozled. . . .

The idea that Britain, France or any other colonial power is holding colonies under "trusteeship" until, in their opinion, the colonies become "capable" of self-government is erroneous and misconceived. Colonial powers cannot afford to expropriate themselves. And then to imagine that these colonial powers will hand freedom and independence to their colonies on a silver platter without compulsion is the height of folly. . . .

The peoples of the colonies know precisely what they want. They wish to be free and independent, to be able to feel themselves on an equal with all other peoples, and to work out their own destiny without outside interference, and to be unrestricted to attain an advancement that will put them on a par with other technically advanced nations of the world. Outside interference does not help to develop their country. It impedes and stifles and crushes not only economic progress, but the spirit and indigenous enterprise of the peoples themselves. . . .

We therefore advance the following programme . . . :

(1) *Political Freedom,* i.e. complete and absolute independence from the control of any foreign government.

Originally published in *Towards Colonial Freedom* (1962) and reprinted in Kwame Nkrumah, *Revolutionary Path* (New York: International Publishers, 1973), 15–16, 40–41.

(2) *Democratic Freedom,* i.e. freedom from political tyranny and the establishment of a democracy in which sovereignty is vested in the broad masses of the people.

(3) *Social Reconstruction,* i.e. freedom from poverty and economic exploitation and the improvement of social and economic conditions of the people so that they will be able to find better means of achieving livelihood and asserting their right to human life and happiness.

6.5
Unity for Africa

Africa ended up a continent of many states, but its elites conceived it in both narrower and broader terms — of the ethnic groups to which they belonged and the regional affinities which provided a basis for cooperation. The sense of regional identity was particularly strong for West Africans. As a student in the United States, Nkrumah associated with other West Africans, contemplating union as one possibility and sharing with them a camaraderie and sense of mission as the young, educated vanguard devoted to liberation. It was thus a small jump for Nkrumah to imagine the advantages of an even broader basis for cooperation. If all of sub-Saharan Africa united, the benefits could be enormous.

A meeting of leaders in Addis Ababa, Ethiopia, in 1963 gave Nkrumah the opportunity to present his audacious proposal. (It would lead to the creation of the Organization of African Unity but little substantive cooperation.) What is Nkrumah's argument for a transcontinental approach? Does he seem aware of the obstacles facing his plan? How do you imagine leaders in the audience reacted?

Kwame Nkrumah
Address to the Conference of African Heads of Government and State
May 24, 1963

On this continent it has not taken us long to discover that the struggle against colonialism does not end with the attainment of national independence. Independence is only the prelude to a new and more involved struggle for the right to conduct our own economic and social affairs, to construct our society according to our aspirations, unhampered by crushing and humiliating neo-colonialist controls and interference. . . .

. . . We have already reached the stage where we must unite or sink into that condition which has made Latin-America the unwilling and distressed prey of imperialism after one-and-a-half centuries of political independence. . . .

The unity of our continent, no less than our separate independence, will be delayed if, indeed, we do not lose it, by hobnobbing with colonialism.

Originally published in *Africa Must Unite* (1963) and reprinted in Nkrumah, *Revolutionary Path,* 234–43.

African Unity is, above all, a political kingdom which can only be gained by political means. The social and economic development of Africa will come only within the political kingdom, not the other way round. . . .

How, except by our united efforts, will the richest and still enslaved parts of our continent be freed from colonial occupation and become available to us for the total development of our continent? Every step in the decolonization of our continent has brought greater resistance in those areas where colonial garrisons are available to colonialism and you all here know that.

. . . When Portugal violates Senegal's border, when Verwoerd[1] allocates one-seventh of South Africa's budget to military and police, when France builds as part of her defence policy an interventionist force that can intervene, more especially in French-speaking Africa, when Welensky[2] talks of Southern Rhodesia joining South Africa, when Britain sends arms to South Africa, it is all part of a carefully calculated pattern working towards a single end: the continued enslavement of our still dependent brothers and an onslaught upon the independence of our sovereign African states. . . .

Our people supported us in our fight for independence because they believed that African Governments could cure the ills of the past in a way which could never be accomplished under colonial rule. If, therefore, now that we are independent we allow the same conditions to exist that existed in colonial days, all the resentment which overthrew colonialism will be mobilized against us.

The resources are there. It is for us to marshal them in the active service of our people. . . .

Our continent is probably the richest in the world for minerals and industrial and agricultural primary materials. From the Congo alone, Western firms exported copper, rubber, cotton, and other goods to the value of 2,773 million dollars in the ten years between 1945 and 1955, and from South Africa, Western gold mining companies have drawn a profit, in the six years between 1947 to 1951, of 814 million dollars.

Our continent certainly exceeds all the others in potential hydroelectric power, which some experts assess as 42 per cent of the world's total. . . .

. . . Our capital flows out in streams to irrigate the whole system of Western economy. . . . Africa provides more than 60 per cent of the world's gold. A great deal of the uranium for nuclear power, of copper for electronics, of titanium for supersonic projectiles, of iron and steel for heavy industries, of other minerals and raw materials for lighter industries — the basic economic might of the foreign Powers — come from our continent.

Experts have estimated that the Congo Basin alone can produce enough food crops to satisfy the requirements of nearly half the population of the whole

---

[1]Hendrik Verwoerd, prime minister of the white-controlled government of South Africa between 1958 and 1966 and a staunch supporter of the policy of apartheid (or racial separation).

[2]Roy Welensky, prime minister of the Federation of Rhodesia and Nyasaland (a British possession) between 1956 and 1963. The Federation was collapsing when this was written in 1963.

world and here we sit talking about regionalism, talking about gradualism, talking about step by step. Are you afraid to tackle the bull by the horn? . . .

We have the resources. It was colonialism in the first place that prevented us from accumulating the effective capital; but we ourselves have failed to make full use of our power in independence to mobilize our resources for the most effective take-off into thoroughgoing economic and social development. We have been too busy nursing our separate states to understand fully the basic need of our union, rooted in common purpose, common planning and common endeavour. . . . It is only by uniting our productive capacity and the resultant production that we can amass capital. And once we start, the momentum will increase. With capital controlled by our own banks, harnessed to our own true industrial and agricultural development, we shall make our advance. We shall accumulate machinery and establish steel works, iron foundries and factories; we shall link the various states of our continent with communications by land, sea and air. We shall cable from one place to another, phone from one place to the other and astound the world with our hydro-electric power; we shall drain marshes and swamps, clear infested areas, feed the under-nourished, and rid our people of parasites and disease. It is within the possibility of science and technology to make even the Sahara bloom into a vast field with verdant vegetation for agricultural and industrial developments. We shall harness the radio, television, giant printing presses to lift our people from the dark recesses of illiteracy.

A decade ago, these would have been visionary words, the fantasies of an idle dreamer. But this is the age in which science has transcended the limits of the material world, and technology has invaded the silences of nature. Time and space have been reduced to unimportant abstractions. . . .

There is hardly any African State without a frontier problem with its adjacent neighbours. . . . [T]his fatal relic of colonialism will drive us to war against one another as our unplanned and uncoordinated industrial development expands, just as happened in Europe. Unless we succeed in arresting the danger through mutual understanding on fundamental issues and through African Unity, which will render existing boundaries obsolete and superfluous, we shall have fought in vain for independence. Only African Unity can heal this festering sore of boundary disputes between our various states. . . . By creating a true political union of all the independent states of Africa, with executive powers for political direction we can tackle hopefully every emergency, every enemy, and every complexity. This is not because we are a race of supermen, but because we have emerged in the age of science and technology in which poverty, ignorance and disease are no longer the masters, but the retreating foes of mankind. We have emerged in the age of socialized planning, where production and distribution are not governed by chaos, greed and self-interest, but by social needs. Together with the rest of mankind, we have awakened from Utopian dreams to pursue practical blueprints for progress and social justice. . . .

Unite we must. Without necessarily sacrificing our sovereignties, big or small, we can here and now forge a political union based on Defence, Foreign

Affairs and Diplomacy, and a Common Citizenship, an African Currency, an African Monetary Zone and an African Central Bank. We must unite in order to achieve the full liberation of our continent. . . .

. . . [M]any Independent African States are involved by military pacts with the former colonial powers. . . . We have seen how the neo-colonialists use their bases to entrench themselves and even to attack neighbouring independent states. Such bases are centres of tension and potential danger spots of military conflict. They threaten the security not only of the country in which they are situated but of neighbouring countries as well. How can we hope to make Africa a nuclear-free zone and independent of cold war pressure with such military involvement on our continent? Only by counter-balancing a common defence force with a common desire for an Africa untrammelled by foreign dictation or military and nuclear presence. This will require an all-embracing African High Command. . . .

We need unified economic planning for Africa. Until the economic power of Africa is in our hands, the masses can have no real concern and no real interest for safeguarding our security, for ensuring the stability of our regimes, and for bending their strength to the fulfillment of our ends. With our united resources, energies and talents we have the means, as soon as we show the will, to transform the economic structures of our individual states from poverty to that of wealth, from inequality to the satisfaction of popular needs. Only on a continental basis shall we be able to plan the proper utilization of all our resources for the full development of our continent. . . .

Our people call for Unity so that they may not lose their patrimony in the perpetual service of neo-colonialism. In their fervent push for Unity, they understand that only its realization will give full meaning to their freedom and our African independence.

6.6

Socialism for Ghana

Nothing was more critical to the fate of the people of Ghana and other newly independent states than the success of economic development programs. Colonial authorities usually left behind some assets (in Ghana's case a lucrative cash crop, cocao, as well as a large budgetary surplus for the new government to draw on). On the other hand, they tended to neglect the countryside, especially in regard to transport, education, and health care. Determined to create a modern society and economy, leaders like Nkrumah and Nasser looked to socialism as the system that could bring quick results. The Soviet and Chinese examples appealed to them powerfully.

Nkrumah's speech launching an ambitious seven-year development plan needs to be read against this backdrop. What did socialism mean to him? How aggressively did he propose pursuing socialist goals? What sort of country did he imagine emerging from the socialist drive?

Kwame Nkrumah
Speech to the National Assembly
March 11, 1964

Our aim, under this Plan, is to build in Ghana a socialist State which accepts full responsibility for promoting the well-being of the masses. Our national wealth must be built up and used in such a way that economic power shall not be allowed to exploit the worker in town or village, but be used for the supreme welfare and happiness of our people. The people, through the State, should have an effective share in the economy of the country and an effective control over it.

A socialist Ghana must also secure for every citizen, at the earliest possible date, an adequate level of education and nutrition and a satisfactory standard of clothing, housing and leisure.

The [Convention People's] Party has always proclaimed socialism as the objective of our social, industrial and economic programmes. Socialism, however, will continue to remain a slogan until industrialization is achieved. . . .

Mr Speaker, in order to accomplish our objectives, we have decided that the economy of Ghana will, for some time to come, remain a mixed economy in which a vigorous public and co-operative sector will operate along with the private sector. . . .

We are determined that the economic independence of Ghana shall be achieved and maintained so as to avoid the social antagonisms resulting from the unequal distribution of economic power. We are equally determined to ensure that the operation of a mixed economy leads to the socialist transformation we envisage, and not to the defeat of our socialist aims. . . .

We welcome foreign investors in a spirit of partnership. They can earn their profits here, provided they leave us an agreed portion for promoting the welfare and happiness of our people as a whole as against the greedy ambitions of the few. From what we get out of this partnership, we hope to be able to expand the health services for our people, to feed and house them well, to give them more and better educational institutions and to see to it that they have a rising standard of living. . . .

One of the worst features of colonialism was that it produced an unbalanced economy in which there was little room for investment of the profits which were made by expatriate firms. In colonial days it was natural that profits made in Ghana should be invested abroad. Today the situation is entirely different. An investor who lays out his money wisely in Ghana is likely to make a larger profit than if he invested it in a more developed country. Nevertheless, old habits of investment persist and there are a considerable number of Ghanaians who still maintain their savings in foreign investments and in property outside Ghana.

Nkrumah, *Revolutionary Path,* 190–96, 202–204.

Under our Exchange Control laws it is, of course, illegal for Ghanaians to have property abroad without having declared this to the appropriate authorities. . . .

We intend that the State should retain control of the strategic branches of the economy, including public utilities, raw materials and heavy industry. The State will also participate in light and consumer goods industries in which the rates of return on capital should be highest. We intend also that those industries which provide the basic living needs of the people shall be State-owned, in order to prevent any exploitation. . . .

The development of Ghana has hitherto not been sufficiently balanced between different parts of the country. . . . [A] special effort has to be made in order to ensure that the rate of progress in the less favoured parts of the country is even greater than the rate of progress in those sections which have hitherto been more favoured. It is only by this means that we can achieve a more harmonious national development.

In the present Plan period it is proposed to pay special attention to the modernizing of agriculture in the savannah areas of the Northern and Upper Regions. It is hoped through secondary industries based on agricultural raw materials, to turn the Northern areas into major sources of food supplies for the whole country. . . .

Mr Speaker, the backbone of Ghana's agriculture has always been its farmers . . . . The developments the Government is proposing in the areas of State and co-operative farming will bring them a share of the local facilities they have so long been denied. More than this: they will have the opportunity also to share in the up-to-date techniques of farming that must be employed if greater yields and diversity of crops are to be attained.

I want our farmers to understand that the State Farms and Co-operative enterprises are not being encouraged as alternatives to peasant farming. The interests of individual peasant farmers will not be made subservient to those of the State Farms and Co-operatives. We need the efforts of our individual Farmers more than ever, along with our State Farms and Co-operatives, if we are to achieve, at an increased pace, the agricultural targets we have set ourselves. . . .

The initiative of Ghanaian businessmen will not be cramped, but we must take steps to see that it is channelled towards desirable social ends and is not expended in the exploitation of the community. The Government will encourage Ghanaian businessmen to join with each other in co-operative forms of organization. In this way Ghanaian businessmen will be able to contribute actively in broadening the vitality of our economy and co-operation, and will provide a stronger form of organization than can be achieved through individual small businesses.

We must also discourage anything that can threaten our socialist construction. For this reason, no Ghanaian will be allowed to take up shares in any enterprise under foreign investment. On the contrary, we shall encourage our people with savings to invest in the State sector and co-operative undertakings. . . .

This Seven-Year Development Plan can only be accounted a success if by 1970 — the year in which we conclude the Plan and the year in which we celebrate the Tenth Anniversary of our Republic — we can truly say that the productive base of the economy has been revolutionized and that the level of technology and productivity in Ghana is approaching modern standards over an adequate area of the national economy.

Mr Speaker, Members of the National Assembly, 1964, the year in which we launch the Seven-Year Development Plan, will be hailed as the turning point in the history of Ghana. In a little over a year from now, we shall be generating electricity from the Volta River Project to feed our expanding factories throughout the country. The Kwame Nkrumah Steel Works in Tema will soon be completed. Tema Harbour itself is already being extended to meet the needs of our expanding economy, and in Tema a growing number of industrial projects are already in production and more are being established. . . .

I can already see, in my mind's eye, a picture of Ghana as it will be by the end of the Plan period. I see a State with a strong and virile economy, its agriculture and industry buoyant and prosperous, an industrialized nation serving the needs of its people.

6.7
Hopes for a Global Black-Power Movement

Nkrumah was in exile and eager to regain power in Ghana when growing black radicalism in the United States caught his attention and prompted the following enthusiastic response. Black power, however, did not develop into an international movement strong enough to restore his authority back home, and Nkrumah died in 1971 still in exile. The general mismanagement and instability under the governments following the 1966 coup restored some luster to Nkrumah's reputation, and he has in recent decades become a celebrated national icon.

How did Nkrumah link global trends to his long-held hopes for true independence, development, and pan-Africanism? How does his notion of black power compare with Stokely Carmichael's (Document 4.11)?

Kwame Nkrumah
The Spectre of Black Power
1968

With a decisiveness and force which can no longer be concealed the spectre of Black Power has descended on the world like a thundercloud flashing its lightning. Emerging from the ghettoes, swamps and cotton-fields of America, it now haunts the streets, legislative assemblies and high councils and has so shocked and horrified Americans that it is only now that they are beginning

Originally published in *The Spectre of Black Power* (1968) and reprinted in Nkrumah, *Revolutionary Path*, 423–28.

to grasp its full significance, and the fact that Black Power, in other manifestations, is in confrontation with imperialism, colonialism, neo-colonialism, exploitation and aggression in many parts of the world. . . .

As the United States grew richer, more powerful and imperialistic, as it expanded and extended its influence and control throughout Latin America and the islands of the Caribbean, its racialism, oppression and contempt for the peoples of African descent became accepted as an American way of life. . . .

In spite of the long and untiring work in education and organization of the pioneers of "Civil Rights"; in spite of the painstaking efforts made by African-American citizens of the United States to educate their children, and by hard work to achieve "acceptance" in American society, African-Americans have remained only barely tolerated aliens in the land of their birth, the vast mass of them outside consideration of basic human justice. . . .

The young African-American "sit-downers" of recent years committed no violence, nor did the many white students who, following their example, poured out of the great northern universities to demonstrate against racialism, segregation and discrimination. But their petitions and pleas for justice were met with violence, with savage beatings, with jail sentences. Some of them died in the struggle.

Then, on August 18th, 1965, in the Negro ghetto of Watts, in the city of Los Angeles, African-Americans took up arms to meet their aggressors. Since then, practically every major city in the United States has seen guns, rifles and fire bombs in the hands of black men, who, with every shot fired, are claiming their birthright. Since 1966, the cry of the rebellion has been "Black Power."

What is Black Power? I see it in the United States as part of the vanguard of world revolution against capitalism, imperialism and neo-colonialism which have enslaved, exploited and oppressed peoples everywhere, and against which the masses of the world are now revolting. Black Power is part of the world rebellion of the oppressed against the oppressor, of the exploited against the exploiter. It operates throughout the African continent, in North and South America, the Caribbean, wherever Africans and people of African descent live. It is linked with the Pan-African struggle for unity on the African continent, and with all those who strive to establish a socialist society. . . .

In Africa, we thought we could achieve freedom and independence, and our ultimate goals of unity and socialism by peaceful means. This has landed us in the grip of neo-colonialism. We could not succeed using non-violent methods. The same power structure which is blocking the efforts of African-Americans in the United States is also now throwing road-blocks in Africa's way. Imperialism, neo-colonialism, settler domination and racialism seek to bring us down and re-subjugate us.

In Africa, Latin America, the Caribbean, the Middle East and South East Asia, imperialists and neo-colonialists, with the help of local stooges, attempt to master with guns. They are united in their determination to extend and prolong their domination and exploitation. So we must fight wherever imperialism, neo-colonialism and racialism exist. We too must combine our strength and co-ordinate our strategy in a unified armed struggle. Non-violent methods are now anachronistic in revolution. And so I say to the progressive, revolutionary forces of the world, in the words of Ernesto Ché Guevara[1]: "Let us develop a true proletarian internationalism, with international proletarian armies; the flag under which we fight shall be the sacred cause of redeeming humanity."

It must be understood that liberation movements in Africa, the struggle of Black Power in America or in any other part of the world, can only find consummation in the political unification of Africa, the home of the black man and people of African descent throughout the world. African-Americans have been separated from their cultural and national roots. Black children overseas are not taught of the glory of African civilization in the history of mankind, of pillaged cities and destroyed tribes. They do not know the millions of black martyrs who died resisting imperialist aggression. The imperialists and neo-colonialists inside or outside the United States designate everything "good" as "white," and everything "bad" as "black." Black Power says: "We will define ourselves." For centuries, African-Americans have been the victims of racialism. They have now taken up arms to abolish it for ever, and to destroy its fertile breeding ground, the capitalist system. For it is only with the building of a socialist society that peace and racial harmony can be ultimately achieved. It is only world socialism which can provide the solution to the problems of the world today.

---

[1]Argentine-born associate of Fidel Castro. See Document 6.14.

6.8
Bitter Reflections on Nkrumah's Failure

Ayi Kwei Armah was Ghanaian-born (1939), near Nkrumah's birthplace on the coast. Like Nkrumah, he attended the prestigious Achimoto School and then left for further studies in the United States (in Armah's case at Groton and Harvard). He worked as a writer and translator and taught at universities in Africa and the United States. *The Beautyful Ones Are Not Yet Born*, Armah's first novel, is the story of an anonymous railway clerk psychologically burdened by the failed promise of the Nkrumah era. His wife and mother-in-law badger him to forget integrity and make his family's life easier by taking up the corrupt practices prevailing under Nkrumah's ruling Convention People's Party. He stubbornly refuses and instead incessantly reflects on the corruption — literal and figurative — around him. The novel closes with Nkrumah falling to a coup, but the protagonist has no hope that a better government is going to take his place.

How do the following reflections from the conclusion of the novel shed light on Nkrumah's goals and his shortcomings? How does the language used by Nkrumah and Armah differ? How might this novel have reflected or shaped opinion in Ghana at the time?

Ayi Kwei Armah
From *The Beautyful Ones Are Not Yet Born*
1969

It was not until after eight o'clock that the other staff started coming in. When, at half past seven, not even the messengers had come, the man had wondered what could have happened, but in a while he took his mind off the matter. The messengers were, as usual, the first to arrive. One of them came in like a ghost, so quietly in fact that the man did not notice him till the other arrived. This one came whistling, which was something of an unusual thing to do, though it did not disturb the man. But the other messenger shut his companion up. The second could not bear the silence long, and, walking around behind the man, he sighed very loudly and exclaimed. "Ei, these *coups!*"

The man did not turn around, but he asked the messenger, "Has there been another one?"

"Yea, man!"

"In Africa or somewhere else?"

"Today, today, here in Ghana!"

Now the other messenger walked out of his corner and joined the two. "So you haven't heard?"

"On the morning shift we can't hear the news," the man said.

"No six o'clock news this morning. Only some strange announcement by a man with a strange name, then *soja* music. They say they have seized power."

"Who?" the man asked.

"Army men and policemen."

"Oh, I see. I thought they always had power. Together with Nkrumah and his fat men."

The messengers said nothing. Even the one who had come in whistling had a sort of second fear in his eyes, the kind of look people have when they are unsure of what they are doing, and want to take care to be able to claim, that it was all a joke, should the need arise. In the man's own mind there was a diffuse uncertainty. What, after all, could it mean? One man, with the help of people who loved him and believed in him, had arrived at power and used it for himself. Now other men, with the help of guns, had come to this same power. What would it mean?

The senior men did not come to work. Fear was a very strong thing in their lives, and it was understandable that they would want to wait when something like this was happening. In the great strike many men had thought the big chance had definitely come, and had rushed to say how much they had fought against the order they thought had been overthrown. When in the end the police came and dragged people off to their jails and everyone knew there would be no change, many senior men had walked around fearing that

Ayi Kwei Armah, *The Beautyful Ones Are Not Yet Born* (Oxford: Heinemann, 1969), 156–59, 162.

someone who had heard them in the red days would remember their words.

The other junior staff came one by one, adding little bits, some very wild indeed, to the news available. They said all big Party men were being arrested and placed in something called protective custody — already a new name for old imprisonment without trial. New people, new style, old dance. When the Time Allocations clerk came in, he greeted everybody loudly and added, in a highly satisfied tone, "Now another group of bellies will be bursting with the country's riches!" The reaction to that, like everything else this day, was a confusion of approval and insecure hesitation.

When the sun had gone up there was the sound of some commotion in the street outside. A man who had been a trade unionist for the overthrown government rushed into the office announcing the *coup* as if he had himself accomplished it. Then he ordered people to go out and show their loyalty to the new men of power. With a silence that spoke everybody's shame, the men in the office went out singly to join the crowd outside. In the same manner they had gone out in fear to hear the farts of the Party men.

The man did not move from his desk. The old–new union man stood staring at him, then said, "Contrey, what about you?"

"Yes, what about what?"

"We are all demonstrating."

"For what?"

"Don't you know there is a new government?"

"They tell me so. But I know nothing about the men. What will I be demonstrating for?"

"Look, Contrey, if you don't want trouble, get out."

"If two trains collide while I'm demonstrating, will you take the responsibility?"

"Oh," said the organizer, "if it is the job, fine. But we won't tolerate any Nkrumaists now."

"You know," said the man slowly, "you know who the real Nkrumaists are."

The unionist turned round and went down to join his crowd. Through the windows their sounds came: old songs with the words changed from the old praise for Nkrumah to insults for him. So like the noises of the Party when all the first promise had been eaten up and it had become a place where fat men found things to swell themselves up some more. The noise moved away up the hill, and then the men who had followed their fear to go and swell it did not come back to work the rest of the day. . . .

. . . In the life of the nation itself, maybe nothing really new would happen. New men would take into their hands the power to steal the nation's riches and to use it for their own satisfaction. That, of course, was to be expected. New people would use the country's power to get rid of men and women who talked a language that did not flatter them. There would be nothing different in that. That would only be a continuation of the Ghanaian way of life. But here was the real change. The individual man of power now shivering, his head filled with the fear of the vengeance of those he had wronged. For him everything was going to change. And for those like him who had grown greasy and fat singing the praises of their chief, for those who had been getting themselves ready for the enjoyment of hoped-for favors, there would be long days of pain ahead. The flatterers with their new white Mercedes cars would have to find ways of burying old words. For those who had come directly against the old power, there would be much happiness. But for the nation itself there would only be a change of embezzlers and a change of the hunters and the hunted. A pitiful shrinking of the world from those days ... when the single mind was filled with the hopes of a whole people. A pitiful shrinking, to days when all the powerful could think of was to use power of a whole people to fill their own paunches. Endless days, same days, stretching into the future with no end anywhere in sight.

CASTRO'S DRIVE TO CREATE A NEW CUBA

Fidel Castro Ruz is the longest-living revolutionary of the postwar era. He burst on the public scene in 1953 as the leader of a coup attempt against dictator Fulgencio Batista. After several years in jail and in exile in Mexico, he returned to the island in 1956 with a small band in a second attempt to overthrow Batista. The revolutionary movement which he led triumphed in 1959, beginning an eventful and tension-filled period in which Castro consolidated his domestic control, introduced far-reaching reforms, and shifted a reliance on the United States to the Soviet Union. Throughout the Cold War and beyond, Castro has remained a staunch proponent of a socialist course at home and an irritant to Washington.

Castro's revolution fits the pattern seen in other third-world cases. A sense of injustice done his country and people drove him. His ideas on the nature of the injustice and the way to correct it were a complex and changing mix. And finally, the tempo of the revolutionary program tended to accelerate as one success fed the hunger for more.

6.9

Fidel Castro: "History Will Absolve Me"

Castro's reputation rested on a dual act of defiance in mid-1953. The attempt by his small band of about a hundred and seventy to seize the Moncada Barracks in eastern Cuba on July 26 and thereby ignite a popular uprising against Batista was daring, even foolhardy. Half of the attacking force died in the fighting or at the hands of their captors. The following October during his trial Castro not only defended the insurrection but also indicted the Batista dictatorship in a long, carefully prepared statement to the presiding judges that at the time must have seemed like pure bravado. In a makeshift courtroom in a hospital out of the public eye, the twenty-seven-year-old spoke for several hours, outlining the story of the attack, the brutality and corruption of the regime in power, and his own dreams for social justice.

This rhetorical tour de force alternately offers detached analysis, rousing patriotic appeals, defiant challenges, and sly insinuations. Thanks to notes kept by reporters attending the trial and Castro's own reconstruction of the speech while serving his prison sentence, an approximation of the text survived and by mid-1954 was in print and in wide circulation. His self-confidence and the power of his appeal evident here laid the foundation for the mystique that would help carry Castro to power and keep him there. Batista for his part underestimated the mettle of this young man and by pardoning him in 1956 set in motion events that would sweep away the old regime. The final words by which this speech is known — "History Will Absolve Me" — ring prophetically. Imagine yourself a Cuban reading Castro's declaration for the first time in 1954. How would you have assessed his goals and political prospects?

Address to the Presiding Trial Judges
October 16, 1953

The plan was drawn up by a group of young men, none of whom had any military experience at all. . . . Half of them are dead, and in tribute to their memory I can say that although they were not military experts they had enough patriotism to have given, had we not been at such a great disadvantage, a good beating to that entire lot of [Batista's] generals together . . . who are neither soldiers nor patriots. Much more difficult than the planning of the attack was our organizing, training, mobilizing and arming men under this repressive regime with its millions of dollars spent on espionage, bribery and information services. Nevertheless, all this was carried out by those men and many others like them with incredible seriousness, discretion and discipline. Still more praiseworthy is the fact that they gave this task everything they had; ultimately, their very lives.

The final mobilization of men who came to this province from the most remote towns of the entire island was accomplished with admirable precision and in absolute secrecy. It is equally true that the attack was carried out with magnificent coordination. It began simultaneously at 5:15 a.m. in both Bayamo and Santiago de Cuba; and one by one, with an exactitude of minutes and seconds prepared in advance, the buildings surrounding the barracks fell to our forces. . . . [D]ue to a most unfortunate error, half of our forces, and the better armed half at that, went astray at the entrance to the city and were not on hand to help us at the decisive moment. Abel Santamaría, with 21 men, had occupied the Civilian Hospital; with him went a doctor and two of our women comrades to attend to the wounded. Raúl Castro, with ten men, occupied the Palace of Justice, and it was my responsibility to attack the barracks with the rest, 95 men. Preceded by an advance group of eight who had

Available online at <http://www.marxists.org/history/cuba/archive/castro/1953/10/16.htm> (January 13, 2003). This Internet version is based on a translation by Pedro Álvarez Tabío, subsequently checked by Andrew Paul Booth against English and Spanish editions.

forced Gate Three, I arrived with the first group of 45 men. It was precisely here that the battle began, when my car ran into an outside patrol armed with machine guns. The reserve group which had almost all the heavy weapons (the light arms were with the advance group), turned up the wrong street and lost its way in an unfamiliar city. . . . Many of them, captured later on, met death with true heroism.

Everyone had instructions, first of all, to be humane in the struggle. Never was a group of armed men more generous to the adversary. From the beginning we took numerous prisoners — nearly twenty — and there was one moment when three of our men . . . managed to enter a barrack and hold nearly fifty soldiers prisoners for a short time. Those soldiers testified before the Court, and without exception they all acknowledged that we treated them with absolute respect, that we didn't even subject them to one scoffing remark. . . .

Discipline among the [government] soldiers was very poor. They finally defeated us because of their superior numbers — fifteen to one — and because of the protection afforded them by the defenses of the fortress. Our men were much better marksmen, as our enemies themselves conceded. There was a high degree of courage on both sides. . . .

When I became convinced that all efforts to take the barracks were now useless, I began to withdraw our men in groups of eight and ten. Our retreat was covered by six expert marksmen . . . . Our losses in the battle had been insignificant; 95% of our casualties came from the Army's inhumanity after the struggle. . . .

We planned to continue the struggle in the mountains in case the attack on the regiment failed. . . . For a week we held the heights of the Gran Piedra range and the Army occupied the foothills. We could not come down; they didn't risk coming up. It was not force of arms, but hunger and thirst that ultimately overcame our resistance. . . . Finally only two comrades remained with me — José Suárez and Oscar Alcalde. While the three of us were totally exhausted, a force led by Lieutenant Sarría surprised us in our sleep at dawn. This was Saturday, August 1st. . . . This officer, a man of honor, saved us from being murdered on the spot with our hands tied behind us. . . .

It was never our intention to engage the soldiers of the regiment in combat. We wanted to seize control of them and their weapons in a surprise attack, arouse the people and call the soldiers to abandon the odious flag of the tyranny and to embrace the banner of freedom; to defend the supreme interests of the nation and not the petty interests of a small clique; to turn their guns around and fire on the people's enemies and not on the people, among whom are their own sons and fathers; to unite with the people as the brothers that they are instead of opposing the people as the enemies the government tries to make of them; to march behind the only beautiful ideal worthy of sacrificing one's life — the greatness and happiness of one's country. To those who doubt that many soldiers would have followed us, I ask: What Cuban does not cherish glory? What heart is not set aflame by the promise of freedom? . . .

. . . Our men were killed not in the course of a minute, an hour or a day. Throughout an entire week the blows and tortures continued, men were thrown from rooftops and shot. All methods of extermination were incessantly practiced by well-skilled artisans of crime. Moncada Barracks were turned into a workshop of torture and death. Some shameful individuals turned their uniforms into butcher's aprons. The walls were splattered with blood. The bullets imbedded in the walls were encrusted with singed bits of skin, brains and human hair, the grisly reminders of rifle shots fired full in the face. The grass around the barracks was dark and sticky with human blood. The criminal hands that are guiding the destiny of Cuba had written for the prisoners at the entrance to that den of death the very inscription of Hell: "Forsake all hope."

They did not even attempt to cover appearances. . . . They felt themselves lords and masters of the universe, with power over life and death. So the fear they had experienced upon our attack at daybreak was dissipated in a feast of corpses, in a drunken orgy of blood. . . .

. . . Remember that today you are judging an accused man, but that you yourselves will be judged not once, but many times, as often as these days are submitted to scrutiny in the future. What I say here will be then repeated many times, not because it comes from my lips, but because the problem of justice is eternal and the people have a deep sense of justice above and beyond the hairsplitting of jurisprudence. The people wield simple but implacable logic, in conflict with all that is absurd and contradictory. Furthermore, if there is in this world a people that utterly abhors favoritism and inequality, it is the Cuban people. To them, justice is symbolized by a maiden with a scale and a sword in her hands. Should she cower before one group and furiously wield that sword against another group, then to the people of Cuba the maiden of justice will seem nothing more than a prostitute brandishing a dagger. My logic is the simple logic of the people. . . .

The right of rebellion against tyranny, Honorable Judges, has been recognized from the most ancient times to the present day by men of all creeds, ideas and doctrines. . . .

. . . How can Batista's presence in power be justified when he gained it against the will of the people and by violating the laws of the Republic through the use of treachery and force? How could anyone call legitimate a regime of blood, oppression and ignominy? . . . With what right do the Courts send to prison citizens who have tried to redeem their country by giving their own blood, their own lives? All this is monstrous to the eyes of the nation and to the principles of true justice!

Still there is one argument more powerful than all the others. We are Cubans and to be Cuban implies a duty; not to fulfill that duty is a crime, is treason. We are proud of the history of our country; we learned it in school and have grown up hearing of freedom, justice and human rights. We were taught to venerate the glorious example of our heroes and martyrs. . . . We were taught to cherish and defend the beloved flag of the lone star, and to sing every afternoon the verses of our National Anthem: "To live in chains is to live in disgrace and in opprobrium," and "to die for one's homeland is to live forever!" All this we learned and will never forget, even though today in our land there is murder and prison for the men who practice the ideas taught to them since the cradle. We were born in a free country that our parents bequeathed to us, and the Island will first sink into the sea before we consent to be the slaves of anyone. . . .

I come to the close of my defense plea but I will not end it as lawyers usually do, asking that the accused be freed. I cannot ask freedom for myself while my comrades are already suffering in the ignominious prison of the Isle of Pines. Send me there to join them and to share their fate. It is understandable that honest men should be dead or in prison in a Republic where the President is a criminal and a thief. . . .

I know that imprisonment will be harder for me than it has ever been for anyone, filled with cowardly threats and hideous cruelty. But I do not fear prison, as I do not fear the fury of the miserable tyrant who took the lives of 70 of my comrades. Condemn me. It does not matter. History will absolve me.

6.10

Fidel Castro on Resisting the United States

Castro's seizure of power in January 1959 set off a cascade of events — revolutionary retribution against criminal elements in the old regime, increasing alienation from Washington culminating in a bitter split, growing rapprochement with the Soviet Union, and radicalization of land and industrial policy at home. Never close to the Communist party before victory, Castro drew closer afterward.

Against this backdrop of revolutionary consolidation and confrontation with the United States, Castro issued this statement. It was a response to the expulsion of Cuba from the Organization of American States at the instigation of the Kennedy administration. But its purpose and audience was broader than merely rebutting American charges. What audience did Castro seem to be speaking to and where was he trying to take it?

Declaration Issued in Havana
February 4, 1962

Cuba has lived three years of the Revolution under the incessant harassment of Yankee intervention in our internal affairs. Pirate airplanes coming from the United States, dropping incendiaries, have burned millions of [pounds] of sugar cane; acts of international sabotage perpetrated by Yankee agents . . . have cost dozens of Cuban lives; thousands of North American weapons have been dropped by parachute by the U.S. military services onto our territory to

---

Martin Kenner and James Petras, eds., *Fidel Castro Speaks* (New York: Grove Press, 1969), 105, 115–16.

promote subversion; hundreds of tons of explosive materials and bombs have been secretly landed on our coast from North American launches to promote sabotage and terrorism; . . . our sugar quota was abruptly cut and an embargo proclaimed on parts and raw materials for factories and North American construction machinery in order to ruin our economy. Cuban ports and installations have been surprise-attacked by armed ships and bombers from bases prepared by the United States. Mercenary troops, organized and trained in countries of Central America by the same government, have in a warlike manner invaded our territories, escorted by ships of the Yankee fleet and with aerial support from foreign bases, causing much loss of life as well as material wealth; counter-revolutionary Cubans are being trained in the U.S. army and new plans of aggression against Cuba are being made. . . .

Great as was the epic of Latin American Independence, heroic as was that struggle, today's generation of Latin Americans is called upon to engage in an epic which is even greater and more decisive for humanity. For that struggle was for liberation from Spanish colonial power, from a decadent Spain invaded by the armies of Napoleon. Today the call for struggle is for liberation from the most powerful imperialist center . . . .

. . . [N]ow in the fields and mountains of America, on its slopes and prairies and in its jungles, in the wilderness or in the traffic of the cities, this world is beginning with full cause to erupt. Anxious hands are stretched forth, ready to die for what is theirs, to win those rights which were laughed at by one and all for 500 years. Yes, now history will have to take the poor of America into account, the exploited and spurned of Latin America, who have decided to begin writing history for themselves for all time. . . .

6.11

A Popular Perspective on Revolutionary Cuba

Revolutions look quite different from the ground level — from the perspective of ordinary people — than they do from heights of power occupied by those leading the revolutions. Gabriel Capote Pacheco (a pseudonym) is one of those ordinary people. Born around 1941, he had grown up in poverty. His father had abandoned the family, and his mother had moved with the children from a village in eastern Cuba to working-class neighborhoods in Havana. After the revolution Capote got a good job as a waiter in upscale hotels now operated by the government. There he made a reputation for himself as a good worker, revolutionary sympathizer, and sometime activist.

This oral history provides a bottom-up perspective on a decade of revolutionary change in Cuba. It is the product of interviews conducted in 1969–1970 by a team led by anthropologist Oscar Lewis working with the backing of Castro himself. To judge from these reflections, in what ways had the Castro revolution changed society and in what ways do older patterns persist? What gaps exist between Castro's conception of the revolution and Capote's experience of it? How might Capote's perspective differ from that of other Cubans, such as the well-to-do who fled the island or rural workers? What gaps or biases might we look for in this oral history?

Gabriel Capote Pacheco
Oral History on Life in Revolutionary Cuba
1970

People ask me, why did I have so many children? Well, I wanted to have them. I like children. The only problem is the way they live. They don't live like human beings. They live like pigs. We all do. The furniture is broken. The wardrobe is held together with boards from the broken bed. We not only don't have beds, we don't have a blanket. My wife and I have only a crib-size sheet to cover us, and we keep pulling it away from each other all night long. . . .

We cook on a small kerosene stove I bought for 8 *pesos* [$8 at the official exchange rate], and also on a tin filled with alcohol; they both stand on the dressing table. We keep the food on the two bedside tables. The rocking chair broke so there's no place to sit. I stand by the bed holding my plate and look at my children flopped down on the floor, eating like puppies.

And I hate the lack of privacy. Sometimes I've come home after being away in the countryside a month or two, wanting to be with my wife, only you can't have intercourse in front of kids — it's too ugly. We have to wait and do it late at night with the light out and with an eye on the kids every minute, in case they wake up. . . .

. . . [I]t's a dog's life, all six of us crammed into that tiny room. When it's hot we practically melt. And then the mosquitoes and cockroaches . . . *ay!* That's no way to live. . . .

The roof leaked so they tarred it over, and now the ceiling is cracked. The door to our room is falling apart; I patched it up with wood from a packing case. The bathroom is out in the hall and is always filthy. I don't want the kids using it so we have a chamber pot for them. [My wife] and I use the toilet but we bathe in our room in a tin tub with water out of a pail. . . .

There's a lot more freedom in Cuba now. Take young people — I see boys and girls walking unchaperoned all over the city. In the old days the *papá* or *mamá* had to go along. And the youngsters go with whoever they please — black with white. Now *there's* a change! . . .

A white woman who goes with a black loses her reputation. I'm no racist but I sure as hell wouldn't want a daughter of mine to marry a black. It would hurt me deeply. Now if a son of mine wanted to marry a Negro girl, that's all right. A man doesn't lose as much by such a marriage. But no one in Cuba want his daughter to marry a black. I've even heard some black girl comrades at work say, "What! Me marry a Negro? I should say not, I'm black enough for two. When I marry, it will be to improve the race." . . .

I'm against women's liberation, too. Most of the older generation are [also]. . . .

Oscar Lewis, Ruth M. Lewis, and Susan M. Rigdon, *Living the Revolution: An Oral History* (Urbana: University of Illinois Press, 1977), vol. 1: *Four Men,* 501–502, 521–22.

The Revolution gave women a lot more freedom by giving them jobs, so now they don't depend so much on their husbands. I think that's not right. And as for this business of married women going alone to work in the country — it won't do. I've known a number of them who have gone to work in the country and put the horns on their husbands [had sexual affairs]. It's the truth. Women are weak, see? When a woman goes away without her husband, the chances are she'll be unfaithful to him. Even if she loves her husband, in a moment of weakness she'll make a slip and the harm's done. The closer she stays to him, the more children she bears him, the better.

. . . I expect [my wife] to stay home and look after the house. She has plenty to do here. She owes herself to me and the children.

SWEEPING VISIONS AND BOLD STRATEGIES

The 1960s marked the most intense period in the postwar development of third-world radicalism. After some delay and intermittent resistance, colonial power was in retreat. The few exceptions in sub-Saharan Africa such as Rhodesia and Angola were, it was widely assumed, on borrowed time. In early 1961 Nikita Khrushchev threw his support behind wars of national liberation as "not only admissible but inevitable, since the colonialists do not grant independence voluntarily." He cited Cuba's "uprising against the internal tyrannical regime supported by U.S. imperialism" as a prime example of a worldwide trend that Khrushchev regarded as favorable to the Soviet Union.[1] While in part a response to Chinese charges that the Soviets were no longer revolutionary, Khrushchev was also recognizing the changing mood in the third world in favor of socialism.

Khrushchev's speech heralded a succession of ever-bolder statements issuing from the third world itself taking up the revolutionary banner. Not only were countries in ferment but the entire global system seemed on the verge of a fundamental shift. The documents that follow give a sense of the wide range of views articulated and the soaring hopes for revolution and socialism that defined the times.

6.12
Frantz Fanon: Liberation and Violence

Frantz Fanon was born in Martinique in 1925 and, like the native intellectuals of whom he would later express such profound suspicions, he studied in France and became a psychiatrist. Working as a doctor in Algeria provided the impetus for his second and best-known work, *The Wretched of the Earth*. In Algeria he witnessed

---

[1]Khrushchev's statement took the form of a speech at the Institute of Marxism-Leninism, January 6, 1961, in *The Sino-Soviet Dispute,* ed. G. F. Hudson et al. (New York: Praeger, 1961), 207–221.

the colonial war (1954–1962) that had turned increasingly ugly as French forces and settlers tried to retain control against armed resistance and terrorist attacks. Fanon's reflections on this conflict appeared in French in 1961, the same year that Fanon died of cancer. It became a classic of third-world literature, appearing widely in translation.

The issues that Fanon addresses are wide-ranging — from pan-Africanism to social divisions within colonial societies to the effects of the capitalist world system on colonies and decolonization. But perhaps most important was Fanon's emphasis on violence as an integral and critical part of decolonization. This is the subject of this excerpt, taken from the opening chapter of *The Wretched of the Earth*. What is the relationship between the colonial population and the colonized, and how does the relationship change during decolonization? How do native intellectuals and peasants figure in Fanon's treatment of decolonization? How do the views laid out here echo other statements on decolonization in this chapter and in chapter 3?

From *The Wretched of the Earth*
1961

National liberation, national renaissance, the restoration of nationhood to the people, commonwealth: whatever may be the headings used or the new formulas introduced, decolonization is always a violent phenomenon. At whatever level we study it — relationships between individuals, new names for sports clubs, the human admixture at cocktail parties, in the police, on the directing boards of national or private banks — decolonization is quite simply the replacing of a certain "species" of men by another "species" of men. Without any period of transition, there is a total, complete, and absolute substitution. . . .

Decolonization, which sets out to change the order of the world, is, obviously, a program of complete disorder. . . . Decolonization is the meeting of two forces, opposed to each other by their very nature . . . . Their first encounter was marked by violence[,] and their existence together — that is to say the exploitation of the native by the settler — was carried on by dint of a great array of bayonets and cannons. The settler and the native are old acquaintances. In fact, the settler is right when he speaks of knowing "them" well. For it is the settler who has brought the native into existence and who perpetuates his existence. The settler owes the fact of his very existence, that is to say, his property, to the colonial system.

Decolonization never takes place unnoticed, for it influences individuals and modifies them fundamentally. It transforms spectators crushed with their inessentiality into privileged actors, with the grandiose glare of history's floodlights upon them. It brings a natural rhythm into existence, introduced by

---

Frantz Fanon, *The Wretched of the Earth*, trans. Constance Farrington (New York: Grove Press, 1968), 35–39, 41–45, 71–74, 88–90, 92–94. Originally published in 1961 as *Les damnés de la terre*.

new men, and with it a new language and a new humanity. Decolonization is the veritable creation of new men. But this creation owes nothing of its legitimacy to any supernatural power; the "thing" which has been colonized becomes man by the same process by which it frees itself.

In decolonization, there is therefore the need of a complete calling in question of the colonial situation. If we wish to describe it precisely, we might find it in the well-known words: "The last shall be first and the first last." . . .

The naked truth of decolonization evokes for us the searing bullets and bloodstained knives which emanate from it. For if the last shall be first, this will only come to pass after a murderous and decisive struggle between the two protagonists. That affirmed intention to place the last at the head of things, and to make them climb at a pace (too quickly, some say) the well-known steps which characterize an organized society, can only triumph if we use all means to turn the scale, including, of course, that of violence. . . .

The colonial world is a world cut in two. The dividing line, the frontiers are shown by barracks and police stations. In the colonies it is the policeman and the soldier who are the official, instituted go-betweens, the spokesmen of the settler and his rule of oppression. . . . In the capitalist countries a multitude of moral teachers, counselors and "bewilderers" separate the exploited from those in power. In the colonial countries, on the contrary, the policeman and the soldier, by their immediate presence and their frequent and direct action, maintain contact with the native and advise him by means of rifle butts and napalm not to budge. It is obvious here that the agents of government speak the language of pure force. The intermediary does not lighten the oppression, nor seek to hide the domination; he shows them up and puts them into practice with the clear conscience of an upholder of the peace; yet he is the bringer of violence into the home and into the mind of the native.

The zone where the natives live is not complementary to the zone inhabited by the settlers. The two zones are opposed . . . . The settlers' town is a strongly built town, all made of stone and steel. It is a brightly lit town; the streets are covered with asphalt, and the garbage cans swallow all the leavings, unseen, unknown and hardly thought about. The settler's feet are never visible, except perhaps in the sea; but there you're never close enough to see them. His feet are protected by strong shoes although the streets of his town are clean and even, with no holes or stones. The settler's town is a well-fed town, an easygoing town; its belly is always full of good things. The settlers' town is a town of white people, of foreigners.

The town belonging to the colonized people; or at least the native town, the Negro village, the medina, the reservation, is a place of ill fame, peopled by men of evil repute. They are born there, it matters little where or how; they die there, it matters not where, nor how. It is a world without spaciousness; men living there on top of each other, and their huts are built one on top of the other. The native town is a hungry town, starved of bread, of meat, of shoes, of coal, of light. The native town is a crouching village, a town on its knees, a town wallowing in the mire. It is a town of niggers and dirty Arabs. The look that the native turns on the settler's town is a look of lust, a look of envy; it expresses his dreams of possession — all manner of possession: to sit at the settler's table, to sleep in the settler's bed, with his wife if possible. The colonized man is an envious man. And this the settler knows very well; when their glances meet he ascertains bitterly, always on the defensive, "They want to take our place." It is true, for there is no native who does not dream at least once a day of setting himself up in the settler's place. . . .

. . . The colonial world is a Manichean world. It is not enough for the settler to delimit physically, that is to say with the help of the army and the police force, the place of the native. As if to show the totalitarian character of colonial exploitation[,] the settler paints the native as a sort of quintessence of evil. . . . All values, in fact, are irrevocably poisoned and diseased as soon as they are allowed in contact with the colonized race. The customs of the colonized people, their traditions, their myths — above all, their myths — are the very sign of that poverty of spirit and of their constitutional depravity. That is why we must put the DDT which destroys parasites, the bearers of disease, on the same level as the Christian religion which wages war on embryonic heresies and instincts, and on evil as yet unborn. The recession of yellow fever and the advance of evangelization form part of the same balance sheet. . . .

At times this Manicheism goes to its logical conclusion and dehumanizes the native, or to speak plainly, it turns him into animal. In fact, the terms the settler uses when he mentions the native are zoological terms. He speaks of the yellow man's reptilian motions, of the stink of the native quarter, of breeding swarms, of foulness, of spawn, of gesticulations. When the settler seeks to describe the native fully in exact terms he constantly refers to the bestiary. . . . Those hordes of vital statistics, those hysterical masses, those faces bereft of all humanity, those distended bodies which are like nothing on earth, that mob without beginning or end, those children who seem to belong to nobody, that laziness stretched out in the sun, that vegetative rhythm of life — all this forms part of the colonial vocabulary. . . . The native knows all this, and laughs to himself every time he spots an allusion to the animal world in the other's words. For he knows that he is not an animal; and it is precisely at the moment he realizes his humanity that he begins to sharpen the weapons with which he will secure its victory.

As soon as the native begins to pull on his moorings, and to cause anxiety to the settler, he is handed over to well-meaning souls who in cultural congresses point out to him the specificity and wealth of Western values. . . . [W]hen the native hears a speech about Western culture he pulls out his knife — or at least he makes sure it is within reach. . . . [T]he native laughs in mockery when Western values are mentioned in front of him. In the colonial context the settler only ends his work of breaking in the native when the latter admits loudly and intelligibly the supremacy of the white man's values. In the period of decolonization, the colonized masses mock at these very values, insult them, and vomit them up.

This phenomenon is ordinarily masked because, during the period of decolonization, certain colonized intellectuals have begun a dialogue with the bourgeoisie of the colonialist country. . . . [T]he colonialist bourgeoisie looks feverishly for contacts with the elite and it is with these elite that the familiar dialogue concerning values is carried on. The colonialist bourgeoisie, when it realizes that it is impossible for it to maintain its domination over the colonial countries, decides to carry out a rearguard action with regard to culture, values, techniques, and so on. Now what we must never forget is that the immense majority of colonized peoples is oblivious to these problems. For a colonized people the most essential value, because the most concrete, is first and foremost the land: the land which will bring them bread and, above all, dignity. But this dignity has nothing to do with the dignity of the human individual: for that human individual has never heard tell of it. All that the native has seen in his country is that they can freely arrest him, beat him, starve him: and no professor of ethics, no priest has ever come to be beaten in his place, nor to share their bread with him. As far as the native is concerned, morality is very concrete; it is to silence the settler's defiance, to break his flaunting violence — in a word, to put him out of the picture.... The intellectual who for his part has followed the colonialist with regard to the universal abstract will fight in order that the settler and the native may live together in peace in a new world. But the thing he does not see, precisely because he is permeated by colonialism and all its ways of thinking, is that the settler, from the moment that the colonial context disappears, has no longer any interest in remaining or in co-existing....

... [I]n the colonial countries the peasants alone are revolutionary, for they have nothing to lose and everything to gain. The starving peasant, outside the class system, is the first among the exploited to discover that only violence pays. For him there is no compromise, no possible coming to terms; colonization and decolonization are simply a question of relative strength. The exploited man sees that his liberation implies the use of all means, and that of force first and foremost. When in 1956 ... the [Algerian] Front de Libération Nationale, in a famous leaflet, stated that colonialism only loosens its hold when the knife is at its throat, no Algerian really found these terms too violent. The leaflet only expressed what every Algerian felt at heart: colonialism is not a thinking machine, nor a body endowed with reasoning faculties. It is violence in its natural state, and it will only yield when confronted with greater violence.

... Non-violence is an attempt to settle the colonial problem around a green baize table, before any regrettable act has been performed or irreparable gesture made, before any blood has been shed. But if the masses, without waiting for the chairs to be arranged around the baize table, listen to their own voice and begin committing outrages and setting fire to buildings, the elite and the nationalist bourgeois parties will be seen rushing to the colonialists to exclaim, "This is very serious! We do not know how it will end; we must find a solution — some sort of compromise."

... The partisans of the colonial system discover that the masses may destroy everything. Blown-up bridges, ravaged farms, repressions, and fighting harshly disrupt the economy. Compromise is equally attractive to the nationalist bourgeoisie, who since they are not clearly aware of the possible consequences of the rising storm, are genuinely afraid of being swept away by this huge hurricane and never stop saying to the settlers: "We are still capable of stopping the slaughter; the masses still have confidence in us; act quickly if you do not want to put everything in jeopardy." One step more, and the leader of the nationalist party keeps his distance with regard to that violence. He loudly proclaims that he has nothing to do with these Mau-Mau,[1] these terrorists, these throat-slitters. At best, he shuts himself off in a no man's land between the terrorists and the settlers and willingly offers his services as go-between; that is to say, that as the settlers cannot discuss terms with these Mau-Mau, he himself will be quite willing to begin negotiations. Thus it is that the rear guard of the national struggle, that very party of people who have never ceased to be on the other side in the fight, find themselves somer-saulted into the van of negotiations and compromise — precisely because that party has taken very good care never to break contact with colonialism. . . .

. . . [H]ow do we pass from the atmosphere of violence to violence in action? What makes the lid blow off? . . . The settler who "understands" the natives is made aware by several straws in the wind showing that something is afoot. "Good" natives become scarce; silence falls when the oppressor ap-proaches; sometimes looks are black, and attitudes and remarks openly ag-gressive. The nationalist parties are astir, they hold a great many meetings, the police are increased and reinforcements of soldiers are brought in. The set-tlers, above all the farmers isolated on their land, are the first to become alarmed. They call for energetic measures.

The authorities do in fact take some spectacular measures. They arrest one or two leaders, they organize military parades and maneuvers, and air force displays. But the demonstrations and warlike exercises, the smell of gunpow-der which now fills the atmosphere, these things do not make the people draw back. Those bayonets and cannonades only serve to reinforce their ag-gressiveness. The atmosphere becomes dramatic, and everyone wishes to show that he is ready for anything. And it is in these circumstances that the guns go off by themselves, for nerves are jangled, fear reigns and everyone is trigger-happy. A single commonplace incident is enough to start the machine-gunning. . . .

The repressions, far from calling a halt to the forward rush of national con-sciousness, urge it on. Mass slaughter in the colonies at a certain stage of the embryonic development of consciousness increases that consciousness . . . . [C]olonialism may decide to arrest the nationalist leaders. But today the gov-ernments of colonized countries know very well that it is extremely dangerous to deprive the masses of their leaders; for then the people, unbridled, fling themselves into *jacqueries* [peasant revolts], mutinies, and "brutish murders." The masses give free rein to their "bloodthirsty instincts" and force colonialism to free their leaders, to whom falls the difficult task of bringing them back to order. . . .

---

[1]A secret organization that violently challenged British control of Kenya in the early 1950s.

... [A]s a result of the colonialist repression and of the spontaneous reaction of the people the parties find themselves out-distanced by their militants. The violence of the masses is vigorously pitted against the military forces of the occupying power, and the situation deteriorates and comes to a head. Those leaders who are free .... suddenly become useless, with their bureaucracy and their reasonable demands; yet we see them, far removed from events, attempting the crowning imposture — that of "speaking in the name of the silenced nation." As a general rule, colonialism welcomes this godsend with open arms, tranforms these "blind mouths" into spokesmen, and in two minutes endows them with independence, on condition that they restore order. . . .

... We have seen that it is the intuition of the colonized masses that their liberation must, and can only, be achieved by force. By what spiritual aberration do these men, without technique, starving and enfeebled, confronted with the military and economic might of the occupation, come to believe that violence alone will free them? How can they hope to triumph?

... When militarist Germany decides to settle its frontier disputes by force, we are not in the least surprised; but when the people of Angola, for example, decide to take up arms, when the Algerian people reject all means which are not violent, these are proofs that something has happened or is happening at this very moment. The colonized races, those slaves of modern times, are impatient. They know that this apparent folly alone can put them out of reach of colonial oppression. A new type of relations is established in the world. The underdeveloped peoples try to break their chains, and the extraordinary thing is that they succeed. It could be argued that in these days of sputniks it is ridiculous to die of hunger; but for the colonized masses the argument is more down-to-earth. The truth is that there is no colonial power today which is capable of adopting the only form of contest which has a chance of succeeding, namely, the prolonged establishment of large forces of occupation. . . .

... The development of violence among the colonized people will be proportionate to the violence exercised by the threatened colonial regime. . . . Terror, counter-terror, violence, counter-violence: that is what observers bitterly record when they describe the circle of hate, which is so tenacious and so evident in Algeria.

In all armed struggles, there exists what we might call the point of no return. Almost always it is marked off by a huge and all-inclusive repression which engulfs all sectors of the colonized people. . . .

When the native is tortured, when his wife is killed or raped, he complains to no one. The oppressor's government can set up commissions of inquiry and of information daily if it wants to; in the eyes of the native, these commissions do not exist. The fact is that soon we shall have had seven years of crimes in Algeria and there has not yet been a single Frenchman indicted before a French court of justice for the murder of an Algerian. In Indo-China, in Madagascar, or in the colonies the native has always known that he need expect nothing from the other side. The settler's work is to make even dreams of liberty impossible for the native. The native's work is to imagine all possible methods for destroying the settler. . . .

The mobilization of the masses, when it arises out of the war of liberation, introduces into each man's consciousness the ideas of a common cause, of a national destiny, and of a collective history. In the same way the second phase, that of the building-up of the nation, is helped on by the existence of this cement which has been mixed with blood and anger. Thus we come to a fuller appreciation of the originality of the words used in these underdeveloped countries. During the colonial period the people are called upon to fight against oppression; after national liberation, they are called upon to fight against poverty, illiteracy, and underdevelopment. The struggle, they say, goes on. The people realize that life is an unending contest. . . .

At the level of individuals, violence is a cleansing force. It frees the native from his inferiority complex and from his despair and inaction; it makes him fearless and restores his self-respect. Even if the armed struggle has been symbolic and the nation is demobilized through a rapid movement of decolonization, the people have the time to see that the liberation has been the business of each and all and that the leader has no special merit. . . . When the people have taken violent part in the national liberation they will allow no one to set themselves up as "liberators." They show themselves to be jealous of the results of their action and take good care not to place their future, their destiny, or the fate of their country in the hands of a living god. Yesterday they were completely irresponsible; today they mean to understand everything and make all decisions.

6.13

Lin Biao: The Maoist Appeal

Privately Mao Zedong in the last decade of his life was frustrated with the ebbing of revolutionary sentiment in China generally and in the Communist Party in particular. The fiasco of the Great Leap Forward, an experiment in economic development launched in 1958, had resulted in massive famine and deaths in the millions. Mao retreated to the background — but only briefly. In 1966, he launched the Great Proletarian Cultural Revolution with the assistance of his wife, Jiang Qing, and Lin Biao, an old associate and head of the army. The goal was to mobilize popular enthusiasm for revolutionary change. Crowds of students chanting slogans from Mao's *Quotations* ("the little red book") and fiery anti-imperialist rhetoric deeply impressed carefully selected foreign visitors and readers of the controlled media. By 1969 the Cultural Revolution had run its course. It had shattered a party leadership that Mao had suspected of losing its ideological fervor but left him still uncertain about the durability of his revolutionary legacy.

Two of the most widely circulated official Cultural Revolution documents follow. Both bear Lin Biao's name and both reflect the Mao cult that reached its height in China and overseas in the late 1960s. The first item is Lin's "Long Live the Victory of People's War!" published in the party newspaper, *People's Daily,* in 1965 on the twentieth anniversary of victory over Japan. The second item is Lin's forward to the second edition of *Quotations from Chairman Mao Tse-tung.* First published in May 1964 by the Chinese army, it is a collection of the chairman's writing going back to 1929 (invariably in highly excerpted form and often revised to suit the politics of the day). The little volume leapt to prominence when young Red Guards, gathered in Tiananmen Square in central Beijing in August 1966, held it aloft like a talisman of their revolutionary faith in Mao's leadership. The rhetoric and expectations of these two documents may seem overblown, so it may be worthwhile to reflect on their appeal at the time. What values did the Cultural Revolution stand for both nationally and internationally? What role is ascribed to the United States and the Soviet Union? It may also be helpful to compare the values exalted in the mid-1960s with those evoked in the earlier phase of the Chinese revolution (treated in chapter 3).

"Long Live the Victory of People's War!"
September 3, 1965

Taking the entire globe, if North America and Western Europe can be called "the cities of the world," then Asia, Africa and Latin America constitute "the rural areas of the world." Since World War II, the proletarian revolutionary movement has for various reasons been temporarily held back in the North American and West European capitalist countries, while the people's revolutionary movement in Asia, Africa and Latin America has been growing vigorously. In a sense, the contemporary world revolution also presents a picture of the encirclement of cities by the rural areas. In the final analysis, the whole cause of world revolution hinges on the revolutionary struggles of the Asian, African and Latin American peoples who make up the overwhelming majority of the world's population. The socialist countries should regard it as their internationalist duty to support the people's revolutionary struggles in Asia, Africa and Latin America. . . .

. . . In the world as a whole, this is the area where the people suffer worst from imperialist oppression and where imperialist rule is most vulnerable. Since World War II, revolutionary storms have been rising in this area, and today they have become the most important force directly pounding U.S. imperialism. The contradiction between the revolutionary peoples of Asia, Africa and Latin America and the imperialists headed by the United States is the principal contradiction in the contemporary world. The development of this contradiction is promoting the struggle of the people of the whole world against U.S. imperialism and its lackeys.

Since World War II, people's war has increasingly demonstrated its power in Asia, Africa and Latin America. The peoples of China, Korea, Viet Nam, Laos, Cuba, Indonesia, Algeria and other countries have waged people's wars against the imperialists and their lackeys and won great victories. . . . [T]he victories in these people's wars have very much weakened and pinned down the forces of imperialism, upset the U.S. imperialist plan to launch a world war, and become mighty factors defending world peace. . . .

Lin Piao (Lin Biao), *Long Live the Victory of People's War!* (Beijing: Foreign Languages Press, 1965), 48–49, 53–59, 69.

Since World War II and the succeeding years of revolutionary upsurge, there has been a great rise in the level of political consciousness and the degree of organization of the people in all countries, and the resources available to them for mutual support and aid have greatly increased. The whole capitalist-imperialist system has become drastically weaker and is in the process of increasing convulsion and disintegration. . . . Since World War II, . . . not only have they been unable to stop a number of countries from taking the socialist road, but they are no longer capable of holding back the surging tide of the people's revolutionary movements in the areas under their own rule.

U.S. imperialism is stronger, but also more vulnerable, than any imperialism of the past. It sets itself against the people of the whole world, including the people of the United States. Its human, military, material and financial resources are far from sufficient for the realization of its ambition of dominating the whole world. U.S. imperialism has further weakened itself by occupying so many places in the world, over-reaching itself, stretching its fingers out wide and dispersing its strength, with its rear so far away and its supply lines so long. As Comrade Mao Tse-tung has said, "Wherever it commits aggression, it puts a new noose around its neck. . . ."

Everything is divisible. And so is this colossus of U.S. imperialism. It can be split up and defeated. The peoples of Asia, Africa, Latin America and other regions can destroy it piece by piece, some striking at its head and others at its feet. That is why the greatest fear of U.S. imperialism is that people's wars will be launched in different parts of the world, and particularly in Asia, Africa and Latin America, and why it regards people's war as a mortal danger. . . .

However highly developed modern weapons and technical equipment may be and however complicated the methods of modern warfare, in the final analysis the outcome of a war will be decided by the sustained fighting of the ground forces, by the fighting at close quarters on battlefields, by the political consciousness of the men, by their courage and spirit of sacrifice. . . .

Viet Nam is the most convincing current example of a victim of aggression defeating U.S. imperialism by a people's war. The United States has made South Viet Nam a testing ground for the suppression of people's war. It has carried on this experiment for many years, and everybody can now see that the U.S. aggressors are unable to find a way of coping with people's war. On the other hand, the Vietnamese people have brought the power of people's war into full play in their struggle against the U.S. aggressors. The U.S. aggressors are in danger of being swamped in the people's war in Viet Nam. They are deeply worried that their defeat in Viet Nam will lead to a chain reaction. They are expanding the war in attempt to save themselves from defeat. But the more they expand the war, the greater will be the chain reaction. The more they escalate the war, the heavier will be their fall and the more disastrous their defeat. The people in other parts of the world will see still more clearly that U.S. imperialism can be defeated. . . .

History has proved and will go on proving that people's war is the most effective weapon against U.S. imperialism and its lackeys. All revolutionary people . . . will take up arms, learn to fight battles and become skilled in waging people's war, though they have not done so before. U.S. imperialism, like a mad bull dashing from place to place, will finally be burned to ashes in the blazing fires of the people's wars it has provoked by its own actions.

The Khrushchov revisionists[1] have come to the rescue of U.S. imperialism just when it is most panic-stricken and helpless in its efforts to cope with people's war. Working hand in glove with the U.S. imperialists, they are doing their utmost to spread all kinds of arguments against people's war and, wherever they can, they are scheming to undermine it by overt or covert means.

The fundamental reason why the Khrushchov revisionists are opposed to people's war is that they have no faith in the masses and are afraid of U.S. imperialism, of war and of revolution. Like all other opportunists, they are blind to the power of the masses and do not believe that the revolutionary people are capable of defeating imperialism. They submit to the nuclear blackmail of the U.S. imperialists and are afraid that, if the oppressed peoples and nations rise up to fight people's wars or the people of socialist countries repulse U.S. imperialist aggression, U.S. imperialism will become incensed, they themselves will become involved and their fond dream of Soviet-U.S. co-operation to dominate the world will be spoiled. . . .

All peoples suffering from U.S. imperialist aggression, oppression and plunder, unite! Hold aloft the just banner of people's war and fight for the cause of world peace, national liberation, people's democracy and socialism! Victory will certainly go to the people of the world!

Long live the victory of people's war!

---

[1]Though out of power by 1965, Nikita Khrushchev is used here as a byword for the Soviet failure to live up to the strong words of support for liberation movements that Khrushchev had expressed in 1961.

Foreword to Quotations from Chairman Mao Tse-tung
December 16, 1966

Comrade Mao Tse-tung is the greatest Marxist-Leninist of our era. He has inherited, defended and developed Marxism-Leninism with genius, creatively and comprehensively and has brought it to a higher and completely new stage.

Mao Tse-tung's thought is Marxism-Leninism of the era in which imperialism is heading for total collapse and socialism is advancing to world-wide victory. It is a powerful ideological weapon for opposing imperialism and for opposing revisionism and dogmatism. Mao Tse-tung's thought is the guiding principle for all the work of the Party, the army and the country.

Available at <http://www.marxists.org/reference/archive/lin-biao/1966/12/16.htm> (August 7, 2002). Based on *Quotations from Chairman Mao Tse-tung,* 2nd ed. (Beijing: Foreign Languages Press, 1967).

Therefore, the most fundamental task in our Party's political and ideological work is at all times to hold high the great red banner of Mao Tse-tung's thought, to arm the minds of the people throughout the country with it and to persist in using it to command every field of activity. The broad masses of the workers, peasants and soldiers and the broad ranks of the revolutionary cadres and the intellectuals should really master Mao Tse-tung's thought; they should all study Chairman Mao's writings, follow his teachings, act according to his instructions and be his good fighters.

In studying the works of Chairman Mao, one should have specific problems in mind, study and apply his works in a creative way, combine study with application, first study what must be urgently applied so as to get quick results, and strive hard to apply what one is studying. In order really to master Mao Tse-tung's thought, it is essential to study many of Chairman Mao's basic concepts over and over again, and it is best to memorize important statements and study and apply them repeatedly. The newspapers should regularly carry quotations from Chairman Mao relevant to current issues for readers to study and apply. . . .

We have compiled *Quotations from Chairman Mao Tse-tung* in order to help the broad masses learn Mao Tse-tung's thought more effectively. In organizing their study, units should select passages that are relevant to the situation, their tasks, the current thinking of their personnel, and the state of their work.

In our great motherland, a new era is emerging in which the workers, peasants and soldiers are grasping Marxism-Leninism, Mao Tse-tung's thought. Once Mao Tse-tung's thought is grasped by the broad masses, it becomes a source of strength and a spiritual atom bomb of infinite power.

6.14

Ché Guevara: The Insurrectionary Impulse

The Argentine-born Ernesto (Ché) Guevara emerged in the 1960s as the embodiment of the revolutionary mystique and a leading advocate of anti-imperialist struggle. A physician with strong social concerns, he had witnessed the U.S. overthrow of the reformist Arbenz regime in Guatemala and threw in his lot with the fledgling Cuban revolution led by Fidel Castro. He won his spurs as a military commander in that revolution, and following its consolidation, the restless Guevara turned his attention overseas. In 1965 he led a Cuban military force in the Congo, and then a year later took a small volunteer force into Bolivia with the hopes of igniting a popular revolution against that country's military dictator. The operation bogged down, and Guevara was killed in October 1967. Now a martyr, he was mourned by the Left around the world.

The document that follows was written in 1966 before Guevara's departure for Bolivia, and appeared the next year in the magazine *Tricontinental*, the publication for the Havana-based Organization of Solidarity with the Peoples of Asia, Africa, and Latin America. His message was encapsulated in the phrase, "Create two, three ... many Vietnams, that is the watchword." What did he mean by that phrase? How does his understanding of the world scene compare with others earlier in this chapter?

"Message to the Tricontinental"
April 16, 1967

We must bear in mind that imperialism is a world system, the last stage of capitalism — and it must be defeated in a world confrontation. The strategic end of this struggle should be the destruction of imperialism. Our share, the responsibility of the exploited and underdeveloped of the world is to eliminate the foundations of imperialism ....

The fundamental element of this strategic end shall be the real liberation of all people, a liberation that will be brought about through armed struggle in most cases and which shall be, in Our America, almost indefectibly [without fail], a Socialist Revolution.

While envisaging the destruction of imperialism, it is necessary to identify its head, which is no other than the United States of America.

We must ... [get] the enemy out of its natural environment, forcing him to fight in regions where his own life and habits will clash with the existing reality. We must not underrate our adversary; the U.S. soldier has technical capacity and is backed by weapons and resources of such magnitude that render him frightful. He lacks the essential ideologic motivation which his bitterest enemies of today — the Vietnamese soldiers — have in the highest degree. We will only be able to overcome that army by undermining their morale — and this is accomplished by defeating it and causing it repeated sufferings.

But this brief outline of victories carries within itself the immense sacrifice of the people, sacrifices that should be demanded beginning today, in plain daylight, and which perhaps may be less painful than those we would have to endure if we constantly avoided battle in an attempt to have others pull our chestnuts out of the fire.

It is probable, of course, that the last liberated country shall accomplish this without an armed struggle and the sufferings of a long and cruel war against the imperialists — this they might avoid. But perhaps it will be impossible to avoid this struggle or its effects in a global conflagration; the suffering would be the same, or perhaps even greater. We cannot foresee the future, but we should never give in to the defeatist temptation of being the vanguard of a nation which yearns for freedom, but abhors the struggle it entails and awaits its freedom as a crumb of victory.

Available online at <http://www.marxists.org/archive/guevara/1967/04/16.htm> (January 7, 2003). Also available in a variant translation in David Deutschmann, ed., *Che Guevara Reader: Writings on Guerilla Strategy, Politics and Revolution* (Melbourne, Australia: Ocean Press, 1997), 313–28.

... [T]he present moment may or may not be the proper one for starting the struggle, but we cannot harbor any illusions, and we have no right to do so, that freedom can be obtained without fighting. And these battles shall not be mere street fights with stones against tear-gas bombs, or of pacific general strikes; neither shall it be the battle of a furious people destroying in two or three days the repressive scaffolds of the ruling oligarchies; the struggle shall be long, harsh, and its front shall be in the guerrilla's refuge, in the cities, in the homes of the fighters — where the repressive forces shall go seeking easy victims among their families — in the massacred rural population, in the villages or cities destroyed by the bombardments of the enemy.

They are pushing us into this struggle; there is no alternative: we must prepare it and we must decide to undertake it.

The beginnings will not be easy; they shall be extremely difficult. All the oligarchies' powers of repression, all their capacity for brutality and demagoguery will be placed at the service of their cause. Our mission, in the first hour, shall be to survive; later, we shall follow the perennial example of the guerrilla, carrying out armed propaganda (in the Vietnamese sense, that is, the bullets of propaganda, of the battles won or lost — but fought — against the enemy). The great lesson of the invincibility of the guerrillas taking root in the dispossessed masses. The galvanizing of the national spirit, the preparation for harder tasks, for resisting even more violent repressions. Hatred as an element of the struggle; a relentless hatred of the enemy, impelling us over and beyond the natural limitations that man is heir to and transforming him into an effective, violent, selective and cold killing machine. Our soldiers must be thus; a people without hatred cannot vanquish a brutal enemy.

We must carry the war into every corner the enemy happens to carry it: to his home, to his centers of entertainment; a total war. It is necessary to prevent him from having a moment of peace, a quiet moment outside his barracks or even inside; we must attack him wherever he may be; make him feel like a cornered beast wherever he may move. Then his moral fiber shall begin to decline. He will even become more beastly, but we shall notice how the signs of decadence begin to appear.

And let us develop a true proletarian internationalism; with international proletarian armies; the flag under which we fight would be the sacred cause of redeeming humanity. To die under the flag of Vietnam, of Venezuela, of Guatemala, of Laos, of Guinea, of Colombia, of Bolivia, of Brazil — to name only a few scenes of today's armed struggle — would be equally glorious and desirable for an American, an Asian, an African, even a European. . . .

How close we could look into a bright future should two, three or many Vietnams flourish throughout the world with their share of deaths and their immense tragedies, their everyday heroism and their repeated blows against imperialism, impelled to disperse its forces under the sudden attack and the increasing hatred of all peoples of the world!

And if we were all capable of uniting to make our blows stronger and infallible and so increase the effectiveness of all kinds of support given to the struggling people — how great and close would that future be!

If we, in a small point of the world map, are able to fulfill our duty and place at the disposal of this struggle whatever little of ourselves we are permitted to give: our lives, our sacrifice, and if some day we have to breathe our last breath on any land, already ours, sprinkled with our blood let it be known that we have measured the scope of our actions and that we only consider ourselves elements in the great army of the proletariat but that we are proud of having learned from the Cuban Revolution, and from its maximum leader, the great lesson emanating from his attitude in this part of the world: "What do the dangers or the sacrifices of a man or of a nation matter, when the destiny of humanity is at stake."

CHAPTER 7

THE COLD WAR COMES
TO A CLOSE

KNOWING THE FUTURE IS A GIFT GIVEN TO FEW, as the surprise end of the Cold War demonstrated. There were attempts as early as the 1950s to defuse the Cold War confrontation, but these attempts ran up against lingering suspicion among leaders in Washington and Moscow. By the early 1980s, Leonid Brezhnev on the Soviet side and Jimmy Carter and Ronald Reagan on the U.S. side were so poorly matched in their outlooks that the Cold War took on a new life. The pervasive assumption was that the nearly thirty-year-old rivalry had decades to go. And then suddenly in a rush between 1989 and 1991 the Cold War came to an end. The international landscape was transformed almost overnight, leaving pundits embarrassed that they had failed to anticipate this geopolitical earthquake and struggling to envision the next phase of international politics.

What accounts for this outcome? What did analysts at the time not see? In broad terms, a convergence of forces set the stage for the end of the Cold War. The American public had been divided by Vietnam and had lost its paranoia about communism. The fear of nuclear war hung heavy, especially over Europe. And both the United States and the Soviet Union encountered economic difficulties — stagflation in one and a struggle to meet consumer demand in the other. These developments set the stage, but it took bold leaders on both sides of the Iron Curtain to find either a new basis for U.S.-Soviet rivalry or a way to transcend that rivalry altogether. A commitment to détente (a lessening of tensions) and domestic reform in the Soviet Union combined to achieve the unexpected: the collapse of socialism in eastern Europe and then of the Soviet Union itself.

THE STRUGGLE OVER DÉTENTE

The Western policy of détente took shape at the end of the tumultuous sixties. A new West German chancellor, Willy Brandt, joined with the new American president, Richard Nixon, in draining some of the fervor from the Cold War rivalry by emphasizing instead a more carefully calculated, negotiated relationship with both the Soviet bloc and China. The initiatives launched by Brandt and Nixon stumbled in the late 1970s and early 1980s as U.S.-Soviet relations deteriorated. Reagan won the White House in 1980 as a sharp critic of détente and proceeded to restore the confrontational style of the early Cold War. The setback, however, proved brief. In 1985 the new leader of the Soviet Union, Mikhail Gorbachev, began pressing for tension-reducing measures essential if he was to make headway on his first priority, domestic renovation. Reagan responded positively. By 1989 talk could be heard of the Cold War being over, and the collapse of the Soviet Union two years later left the matter in no doubt.

What is striking in retrospect is how publicly the rising doubts about the Cold War were discussed and how vigorously they were opposed. The following speeches provide an opportunity to follow the thinking of those confronting the Cold War in its last stage and to appraise once more the virtues and defects of public rhetoric as a kind of historical source. How much can we depend on it for insights on the thinking of its author? How much did it speak to or play back concerns of the broader public or to particular audiences such as the Soviet Communist Party or evangelical Christians?

7.1

West German Chancellor Willy Brandt Proposes Bridging the Two Germanys and the Two Europes

With the memory of two world wars still fresh, western Europeans were especially averse to the risks of a third, far more devastating conflict. In 1969 the West German chancellor Willy Brandt spoke out forcefully for reaching across the European political divide. Sustained contact could, in his view, help create a new, integrated, and more assuredly stable Europe. Brandt had good reason to take that position. His country stood on the front line of the Cold War, and would serve as the main battlefield in the opening hours of any hot war. His was also a divided nation, cut in two in the first years of the Cold War and dependent on an end to the Cold War for reunification to have any chance of success. Finally, West Germany bore the burden of its past aggression, a specter that still worried its neighbors. By embracing NATO and the European Community, West German leaders in Bonn had largely resolved Western Europeans' fears. But Bonn had taken no comparable initiatives to explicitly recognize the legitimacy of the East German state or formally accept the loss of German territory at the end of World War II. In 1969 following his victory over the conservative Christian Democrats, Brandt stepped forward with an offer — to become known as *Ostpolitik* — to regularize West Germany's relationship to its neighbors to the east.

Reading Brandt reminds us that perspectives on the Cold War varied considerably from region to region. In fact, in this excerpt Brandt does not use the term *Cold War* or allude to the superpower rivalry. What seems to guide his approach to relations among European states divided by the Iron Curtain? How much do his concerns diverge from those of Soviet and American leaders treated earlier (in chapters 1 and 4)?

Statement to the West German Bundestag

Bonn, October 28, 1969

This Government works on the assumption that the questions which have arisen for the German people out of the Second World War and from the national treachery committed by the Hitler régime can find their ultimate answers only in a European peace arrangement. However, no one can dissuade us from our conviction that the Germans have a right to self-determination just as has any other nation. The object of our practical political work in the years immediately ahead is to preserve the unity of the nation by ending the present deadlock in the relationship between the two parts of Germany.

The Germans are one not only by reason of their language and their history, with all its splendour and its misery; we are all at home in Germany. And we still have common tasks and a common responsibility: to ensure peace among us and in Europe.

Twenty years after the establishment of the Federal Republic of Germany [West Germany] and of the G.D.R. [German Democratic Republic, or East Germany], we must prevent any further alienation of the two parts of the German nation — that is, arrive at a regular *modus vivendi* [a way of getting along] and from there proceed to co-operation. This is not just a German interest; it is of importance also for peace in Europe and for East–West relations. . . .

. . . International recognition of the G.D.R. by the Federal Republic is out of the question. Even if there exist two States in Germany, they are not foreign countries to each other; their relations with each other can only be of a special nature.

Following up the policy of its predecessor, the Federal Government declares that its readiness for binding agreements on the reciprocal renunciation of the use or threat of force applies equally with regard to the G.D.R.

The Federal Government will advise the United States, Britain, and France to continue energetically the talks begun with the Soviet Union on easing and improving the situation in [divided] Berlin. The status of the City of Berlin under the special responsibility of the Four Powers must remain untouched. This must not be a hindrance to seeking facilities for traffic within and to Berlin. We shall continue to ensure the viability of Berlin. West Berlin must be placed in a position to assist in improving the political, economic and cultural relations between the two parts of Germany. . . .

The Federal Government will promote the development of closer political co-operation in Europe with the aim of evolving step by step a common

Keesing's Research Report, *Germany and Eastern Europe Since 1945* (New York: Charles Scribner's Sons, 1973), 229–31.

attitude in international questions. Our country needs co-operation and co-ordination with the West and understanding with the East. The German people need peace in the full sense of that word also with the peoples of the Soviet Union and of the European East. We are prepared to make an honest attempt at understanding, in order to help overcome the aftermath of the disaster brought on Europe by a criminal clique [the Hitler regime]. . . .

In continuation of its predecessor's policy, the Federal Government aims at equally binding agreements on the mutual renunciation of the use or threat of force. Let me repeat: This readiness also applies as far as the G.D.R. is concerned. And I wish to make it unmistakably clear that we are prepared to arrive with Czechoslovakia — our immediate neighbour — at arrangements which bridge the gulf of the past. . . .

. . . [The Federal Government] is well aware that there will be no progress unless the Governments in the capitals of the Warsaw Pact countries adopt a co-operative attitude.

7.2
President Richard Nixon Argues for a Policy of Détente

The Nixon presidency was so badly tarnished by impeachment and resignation that many now automatically associate the disgraced president with the five o'clock shadow across his face, an awkward public style, and a "Tricky Dick" reputation. This popular image overlooks Nixon's signal success at mitigating the Cold War. The effort began when he entered the White House in January 1969, and by 1971 he had begun arms-control talks with the Soviets and initiated promising contacts with Mao's China.

In July 1971, with Nixon's assistant Henry Kissinger just back from a secret visit to Beijing, the president delivered some informal remarks to news media executives that reveal his thinking on U.S. Cold War policy at a critical time in his own presidency. What is his sense of the problems confronting the United States? What are the solutions? How profound and far-reaching is this appraisal? What characteristics of Nixon's style and personality come through in this document?

Remarks to Media Executives
Kansas City, July 6, 1971

[L]et's look at the situation today. . . .

First, instead of just America being number one in the world from an economic standpoint, the preeminent world power, and instead of there being just two super powers, when we think in economic terms and economic potentialities, there are five great power centers in the world today. . . .

Available on the website maintained by the Richard Nixon Library and Birthplace: <http://www.nixonfoundation.org/Research_Center/1971_pdf_files\1971_0222.pdf> (August 5, 2002). Copy also in *Public Papers of the Presidents of the United States: Richard Nixon, 1971* (Washington, D.C.: Government Printing Office, 1972), 804–812.

There is, of course, the United States of America. There is, second, Western Europe — Western Europe with Britain in the Common Market. That means 300 million of the most advanced people in the world, with all the productivity and all the capacity that those people will have and, of course, with the clout that they have when they will act together, as they certainly will. . . .

Then in the Pacific, looking also at free world countries, we have a resurgent Japan. . . .

So now we have three power centers — the United States, Western Europe, Japan, noting that both Western Europe and Japan are very potent competitors of the United States — friends, yes; allies, yes — but competing and competing very hard with us throughout the world for economic leadership.

Now we turn to the other two super powers, economic super powers I will say for the moment. The Soviet Union, of course, first comes to mind. Looking at the Soviet Union, we are entering a period which only time will tell may be successful in terms of creating a very new relationship or a very different relationship than we have had previously.

. . . The important thing is that we are negotiating rather than confronting in many areas of the world where confrontation could lead to explosion. Whether it is on the limitation of nuclear arms, whether it is on the central issue of Europe, or whether it is on the Mideast, negotiations are going on.

. . . [W]e must recognize that the Soviet Union will continue to be a very potent, powerful, and aggressive competitor of the United States of America. . . . [I]f we have a limitation in nuclear arms, if we are able to turn our eyes more toward our economic development and our economic problems, it simply means that the competition changes and becomes much more challenging in the economic area than it has been previously. . . .

. . . [W]hether in Hong Kong, or whether in Taiwan, or whether they are in Singapore or Bangkok, any of the great cities, Manila, where Chinese are there — they are creative, they are productive, they are one of the most capable people in the world. And 800 million Chinese are going to be, inevitably, an enormous economic power, with all that that means in terms of what they could be in other areas if they move in that direction. . . .

. . . [T]he goal of U.S. policy must be, in the long term, ending the isolation of Mainland China and a normalization of our relations with Mainland China because, looking down the road — and let's just look ahead 15 to 20 years — the United States could have a perfectly effective agreement with the Soviet Union for limitation of arms; the danger of any confrontation there might have been almost totally removed.

But Mainland China, outside the world community, completely isolated, with its leaders not in communication with world leaders, would be a danger to the whole world that would be unacceptable, unacceptable to us and unacceptable to others as well. . . .

. . . [These five great economic super powers, the United States, Western Europe, Japan, the Soviet Union, and China] will determine the economic future and, because economic power will be the key to other kinds of power, the future of the world in other ways in the last third of this century. . . .

. . . [T]he United States no longer is in the position of complete preeminence or predominance. That is not a bad thing. As a matter of fact, it can be a constructive thing. The United States, let us understand, is still the strongest nation in the world, it is still the richest nation in the world. But now we face a situation where four other potential economic powers have the capacity, have the kind of people — if not the kind of government, but at least the kind of people — who can challenge us on every front.

That brings us back home . . . for a hard look at what America needs to do if we are going to run this race economically and run it effectively and maintain the position of world leadership, a position that can only be maintained if the United States retains its preeminent position in the economic field.

I could sum it up briefly this way: First, in personal terms, we need a healthy people. . . .

We need a healthy environment. . . .

We need, also, a healthy economy. . . .

. . . We have got to thin [the government] down; we have got to get it ready for the race. . . .

. . . This Nation [also] needs moral health. . . .

We have been in four wars in this century, and four times young Americans have gone abroad. We have done so without any idea of conquest or domination. We have lost hundreds of thousands of lives and we have not gotten a thing out of any of it. And we have helped each of our enemies, after each of the wars, get on his feet again.

Oh, we have made our mistakes. . . . But . . . [w]hat other nation in the world would you like to have in the position of preeminent power? . . .

I think of what happened to Greece and to Rome and, as you see, what is left — only the pillars. What has happened, of course, is that great civilizations of the past, as they have become wealthy, as they have lost their will to live, to improve, they then have become subject to the decadence which eventually destroys a civilization.

The United States is now reaching that period. I am convinced, however, that we have the vitality, I believe we have the courage, I believe we have the strength out through this heartland and across this Nation that will see to it that America not only is rich and strong, but that it is healthy in terms of moral strength and spiritual strength.

7.3

Ronald Reagan Dubs the Soviet Union the "Focus of Evil"

The headway that Nixon had made toward easing superpower tensions suffered repeated reversals in the late 1970s and early 1980s. Soviet-backed Communists made inroads in the third world and Soviet troops invaded Afghanistan. President Jimmy Carter's stand on human rights and difficulties over arms control created more acrimony. These developments fed disillusion with détente and found fullest expression in Ronald Reagan's first presidential term (1981–1985). Reagan continued the military build up begun by Carter, fought leftist gains in Central America, and lent his personal prestige to the creation of a high-tech shield against missile attack (popularly known as "Star Wars" for its resemblance to science fiction). Reagan's anti-communism and arms buildup helped ignite a broad-based movement in western Europe calling for a freeze on nuclear programs by both superpowers. By spring 1982 the freeze movement had crossed the Atlantic and won broad popular backing in the United States and support in Congress.

Underlying Reagan's policies was a long-standing and often-expressed view of the Soviet Union summed up in what is perhaps his best-known speech, excerpted here. How does Reagan's view differ from the détente thinking of Brandt and Nixon? On what basis does he seem to want to place U.S. policy? Consider for example moral principles, religious values, and national mission. How might the president have tailored his words to his audience? Can we be sure this speech represents Reagan's views?

Remarks at the Annual Convention
of the National Association of Evangelicals
Orlando, Florida, March 8, 1983

[A]s good Marxist–Leninists, the Soviet leaders have openly and publicly declared that the only morality they recognize is that which will further their cause, which is world revolution. . . . Morality is entirely subordinate to the interests of class war. And everything is moral that is necessary for the annihilation of the old, exploiting social order and for uniting the proletariat.

Well, I think the refusal of many influential people to accept this elementary fact of Soviet doctrine illustrates an historical reluctance to see totalitarian powers for what they are. We saw this phenomenon in the 1930's. We see it too often today.

This doesn't mean we should isolate ourselves and refuse to seek an understanding with them. I intend to do everything I can to persuade them of our peaceful intent, to remind them that it was the West that refused to use its nuclear monopoly in the forties and fifties for territorial gain and which now proposes [a] 50-percent cut in strategic ballistic missiles and the elimination of an entire class of land-based, intermediate-range nuclear missiles.

At the same time, however, they must be made to understand we will never compromise our principles and standards. We will never give away our freedom. We will never abandon our belief in God. And we will never stop searching for a genuine peace. But we can assure none of these things America stands for through the so-called nuclear freeze solutions proposed by some.

The truth is that a freeze now would be a very dangerous fraud, for that is merely the illusion of peace. The reality is that we must find peace through strength.

From the Reagan Presidential Library website: <http://www.reagan.utexas .edu/resource/speeches/1983/30883b.htm> (April 2, 2002). Also available in *Public Papers of the Presidents of the United States: Ronald Reagan, 1983* (Washington, D.C.: GPO, 1984), 1:359–64.

I would agree to a freeze if only we could freeze the Soviets' global desires. . . .

A freeze would reward the Soviet Union for its enormous and unparalleled military buildup. It would prevent the essential and long overdue modernization of United States and allied defenses and would leave our aging forces increasingly vulnerable. And an honest freeze would require extensive prior negotiations on the systems and numbers to be limited and on the measures to ensure effective verification and compliance. And the kind of a freeze that has been suggested would be virtually impossible to verify. Such a major effort would divert us completely from our current negotiations on achieving substantial reductions.

A number of years ago, I heard a young father, a very prominent young man in the entertainment world, addressing a tremendous gathering in California. It was during the time of the cold war, and communism and our own way of life were very much on people's minds. And he was speaking to that subject. And suddenly, though, I heard him saying, "I love my little girls more than anything —" And I said to myself, "Oh, no, don't. You can't — don't say that." But I had underestimated him. He went on: "I would rather see my little girls die now, still believing in God, than have them grow up under communism and one day die no longer believing in God."

There were thousands of young people in that audience. They came to their feet with shouts of joy. They had instantly recognized the profound truth in what he had said, with regard to the physical and the soul and what was truly important.

Yes, let us pray for the salvation of all of those who live in that totalitarian darkness — pray they will discover the joy of knowing God. But until they do, let us be aware that while they preach the supremacy of the state, declare its omnipotence over individual man, and predict its eventual domination of all peoples on the Earth, they are the focus of evil in the modern world. . . .

. . . I believe that communism is another sad, bizarre chapter in human history whose last pages even now are being written. I believe this because the source of our strength in the quest for human freedom is not material, but spiritual. And because it knows no limitation, it must terrify and ultimately triumph over those who would enslave their fellow man. . . .

7.4

Mikhail Gorbachev Reassesses Soviet Foreign Policy

The selection of Mikhail Gorbachev in early 1985 to head the Soviet Communist Party was in itself a bit of a surprise to outsiders accustomed to aged, ill, plodding figures in charge in the Kremlin. Young, dynamic, and well-educated, he promoted policies at home and abroad that proved even more surprising. Domestic reform was, he reasoned, impeded by Cold War spending and preoccupations. Thus a return to détente if not an outright end to the Cold War was high on his agenda from the outset. In another surprise, he quickly won Reagan to the cause of negotiations. From 1986 to 1988 a string of summit meetings between the two leaders (followed by still others between Gorbachev and Reagan's successor, George H. W. Bush) focused on arms control and in the process sharply reduced Cold War tensions.

One of the earliest and fullest expressions of Gorbachev's views appeared almost a year after he assumed power. How does Gorbachev assess the international situation generally and the position of the Reagan administration? In what respect are his views innovative? How do they both build on and depart from Khrushchev's position (see chapter 4)? How does his understanding of détente compare with Brandt's and Nixon's? How might Reagan's advisers have interpreted this speech?

Report to the Twenty-Seventh Congress of the Communist Party of the Soviet Union
Moscow, February 25, 1986

[CAPITALISM IN CONFLICT WITH SOCIALISM]

Capitalism regarded the birth of socialism as an "error" of history which must be "rectified." It was to be rectified at any cost, by any means, irrespective of law and morality: by armed intervention, economic blockade, subversive activity, sanctions and "punishments," or rejection of all cooperation. But nothing could interfere with the consolidation of the new system and its historical right to live. . . .

Today . . . the right wing of the US monopoly bourgeoisie regards the stoking up of international tensions as something that justifies military spending, claims to global supremacy, interference in the affairs of other states, and an offensive against the interests and the rights of the American working people. . . .

The policy of total contention, of military confrontation has no future. . . . We, for our part, are ready to do everything we can in order radically to improve the international situation. To achieve this, socialism need not renounce any of its principles or ideals. It has always stood for and continues to stand for the peaceful coexistence of states with different social systems.

. . . Today, too, we are firmly convinced that promoting revolutions from outside, and even more so by military means, is futile and inadmissible.

The problems and crises experienced by the capitalist world arise within its own system and are a natural result of the internal antagonistic contradictions of the old society. . . .

The myth of a Soviet or communist "threat" that is being circulated today is meant to justify the arms race and the imperialist countries' own aggressiveness. But it is becoming increasingly clear that the path of war can yield no sensible solutions, either international or domestic. . . . Now that the world has huge nuclear stockpiles and the only thing experts argue about is how

Mikhail Gorbachev, *The Challenges of Our Time: Disarmament and Social Progress* (New York: International Publishers, 1986), 10–12, 16–22, 73, 77.

many times or dozens of times humanity can be destroyed, it is high time to begin an effective withdrawal from the brink of war, from the equilibrium of fear, to normal, civilised forms of relations between the states of the two systems. . . .

[Tensions among the Capitalist Powers]

The economic, financial, and technological superiority which the USA enjoyed over its closest competitors until the end of the 1960s has been put to a serious trial. Western Europe and Japan managed to outdo their American patron in some things, and are also challenging the United States in such a traditional sphere of US hegemony as that of the latest technology. . . .

. . . For the first time, governments of some West European countries, the social democratic and liberal parties, and the public at large have begun to discuss openly whether present US policy coincides with Western Europe's notions about its own security and whether the United States is going too far in its claims to "leadership"? The partners of the United States have had more than one occasion to see that someone else's spectacles cannot substitute for one's own eyes. . . .

[Imperialists at Odds with the Developing World]

. . . The developing countries with a population of more than two billion, have, in effect, become a region of wholesale poverty. In the early 1980s, the per capita income in the newly free countries was, on the whole, less than 10 per cent that of the developed capitalist states. And in the past thirty years, far from shrinking, the gap has grown wider. Nor is it a question of just comparative poverty. There is illiteracy and ignorance, chronic undernourishment and hunger, appalling child mortality, and epidemics that afflict hundreds of millions of people.

This is a disgrace for civilised humanity! And its culprit is imperialism. Not only from the point of view of history, that is, of colonial plunder on entire continents which left behind a heritage of unbelievable backwardness, but equally in terms of present-day practices. In just the past ten years, the profits squeezed out of the developing countries by US corporations exceeded their inputs four-fold. And in Latin America and the Caribbean, in the same period, the profits of US monopolies were over eight times greater than their inputs. . . .

The distressing condition of the developing countries is a major world-wide problem. This and nothing else is the true source of many of the conflicts in Asia, Africa, and Latin America. Such is the truth, however hard the ruling circles of the imperialist powers may invoke the "hand of Moscow" in order to vindicate their neocolonialist policy and global ambitions. . . .

. . . Sooner or later, in this area too, capitalism will have to choose between the policy of force and shameless plunder, on the one hand, and the opportunity for cooperation on an equitable basis, on the other. The solutions must be radical — in the interests of the peoples of the developing states.

[STRESSES WITHIN THE GLOBAL SYSTEM]

. . . This refers first of all to pollution of the environment, the air and ocean, and to the depletion of natural resources. The problems are aggravated not just by the excessive loads on the natural systems as a consequence of the scientific and technological revolution and the increasing extent of man's activity. Engels,[1] in his time, foresaw the ill effects of subordinating the use of natural resources to the blind play of market forces. The need for effective international procedures and mechanisms, which would make for the rational use of the world's resources as an asset belonging to all humanity, is becoming increasingly apparent.

The global problems, affecting all humanity, cannot be resolved by one state or a group of states. This calls for cooperation on a worldwide scale, for close and constructive joint action by the majority of countries. . . .

Capitalism also causes an impoverishment of culture, an erosion of the spiritual values created over the centuries. Nothing elevates man more than knowledge. But in probably no other period of history has mankind experienced any stronger pressure of falsehood and deceit than it does now. Bourgeois propaganda foists cleverly doctored information on people all over the world, imposing thoughts and feelings, and inculcating a civic and social attitude advantageous to the ruling forces. . . .

. . . The US President said once that if our planet were threatened by a landing from another planet, the USSR and the USA would quickly find a common language. But isn't a nuclear disaster a more tangible danger than a landing by extra-terrestrials? Isn't the ecological threat big enough? Don't all countries have a common stake in finding a sensible and fair approach to the problems of the developing states and peoples?

. . . What does the United States hope to win in the long term by producing doctrines that can no longer ensure US security within the modest dimensions of our planet?

Imperialism is resorting to all possible means to keep in the saddle of history, but such a policy is costing the world dearly. The nations are compelled to pay an ever higher price for it. To pay both directly and indirectly. To pay with millions of human lives, with a depletion of national resources, with the waste of gigantic sums on the arms race. . . .

The US ruling circles are clearly losing their realistic bearings in this far from simple period of history. Aggressive international behaviour, increasing militarisation of politics and thinking, contempt for the interests of others — all this is leading to the inevitable moral and political isolation of US imperialism, widening the abyss between it and the rest of humanity. It is as though the opponents of peace in that country are unaware that when nuclear weapons are at the ready, for civilisation time and space lose their habitual contours, and mankind becomes the captive of an accident.

---

[1]Friedrich Engels (1820–1895), German philosopher, who is along with Karl Marx considered the fountainhead of Soviet ideology.

Will the ruling centres of the capitalist world manage to embark on the path of sober, constructive assessments of what is going on? The easiest thing is to say: maybe yes and maybe no. But history denies us the right to make such predictions. We cannot take "no" for an answer to the question: will mankind survive or not? We say: the progress of society, the life of civilisation, must and will continue.

We say this not only by dint of the optimism that is usual for Communists, by dint of our faith in people's intelligence and common sense. We are realists and are perfectly well aware that the two worlds are divided by very many things, and deeply divided, too. But we also see clearly that the need to re-solve the most vital problems affecting all humanity must prompt them to-wards interaction, awaken humanity's heretofore unseen powers of self-preservation. And here is the stimulus for solutions commensurate with the realities of our time.

The course of history, of social progress, requires ever more insistently that there should be **constructive and creative interaction between states and peoples on the scale of the entire world.**[2] . . .

There is no alternative to this policy. This is all the more true in periods of tension in international affairs. It seems that never in the decades since the war [World War II] has the situation in the world been so explosive, and consequently complex and uncongenial as in the first half of the 1980s. The right-wing group that came to power in the USA and its main NATO fel-low-travellers made a steep turn from detente to a policy of military strength. They have adopted doctrines that reject good-neighbourly relations and co-operation as principles of world development, as a political philosophy of international relations. The Washington administration remained deaf to our calls for an end to the arms race and an improvement of the situation. . . .

. . . In the military sphere we intend to act in such a way as to give nobody grounds for fears, even imagined ones, about their security. But to an equal extent we and our allies want to be rid of the feeling that we are threatened. The USSR undertook the obligation not to be the first to use nuclear weap-ons and it will abide strictly by that obligation. But it is no secret that sce-narios for a nuclear strike against us do exist. We have no right to overlook this. The Soviet Union is a staunch adversary of nuclear war in any variant. Our country stands for removing weapons of mass destruction from use, for limiting the military potential to reasonable adequacy. But the character and level of this ceiling continue to be restricted by the attitudes and actions of the USA and its partners in the blocs. Under these conditions we repeat again and again: **the Soviet Union lays no claim to more security, but it will not settle for less.**[3]

---

[2]Text in bold in the original.
[3]Text in bold in the original.

GORBACHEV'S REFORMS

Mikhail Gorbachev did not create the reform impulse within the Soviet system but he came quickly to embody its hopes when he became the head of the Soviet Communist Party. Gorbachev had joined the party in 1953 and advanced rapidly. His notions of reform, influenced by his predecessors, were at first limited to upgrading technology and raising economic efficiency. But by degrees he began thinking of sweeping economic restructuring (*perestroika*) reinforced by greater political and cultural openness (*glasnost*).

Translating innovative ideas into effective policy is never easy, and in Gorbachev's case the process led to disaster. His reform program encountered resistance within the party, unleashed disruptive political forces on the periphery of the Soviet Union, and damaged the economy. By 1989 Gorbachev was on the defensive, less and less popular even as he won accolades abroad for his foreign policy. He was finally discredited in 1991 when associates attempted a coup. He survived the challenge, but it was a hollow victory. By then the Soviet Union was coming apart and Gorbachev had lost all credibility.

7.5
Gorbachev Outlines *Glasnost* and *Perestroika*

By early 1987 Gorbachev's notions of reform — associated with the terms *glasnost* and *perestroika* — had evolved from a tentative approach to a robust, far-reaching set of policies. At a meeting of the entire Central Committee of the Soviet Communist Party in January, he presented a report calling for an ambitious makeover of the Soviet system. By the summer of 1988 his vision had evolved even further — to what amounted to democratic socialism in which the party's power would be strictly limited.

Gorbachev's notions of reform are slippery, in part because they were a work in progress and in part because his own formulations could be fuzzy. So grasping his views may require a bit of effort. What did Gorbachev see as the sources of Soviet problems that required reform? How did he understand *perestroika* and *glasnost* and how were these notions to address those problems? How fundamental a break with the past did he see his reforms?

Report to the Central Committee
of the Soviet Communist Party
Moscow, January 27, 1987

We have irrevocably begun restructuring and have taken the first steps on this path. . . .

At the same time, we see that changes for the better are taking place slowly, that the task of restructuring has turned out to be more difficult than it had seemed to us earlier, and that the causes of the problems that have accumu-

---

Translation in *Current Digest of the Soviet Press* 39 (February 25, 1987), 1–2, 4–6; (March 4, 1987), 8–11; (March 11, 1987), 14.

lated in society are more deep-rooted than we had thought. The more deeply we go into restructuring work, the clearer its scale and importance become; more and more new unsolved problems inherited from the past are coming to light. . . .

. . . At a certain stage the country began to lose momentum, difficulties and unsolved problems began to pile up, and stagnation and other phenomena alien to socialism appeared. All of this had a serious effect on the economy and on the social and spiritual spheres. . . .

Comrades, all this had a negative effect on the development of many spheres of the life of society. Take material production. Over the past three five-year plans, the growth rates of national income declined by more than 50%. For most indices, plans had not been fulfilled since the early 1970s. The economy as a whole became unreceptive to innovations and sluggish, the quality of a large part of output no longer met current demands, and disproportions in production became exacerbated. . . .

. . . While successfully resolving questions of the population's employment and providing for fundamental social guarantees, we have at the same time been unable to fully realize the possibilities of socialism in improving living conditions and the food supply, in organizing transportation, medical service and education and in solving a number of other urgent problems.

Violations of the most important principle of socialism — distribution according to work — appeared. The struggle against unearned income was waged indecisively. The policy of providing material and moral incentives for highly productive labor was inconsistent. Large sums of money were paid out in unwarranted bonuses and in various kinds of additional incentives, and reports were padded for the sake of personal gain. A dependent mind-set grew, and a "wage-leveling" mentality began taking root in people's minds. This hit at those toilers who were able and wanted to work better, while at the same time it made life easier for those whose idea of working involves little effort. . . .

The elements of social corrosion that emerged in recent years had a negative effect on society's spiritual temper and imperceptibly sapped the lofty moral values that have always been inherent to our people and in which we take pride — ideological conviction, labor enthusiasm and Soviet patriotism.

The inevitable consequence of this was a falloff in interest in public affairs, manifestations of spiritual emptiness and skepticism, and a decline in the role of moral incentives to labor. The stratum of people, including young people, whose goal in life came down to material well-being and personal gain by any means increased. Their cynical position took on increasingly militant forms, poisoned the minds of those around them, and gave rise to a wave of consumerism. The growth of drunkenness, the spread of drug addiction and the increase in crime became indices of the falloff in social mores.

Instances of a scornful attitude toward laws, hoodwinking, bribetaking and the encouragement of servility and glorification had a pernicious effect on the moral atmosphere in society. Genuine concern for people, their living and working conditions and their social well-being was frequently supplanted by political ingratiation — the mass handing out of awards, titles and bonuses.

An atmosphere of all-forgivingness took shape, while exactingness, discipline and responsibility declined. . . .

Today there is a need to state once again what we mean by restructuring.

Restructuring means resolutely overcoming the processes of stagnation, scrapping the mechanism of retardation, and creating a reliable and effective mechanism of accelerating the social and economic development of Soviet society. The main idea of our strategy is to combine the achievements of the scientific and technological revolution with a planned economy and to set the entire potential of socialism in motion.

Restructuring means reliance on the vital creativity of the masses, the all-round development of democracy and socialist self-government, the encouragement of initiative and independent activity, the strengthening of discipline and order, and the expansion of openness, criticism and self-criticism in all spheres of the life of society; it means respect, raised on high, for the value and worth of the individual.

Restructuring means steadily enhancing the role of intensive factors in the development of the Soviet economy; restoring and developing Leninist principles of democratic centralism in the management of the national economy, introducing economic methods of management everywhere, renouncing the peremptory issuing of orders and administrative fiat, ensuring the changeover of all elements of the economy to the principles of full economic accountability and to new forms of the organization of labor and production, and encouraging innovation and socialist enterprise in every way.

Restructuring means a decisive turn toward science. . . .

Restructuring means the priority development of the social sphere and the ever fuller satisfaction of Soviet people's requirements for good working, living, recreational, educational and medical-service conditions . . . .

Restructuring means the energetic elimination from society of distortions of socialist morality, and the consistent implementation of the principles of social justice . . . .

The ultimate aim of restructuring is clear, I think — a thoroughgoing renewal of all aspects of the country's life, the imparting to socialism of the most up-to-date forms of social organization, and the fullest possible disclosure of the humanistic nature of our system in all its decisive aspects — economic, social, political and moral. . . .

Apparently it is difficult for some comrades to understand that democracy is not just a slogan but the essence of restructuring. They much change their views and habits, if they are not to be left outside the mainstream of life. This is our insistent advice to all doubters and laggards.

The question of the election of managers of enterprises and production facilities, the superintendents of shops, divisions and sections, the heads of livestock sections and teams, brigade leaders and foremen should be singled out. The present stage of restructuring and the transition to new methods of economic management, economic accountability, self-financing and paying one's own way are moving this problem onto a practical plane. This measure is important and necessary, and there is no doubt that it will meet with the working people's approval. . . .

On the political level, the matter at hand is deepening democracy in the electoral system and achieving the more effective and more active participation of voters at all stages of preelection and election campaigns. . . .

It is quite natural that questions of expanding inner-Party democracy be examined within the overall context of the future democratization of Soviet society. . . .

There is . . . a need to give some thought to changing the procedure for the election of secretaries of district, region, city, province and territory Party committees and of Union-republic Communist Party Central Committees. Here comrades suggest that secretaries, including first secretaries, could be elected by secret ballot at plenary sessions of the appropriate Party committees. In the process, the members of the Party committee would have the right to enter any number of candidates on the ballot. This measure ought to significantly enhance the responsibility of secretaries to the Party committees that elected them, give them more confidence in their work, and make it possible to more accurately determine the extent of their prestige.

Needless to say, the Party's statutory principle according to which the decisions of higher agencies are binding on all lower-level Party committees, including decisions on personnel questions, should remain immutable.

In the Politburo's opinion, further democratization should extend to the formation of the Party's central leadership bodies as well. I think this is perfectly logical. Apparently it would be logical to democratize elections of leadership bodies in other public organizations as well. . . .

In improving the social atmosphere, it is also necessary to continue to develop openness. It is a powerful lever for improving work in all sectors of our construction and an effective form of control by all the people. . . .

Obviously, the time has come to begin the drafting of legal documents guaranteeing openness. They should ensure maximum openness in the activities of state and public organizations and give working people a real opportunity to express their opinion on any question of the life of society. . . .

. . . [W]e continue to encounter not only hostility toward criticism but also instances of persecution for it and the outright suppression of critical statements. Frequently . . . the Central Committee has to intervene in order to restore truth and justice and to support honest people who back the interests of the cause. . . .

In this connection, the efforts of the mass news media to develop criticism and self-criticism in our society must be supported. . . .

Socialist democracy has nothing in common with an "everything goes" attitude, irresponsibility or anarchy. Genuine democracy serves every person, protecting his political and social rights, and at the same time it serves every collective and society as a whole, upholding their interests. . . .

We want to transform our country into a model of a highly developed state, into a society of the most advanced economy, the broadest democracy and the most humane and lofty morality, where the working person will feel himself to be a full-fledged proprietor and can enjoy all the benefits of material and spiritual culture, where his children's future will be secure, and where he will possess everything he needs for a full, meaningful life. We want to force even the skeptics to say: Yes, the Bolsheviks can do anything. Yes, the truth is on their side. Yes, socialism is a system that serves man, his social and economic interests and his spiritual elevation.

7.6
Elite Supporters Reflect on the Reform Program

Gorbachev's staunchest supporters were party intellectuals of his generation. Like him, they had gone to school in the late Stalin years, joined the party in the early 1950s, and welcomed Khrushchev's attack on Stalin in 1956. They thought of themselves as "children of the twentieth party congress" at which Khrushchev delivered that attack. Tatyana Zaslavskaya, a leading sociologist, was one of those well-known supporters. From an academic family, she had been schooled at the prestigious Moscow State University as an economist and then moved into the more politically sensitive discipline of sociology. No less prominent was Fyodor Burlatsky, a close Gorbachev adviser and long-time reformist gadfly within the Communist Party. He came from a committed Bolshevik family and after studying law went to work for the Central Committee under Khrushchev.

Stephen Cohen and Katrina vanden Heuvel conducted multiple taped interviews with these two reformers between June 1987 and April 1989, at the height of the reform process. The questions posed in these interviews (marked here in italics) evoked responses that provide a behind-the-scenes sense of the goals Gorbachev was pursuing and the obstacles he faced. Do these two reformers agree with Gorbachev on the meaning of *glasnost* and *perestroika?* What obstacles do they see standing in the way of reform? Putting Gorbachev's own statement together with these interviews, would you say that his reforms were well conceived? And were they within a socialist framework? How would Djilas, the Yugoslav critic of the new Communist class (Document 4.3), have reacted to the views expressed here?

Stephen Cohen and Katrina vanden Heuvel
Interview with Tatyana Zaslavskaya

I wept and felt terrible when Stalin died in 1953. I think almost everybody did. Like many young people, I felt that I had to join the party to make up for the loss of Stalin. Or something like that. I applied for membership in the spring of 1953 and became a member in 1954. And yet I joined with terribly contradictory feelings. It was impossible not to see some of the terrible things that had been going on. . . .

Stephen F. Cohen and Katrina vanden Heuvel, *Voices of Glasnost: Interviews with Gorbachev's Reformers* (New York: W. W. Norton, 1989), 120, 122–23, 126–30, 132–34, 137–38.

After four years of Gorbachev's policies, do you, as a sociologist, have an understanding of the process of perestroika that differs in any fundamental way from what we usually read in the Soviet press?

Everyone understands that we began these revolutionary reforms because we had reached an economic dead end and we had to find a road to real progress. The country had entered a crisis. It was lagging behind the world economically, technologically, and scientifically, and mass dissatisfaction was growing more acute. So everyone also understands that restructuring the economy is our most pressing task. But I remain convinced that the primary reasons for the need for perestroika were not the sluggish economy and rate of technological development but an underlying mass alienation of working people from significant social goals and values. This social alienation is rooted in the economic system formed in the 1930s, which made state property, run by a vast bureaucratic apparatus, the dominant form of ownership. By the 1980s, 15–18 million functionaries administered this statist system, from Moscow to the thousands of enterprises. For fifty years it was said that this was public property and belonged to everyone, but no way was ever found to make workers feel they were the co-owners and masters of the factories, farms, and enterprises. They felt themselves to be cogs in a gigantic machine.

Maybe this system was necessary in the 1930s, when the country was so terribly backward. The majority of the working class came from the countryside. Workers were uneducated, knew only their narrow slice of life, and had nothing. I don't know. Personally, I think the Stalinist 1930s were our Thermidor,[1] when the socialist revolution was thwarted and Stalin carried out an anti-Leninist coup d'état. The claim that socialism was being built camouflaged the emergence of some other kind of system, maybe some kind of Asiatic despotism. Now we have to squeeze Stalinism out of ourselves drop by drop.

I do know that this system no longer works because people have changed enormously in the last fifty years. Now they are educated and well informed. They have a much higher standard of living, apartments, free medicine, free education, and they don't have to work hard to get it. The bureaucratic-command system can no longer direct and control them. Man is resilient — you push and he pushes back. The bottom is no longer willing to work efficiently, and the top can no longer force it to do so.

Therefore, if we want people to be creative, productive, and efficient, we have to change the whole system of social relations. That is why I say perestroika must be a social revolution. It must bring about a fundamental redistribution of power, rights, freedoms, wealth, and control of property among the various strata and groups that make up the Soviet Union. It must democratize social

---

[1] Following the triumph of the French Revolution when moderate leaders turned on their radical colleagues and purged them from power.

relations. That is also why perestroika cannot be carried out only from above. It requires broad participation and activism on the part of the masses. . . . What I want for my country is real not fictional socialism, where people can be happy as creators, not just as consumers, and where they will be able to pursue all of their talents. Where people will feel like human beings and not feel constantly oppressed.

In particular, we have to open up new social-economic roads for millions of people that will allow them to identify with the means of production — to feel they are the owners and masters of property and that their income depends on how it is used. To do this, we must have economic pluralism — not just state ownership but also cooperative and individual ownership. And there must be real competition among these forms. . . .

. . . [T]here has been a colossal, just colossal, corruption of our whole legal apparatus — so many very unjust legal decisions and sentences. And this has had a terrible influence on the way people work and live. They have lost faith in the justness of the whole system. When people believe that evil triumphs, they just give up.

. . . [P]eople born in the countryside have many fewer opportunities to develop their innate abilities. City children have far greater access to child care, high quality schools, and cultural life. A survey at Novosibirsk University showed that only 3 percent of the students came from rural areas. Rural students take the entrance exams, but they can't pass them. And when students do graduate from higher educational institutions, who actually gets which jobs? Are decisions really made on the basis of their abilities? An enormous social mechanism of family connections, social ties, string-pulling, obedience, and conformity is at work here. Theoretically, people with ability and talent rise. In practice, those who are gray and mediocre rise more easily and swiftly. Even then, people aren't able to work to their full creative ability because their hands and feet are tied by bureaucratic instructions and prohibitions. To say nothing of our very skewed wage and salary system, which is strictly regulated by a state committee. Engineers, doctors, teachers, and others are badly underpaid. Service industries pay far less than manufacturing. I could mention many more examples of injustices.

And yet, the perestroika advocated by you and by most reform economists is certain to lead to other kinds of social injustices. . . .

I know that the economic reforms will produce some new injustices. We are not going to be able to exercise strict control over private enterprise. Some people will amass great fortunes, sometimes through sneakiness and machinations. Some people will have to be laid off and find new jobs. This is an organic social price we will have to pay, but existing injustices are so much greater.

Moreover, why shouldn't people who are more able live better than those who are not? The people who live best today are not those who do the best work. Is that just? Anyway, you can't escape the fact that people are born with different levels of ability. . . .

. . . The changes you and evidently Gorbachev himself are proposing — perestroika as a "social revolution" — are so fundamental that they would profoundly affect the longstanding social contract in the Soviet Union, the explicit or implicit relationship between state and society. And that, of course, could affect the political stability of the Soviet system. For years, you have had, for example, a kind of cradle-to-grave welfare state, which guaranteed citizens all sorts of free or cheap benefits if they complied with the rules of the game. Now, you say these guarantees are part of the problem because they have deprived people of incentives to be productive. You are telling people that there will be less guarantees in economic and social life and they must take more risks. But if you affect people's psychology in those ways, they may decide to take more political risks as well. They may stop being so obedient and deferential to the state in other areas.

Yes, that is possible and maybe inescapable. As I see it, people will develop the habit of taking their fate into their own hands, first of all in economic life. They will turn into different kinds of people, confident and energetic in their work. And that will have positive political consequences. It is hard to imagine such energetic, economically independent people voting for just anyone. It will contribute to the general process of democratization by enhancing the importance of opinion from below, as people overcome their political alienation. If you have a passive citizenry, with 99.9 percent of the people voting for the same person, as we had in the past, you have the stability of a cemetery. If you want real life, you have to have conflicting interests and democracy. Without democratization, you can't have perestroika. . . .

The problem is that people were made so passive by what happened under Stalin and Brezhnev that there is essentially no public opinion on many vitally important questions. Under the old system, nobody cared what the people thought. I don't mean that public opinion doesn't exist but that it isn't expressed, except by the intelligentsia. Broad masses of people didn't have enough information to think about things. Our hope is that glasnost and public discussion of ideas and policies will compel more and more people to think, take a position, become active, and therefore support perestroika. In a country where the rulers have long lost the habit of any sort of dialogue with the population, where they have viewed the population as simply an object to be manipulated, this kind of public opinion is very important. . . .

. . . Marxism taught that there would be no exploiting class under socialism because there would be no private ownership of the large-scale means of production. And yet, our nomenklatura[2] of bureaucrats and apparatchiks has acquired some of the characteristics that Lenin attributed to such a class. He emphasized the class's control over the means of production, access to a disproportionate part of the social wealth, and economic exploitation of the population. From what we now know about how our system functioned un-

---

[2]The powerful and privileged class of officials who head major economic and political organizations.

der Stalin and Brezhnev, it is possible to say that a layer or strata of the nomenklatura indirectly exploits the basic mass of the population. . . .

I do know that perestroika conflicts with the interests of a sizable part of the administrative bureaucracy, which is full of groups whose interests and attitudes are very conservative. One reason that perestroika is proceeding with such great difficulty is that officials of most of the state ministries are trying to strangle the economic reforms. They are finding ways to use the reforms, which are supposed to free enterprises from ministerial control, to tighten their hold on the enterprises. And don't forget the outright reactionaries in the state bureaucracy and party apparatus. Some of them are mafiosi types with ties to organized crime on a grand scale, as we have seen in Uzbekistan. If they had the chance they'd shoot Gorbachev and perestroika five times over. . . .

. . . Gorbachev, his aides, and some other political leaders do have the historic vision, will, and courage to see perestroika through to the end. But many political leaders do not. They were formed by past practices, they remain profoundly authoritarian, they lack the ability to govern the country in new democratic ways, and they have done things in the past that cannot be forgotten. The whole party apparatus must be greatly reduced, rejuvenated, and radicalized. And this is true also of the ruling group of political leaders. . . .

But whether we are talking about men or women, perestroika has to give people faith in its goals and the freedom to be active and creative. Otherwise there will be no social revolution in our country. Working people are watching and waiting to see if the changes are really going to affect their lives. They've grown accustomed to a discrepancy between words and deeds. The greatest danger is that we will disappoint them again and lose their support. . . .

Maybe that is what your conservative officials really fear — that if Soviet citizens are unbound, they will run very fast and in extreme directions. The policies of perestroika have already unleashed kinds of unrest and turbulence that many ordinary citizens also seem to find objectionable. . . .

In general, the apparatus is scared of all forms of conflict — it's afraid of protests, of strikes, of everything. But we cannot rule out the possibility of even more acute political, social, and nationality conflicts as perestroika goes on. They are growing not only in the Baltic republics and the Transcaucasus but also in a number of large Russian cities. Some of them, alas, have taken extreme forms — hunger strikes and even people setting themselves on fire. These things reflect the country's low level of political culture and lack of democratic traditions. That is why the Soviet Union faces a choice: either carry through the radical reforms we have begun in all social relations or return to the repressive methods that produced this situation. Meanwhile, as perestroika goes on, the party and the state have to find ways to maintain a balance between constitutional procedures and social order, on the one hand, and the growth of democratic mass activism, on the other.

Cohen and vanden Heuvel
Interview with Fyodor Burlatsky

I've been struggling against Stalinism and for the democratization of my country for more than thirty-five years, ever since 1953. There have been ups and downs in my life — times when I worked closely with Soviet leaders and times when I had to resign or I lost my job. . . .

I don't think you can say that our dissidents prepared the way for perestroika. Perestroika was prepared by people within the system who continued to speak out for revolutionary structural reforms. First and foremost, Khrushchev had a great and lasting influence, but there was a whole galaxy of Soviet editors and writers . . . . These were people who did not allow themselves to be pushed outside the political system, who did not retreat into dissidence. . . .

Are you saying that the progressive wing of the Soviet Communist Party came to power with Gorbachev?

No doubt about it. But this meant, first and foremost, Gorbachev himself and his circle of close associates. It will take time for the progressive wing to come to power throughout the party and at all levels of society. This process is underway, but it is a struggle, and it will take many years. . . .

As someone who has thought about and struggled for reforms in the Soviet system for so many years, how would you explain the essence or essential purpose of perestroika?

. . . We need economic and political reforms that will enable Soviet society to achieve the highest possible living standards, to reach the technological level of the most advanced industrialized countries, to express moral values and people's abilities, and to have democratic mechanisms through which public opinion can shape major decisions and individuals will be free. Essentially, this means that the Soviet state must give up much of its power and many of its functions to society and organizations. Instead of a state-run economy, this means a self-managed economy based on market relations and competition among state, cooperative, and private enterprises. Instead of bureaucratic dictates, this means democratic political procedures based on mass participation and competitive elections. That is why I call perestroika a transition from state socialism to civil socialist society — to a more efficient, democratic, and humane model of socialism. . . .

. . . The magnitude of our problems, what Gorbachev calls stagnation, is clear. Our standard of living and technological development lag behind not only Western countries but even Eastern European ones. We have shortages of everything, from food and razors to personal computers. Bureaucratization and corruption are pervasive, and in some places we even have mafias. And the decline in morale and the loss of socialist values among our young people is serious. These are the objective preconditions for perestroika. On another

---

Cohen and vanden Heuvel, *Voices of Glasnost,* 175, 180, 184–87, 193–96.

level, people have changed and are ready to live differently. All of their abilities and demands are greater — economic, cultural, informational, and psychological. They are ready for the new model of socialism. . . .

. . . [W]e must accept the basic principle of a division of executive, legislative, and judicial powers — the need for separation and sharing of power. . . . The general secretary of the Communist Party should be elected by a party congress and then submit himself to direct election as president by all citizens in secret ballot. He and all other elected officials should be limited to two five-year terms in office. This presidential reform must be accompanied by reforms that will transform the Supreme Soviet from a ceremonial institution into a working Soviet parliament of deputies chosen in multi-candidate elections. . . . Judges and courts must be made independent of party and state bodies. Defendants should have the help of a defense attorney immediately. Jury trials should be introduced for major offenses. Punishment for most crimes should be made less harsh. Capital punishment should be abolished . . . . And we should have laws guaranteeing and protecting glasnost and the freedom of opinion, speech, organization, and orderly demonstrations. . . .

And if all these political reforms work out, will Soviet democracy eventually resemble American democracy?

They will have some things in common, such as mass media that reflect public opinion, elections, and other forms of mass participation. But what you Americans don't seem to understand is that there are various kinds of democracy. Democracy isn't just a constitutional or legal system but a form of politics that rests upon a nation's historical traditions and political culture. Therefore, it is naive to think that there should be only one kind of democracy everywhere in the world. It is also naive to expect the Soviet Union, which inherited antidemocratic traditions from tsarist Russia, to develop in the way the United States did. We have had centuries of patriarchal, authoritarian culture in Russia, which had no liberal tradition. Stalin's personality cult was not merely imposed from above. It also grew from below.

Another important difference is that we want democracy in economic life, so that the economy is not controlled by an elite. We want workers to control state-owned enterprises and to have economic power, something that does not exist in America. But I don't think we will achieve economic democracy in the next decade or so because of the diseases of bureaucratization and centralization, which plague both of our systems.

Another difference is that we will preserve the one-party system. Our problem is to find some combination of traditional and nontraditional ways to develop democracy within our one-party system. . . .

. . . Isn't democratization in effect an assault on the whole nomenklatura system of appointing officials from above? Therefore, isn't opposition bound to be very large-scale and powerful — perhaps too much so to be overcome?

Certainly the system of elections will clash with the system of appointments from above. And certainly a large part of the nomenklatura wants to retain its power and privileges. But there is a struggle underway in the nomenklatura class between democratic and bureaucratic forces. After all, the reform ideas themselves emerged from segments of this nomenklatura class, under Khrushchev and Gorbachev. Even our present ideas about democratization came from above. So there is a struggle between these two trends. The Gorbachev leadership must try to guide this process, and the masses should strive to democratize it. It is true that opposition to democratization is strong within the nomenklatura, particularly in the managerial ranks. But there are also forces in the nomenklatura that want to change the balance of power and thus will support democratization. For example, in lower party organizations there are younger, more capable people who want to replace the old guard, and they see democratization as a way to do so. . . .

Where are the neo-Stalinists in all this? During our dozen or so trips to Moscow since 1985, we have gotten the impression that they are growing increasingly strong or at least clamorous.

. . .There are two reasons why neo-Stalinist moods are widespread. One is that many people still want simplistic answers to all of our problems. For Stalin or against Stalin. So naturally, given the complexity of our problems, a sizable number of people are for Stalin. . . . Stalin's name is linked to thirty years in the lives of many people — to events that shaped several generations. And there were so many different events during those years. So if you ask people what they think about Stalin's mass repressions, a large majority may be against them. But if you ask about Stalin's leadership in World War II, a large majority may be in favor of it. Again, don't forget our authoritarian-patriarchical traditions and the fact that Stalinism came from above and from below.

That raises the very large question of whether or not Soviet political culture has really changed fundamentally — whether or not it now is high enough to support the kind of democratization you are advocating. . . .

We are faced with a paradox. We must democratize power in order to democratize society, but in order to democratize power we need a democratic society. You are right that democratization is a long march, but I think that the Soviet leadership and the Soviet people have already traveled a long way toward it. . . .

I don't deny the huge problems that remain. Even though Soviet society is ridding itself of Stalinism and stagnation, those decades of experience have left deep scars. Look at the lack of tolerance, even among educated political people. Too many of them don't know how to live with an opponent. They want to deprive him of the right to speak, destroy him, or put him in a concentration camp. Tolerance of pluralism, the ability to understand another person's interests and viewpoints, are true signs of a democratic culture. And look at the intense national feelings and hatreds that are erupting around the country. All these problems were created by the authoritarian past, including Stalin's genocide of entire nationalities, and yet they erupt just as perestroika holds out the possibility of democratic solutions. We are paying the price for decades of graveyard silence.

Nothing seems to test the tolerance of Soviet citizens as much as glasnost. Apparently, many people are sincerely outraged that Soviet newspapers, magazines, and tele-

vision are openly discussing so many formerly taboo subjects, from prostitution, homo-
sexuality, drug addiction, and AIDS to Stalin's terror and the persecution of noncon-
formists in the 1970s. . . .

Perestroika began with glasnost, and it cannot exist without it. Glasnost is giving birth to independent public opinion in the Soviet Union, which is a prerequisite of democratization. We have achieved quite a lot in this area since 1985. . . . The media are beginning to play their proper role in promoting openness and information. And a significant pluralism of opinions is emerging. . . .

To tell you the truth, I am worried that we may already have more glasnost than society can stand. There is already a great imbalance between what glasnost is promising and actual political and economic changes. When a worker is free to criticize his manager, for example, but nothing changes in his economic situation, I worry that will be a source of additional social tension. Faster economic changes would eliminate this imbalance, but meanwhile there is a danger that glasnost could go too far.

What do you mean "too far"? As a writer who has criticized abuses of power and policies of the past, wouldn't you like to have enough glasnost so that the press would be free to criticize the Politburo or the top leadership today?

. . . We still lack the kind of traditions that would enable such criticism of our leaders to be constructive and positive. Ideally, yes, it would be good to have glasnost like that. But we must live and carry out perestroika in the conditions that we have inherited from the past. We are overcoming those traditions, they aren't dead yet. And you know the old saying: The dead always seize the living by the throat.

7.7
Gorbachev Resigns as President of the USSR

In late 1991 after a failed coup against him by party hardliners and amidst economic crisis and separatist pressures tearing the Soviet Union apart, Gorbachev made a painful public admission of defeat. In his resignation, he remained defiantly optimistic about the long-term effects of reform.

How does Gorbachev assess his reform program — its origins, development, and outcome? What has he learned about reform in the Soviet Union that he might not have understood initially? What kind of resignation speech might Reagan or the senior Bush (or for that matter Stalin or Khrushchev) have written for Gorbachev on this occasion?

Televised Speech
December 25, 1991

A policy aimed at dismembering the country and disuniting the state has prevailed, something that I cannot agree with. . . .

Fate ordained that when I became head of state it was already clear that things were not going well in the country. We have a great deal of everything — land, petroleum, gas and other natural resources — and God has endowed us with intelligence and talent, too, but we live much worse than people in the developed countries do, and we are lagging further and further behind them.

The reason was evident — society was suffocating in the grip of the command-bureaucratic system. Doomed to serve ideology and to bear the terrible burden of the arms race, it had been pushed to the limit of what was possible.

All attempts at partial reforms — and there were a good many of them — failed, one after the other. The country had lost direction. It was impossible to go on living that way. Everything had to be changed fundamentally.

That is why I have never once regretted that I did not take advantage of the position of General Secretary just to "reign" for a few years. I would have considered that irresponsible and immoral.

I realized that to begin reforms on such a scale and in such a society as ours was an extremely difficult and even risky endeavor. But even today I am convinced of the historical correctness of the democratic reforms that were begun in the spring of 1985. . . .

— The totalitarian system, which for a long time deprived the country of the opportunity to become prosperous and flourishing, has been eliminated.

— A breakthrough has been achieved in the area of democratic transformations. Free elections, freedom of the press, religious freedoms, representative bodies of power and a multiparty system have become a reality. Human rights have been recognized as the highest principle.

— Movement toward mixed economy has begun, and the equality of all forms of ownership is being established. Within the framework of a land reform, the peasantry has begun to revive, private farming has appeared, and millions of hectares of land are being given to rural and urban people. The economic freedom of the producer has been legalized, and entrepreneurship, the formation of joint-stock companies and privatization have begun to gather momentum.

— In turning the economy toward a market, it is important to remember that this is being done for the sake of human beings. In this difficult time, everything must be done for their social protection, and this applies especially to old people and children.

We are living in a new world:

— An end has been put to the cold war, and the arms race and the insane militarization of the country, which disfigured our economy and the public consciousness and morals, have been halted. The threat of a world war has been removed. . . .

Translation in *Current Digest of the Soviet Press* 43 (January 29, 1992), 1, 3. Audio version available online at <http://www.historychannel.com/speeches/archive/speech_525.html> (January 17, 2003).

All these changes required enormous effort and took place in an acute struggle, with mounting resistance from old, obsolete and reactionary forces — both the former Party-state structures and the economic apparatus — and also from our habits, ideological prejudices, and a leveling and parasitic mentality. The changes ran up against our intolerance, low level of political sophistication and fear of change.

For this reason, we lost a great deal of time. The old system collapsed before a new one had time to start working.

THE REVOLUTIONS OF '89 IN EUROPE

In the course of 1989 the Soviet-backed socialist regimes of eastern Europe one by one came tumbling down. They approached their moment of collapse by different routes beginning at different points, though in all cases outsiders helped push the process along. From the West came the Helsinki accords of 1975, guaranteeing civil and political rights across Europe. The Soviet Union and its client states signed, thinking that the rights were mere formalities, whereas they proved in fact to cast a blanket of legitimacy over dissent and to put repression in the international spotlight. From the East a decade later came Gorbachev's public renunciation of force to prop up those clients, demoralized Communist party leaders already isolated and under attack from dissidents within their own countries.

The readings below — from Poland, Czechoslovakia, and East Germany — capture the rising pressure, especially strong among intellectuals and workers. The upheaval of 1989 was a complex event in each of these countries, and these three cases, each with their own peculiarities, diverge from the events elsewhere in eastern Europe — in Hungary, Romania, Bulgaria, and even Yugoslavia (not Soviet controlled but still Communist run). The first two documents highlight how long the discontent had been simmering, while the third reveals that change, when it finally came in 1989, could leave its advocates feeling disappointed, even betrayed. It is worth considering what distinguishes the opposition in these three national cases, what unites them, and how far they each go in repudiating socialism.

7.8

A Critique of the Polish Communist Party

In Poland what would prove to be the final challenge to party authority took shape in the late 1970s and early 1980s and on a broad front, including dissident intellectuals, discontented workers, and the Catholic Church. This coalition eroded the capacity of the Communists to govern and stripped them of the last shreds of their legitimacy. When the demoralized party finally agreed to elections, held in June 1989, its candidates suffered a crushing defeat at the hands of Solidarity.

Organized in 1980 and led by Lech Walesa, this worker-dominated movement had become the leading political force within Poland.

The Workers' Defense Committee, best known by its acronym KOR, was the forerunner to and model for Solidarity. Worker strikes in 1976 protesting a government-imposed increase in food prices led to the creation of KOR. Like Solidarity later, it brought intellectuals and workers into a cooperative relationship. Also like Solidarity, support for KOR spread rapidly and included the backing of the Catholic Church. Two years after its founding KOR issued this indictment. While it would fall to Solidarity to press the attack on Communist control to a successful conclusion, we can see already here the depth of the discontent with socialist rule. What problems prompted this attack? What political vision animates the KOR critique? Does this document represent a call for reform or the end of one-party rule? How did KOR imagine advancing its agenda?

Workers' Defense Committee (KOR)
"Appeal to Society"
October 10, 1978

Growing disorganization and chaos have ravaged the economic, social, and cultural life of the country. In this serious situation, we consider it our responsibility to present to Polish society an evaluation of the situation, together with an attempt to indicate what possible remedies are available to society. We would also like our statement to serve as a warning to the authorities against continuing their policy of deliberate disregard for genuine social problems, and against their evasion of the responsibility for solving these problems. The results of such policies have on many occasions proven tragic for society, and the entire responsibility for this rests with the authorities.

I

1. The increase in prices for foodstuffs that was rejected by the public in 1976 has been replaced by hidden price increases. . . .

Difficulties with supplies are constantly increasing, both in the area of industrial goods and of foodstuffs. It is impossible to purchase many items in the stores without standing in lines, an enormous waste of time, or engaging in bribery or nepotism. . . .

2. The state of health services is alarming. Chronic underinvestment over a period of years has recently been reflected in a decrease in the number of hospital beds. . . . The overcrowding and the technical conditions in a great many hospitals, which have never been renovated since the prewar period, create sanitary conditions that endanger the health of patients.

Insufficient nutrition and the lack of medications available in the hospitals and on the market are also obstacles to treatment. . . .

Jan Józef Lipski, *KOR: A History of the Workers' Defense Committee in Poland, 1976–1981* (Berkeley: University of California Press, 1985), 474–82.

3. The past several years have also brought about no improvement in the dramatic situation in housing. The number of people waiting for apartments grows larger every year, while the waiting period grows longer. This is coupled with a systematic increase in the cost of housing, which significantly burdens family budgets. . . .

4. The authorities are attempting to make up for the disorganization of the economy through an increased exploitation of the workers. The average working day of many occupational groups has often been lengthened. Drivers, miners, construction workers, many other occupational groups now work ten to twelve hours a day. . . .

5. . . . There are enormous differences in retirement benefits. We have now in Poland families who are struggling under extremely difficult living conditions, and a small number of families who have no financial worries whatsoever. Another factor deepening social inequalities is the extensive system of privileges for groups associated with the authorities: privileged supplies, special health services, allocation of housing and building lots, foreign currency, and special recreational areas. . . .

More and more often, one can observe children inheriting the privileged position of their parents. The principle of equal opportunity for all young people is becoming illusory.

In a situation where the economic crisis threatens all of society, and especially the underprivileged groups, the assurance of special privileges to the governing groups provokes righteous anger and moral indignation.

6. The deepening crisis in agriculture is a fundamental factor in the economic, political, and social situation in the country. The consequences of a policy of discrimination and destruction of family farming, which has been conducted for thirty years, are now becoming visible. In spite of this, the production from one hectare of arable land in private hands is still higher than the production from one hectare of arable land in state agriculture. Still, gigantic investments are directed to the State Agricultural Farms and to production cooperatives despite the fact that the costs of maintaining State Agricultural Farms exceeds the value of their production.

Over the past several years, difficulties connected with the general state of the economy have been particularly evident: lack of coal, fertilizers, cattle feed, farming machinery, and building materials. This limits to a great extent the investment possibilities of peasant farms, and leads to the exodus of young people to the cities.

Disorganization and corruption in the purchasing centers cause wastage of already produced farm goods. . . .

7. . . . Beatings of detainees by organs of the police are not isolated cases, but constitute a form of police mob rule which is sanctioned by the higher authorities. . . .

8. The usurpation by the party of the exclusive and totally arbitrary right to issue and impose judgments and decisions in all areas of life without exception has created a particular threat to Polish science and culture. Drastic limitations of the extent and freedom of scientific research and the publica-

tion of its results, especially in the humanities and social sciences such as philosophy, economy, sociology, and history; the stiff demands of the imposed doctrine, which has lost all the characteristics of an ideology and been transformed into a system of dogmas and unrestricted commands dictated by the authorities; the staffing of scientific positions with incompetent people who simply comply with the directives of the rulers — all of this brings harm to Polish culture, and not only hinders its development but also the preservation and cultivation of its former achievements. Literature, theater, and film — those branches of culture dominated by language — are especially vulnerable to the arbitrary throttling of the freedom of thought and to the annihilation of creative activities. Under these conditions, culture is being deadened, while literature, an enormously important element in the spiritual life of the nation, though unmensurable [unmeasurable?] in its effectiveness, is either reduced to the role of an executor of the orders of the authorities or forced to divorce itself completely from expressing the truth about the surrounding reality. . . .

The system of preventive censorship harms not only culture and science, but the entire social and economic life of the country. Censorship stifles not only all signs of criticism, but also all authentic information that could equip society with self-knowledge about its actual situation, which could prove undesirable for the authorities. . . .

The system of disinformation constitutes a vicious circle that does not spare even the authorities who created it. . . . It is impossible to make correct decisions on the basis of false information. Under these circumstances, paralysis must overwhelm the entire life of the country.

The authorities fear society, and are therefore unable to provide it with the truth about the current situation. . . .

The system based on arbitrary and irrevocable decisions by state and party authorities who see themselves as infallible has caused immeasurable damage to the social consciousness of the nation. The persecution of independent views, together with the use of coercion to extort an unconditional compliance with all directives coming from above, has formed attitudes that lack all ideals, and has fostered duplicity; the spread of conformism, servility, and careerism has been encouraged throughout society. These characteristics serve as recommendations in the staffing of leadership positions. Competent, enlightened, and independently minded people are deprived of the possibility of advancement, and often even of a job.

The total lack of consideration for public opinion means that an overwhelming majority of the citizens have ceased to identify themselves with the state, and feel no responsibility for it.

Radical economic reform is necessary. But even the most thoroughly developed and most consistent reforms will not be able to change anything if they run up against a barrier of public indifference and despair. . . .

II

Polish society possesses tremendous reserves of initiative, activity, and energy which are capable of overcoming the present crisis. The one condition which is necessary to free them is to allow for the creation of true representation for all social groups. It is also necessary to publish accurate data concerning the economic and social situation. Only when these conditions are met (in cooperation between the authorities and society) can a detailed program be formulated for the repair of the economic system and the social situation. Such a program could be worked out in the course of a broad public discussion involving the participation of independent experts. Without the realization of these conditions, all attempts to establish contact with society will only be transformed into a dialogue between the authorities and themselves. . . .

III

The independent social activity reemerging in the course of the past several years is based above all on the organization of authentic public opinion, on the defense against reprisals, on the formulation of genuine social demands, and on the interruption of the state monopoly over the dissemination of information. Participation in these activities is open to everyone.

1. There is a need for the broadest possible discussion of the social and economic situation in the country. . . .

2. It is necessary to organize to defend one's rights. Only the organized can elect their own genuine representatives. All Polish citizens who are members of trade unions or corresponding farmers' organizations have the possibility of electing authentic representatives to all trade union posts and of formulating a program for defending the interests of the employees. For example, miners who are waiting to no avail for the elimination of required work on Sundays and of the twelve-hour working day could make these problems into a union election issue, voting only for those candidates who promise to undertake to implement their demands. Citizens who are denied the possibility of action through generally discredited official organizations have the option of organizing new associations. . . .

3. It is always easier to fight in an organized manner. Every strike, every collective action on the part of factory workers or villagers can achieve its goal if it will act in solidarity and in a disciplined manner. This is especially important when coercion on the part of the authorities leads to indignation, anger, and despair. The participants in the struggle have to be defended with even more decisiveness than the demands that have been made. Without organization and solidarity we can achieve nothing.

7.9

A Czech Dissident Explores the Moral Basis for National Renewal

As in Poland so too in Czechoslovakia, the signs of a Communist regime in trouble were early and pervasive. The 1968 Soviet invasion, ending the Prague Spring, had checked the demands for change coming from within the party itself. Thereafter dissident intellectuals led the charge against Communist control, and one played an unusually prominent role. Václav Havel was a playwright who had plunged into politics in the 1960s. As a thorn in the side of Soviet-backed Communist hardliners after 1968, he suffered harassment and detention but continued to speak out against injustice. His grace and determination during the difficult post-1968 period made him a leader when in the fall of 1989 Czechoslovakia experienced its own liberation, known as the "velvet revolution" for its relatively nonviolent character. In December Havel was elected the first president of the post-Communist era, and he continued to serve in that post until 2003 — to the end a popular figure.

Havel insisted that politics was fundamentally about ethical choices, not programs. The moral quality of his approach is reflected in the following essay, published a full decade before the vindication of his cause and widely read by dissidents throughout eastern Europe. Consider the way this essay is argued. What is the essential point that Havel is making? How does he drive home his point when, to many people, resistance seemed a lost cause?

Václav Havel
"Power of the Powerless"
1979

The manager of a fruit-and-vegetable shop places in his window, among the onions and carrots, the slogan: "Workers of the world, unite!" Why does he do it? What is he trying to communicate to the world? Is he genuinely enthusiastic about the idea of unity among the workers of the world? Is his enthusiasm so great that he feels an irrepressible impulse to acquaint the public with his ideals? Has he really given more than a moment's thought to how such a unification might occur and what it would mean?

I think it can safely be assumed that the overwhelming majority of shopkeepers never think about the slogans they put in their windows, nor do they use them to express their real opinions. That poster was delivered to our greengrocer from the enterprise headquarters along with the onions and carrots. He put them all into the window simply because it has been done that way for years, because everyone does it, and because that is the way it has to be. If he were to refuse, there could be trouble. He could be reproached for not having the proper decoration in his window; someone might even accuse him of disloyalty. He does it because these things must be done if one is to get along in life. It is one of the thousands of details that guarantee him a relatively tranquil life "in harmony with society," as they say. . . .

Let us now imagine that one day something in our greengrocer snaps and he stops putting up the slogans merely to ingratiate himself. He stops voting in elections he knows are a farce. He begins to say what he really thinks at political meetings. And he even finds the strength in himself to express solidarity with those whom his conscience commands him to support. In this revolt the greengrocer steps out of living within the lie. He rejects the ritual

Václav Havel, "Power of the Powerless," trans. Paul Wilson, in Havel, *Open Letters: Selected Writings, 1965–1990,* ed. Paul Wilson (New York: Knopf, 1991), 132, 146–47, 153, 162.

and breaks the rules of the game. He discovers once more his suppressed identity and dignity. He gives his freedom a concrete significance. His revolt is an attempt to live within the truth.

The bill is not long in coming. He will be relieved of his post as manager of the shop and transferred to the warehouse. His pay will be reduced. His hopes for a holiday in Bulgaria will evaporate. His children's access to higher education will be threatened. His superiors will harass him and his fellow workers will wonder about him. Most of those who apply these sanctions, however, will not do so from any authentic inner conviction but simply under pressure from conditions, the same conditions that once pressured the greengrocer to display the official slogans. They will persecute the greengrocer either because it is expected of them, or to demonstrate their loyalty, or simply as part of the general panorama, to which belongs an awareness that this is how situations of this sort are dealt with, that this, in fact, is how things are always done, particularly if one is not to become suspect oneself. The executors, therefore, behave essentially like everyone else, to a greater or lesser degree: as components of the post-totalitarian system, as agents of its automatism, as petty instruments of the social auto-totality.

Thus the power structure, through the agency of those who carry out the sanctions, those anonymous components of the system, will spew the greengrocer from its mouth. The system, through its alienating presence in people, will punish him for his rebellion. It must do so because the logic of its automatism and self-defense dictate it. The greengrocer has not committed a simple, individual offense, isolated in its own uniqueness, but something incomparably more serious. By breaking the rules of the game, he has disrupted the game as such. He has exposed it as a mere game. He has shattered the world of appearances, the fundamental pillar of the system. He has upset the power structure by tearing apart what holds it together. He has demonstrated that living a lie is living a lie. He has broken through the exalted facade of the system and exposed the real, base foundations of power. He has said that the emperor is naked. And because the emperor is in fact naked, something extremely dangerous has happened: by his action, the greengrocer has addressed the world. He has enabled everyone to peer behind the curtain. He has shown everyone that it *is* possible to live within the truth. Living within the lie can constitute the system only if it is universal. The principle must embrace and permeate everything. There are no terms whatsoever on which it can co-exist with living within the truth, and therefore everyone who steps out of line denies it in principle and threatens it in its entirety. . . .

The profound crisis of human identity brought on by living within a lie, a crisis which in turn makes such a life possible, certainly possesses a moral dimension as well; it appears, among other things, as a deep moral crisis in society. A person who has been seduced by the consumer value system, whose identity is dissolved in an amalgam of the accouterments of mass civilization, and who has no roots in the order of being, no sense of responsibility for anything higher than his own personal survival, is a demoralized person. The system depends on this demoralization, deepens it, is in fact a projection of it into society.

Living within the truth, as humanity's revolt against an enforced position, is, on the contrary, an attempt to regain control over one's own sense of responsibility. In other words, it is clearly a moral act, not only because one must pay so dearly for it, but principally because it is not self-serving: the risk may bring rewards in the form of a general amelioration in the situation, or it may not. . . . [I]t is difficult to imagine a reasonable person embarking on such a course merely because he reckons that sacrifice today will bring rewards tomorrow, be it only in the form of general gratitude. . . .

. . . If a better economic and political model is to be created, then perhaps more than ever before it must derive from profound existential and moral changes in society. This is not something that can be designed and introduced like a new car. . . . A better system will not automatically ensure a better life. In fact the opposite is true: only by creating a better life can a better system be developed.

7.10

East German Workers on Socialism and National Reunification

In East Germany, a Communist party with a seemingly secure hold on power came under belated challenge in fall 1989, initially from intellectuals. But demonstrations soon began in the streets, attracting more and more participants. These popular signs of disaffection proved doubly decisive: They pushed the party into making belated concessions and then, with the party's grip on power slipping, pushed East Germany toward reunification with West Germany on the latter's terms.

This outcome was, from the perspective of East German workers, bittersweet as shown by the following interviews conducted in August 1990 by Dirk Philipsen, himself a worker and low-level union functionary in West Germany before attending university in Berlin and doing graduate work in the United States. He did his interviews at a fascinating moment of transition — integration between the two Germanys was under way and plant closings in the East along with massive job losses were looming. The excerpts that follow begin with a group of workers in East Berlin's largest heavy machinery plant, where the elite of the working class under the old regime would have been found, and they end with the ranking union official at East Germany's second largest heavy machinery plant, located in Magdeburg. How do these workers assess conditions under socialism — its virtues and defects? What is their view of reunification in 1989, beginning with demonstrations and ending with West Germany taking over the East? How well do these views fit the commonplace outlook in the west condemning the old regime and celebrating its fall? Which perspective makes more sense?

Dirk Philipsen
Interviews with Industrial Workers
August 1990

BERND K.: [born 1935, began work as a factory apprentice in 1950, joined the Communist party in 1975, and became a full-time union official in 1980]: . . . [W]hy did this revolution happen so peacefully? It could only happen so peacefully, not because so many people came together on the streets, but because the whole system was so rotten, was so finished at that point, that everybody, even in the party, all the way up to the central leadership, must have realized that things could not continue like that. . . .

RUDI E.: [born 1938, worked as a boiler and tank worker, then studied engineering; joined the party in 1957]: . . . In August [1989] the big wave of emigrations via Hungary and Czechoslovakia began, and they brought things into the press, such as that people were "abducted by Western agents," and "these are the methods the West is employing". . . .

DORIS C.: [born 1934, apprenticed in 1949 as a lathe operator, later employed as an assistant engineer, active as a party member in the unions, especially in women's issues]: . . . We had a lot of big laughs at the time about all the ludicrous stories they were making up. . . .

RUDI E.: . . . About people who had been drugged and did not wake up until they got to Vienna. You have to imagine that such things were on the front page of the official party newspaper. They were actually trying to convince us that the West was employing such methods in order to worsen the situation in our country. Of course, we usually found out, as most people had already suspected, that there was no truth to such accounts. . . . [T]his was their method of telling us that we should not worry, and that we could easily live without those people. . . .

DORIS C.: The straw that finally broke the camel's back was Honecker's[1] statement that "we are not going to shed a tear for these people." We were simply outraged, everywhere, young people and old people alike. This statement was just impertinent. Every evening we saw on Western television thousands of young GDR citizens who had fled to the West German embassies or had made it across the border in some way, and then this comment "we are not going to shed a single tear." . . .

BERND K.: . . . You have to understand how completely we were walled in; very few people had been allowed to travel and to see for themselves what the West was like. And those who were allowed usually did not talk about it much because they did not want to risk their chance of getting a [travel] permit again. . . .

---

[1]Erich Honecker, the leader of the German Communist party (1971–1989).

Dirk Philipsen, *We Were the People: Voices from East Germany's Revolutionary Autumn of 1989* (Durham, N.C.: Duke University Press, 1993), 120–28, 281, 283–86, 380–81.

DORIS C.: . . . And sometimes people simply did not believe what they told us after they had returned. Or people were accused of just wanting to bitch and complain about the GDR when they told us how things looked in the West, when they conveyed such golden pictures of the West.

How much and how openly could you, and did you, discuss such matters in the work-place?

LEONHARD B.: [born 1948, apprenticed as a machinist in 1965, joined the party in 1967, and left it in 1978]: In the shops we discussed these things a lot.

I guess one thing I still don't quite understand is that there was such a debate about this. After all, you could all receive Western radio and TV, so you should have had a pretty good impression as to how things looked in the West, didn't you?

DORIS C.: Yes, everybody watched Western TV. . . .

BERND K.: . . . But you simply could not imagine the dimensions of it all, the technological level, the availability of consumer goods. . . . But whereas we had to wait for an apartment or a house for more than 15 years and had to pay these incredibly overpriced amounts for certain goods, or simply could not get certain basic goods or had to wait for them forever, it was just mind-boggling, at least to me, when I went over there for the first time.

. . . Of course we watched Western TV, saw Western advertisements, and such, but the reality of it all just blew me away. When I went to a home appliance store in the West for the first time, I walked through the aisles and just mumbled to myself, like a senile old man, "This can't be true, this is unbelievable, I must be dreaming." They had all the things I had been trying to get at home for years, and not just in one kind, but in hundreds of variations. . . . The same was true with grocery stores. We never had to go hungry in the GDR, never, but we had to stand in line for cheese or meat, and often had no selection, and certain things we just never saw. And if you then went to KaDeWe [a large West Berlin department store with a well-stocked food department], you just thought you were on another planet.

RUDI E.: I think the main thing is that we were never exposed to any of this. We were walled in, things were kept away from us, we were lied to. And then, all of a sudden, we realized things could also be done or organized differently, and that's when it all began, when we began to rethink every-thing. . . . [After 1987] more people were allowed to travel, from some 400,000 before to some 1.5 or 2 million per year afterward. But that way, people could get their own personal impressions, and that had to have some consequences sooner or later.

Let me put it in a provocative and oversimplified way then. Why couldn't one say that, in the last analysis, the gap in consumer standards and the desire of the GDR citizens for more consumption has led to the Wende [literally "turn" or "turn-about," a fairly neutral term suggesting the less hopeful reading of the situation in 1990 than had prevailed in 1989]?

DORIS C.: No, no, not at all. . . .

LEONHARD B.: . . . No, I would not put it like that at all. Of course, this question of consumer items plays a certain role, but it was not the key issue. You see, we had people in the GDR who also had everything. In fact, as we later found out, some of the party hacks had far higher living standards than anything we had ever suspected. Or, for example, if somebody had a dacha [country home], and his neighbor turned out to have everything your heart could desire, all Western stuff at that, well, then you knew, first of all, this guy is probably with the Stasi [secret police] and, secondly, he could therefore get everything he wanted.

Over the years, more and more people found out that there were those who had no problems acquiring anything. I met a construction supervisor once who told me that they were sometimes asked, for an extra 1,000 Marks a weekend [about the average monthly income of a worker in East Germany], to leave their real jobs and build houses for functionaries, mostly with Western material.

So you are saying it was more a sense of injustice than the desire for consumption?

LEONHARD B.: Yes, precisely. There was just an incredible degree of injustice everywhere.

RUDI E.: This injustice was really quite unbelievable. Some people had everything and hence did not give a damn about what common folks at the bottom of society had. Nothing has changed on that level over the last few years. . . .

LEONHARD B.: . . . Of course it has — it has gotten considerably worse. . . .

. . . Well, as you have been told many times, and as many Western critics believe, social injustice is far worse in the West. . . .

DORIS C.: . . . Yes, yes, but there it did not touch me, it didn't make any difference to me. But here, with a socialist government, claiming to be just dyed in red, always ready to quote Karl Marx, and then acting like this, that just drove us mad. And it got worse and worse; after a while, they did not even make an attempt anymore to cover it up, like they had previously done, and they got increasingly excessive in their consumption trips. . . .

And, you know, the election in May [1989] was decisive for a lot of people, because we simply said to ourselves that most governments in the world that receive 10 to 15 percent no-votes would kiss their own feet. After all, what government receives 80 to 85 percent support? But that they even had to lie about these 10 to 15 percent — we were really deeply upset about that. . . . [W]e no longer knew what to do with our bottled-up anger. . . . We deeply believed that there was nothing we could possibly do. An individual can't change anything anyway. And if we had tried as a group, we immediately would have been treated like criminals.

But this election fraud just pushed things beyond the breaking point. After that, a lot of people just thought: "It doesn't matter anymore. Let them come, let them accuse me of crimes, let them arrest me, I just can't take it anymore. I will no longer say 'yes' to all this."

When you say there was "nothing one could do anyway," how did things go in the factory, at the workplace? Did you have specific work-related problems as well, and could you talk about them?

DORIS C.: Oh yes, we talked, we copied things or wrote petitions ourselves that we posted in the shops, but usually these things were immediately torn down again. There was an incredible atmosphere in the shops; people were totally fed up. . . .

 . . . You certainly tried to check out very well with whom you were talking, but you could still never be certain that one of them was not a Stasi informant. But we still began to risk it, because we just felt too stupid carrying on not saying anything. Until this very day we are not sure as to who exactly was a Stasi informant. . . .

What is surprising to me about all of this is how long you continued to invest trust and hope that you could change something by appealing to official organs or party functionaries.

DORIS C.: Yes, you are absolutely right about that. But you have to understand the basis for this, which was our work. We all had work; in fact, we did not know any unemployment. Families with a lot of children were supported. We had a comprehensive child care and kindergarten system. We had a decent educational system for everybody. All of this was very well-established, nobody had to live in poverty or great need, everybody enjoyed a sense of security, had enough to eat, a place to live, and clothes to wear. Basically, we always got everything we really needed. . . .

 Everybody always bought everything he could get his hands on, whether he needed it or not, and then we exchanged things among ourselves. We had a lively barter economy going. It usually took quite a long time to get what you needed or wanted, but you almost always got it at some point. In that sense, we were all pretty satisfied, and that's why we did not have this blazing dissatisfaction around here. We swallowed a lot and protested a little every once in a while. . . .

RUDI E.: . . . It is true that the productivity was really quite low. We had a lot of patchwork in the factories, much was only solved through extra shifts, which cost more and ate away the financial substance of a given enterprise. . . .

BERND K.: . . . The whole production process was just very badly organized. Often we had to work on Sunday, with all the extra payments and benefits involved, and on Monday we just stood around because a certain part was missing, so we couldn't continue to work.

LEONHARD B.: What we also experienced a lot was that they invested millions in setting up some new shop, and as soon as work was completed, the whole thing was already outdated again, or nobody needed it anymore. So many rank-and-file workers began to wonder whether we had idiots organizing our production. We constantly asked ourselves "don't they, can't they comprehend what is going on?" If we as workers understood that things like that should not happen, one would assume that someone who went to college should be able to grasp that as well. . . .

What was your response to [the breaching of the Berlin Wall on] 9 November 1989?

MARIA C.: [born 1940, worked as an industrial photographer, active in the union but not a party member]: I really think they never should have opened the Wall. . . .

All we wanted was to be able to travel. We wanted a passport. . . . We wanted to be able to go wherever we felt like, and for as long as we wanted, that's all. . . . But this kind of open Wall, well, let me tell you, that is not what I wanted. And I also did not want to get rid of socialism. It is true, I did not want *this kind* of socialism, not one with the likes of Erich Honecker, but rather another kind of socialism.

You have to realize, we looked wide-eyed at Gorbachev, what he was trying to do in the Soviet Union. That came right out of our own hearts; that's what we wanted to happen here. We did not want these senile old men with their hunting lodges; we wanted young men who were willing to work together with all of us on something like glasnost and perestroika. . . .

LEONHARD B.: . . . The tragedy is that things went backward instead of forward. We wanted a development within socialism, and not away from it. At least, I think that's what most people wanted.

Well, and when we took to the streets and such, we noticed over and over again that there were virtually no people who were capable of carrying out the kind of socialism we wanted. It was a big problem that all the positions through which one could have changed something were not filled with the right people during the first phase of this revolution. The senile old men were still sitting up there and continuing their mush. Only at the lower ranks did change actually take place.

All of this, in my opinion, pushed the cart so forcefully in one direction that it began to pick up speed by itself, and then it had to end up in the ditch. In the end, nobody could have implemented what we actually wanted anymore. . .

. . . *Who exactly are you referring to when you say "we"?*

LEONHARD B.: Well, the people in this room, and then, of course, most other people in a similar situation. Most workers, I would say. . .

DORIS C.: . . . The same people who served Honecker for decades, as directors, supervisors, or managers . . . are precisely the ones who are currently in the process of selling off our enterprises — I say *our* because that's what they really should be — to people from the West. And they sell it for little more than they would ask for a piece of apple pie, while we stand around like complete idiots and just let it happen. Once again we are saying, "What can we do? There is nothing that we can do." . . .

PETER R.: [a worker about whom no additional information is available]: . . . This pushing us around like children, this ordered repression, was just simply unbearable; it was so depressing. Every report you submitted to the union leadership or the plant management had to end with a "hurrah" to the party. We had to claim 150 percent success, even though everyone knew that this was a complete swindle. We were all part of this big lie; it was so frustrating, one could not really avoid it, as comrade, as colleague, as communist.

At some point we all began to say to ourselves, "Why, why does it have to be this way? These are my comrades, my colleagues. Why do I have to lie to them? Don't you understand, why, in God's name, don't you understand that?"

And then this valve opened, and we had so much hope that we could perhaps still save the whole thing. And then we got Egon Krenz,[2] who had been fed the same shit, who *was,* in fact, the same old shit. Nothing, absolutely nothing, was possible with him. . . .

LEONHARD B.: The opening of the Wall was also the opening of a valve. All the anger we had built up was gone at the moment we crossed the border. We had so much in our heads, new impressions and all. Everybody thought about all sorts of things, but not about the fact that we should now pay close attention to the political developments in our own country. So our chance really sort of slipped away. . . .

DORIS C.: . . . Many new groups — New Forum,[3] for example — who had been active in the neighborhoods, in the factories, everywhere, simply disintegrated after the opening of the Wall.

An incredible number of young people simply took off to the West, stayed there for a couple of nights, came back, then stayed another couple of nights, and so on. The interest of a lot of people in changing things in the GDR simply disappeared for a decisive period of time.

I am afraid many people thought: "Now we have achieved what we always wanted, and the rest will happen by itself." So large portions of a necessary political potential were gone all of a sudden, simply gone . . .

RUDI E.: . . . And of course we were also not prepared for those politicians from the West who suddenly invaded our country. With this big show they put on, they successfully cajoled many of us into believing that their way was the only way of doing things. They promised us the West German Mark, they promised us the good life, and . . .

MARIA C.: . . . When I saw the pictures from [the demonstrations in] Leipzig, I was so angry I almost blew up. I could have gone to Leipzig and beat the shit out of them, with their placards and mottoes and "Germany, united fatherland."

I don't mind "Germany, united fatherland" in the long run, but, please, not so quickly. . . .

WOLFGANG K.: [newly elected trade union secretary at a large heavy machinery plant in Magdeburg]: I don't have any hope that we can save this factory. I think total bankruptcy is now inevitable. More than 20,000 people are going to lose their jobs, and for many colleagues those will have been the last decent jobs they will have ever had. . . .

You know, we were never really asked whether we wanted all this, and I guess we never had the guts to stand up and fight for our own rights.

---

[2]Egon Krenz, a Honecker protégé who took charge of the party in October 1989 in the midst of growing protests.

[3]An organization created in early September 1989 as a voice for democratic socialism. It was intent on persuading the ruling party to undertake reforms.

Anyway, I am not at all sure things will really get better for us now. On the contrary, I think for many of us things will get a lot worse. But we will see. . . .

We should never have given up as much as we did. Despite all the failures and shortcomings, you know, we had achieved quite a bit. . . . What? A basic security, much more equality — we used to help each other out. I don't know, we were just all in the same boat together, not all fighting against each other all the time — which is, as far as I can tell, exactly what we are going to get now. . . .

Look, now the boss of the West German unions is going to come visit us. It's the very first time he has ever made it over here; he doesn't know much about our situation. They don't even know how to talk to us. Yes, they feel sorry for us, and somehow I guess they really want to help. But do they take us seriously? I don't think so. And when push comes to shove, I am not sure they will look out for our interests very well. . . .

I think we need to look out for ourselves. In fact, we should have done that all along. You see, in the opinion of West Germans pretty much everything we've done, everything we've had here, was somehow wrong, or at least deficient. In their eyes we are basically all failures, whether it was our fault or not. I don't think that's correct, and I certainly don't think it's fair. I am not going to let them steal my whole past, and I don't want to be a second-class citizen for the rest of my life.

CHAPTER 8

GLOBAL MARKETS: ONE SYSTEM, THREE CENTERS

TWO INTERSECTING TRENDS SHAPED THE INTERNATIONAL ECONOMY from the 1970s onward as globalization of production, trade, and investment gained headway. One was the growing influence of free market principles. In the United States a bipartisan consensus began to emerge that international free trade and investment served the country well, indeed that in an age of globalization Americans had no choice but to embrace the free market regime if they wished to enjoy strong economic growth. U.S. leaders and their overseas allies worked to make the market an international orthodoxy and persuade countries around the world to conform to its rules.

The other significant trend was the increased reliance on regional economic groupings. In the lead was the European Community, which won new members and in 1993 made the transition to the more tightly integrated European Union. The economies of Canada, the United States, and Mexico also moved toward association under NAFTA (the North American Free Trade Agreement). Compared to the EC, it was not only late but limited. While making the region one free economic market, it ignored the social, cultural, political, and environmental policies that had become increasingly prominent in an integrated Europe. East Asia was emerging as a third bloc but one that was notable for its informal integration and (as the Chinese case suggests) pronounced state guidance within national economies.

CHAMPIONING FREE MARKET ORTHODOXY

Free market principles had flourished during the first phase of globalization in the nineteenth century. But between 1914 and 1945, two world wars and a prolonged economic depression eclipsed the free market cause. During that time champions of state intervention won a large following by detailing the defects of unregulated marketplace activity. The British economist John Maynard Keynes triumphed over his rival Friedrich Hayek (see Documents

2.5 and 2.6), and so the balance of influence continued until the 1970s when the proponents of the market (commonly called neo-liberals) rallied. They enjoyed a resurgence as a result of the Keynesians' failure to find a remedy for the economic stagnation and inflation of the time.

The election of conservative governments — Margaret Thatcher's in Britain and Ronald Reagan's in the United States — gave free market ideas a new public prominence. That those ideas fixed a firm grip in the United States was particularly important. Not only was the U.S. economy the world's largest and most attractive for exporters and investors around the globe, but in addition Washington spoke the loudest in defining the terms by which the international economy would run. U.S. leaders fought for minimizing state or other interference in the market in the name of optimal efficiency and freedom.

8.1

Milton Friedman on the Critical Relationship between Economic and Political Freedom

Milton Friedman was the herald of the new age of market orthodoxy. Born in 1912 in Brooklyn, New York, he taught at the University of Chicago from 1946 to 1977 and won the Nobel Prize in economics in 1978. His timing as a critic of Keynes was perfect. He published the best known of his works, *Capitalism and Freedom*, in 1962, and by the end of the decade — just as the Keynesian reliance on the state was running into trouble — Friedman's case against Keynes and against state interference in the economy had won an influential following.

Consider Friedman's position with some care because it represents what has become the reigning orthodoxy in the United States and Britain and in the regulatory agencies of the international economy. What is Friedman arguing about the relationship among freedom, the economy, and the state? How does his position link him to Hayek (Document 2.5)? Precisely because his argument seems to many self-evident truths rather than a set of debatable propositions, it deserves critical examination. Do you accept his position on the nature of social justice, definitions of the good life, the relation of the individual to the group, and the role of the state? Does the daily news support Friedman's confidence in the market as a regulatory mechanism? How does the case Friedman makes compare with other economic philosophies treated in chapters 2 and 5, especially Documents 2.6 to 2.8, 5.6, and 5.7? Which seems to you most compelling — and why? What obstacles or criticism might your preferred approach encounter were it applied in the United States today?

From *Capitalism and Freedom*
1962

[THE MEANINGS OF LIBERALISM]

It is extremely convenient to have a label for the political and economic viewpoint elaborated [here]. The rightful and proper label is liberalism. Unfortunately, "As a supreme, if unintended compliment, the enemies of the system of private enterprise have thought it wise to appropriate its label,"[1] so that liberalism has, in the United States, come to have a very different meaning than it did in the nineteenth century or does today over much of the Continent of Europe.

As it developed in the late eighteenth and early nineteenth centuries, the intellectual movement that went under the name of liberalism emphasized freedom as the ultimate goal and the individual as the ultimate entity in the society. It supported laissez faire at home as a means of reducing the role of the state in economic affairs and thereby enlarging the role of the individual; it supported free trade abroad as a means of linking the nations of the world together peacefully and democratically. In political matters, it supported the development of representative government and of parliamentary institutions, reduction in the arbitrary power of the state, and protection of the civil freedoms of individuals.

Beginning in the late nineteenth century, and especially after 1930 in the United States, the term liberalism came to be associated with a very different emphasis, particularly in economic policy. It came to be associated with a readiness to rely primarily on the state rather than on private voluntary arrangements to achieve objectives regarded as desirable. The catchwords became welfare and equality rather than freedom. The nineteenth-century liberal regarded an extension of freedom as the most effective way to promote welfare and equality; the twentieth-century liberal regards welfare and equality as either prerequisites of or alternatives to freedom. In the name of welfare and equality, the twentieth-century liberal has come to favor a revival of the very policies of state intervention and paternalism against which classical liberalism fought. . . .

. . . [T]he twentieth-century liberal favors centralized government. He will resolve any doubt about where power should be located in favor of the state instead of the city, of the federal government instead of the state, and of a world organization instead of a national government.

Because of the corruption of the term liberalism, the views that formerly went under that name are now often labeled conservatism. But this is not a satisfactory alternative. The nineteenth-century liberal was a radical, both in the etymological sense of going to the root of the matter, and in the political sense of favoring major changes in social institutions. So too must be his modern heir. We do not wish to conserve the state interventions that have interfered so greatly with our freedom, though, of course, we do wish to conserve those that have promoted it. Moreover, in practice, the term conservatism has come to cover so wide a range of views, and views so incompatible with one another, that we shall no doubt see the growth of hyphenated designations, such as libertarian-conservative and aristocratic-conservative.

---

[1]Note in original: Joseph Schumpeter, *History of Economic Analysis* (New York: Oxford University Press, 1954), 394.

Milton Friedman with the assistance of Rose D. Friedman, *Capitalism and Freedom* (Chicago: University of Chicago Press, 1962), 5–10, 12–13, 15–16, 199–201.

Partly because of my reluctance to surrender the term to proponents of measures that would destroy liberty, partly because I cannot find a better alternative, I shall resolve these difficulties by using the word liberalism in its original sense — as the doctrines pertaining to a free man. . . .

[ECONOMIC FREEDOM AND POLITICAL FREEDOM]

Economic arrangements play a dual role, in the promotion of a free society. On the one hand, freedom in economic arrangements is itself a component of freedom broadly understood, so economic freedom is an end in itself. In the second place, economic freedom is also an indispensable means toward the achievement of political freedom.

The first of these roles of economic freedom needs special emphasis because intellectuals in particular have a strong bias against regarding this aspect of freedom as important. They tend to express contempt for what they regard as material aspects of life, and to regard their own pursuit of allegedly higher values as on a different plane of significance and as deserving of special attention. For most citizens of the country, however, if not for the intellectual, the direct importance of economic freedom is at least comparable in significance to the indirect importance of economic freedom as a means to political freedom. . . .

The citizen of the United States who is compelled by law to devote something like 10 per cent of his income to the purchase of a particular kind of retirement contract, administered by the government, is being deprived of a corresponding part of his personal freedom. . . .

A citizen of the United States who under the laws of various states is not free to follow the occupation of his own choosing unless he can get a license for it, is likewise being deprived of an essential part of his freedom. So is the man who would like to exchange some of his goods with, say, a Swiss for a watch but is prevented from doing so by a quota. So also is the Californian who was thrown into jail for selling Alka Seltzer at a price below that set by the manufacturer under so-called "fair trade" laws. So also is the farmer who cannot grow the amount of wheat he wants. And so on. Clearly, economic freedom, in and of itself, is an extremely important part of total freedom.

. . . The kind of economic organization that provides economic freedom directly, namely, competitive capitalism, also promotes political freedom because it separates economic power from political power and in this way enables the one to offset the other. . . .

Because we live in a largely free society, we tend to forget how limited is the span of time and the part of the globe for which there has ever been anything like political freedom: the typical state of mankind is tyranny, servitude, and misery. The nineteenth century and early twentieth century in the Western world stand out as striking exceptions to the general trend of historical development. Political freedom in this instance clearly came along with the free market and the development of capitalist institutions. So also did political freedom in the golden age of Greece and in the early days of the Roman era.

History suggests only that capitalism is a necessary condition for political freedom. Clearly it is not a sufficient condition. Fascist Italy and Fascist Spain, Germany at various times in the last seventy years, Japan before World Wars I and II, tzarist Russia in the decades before World War I — are all societies that cannot conceivably be described as politically free. Yet, in each, private enterprise was the dominant form of economic organization. It is therefore clearly possible to have economic arrangements that are fundamentally capitalist and political arrangements that are not free. . . .

The basic problem of social organization is how to co-ordinate the economic activities of large numbers of people. Even in relatively backward societies, extensive division of labor and specialization of function is required to make effective use of available resources. In advanced societies, the scale on which co-ordination is needed, to take full advantage of the opportunities offered by modern science and technology, is enormously greater. Literally millions of people are involved in providing one another with their daily bread, let alone with their yearly automobiles. The challenge to the believer in liberty is to reconcile this widespread interdependence with individual freedom.

Fundamentally, there are only two ways of co-ordinating the economic activities of millions. One is central direction involving the use of coercion — the technique of the army and of the modern totalitarian state. The other is voluntary co-operation of individuals — the technique of the market place.

The possibility of co-ordination through voluntary co-operation rests on the elementary — yet frequently denied — proposition that both parties to an economic transaction benefit from it, *provided the transaction is bi-laterally voluntary and informed.*

Exchange can therefore bring about co-ordination without coercion. A working model of a society organized through voluntary exchange is a *free private enterprise exchange economy* — what we have been calling competitive capitalism. . . .

Indeed, a major source of objection to a free economy is precisely that it does this task so well. It gives people what they want instead of what a particular group thinks they ought to want. Underlying most arguments against the free market is a lack of belief in freedom itself.

The existence of a free market does not of course eliminate the need for government. On the contrary, government is essential both as a forum for determining the "rules of the game" and as an umpire to interpret and enforce the rules decided on. What the market does is to reduce greatly the range of issues that must be decided through political means, and thereby to minimize the extent to which government need participate directly in the game. The characteristic feature of action through political channels is that it tends to require or enforce substantial conformity. The great advantage of the market, on the other hand, is that it permits wide diversity. It is, in political terms, a system of proportional representation. Each man can vote, as it were, for the color of tie he wants and get it; he does not have to see what color the majority wants and then, if he is in the minority, submit.

It is this feature of the market that we refer to when we say that the market provides economic freedom. But this characteristic also has implications that go far beyond the narrowly economic. Political freedom means the absence of coercion of a man by his fellow men. The fundamental threat to freedom is power to coerce, be it in the hands of a monarch, a dictator, an oligarchy, or a momentary majority. The preservation of freedom requires the elimination of such concentration of power to the fullest possible extent and the dispersal and distribution of whatever power cannot be eliminated — a system of checks and balances. By removing the organization of economic activity from the control of political authority, the market eliminates this source of coercive power. It enables economic strength to be a check to political power rather than a reinforcement.

Economic power can be widely dispersed. There is no law of conservation which forces the growth of new centers of economic strength to be at the expense of existing centers. Political power, on the other hand, is more difficult to decentralize. There can be numerous small independent governments. But it is far more difficult to maintain numerous equipotent small centers of political power in a single large government than it is to have numerous centers of economic strength in a single large economy. There can be many millionaires in one large economy. But can there be more than one really outstanding leader, one person on whom the energies and enthusiasms of his countrymen are centered? If the central government gains power, it is likely to be at the expense of local governments. There seems to be something like a fixed total of political power to be distributed. Consequently, if economic power is joined to political power, concentration seems almost inevitable. On the other hand, if economic power is kept in separate hands from political power, it can serve as a check and a counter to political power. . . .

[THE THREAT POSED BY THE STATE]

The greater part of the new ventures undertaken by government in the past few decades have failed to achieve their objectives. The United States has continued to progress; its citizens have become better fed, better clothed, better housed, and better transported; class and social distinctions have narrowed; minority groups have become less disadvantaged; popular culture has advanced by leaps and bounds. All this has been the product of the initiative and drive of individuals co-operating through the free market. Government measures have hampered not helped this development. We have been able to afford and surmount these measures only because of the extraordinary fecundity of the market. The invisible hand has been more potent for progress than the visible hand for retrogression.

Is it an accident that so many of the governmental reforms of recent decades have gone awry, that the bright hopes have turned to ashes? Is it simply because the programs are faulty in detail?

I believe the answer is clearly in the negative. The central defect of these measures is that they seek through government to force people to act against their own immediate interests in order to promote a supposedly general interest. They seek to resolve what is supposedly a conflict of interest, or a difference in view about interests, not by establishing a framework that will eliminate the conflict, or by persuading people to have different interests, but by forcing people to act against their own interest. They substitute the values of outsiders for the values of participants; either some telling others what is good for them, or the government taking from some to benefit others. These measures are therefore countered by one of the strongest and most creative forces known to man — the attempt by millions of individuals to promote their own interests, to live their lives by their own values. This is the major reason why the measures have so often had the opposite of the effects intended. It is also one of the major strengths of a free society and explains why governmental regulation does not strangle it.

The interests of which I speak are not simply narrow self-regarding interests. On the contrary, they include the whole range of values that men hold dear and for which they are willing to spend their fortunes and sacrifice their lives. . . .

The preservation and expansion of freedom are today threatened from two directions. The one threat is obvious and clear. It is the external threat coming from the evil men in the Kremlin who promise to bury us. The other threat is far more subtle. It is the internal threat coming from men of good intentions and good will who wish to reform us. Impatient with the slowness of persuasion and example to achieve the great social changes they envision, they are anxious to use the power of the state to achieve their ends and confident of their own ability to do so. Yet if they gained the power, they would fail to achieve their immediate aims and, in addition, would produce a collective state from which they would recoil in horror and of which they would be among the first victims. Concentrated power is not rendered harmless by the good intentions of those who create it.

8.2
Margaret Thatcher Promises Free Market Prosperity for Britain

Margaret Thatcher was the first British prime minister to be a woman and the longest tenured in the twentieth century (1979–1990). Educated at Oxford, she worked as a research chemist and as a lawyer before becoming active in the Conservative Party. She gained a seat in Parliament in 1953 and served as education minister between 1970 and 1974, the year she took over leadership of the party.

This major statement made as party leader laid out the approach that Thatcher would follow when she became prime minister. She spoke against a backdrop of crisis within the British economy. So dire had the situation become that the Labour government had had to seek help from the International Monetary Fund and accept in turn stiff cuts in government spending. Thatcher saw in this greater discipline hope that a new age of market-inspired prosperity was around the corner. What economic and moral principles emerge as the touchstones for Thatcher's views on the free market? What points of overlap do you see between the case made by Thatcher and those made earlier by Friedrich Hayek, whose *Road to Serfdom* she had read as an Oxford undergraduate (Document 2.6), and by Milton Friedman (Document 8.1)? Are there points of divergence?

Speech to Zurich Economic Society
March 14, 1977

I have reason to believe that the tide is beginning to turn against collectivism, socialism, statism, dirigism, whatever you call it. And this turn is rooted in a revulsion against the sour fruit of socialist experience. It is becoming increasingly obvious to many people who were intellectual socialists that socialism has failed to fulfil its promises, both in its more extreme forms in the Communist world, and in its compromise versions. . . .

It is up to us to give intellectual content and political direction to these new dissatisfactions with socialism in practice, with its material and moral failures, we must convert disillusion into understanding.

If we fail, the tide will be lost. But if it is taken, the last quarter of our century can initiate a new renaissance matching anything in our island's long and outstanding history. . . .

. . . [S]enior socialist politicians have continued to affirm their faith in the mixed economy. But in the mixed economy, as in a cocktail, it is the mix that counts. In their favoured mix, collectivism has taken an ever larger proportion. The words of these politicians expressed a belief that private enterprise had a major role to play in the economy. But their deeds extended government into almost every part of business life. The "progressives" had their way.

The nationalized sector of the economy has been extended far beyond the major industries of fuel, transport and steel. In the next few weeks the aircraft and shipbuilding industries will be nationalized; whilst the Labour Party's programme for the future, published last year, includes plans for taking over banks and insurance companies. Private firms in difficulties have been taken into public ownership. More and more of the taxpayer's money has been pumped into companies that no prudent banker could go on supporting for long, because instead of creating wealth, they use up wealth created by others. The state sector has come to dominate the mixed economy. Its insatiable demand for finance has inhibited the operation of the market sector. Yet the public sector can only live on private enterprise on whose surplus it relies.

Indeed a flourishing private enterprise is the surest base on which to erect a healthy public sector. The profits[,] wages and salaries of private business

Based on the speaking text on the Margaret Thatcher Foundation website: <http://www .margaretthatcher.org/speeches/displaydocument.asp?docid=103336> (February 13, 2003). Minor amendments made here on the basis of the copy in *The Collected Speeches of Margaret Thatcher,* ed. Robin Harris (New York: HarperCollins, 1997), 49–54.

provide the tax base for financing welfare services, like health and education and for supporting the old, the unemployed and the unfortunate.

Socialism promised to raise the provision of education, health, and housing. As is becoming patent to almost everyone, the result has been the opposite. . . .

Socialism whetted appetites for more, but has resulted in less being available. . . .

There is a growing realization in Britain that the "progressives" were wrong. They are being proved wrong by the failure of the very system they advocated. To finance the extension of socialism on so vast a scale, taxation has risen to penal levels. We have all seen the results — for living standards, for incentive and for enterprise — of the excessive tax burden in Britain. . . .

. . . [I]t is our system, the free enterprise system, which delivers the goods to the great mass of the people. We may have been remiss in not saying this with sufficient vigor in the past; well, I shall not be remiss this evening.

For it is not only in my country that socialism has failed the nation. It is well known that the ultimate aspiration of every Soviet planner is for his country to equal the levels of production in the USA. It is the West, not the East, which sells off surpluses of grain and other foodstuffs to the planned economies, and also gives them to the countries of the third world. It is Western technology which the East seeks to acquire. And it is the Western world, those countries with essentially capitalist economies, from which the British Government has recently sought, and received, help for the pound. The socialist countries do not attempt to conceal their admiration for the productive achievements of the free market economy. But what they do argue is that the avalanche of goods which the capitalist system produces is available only for the well-to-do.

This is totally false. It misconceives the very essence of capitalist achievement. As Josef Schumpeter[1] put it:

> The capitalist engine is first and last an engine of mass production, which unavoidably means also production for the masses. . . . It is the cheap cloth, the cheap fabric, boots[,] motor cars and so on that are the typical achievements of capitalist production and not as a rule improvements that would mean much to the rich man.

In brief, the material superiority of the free society gives its main benefits to the very people the Socialists claim to cherish.

Continuing benefits depend upon innovation. It is innovation which lies at the heart of economic progress. And only the free economy can provide the conditions in which it will flourish. . . .

. . . Collectivists may flatter themselves that wise men at the center — with whom they identify — can make better decisions, and waste fewer resources

---

[1] The Austrian economist (also quoted approvingly above by Friedman) who spent most of his distinguished career in the United States.

than a myriad of individual decision-makers and independent organisations all over the country. Events in Britain have shown that, wise or not, those at the centre lack the knowledge, foresight and imagination required. They are overworked and overwhelmed. They are certainly surprised by events. . . .

The economic success of the Western world is a product of its moral philosophy and practice. The economic results are better because the moral philosophy is superior. It is superior because it starts with the individual, with his uniqueness, his responsibility, and his capacity to choose. Surely this is infinitely preferable to the Socialist-statist philosophy which sets up a centralised economic system to which the individual must conform, which subjugates him, directs him and denies him the right to free choice.

Choice is the essence of ethics: if there were no choice, there would be no ethics, no good, no evil; good and evil have meaning only insofar as man is free to choose. In our philosophy the purpose of the life of the individual is not to be the servant of the state and its objectives, but to make the best of his talents and qualities. The sense of being self-reliant, of playing a role within the family, of owning one's own property, of paying one's way, are all part of the spiritual ballast which maintains responsible citizenship, and provides the solid foundation from which people look around to see what more they might do, for others and for themselves. That is what we mean by a moral society; not a society where the state is responsible for everything, and no one is responsible for the state.

I said earlier that the better moral philosophy of the free society underlies its economic performance. In turn the material success of the free society enables people to show a degree of generosity to the less fortunate — unmatched in any other society. It is noteworthy that the Victorian era — the heyday of free enterprise in Britain — was also the era of the rise of selflessness and benefaction.

The second reason why the free society is morally better is because it entails dispersal of power away from the centre to a multitude of smaller groups, and to individuals. On the other hand, the essence of collectivism, is the concentration of power in large groups, and in the hands of the State at the centre: as Lord Acton[2] reminded us, all power corrupts and absolute power corrupts absolutely! . . .

Experience has shown that socialism corrodes the moral values which form part of a free society. Traditional values are also threatened by increasing state regulation.

The more the state seeks to impose its authority, the less respect that authority receives. The more living standards are squeezed by taxation, the greater is the temptation to evade that taxation. The more pay and prices are controlled, the more those controls are evaded. In short, where the state is too powerful, efficiency suffers and morality is threatened.

---

[2]Nineteenth-century English historian and Cambridge academic.

8.3

Worker Anxiety in Reagan's Free Market America

The economic malaise that dominated the United States in the 1970s hit workers especially hard. The 1980s and 1990s witnessed a shift toward free market policies and an improvement in overall economic conditions, but workers still lagged behind. The last third of the century brought declining unions, declining wages, declining aspirations, even a sense of the American dream glimmering away. Brian Devlin gave voice to this pessimism when in the mid-1980s he talked to the leading American practitioner of oral history, Studs Terkel. Devlin was then a twenty-two-year-old union member employed in the wrecking and maintenance business and living in a working-class Chicago neighborhood with his mother and two sisters.

What are Devlin's views of his life's prospects? How do they correspond to Friedman's and Thatcher's promise of the general benefits of a free market economy? How might Friedman or Thatcher have responded to Devlin's pessimism?

Studs Terkel
Interview with Brian Devlin
Mid-1980s

The thing that scares me is that someday the work will run out. I feel sorry for these guys who've worked twenty years for a company and all of a sudden they get the axe. That's the worst that can happen in a country. And farmers gettin' a raw deal. That's the kinda stuff we could do with the money instead of throwin' it into defense.

That doesn't always make sense to me why some guy has five million, ten million, a hundred million dollars and other people are broke. It seems like my class of people, my neighborhood, are the ones payin' for those people that aren't workin'. And the people makin' millions are loopholin' here and there and not givin' a thing back. They say they're puttin' money back by buildin' plants. The trickle-down theory, that garbage. . . .

Older guys, twenty-five, thirty years ago, they got outa high school, they could just pick a job. Do I want to be an electrician, a plumber? They had a choice on what they were gonna do with their life. Nowadays you don't have a choice. You get out and scrape for whatever you can get. In back of your head's the feeling that someday it could even get worse. I don't know what I'd do if fifteen years from now, after I get a family started, I suddenly get my pay cut in half because the unions go.

Studs Terkel, *The Great Divide: Second Thoughts on the American Dream* (New York: Pantheon Books, 1988), 196–97.

You're used to livin' at a certain standard and all of a sudden you're chopped. You know most people are livin' on borrowed money anyway (laughs). That's my biggest worry in life. Jobs are gonna be taken over by technology.

I think the workin' class is goin' down. There's not gonna be any middle class too long. You're either makin' big bucks or little bucks. There's nothin' in between. That's what I always wanted with my life. Have my family, take it light, and maybe have the enjoyment of a little cottage in Wisconsin. No mansion anywhere. I never expected to be rich. But I expected to have what a workin' man has.

It scares me that fifteen years from now it's not gonna be like that. You're gonna be menial labor for peanuts. Even my buddies think about that. Why can't I be like my old man? It was so easy for them and so hard for us.

Every generation was always better. My kid will have it better than me and his kid will have it better than him. Now it's the reverse. You're not gonna have it as good as your old man. Maybe if you go to school, you have a chance, but if you don't . . .

My old man worked hard to get where he's at. I don't want to come along and in fifteen years I end up bein' a lower-class broke person. You'd feel like a bum. It's the fear about maybe takin' a step down in society. Everyone's got that fear.

8.4

President Bill Clinton Endorses NAFTA and Praises International Free Trade

In December 1992 the leaders of the United States, Canada, and Mexico signed an agreement intended to reap the benefits of a single continental market, already partially realized by the 1988 U.S.-Canada free trade pact. The new, broader agreement removed obstacles to trade and investment. It sparked a lively debate, especially over the impact of the agreement on U.S. labor (threatened by jobs moving to low-wage Mexico) and on the environment (threatened by lax Mexican standards). During the 1992 U.S. presidential election, candidate Bill Clinton expressed reservations about NAFTA, which was the handiwork of his opponent, President George H. W. Bush. His doubts were shared by labor unions, environmentalists, and human rights advocates and also by strong nationalists, such as the independent presidential candidate Ross Perot, who were jealous of U.S. sovereignty. Following his election, Clinton gradually reversed himself and then in fall 1993 energetically campaigned to win congressional approval.

As part of that campaign, Clinton delivered the following remarks to an audience of business leaders and other NAFTA supporters at the White House. What are the essential arguments that Clinton uses to justify the agreement? How does he handle charges that NAFTA would seriously harm workers and the environment? Does Clinton make an effective case and a compelling response to the critics? Would Bill Devlin have been persuaded? How closely does he align himself with the free market arguments of Friedman and Thatcher?

Public Remarks
Washington, D.C., November 9, 1993

The American economy is changing very rapidly. For 20 years the wages of the bottom 60 percent of our work force, more or less, have been stagnant as people work harder for the same or lower wages. We know that over the last 20 years, as we've become more and more enmeshed in the global economy, the jobs have been changing more rapidly. . . .

We know that through the discipline of the market economy our productivity now is the highest in the world again in manufacturing and in many other areas. But we also know that there's been a whole lot of reduction of employment in many areas to get that higher productivity, with fewer people producing more output. So this is a time of enormous opportunity and enormous insecurity. . . .

. . . [N]o one has shown how a wealthy country can grow wealthier and create more jobs unless there is global economic growth through trade. There is simply no evidence that you can do it any other way. About half America's growth in the last 7 years has come from trade growth. And the jobs that are tied to trade, on average, pay about 17 percent more than jobs which are totally within the American economy, so that . . . creating more jobs, more growth, and higher incomes [becomes impossible] unless there is a level of global economic growth financed through expanded trade that Americans can take advantage of. . . .

So that brings us to NAFTA. . . . This agreement will, as all of you know, lower American tariffs but will lower Mexican tariffs and trade barriers more than American tariffs, because ours are lower anyway. This agreement will help us to gain access to a market of 90 million people, which has shown a preference for American products unprecedented in all the world. Seventy percent of all the purchases by Mexican consumers of foreign products go to American products. This agreement will unite Canada, Mexico, and the United States in a huge trading bloc which will enable us to grow and move together.

This agreement will also — and this is very important — produce most of its jobs by enabling us to use the Mexican precedent to go into the whole rest of Latin America, to have a trading bloc of well over 700 million people . . . .

It will also make a statement that America intends to go charging into the 21st century still believing we can compete and win and that we intend to lead the world in expanding horizons, not in hunkering down. . . . This is why the NAFTA agreement has acquired a symbolic and larger significance even than the terms of the agreement, because we know that if the United States turns away from open markets and more trade and competition, how can we

---

Public Papers of the Presidents of the United States: William J. Clinton, 1993, vol. 2 (Washington, D.C.: Government Printing Office, 1994), 1934–35, 1937. Also available at the website for the GPO beginning at <http://www.gpo.gov/nara/pubpaps/photoidx.html> (July 15, 2003).

then say to the Europeans and the Japanese they must open their markets to us, they must continue to expand? So the stakes here are very large indeed.

Now, let's deal with the arguments against NAFTA. The people who are against it say that if this agreement passes, more irresponsible American companies will shut their doors in America and open doors in Mexico because the costs are cheaper and this agreement allows them to do that all over the country. To that I answer the following: Number one, I was the Governor of a State for 12 years that had almost 22 percent of its work force in manufacturing. I saw plants close and go to Mexico, brought one back before I left office. I know why they did it. I know how they did it. I understand the pressures, particularly on the lower wage companies with low margins of profit.

. . . If anybody wants to go down there to produce for the American market, they can do that now. And if we defeat NAFTA, they can continue to do that, and it will be more likely that they will do that. Why? This is the nub of the argument: Because clearly, with the agreements we have on labor committing Mexico to enforce its own labor code and make that a part of an international commission on the environment, clearly, we're going to raise the cost of production in Mexico. . . .

. . . [T]he more people down there who have jobs and the better the jobs are, the more they can buy American products and the less they will feel a compulsion to become part of America's large immigration problem today. So that is good for us.

. . . I would never knowingly do anything to hurt the job market in America. I have spent my entire life, public life, trying to deal with the economic problems of ordinary people. I ran for this job to alleviate the insecurity, the anxiety, the anger, the frustration of ordinary Americans. . . .

Q. . . . I'm very concerned about the environment on the border. How will NAFTA affect the borders?

THE PRESIDENT. It will improve the environment on the border. That's why we've gotten so many environmental organizations to endorse this. Not all the environmental groups are for it, but most of the environmental groups that are against it are against it for something that often happens to progressives: They're making the perfect, the enemy of the good. That is, they think it ought to be better, but it's very good.

This agreement, first of all, requires every nation to enforce its own environmental laws and can make the failure to do so the subject of a complaint through the trade system. Secondly, to support this agreement, the World Bank has committed about $2 billion in financing, and we have agreed to set up a North American development bank to have $2 to $3 billion worth of infrastructure projects in the beginning on both sides of the border.

8.5

A Critical Mexican Perspective on NAFTA

For the Mexican economy, NAFTA represented one of a series of steps away from a policy strongly biased toward import substitution (promoting domestic industry and protecting it against foreign competition) and a strong state presence in the economy. Mexican president Carlos Salinas de Gortari gave his backing to NAFTA as an impetus to a more vibrant economy. Businesses would move south to take advantage of lower labor costs and less regulation. Investors would gain confidence to put their capital to productive uses. Mexican producers would gain access to the U.S. market for their own products.

These economic gains were illusory, according to two Mexican critics. Both were public intellectuals — well trained and well connected academics who regularly commented in the media and enjoyed political prominence. One, Jorge Castañeda, would later become foreign minister, while the other, Carlos Heredia, would serve in the legislature and in the cabinet of the governor of Mexico City. What are their doubts about the workings of a regional free market? How does their view diverge from Clinton's? What about the European model of economic integration appeals to them? Having read Clinton's statement of support and the Castañeda-Heredia critique, how would you have voted on NAFTA? (It in fact passed the U.S. Senate on November 17, 1993, by a 61 to 38 margin, and the House three days later 234 to 200.)

Jorge G. Castañeda and Carlos Heredia
"Another NAFTA:
What a Good Agreement Should Offer"
1992

Do we Mexicans really want a market economy like the one the United States has? No one has asked us. . . .

. . . In reality, the choice is between the agreement already negotiated, a right-wing agreement of a neo-liberal Republican cast, and an agreement of some other kind, more like a social-democratic agreement, with a strong dose of regulation and planning, inspired by an emerging progressive social compact for a new North America. The choice is between what is called an exclusively commercial agreement, proper to the Anglo-Saxon world's individualistic and deregulated capitalism, and an accord that would go beyond the strictly commercial, also encompassing social issues and the relation between the state and the market. The contrast between those two agreements, the "bad" one we have and the "good" one we want, reflects the difference between the kinds of market economies that exist in the world today. . . .

What is the bad agreement all about? Its conceptual premise is to leave free trade exclusively to the free market. In Mexico, leaving everything to the market means giving free rein to those who command it: the most powerful, the richest. Second, the agreement supposedly covers only economic issues. In reality, NAFTA is an agreement that encompasses not only financial matters, investment, intellectual property, and of course commerce, but also dispute-resolution, banking, transport, and services. Clearly, the agreement is not solely commercial.

Jorge G. Castañeda and Carlos Heredia, "Another NAFTA: What a Good Agreement Should Offer," *World Policy Journal* 9 (Fall/Winter 1992), 673, 675–82, 684–85.

But it *is* a strictly economic agreement, one that does not include other possible issues: social, political, environmental, cultural. What we have here is an accord that is fundamentally opposed to the idea of planning, to choosing what each country will produce, to defining how established goals will be met, and to clarifying how certain sectors will be protected or exposed in order to reach long-term objectives.

Just as deregulation was a major feature of the economic policy of both the Bush administration and the Salinas government, so, too, NAFTA lacks a strict regulatory framework. To the greatest extent possible, it seeks to eliminate all social, economic, consumer-protection, and environmental regulations. True, that is no easy task, since the United States and Canada have legislative bodies, courts, and citizens' organizations that have struggled for years to pass the present regulatory framework.

Here, the Salinas government stands to the right even of the Bush administration. It was the Mexicans who insisted on dismantling the various regulations in force in the United States, alleging that they constituted disguised forms of protection (in some cases true). Ironically, Mexico, completely lacking in effective regulation of anything, lacking a minimum regulatory framework in any area, now opposes the preservation of the U.S. regulatory framework, arguing that it is contrary to the market and free trade. . . .

The premise underlying a good agreement is that there is no single model of formal economic integration, just as there is no single model of a market economy. . . . [T]he differences between individualistic, predatory Anglo-Saxon capitalism and the social-democratic market capitalism of Germany (or of the Rhineland, as some European observers have put it) or the public-private capitalism of Japan are striking. The U.S. model, presently under severe strain, is highly dynamic but anti-social, short-term oriented, anti-interventionist, and tends to exacerbate inequalities. The European and Japanese models — looking beyond their differences — are less dynamic but more socially oriented and regulated with a more active and dominant role for the state, and tend to forge more egalitarian homogeneous societies.

There are also various models of formal economic integration, from the U.S.-Canada model of 1988, which leaves almost everything to the will of the market, to the European plan of Jean Monnet and the Treaty of Rome, which emphasizes the state's role in planning, regulation, and social policymaking. . . .

The European Community established structural adjustment funds to mitigate economic and social differences and strengthen economic and social cohesion. EC members seek to stimulate productivity and enhance development in depressed areas by strengthening infrastructure, training workers, and introducing appropriate technology. This is a policy specifically designed to redistribute wealth to the poor . . . .

. . . Ireland, perhaps the European country that has benefited most from regional funds, receives 8 percent of its annual GDP from community aid. It is as if Mexico were to receive $20 to $25 billion a year from the governments of the United States and Canada. . . .

A good agreement includes the idea of a trilateral industrial policy — a strategic alliance between the private sector and states to capture markets, develop technologies, achieve dynamic competitive advantages, and reach new levels of competitiveness.

. . . It is not enough to expand physical infrastructure and make things easier for the transnational corporations whose investments are being courted. Each country must invest in social infrastructure to improve wages and standards of living. . . .

If NAFTA is to improve access to the United States market for our exports, then two major exports have been left out of the agreement: drugs and people. Call it what you will, but Mexico has been exporting Mexicans for over a century now. Yet those who negotiated NAFTA almost completely ignored this situation.

It is not true that it is impossible to legalize migration from a poor to a rich country. On the contrary, the great discovery of the Europeans was legalizing the previously existing movements of undocumented people. When the Treaty of Rome [creating the EC in 1957] entered into force there was already a very large number of workers from southern Italy working in Germany, Belgium, Holland, and France. Most were undocumented. The only solution was to give them papers, granting them entitlements, rights, and power. . . .

The free-trade agreement says little about the free movement of unskilled labor. Only some provisions concerning temporary and limited entry for professionals have been included. The Mexican authorities have been unable to explain why the negotiations resulted in free entry for officials, bankers, or consultants, but not for everybody else. Worse, entry for professionals from the United States and Canada into Mexico was significantly liberalized. The governments are opening borders to goods and capital flows, while labor, Mexico's main export, is barred from entry. . . .

A good agreement will provide for upward harmonization of labor standards and rights — not just labor legislation but also implementation of standards. . . .

One reason why [Mexican] workers at factories belonging to the same company, producing the same cars with the same quality and productivity, earn 20 times less [than their U.S. counterparts], is that the right to strike in Mexico is more a metaphor than anything else. . . . [T]he workers' ability to use the strike as a weapon is negligible. Although it is difficult to legislate equal pay . . . , it is possible to harmonize standards for collective bargaining, labor tribunals, the right to strike, and wider union freedom. With such power the workers themselves can achieve, over time, those levels of wages and benefits, as well as dignity in the workplace.

Beyond harmonization of labor standards, a free-trade agreement should promote workers' rights. One way to do this is to allow workers to organize and negotiate collectively at a continental level. NAFTA allows General Motors to decide what to produce in North America and where, but does not create conditions so that workers in Michigan and Coahuila can act jointly to influence industrial policy and wages in their areas. . . . [A] social charter should include the adoption of workers' councils, establishing the right of workers' representatives to participate in decisions regarding contracts or lay-offs, assignment of workers to a particular place of work, matters of health and safety in the workplace, and access to training. The idea is that all of these rights go hand in hand with the commitment to increase productivity.

Other elements of the social charter might include: no favorable tariff treatment for goods whose production fails to comply with given conditions; prohibiting child labor (under age 16); and requiring employers to provide a healthy workplace, without exposure to toxic substances. . . .

One of the biggest incentives for U.S. companies to move to Mexico is to evade environmental protection laws. In Mexico, the environment is not protected, nor is society itself very comfortable with the idea. Harmonizing consumer protection and environmental standards, which tend to be similar, is intended to prevent Mexico from becoming like the border — a toxic waste-dump for the United States. . . .

The elements of a good agreement do not amount to a list of protectionist measures or suggest that workers should be a privileged group. The idea is simply to put into practice the principle that governments often repeat, but seldom live up to, that a country's most valuable asset is its work force, the majority of the population who are systematically left out of decision making circles but are affected by what the elites decide. The idea is also to go beyond the myopic vision that seeks to divorce the free-trade agreement from labor, emigration, environmental, or human rights provisions on the ground that it is only a commercial agreement. This narrow view overlooks an incontrovertible truth: flows of trade, capital, and investment bring with them social implications that cannot be divorced from their causes and have to be addressed. . . .

A new, progressive North American social compact could become an example for the rest of Latin America; a bad agreement is merely a Trojan horse for the most reactionary sectors in the United States and the rest of the hemisphere. A conservative covenant can never become a step toward a progressive program; on the contrary, it makes such an agreement all the more difficult and remote a prospect. NAFTA should not become a legacy of the Reagan-Bush era, but a precedent for a different North America.

FROM THE EC TO THE EU: TIGHTENING EUROPEAN BONDS

The Schuman declaration of 1950 (Document 5.5) and the European Coal and Steel Community that emerged from it were the harbingers of a dramatic process of regional integration that would change the face of Europe. Next, the Treaty of Rome of 1957 created the European Community made up of the six core countries of Belgium, France, Italy, Luxembourg, the Netherlands, and West Germany. In the following decades new members would join them, while at the same time integration of activities — economic, cultural, judicial, and so forth — would deepen the relationship among the member countries and begin to create an increasingly distinct European entity. In 1986 the Single Europe Act set community goals in simple, clear terms and paved the way for fresh action in a wide range of fields — from environmental protection to workers' rights to common business standards. The collapse of the socialist regimes in eastern Europe brought a flock of new applicants for a place in the new Europe. Finally, the negotiation of the Maastricht treaty in late 1991 led to creation of the European Union just as the Treaty of Rome had founded the European Community.

The advance of integration depended heavily on the leaders of France and West Germany. They combined to launch the European Coal and Steel Community early in the process and later pressed for deepening integration in areas such as monetary policy. On the other side, British leaders found themselves regularly playing the role of naysayers. London at first doubted that the European Community would work and then after belatedly applying for membership found its way blocked by Charles de Gaulle, who pointedly asked whether Britain's attachments to its imperial legacy and to the United States outweighed its continental identity and commitment. Even after Britain managed to gain entry in 1973, its leaders remained "Euroskeptics" in the face of increasingly robust EC and EU policies and institutions.

8.6
Margaret Thatcher Defines the Limits of European Integration

As party leader, Margaret Thatcher initially supported closer links to Europe but by the latter part of her tenure as prime minister, she had developed doubts about the EC. Her doubts reflected perennial and widely felt attachment to British national identity and political autonomy.

Thatcher offered the best statement of her views in a speech delivered to the College of Europe in Bruges, Belgium, at a time when fresh steps toward integration were gaining momentum. How does she define Europe? In which areas does she favor cooperation and in which does she oppose it? How does she seek to sugarcoat her opposition to a more wide-ranging integration? How do Thatcher's views below mesh with her free market principles laid out in her 1977 Zurich statement (Document 8.2)?

Speech to the College of Europe
Bruges, Belgium, September 20, 1988

Europe is not the creation of the Treaty of Rome. Nor is the European idea the property of any group or institution.

Based on an audiotape of the speech, available at the Margaret Thatcher Foundation website at: <http://www.margaretthatcher.org/Speeches/displaydocument.asp?docid =107332> (March 11, 2003). Minor amendments made here on the basis of the copy in *The Collected Speeches of Margaret Thatcher*, 315–25.

We British are as much heirs to the legacy of European culture as any other nation. Our links to the rest of Europe, the continent of Europe, have been the *dominant* factor in our history. . . .

. . . [F]rom our perspective today surely what strikes us most is our common experience. For instance, the story of how Europeans explored and colonised — and yes, without apology — civilised much of the world is an extraordinary tale of talent, skill and courage.

But we British have in a very special way contributed to Europe. Over the centuries we have fought to prevent Europe from falling under the dominance of a single power. We have fought and we have died for her freedom. . . .

The European Community is *one* manifestation of that European identity, but it is not the only one. We must never forget that east of the Iron Curtain, people who once enjoyed a full share of European culture, freedom and identity have been cut off from their roots. We shall always look on Warsaw, Prague and Budapest as great European cities. Nor should we forget that European values have helped to make the United States of America into the valiant defender of freedom which she has become. . . .

. . . Europe never would have prospered and never will prosper as a narrow-minded, inward-looking club.

The European Community belongs to *all* its members. It must reflect the traditions and aspirations of *all* its members.

And let me be quite clear. Britain does not dream of some cosy, isolated existence on the fringes of the European Community. Our destiny is in Europe, as part of the Community.

That is not to say that our future lies only in Europe, but nor does that of France or Spain or, indeed, of any other member.

The Community is not an end in itself. Nor is it an institutional device to be constantly modified according to the dictates of some abstract intellectual concept. Nor must it be ossified by endless regulation. The European Community is a practical means by which Europe can ensure the future prosperity and security of its people in a world in which there are many other powerful nations and groups of nations.

. . . Europe has to be ready both to contribute in full measure to its own security and to compete commercially and industrially in a world in which success goes to the countries which encourage individual initiative and enterprise, rather than those which attempt to diminish them.

This evening I want to set out some guiding principles for the future which I believe will ensure that Europe does succeed, not just in economic and defence terms but also in the quality of life and the influence of its peoples.

My first guiding principle is this: willing and active cooperation between independent sovereign states is the best way to build a successful European Community. To try to suppress nationhood and concentrate power at the centre of a European conglomerate would be highly damaging and would jeopardise the objectives we seek to achieve. Europe will be stronger precisely because it has France as France, Spain as Spain, Britain as Britain, each with its own customs, traditions and identity. It would be folly to try to fit them into some sort of identikit European personality. . . .

I am the first to say that on many great issues the countries of Europe should try to speak with a single voice. I want to see us work more closely on the things we can do better together than alone. Europe is stronger when we do so, whether it be in trade, in defence or in our relations with the rest of the world.

But working more closely together does not require power to be centralised in Brussels or decisions to be taken by an appointed bureaucracy. Indeed, it is ironic that just when those countries such as the Soviet Union, which have tried to run everything from the centre, are learning that success depends on dispersing power and decisions away from the centre, there are some in the Community who seem to want to move in the opposite direction. We have not successfully rolled back the frontiers of the state in Britain, only to see them re-imposed at a European level with a European super-state exercising a new dominance from Brussels. . . .

My second guiding principle is this: Community policies must tackle present problems in a *practical* way, however difficult that may be. If we cannot reform those Community policies which are patently wrong or ineffective and which are rightly causing public disquiet, then we shall not get the public support for the Community's future development.

. . . It was not right that half the total Community budget was being spent on storing and disposing of surplus food. Now those stocks are being sharply reduced. It was absolutely right to decide that agriculture's share of the budget should be cut in order to free resources for other policies, such as helping the less well-off regions and helping training for jobs. It was right too to introduce tighter budgetary discipline to enforce these decisions and to bring the Community spending under better control.

. . . Certainly, Europe needs a stable and efficient farming industry. But [the EC policy of support for agriculture] has become unwieldy, inefficient and grossly expensive. Production of unwanted surpluses safeguards neither the income nor the future of farmers themselves. We must *continue* to pursue policies which relate supply more closely to market requirements, and which will reduce over-production and limit costs. Of course, we must protect the villages and rural areas which are such an important part of our national life, but not by the instrument of agricultural prices.

My third guiding principle is the need for Community policies which encourage enterprise. If Europe is to flourish and create the jobs of the future, enterprise is the key. . . .

The lesson of the economic history of Europe in the 70's and 80's is that central planning and detailed control *do not* work and that personal endeavour and initiative *do*. That a state-controlled economy is a recipe for low growth and that free enterprise within a framework of law brings better results.

. . . By getting rid of barriers, by making it possible for companies to operate on a European scale, we can best compete with the United States, Japan and other new economic powers emerging in Asia and elsewhere.

And that means action to *free* markets, action to *widen* choice, action to *reduce* government intervention. Our aim should *not* be more and more detailed regulation from the centre: it should be to deregulate and to remove the constraints on trade. . . .

Regarding *monetary matters,* let me say this. The key issue is *not* whether there should be a European Central Bank. The immediate and practical requirements are: to implement the Community's commitment to free movement of capital — in Britain, we have it; and to the abolition through the Community of exchange controls — in Britain, we abolished them in 1979; [and] to establish a genuinely free market in financial services in banking, insurance, investment . . . . These are the *real* requirements because they are what the Community business and industry need if they are to compete effectively in the wider world. And they are what the European consumer wants, for they will widen his choice and lower his costs. . . .

It is the same with *frontiers* between our countries. Of course, we want to make it easier for goods to pass through frontiers. Of course, we must make it easier for people to travel throughout the Community. But it is a matter of plain common sense that we cannot totally abolish frontier controls if we are also to protect our citizens from crime and stop the movement of drugs, of terrorists and of illegal immigrants. . . .

And before I leave the subject of a single market, may I say that we certainly do not need new regulations which raise the cost of employment and make Europe's labour market less flexible and less competitive with overseas suppliers. . . .

My fourth guiding principle is that Europe should not be protectionist. The expansion of the world economy requires us to continue the process of removing barriers to trade. . . . It would be a betrayal if, while breaking down constraints on trade within Europe, the Community were to erect greater external protection. We must ensure that our approach to world trade is consistent with the liberalisation we preach at home. We have a responsibility to give a lead on this, a responsibility which is particularly directed towards the less developed countries. They need not only aid; more than anything, they need improved trading opportunities if they are to gain the dignity of growing economic strength and independence.

My last guiding principle concerns the most fundamental issue — the European countries' role in defence. Europe must continue to maintain a sure defence through NATO. . . .

It is to NATO that we owe the peace that has been maintained over 40 years. The fact is things *are* going our way: the democratic model of a free enterprise society *has* proved itself superior; freedom *is* on the offensive, a peaceful offensive the world over, for the first time in my life-time. . . .

Let Europe be a family of nations, understanding each other better, appreciating each other more, doing more together but relishing our national identity no less than our common European endeavour. Let us have a Europe which plays its full part in the wider world, which looks outward not inward, and which preserves that Atlantic community — that Europe on both sides of the Atlantic — which is our noblest inheritance and our greatest strength.

8.7
Jacques Delors Offers His Vision for European Integration

Jacques Delors had signal success in energizing the integrationist cause as president of the European Commission, the executive body that took direction from the Council of Ministers made up of representatives from the member states. Delors's background was in French banking and state planning, including service as his country's economics and finance minister (1981–1983). Elected to the Commission presidency in 1985, Delors pushed to create Europe-wide social legislation, a single integrated market, and a single currency and central bank. The remarkable progress that he made owed much to backing from French president François Mitterand (with whom Delors was on close terms) and German chancellor Helmut Kohl.

This speech was a response to Thatcher's case for Euroskepticism offered in the same setting in Bruges a year earlier. What does Delors mean by his key term "subsidiarity"? What are the leading justifications he advances for pursuing a wider and deeper integration? Where is his disagreement with Thatcher sharpest? Are there areas of agreement?

Speech to the College of Europe
Bruges, Belgium, October 17, 1989

[A]s a militant European, . . . I see [the principle of subsidiarity] as a way of reconciling what for many appears to be irreconcilable: the emergence of a united Europe and loyalty to one's homeland; the need for a European power capable of tackling the problems of our age and the absolute necessity to preserve our roots in the shape of our nations and regions; and decentralization of responsibilities, so that we never entrust to a bigger unit anything that is best done by a smaller one. This is precisely what subsidiarity is about. . . .

Politically speaking, power is not necessarily the obverse of freedom. Neither the European Community — nor the peoples and nations that form it — will truly exist unless it is in a position to defend its values, to act on them for the benefit of all, to be generous. Let us be powerful enough to command respect and to uphold the values of freedom and solidarity. In a world like ours, there is no other way. . . .

. . . Our present concerns — be it the social dimension or the new frontier represented by economic and monetary union — offer a golden opportunity

Bulletin of the European Communities, vol. 22, no. 10 (November 1989), 110–12, 114–16, 118.

for the joint exercise of sovereignty, while respecting diversity and hence the principles of pluralism and subsidiarity.

There is a need for urgency, for history does not wait. As upheavals shake the world, and the other [eastern] "Europe" in particular, our reinvigorated Community must work for increased cohesion and set objectives commensurate with the challenges thrown down by history. . . .

. . . The founding fathers wanted to see an end to the internecine strife in Europe. But they also sensed that Europe was losing its place as the economic and political centre of the world. . . .

. . . Since the turn-around of 1984–87 our achievements are there for all to see. . . . Europe is once again a force to be reckoned with and is arousing interest everywhere: in America, in Asia, in Africa, in the North and in the South. . . .

. . . The Twelve [states making up the EC] cannot control history but they are now in a position to influence it once again. They did not want Europe to be cut in two at Yalta[1] and made a hostage in the Cold War. They did not, nor do they, close the door to other European countries willing to accept the terms of the contract in full. . . .

. . . By its very nature, economic and monetary union is the interface between economic integration and political integration. It is the political crowning of economic convergence. It is a perfect illustration of the joint exercise of sovereignty because a single market for capital and financial services in a world dominated by financial matters calls for a monetary policy which is sufficiently coordinated and sufficiently tight to allow us to make the most of it. Without such a policy we would be prey to international speculation and the instability of dominant currencies.

Monetary union will be acceptable and feasible only if there is parallel progress towards increased convergence of our economies so that policies are more consistent and harnessed to agreed objectives. There is consensus on economic expansion against a background of stability, on qualitative growth to generate new jobs. In a democratic society objectives can only be defined by political authorities which have democratic legitimacy. We therefore need to combine an independent monetary authority — the guarantor of stability — with the subsidiarity which is vital if each nation is to pursue it[s] own policies in areas which are a matter for it alone, and control by our elected representatives in the shape of the European Parliament, our governments and our national parliaments. . . .

Acceptance of subsidiarity implies respect for pluralism and, by implication, diversity.

This is evident not only in discussions on economic and monetary union, but also in what we call the Community's social dimension.

The facts are clear. Our 12 countries have differing traditions in the areas of industrial relations. Major disparities persist in terms of living standards,

---

[1]Site of the meeting of the Allied leaders toward the close of World War II in Europe.

although our common policies are designed to reduce these gradually. There can be no question, therefore, of artificially forcing standards upwards, or, conversely, of provoking the export of social problems. Last but not least, our governments have differing, and in some cases, opposing, points of view. . . .

The social dimension permeates all our discussions and everything we do: our efforts to restore competitiveness and cooperate on macroeconomic policy to reduce unemployment and provide all young Europeans with a working future; common policies designed to promote the development of less-prosperous regions and the regeneration of regions hit by industrial change; employment policy and the concentration of efforts on helping young people to gain a foothold in the labour market and combating long-term unemployment; and the development of rural regions threatened by the decline in the number of farms, desertification and demographic imbalances.

Think what a boost it would be for democracy and social justice if we could demonstrate that we are capable of working together to create a better-integrated society open to all. . . .

. . . I know that our task is to unite old nations with strong traditions and personalities. There is no conspiracy against the nation state. Nobody is being asked to renounce legitimate patriotism. I want not only to unite people, as Jean Monnet[2] did, but also to bring nations together. As the Community develops, as our governments emphasize the need for a people's Europe, is it heresy to hope that all Europeans could feel that they belong to a Community which they see as a second homeland? If this view is rejected, European integration will founder and the spectre of nationalism will return to haunt us, because the Community will have failed to win the hearts and minds of the people, the first requirement for the success of any human venture. . . .

As I stand before a predominantly young audience, I find myself dreaming of a Europe which has thrown off the chains of Yalta, a Europe which tends its immense cultural heritage so that it bears fruit, a Europe which imprints the mark of solidarity on a world which is far too hard and too forgetful of its underdeveloped regions.

---

[2]One of the early architects of integration and the author of the Schuman declaration (see document 5.5).

8.8

François Mitterand Reflects on the Prospects for an Integrated Europe

François Mitterand, a politician on France's moderate Left, was coming to the end of a long political career when he delivered this speech in 1996. Born eighty years earlier, the son of a railway station manager, Mitterand had become a familiar figure in postwar French politics, a popular president of France during the 1980s, and a strong supporter of European cooperation. He shared the view, popular among French leaders, that an integrated Europe was the best, perhaps only way to make the region a force in the world with the capacity to protect its interests. Like many in France, he viewed binding Germany to the rest of Europe the surest way to avoid a revival of past rivalry.

Mitterand made this speech before the European Parliament, a body composed of members elected from within their own countries and eager to achieve parity of influence alongside the European Commission and the European Council of Ministers. The confident tone of the speech is understandable if set against the recent successes for integration: the addition of East Germany in 1990; the opening of negotiations for membership by Hungary, Czechoslovakia, and Poland; the implementation of the Maastricht treaty in 1993 creating the EU; and the admission of Austria, Finland, and Sweden the year he spoke. What are the elements in Mitterand's conception of an integrated Europe? How did the experience of his generation provide the impetus for integration? In what key ways does his appraisal of an integrated Europe differ from Thatcher's?

Speech to the European Parliament
Strasbourg, France, January 17, 1995

[W]hat is at stake, what we must discuss, is the means of assuring Europe's rightful role and place in a world waiting to be built: a Europe which is economically and commercially strong, a Europe which is unified in monetary terms, active on the international scene, able to guarantee its own security, and culturally fertile and diverse. Such a Europe will be both more mindful of other peoples and more self-assured. . . .

[Strong economic growth in Europe depends on] using three of our major assets to the full. What is the first of those assets? It is the size of our internal market. So far, we have essentially succeeded in removing the administrative, customs and regulatory barriers which partitioned this vast economic area. That is the task that was accomplished by means of the Single European Act. We now have to eliminate or reduce the remaining barriers — which are far from insignificant — including the physical barriers which still restrict the free movement of people, goods and ideas. . . .

Our second major asset is, of course, economic and monetary union, which is the natural and essential complement, in my view, to the single market, and without which the single market . . . would be a recipe for anarchy and the worst forms of unfair competition.

. . . [T]he introduction of a single currency is the only means of ensuring that Europe remains a great economic and monetary power, and it is the best means of ensuring the sustained growth of our economies. . . .

Our third major asset is the European Union's technological excellence. Our research scientists have been responsible for countless innovations. Such capital cannot fail to yield a profit if we prove capable of utilizing it properly, and on a European scale. . . .

Let us make no mistake: markets are no more than instruments, no more than mechanisms which are all too often governed by the law of the strongest, mechanisms which can lead to injustice, exclusion and dependence, unless the necessary counterweight is provided by those who can assert their democratic legitimacy. Alongside the markets, there is room for economic and social activities based on the concepts of solidarity, cooperation, partnership, reciprocity and the common interest — in short, public services. So far, we have drawn the outline of a social Europe, but it has no content. And will it not be an exciting, exhilarating venture to provide that content? Will it not be the task of the coming months and years? . . .

Such a Europe, our Europe, must be embodied in something more than simply balance sheets and freight tonnages. I would go as far as to say, while not wishing to become too rhetorical, that it needs a soul, so that it can give expression — and let us use more modest language here — to its culture, its ways of thinking, the intellectual make-up of its peoples, the fruits of the centuries of civilization of which we are the heirs. The expressions of Europe's many forms of genius are rich and diverse; and, as in the past, we must share with the whole world — while not seeking to impose them, somewhat differently from in the past — our ideas, our dreams and, to the extent that they are of the right kind, our passions. . . .

. . . There is a need for Europe to be better known — I would go so far as to say better loved — by its people. . . . The people of Europe must love Europe. Why, in the past, have they defended their native land — and they must continue to do so if necessary? Because they love it. And why do they love their native land? Because it represents their home, their scenery, their landscape, their friends, their identity. If Europe lacks all this, there will be no Europe. . . .

. . . [T]he cultural identity of nations is reinforced by the process of European integration. The Europe of cultures, ladies and gentlemen, is a Europe of nations as opposed to a Europe of nationalism. . . .

. . . I was born during the First World War and fought in the Second. I therefore spent my childhood in the surroundings of families torn apart, all of them mourning loved ones and feeling great bitterness, if not hatred, towards the recent enemy, the traditional enemy. . . .

. . . [M]y generation has almost completed its work; it is carrying out its last public acts, and this will be one of my last. It is therefore vital for us to pass on our experience. Many of you will remember the teaching of your parents, will have felt the suffering of your countries, will have experienced the grief, the pain of separation, the presence of death — all as a result of the mutual enmity of the peoples of Europe. It is vital to pass on not this hatred but, on the contrary, the opportunity for reconciliation which we have, thanks — it must be said — to those who, after 1944–1945, themselves bloodstained and with their personal lives destroyed, had the courage to envisage a more radiant future which would be based on peace and reconciliation. That is what we have done.

8.9

Citizens of the EU Reflect on Life in an Integrated Europe

The evolving European community has sought to track the views of its citizens in a systematic way since the early 1970s. The resulting public opinion surveys provide a snapshot of changing levels of support for integration and a revealing sense of the concerns of people living in the fifteen countries composing the EU at the end of the 1990s.

These surveys offer a kind of overall view of the situation that is hard to get in any other way. What are the general values and concerns prevailing within the EU? How broad is the support for integration? Where is it strongest and where weakest? How much is integration an elite-driven project? How much do the values and priorities registered here echo the caution and free market, anti-statist preferences of Thatcher or the soaring hopes and social ideals of Delors and Mitterand? Interpreting poll data is perhaps more an art than a science despite the fact that they appear as rows of crisp numbers. What problems or ambiguities do you see in these surveys?

The Values of Europeans[1]

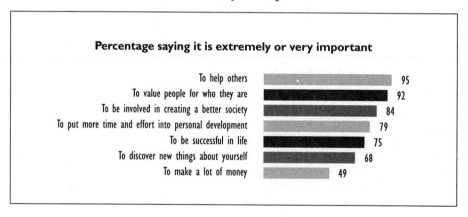

Percentage saying it is extremely or very important

To help others	95
To value people for who they are	92
To be involved in creating a better society	84
To put more time and effort into personal development	79
To be successful in life	75
To discover new things about yourself	68
To make a lot of money	49

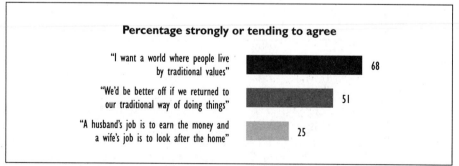

Percentage strongly or tending to agree

"I want a world where people live by traditional values"	68
"We'd be better off if we returned to our traditional way of doing things"	51
"A husband's job is to earn the money and a wife's job is to look after the home"	25

---

[1]Based on surveys in August–September 1997.

European Commission, *How Europeans See Themselves: Looking through the Mirror with Public Opinion Surveys* (Luxembourg: Office for Official Publications of the European Communities, 2001), 8, 11, 20–21, 30, 41, 50–51. Copy available online at the EU website: <http://europa.eu.int/comm/publications/booklets/eu_documentation/05/index_en.htm>.

Identity: European, National, or Mixed?[2]

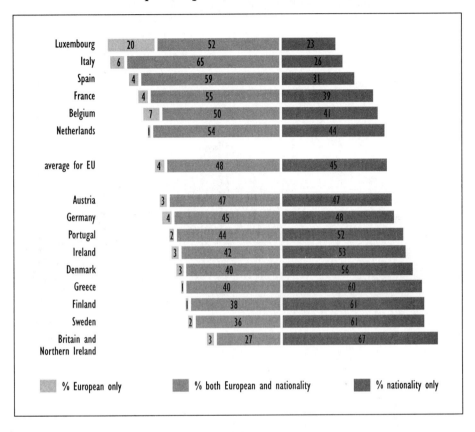

	% European only	% both European and nationality	% nationality only
Luxembourg	20	52	23
Italy	6	65	26
Spain	4	59	31
France	4	55	39
Belgium	7	50	41
Netherlands	1	54	44
average for EU	4	48	45
Austria	3	47	47
Germany	4	45	48
Portugal	2	44	52
Ireland	3	42	53
Denmark	3	40	56
Greece	1	40	60
Finland	1	38	61
Sweden	2	36	61
Britain and Northern Ireland	3	27	67

[2]Based on surveys in October–November 1999. Percentage of "don't know" responses not shown.

Support for European Community Membership, 1981–1999[3]

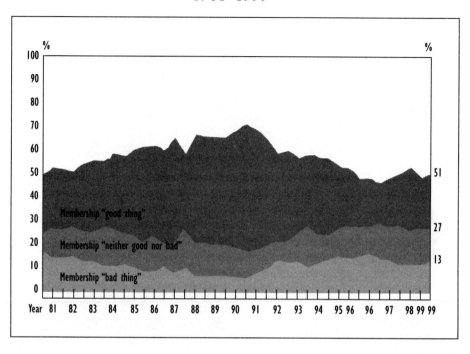

[3]The surveys before 1995 cover the twelve member countries; thereafter the three new members were included in the survey. Percentage of "don't know" responses not shown.

Support for European Community Membership by Country in 1999[4]

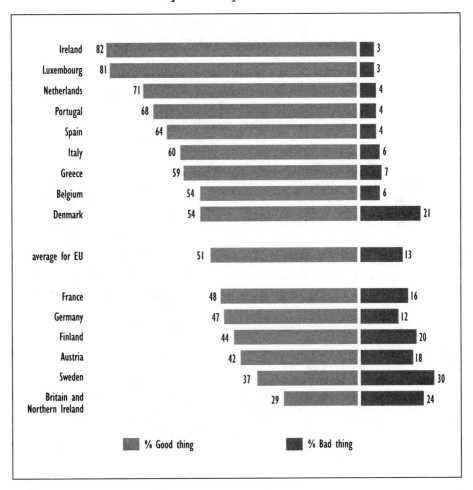

Decisions Best Made at the National or Joint EU Level?[5]

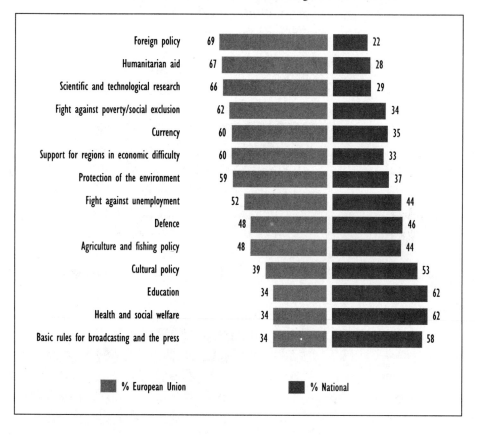

	% European Union		% National
Foreign policy	69		22
Humanitarian aid	67		28
Scientific and technological research	66		29
Fight against poverty/social exclusion	62		34
Currency	60		35
Support for regions in economic difficulty	60		33
Protection of the environment	59		37
Fight against unemployment	52		44
Defence	48		46
Agriculture and fishing policy	48		44
Cultural policy	39		53
Education	34		62
Health and social welfare	34		62
Basic rules for broadcasting and the press	34		58

[5]Based on surveys in October–November 1999. Percentage of "don't know" responses not shown.

The Worries of Europeans[6]

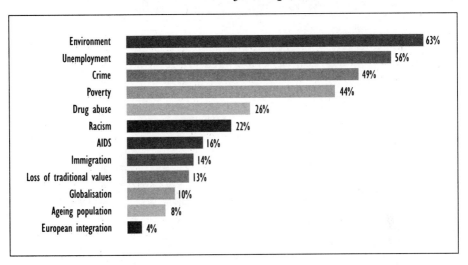

[6]Based on surveys in March–April 1997. Pollsters gave respondents a list of possible answers to select from.

*Elite vs. General Public on Support for EU Membership
and on Resulting National Benefits*[7]

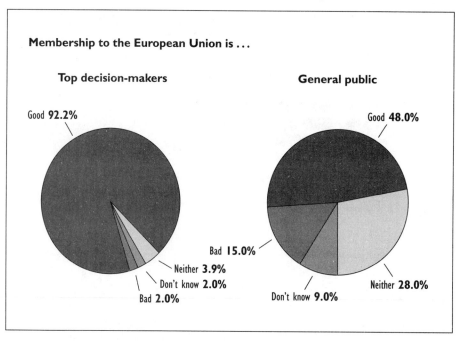

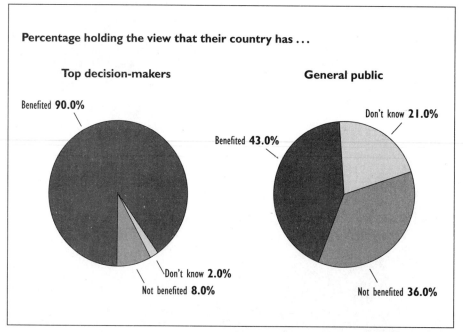

---

[7]Based on surveys in May 1996. "Top decision-makers" here means civil servants; elected politicians; business and labor leaders; and academic, cultural, and religious leaders.

CHINA'S AUTHORITARIAN CAPITALISM

Market- and export-oriented development strategies made relentless head-way in East Asia from the 1950s onward. Japan took the lead and offered a model for those that followed, notably at first South Korea and Taiwan. Hong Kong and Singapore joined the charmed circle of prosperity by serving as entrepôts for the rising trade of the region. In the mid-1980s both China and Vietnam began the shift from a command to a market economy. Countries on the East Asian periphery such as Indonesia, Thailand, and Malaysia were by then also participating in the economic reorientation and reaping its benefits. Of all those to shift, China was along with Japan the most important. The stunning changes in the region's largest and once militantly socialist country should not hide a fundamental continuity: A Chinese Communist Party de-voted to making China strong and prosperous engineered the country's eco-nomic revolution every bit as much as it had led its political revolution of 1949.

The Chinese experiment in combining market with authoritarian politics proved wildly successful. In a record matched by no other third-world coun-try in the post-1945 period, China achieved high levels of economic growth through the 1980s and 1990s and into the new century. By 1999 China's gross domestic product (GDP) had passed the four billion dollar mark. Per capita GDP, which had roughly doubled between 1949 when Mao Zedong had come to power and the late 1970s when the market strategy made its debut, tripled over the next twenty years, reaching $3,259 in 1999. Industry, agriculture, cityscapes, private lives, and cultural practices all underwent an astounding transformation over those two decades. But the transformation produced serious social strains as party members exploited new economic opportunities created by markets, as previously favored groups such as indus-trial workers lost ground, and as demands for greater political accountability if not democratization gained ground.

8.10
Deng Xiaoping Champions Market Reforms

If the first political revolution was Mao's, the second economic one belonged to Deng Xiaoping. He was an early member of the Communist Party who studied in France and in the 1930s threw in his lot with Mao. By the 1950s Deng was one of the handful of leading figures within Communist leadership. Targeted during the Cultural Revolution, he survived and gained command of the party soon after Mao's death in 1976.

As Deng launched his economic reforms during the late 1970s and early 1980s, he offered no single grand theoretical pronouncement reconciling growing em-phasis on the market mechanism and on international trade with socialism and the leading role of the party. In keeping with his cautious, step-by-step approach, he limited himself to occasional and fairly informal comments about his reform policy. A selection from those comments follows. How does Deng describe his market reforms in relation to long-standing party positions on the superiority of socialism to capitalism? How does he define socialism? By what stages does Deng's thinking evolve in these years? What were some of his abiding concerns? Can we tell from these statements whether Deng thought he was staying within a socialist framework, creating some uniquely Chinese mix of socialism and capitalism, or simply abandoning socialism for capitalism? How does Deng's approach to the reform of socialism compare with Gorbachev's (see Document 7.5)?

Speech at a Party Forum on Theoretical Work
March 30, 1979

[A]lthough it is a fact that socialist China lags behind the developed capitalist countries in its economy, technology and culture, this is not due to the socialist system but basically to China's historical development before Liberation [in 1949]; it is the result of imperialism and feudalism. The socialist revolution has greatly narrowed the gap in economic development between China and the advanced capitalist countries. Despite our errors, in the past three decades we have made progress on a scale which old China could not achieve in hundreds or even thousands of years. Our economy has attained a fairly high rate of growth. Now that we have summed up experience and corrected errors, it will undoubtedly develop more rapidly than the economy of any capitalist country, and the development will be steady and sustained. . . . The socialist economy is based on public ownership, and socialist production is designed to meet the material and cultural needs of the people to the maximum extent possible — not to exploit them. These characteristics of the socialist system make it possible for the people of our country to share common political, economic and social ideals and moral standards. All this can never happen in a capitalist society. There is no way by which capitalism can ever eliminate the extraction of super-profits by its millionaires or ever get rid of exploitation, plundering and economic crises. It can never generate common ideals and moral standards or free itself from appalling crimes, moral degradation and despair. On the other hand, capitalism already has a history of several hundred years, and we have to learn from the peoples of the capitalist countries. We must make use of the science and technology they have developed and of those elements in their accumulated knowledge and experience which can be adapted to our use. While we will import advanced technology and other things useful to us from the capitalist countries — selectively and according to plan — we will never learn from or import the capitalist system itself, nor anything repellent or decadent. . . . We should introduce to our people, and particularly to our youth, whatever is progressive and useful in the capitalist countries, and we should criticize whatever is reactionary and decadent.

Selected Works of Deng Xiaoping (Beijing: Foreign Languages Press, 1984–1994), 2:174–76. Available on the website for the party's newspaper, *People's Daily:* <http://english.peopledaily.com.cn/dengxp/vol2/text/b1290.html> (February 16, 2003).

Interview
August 21 and 23, 1980

Question [by Italian journalist Oriana Fallaci]: The four modernizations[1] will bring foreign capital into China, and this will inevitably give rise to private investment. Won't this lead to a miniaturized capitalism?

Answer: In the final analysis, the general principle for our economic development is still that formulated by Chairman Mao, that is, to rely mainly on our own efforts with external assistance subsidiary. No matter to what degree we open up to the outside world and admit foreign capital, its relative magnitude will be small and it can't affect our system of socialist public ownership of the means of production. Absorbing foreign capital and technology and even allowing foreigners to construct plants in China can only play a complementary role to our effort to develop the socialist productive forces. Of course, this will bring some decadent capitalist influences into China. We are aware of this possibility; it's nothing to be afraid of.

Question: Does it mean that not all in capitalism is so bad?

Answer: It depends on how you define capitalism. Any capitalism is superior to feudalism. And we cannot say that everything developed in capitalist countries is of a capitalist nature. For instance, technology, science — even advanced production management is also a sort of science — will be useful in any society or country. We intend to acquire advanced technology, science and management skills to serve our socialist production. And these things as such have no class character.

---

[1]A term popularized by Premier Zhou Enlai in 1975 (just before his death) that stood for the modernization of agriculture, industry, national defense, and science and technology. Deng made the four modernizations his slogan, and they became the bedrock of his domestic policy.

Based on the Chinese transcript of the interview. *Selected Works of Deng Xiaoping,* 2:332–33. Available online at <http://english.peopledaily.com.cn/dengxp/vol2/text/b1470.html> (February 16, 2003).

Talk to State Officials Involved in Economic Affairs
January 12, 1983

Some people in rural areas and cities should be allowed to get rich before others. It is only fair that people who work hard should prosper. To let some people and some regions become prosperous first is a new policy that is supported by everyone. It is better than the old one. In agriculture I favour the system of contracted responsibility for larger tracts of land. This system should

---

Selected Works of Deng Xiaoping, 3:33. Available online at <http://english.peopledaily.com.cn/dengxp/vol3/text/c1080.html> (February 16, 2003).

be adopted more widely. In short, our work in all fields should help to build socialism with Chinese characteristics, and it should be judged by the criterion of whether it contributes to the welfare and happiness of the people and to national prosperity.

Talk to Leading Members of the Party Central Committee
July 8, 1983

We should make use of the intellectual resources of other countries by inviting foreigners to participate in key development projects and other construction projects in various fields. . . . In the matter of modernization we have neither experience nor technical knowhow. We should not be reluctant to spend money on recruiting foreigners. . . .

We should open our country wider to the outside world. Now that the West European countries are beset with economic difficulties, we should lose no time in seeking their cooperation, so as to speed up our technological transformation. We should do the same with the East European countries, because some of their techniques are more advanced than ours and some of ours are needed by them. China provides a huge market, so many countries wish to develop cooperation or do business with us. We should seize this opportunity. It is a matter of strategic importance.

Selected Works of Deng Xiaoping, 3:43. Available online at <http://english.peopledaily.com.cn/dengxp/vol3/text/c1130.html> (February 16, 2003).

Speech at a Session of the Party's
Central Advisory Commission
October 22, 1984

Since [some of our veteran comrades] have been devoted to socialism and communism all their lives, they are horrified by the sudden appearance of capitalism. They can't stand it. But it will have no effect on socialism. No effect. Of course, some negative elements will come in, and we must be aware of that. But it will not be difficult for us to overcome them; we'll find ways of doing so. If we isolate ourselves and close our doors again, it will be absolutely impossible for us to approach the level of the developed countries in 50 years. Even if our country remains as open as it is now, and even when our per capita GNP reaches several thousand dollars, no new bourgeoisie will emerge, because the basic means of production will still be state-owned or collectively owned — in other words, publicly owned. And if the country prospers and the people's material and cultural life continually improves, what's wrong with that? However much we open up in the next 16 years until the end of the century, the publicly owned sector of the economy will remain predominant. Even in a joint venture with foreigners, half is socialist-owned. And we shall take more than half of the earnings of joint ventures. So, don't be afraid. It is the country and the people who will benefit most from them, not the capitalists.

Selected Works of Deng Xiaoping, 3:97. Available online at <http://english.peopledaily.com.cn/dengxp/vol3/text/c1280.html> (February 16, 2003).

Talk with a Chinese University Professor
May 20, 1985

The mainland will maintain the socialist system and not turn off onto the wrong road, the road to capitalism. One of the features distinguishing socialism from capitalism is that socialism means common prosperity, not polarization of income. The wealth created belongs first to the state and second to the people; it is therefore impossible for a new bourgeoisie to emerge. The amount that goes to the state will be spent for the benefit of the people, a small portion being used to strengthen national defence and the rest to develop the economy, education and science and to raise the people's living standards and cultural level.

. . . [A]n ideological trend has appeared that we call bourgeois liberalization. Its exponents worship the "democracy" and "freedom" of the Western capitalist countries and reject socialism. . . . We must keep this evil trend in check. . . . Without ideals and a strong sense of discipline it would be impossible for China to adhere to the socialist system, to develop the socialist economy and to realize the modernization programme.

Selected Works of Deng Xiaoping, 3:129–30. Available online at <http://english.peopledaily.com.cn/dengxp/vol3/text/c1400.html> (February 16, 2003).

Remarks to Leading Members of the Party Central Committee
December 30, 1986

The struggle against bourgeois liberalization will last for at least 20 years. Democracy can develop only gradually, and we cannot copy Western systems. If we did, that would only make a mess of everything. Our socialist construction can only be carried out under leadership, in an orderly way and in an environment of stability and unity. That's why I place such emphasis on the need for high ideals and strict discipline. Bourgeois liberalization would plunge the country into turmoil once more. Bourgeois liberalization means rejection of the Party's leadership; there would be no centre around which to unite our one billion people, and the Party itself would lose all power to fight. A party like that would be no better than a mass organization; how could it be expected to lead the people in construction? . . .

The struggle against bourgeois liberalization is indispensable. We should not be afraid that people abroad will say we are damaging our reputation. We must take our own road and build a socialism adapted to conditions in China — that is the only way China can have a future. We must show foreigners that China's political situation is stable. If our country were plunged into disorder and our nation reduced to a heap of loose sand, how could we ever accomplish anything? The reason the imperialists were able to bully us in the past was precisely that we were a heap of loose sand.

Selected Works of Deng Xiaoping, 3:196–97. Available online at <http://english.peopledaily.com.cn/dengxp/vol3/text/c1630.html> (February 16, 2003).

8.11

Students Criticize the Communist Regime and Its Market Reforms

The strains inherent in the Deng reforms burst into the open in 1989. Economic growth was fueling inflation that hurt those on fixed income such as students and teachers. At the same time peasants and a new class of entrepreneurs were enjoying unprecedented prosperity. Corruption in the party was rife as members traded on their insider position to make money. The charges of misbehavior extended even to leaders' relatives, a serious blow to the prestige of a party long claiming selfless service to the people. Discontent began building on Beijing campuses in late April, setting in motion a public confrontation between the party and an array of urban critics.

Four student statements provide a flavor of views during the earliest phase of the protest in Beijing. To judge from these examples, what concerns prompted the protest? How much are these statements about democracy (the interpretive frame applied by most Western observers at the time) and how much about the problems associated with Deng's economic reform? How do the concerns of these Chinese youths compare to those of their European and North American counterparts from 1968 (see Documents 4.11 through 4.13)? Why would students on both these occasions have led the protests?

The following selections draw from Han Minzhu (pseudonym), ed., *Cries for Democracy: Writings and Speeches from the 1989 Chinese Democracy Movement* (Princeton: Princeton University Press, 1990). Explanatory footnotes supplied by Han Minzhu unless otherwise indicated.

A Student from Beijing Industrial University
Poster Placed in Tiananmen Square
Circa April 15–22, 1989

Comrade [Deng] Xiaoping, I'd like to know:

You realized early on that it doesn't matter if a cat is black or white; as long as it catches mice, it's a good cat. Doesn't it follow that insistence on distinguishing between "red" [politically correct] and "yellow" [liberal or bourgeois Western] thinking shows a lack of careful reflection?

Reform in the political arena is an absolute necessity. But if we hear only words and see no actions, how will there be any results? Cars and residences, I want them all — and a computer to boot; so how is it that your policy of "getting rich together" has turned out to be nothing but the same old empty promises? Democracy and freedom, the people want; how can you claim that we are too childish by this much or that much? . . . [S]o just what makes it so tough to clean up corruption in the Party?

Han, *Cries for Democracy,* 13–15.

Handbill at Beijing University
Circa April 15–23, 1989

Dear soldiers, please ask yourselves how come in these days of wild inflation, your food stipend remains at 1.65 yuan.[1] I suggest that you take a look at the profiteering going on among government officials!

What does it mean when people talk about "profiteering by government officials"? To describe it simply, it refers to officials using their power to acquire things such as goods at low state-fixed prices, import and export licences (or documents), loans, and foreign currency at special low exchange rates, so that they can reap huge profits. These officials do business in the name of their companies. These companies can be categorized into two kinds: those run by the government and those run by the sons and daughters of high-level cadres [officials].[2] . . .

. . . [L]et me tell you, our lord officials are no monks who have taken a vow of abstinence. Who cares that the people are suffering hardships, who cares

---

[1] Although in the early 1980s one yuan was sufficient to buy a modest meal of noodles or dumplings, or a plate of meat, by 1989 it barely bought a small snack.

[2] The Chinese term *ganbu,* or cadre, refers to all those who are state and Party officials, from low-level functionaries to the top leaders of the government and Party. Since the term *ganbu* does not carry the slightly pejorative meaning that "bureaucrat" has in English, it is generally translated here as "cadre" rather than "bureaucrat."

Han, *Cries for Democracy.* 28, 30–31.

that there are urgent telegrams from disaster areas? You show them cash, their heads go dizzy. . . .

Mind you, these profiteering officials are not nobodies. They have power and extraordinary IQs, and you name it, they know from A to Z the 1,001 ways to make a profit. . . .

Turning your head to one side, you hear people with hungry stomachs complaining, and turning it to the other, you see others squandering money without a second thought. And the general state of economic depression persists alongside the ever-expanding pockets of a few individuals. Why is China's foreign debt so immense? Why is China's economy such a mess? Why does the daily stipend of a soldier remain at 1.65 yuan after all these years, despite rocketing prices? Nowhere else can one find the answer to these questions except in the word "official." One official takes the lead, another follows, and very soon each official acts as a protective shield for another's crimes. . . . We want to build our country and we want to bring prosperity to the people, but allowing these corrupt officials to have their way will reduce all this to empty rhetoric. Trees must be chopped down when they are rotten, and parasites exterminated. . . .

Poster at People's University in Beijing
April 24, 1989

Only if we implement widespread democracy and more flexible economic policies will China have a way out. Democracy will check the hereditary system [that breeds corruption]; limited privatization will accelerate the development of the economy; freedom of speech and freedom of the press will provide effective supervision over the government; and equality will unite people into a greater force. But none of this will come to us: we must reach out and struggle for it.

Han, *Cries for Democracy*, 35.

Poster at Beijing Normal University
April 24, 1989

The privileged class, "officials of the people,"
    you live a life to make the immortals envious;
Opening up, reform — what good opportunities —
    if you don't make money now, then you never will.
Children of officials violate the law and run wild,
    but the law barely touches them.

Han, *Cries for Democracy*, 41–42.

Although their sons and daughters are idiots,
    they can still chose [sic] between [prestigious] Beijing and
        Qinghua universities.
These privileged accompany foreign guests, eating and drinking for
    free,
    And what's more, they receive a "subsidy" of hundreds of yuan.
Not bothering to separate official business from private affairs,
    they ride gratis in airplanes and cars.
Everyone has a "special purchasing card,"
    which buys them high-quality products at low prices.
Chartered planes and trains deliver gifts,
    delicacies from every land, fresh year round. . . .
The whole family happily resides in Zhongnanhai,[1]
    their palatial second homes and villas scattered from the
        mountains to the sea.
Luxurious gleaming buildings, clubs, and hotels —
    the people can only look and sigh!
Well-known and clandestine "pleasure nests" —
    ordinary folks cannot even approach them in their lifetime.
A cluster of "public servants" for private masters,
    cooks, doctors, bodyguards;
"Staff workers" line up in front and back,
    beautiful ladies, "courtesans," await them on both sides.
"Limited-distribution movies" with sex and violence,
    only within the palaces are they not prohibited. . . .
The mighty Mercedes Benz moves through the staring red traffic
    light.
Tourists and travelers are driven out from parks and beaches,
    only because some senior official has entered the park to play.
During their lives they enjoy to the hilt days of honor and glory,
    after death, they ascend to Babaoshan cemetery.[2]

---

[1] Compound reserved for the highest party leaders located in central Beijing. — M.H.
[2] Babaoshan cemetery in western Beijing is the burial place for China's top military and political leaders. — M.H.

8.12
Deng's Response to the Protests

Deng reacted hostilely to student-led protests, condemning them both privately and publicly in late April. They nonetheless intensified, spreading to other cities and attracting workers and other ordinary citizens. On May 13 in a dramatic act of defiance, students occupied Tiananmen Square in central Beijing and started a hunger strike. Deng briefly had his hands tied by a split within the party leadership over how to deal with this challenge but finally insisted on a hard line. On the night of June 4 he had troops clear the square and nearby streets. In the ensuing violence several hundred died.

Following these traumatic events, Deng appeared before senior officers charged with enforcing martial law in Beijing to offer a justification for the crackdown. How did Deng see the student challenge? What are the implications of his remarks for his earlier conception of economic reform? And what impact had the protest had on his plans for economic reform?

Remarks to Military Commanders
June 9, 1989

The nature of the incident should have been obvious from the very beginning. The handful of bad people had two basic slogans: overthrow the Communist Party and demolish the socialist system. Their goal was to establish a bourgeois republic, an out-and-out vassal of the West. Naturally, we accepted the people's demand for a fight against corruption. We even had to accept as well-intentioned the so-called anti-corruption slogans of the bad individuals. Of course, these slogans were simply pretexts, and their ultimate aim was to overthrow the Communist Party and demolish the socialist system. . . .

What about . . . keeping to the policies of reform and opening to the outside world? Is that wrong or not? It is not wrong. How could we have achieved the success we have today without the reform and the open policy? During the last ten years living standards have been raised considerably, or in other words, our economy has been raised to a new stage. Although there have been inflation and other problems, we must not underestimate our achievements in the past decade. Naturally, in the process of carrying out these policies many bad influences from the West are making themselves felt in China. We have never underestimated this trend. . . .

. . . [W]e must continue to combine economic planning with regulation by market forces. . . . The combination of planning and market regulation will be continued. The important thing is that we must never turn China back into a country that keeps its doors closed. A closed-door policy would be greatly to our disadvantage; we would not even have quick access to information. People say that information is important, right? It certainly is. If an administrator has no access to information, it's as if he was purblind and hard of hearing and had a stuffed nose. And on no account must we go back to the old practice of keeping the economy under rigid control.

Selected Works of Deng Xiaoping, 3:295, 298. Available online at <http://english.peopledaily.com.cn/dengxp/vol3/text/c1990.html> (February 16, 2003).

8.13
Peasants Approve of Market Reforms and Stability

With all eyes fixed on urban protest, it was easy to lose sight of the views of the half of the population living in the countryside. *New York Times* reporter Nicholas Kristof (who produced prize-winning dispatches during 1989) sought to remedy the oversight by going on a five-day tour to Gansu, a remote and relatively poor province to gauge reaction there to the student demonstrations and the government crackdown.

    Journalism of the sort that follows can serve as a primary source. It is especially valuable if the reporter knows the country and speaks the language. How much did the peasants interviewed here know about the student protest and the government repression? Did they accept the concerns and goals of the protesters? What is the peasants' verdict on Deng's economic reforms?

Nicholas D. Kristof
Report from the Countryside
November 14, 1989

Xincheng, China — With the indulgent air of someone who missed a trivia question, but doesn't much care, Li Huifang cheerfully admitted that she could not remember the names of China's leaders. . . .

    Two local party officials, responsible for ideology in the area, flinched and shuffled their feet in the background as Miss Li laughingly dismissed such matters and turned to what she regarded as the important matter at hand: Should she buy a refrigerator, or should she save the money for her children's weddings?

    "What I'm concerned about is a good crop, not politics," said Miss Li, a 43-year-old mother of four, whose face and hands are etched with the creases that come from a lifetime of toil in this village set in the dry moonscape of Gansu Province, in the north-central part of China. "My job is cooking and caring for the children and seeing that they get married. I just don't care about politics." . . .

    "What we care about is getting rich quickly," said Sheng Jinling, a 27-year-old farmer who was leading a donkey cart near Jiayuguan village, not far from the western end of the Great Wall. "I want a good grain harvest, and I want stability in the country and continuation of the open-door policies. If I can just get rich, I want to buy absolutely everything — especially a motorcycle."

    Mr. Sheng's comments about getting rich and about stability were echoed frequently. While in the large cities many intellectuals and workers seethed with indignation at corruption and described in interviews their yearning for

Nicholas D. Kristof, "Xincheng Journal: Far From Beijing, Good Life Is Goal," *New York Times,* November 14, 1989, p. 4.

a more democratic life, the attitude in these villages was both more content-ment and more indifference to the upheavals in Beijing. . . .

. . . Xing Yisheng, a 74-year-old man with a wispy beard, had no idea who China's leaders were, but he spoke with animation about the generation gap these days.

"Last year, this young man wanted to buy a stereo cassette player for 700 yuan," or about $190, Mr. Xing said, gesturing indignantly toward his grown son in another chair in their living room. "I said no, that's too much. We should buy a mule. A mule can work. It's useful. A stereo isn't. And a mule is so big, while a stereo is so small."

Mr. Xing recalled that before the 1949 Communist revolution he was a landless peasant, mired in poverty. In the 1940's, he survived only by selling two of his sons for a total of 880 pounds of wheat.

"I say, 'Young man, you're now living in heaven!'" Mr. Xing said, gazing sternly at his other son, born after his brothers were sold. The son hung his head, but paid little heed. Not only did he buy the stereo, but he is now dreaming of a motorcycle as well.

CHAPTER 9

DIVERGENT PATHS
IN THE THIRD WORLD

FROM THE 1970s ONWARD, radical notions of transformation lost their appeal in the third world, and the sense of shared history and common problems, so important earlier in the outlook of third-world leaders, began to fade. Indeed, so diverse were the conditions in the third world that the notion of a shared outlook or condition lost meaning. A few remnants of the socialist dream survived in Cuba or flared in Cambodia, but China's turning from Mao to the market reflected the broader trend at the end of the twentieth century.

That trend was shaped by three fresh forces operating in what might now be better called the developing world. One was an Islamic ideological fervor, pronounced in the Middle East but also evident from Morocco all the way to the Philippines. Iran proved dramatically that Mohammed could inspire revolutionary change as well as Marx or Mao. Another force was an upsurge in resistance by indigenous peoples dispossessed by outsiders (a condition known as settler colonialism). Intractable cultural differences, usually aggravated by mutually exclusive claims to land, caused prolonged civil violence in places as different as Guatemala, Palestine, and South Africa. Finally, the dwindling appeal of socialism left the international market economy the default option for most developing countries. For some, such as China (treated in chapter 8), a market strategy proved a good gamble, while for others the results fell short.

THE IRANIAN REVOLUTION

The history of Iran until the 1970s provided ample evidence for an irreversible secular and Westernizing process. Reza Khan, an ambitious military man who maneuvered his way to national power, was the pivotal figure in this process. In 1926 he founded the new Pahlevi dynasty and began centralizing power and pushing socioeconomic change. His son, Mohammed Reza, commonly known as the shah, followed suit once his throne was secure in the early 1950s. Thanks to a quickening stream of oil revenue, the shah pressed to create industry, spread literacy, promote higher education, impose land reform, and establish Iran as a regional power. Like his father, he moved to reduce the influence of the Islamic clergy and Islamic law.

Then to the surprise of many, a broad coalition led by Islamists challenged the shah's grip on power in the 1970s. The reasons for the coalition's ultimate triumph bears close examination. The following documents capture the concerns of the shah and the leader of the opposition, Ayatollah Ruhollah Khomeini, as well as some of the ordinary people caught up in the revolution and should provide some insights into a revolution that bears little resemblance to those considered earlier in this volume.

9.1

Mohammed Reza Shah Pahlevi Reflects
on the Problems of His Regime

Mohammed Reza Shah Pahlevi came to power in 1941 after the Soviets and the British had sent his father into exile for his pro-German views. For the following decade the son struggled to maintain control, and in the early 1950s he confronted a nationalist coalition led by Mohammed Mossadeq that wanted to curb the court's power and nationalize the British company monopolizing the country's oil. An alarmed Eisenhower administration threw its support behind the British, and in 1953 a CIA-orchestrated coup restored the shah to power. Now with U.S. backing, he established strongman rule and used rising oil revenues to industrialize and build up his military. As the 1970s began, his hold on power at home and his influence in the region seemed beyond question.

The entries that follow reveal the shah's thinking during the closing years of his rule. They come from a daily, detailed diary kept by Asadollah Alam, a close and loyal adviser to the shah. Descended from an aristocratic family, Alam had supported the young shah in the 1940s and went on to serve him in a variety of capacities including prime minister between 1962 and 1964 and minister of court and the shah's confidant from 1966 until 1977 (the year before Alam's death). In almost daily meetings they discussed family matters and affairs of the heart as well as politics. Once Alam had filled a diary volume with impressions derived from these contacts, he would send it away for safekeeping in a Swiss bank vault. Following the revolution, the family agreed to publish portions of the diary. What do these entries reveal about the shah's perceptions of domestic problems and international relations? What do they tell us about his regime's vulnerability to a revolutionary challenge? In what ways might the diary be suspect as evidence of the shah's state of mind?

Asadollah Alam
The Confidential Diary of the Minister of Court
1970–1977

APRIL 19, 1972

"Your Majesty is always saying that he wishes to be ahead of events," I said, "why not then implement change before change is forced upon us?" "But what more do you expect me to do?," he replied; "No one could have accomplished more than us." He then went on to say that he has discovered the root cause of discontent amongst the younger generation; the disparity between their wages and those of men already in established positions. I suggested that this is only one of several factors at work. If people could be persuaded that they are working to achieve some basic goal, a goal respected by the ruling class, they would be prepared to put up with any amount of deprivation, even real hunger. "But what principles do you suggest we put to the nation?," asked HIM [His Imperial Majesty]. I replied that the public must feel that they are more than mere spectators of the political game. We must prepare the ground for their greater integration into this game; only then will they be satisfied and learn to play by the rules. HIM totally lost track of what I was saying, since he objected: "But we lack the equipment; our department of physical education hasn't enough sports fields, trainers or even simple cash." I explained that this wasn't exactly what I had in mind; that I was talking about popular participation in the game of politics. For example, why does the government continue to meddle in local elections? Leave the public to fight their own political contests and to choose whatever local representatives they prefer. Parliamentary elections may still require a degree of management, but surely this is untrue of elections in the municipalities. Why not allow the people free discussion of their local cares and concerns? What harm could it possibly do? "What are you talking about; of course it would be harmful," he declared, "they'd begin moaning about inflation, or some such rot." "Sadly," I replied, "what they say about inflation is all too true. But even assuming it to be nonsense, why not open the safety valve and allow them to talk nonsense, freely, amongst themselves?" "Precisely the reason I've allowed the opposition party to continue in existence," he replied. "Yes," I said, "but an opposition deprived of free discussion is surely no opposition at all?" At this point he asked [me] why the people pay so little attention to the progress we have made. "Because" I told him, "our propaganda is applied in quite the wrong directions. So much of our self-advertisement is patently untrue, and for the rest it's so mixed up with adulation of Your Majesty's own person that the public grows tired of it. . . ."

Asadollah Alam, *The Shah and I: The Confidential Diary of Iran's Royal Court, 1969–1977*, ed. Alinaghi Alikhani and trans. Alikhani and Nicholas Vincent (New York: St. Martin's Press, 1992), 210–11, 323, 341, 360, 544.

OCTOBER 7, 1973

Referring to a recent broadcast on the BBC [British Broadcasting Corporation], he [the shah] declared, "The bastards have the audacity to state that the chances of a revolution in Iran have receded, since our army will be able to crush any rising, now that we've purchased so many new weapons. What the hell do they mean 'the chances of a revolution'? Our farmers and workers are far too happy ever to contemplate becoming revolutionaries." In the same way, he's outraged by an article in the [London] *Financial Times,* describing the problems we face with inflation.

DECEMBER 9, 1973

[The shah] is extremely anxious about student unrest which has now infected every campus save the Pahlavi University at Shiraz. "Mark my words, Moscow is behind it all," he said. I replied that this might be so, but that we should bear in mind that they would have to be sowing fertile ground if their success is to be explained. For my own part, I'm convinced that the university authorities have made the mistake of refusing any sort of dialogue with the students. The same goes for the country at large; our government behaves like the conqueror of a vanquished land. As I said to HIM, for all his achievements and his tireless endeavour, there's a growing sense of alienation between regime and people. "I'm afraid you're right," he replied. "I've sensed the same thing myself. Something must be done."

MARCH 22–APRIL 3, 1974

I remarked to him [the shah] that every one of his dreams seems to have come true. It's almost unbelievable, but our oil income has rocketed from $2 billion to $16 billion; heavy rainfall suggests a bumper harvest, and HIM is now unrivalled amongst Middle Eastern statesmen. "But I have so many more aspirations," he replied. "To be first in the Middle East is not enough. We must raise ourselves to the level of a great world power. Such a goal is by no means unattainable."

MAY 21, 1977

Much to HIM's disgust the new US ambassador, William Sullivan, has issued a statement to Congress, referring to the existence of religious opposition groups here in Iran . . . "Doesn't he realize these people are Islamic Marxists, mere Soviet puppets," HIM said. I replied that, whilst various of them may well be manipulated by the Soviets, or for that matter by Washington, there are others who act solely out of ignorant fanaticism . . . HIM remarked that he had no objection to girls wearing scarves at school or university; "But veils are out of the question . . . Tell my private secretariat to inform the government accordingly."

9.2
Ayatollah Ruhollah Khomeini's Islamic Challenge

The author of the stunningly successful revolution against the shah was an obscure Islamic cleric, the Ayatollah Ruhollah Khomeini. In 1963, the sixty-one-year-old-Khomeini chastised the shah publicly, setting in motion a contest between two seemingly ill-matched political forces. Exiled in 1965, Khomeini exploited the simmering discontent within Iran, using his own considerable charisma as well as an effective network of clerical supporters. Anti-regime demonstrations grew in force during 1978 and finally drove a demoralized and isolated shah into his own exile in January 1979. Khomeini returned home the next month. From his leading position within the revolutionary coalition, he would go on to purge secular allies, create an Islamic Republic at home, and confront the United States and Iraq.

Khomeini differs so dramatically from the third-world leaders discussed earlier in this volume that it is difficult to know how to label him. Fundamentalist, patriot, revolutionary, populist, and nationalist are only some of the more obvious choices. In searching for the most appropriate label, consider Khomeini's appeals in the statements and sermons that follow. Do you see elements of continuity in these appeals? Is there any shift in content or tone between the first challenges of the mid-1960s and the moment of triumph in 1979–80? In exploring the views of the shah's chief antagonist, we have nothing like the Alam diary to turn to. We have to use instead public statements and imagine ourselves in the place of one of the faithful listening to Khomeini delivering a sermon, a theological student in a seminary taking notes as Khomeini lectures, or one of the urban poor hearing Khomeini on an audiotape smuggled into the country. Which concerns and themes would you guess had the greatest appeal to his audience? How might the public nature of these statements skew our understanding of Khomeini?

Sermons and Writings
1963-1980

SERMON DELIVERED IN QUM, IRAN, JUNE 3, 1963

Iranian nation! Those among you who are thirty or forty years of age or more will remember how three foreign countries attacked us during World War II. The Soviet Union, Britain, and America invaded Iran and occupied our country. The property of the people was exposed to danger and their honor was imperilled. But God knows, everyone was happy because the Pahlavi had gone![1]

Shah, I don't wish the same to happen to you; I don't want you to become like your father. Listen to my advice, listen to the *'ulama* [learned clergy] of Islam. They desire the welfare of the nation, the welfare of the country. Don't listen to Israel; Israel can't do anything for you. You miserable wretch, forty-

---

[1] A reference to the 1941 abdication of the shah's father on the demand of Britain and the Soviet Union.

Hamid Algar, ed. and trans., *Islam and Revolution: Writings and Declarations of Imam Khomeini* (Berkeley: Mizan Press, 1981), 29–30, 115, 120, 126–27, 132, 178–79, 181–82, 185, 240, 286–87, 303, 305.

five years of your life have passed; isn't it time for you to think and reflect a little, to ponder about where all this is leading you, to learn a lesson from the experience of your father? If what they say is true, that you are opposed to Islam and the religious scholars, your ideas are quite wrong. If they are dictating these things to you and then giving them to you to read, you should think about it a little. Why do you speak without thinking? Are the religious scholars really some form of impure animal? If they are impure animals, why do the people kiss their hands? Why do they regard the very water they drink as blessed? Are we really impure animals?

SERMON DELIVERED IN QUM, IRAN, OCTOBER 27, 1964

A law has been put before the Majlis [parliament] . . . that all American military advisers, together with their families, technical and administrative officials, and servants — in short, anyone in any way connected to them — are to enjoy legal immunity with respect to any crime they may commit in Iran.

If some American's servant, some American's cook, assassinates your *marja'*[2] in the middle of the bazaar, or runs over him, the Iranian police do not have the right to apprehend him! Iranian courts do not have the right to judge him! The dossier must be sent to America, so that our masters there can decide what is to be done!

. . . If someone runs over a dog belonging to an American, he will be prosecuted. Even if the Shah himself were to run over a dog belonging to an American, he would be prosecuted. But if an American cook runs over the Shah, the head of state, no one will have the right to interfere with him.

. . . The government has sold our independence, reduced us to the level of a colony, and made the Muslim nation of Iran appear more backward than savages in the eyes of the world! . . .

I don't know where this White Revolution[3] is that they are making so much fuss about. God knows that I am aware of (and my awareness causes me pain) the remote villages and provincial towns, not to mention our own backward city of Qum. I am aware of the hunger of our people and the disordered state of our agrarian economy. Why not try to do something for this country, for this population, instead of piling up debts and enslaving yourselves?

LECTURES DELIVERED TO SEMINARY STUDENTS,
NAJAF, IRAQ, JANUARY–FEBRUARY 1970[4]

At a time when the West was a realm of darkness and obscurity — with its inhabitants living in a state of barbarism and America still peopled by half-savage redskins — and the two vast empires of Iran and Byzantium were un-

---

[2]A scholar of proven learning and piety whose rulings are authoritative in matters of religious practice.

[3]A broad-gauge government program to modernize Iran. It included prominently the promotion of industry, the liberation of women, the advancement of higher education as well as basi=c literacy, the implementation of land reform, and the establishment of civil law in place of Islamic law.

[4]A student recorded these lectures, subsequently published as a book titled *Islamic Government*.

der the rule of tyranny, class privilege, and discrimination, and the powerful dominated all without any trace of law or popular government, God, Exalted and Almighty, by means of the Most Noble Messenger [the prophet Mohammed] (peace and blessings be upon him), sent laws that astound us with their magnitude. He instituted laws and practices for all human affairs and laid down injunctions for man extending from even before the embryo is formed until after he is placed in the tomb. In just the same way that there are laws setting forth the duties of worship for man, so too there are laws, practices, and norms for the affairs of society and government. Islamic law is a progressive, evolving, and comprehensive system of law. . . .

. . . Huge amounts of capital are being swallowed up; our public funds are being embezzled; our oil is being plundered; and our country is being turned into a market for expensive, unnecessary goods by the representatives of foreign companies, which makes it possible for foreign capitalists and their local agents to pocket the people's money. A number of foreign states carry off our oil after drawing it out of the ground, and the negligible sum they pay to the regime they have installed returns to their pockets by other routes. As for the small amount that goes into the treasury, God only knows what it is spent on. . . .

Our wretched people subsist in conditions of poverty and hunger, while the taxes that the ruling class extorts from them are squandered. They buy Phantom jets so that pilots from Israel and its agents can come and train in them in our country . . . — Israel, which is in a state of war with the Muslims . . . .

. . . It is our duty to begin exerting ourselves now in order to establish a truly Islamic government. We must propagate our cause to the people, instruct them in it, and convince them of its validity. We must generate a wave of intellectual awakening, to emerge as a current throughout society, and gradually, to take shape as an organized Islamic movement made up of the awakened, committed, and religious masses who will rise up and establish an Islamic government. . . .

. . . So, courageous sons of Islam, stand up! Address the people bravely; tell the truth about our situation to the masses in simple language; arouse them to enthusiastic activity, and turn the people in the street and the bazaar, our simple-hearted workers and peasants, and our alert students into dedicated *mujahids* [those engaged in jihad or holy struggle]. The entire population will become *mujahids*. All segments of society are ready to struggle for the sake of freedom, independence, and the happiness of the nation, and their struggle needs religion. Give the people Islam, then, for Islam is the school of *jihad,* the religion of struggle; let them amend their characters and beliefs in accordance with Islam and transform themselves into a powerful force, so that they may overthrow the tyrannical regime imperialism has imposed on us and set up an Islamic government.

DECLARATION ON THE ANTI-SHAH DEMONSTRATIONS,
ISSUED IN PARIS, OCTOBER 11, 1978

Great people of Iran! The history of Iran, even world history, has never witnessed a movement like yours; it has never experienced a universal uprising like yours, noble people!

Today primary school children of seven or eight stand ready to sacrifice themselves and shed their blood for the sake of Islam and the nation; when has anything like that been seen? Our lion-hearted women snatch up their infants and go to confront the machine guns and tanks of the regime; where in history has such valiant and heroic behavior by women been recorded? Today the thunderous cry of "Death to the Shah!" arises from the heart of the primary school child and the infirm old man alike, and it has blackened the days of this vile Pahlavi regime and so shattered the nerves of the Shah that he seeks to calm himself with the blood of our children and young people.

Beloved sisters and brothers! Be steadfast; do not weaken or slacken your efforts. Your path is the path of God and His elect. Your blood is being shed for the same cause as the blood of the prophets and the Imams [recognized religious leaders] and the righteous. You will join them, and you have no cause to grieve, therefore, but every reason for joy.

MESSAGE ON OCCASION OF THE IRANIAN NEW YEAR,
TEHRAN, MARCH 21, 1980

We must strive to export our Revolution throughout the world, and must abandon all idea of not doing so, for not only does Islam refuse to recognize any difference between Muslim countries, it is the champion of all oppressed people. Moreover, all the powers are intent on destroying us, and if we remain surrounded in a closed circle, we shall certainly be defeated. We must make plain our stance toward the powers and the superpowers and demonstrate to them that despite the arduous problems that burden us, our attitude to the world is dictated by our beliefs. . . .

Once again, I declare my support for all movements and groups that are fighting to gain liberation from the superpowers of the left and the right. I declare my support for the people of [Israeli] Occupied Palestine and Lebanon. I vehemently condemn once more the savage occupation of Afghanistan by the aggressive plunderers of the East [the Soviet Union], and I hope that the noble Muslim people of Afghanistan will achieve victory and true independence as soon as possible, and be delivered from the clutches of the so-called champions of the working class.

MESSAGE TO PILGRIMS, ISSUED IN TEHRAN, SEPTEMBER 12, 1980

Part of the extensive propaganda campaign being waged apparently against Iran, but in reality against Islam, is intended to show that the Revolution of Iran cannot administer our country or that the Iranian government is about to fall . . . . But by the blessing of Islam and our Muslim people, in the space of less than two years, we have voted on, approved, and put into practice all the measures necessary for the administration of the country. Despite all the difficulties that America and its satellites have created for us — economic boycott, military attack, and the planning of extensive coups d'etat — our valiant people have attained self-sufficiency in foodstuffs. Soon we will transform the imperialist-inspired education system that existed under the previous regime into an independent and Islamic education system. The armed forces, the Revolutionary Guards, the gendarmerie, and the police stand ready to defend the country and uphold order, and they are prepared to offer their lives in *jihad* for the sake of Islam. In addition, a general mobilization of the entire nation is under way, with the nation equipping itself to fight for the sake of Islam and the country. Let our enemies know that no revolution in the world was followed by less bloodshed or brought greater achievements than our Islamic Revolution, and that this is due entirely to the blessing of Islam. . . .

America is the number-one enemy of the deprived and oppressed people of the world. There is no crime America will not commit in order to maintain its political, economic, cultural, and military domination of those parts of the world where it predominates. . . .

Iran has tried to sever all its relations with this Great Satan and it is for this reason that it now finds wars imposed upon it. America has urged Iraq to spill the blood of our young men [in border clashes that preceded the Iran-Iraq war, 1980–1988], and it has compelled the countries that are subject to its influence to boycott us economically in the hope of defeating us. . . . This is a result of the Islamic content of our Revolution, which has been established on the basis of true independence. Were we to compromise with America and the other superpowers, we would not suffer these misfortunes. But our nation is no longer ready to submit to humiliation and abjection; it prefers a bloody death to a life of shame.

9.3

The Villagers of Deh Koh Come to Terms with the Islamic Revolution

A revolutionary upheaval has many facets. We can read the statements of the leaders and imagine the shocked reaction of foreign observers. Perhaps the facet most difficult to grasp is revolution's impact on ordinary people. Thanks to the account of a German-born, U.S.-based anthropologist, we have a picture of the Iranian revolution from the bottom up. Erika Freidl spent five years during the 1970s and 1980s living among the two thousand villagers of Deh Koh (literally "mountain village," an invented name). It is a six-hour drive to this uplands village from the closest city, Shiraz. Freidl writes from the perspective of five village women whose pseudonyms (Aftab, Begom, Maryam, Hakime, and Gouhar) hide their real identity.

How do these women react to the anti-shah protests in late 1978, the arrival of revolutionary activists in the village, and the war with Iraq that began in September 1980? How much of their reaction is shaped by village insularity and suspicion of outsiders? As with the earlier anthropological account, *Village in the Vaucluse*, we need to ask how the anthropologist-observer might bias our understanding. That Freidl had to limit intimate contact to women creates one kind of bias. How might the perceptions of men in the village have differed from those presented here? Does Freidl interpret so much for us that we in fact cannot regard this as a primary source? If so, how do we gain direct access to the views of villagers such as these?

Erika Friedl
From *Women of Deh Koh*
1989

[I]n early fall [1978], the rumblings of the revolution started to roll over the village, and Aftab got a most exciting spectacle. For a long time, rumors had been going around in the village about secret service agents. Aftab was not quite sure what the secret service meant, except that it was bad and that Tamas's son Rahmat and a few other schoolboys kept saying that once the Shah and his secret police and his thieving servants were gone, everybody in Iran would get seventy Toman [about ten dollars] a day forever. Like all her neighbors, including Rahmat's own mother, Aftab wisely reserved judgment about this. Begom even told the lad that as long as she had her lentils (which she was washing at the time) she would be content, and he could, with all due respect, feed his seventy Toman to his donkey. But then the news spread that a teacher in Deh Rud had been accused of being a secret service informer and then was beaten up and dragged away, thrown into prison, or maybe even killed, who was to know, and people everywhere put their heads together, whispering. A few days later five or six bearded young men in blue jeans and green jackets came storming up the lane, shouting something about the glories of the revolution and the destruction of the country's enemies; they burst through the Haji's wooden gate, and a great tumult arose in the courtyard. Aftab left her cradle and the tray with rice she was just cleaning and flew down her steep stairs and across the lane and the water channel to be where the action was.

The open gate was clogged with people. Inside there was shouting and banging about, topped by the Haji's staccato shouts and [his wife] Gouhar's shrill wailing. People appeared on rooftops, in the lane, in doorways. Aftab was pushed back out into the lane by a dense pack of human bodies squeezing a struggling and flailing Haji through the gate. His hat was gone, his face scratched, his pyjama-pants torn. "It's a lie, all lies!" he shouted. Gouhar, in the rear, was thrashing around with a broomstick, and the Haji's daughter was screeching and throwing things at the young men. On the Haji's bridge, right outside the door, the struggle intensified; the pushing and shoving mass swayed and teetered, lost its collective balance, and stumbled into the shallow, muddy bed of the water channel. Aftab got a close view of the rumpled, mud-smeared Haji clambering to his feet and of Gouhar swinging a copper toilet can by its spout onto some broad padded shoulders at her feet. The Haji's son was pelting the group with rocks from the roof. As the men were climbing out of the slimy channel, the flabbergasted spectators retreated behind the safety of their own walls. The dense group slowly moved down the lane in a cloud of dust

Erika Friedl, *Women of Deh Koh: Lives in an Iranian Village* (New York: Penguin, 1991), 69–71, 73, 77–78. First published as *The Women of Deh Koh: Stories from Iran* (Washington, D.C.: Smithsonian Institution Press, 1989).

and noise, followed at a safe distance by the Haji's son hurling rocks. Gouhar collapsed on Aftab's shoulder. "He isn't a secret service agent, it is a lie," she wailed. When the dark cluster with the hapless Haji was out of sight, the women reappeared. Aftab led Gouhar back into her house, followed by the neighbors, who talked, consoled, and tried to get the story. So it was true that the Haji was a paid agent? So that was how he got rich? But what in the world did he report on — how many sheep Akbar had, maybe? How much bread Maryam ate? How often Tamas and Hakime fought? Who had debts? (A lot to report on that topic, Hakime said.) Or who still used the barn as an outhouse although the doctor and the Shah had forbidden it? Gleefully they winked at each other....

As had been the custom until then, Gouhar went to the gendarmerie to complain about her husband's abduction. She even took a gold coin with her, a very small one, to give her claim more persuasive force if need be.... The gendarme at the gate turned Gouhar away, saying that these matters were none of their business and that she should go elsewhere to complain, to town or to the prison or to the governor. Gouhar went to her brothers for help, but none of them was eager to get involved in what was clearly a touchy situation in most opaque circumstances. They all told her to wait a few days. Sure enough, after three days the Haji came home as a passenger on his own minibus, dirty and unshaven, with a bare head and black smudges under his eyes. Shoulders bent and limping slightly, he hurried up the lane accompanied by stares and whispers. Fortunately for his pride, he met no men, only a few boys he could as easily ignore as the nosy women....

...Things were becoming scarcer and more expensive month after month. "It is because of the war [with Iraq]," said the people, echoing the radio and television. They sighed and grumbled although the mullahs in their television sermons told them that the Islamic Revolution was not meant to make more watermelons but to spread the true faith. Aftab, who did not own a watermelon patch or a television set, did not feel her faith becoming any truer than before. Like Begom, and Maryam, and Hakime, and Gouhar, she said so, only a little more often and louder, until one day, when she and a few other neighbors were talking around the water faucet, Rahmat happened to come their way. Young as he was, he had become a revolutionary guard, sporting an unshaven look and a gun, much to his father's bewilderment and his mother's misgivings. Although usually he never as much as looked at any of the women when passing through the lane, today he stopped in front of Aftab and, steadfastly looking sideways and far over Aftab's head (she was much shorter than he), addressed her with visible embarrassment. "Sister," he said hurriedly, "with your talk you show great ignorance of the important matters of the revolution. You should come to the sermons, you should better yourself." So he said and disappeared. The women were stunned for a few moments.

"Impudent ass," someone in the group said after him, and Aftab, recovered, even shouted an obscenity. But Maryam hissed, "Shut up," and Gouhar shook her head at Aftab and motioned silence. From then on Aftab, like the other women, looked over her shoulder before she gave her opinion out in the open.

Slowly a new order was creeping into the village. Some women changed the cap and light scarf of the traditional costume for a heavy headscarf pulled way down over the forehead. Whoever needed a new veil-wrap made sure it was of dark fabric. The village was swarming with strangers now: revolutionary guards coming and going, mullahs, Afghani refugees working for cheap wages for a local contractor, a few families from the south displaced by the war, local men returning from the cities after many years because of lack of work there. Self-respecting women wrapped themselves tightly in their long veils when they had to be outside or else stayed home. . . .

Despite the many rumors and promises by revolutionary sympathizers, the poor in the village had not gotten any richer since the revolution, nor had teachers or other government employees. Everybody was urged constantly to work hard, to be patient, to pray, to donate money to the war chest, to help the soldiers, to volunteer for front service (if a man) and to rejoice over the martyred (if a woman). Everybody was in debt. But while the war and the difficult economic conditions put a heavy burden on the have-nots, it was generally felt that the rich — the merchants, those with access to capital and to the black market, those who managed in a thousand ways to profit from the wants and needs of the poor now as before, those who could buy their way through this world and, people like Begom suspected, into heaven as well — did not suffer at all. A feeling of prevailing injustice and resentment was growing everywhere. Speeches and homilies extolled the virtues of poverty and chastised greed and avarice. In the cities, in exemplary fashion, many of the houses of old wealth were destroyed by revolutionary guards, valuables confiscated, owners killed as enemies of the state. The old moneyed elite fled, and those who stayed behind took on a crumpled, unshaven demeanor and kept a very low profile while trying to send abroad as many of their assets as possible.

The Haji, well connected in the city, became rather nervous at this news. He was a good Muslim . . . , but he did have to bear the stigma of being a former agent and he was, by local standards at least, a rich man. What prevented one of the revolutionary hotheads, one of the misguided robbers, to close in on him again and loot his house and destroy his wealth, which, small as it was, he had scratched together by the efforts of his own hands and his own head over decades with the help of God? To Gouhar with whom he discussed his fears, the issue was just as burning: a good deal of the Haji's assets was in gold coins, and, gratifying for her, in the form of her jewelry. Both, she knew, were much more vulnerable to theft or looting or confiscation than shares in sheep or houses or a tractor. Finding a safe hiding place for their treasure became a concern of great moment. To safeguard the money outside their house was next to impossible, they realized. Her people, Gouhar knew, either would refuse the thankless burden of guarding her gold with a thousand polite reasons and excuses, or, if pressed, would expect a very heavy cut which the Haji, even if he promised it in the clutches of pressing necessity, would hotly contend later. The Haji himself had no trustworthy relative close by. His only kinsman, Nur Ahmad, a distant nephew, was his most successful and bitter competitor, not an ally. There were no faithful servants, no beholden retainers. Times had changed: everybody was on his own now, even the rich, and one had to pay dearly for help and loyalty.

GUATEMALA'S BRUTAL CIVIL WAR

Civil violence convulsed Guatemala through the 1970s and 1980s. The conflict began in earnest in 1972 when the leading insurgent group, the Guerrilla Army of the Poor, crossed from Mexico into Guatemala demanding reform of a society marked by gross inequalities and discrimination against the indigenous Mayan people (roughly half the population). Several other armed groups and labor organizations joined the challenge to a repressive government dominated by the national army and affluent families of European descent (mostly Spanish hence the name given them, Ladino). Government forces struck back in a campaign of repression directed at anyone suspected of subversion. In the mid-1980s with the country in deadlock, the military government yielded power to an elected civilian president, who in 1991 began negotiations to end the conflict. In 1996 the parties on both sides agreed to free elections, social reforms, and guarantees for Mayan autonomy and respect.

Two themes shed light on this destructive time. One is the ethnic and class identities that polarized Guatemala's two peoples, with the majority of poor and landless Maya in contrast to a small number of Ladino rich. Ladinos had seized most of the land as part of the Spanish conquest in the sixteenth century, and over the following three hundred years they extended their control and either marginalized the native Mayan population or integrated it into plantation agriculture. The second theme is the brutality of the instruments of political repression that the small but powerful Ladino elite employed to protect their privileged position against popular demands for reform, increasingly insistent since the mid-1940s. In the conflict of the 1970s and 1980s some 90 percent of 200,000 wrongful deaths was the work of government or pro-government right-wing forces.

9.4

Mayan Women Reflect on Poverty and Cultural Autonomy

The Maya survived the Spanish conquest and Ladino domination as multiple communities. They are divided by dialect and by their degree of integration into the Ladino-dominated world of commercial agriculture and urban life. The three oral histories that follow reflect this diversity. The first interviewee, Margarita, tells of her time on the plantations (*fincas*) that grew export crops such as coffee and cotton. When interviewed, she was thirty years old, single, and employed in Guatemala City as a live-in servant. She was still returning once a month to her village several hours west of Guatemala City. The second interviewee, also named Margarita (hence Margarita II) and also from an area immediately west of Guatemala City, was twenty-four years old when she described her life as a domestic. The third account comes from Victoria, a twenty-seven-year-old primary school teacher from an area just north of Guatemala City. She articulates the view of those Maya fighting to preserve their community's values and customs against the pressures to assimilate into the dominant Ladino world. At the time of the interview she was living with her husband (also Maya) in cramped quarters in a squatter settlement on the outskirts of Guatemala City. She insisted on being interviewed outdoors so that no one could overhear her.

What kinds of identities define these three women? How do they handle the tension between a commitment (sometimes militant) to their native community and culture, and the lure of individualism and a better (read Westernized) life that would make them more Ladino and less Maya? How do the views expressed here help us understand the sources of Guatemala's social and political conflict?

Margaret Hooks
From *Guatemalan Women Speak*
1991

MARGARITA RECALLS HER YOUTH WORKING ON THE *FINCA*

I went for three months towards the end of every year — to pick coffee if possible, if not, to clear the fields after the other pickers. We had to get up at three o'clock in the morning to make breakfast and walk the long way to the coffee fields, arriving by seven o'clock in the morning. We had to get there early in order to finish the work by one o'clock, when it's getting too hot to do anything.

At two o'clock they would sound the loudspeaker so that we would leave the fields and get what we had cut weighed. We had to carry the bags of coffee on our backs. The strongest men carried 100 pounds, and so did the women who had the strength. I could only carry 60 pounds.

There were always long queues at the place where they weighed the coffee. If a woman was with her husband or brothers, then the men would wait to do the weighing and the women could go on ahead to prepare something to eat. But if she didn't have anyone to help her, then she would have to wait too, even though she would sometimes have to go back after dark. This is one of the problems of single women working on a *finca*. It's frightening walking around after dark. If you have other women friends you can make an arrangement with them and all go together. But if you have no friends or family you feel very alone.

We were all housed together in long sheds — there's no privacy. About 40 to 50 people, sleeping in groups. One night I woke up at about midnight and felt a man on top of me. I hit him hard and screamed but none of the other people helped me. I had to take care of myself.

Margaret Hooks, *Guatemalan Women Speak* (London: Catholic Institute for International Relations, 1991), 3–4, 43–46, 49–52.

When you get back to the sheds in the evening you have to wash your clothes and go for the *tortillas*. The only thing they gave us to eat was *tortillas* and beans. Sixteen *tortillas* a day: eight in the morning and eight in the evening.

In one *finca* where I picked coffee there was no running water so they kept the water in drums that had been used to store petrol, and then they used this water to make our *tortillas*. We had to eat *tortillas* that tasted of petrol. It was awful, but we were hungry. There was no water anywhere there, no rivers, no drinking water; only a trickle in a gully but it smelt of skunk. We had to get right into the gully to collect it, and the smell of skunk, ugh!

On Sundays we had a day off. We were given a small advance on our wages to buy potatoes or a bit of meat and then we prepared our own meals. You get so tired of beans, beans, beans. So on Sundays you make stew, even though it's a very long walk to the butchers.

The one thing I couldn't stand about the *finca* was the dirt. Picking the coffee wasn't so bad, but there were no toilets — not even a ditch where we could go. I really noticed the dirt, there were flies on the *tortilla* dough, on the dishes, everywhere. So much poverty that it was depressing. Some people were aware of the situation and were careful to move away from the rest of us if they needed to go to the toilet, but others didn't care and went anywhere. There must have been a lot of germs, and people became sick with fevers and coughs.

Another horrible thing is fumigation, but this only happened to me when I was picking cotton, not coffee. They never warned us beforehand, they would just cover the food. But the smell of the poison was very, very, strong — dreadful — and when the planes passed overhead it fell on us, leaving marks on our hands, like milk, some kind of liquid . . .

You never see the owners of these *fincas*. They don't even come to pay you. There's a foreman. People would say, "Hurry up, get a move on. Here he comes." There are good and bad foremen — some will help the women to reach the coffee on the topmost branches but others (and our own people are sometimes the worst) only ill-treat you.

The reason I went to work on the *fincas* was to pay for fertiliser. Since my family has only a little plot of land, and we didn't have the cash to buy fertiliser, we had to get it on credit from the contractor. He gave a hundredweight to each of us and then we had to pay off the debt by going to work on the *finca*. The contractor works for the *finca* owner. At times we earned enough to pay back our debt and have a little bit over to buy clothes.

Margarita II Describes Working as a Live-In Maid in the City

I came to the capital to work when I was eight years old, as my parents are very poor and they weren't able to support us all. . . .

. . . The first thing the *señora* [lady of the house] did was to teach me housework. I had to do the shopping, the cleaning and wash the dishes. I worked in the mornings and in the afternoon I would go to school for a few hours. The family was fond of me, but they were very strict about everything, very demanding. I was supposed not to think too much, just to do things as fast as possible. I would often have to get up at around 3 or 4 o'clock in the morning because of the water shortages. There was usually only water at that time of the day, and I had to fill all the buckets. It was really hard because I normally had to work until 9 or 10 o'clock at night — virtually the only thing I thought about was work. When I was about 12 years old, I stopped going to school because there was no time. I was so tired that I couldn't apply my mind to studying. . . .

. . . Sometimes the people I first worked for beat me and treated me badly. At times I would answer back and they would punish me. "Your parents didn't bring you up, we did," they said, "and you have to obey us if you want to stay here. If you don't, then find somewhere else to go." They know that you need the work — the money — and they try to make you suffer even more than you're already suffering.

It's really only now that I am meeting other people that I realise the difference between people here and people in my village. I don't want to speak badly of the people in the capital, but I've suffered this treatment in the flesh — the disdain that always exists because you are Indian. They think they have to crush you because you work for them. For example, I had to eat first, then the family ate; if I ate off a plate then it mustn't be touched; these plates were theirs and this plate was mine — everything was kept separate.

In the beginning, I really missed my family. It was very difficult to adjust to life here in Guatemala City. But the family I worked for had a little girl and she really loved me. We played together and as time passed I forgot nearly everything about my life in the village. The little girl was a *ladina,* obviously, and we were always treated differently. Her mother used to tell her that I was different. Later she got married and I went to work in her house. But she married into a family with a lot of money and she became more demanding, more arrogant. She began to treat me differently. It was money that made her change. I hardly ever see her now. But I still think of her family as my second parents — they were the ones who gave me some education, after all.

Nearly every Sunday I go to my village to see my parents. I love my family, my people and my village, and I've always loved going there. I like their traditions and customs, but I grew up in another environment, I didn't grow up in the countryside, cultivating the land. If you asked me how I would feel if I went back there permanently, I would have to say that I wouldn't be happy, because I am used to things here in the city.

Very few village people really know the capital. They are very poor, and there are few possibilities for them to come here. Many of them view coming here in a negative light. They say that if you come here to live, you are a lost cause. . . .

The life of an Indian woman in the countryside is to work the land, collect firewood, carry water, wash the clothes in the river and take the animals to pasture. I haven't done any of this. The only tradition I retain is wearing my *traje* [wraparound, ankle-length woven skirt] and speaking my native language.

I like to wear my *traje,* and I think I ought to, since all my family still wears it. . . .

Indian customs demand that we marry our own people. . . . In fact, my boyfriend is from my village, but he is studying in the city to be an engineer. He would like us to get married and live here, going back to our village every week or so to see our families. In other words, he no longer wants to adjust to life in the village. It would be very difficult for people like us to adapt to the customs of the village indigenous people.

Men like him, who have been educated and have more experience, tend to have relationships with women like me who are able to speak Spanish well. . . . So marrying someone who has never left the village would be very difficult. They wouldn't know what it is to have a house, to have things like an electric stove or a television, though many Indians nowadays would like the chance. Our intention is to take the good things from the *ladino* way of life.

VICTORIA CALLS FOR DEFENDING MAYAN CULTURE

My village is so wonderful, you can't imagine . . . to me it is such a special place. It's where I spent my childhood, and I left part of my life there. I have good memories of it, but also very bad ones because it was there that my two brothers disappeared.[1]

. . . The military commander who is responsible for so many deaths still lives there. These are the negative things that prevent us from going back. But it's where our land is, our home — everything. Our house has been ransacked, there is nothing left. The heads of the civil defense patrols divided everything up between them and took over our land as well. . . .

Although I live in the capital, I still speak my native language. We don't speak Spanish at home because it's not our language, and my husband is Indian from the same ethnic group as me. When I was born, my father and my grandfather made a pact. My grandfather wanted to preserve our Indian traditions for ever, so he asked my father to promise that we wouldn't alter our customs or our culture. Even if someone tried to force me to change my *traje* for *ladino* clothes on pain of death I wouldn't do so.

I first met *ladinos* when I was seven, when I tried to enrol in primary school. I received a rebuff at the time that I've never forgotten. The teacher was a *ladina* and by chance I was the last child to enrol, but they wouldn't let me because there were no desks left. My father went to see the teacher and begged her to let me stay in the class. She refused and said, "She's just one more Indian who wants an education." . . .

According to *ladinos,* we Indians have no God. I thought it was very strange once when I heard a priest say that for Indians, Christ had never been born. I thought very deeply about this. Did this mean to say that my people were just

---

[1] Ages seventeen and twenty-five, they were abducted by government or local right-wing groups and never heard from again.

savages, that they had no God? I couldn't accept this because I had seen how my grandmother carried out animal sacrifices, how she worshipped St. Anthony of the Mountain who was her saint of animals and the land. We Indians are 100 per cent religious, we believe in divine works. According to the historians, the Mayans were polytheistic. They believed in the God of the Rain, the God of the Sun, the God of the Moon. But this isn't true polytheism. Indians have only one God, it is just that we identify him with different aspects of nature.

There are two kinds of Indian: true Indians and those who are Indian in terms of blood and nationality, but who want to be better than others, so start to use things that are inappropriate to us. There are Indians, for example, who say that it is bad for you to have a lot of children, so they take contraceptives. The true Indian doesn't use contraceptives. We accept children as they come.

These days, there are also Indian women who use their bodies commercially, like the Rabina Hau [the winner of a beauty-queen contest for Indian women], who makes an exhibition of herself for a few dollars. In other words, not all Indians value our culture. There are many of us who for a title or a job stop being what we are.

I'm careful not to put a foot wrong because there are many eyes on me: not just my husband or my family, but also members of my community. I feel part of this community, and I don't want to let people down.

I have no hope in *ladinos*. I have no hope because it would be very difficult to civilise the *ladino* into our way of thinking. It is difficult for us to understand each other. I put my hopes, my faith and my trust in those of my Indian people who are fighting for change.

9.5

Ladina Elites Reflect on Their Privileged World

The next three interviews capture the outlook of Ladinas in positions of power and privilege. Amparo, in her late seventies when interviewed, conveys the attachment to large landed estates common among her class and the resistance, often violent, to even minor agrarian reform. In the climate of mounting violence, guerrillas executed her husband in 1975. Marta, the second interviewee, was a forty-nine-year-old lawyer prominent in one of the country's right-wing political parties that are staunchly anti-communist, anti–trade union, authoritarian, and protective of the interests of a privileged few. The last account is from an anonymous journalist (a forty-year-old woman) who provides an insider commentary on Ladino views of the Maya.

How do Ladinas define themselves and view life in Guatemala? Can we assume their male counterparts would have the same outlook? How does the addition of the Ladina perspective add to our understanding of the divisions that underlay Guatemala's violent history?

Margaret Hooks
From *Guatemalan Women Speak*
1991

AMPARO GIVES THE OWNER'S VIEW ON COFFEE PLANTATION LIFE

I was born in Quetzaltenango [in southwestern Guatemala] but soon afterwards my parents took me to Spain. I grew up there, and came back to Guatemala when I was 19. A year later I married a Guatemalan of Colombian origin.

I started work on the *finca* at my husband's side. But he would often be out in the fields and I would stay in the house. I never felt lonely because I had very good servants. When my husband had to go to Guatemala City I stayed behind and supervised the workers. . . .

We had a very nice house with many patios. It had six bedrooms. We never had time to make it as pretty as we had planned. And, although I had come from Europe, I got used to this way of life. . . .

[My husband] had a very harsh character, but he was good to his people. They killed my husband. . . . He was paying people when suddenly six or seven men arrived. . . . They didn't steal any of the money, but they shot him down. He was buried on the *finca*. After this my sons took over the *finca*.

We don't have any labour problems, the *finca* has electricity and very good machinery. People have their little houses, and they live well. More than a thousand people live and work on the *finca*. It is enormous. Most of the land is wild and very fertile because there are many rivers and it rains a lot. . . .

The people who work on the *finca* are Indians. I have never had any problems with them; they are good people. The women have a lot of children — 10, 11, 12, 14 and many of them die. People are Catholic, but what sort of Catholicism is it? They are Catholics, but they baptise their children and nothing else. There are no priests in this area. Early on there was no church, but we had one built and some American Evangelicals are now constructing a hospital.

. . . I have always been very concerned about my people. There is a school on the *finca* and we always try to help anyone who is sick. For example, on one occasion when there was a government amnesty for guerrillas, over 2,000 people arrived at the *finca* in a very bad state, very ill and really thin. They had been in the mountains. They were asked why they had gone with the guerrillas and they said that they had been told that Guatemala was going to be theirs, that the crops would be theirs, the light planes, everything. But there was none of that. There they were in the mountains and all they had to eat were plants, no salt, and their clothes were ruined. When the army went after them they had to hide, and many children died. So they came to the *finca*. We built them houses — well, one big shed for all of them. They were given corn, beans, salt, coffee and molasses, pretty good, eh? . . .

Hooks, *Guatemalan Women Speak,* 6–9, 48, 114, 116–17.

There is a lot of social work to be done in Guatemala, without a doubt. I think we must all get together and form committees so that there are fewer illiterate people and fewer starving children. . . .

The economic situation is not good. This government redistribution of land is a very complicated issue. It's not just a question of taking away a *finca* and giving it to someone else. You give them the land and what do they do with it? They can't do anything. . . .

These people don't want virgin land that they would have to work. When I first came to the *finca* there wasn't anything — no road, no doctor, no medicine. So why don't they do the same? You know why? Because they have no proper management.

I have learnt what it is to love land. If you come to love the land then it doesn't matter what sacrifices you have to make, as long as you save the land. There is a point at which profit is not so important. What is important is your land, your people. . . . My family is my reality, but the land is my roots. I went to see the film *Gone with the Wind* and I understood it very well. My life has been a bit like that film.

Marta Describes Her Right-Wing Political Views

My family was well-to-do. My great-grandfather owned some properties, so we had enough money to "get by." We weren't multi-millionaires, but we had enough. My great-uncle was President Jorge Ubico [the dictator overthrown in 1944]. . . . I think that his was the last honest government in Guatemala. . . .

Central America seems to be in increasing danger of invasion by totalitarian groups. Communism is currently the worst threat, and we definitely don't want that for our countries. We believe in freedom, and we have seen that it is the poor who suffer most from totalitarianism, especially Marxism.

. . . Our party believes in a civilian government, but with a place for the army, since we are under a constant threat. We feel that we should have a strong, professional army dedicated to protecting the territory and the population from foreign invasion, and to supporting the Constitution and whoever is legally and freely elected. . . .

My party also feels that we need to stimulate and provide security for local and foreign investment. We would propose freezing taxes for at least five years. If we gave investors the security of knowing that they can get their money out of the country (after paying any taxes that they should pay under Guatemalan law), it would stimulate both foreign and local investment. People like to be sure that their money is safe, that nobody will take it away. . . .

On the question of the indigenous population, something that should have been done a long time ago is to provide bi-lingual education during the first three years of schooling so that Indian children can start learning Spanish. This is the only way for them to communicate and gradually increase their knowledge. As long as they don't speak Spanish, how are we to get our message across or give them information about anything? Even political parties run into this problem — we have to find interpreters to convey messages in the 22 different languages. The make-up of this country is really absurd. I can understand why it is so difficult for Europeans to comprehend what is happening here.

With sufficient education Indians will probably gradually abandon their customs and their language. If it were possible for them still to speak their own language as well as Spanish, then fine. But the natural tendency would be for it to disappear. To tell you the truth, I've always felt that it is very cruel to assume that Indians should keep to their local customs. We have to catch up with the times, with the 20th century. I wouldn't want to impose anything on anyone, but I think that they would want to be educated if they realised that they could trade more profitably if they were familiar with numbers and knew how to do business in Spanish. They are bound to want to. They are not stupid or different from the rest of us. There are very bright people among them. They just don't have opportunities.

A Journalist Reflects on Ladino Views of Indians

I believe that one of the reasons why the repression [by the government] did not cause too big a commotion among Guatemalans in the capital was because it was mainly Indians that were affected. All the suffering that took place was not *really* suffering because it happened to Indians. The Guatemalan upper class believes that Indians cannot really feel, that an Indian woman will not truly suffer if her husband or children are killed because she is not "the same as us." They say, "Well, they were Indians weren't they?"

One of the things that most shocks foreigners is that people in the capital were unaware of what went on. I was once invited to lunch by a woman who asked me if it was true that there were war orphans. Another upper class woman asked me if Indians ever laughed.

There are really two societies in Guatemala, *ladino* and indigenous, and I don't think that they are ever going to become one because neither is interested in achieving this. Politicians pay lip service to the idea, because the Indians represent five million votes. But that is their only value — votes.

9.6

Government Torturer Describes His Work

For a chilling insight into the repression that was the ultimate defense of the Guatemalan privileged class, we turn to this interview with an anonymous government torturer conducted by Jennifer Schirmer, an academic studying the Guatemalan military. The torturer was recruited into G-2 (army intelligence) at age sixteen while already a sergeant in the army. He was drawn to the job by the chance for better living conditions, access to a car, and the right to carry a gun. From 1978 to 1987 he worked in a patrol unit that normally consisted of four to eight men and was commanded by a major or captain.

For repression to work, it needs to be systematic (to sweep up anyone suspected of subversion) and intimidating (to silence sympathizers and deplete the ranks of resistance). How does the system actually function? How does someone whose poverty should set him at odds with the government come to work seemingly against his own class interests? Is this in general a reliable account? What particular points made here seem questionable?

Jennifer Schirmer
Interview with a G-2 Investigator

To become an *elemento* of the G-2, one must go through a course, to be trained. So one goes but [he hesitates], [it is a] training course in which one is taken to one of the cells (we call them *calabozos*) where they have people destined to be killed, okay? The major or captain (never a colonel) takes you to the cell, gives you a knife and throws you together to see how, how you react against that person, while he watches.

Q: As a kind of training exercise?

Yes, in other words, it is to prove your tolerance for such things, to prove that you are cold-blooded, if you have sufficient courage to torture and kill any person.

Q: With a knife?

With a knife, with whatever [they give you]. But there [in the cell], the only thing they give you is a knife, nothing else, and one has to figure out for oneself how to torture that person, how to kill that person and if you have enough courage to do so. . . . And then, from there, you begin to do your work, making pieces of that person, to do it like one cuts up an animal. And if one does [the job] well and they think you have enough courage to do these things, then they give you a position. . . . This lasts only one or two hours. It makes me uneasy at times to relate this. I have always asked God's forgiveness and the forgiveness of some of the people I've killed for what I've done.

Q: What do they tell you about these people in the cells? Who are they?

Frankly, when one is doing this [work], one isn't interested whether the person is a *guerrillero* or not. . . .

Each military zone and garrison has a G-2 section and secret torture cells. . . . At the garrison level, with an order signed by the commanding officer one goes out to kidnap or investigate a person. The mission is to bring that person back alive to base headquarters, where he will be tortured. If that person resists with gunshots, then one can assassinate that person then and there. . . .

Q: A *comisionsita* is a G-2 mission to kidnap?

There exist various types of *comisiones*. It can consist of being ordered to just investigate. That's when one works in civilian clothes, drinks beer with those close to the person or directly with him if possible. You never say "I'm from the G-2"; on the contrary, you say, "I don't work with either the Army or the Police, I don't work for anyone. I work with the guerrilla, or that one is a criminal (*asaltante*) and that one is looking for one or two people to

---

Jennifer Schirmer, *The Guatemalan Military Project: A Violence Called Democracy* (Philadelphia: University of Pennsylvania Press, 1998), 285–92. Schirmer is not explicit on the date of this interview. In general the interviews for her book were done between 1984 and 1997.

collaborate with [on a crime], something like that." . . . When one goes to kidnap a person it is also a *comisión:* one's mission is to bring this person back alive, or if they resist, dead. . . .

Q: So, one goes out in civilian clothes?

Yes, tennis shoes, regular shoes . . .

Q: In private cars?

Civilian cars of the government of whatever color. But it must be large, with six or eight cylinders, in case it is pursued.

Q: At night?

At any hour. This [work] has no [fixed] hour.

Q: How does one enter a house to kidnap someone?

It's not easy. You don't say, "I've come to kidnap you." That's because you've already been there and investigated [the scene].

Q: But aren't there witnesses?

Yes, many people see what is going on when one does one's job, but they cannot say that it is the G-2. Because one is in civilian clothes. So people can say it is criminals, guerrillas, or the army. But who is going to say, who would *dare* say: "It was the army, it was G-2"? No one. Everyone says, "Well, there were some civilians who came, entered [the house], and took him away." . . .

The reason G-2 *exists* is to kidnap and torture until our subjects are wretched and maimed. Then they are assassinated, thrown in a ravine, buried, or left by the side of the road. That's the work we do.

Q: Are you saying it is the same thing as a death squad?

G-2 *is* a death squad; it is a squad that is directly for killing. . . . [W]e torture everyone the same. There are persons who have been grabbed (*agarrado*) and killed who are white, tall and everything, and many times one believes they are Americans. But legally, one doesn't know where they come from because their identification is never revealed. . . .

Q: What kinds of torture methods does G-2 use?

We use the most painful we can find in order to pull out [as much] information from the person: sewing needles, electric cables; one places an electric battery in water and electrifies the water; there are many forms . . . pulling out fingernails.

Q: Who decides which methods to use?

It depends on the person [being tortured]. There are persons who one has only to prick them with a needle and he says, "*Un momento, no me matan* (don't kill me). I'm going to help you." So one stops torturing that person. . . . When they say no, they give no information. It's someone who you cut off at least a finger and he says, "Kill me, I will say nothing." Then you cut off an ear and he still refuses to speak; you cut off another finger, and he still refuses. And you realize that you could cut this person into a thousand pieces and he won't give you anything (*este no da nada*). So, why bother torturing him? So in one stroke you eliminate him.

Q: And are there times when the *jefe del cuartel* or *jefe del destacamento* (G-2 military zone or garrison chief) comes in when you are torturing to see how you are doing your job? Does he supervise?

Yes, sometimes. And at times, when he sees that one is trying to tear out information from a person that is giving us nothing, he says, "No, this one will give [up] nothing," and he pulls out his 9mm gun, grabs the prisoner, and shoots him in the head right there. And he says, "Go on and throw this one away . . ." . . .

Q: As a G-2 *elemento,* did torturing a woman include raping her?

Yes, this is normal. But it depends on the women, too. Because there are many women who aren't worth the effort to look at. Some even make you sick. But at times, the opportunity arose to be able to kidnap a young woman, to investigate a young woman, or for a young woman combatant to be wounded in combat, or an excellent woman. . . . Well, that woman couldn't escape. That woman, the first, the first, the first thing would be to rape her, right? That's the very first thing!

Q: By everyone?

Yes. Everyone. Ay! *El jefe* is the first [laughs]. And then the lieutenant or *el comandante* of G-2 or *el jefe de la patrulla.* If I were *el jefe de la patrulla,* then it would be my turn. Ay! This woman I like and so I would tell them, "Leave her over here" or "Cover me." [laughs] Yes, the rapes occur [as normal procedure]. . . .

Q: Was there much [drug] trafficking within G-2?

Yes, we would sell it, we would smoke marijuana and take cocaine. We often went to the border checkpoint where they wouldn't register our cars or our drugs. . . . We would also contract out to kill and rob. . . .

. . . The fact is we enjoyed our work. At least that was true for me; I liked it because I brought to it much of the resentment from my earlier life when I was younger. So, I'll tell you, placing myself in the G-2 I thought to myself, "I'm going to have the opportunity to revenge myself [on others], to kill people [to get back at] those who had killed my parents."

ISRAELIS AND PALESTINIANS IN A "FATAL EMBRACE"

At the heart of the conflict over Palestine is land. The quarrel between Jews and Arabs living in Palestine has evolved into a nationalist battle for territory with military power playing a central though not decisive role. By the 1940s Jews with a Zionist faith had gained a foothold, mobilized international support, and created a nation in arms. The success of those arms was repeatedly demonstrated, with great consequences in the late 1940s and again in 1967. In the first instance Jews asserted their right to a state, fought off Arab armies, and drove out a substantial part of the Arab population living within Israel's borders. In the second, Israeli forces once more repelled Arab armies and then occupied the remaining Palestinian territories. In reaction, the Arabs, first dispossessed and then subjected to occupation, developed their own nationalism. The contest over Palestine was now between two nationalist movements strongly tinged with religious ideology. Palestinians employed both passive resistance and surprise attacks on civilians as well as soldiers, frustrating Israeli claims to full control and winning international legitimacy. Perhaps the Palestinians' greatest hope — and expansionist Israelis' greatest nightmare — was demographic: the prospect that Palestinian population growth in Israel and the occupied territory would outstrip that of the Jews and leave the Jews a minority in an Israel that had annexed those territories.

The following documents trace the claims that both sides have made to the land and the way each has imagined national community. They allow us to follow an often violent debate between two deeply entrenched, seemingly intractable positions and to consider the historical, legal, moral, cultural, and geographical elements in the case that each makes.

9.7
The Arab Case against a Jewish State

Between the two world wars, Jewish settlers in Palestine were energetically acquiring land and organizing politically and militarily to stake a claim for a Jewish state. The Holocaust during World War II added a moral dimension to their claim to statehood. Finally, after the war's end, Britain's withdrawal from Palestine opened the way for the settlers to make good on that claim.

Against these developments Arab representatives protested vigorously before an Anglo-American team sent in 1946 to survey the situation in Palestine and report to the United Nations, into whose lap Britain was dropping the problem. What was the Arab vision of Palestine's future? On what grounds did the Arabs rest their claim to self-determination and support of the West? How much did the Arab case at this point arise from a nationalist (or some other) point of view?

Statement of Arab Views to the
Anglo-American Committee of Inquiry
Jerusalem, March 1946

1. The whole Arab people is unalterably opposed to the attempt to impose Jewish immigration and settlement upon it, and ultimately to establish a Jewish State in Palestine. Its opposition is based primarily upon right. The Arabs of Palestine are descendants of the indigenous inhabitants of the country, who have been in occupation of it since the beginning of history; they cannot agree that it is right to subject an indigenous population against its will to alien immigrants, whose claim is based upon a historical connection which ceased effectively many centuries ago. Moreover they form the major-

---

Walter Laqueur and Barry Rubin, eds., *The Israel-Arab Reader: A Documentary History of the Middle East Conflict,* 5th ed. (New York: Penguin Books, 1995), 80–83, 86–88. A partial copy of this document can be found at <http://www.mideastweb.org/araboffice.htm> (August 12, 2002).

ity of the population; as such they cannot submit to a policy of immigration which if pursued for long will turn them from a majority into a minority in an alien state; and they claim the democratic right of a majority to make its own decisions in matters of urgent national concern. . . .

2. . . . Geographically Palestine is part of Syria; its indigenous inhabitants belong to the Syrian branch of the Arab family of nations; all their culture and tradition link them to the other Arab peoples; and until 1917 Palestine formed part of the Ottoman Empire which included also several of the other Arab countries. The presence and claims of the Zionists, and the support given them by certain Western Powers have resulted in Palestine being cut off from the other Arab countries and subjected to a regime, administrative, legal, fiscal and educational, different from that of the sister-countries. . . .

. . . Zionism is essentially a political movement, aiming at the creation of a state: immigration, land-purchase and economic expansion are only aspects of a general political strategy. If Zionism succeeds in its aim, the Arabs will become a minority in their own country; a minority which can hope for no more than a minor share in the government, for the state is to be a Jewish state . . . .

4. . . . Zionism has become in Arab eyes a test of Western intentions towards them. So long as the attempt of the Zionists to impose a Jewish state upon the inhabitants of Palestine is supported by some or all of the Western Governments, so long will it be difficult if not impossible for the Arabs to establish a satisfactory relationship with the Western world and its civilization, and they will tend to turn away from the West in political hostility and spiritual isolation; this will be disastrous both for the Arabs themselves and for those Western nations which have dealings with them. . . .

9. . . . [T]he Arabs urge the establishment in Palestine of a democratic government representative of all sections of the population on a level of absolute equality; the termination of the Mandate once the Government has been established; and the entry of Palestine into the United Nations Organization as a full member of the working community. . . .

10. The Arabs are irrevocably opposed to political Zionism, but in no way hostile to the Jews as such nor to their Jewish fellow-citizens of Palestine. Those Jews who have already entered Palestine, and who have obtained or shall obtain Palestinian citizenship by due legal process will be full citizens of the Palestinian state, enjoying full civil and political rights and a fair share in government and administration. . . .

It is to be hoped that in course of time the exclusiveness of the Jews will be neutralized by the development of loyalty to the state and the emergence of new groupings which cut across communal divisions. This however will take time; and during the transitional period the Arabs recognize the need for giving special consideration to the peculiar position and the needs of the Jews. No attempt would be made to interfere with their communal organization, their personal status or their religious observances. Their schools and cultural institutions would be left to operate unchecked except for that general control which all governments exercise over education. In the districts in which they are most closely settled they would possess municipal autonomy and Hebrew would be an official language of administration, justice, and education.

11. The Palestinian State would be an Arab state not (as should be clear from the preceding paragraph) in any narrow racial sense, nor in the sense that non-Arabs should be placed in a position of inferiority, but because the form and policy of its government would be based on a recognition of two facts: first that the majority of the citizens are Arabs, and secondly that Palestine is part of the Arab world and has no future except through close cooperation with the other Arab states. . . .

14. . . . (1) The idea of partition and the establishment of a Jewish state in a part of Palestine is inadmissible . . . . Zionism is a political movement aimed at the domination at least of the whole of Palestine; to give it a foothold in part of Palestine would be to encourage it to press for more and to provide it with a base for its activities. Because of this, because of the pressure of population and in order to escape from its isolation it would inevitably be thrown into enmity with the surrounding Arab states and this enmity would disturb the stability of the whole Middle East.

9.8

The Zionist Claim to Land and Political Identity

While the Arabs of Palestine made no significant preparation to create a state of their own, the British withdrawal found the executive committee of the Jewish community ready to move despite threats from the neighboring states to invade and crush any statehood initiative. The Jews did, however, have the support of U.S. president Harry Truman. In May 1948 the state of Israel came into existence when David Ben Gurion, the leading Jewish political figure and the first prime minister, read the declaration of independence. In the fighting that followed in 1948 and 1949, Israeli forces secured not only the land promised under a UN partition plan but also additional territories, while driving out roughly 700,000 Palestinians. Some 150,000 were left behind, now a minority in a state containing some 700,000 Jews.

On what basis does the declaration of independence ground its claim to creating a Jewish state? What are the key points of conflict with the 1946 Arab statement above? Are there any points of compatibility between the two documents?

Israel's Provisional State Council
Declaration of Independence
Tel Aviv, May 14, 1948

The land of Israel was the birthplace of the Jewish people. Here their spiritual, religious and national identity was formed. Here they achieved independence and created a culture of national and universal significance. Here they wrote and gave the Bible to the world.

Exiled from Palestine, the Jewish people remained faithful to it in all the countries of their dispersion, never ceasing to pray and hope for their return and the restoration of their national freedom.

Impelled by this historic association, Jews strove throughout the centuries to go back to the land of their fathers and regain their statehood. In recent decades they returned in masses. They reclaimed the wilderness, revived their language, built cities and villages and established a vigorous and ever-growing community with its own economic and cultural life. They sought peace, but were always prepared to defend themselves. They brought the blessing of progress to all inhabitants of the country. . . .

. . . It is . . . the self-evident right of the Jewish people to be a nation, as all other nations, in its own sovereign State.

ACCORDINGLY, WE, the members of the National Council, representing the Jewish people in Palestine and the Zionist movement of the world, met together in solemn assembly today, the day of the termination of the British mandate for Palestine, by virtue of the natural and historic right of the Jewish and of the Resolution of the General Assembly of the United Nations,

HEREBY PROCLAIM the establishment of the Jewish State in Palestine, to be called ISRAEL. . . .

THE STATE OF ISRAEL will be open to the immigration of Jews from all countries of their dispersion; will promote the development of the country for the benefit of all its inhabitants; will be based on the precepts of liberty, justice and peace taught by the Hebrew Prophets; will uphold the full social and political equality of all its citizens, without distinction of race, creed or sex; will guarantee full freedom of conscience, worship, education and culture; will safeguard the sanctity and inviolability of the shrines and Holy Places of all religions; and will dedicate itself to the principles of the Charter of the United Nations. . . .

We offer peace and unity to all the neighboring states and their peoples, and invite them to cooperate with the independent Jewish nation for the common good of all.

Our call goes out [to] the Jewish people all over the world to rally to our side in the task of immigration and development and to stand by us in the great struggle for the fulfillment of the dream of generations — the redemption of Israel.

From the Mideast Web website: <http://www.mideastweb.org/israeldeclaration.htm> (August 12, 2002). Also available on the Avalon website: <http://www.yale.edu/lawweb/avalon/mideast/israel.htm> (July 17, 2003). A variant version appears in Charles D. Smith, *Palestine and the Arab-Israeli Conflict: A History with Documents,* 4th ed. (Boston: Bedford/St. Martin's, 2001), 219–22.

9.9

Palestine Liberation Organization Asserts a National Identity and the Imperative of Armed Struggle

Through the 1950s and much of the 1960s, Palestinians were scattered and ill-organized. Some had resettled elsewhere in the Middle East after losing home and land in 1948. Others had become refugees in camps in the Jordan-controlled West Bank, in the Gaza Strip under Egyptian oversight, and in adjoining Arab states. Yet others remained in familiar family settings in the West Bank and Gaza. The first sure signs of politicization came in 1964 with the creation of the Palestine Liberation Organization (PLO), a coordinating body for a variety of resistance groups. The Israeli occupation of the West Bank (including East Jerusalem) and Gaza in the Six-Day War of 1967 gave fresh impetus to PLO activism. Yasir Arafat, himself the head of one of the PLO's constituent factions, emerged as the leader of the organization. Palestinian militants lashed out in cross-border attacks and assaults on Israelis overseas.

The new militant current is reflected in the PLO's fundamental document, its charter approved by delegates attending a PLO meeting in Cairo, Egypt, in July 1968. To what extent does this charter echo claims made in 1946 and to what extent does it move beyond them to make new claims about the rights and duties of Palestinians and their relationship to other Arabs?

The Palestinian National Charter

July 1968

ARTICLE 1: Palestine is the homeland of the Arab Palestinian people; it is an indivisible part of the Arab homeland, and the Palestinian people are an integral part of the Arab nation.

ARTICLE 2: Palestine, with the boundaries it had during the British Mandate, is an indivisible territorial unit.

ARTICLE 3: The Palestinian Arab people possess the legal right to their homeland and have the right to determine their destiny after achieving the liberation of their country in accordance with their wishes and entirely of their own accord and will. . . .

ARTICLE 5: The Palestinians are those Arab nationals who, until 1947, normally resided in Palestine regardless of whether they were evicted from it or have stayed there. Anyone born, after that date, of a Palestinian father — whether inside Palestine or outside it — is also a Palestinian.

ARTICLE 6: The Jews who had normally resided in Palestine until the beginning of the Zionist invasion will be considered Palestinians.

From the website of the Mideast Web: <http://www.mideastweb.org/plocha.htm> (August 8, 2002), based on English rendition published in Leila S. Kadi, ed., *Basic Political Documents of the Armed Palestinian Resistance Movement* (Beirut: Palestine Research Centre, December 1969), 137–41. Also available on the Avalon website: <http://www.yale.edu/lawweb/avalon/mideast/plocov.htm> (May 29, 2003).

ARTICLE 7: That there is a Palestinian community and that it has material, spiritual, and historical connection with Palestine are indisputable facts. It is a national duty to bring up individual Palestinians in an Arab revolutionary manner. All means of information and education must be adopted in order to acquaint the Palestinian with his country in the most profound manner, both spiritual and material, that is possible. He must be prepared for the armed struggle and ready to sacrifice his wealth and his life in order to win back his homeland and bring about its liberation. . . .

ARTICLE 9: Armed struggle is the only way to liberate Palestine. . . .

ARTICLE 15: The liberation of Palestine, from an Arab viewpoint, is a national duty and it attempts to repel the Zionist and imperialist aggression against the Arab homeland, and aims at the elimination of Zionism in Palestine. Absolute responsibility for this falls upon the Arab nation — peoples and governments — with the Arab people of Palestine in the vanguard. Accordingly, the Arab nation must mobilize all its military, human, moral, and spiritual capabilities to participate actively with the Palestinian people in the liberation of Palestine. It must, particularly in the phase of the armed Palestinian revolution, offer and furnish the Palestinian people with all possible help . . . .

ARTICLE 19: The partition of Palestine in 1947 and the establishment of the state of Israel are entirely illegal, regardless of the passage of time, because they were contrary to the will of the Palestinian people and to their natural right in their homeland, and inconsistent with the principles embodied in the Charter of the United Nations, particularly the right to self-determination.

ARTICLE 20: . . . Claims of historical or religious ties of Jews with Palestine are incompatible with the facts of history and the true conception of what constitutes statehood. Judaism, being a religion, is not an independent nationality. Nor do Jews constitute a single nation with an identity of its own; they are citizens of the states to which they belong. . . .

ARTICLE 22: Zionism is a political movement organically associated with international imperialism and antagonistic to all action for liberation and to progressive movements in the world. It is racist and fanatic in its nature, aggressive, expansionist, and colonial in its aims, and fascist in its methods. Israel is the instrument of the Zionist movement, and geographical base for world imperialism placed strategically in the midst of the Arab homeland to combat the hopes of the Arab nation for liberation, unity, and progress. . . . Since the liberation of Palestine will destroy the Zionist and imperialist presence and will contribute to the establishment of peace in the Middle East, the Palestinian people look for the support of all the progressive and peaceful forces and urge them all, irrespective of their affiliations and beliefs, to offer the Palestinian people all aid and support in their just struggle for the liberation of their homeland. . . .

ARTICLE 26: The Palestine Liberation Organization, representative of the Palestinian revolutionary forces, is responsible for the Palestinian Arab people's movement in its struggle — to retrieve its homeland, liberate and return to it and exercise the right to self-determination in it — in all military, political, and financial fields and also for whatever may be required by the Palestine case on the inter-Arab and international levels.

9.10
The Likud Coalition Commitment to Hold Occupied Land

The Six-Day War was as important in Israeli politics as it was in Palestinian. The occupation of the West Bank brought within the realm of the possible the Zionist dream of incorporating all of the land historically associated with the Jews. Expansionists particularly had their eyes on the West Bank, to which they referred by its Biblical names of Judea and Samaria. The way to win this territory, expansionists argued, was to mount a campaign of settlement. By moving rising numbers of Jews on the best land and securing it by the Israeli army, Jews would gain permanent control. The Likud Party, which came to power in 1977 and remained the dominant political force in the following decades, embraced this settlement policy.

Likud's approach is evident in the platform laid down by its leader, Menachem Begin, on the eve of his party's first national election victory. How does this campaign statement make the case for Israeli control? What is to be the fate of Palestinians (nearly a million living in the West Bank and Gaza at the time of the 1967 occupation)? How seriously should we treat this document — as merely a ploy to win votes but without any serious policy implications?

Platform for Menachem Begin's Election Campaign
March 1977

THE RIGHT OF THE JEWISH PEOPLE TO THE LAND OF ISRAEL (ERETZ ISRAEL)

The right of the Jewish people to the land of Israel is eternal and indisputable and is linked with the right to security and peace; therefore, Judaea and Samaria will not be handed to any foreign administration; between the sea and Jordan there will only be Israeli sovereignty.

A plan which relinquishes parts of western Eretz Israel, undermines our right to the country, unavoidably leads to the establishment of a "Palestinian State," jeopardizes the security of the Jewish population, endangers the existence of the State of Israel, and frustrates any prospect of peace.

GENUINE PEACE — OUR CENTRAL OBJECTIVE

The Likud government will place its aspirations for peace at the top of its priorities and will spare no effort to promote peace. The Likud will act as a genuine partner at peace treaty negotiations with our neighbors. . . .

SETTLEMENT

Settlement, both urban and rural, in all parts of the Land of Israel is the focal point of the Zionist effort to redeem the country, to maintain vital security areas and serves as a reservoir of strength and inspiration for the renewal of the pioneering spirit. The Likud government will call the younger generation in Israel and the dispersions [Jewish diaspora] to settle and help every group and individual in the task of inhabiting and cultivating the wasteland, while taking care not to dispossess anyone.

Laqueur and Rubin, *The Israel-Arab Reader,* 388–89.

ARAB TERROR ORGANIZATIONS

The PLO is no national liberation organization but an organization of assassins, which the Arab countries use as a political and military tool, while also serving the interests of Soviet imperialism, to stir up the area. Its aim is to liquidate the State of Israel, set up an Arab country instead and make the Land of Israel part of the Arab world. The Likud government will strive to eliminate these murderous organizations in order to prevent them from carrying out their bloody deeds.

9.11

The Islamic Resistance Movement Promotes the First *Intifada*

The daily irritations and humiliations of occupation along with the Likud settlement drive antagonized Palestinians. Their anger exploded in late 1987 in the first *intifada* (or uprising). Two decades of PLO struggle from outside the occupied areas had done nothing to shake the Israeli grip. Now Palestinians under the occupation began to challenge the Israeli presence. Views on how to proceed varied widely — from passive resistance and appeals to the international community to armed attacks. One element within the *intifada* was, like the PLO itself, secular. But another element introduced a militant Islamic approach to the conflict. Indeed, the Islamic Resistance Movement (or Hamas) had sparked the *intifada* among Gaza youth. Hamas was an offshoot of the Muslim Brothers, an Islamic organization with a presence in the Gaza Strip during Egyptian control between 1948 and 1967. Hamas won broad support for its courageous challenge to the occupiers as well as for its social services.

The document that follows was the first bulletin Hamas issued to guide the *intifada*. What are its goals? How does its appeal compare to the Arab statement in 1946 and the PLO charter from 1968? How does its strong Islamic flavor square with the idea of an emergent Palestinian nationalism?

Hamas
Leaflet No. 1
January 1988

O murabitun[1] on the soil of immaculate and beloved Palestine: O all our people, men and women. O our children: the Jews — brothers of the apes, assassins of the prophets, bloodsuckers, warmongers — are murdering you, depriving you of life after having plundered your homeland and your homes. Only Islam

---

[1] Muslims who settled in outlying areas during the initial period of the Muslim conquests in order to defend the borders.

Shaul Mishal and Reuben Aharoni, *Speaking Stones: Communiques from the Intifada Underground* (Syracuse, N.Y.: Syracuse University Press, 1994), 201–203. Footnotes supplied by Mishal and Aharoni. The same version of this document can be found in Esther Webman, "Anti-Semitic Motifs in the Ideology of Hizballah and Hamas," July 9, 1998, available at <http://www.ict.org.il/articles/articledet.cfm?articleid=51#APPENDIX I> (August 9, 2002).

can break the Jews and destroy their dream. Therefore, proclaim to them: Allah is great, Allah is greater than their army, Allah is greater than their airplanes and their weapons. When you struggle with them, take into account to request one of two bounties: martyrdom, or victory over them and their defeat.[2] ...

Let the whole world hear that the Muslim Palestinian people rejects the surrender solutions, rejects an international conference, for these will not restore our people's rights in its homeland and on its soil.... Liberation will not be completed without sacrifice, blood and *jihad* that continues until victory.

Today, as the Muslim Palestinian people persists in rejecting the Jews' policy, a policy of deporting Palestinians from their homeland and leaving behind their families and children — the people stresses to the Jews that the struggle will continue and escalate, its methods and instruments will be improved, until the Jews shall drink what they have given our unarmed people to drink.

The blood of our martyrs shall not be forgotten. Every drop of blood shall become a Molotov cocktail, a time bomb, and a roadside charge that will rip out the intestines of the Jews. [Only] then will their sense return. ...

To you our Muslim Palestinian people, Allah's blessing and protection! May Allah strengthen you and give you victory. Continue with your rejection and your struggle against the occupation methods, the dispossession, deportations, prisons, tortures, travel restrictions, the dissemination of filth and pornography, the corruption and bribery, the improper and humiliating behavior, the heavy taxes, a life of suffering and of degradation to honor and to the houses of worship.

Forward our people in your resistance until the defeat of your enemy and liquidation of the occupation.

---

[2] In Islamic tradition, one of two bounties requested from Allah: victory or martyrdom in battle.

9.12

Hanan Ashrawi's Challenge to Those Responsible for the "Fatal Embrace"

Hanan Ashrawi has been an articulate voice for a more secular and Western-oriented Palestinian nationalism. Like others of her generation, she was deeply influenced by the 1967 Israeli occupation of the West Bank and Gaza. A college student in Beirut at the time, she recalls how the occupation intensified the sense of outraged nationalism among her circle of relatively well-to-do, cosmopolitan Palestinian friends. Ashrawi herself comes from a Christian family, earned her doctorate in English literature at the University of Virginia, and returned home to teach. She rose to sudden prominence as the spokesperson for occupied Palestine after the first *intifada* broke out in December 1987. She later served as a member of the Palestinian Legislative Council, part of a Palestinian government in embryo created in 1994 as a result of international negotiations.

The following statement reveals her frustration following the outbreak of a second *intifada* in September 2000. Try to read through the lines of this carefully worded statement. What seems to be her view of Arafat and the PLO-run administration in parts of the West Bank, the Islamists bent on a campaign of violence, the Likud government headed by Ariel Sharon, and an immobile international community?

"Challenging Questions"
December 11, 2001

The dynamic of violence, revenge, and all other forms of dehumanization seems to have taken hold as both Palestinians and Israelis are locked in a fatal embrace that promises to plunge both peoples into the abyss. . . .

While immobilizing his "adversary," Sharon is repeatedly calling on Arafat to do more to "end the violence and rein in the terrorists." With mindless monotony, Israeli and American officials continue to chant this refrain like a blind chorus in a Greek tragedy, though lacking any critical distance or insight.

This bizarre and painful condition is no act of fate, no accident of history. Rather, it is the natural outcome of the deliberate distortion of history in the form of a festering colonial malady that has been allowed to infect both body and mind with no remedy in sight.

How else can one interpret the victimization of a whole captive and defenseless nation, with a no-holds-barred assault on their lives, lands, rights, freedoms, and aspirations?

How else can one interpret this incessant shelling, pounding, beating of a people who have nowhere to go beyond their homes and whose very homes are being demolished, burned, and besieged? . . .

How else can one interpret the blinders that have suddenly and collectively warped the vision of most Israeli media, simultaneously distorting their perspective, scope, depth, and field of vision? The banal litany of official jargon, processed language, and uniform allocation of blame seem to have had a fatal impact on their own critical perceptions as well as on the conscience of their readers/viewers/audience.

How else can one interpret the self-destruct[ive] political sado masochism that has rendered most of the Israeli "peace camp" both voiceless and powerless . . . ? . . .

As Palestinians, albeit the victims, we too have to admit our share of the blame and ask ourselves those questions that have remained silent or whispered in the privacy of closed-door discussions.

Why and when did the drive for revenge overtake our pursuit of human rights and the struggle for human dignity and liberty, thereby making us fall in the trap of the reactive mode as deliberately set up by the occupation?

From Arabic Media Internet Network at <http://www.amin.org/eng/hanan_ashrawi/2001/11dec2001.html> (July 16, 2002).

How did we allow Sharon to formulate our agenda and dictate our timing by responding to his calculated provocations specifically designed to draw us within his cycle of retribution? Pain, grief, and the impulse for revenge are negative motivations that give rise to mutually destructive acts of desperation. No relief and no remedy can be found in that course.

Why and when did we allow a few from our midst to interpret Israeli military attacks on innocent Palestinian lives as license to do the same to their civilians? Where are those voices and forces that should have stood up for the sanctity of innocent lives (ours and theirs), instead of allowing the horror of our own suffering to silence us? . . .

How did we leave a whole people vulnerable, at the mercy of rhetorical bombast on the one hand and relentless military assaults on the other, with no political strategy and no reprieve or protection?

When and why did international public opinion become desensitized to the plight of Palestinians under occupation, with the silence of the Arabs and the duplicity of the rest? . . .

Whether targeted by an immoral and brutal occupation, or suffering silently from internal inequities, the people of Palestine do not deserve their perpetual victimization.

Whether deafened and terrorized by exploding shells and missiles, or stunned by the silence of their officials and allies, the Palestinian people deserve better.

Whether grieving for their murdered children and their destroyed homes and crops, or smarting at the indignity and deliberate humiliation of the siege and checkpoints, the Palestinian people will not be dehumanized.

Who has the courage now to restore hope to a people whose spirit has never been broken and whose will remains undefeated despite intolerable adversity?

Who has the courage once again to intervene in the course of history and to change its direction from death and destruction to the promise and release of a just peace?

The current dynamic generated by the occupation and the Sharon government's lethal agenda must not be allowed to run its course.

Freedom, democracy, statehood and human dignity are rights that can no longer be put on hold.

9.13

Prime Minister Ariel Sharon on the Palestinian Threat

The Likud Party lost control of the government in June 1992 to the opposition Labor Party, which embarked on negotiations with the Palestinians to end the first *intifada*. The prospects for peace were undercut by the assassination of the Labor prime minister by an angry expansionist (November 1995), by the election of a Likud government (May 1996) supportive of settlements, and by the difficulties a new Labor government (May 1999) encountered in talks with Arafat. The outbreak of the second *intifada* led a fearful Israeli electorate in June 2001 to turn back to the Likud, now led by Ariel Sharon. Hostile to the PLO and Arafat, Prime Minister Sharon embarked on a policy of armed force to tame the restive Palestinians and a policy of intensified settlement, while aligning closely with the U.S. war on terrorism in the Middle East following the September 11 attacks on New York and Washington.

To what extent are Sharon's views expressed here consistent with the ideals and goals of the Israeli declaration of 1948 and the Likud campaign platform of 1977? To what extent does he factor in the growing militancy of Palestinians subjected to Israeli occupation? Does his position close off the possibility of a negotiated peace?

Address to the 34th Zionist Congress
Jerusalem, June 20, 2002

Since the age of 17, I have stood in the service of the Jewish people. I have passed the most terrible fields of destruction, I have beheld the scenes of the terrors of war, I have held the hand of comrades bleeding to death, I have closed the eyes of the fallen — and I have never seen anything so horrific as what I saw on Tuesday in Jerusalem [following a suicide bombing on a bus], the horror of crushed bodies, dismembered and wallowing in blood — the horror of victims whose despicable murderer tried to rob them not only of their lives, but also of their dignity.

This is a time of emergency for our people. Over the past 21 months, Israel has been subject to a severe terror offensive, while another wave of wretched hatred of Israel is surging around the world, the criminal expression of which can be seen in attacks on synagogues, community centers and Jews in many countries. . . .

This is not the first terror offensive that we have known in the Land of Israel since the start of Jewish settlement. In fact, this is just one more wave in a campaign that has continued more than 120 years. The difference is the fact that this time, behind the terror and murder activities, stands a terrorist Palestinian authority, by an axis of global terror, Teheran-Damascus-Bin Laden.

Israel will not stop, even at the height of this campaign, to search for paths to peace with its neighbors. But one iron rule must be set if we desire to live in this region: The destruction of terror and the complete cessation of violence and incitement are the preconditions for any possibility of achieving peace, and on this we will insist with all our strength. . . .

. . . The State of Israel has enabled Jews around the world to hold their heads up high and saved the Jewish people from crumbling after the Holocaust. Today, Israel is the Jewish axis, anchor and center of existence. Israel accepts upon itself the responsibility for the fate of Jews around the world.

From the Israeli prime minister's website: <http://www.pmo.gov.il/english/ts .exe?tsurl=0.41.6286.0.0> (August 12, 2002).

GLOBALIZATION ASCENDANT: THE 1990s AND BEYOND

BY THE 1990s THE WORLD HAD BECOME SUBSTANTIALLY GLOBALIZED. That often-used term meant at heart that patterns of trade and investment were truly worldwide. As economic integration intensified, workers moved to areas of higher wages, and most of the developing world oriented toward the international market economy. The collapse of the Soviet Union not only ended the Cold War division of the world but also left the United States its sole policeman and an unfettered advocate of free-market values. Other developments as dramatic were the rapid movement of disease; the proliferation of popular culture and consumer values; and the growing prominence of international institutions such as the UN and concerted international action on such issues as the environment and human rights.

As this barebones summary of globalization suggests, the phenomenon was complex, and not surprisingly it played out in complex ways. The system generated unprecedented levels of wealth. Total world output jumped from $3 trillion to $30 trillion in the half-century following World War II. But the welcome generation of wealth created problems worrisome to increasingly outspoken critics. Integration of parts of the developing world was proving especially problematic. An Islamic resurgence, especially strong in the Middle East, was one challenge to globalization; sub-Saharan Africa, severely stressed by the AIDS epidemic, was another. Both regional crises had global ramifications. Finally, states and increasingly influential non-governmental organizations (NGO's) engaged in a sustained international conversation over human rights that forced people from diverse cultures and faiths to consider human dignity and welfare in universal as well as specifically local terms.

THE BACKLASH AGAINST GLOBALIZATION

By century's end the neo-liberal orthodoxy was dominant globally. Economists such as Milton Friedman and Anglo-American political leaders such as

Margaret Thatcher had made a sustained, coherent, and ultimately persuasive case that free markets produced not only free but also prosperous societies. This view had generally prevailed in the leading economies, dominated the policies of the leading international economic institutions such as the International Monetary Fund (IMF), and enjoyed at least lip service from leaders of developing countries.

In the realm of ideas, few orthodoxies stand long unchallenged, especially as practical application reveals their shortcomings. The global spread of a market model had a variety of undesirable effects — political, cultural, and social as well as economic — that began to worry critics. By the end of the 1990s the backlash had grown significantly and came from diverse constituencies including notably environmentalists, advocates of more balanced and socially just development, proponents of cultural diversity, and nationalists angered by the loss of sovereignty to international bureaucracies. Whether these critics will form into an effective coalition and mount a fundamental challenge to globalization remains to be seen. That there is no coherent overarching alternative ideology to neo-liberalism would suggest that the critics may effect reforms on the margins but not overthrow the current system. But that assumption rests on a static view of what has been in fact a dynamic and unpredictable response to the effects of globalization. The end of this story is by no means clear.

10.1

On Inequality

As an engine of wealth production, the global economy functioned impressively. But the benefits of growth were distributed in a grossly unequal fashion. The trend toward inequality is not new, but there is evidence that the spread between rich and poor has grown faster in recent decades. In the 1820s the top 20 percent of income earners were three times better off than the bottom 20 percent. By 1970 that ratio was 30:1, and by 1990 it was 60:1. During the 1990s the gap continued to widen not only among countries but within them. The wealthiest, blessed with skills and capital, flourished, while the poorest, lacking all resources but their labor, lagged ever farther behind.

Nothing illustrates the international gap so well as the conditions of families in different parts of the world. Thanks to Peter Menzel, we have precisely such a picture. In the early 1990s he photographed selected families from around the world in front of their homes surrounded by their worldly possessions. In addition, he asked them about their income and aspirations. The table that follows shows three of Menzel's families — from the developed, developing, and least developed worlds. What resources does each have for subsistence, education, health care, and leisure as well as a cushion against adversity? What single feature best captures the differences among these families? Are there any commonalities that appear across the range of richest to poorest? How might a neo-liberal defend the inequalities evident here? What practical changes might an advocate of social justice and equality propose?

Three Families, Three Worlds
1993–1994

	Pfitzner family in Cologne, Germany	de Goes family in São Paulo, Brazil	Yadev family in Ahraura, India
Size of household	4	6	6
Size of dwelling	926 square feet	1,100 square feet	334 square feet
Hours of work per week	Father: 40 Mother: about 50 (in the home)	Father: 60 Mother: "constant" (in the home?)	Father: 56 (when work is available) Mother: 84 (in the home)
Total family income	$76,816	$17,520	$1,980
Disposal of income	40 percent on rent; 30 percent on food, clothing, and household goods	55 percent on food; 15 percent on auto; 0 percent to savings	[Not indicated but likely 100 percent on essentials]
Wishes for future	New refrigerator, house in the country, cleaner environment	Better car, better stereo, better home	1 or 2 new cows for milk
Number of high-tech possessions	3 radios, 1 tape recorder, 1 TV, 1 VCR, 1 video camera, 1 motor-cycle, 1 auto	1 radio, 1 stereo, 1 TV, 1 VCR, 1 auto	1 bicycle (broken)
Most valued possessions	Mother and Father: basket with family memorabilia Oldest son: pocket-knife Youngest son: toy truck	[Not indicated]	Father: print of Hindu gods Mother: sculptures of gods and goddesses protecting family and home
Number of possessions appearing with the family posing in front of their homes	35 items	25 items	18 items

Peter Menzel, *Material World: A Global Family Portrait* (San Francisco: Sierra Club Books, 1994), 65–71, 126–33, 180–85.

10.2
On Fundamental Structural Flaws

Global capitalism is a dynamic system. Its adaptability to changing circumstances is one of its prime strengths. But dynamism carries costs. Overnight, workers can lose their livelihood and communities can collapse as businesses shift production to low wage areas. Even more devastating, surging money flows (surpassing a trillion dollars a day by the 1990s) can capsize national economies, inflicting widespread hardship. Overseeing this dynamic system — enforcing the rules of the market and containing the periodic crises — are bankers and economists, above all in the IMF and the World Trade Organization (WTO). But their decisions are not subject to review or recall by any electorate even though they might have more far-reaching political and social impact than any piece of national legislation. What then, critics asked, happened to vaunted democratic rights of peoples in the face of decisions made by faceless, unelected bureaucrats? Furthermore, these critics contend that a world defined by market forces and a society shaped by market metaphors was a threat to nature and ultimately to human life.

The International Forum on Globalization — a coalition of non-governmental organizations, scholars, activists, and writers — issued the following indictment after a major financial crisis swept through Asia, hitting Indonesia, Thailand, and South Korea especially hard. What are the main charges lodged here? Is there a common thread that runs through this critique, or is it a mish-mash of criticisms? Is it a reformist document, and if so, what reforms does it envision? How persuasive is it?

The International Forum on Globalization
"The Siena Declaration"
September 1998

1. The undersigned have long predicted that corporate-led economic globalization, as expressed and encouraged by the rules of global trade and investment, would lead to an extreme volatility in global financial markets and great vulnerability for all nations and people. These rules have been created and are enforced by the World Trade Organization (WTO), the International Monetary Fund (IMF), the General Agreement on Tariffs and Trade (GATT), the North American Free Trade Agreement (NAFTA), the Maastricht Agreement [advancing European integration], the World Bank and other global bureaucracies that currently discipline governments in the area of trade and financial investment. This volatility is bringing massive economic breakdown in some nations, insecurity in all nations, unprecedented hardships for millions of people, growing unemployment and dislocation in all regions, direct assaults on environmental and labor conditions, loss of wilderness and biodiversity, massive population shifts, increased ethnic and racial tensions, and other disastrous results. Such dire outcomes are now becoming manifest throughout the world, and are increasing daily.

The declaration appeared as an advertisement in the *New York Times,* November 24, 1998, A7. Also available at the website for the Third World Network: <http://www.twnside.org.sg/title/siena-cn.htm> (January 24, 2003).

2. The solutions to the crises that are currently being offered by the leadership of the above-named trade bureaucracies, and the leaders of most western industrialized states, as well as bankers, security analysts, corporate CEO's and economists — the main theoreticians, designers and promoters of the activities that have led us to this point — are little more than repetitions, even expansions, of the very formulas that have already proven socially, economically and environmentally disastrous. The experts who now propose solutions to the financial meltdown are the very ones who, only months ago, were celebrating Indonesia, Thailand, South Korea and other "Asian Tigers" as poster-children for the success of their designs. . . .

Now these "leaders" advocate that we solve the problem by further opening markets, further opening and liberalizing the rules of investment . . . further suppressing the options of nation-states and communities to regulate commerce for the good of their own publics and environments, further discouragement of such models as "import substitution"[1] that have the chance to enable nations to feed and care for themselves, and further centralization of control within the same governing bodies as at present. In other words, more of the same.

According to these architects of globalization, it is only a matter of "fine tuning" or "first aid" while on the way to continued expansion of the same failed dream of theirs. They cite "cronyism" among the Third World's nations as contributing to the problem, but say nothing of the cronyism exhibited by the U.S. Treasury–Wall Street–IMF collaborations by which western bankers bail out other western bankers for their disastrous policies.

Clearly, the architects of the present crisis have not understood what they have wrought, or, if they have understood it, cannot afford to admit it.

3. As for the tens of millions of people who now suffer from this experiment, the expert solutions include no bailouts. Many of these people, formerly self-sufficient in food, are now dependent on the absentee-ownership system of the global economy. Now abandoned, they are left to seek solutions outside the system, from foraging in the (fast disappearing) forests, to barter systems, to social upheaval as means of expression. Many are finding that their attempts to return to prior means of livelihood — such as small scale local farming — are impossible, as their former lands have been converted to industrial corporate agricultural models for export production. Land on which people formerly grew food to eat has been converted to corporate production of luxury commodities — e.g., coffee, beef, flowers, prawns — to be exported to the wealthy nations. Poverty, hunger, landlessness, homelessness, and migration are the immediate outcome of this. Insecure food supplies, lower food quality, and often dangerous contaminated foods are a secondary outcome. The situation is unsustainable.

4. Its creators like to describe the global economic system as the inevitable outgrowth of economic, social and technological evolution. They make

---

[1] Economic development strategy giving the leading role to government promotion and protection of domestic industry.

the case that centralized global economies that feature an export-oriented free trade model, fed by massive deregulation, privatization, and corporate-led free market activity in both commodity trade and finance — free of inhibiting environmental, labor and social standards — will eventually bring a kind of utopia to all people of the planet. Now it is clear that it is a corporate utopia they have in mind. But even this will fail to achieve its goals, as the entire process is riven with structural flaws. No system that depends for its success on a never ending expansion of markets, resources and consumers, or that fails to achieve social equity and meaningful livelihood for all people on the planet, can hope to survive for very long. Social unrest, economic and ecological breakdown are the true inevitabilities of such a system.

5. It is appropriate to recall that the present structures of globalization did not grow in nature as if they were part of a natural selection, evolutionary process. Economic globalization in its present form was deliberately designed by economists, bankers, and corporate leaders to institute a form of economic activity and control that they said would be beneficial. It is an invented, experimental system; there is nothing inevitable about it. Globalization in its recent form even had a birthplace and birthdate: Bretton Woods, New Hampshire, 1944. It was there that a design was agreed to by the leading industrial nations. The WTO, the IMF, the World Bank, et al. were instruments that grew out of the design plan, to facilitate and further the process.

Great expectations have led to despair. After 50 years of this experiment, it is breaking down. Rather than leading to economic benefits for all people, it has brought the planet to the brink of environmental catastrophe, social unrest that is unprecedented, economies of most countries in shambles, an increase in poverty, hunger, landlessness, migration and social dislocation. The experiment may now be called a failure.

6. ... [M]any peoples of the world, and many nation-states, have begun ... to specifically ask if globalization — especially free trade in financial flows — is in the best interest of their own nation, or any nation. We have seen serious corrective actions recently taken by China, India, Hong Kong, Malaysia, Russia and Chile which, by various means, have tried to counter the destabilizing force of unregulated private investment that has proved to benefit no one but the crony capitalists who advocate it. As we write, many more nations are showing renewed interest in these expressions of resistance and withdrawal from uncontrolled global capital. Importantly, the nations that have put, or maintained, controls on capital have demonstrated a higher degree of stability, and are better able to act successfully in the interests of their own resource and economic bases and in the interests of their own populations. ...

7. ... All peoples of the world have been made tragically dependent upon the arbitrary, experimental acts of giant self interested corporations, bankers and speculators. This is the result of the global rules that remove real economic power from nations, communities and citizen democracies, while giving new powers to corporate and financial speculators that act only in their own interests; and that suppress the abilities of local economies, regions and nations to protect resources, public health and human rights. This has left the

peoples of the world in a uniquely isolated, vulnerable condition; dependent upon the whims of great, distant powers. This too is an unsustainable condition.

8. Any truly effective solution to the current financial crisis, and the larger crises of economic globalization, must include the following ingredients, among others:

a) Recognition and acknowledgment that the current model, as designed and implemented by present-day, corporate led global trade bureaucracies is fundamentally flawed, and that the current crises are the inevitable, predictable result of these flaws.

b) Convening of a new Bretton Woods-type international conference which would bring to the table not only representatives of nation-states, bankers and industry, but an equal number of citizen organizations from every country to design economic models that turn away from globalization and move toward localization, re-empower communities and nation-states, place human, social and ecological values above economic values (and corporate profit), encourage national self sufficiency (wherever possible) including "import substitution," and operate in a fully democratic and transparent manner.

c) Efforts to build on the experiences of Chile, Malaysia, India and the other countries that have placed controls on capital investment and currency speculation. Encourage all activity that reverses present policies that expand the freedoms of finance capital and transnational corporations, while suppressing the freedoms of individuals, communities, and nation-states to act in their own behalf.

d) Immediately cancel all efforts . . . that give added freedom to finance capital to operate free of national controls.

Finally, the undersigned wish to state that we are not opposed to international trade and investment, or to international rules that regulate this trade and investment, so long as it complements economic activity that nation-states can achieve for themselves, and so long as the environment, human rights, labor rights, democracy, national sovereignty and social equity are given primacy.

10.3

On Environmental Damage

Mounting levels of production and trade had inflicted potentially catastrophic environmental degradation, felt mostly in poor neighborhoods within developed countries and poorer countries within the international economy. But the rich could not escape some problems, such as global warming and the erosion of the earth's protective ozone shield. Like the social costs to families and communities when jobs moved abroad, environmental costs were not counted as part of the price of production in the free market system.

The delegates to the 1999 WTO meeting arrived in Seattle unaware that discontent with this arrangement had reached a critical mass. Protestors turned out in numbers that overwhelmed the police and disrupted the meeting. The train of globalization had seemingly suffered a temporary derailment. Here are interviews with two protest organizers. What personal experiences led these individuals to take their public stand? Do their views have mainstream appeal in either the developed or developing world, or are they expressing marginal discontents? How threatening is their position to globalization?

The University of Washington's WTO History Project
Interviews with Activists

JENNIFER KRILL, RAINFOREST ACTION NETWORK[1]

Can you go through some of the main points and highlights of your activism career that led to the WTO protests . . . ?

. . . I've been an environmental activist for six years, and in that time I've worked for several organizations, including Greenpeace, Earth Island Institute, and Rainforest Action Network. While I worked for Earth Island Institute, I worked on the Sea Turtle Restoration Project, which is the organization that originally brought the lawsuit that forced the United States to change the Endangered Species Act and protect sea turtles from other countries from being caught in shrimp nets.

This is a really important lawsuit, because sea turtles don't know borders. They don't know the difference between the United States and Mexico, and they don't understand that laws are different from country to country. . . . We won our lawsuit, and the United States amended the Endangered Species Act to protect sea turtles who were getting caught and dying in shrimp nets in amazing numbers every year. The United States would not import shrimp from countries that did not have sea turtle protection on the books.

. . . [N]ations that didn't have sea turtle protection on the books sued the United States under the WTO and won, and forced the United States to change their law protecting a highly endangered species, the endangered sea turtle.

. . . I was the Outreach Director for the sea turtle project at that time, and was well aware in 1997/98 as this decision came down the pike, just how devastating the WTO could be for our laws and our environmental protection. Later I came to work for Rainforest Action Network, and here, while I was here at RAN, I was studying the effects that the WTO would have on the world's forests. . . .

---

[1]Interview by Miguel Bocangera (no interview date supplied) as part of the University of Washington's WTO History Project, available at <http://depts.washington.edu/wtohist/Interviews/Krill.htm> (March 30, 2003).

... [It is] said that the WTO's global free logging agreement, what we call the package of tariff loosening that would happen in the forestry sector, was expected to increase global logging by five to six percent. You're fighting to save the world's old growth forests, then one of the first things you realize is that we hardly have none left. We're talking about 20 percent of the world's old growth forests left after the last couple of centuries of devastating logging, and the last 20 years or so of clear-cutting and industrial scale logging. So increasing our logging by that much will hasten the decline of the millions of species that live in old growth forests. It will hasten the decline of water quality . . . in tropical countries . . . , especially countries which are very corrupt, [and] welcome and love the idea of having increased incentives to log their forests[,] and the corporations who are doing the logging love the idea of making more money.

All of this is bad for the environment and it's bad for species and it's very bad for Labor, so that's why we got involved with the WTO protests in November in such a big and important way. . . .

Why did RAN decide to put so much effort into shutting down the meetings[?] . . .

. . . [T]he WTO ministerial is the meeting at which they, the WTO, was determining the fate of the world's forests, and it was a meeting in which corporations were involved and non-democratically-elected representatives were involved, and there were not spokespeople for the environment and there were not spokespeople for labor. . . .

If the world's forests disappear, then our human future on the planet is in jeopardy. So if the WTO is trying to increase logging in the world's forests with no representation by the people who are affected by this, much less the species that are affected by this, then it has to be shut down, and something new has to be built, some kind of new world ministerial that is going to make more sense for long-term human sustainability on the planet. The WTO is only representing long-term corporate and economic interests at the expense of labor issues and of environmental issues.

KRISTINE WONG, COMMUNITY COALITION FOR ENVIRONMENTAL JUSTICE[2]

How and why did you get involved in the WTO mobilization?

As an activist that has been working on environmental health and justice issues primarily affecting low income communities and communities of color in the Seattle area, I saw how the World Trade Organization was going to take apart a lot of local, state and federal safety and health regulations that protected, to at least some extent, low income communities and communities of color from pollution.

---

[2]Interview by Monica Ghosh, July 28, 2000, as part of the University of Washington's WTO History Project, available at <http://depts.washington.edu/wtohist/Interviews/Wong.htm> (March 30, 2003).

The World Trade Organization has allowed corporations to nullify any of these regulations and laws that have protected these folks from pollutants. In the larger anti-globalization movement in the U.S., I foresaw how this [the WTO mobilization] was going to be a very white dominated protest. I saw . . . that the people who were going to be most affected by unfair trade policies were people living in the Global South, and that disenfranchised communities in the United States would also be affected.

I found that if we did not get involved, then this message would never get out to the public at large, and that because of the work that we do on an everyday basis, it was absolutely essential that we had to make our voice heard on the issue of globalization.

So can you tell me just a little bit about Community Coalition for Environmental Justice and what it does?

The Community Coalition for Environmental Justice is a non-profit organization led by people of color, women of color in particular, and is a multiracial group. We are an organization that was founded in 1993 in Seattle by a diverse coalition of groups . . . .

Our organization seeks to mobilize grassroots people and folks who live by toxic waste sites who are unjustly and disproportionately affected by these sites. We work to get them to the table so that their voices can be heard by the decision-makers who have much influence on who bears the brunt of pollution in Seattle.

Since I've been at the Community Coalition for Environmental Justice, one of our greatest victories was a campaign that I organized alongside local residents to shut down a medical waste incinerator in the Beacon Hill area of Seattle. Beacon Hill is the neighborhood that is 70% people of color, the largest Asian Pacific Islander community in Seattle. The incinerator campaign involved a lot of grassroots politicking that we had to do to get beyond the usual closed doors when important decisions were being made. . . .

So then what motivated you guys to mobilize against the WTO?

There is definitely a lack of understanding, I think, in a lot of people's minds that the local does really affect the global, and vice versa. . . .

. . . We had talked to people about the fact that there are all these public education materials talking about sea turtles and labor rights, but we also need to look at how globalization is affecting environmental racism in local communities. . . .

We had planned to have an environmental justice march. For example, we organized on the issue of dioxin, which is one of the most toxic chemicals known to science, and it's actually produced through the burning of paper and polyvinyl chloride plastic. This chemical is very persistent in the local environment and is difficult to break down. It can actually circulate the globe and get into the body fat of people all over the world, so ultimately it can cross borders and cultures and communities. Its toxic impact, therefore, is global.

AN EMERGING CLASH OF CIVILIZATIONS?

The phrase "clash of civilizations" came into currency early in the 1990s after Samuel P. Huntington, a senior Harvard professor of government, published an essay with that title in *Foreign Affairs*.[1] Huntington disagreed with the dominant view, occasioned by the end of the Cold War, that the world had entered an era of international harmony, and he doubted the emerging conventional wisdom that global economic forces would draw countries together. He saw instead deep, fundamental fault lines dividing peoples and countries around the world into distinct, competing civilizations defined by divergent cultural values. His essay emphasized the West's unique qualities (above all, democracy and liberalism) and its obligation to protect its values in a struggle between (to use the phrase that he invoked) "the West and the Rest." Huntington nominated the United States as the leader of the West with a special responsibility to protect Western values, especially in the face of resurgent Asian/Confucian states, chiefly China, and strong Islamic currents running through a wide swath of territory running from North Africa eastward.

In the wake of its publication, the Huntington thesis gained support from the outbreak of civil wars and ethnic quarrels in Bosnia and Rwanda, from failed democratic initiatives, and from proliferating weapons of mass destruction. The post–Cold War order did indeed seem as conflict prone as any earlier time. After the September 11 attacks on the United States and the initiation of an international war on terrorism, Huntington looked to many like a prophet providing a key to the understanding of such pressing Middle East issues as Israel's occupation of Palestinian land, Iraq under U.S.-British tutelage, the clerical regime in Iran, and foreign control of regional oil. The region did indeed look like it had become the focus of the clash of civilizations.

Huntington's critics pointed to historical complexities and social problems that his argument ignored. In particular, they contended that the widening appeal of political Islam over the last several decades was the result of specific grievances and aspirations that differed from place to place, not the expression of some cosmic civilizational force. The resulting debate raised pointedly the question of whether globalization was going to create a culturally uniform world, was it giving rise to tensions, or was it proving a relatively weak force vulnerable to local challenge or malleable into regional forms of modernity.

10.4

Osama bin Laden Blames the "Western Crusaders"

Osama bin Laden, founder and leader of the organization known as Al Qaeda (literally "the base"), was born in Riyadh, Saudi Arabia, in 1957. His father was of Yemeni origins but moved to Saudi Arabia where he operated a construction business. The father's pride in his work on holy sites in Mecca, Saudi Arabia, and in East Jerusalem suggests the atmosphere of piety in which bin Laden was raised. At

---

[1]Samuel P. Huntington, "The Clash of Civilizations?" *Foreign Affairs* 72 (Summer 1993): 22–49.

university he studied economics before going to work for his father's company. When the Soviets invaded Afghanistan in 1979, bin Laden organized Al Qaeda to help Muslim volunteers to join the resistance. Hardly had the last Soviet troops departed in 1989 than the Americans began setting up military bases in his homeland as part of the first Gulf War. This intrusion into the land of Islam's most holy shrines sharpened bin Laden's alienation from the Saudi ruling family and hostility toward the United States. Al Qaeda launched a series of bombings directed at U.S. embassies, ships, and barracks, capped by the attacks on New York and Washington in 2001.

Who or what does bin Laden see as the main threat to the region and to Muslims? Does his statement serve to support the Huntington thesis? How do the views articulated here compare to those of Khomeini and Hamas treated earlier? To extend the comparison: Is bin Laden a reincarnation of the third-world radicals of the 1960s (treated in chapter 6)?

Al-Jazeera Television Interview
December 1998

We demand that our land be liberated from enemies. That our lands be liberated from the Americans. . . .

Our enemies roam and meander in our seas and lands and skies, attack and assault without seeking permission from anyone . . . . The present [Arab] regimes no longer have the power. Either they are collaborators or have lost the power to do anything against this contemptible occupation. So Muslims should immigrate somewhere where they can raise the symbol of *jihad* [struggle] and protect their religion and world, otherwise they will lose everything. Are they incapable of appreciating the calamity that befell our brothers in Palestine and forgetting how the Palestinian people . . . have become a refugee people, turned into slaves of those colonialist Jews who dictate their movements? The situation is dangerous and if we do not move now, when the ancient holy site of 1.2 billion Muslims has been usurped, then when should people stir? Those who believe that such attacks [against Iraq] will terrorize the Islamic movements are deluding themselves. We Muslims believe that our time of death is fixed. Our fortunes are in the hand of God. . . .

. . . [E]very American man . . . is an enemy of ours whether he fights us directly or merely pays his taxes. You might have heard those who supported Clinton's [air] attacks against Iraq formed three-quarters of the American population. A people that regards its president in high favor when he kills innocent people is a decadent people with no understanding of morality. . . .

We are seeking to drive them [the Americans] out of our Islamic nations and prevent them from dominating us. We believe that this right to defend oneself is the right of all human beings. At a time when Israel stocks hundreds of nuclear warheads and when the Western crusaders control a large percent-

Reproduced in Barry Rubin and Judith Colp Rubin, eds., *Anti-American Terrorism and the Middle East: A Documentary Reader* (New York: Oxford University Press, 2002), 152–55, 157.

age of this [type of] weapon, we do not consider this an accusation but a right . . . . We congratulated the Pakistani people when they achieved this nuclear weapon, and we consider it the right of all Muslims to do so. . . .

Those Muslims who say that these are not the times for *jihad* are gravely wrong. Following the absence of *jihad* from our *umma* [world community of Muslims] for such a long time, we acquired a generation of people seeking education who had not experienced the reality of *jihad,* and they have been influenced by the American culture and media invasion that stormed the Muslim countries. Without even participating in a military war, we find this generation has already been psychologically beaten. What is true is that God granted the chance of *jihad* in Afghanistan, Chechnya, and Bosnia, and we are assured that we can wage a *jihad* against the enemies of Islam, in particular against the greater external enemy — the crusader-Jewish alliance.

Those who carried out the *jihad* [against Soviet forces] in Afghanistan did more than was expected of them because with very meager capacities they destroyed the largest military force and in doing so removed from our minds this notion of stronger nations. We believe that America is weaker than Russia, and from what we have heard from our brothers who waged *jihad* in Somalia, they found to their greatest surprise the weakness, frailty, and cowardliness of the American soldier. When only eight of them were killed[,] they packed up in the darkness of night and escaped without looking back. . . .

. . . [T]his is our aim — to liberate the lands of Islam from the sinners. America and some of its agents in the region bargained with me more than ten times to keep quiet and silence this small tongue of mine. "Shut up" and we will return to you your money. They believe that people only live for worldly matters, and they forgot that our lives are meaningless if we do not seek to please the goodwill and pleasure of Allah.

Finally, I advise all Muslims to adhere to the Koran. This is the way out from our present predicament. Our cure is the Koran. When one reads the Koran one wonders: Do they not read the Koran, or do they actually read but not understand as they should?

10.5

Edward Said Rejects the Clash Thesis and the Call to *Jihad*

When Huntington's views gained a new lease on life after September 11, Edward Said, a literature specialist at Columbia University, had perhaps the best reason of any of the critics to respond. Born into a Palestinian family driven into exile by Israeli expansion, his roots were in the region. He was an outspoken supporter of the Palestinian cause as well as an influential writer on the biases that Americans and Europeans had carried to the region across several centuries and that were still evident in Huntington's perspective. While Americans might see themselves as different, they were in fact deeply implicated in what Said called "orientalism," the persistent and largely unconscious pattern of Western stereotyping and demeaning of the peoples and cultures of the Middle East. Finally, Said had long done intellectual battle with one of Huntington's main sources on the Middle East, Bernard Lewis, a historian at Princeton.

How does Said seek to undercut the emphasis on civilizational conflict? What sort of policy does he seem to suggest as a substitute for the "war on terror"? How might Huntington have responded to Said's argument? In the final analysis who is more compelling — Huntington or Said? Imagine an exchange between bin Laden and Said: Is the gap between those two as great as between Said and Huntington?

"The Clash of Ignorance"
October 2001

[In Huntington's argument] the personification of enormous entities called "the West" and "Islam" is recklessly affirmed, as if hugely complicated matters like identity and culture existed in a cartoonlike world where Popeye and Bluto bash each other mercilessly, with one always more virtuous pugilist getting the upper hand over his adversary. Certainly neither Huntington nor [Bernard] Lewis has much time to spare for the internal dynamics and plurality of every civilization, or for the fact that the major contest in most modern cultures concerns the definition or interpretation of each culture, or for the unattractive possibility that a great deal of demagogy and downright ignorance is involved in presuming to speak for a whole religion or civilization. No, the West is the West, and Islam Islam.

. . . In fact, Huntington is an ideologist, someone who wants to make "civilizations" and "identities" into what they are not: shut-down, sealed-off entities that have been purged of the myriad currents and countercurrents that animate human history, and that over centuries have made it possible for that history not only to contain wars of religion and imperial conquest but also to be one of exchange, cross-fertilization and sharing. This far less visible history is ignored in the rush to highlight the ludicrously compressed and constricted warfare that "the clash of civilizations" argues is the reality. . . .

The basic paradigm of West versus the rest (the cold war opposition reformulated) remained untouched, and this is what has persisted, often insidiously and implicitly, in discussion since the terrible events of September 11. The carefully planned and horrendous, pathologically motivated suicide attack and mass slaughter by a small group of deranged militants has been turned into proof of Huntington's thesis. . . .

But why not instead see parallels, admittedly less spectacular in their destructiveness, for Osama bin Laden and his followers in cults like the Branch Davidians or the disciples of the Rev. Jim Jones at Guyana or the Japanese Aum Shinrikyo? . . .

Edward W. Said, "The Clash of Ignorance," appeared in *The Nation,* October 22, 2001, and widely on the web. This copy is drawn from *The Nation* website: <http://www.thenation.com/doc.mhtml?i=20011022&s=said> (May 31, 2003).

Uncountable are the editorials in every American and European newspaper and magazine of note adding to this vocabulary of gigantism and apocalypse, each use of which is plainly designed not to edify but to inflame the reader's indignant passion as a member of the "West," and what we need to do. Churchillian rhetoric is used inappropriately by self-appointed combatants in the West's, and especially America's, war against its haters, despoilers, destroyers, with scant attention to complex histories that defy such reductiveness and have seeped from one territory into another, in the process overriding the boundaries that are supposed to separate us all into divided armed camps.

This is the problem with unedifying labels like Islam and the West: They mislead and confuse the mind, which is trying to make sense of a disorderly reality that won't be pigeonholed or strapped down as easily as all that. I remember interrupting a man who, after a lecture I had given at a West Bank university in 1994, rose from the audience and started to attack my ideas as "Western," as opposed to the strict Islamic ones he espoused. "Why are you wearing a suit and tie?" was the first retort that came to mind. "They're Western too." He sat down with an embarrassed smile on his face, but I recalled the incident when information on the September 11 terrorists started to come in: how they had mastered all the technical details required to inflict their homicidal evil on the World Trade Center, the Pentagon and the aircraft they had commandeered. Where does one draw the line between "Western" technology and, as [Italy's prime minister Silvio] Berlusconi declared, "Islam's" inability to be a part of "modernity"?

One cannot easily do so, of course. How finally inadequate are the labels, generalizations and cultural assertions. At some level, for instance, primitive passions and sophisticated know-how converge in ways that give the lie to a fortified boundary not only between "West" and "Islam" but also between past and present, us and them, to say nothing of the very concepts of identity and nationality about which there is unending disagreement and debate. A unilateral decision made to draw lines in the sand, to undertake crusades, to oppose their evil with our good, to extirpate terrorism and, in Paul Wolfowitz's[1] nihilistic vocabulary, to end nations entirely, doesn't make the supposed entities any easier to see; rather, it speaks to how much simpler it is to make bellicose statements for the purpose of mobilizing collective passions than to reflect, examine, sort out what it is we are dealing with in reality, the interconnectedness of innumerable lives, "ours" as well as "theirs."

In a remarkable series of three articles published between January and March 1999 in *Dawn,* Pakistan's most respected weekly, the late Eqbal Ahmad, writing for a Muslim audience, analyzed what he called the roots of the religious right, coming down very harshly on the mutilations of Islam by absolutists and fanatical tyrants whose obsession with regulating personal behav-

---

[1]One of a number of neo-conservatives influential in the Bush administration's march to war against Iraq in 2003.

ior promotes "an Islamic order reduced to a penal code, stripped of its humanism, aesthetics, intellectual quests, and spiritual devotion." . . . The modern Islamists, Ahmad concludes, are "concerned with power, not with the soul; with the mobilization of people for political purposes rather than with sharing and alleviating their sufferings and aspirations. Theirs is a very limited and time-bound political agenda." What has made matters worse is that similar distortions and zealotry occur in the "Jewish" and "Christian" universes of discourse. . . .

. . . Think of the populations today of France, Italy, Germany, Spain, Britain, America, even Sweden, and you must concede that Islam is no longer on the fringes of the West but at its center. But what is so threatening about that presence? Buried in the collective culture are memories of the first great Arab-Islamic conquests, which began in the seventh century and which . . . shattered once and for all the ancient unity of the Mediterranean, destroyed the Christian-Roman synthesis and gave rise to a new civilization dominated by northern powers (Germany and Carolingian France) whose mission . . . is to resume defense of the "West" against its historical-cultural enemies. . . . [I]n the creation of this new line of defense the West drew on the humanism, science, philosophy, sociology and historiography of Islam, which had already interposed itself between Charlemagne's world and classical antiquity. Islam is inside from the start, as even Dante, great enemy of Mohammed, had to concede when he placed the Prophet at the very heart of his *Inferno*. . . .

. . . These are tense times, but it is better to think in terms of powerful and powerless communities, the secular politics of reason and ignorance, and universal principles of justice and injustice, than to wander off in search of vast abstractions that may give momentary satisfaction but little self-knowledge or informed analysis. "The Clash of Civilizations" thesis is a gimmick . . . better for reinforcing defensive self-pride than for critical understanding of the bewildering interdependence of our time.

10.6

Elite Opinion around the World Following the September 11 Attacks

After the September 11 attacks, Americans took solace in the expressions of sympathy and solidarity from around the world. However, a survey taken between mid-November and mid-December painted a more complex picture of how elites in twenty-four countries (including the United States and Russia as well as countries in Europe, Latin America, Asia, the Middle East, and sub-Saharan Africa) viewed the clash thesis and the United States. The interviewees consisted of 275 influential people in media, politics, business, and cultural affairs. Four of the more revealing questions asked appear below — whether they see the September 11 attacks

From the website for the Pew Research Center for the People and the Press: <http://people-press.org/reports/display.php3?ReportID=59and145> (May 21, 2003).

as part of a clash of civilizations, how they think people in their country generally view the attacks, what they themselves like least about the United States, and what they like best.

What do these poll results suggest about a gulf between "the West" led by the United States and "the rest" consisting of non-Western regions? Do foreign views of U.S. policy and culture suggest a major gap that amounts to something like a civilizational clash of differences? How do elite perceptions in the United States differ from those overseas? How reliable are the results given the relatively small number sampled?

Pew Polls

December 2001

Clash of Civilizations?			
	Major conflict between West and Islam %	Conflict only between West and Al Qaeda %	Don't know %
U.S.	28	52	20
Total Non-U.S.	27	59	14
Western Europe	20	63	17
E. Europe/Russia	40	40	20
Latin America	34	41	25
Asia	12	76	12
Mid-East/Conflict Area	41	54	5
All Islamic states	29	64	7

Perceived Popular Views of Terrorist Attacks		
	Most/Many People Believe	
	U.S. policy caused attacks %	good for U.S. to feel vulnerable %
U.S.	18	*n/a*
Total Non-U.S.	58	70
Western Europe	36	66
E. Europe/Russia	71	70
Latin America	58	71
Asia	60	76
Mid-East/Conflict Area	81	65
All Islamic states	76	73

Major Reasons for Disliking the U.S.				
	Resent- ment of U.S. power %	Causes rich/poor gap %	U.S. support of Israel %	Power of multinat'l corps. %
U.S.	88	43	70	40
Total Non-U.S.	52	52	29	36
Western Europe	66	61	22	59
E. Europe/Russia	64	53	17	47
Latin America	58	51	7	44
Asia	38	42	36	21
Mid-East/Conflict Area	54	59	57	17
All Islamic states	41	45	57	17

Major Reasons for Liking the U.S.				
	U.S. does a lot of good %	Democra- tic ideas appealing %	Land of oppor- tunity %	Tech/ Science advances %
U.S.	52	70	83	32
Total Non-U.S.	21	63	75	67
Western Europe	22	68	73	63
E. Europe/Russia	23	67	76	66
Latin America	12	66	66	71
Asia	23	63	76	58
Mid-East/Conflict Area	22	49	81	86
All Islamic states	20	48	81	73

THE HIV/AIDS CRISIS

The escalating health crisis associated with AIDS (acquired immune deficiency syndrome) coincides roughly with the rising tide of globalization. Though it probably had its origins in the 1930s when the blood of an infected chimpanzee passed to a human, HIV (the human immunodeficiency virus) did not become widespread in parts of Africa until the late 1970s. Usually transmitted through sexual contact or infected blood, HIV can lay dormant for months or years before AIDS develops, leaving the host vulnerable to a wide range of ultimately deadly infections.

The AIDS crisis itself is marked by the paradoxes that attend globalization. The technology that made airplane travel commonplace, tourism a mass phenomenon, and transport of goods cheap and easy also made it possible for disease to travel far and fast. By 2002 an estimated 25 million people had died of AIDS; 20 million of them were in the epicenter of this catastrophe, sub-Saharan Africa. The growing scale of this disaster soon engaged researchers in a quest for a treatment. But — and here is another paradox — the headway they made in devising drug therapies benefited wealthy individuals and states, not those in poor countries with weak governments and with already vulnerable societies. In a sign of the times, the leading international institution, the United Nations, stepped in to play a critical corrective role. Its agencies, the World Health Organization and the UN Programme on HIV/AIDS (UNAIDS), gathered information on the state of the epidemic, pressed for effective countermeasures in the poor countries worst hit, and lobbied the affluent for funds to support their programs.

10.7
Grim Statistics on a Global Contagion

Determining the magnitude of the crisis has proven a critical task but one plagued by difficulties. It has fallen heavily on the UN agencies to gather and interpret the data based on their own information and that supplied by research institutes and experts working for national HIV/AIDS programs. There is no single survey that supplies a consistent, across-the-board picture. Estimates often have to be made on the basis of partial or fragmentary data. HIV can take up to a decade to manifest itself as AIDS, thus leaving unclear when a latent problem will become a life-and-death crisis. Those surveyed may not wish to admit their illness. Health care records may be rudimentary or fragmentary. Programs may be tempted to exaggerate the crisis as a way of commanding donor attention; governments, to minimize it to avoid panic or reallocation of scarce resources. Finally, the ground rules for surveys tend to change over time, making comparisons between statistical snapshots of the crisis difficult.

Data about an epidemic is a kind of primary source — one that needs to be interpreted and evaluated as much as other, more literary sources. What pattern of geographical spread does the data provided here suggest? Where has the impact of the crisis been greatest? How is the impact best measured: for example, in

Estimates based on most recent data reported by the Joint United Nations Programme on HIV/AIDS and World Health Organization, "AIDS Epidemic Update," December 2002 (online at <http://www.who.int/hiv/pub/epidemiology/epi2002/en/> [April 8, 2003]), 2, 6, 41.

terms of absolute numbers, of the percentage of infected and dead, or of the impact on segments of the population (adults versus children and men versus women)? Why are children and women more affected in some places than in others? What is the most common means of transmission? Do the means of transmission relate in any significant way with the degree of prevalence? Are the problems attending the collection of this data so great that we should side step these sorts of questions?

UN Statistics
End of 2002

Region	Epidemic started	Adults and children living with HIV/AIDS	Adults and children newly infected with HIV	Adult prevalence rate[1]	% of HIV-positive adults who are women	Main modes of transmission for adults living with HIV/AIDS[2]	Estimated adult and children deaths due to HIV/AIDS during 2002
Sub-Saharan Africa	late '70s early '80s	29.4 million	3.5 million	8.8%	58%	Hetero	2.4 million
North Africa & Middle East	late '80s	550,000	83,000	0.3%	55%	Hetero, IDU	37,000
South & Southeast Asia	late '80s	6.0 million	700,000	0.6%	36%	Hetero, IDU	440,000
East Asia & Pacific	late '80s	1.2 million	270,000	0.1%	24%	IDU, Hetero MSM	45,000
Latin America	late '70s early '80s	1.5 million	150,000	0.6%	30%	MSM, IDU, Hetero	60,000
Caribbean	late '70s early '80s	440,000	60,000	2.4%	50%	Hetero, MSM	42,000
Eastern Europe & Central Asia	early '90s	1.2 million	250,000	0.6%	27%	IDU	25,000
Western Europe	late '70s early '80s	570,000	30,000	0.3%	25%	MSM, IDU	8,000
North America	late '70s early '80s	980,000	45,000	0.6%	20%	MSM, IDU, Hetero	15,000
Australia & New Zealand	late '70s early '80s	15,000	500	0.1%	7%	MSM	Less than 100
TOTAL		**42 million**	**5 million**	**1.2%**	**50%**		**3.1 million**
total adults		38.6	4.2				2.5
total women		19.2	2.0				1.2
total children (under 15 yrs)		3.2	0.8				0.61

---

[1]The proportion of adults (15 to 49 years of age) living with HIV/AIDS in 2002, using 2002 population numbers.

[2]Hetero = heterosexual transmission, IDU = transmission through injecting drug use, MSM = sexual transmission among men who have sex with men.

10.8
The Human Face of an Epidemic

Nothing brings home the disaster that is the AIDS epidemic better than a close look at the individuals in its grip. Johanna McGeary, a journalist writing for *Time* magazine in 2001, composed the following portraits of the hardest-hit people in southern Africa struggling to save themselves and their families.

From these case studies some of the causes and consequences of the epidemic can be deduced. What seem the most important reasons for the spread of the disease? What are the societal effects evident here? What recommendations would you make for policy changes to stop the epidemic and help its victims? With available funds in short supply, what initiatives deserve priority? For example, would you focus on care for the infected? Which ones? Or would you channel limited resources to prevention? On which parts of the population would you focus an awareness campaign? Would you consider long-term social changes or settle for immediate medical initiatives with short-term pay off?

Johanna McGeary
"Death Stalks a Continent"
February 12, 2001

Fundisi Khumalo in Personal Denial

Case no. 309 in the Tugela Ferry home-care program shivers violently on the wooden planks someone has knocked into a bed, a frayed blanket pulled right up to his nose. He has the flushed skin, overbright eyes and careful breathing of the tubercular. He is alone, and it is chilly within the crumbling mud walls of his hut at Msinga Top, a windswept outcrop high above the Tugela River in South Africa's KwaZulu-Natal province. The spectacular view of hills and veld would gladden a well man, but the 22-year-old we will call Fundisi Khumalo, though he does not know it, has AIDS, and his eyes seem to focus inward on his simple fear.

Before he can speak, his throat clutches in gasping spasms. Sharp pains rack his chest; his breath comes in shallow gasps. The vomiting is better today. But constipation has doubled up his knees, and he is too weak to go outside to relieve himself. He can't remember when he last ate. He can't remember how long he's been sick — "a long time, maybe since six months ago." Khumalo knows he has TB, and he believes it is just TB. "I am only thinking of that," he answers when we ask why he is so ill.

But the fear never leaves his eyes. He worked in a hair salon in Johannesburg, lived in a men's hostel in one of the cheap townships, had "a few" girlfriends. He knew other young men in the hostel who were on-and-off sick. When

Johanna McGeary, "Death Stalks A Continent," *TIME* 157 (February 12, 2001), 36–42, 44, 53. Available online at the *TIME* magazine website: <http://www.time.com/time/2001/aidsinafrica/cover.html> (March 2003).

they fell too ill to work anymore, like him, they straggled home to rural villages like Msinga Top. But where Khumalo would not go is the hospital. "Why?" he says. "You are sick there, you die there."

"He's right, you know," says Dr. Tony Moll, who has driven us up the dirt track from the 350-bed hospital he heads in Tugela Ferry. "We have no medicines for AIDS. So many hospitals tell them, "You've got AIDS. We can't help you. Go home and die." No one wants to be tested either, he adds, unless treatment is available. "If the choice is to know and get nothing," he says, "they don't want to know."

LAETITIA HAMBAHLANE FACES SOCIAL REJECTION

To acknowledge AIDS in yourself is to be branded as monstrous. Laetitia Hambahlane (not her real name) is 51 and sick with AIDS. So is her brother. She admits it; he doesn't. In her mother's broken-down house in the mean streets of Umlazi township [in South Africa], though, Laetitia's mother hovers over her son, nursing him, protecting him, resolutely denying he has anything but TB, though his sister claims the sure symptoms of AIDS mark him. Laetitia is the outcast, first from her family, then from her society.

For years Laetitia worked as a domestic servant in Durban and dutifully sent all her wages home to her mother. She fell in love a number of times and bore four children. "I loved that last man," she recalls. "After he left, I had no one, no sex." That was 1992, but Laetitia already had HIV.

She fell sick in 1996, and her employers sent her to a private doctor who couldn't diagnose an illness. He tested her blood and found she was HIV positive. "I wish I'd died right then," she says, as tears spill down her sunken cheeks. "I asked the doctor, 'Have you got medicine?' He said no. I said, 'Can't you keep me alive?'" The doctor could do nothing and sent her away. "I couldn't face the word," she says. "I couldn't sleep at night. I sat on my bed, thinking, praying. I did not see anyone day or night. I ask God, Why?"

Laetitia's employers fired her without asking her exact diagnosis. For weeks she could not muster the courage to tell anyone. Then she told her children, and they were ashamed and frightened. Then, harder still, she told her mother. Her mother raged about the loss of money if Laetitia could not work again. She was so angry she ordered Laetitia out of the house. When her daughter wouldn't leave, the mother threatened to sell the house to get rid of her daughter. Then she walled off her daughter's room with plywood partitions, leaving the daughter a pariah, alone in a cramped, dark space without windows and only a flimsy door opening into the alley. Laetitia must earn the pennies to feed herself and her children by peddling beer, cigarettes and candy from a shopping cart in her room, when people are brave enough to stop by her door. "Sometimes they buy, sometimes not," she says. "That is how I'm surviving."

Her mother will not talk to her. "If you are not even accepted by your own family," says Magwazi, the volunteer home-care giver from Durban's Sinoziso project who visits Laetitia, "then others will not accept you." When

Laetitia ventures outdoors, neighbors snub her, tough boys snatch her purse, children taunt her. Her own kids are tired of the sickness and don't like to help her anymore. "When I can't get up, they don't bring me food," she laments. One day local youths barged into her room, cursed her as a witch and a whore and beat her. When she told the police, the youths returned, threatening to burn down the house.

But it is her mother's rejection that wounds Laetitia most. "She is hiding it about my brother," she cries. "Why will she do nothing for me?" Her hands pick restlessly at the quilt covering her paper-thin frame. "I know my mother will not bury me properly. I know she will not take care of my kids when I am gone."

Louis Chikoka Accepts the Risks of Being a Man

He regularly drives the highway that is Botswana's economic lifeline and its curse. The road runs for 350 miles through desolate bush that is the Texas-size country's sole strip of habitable land, home to a large majority of its 1.5 million people. It once brought prospectors to Botswana's rich diamond reefs. Now it's the link for transcontinental truckers like Chikoka who haul goods from South Africa to markets in the continent's center. And now the road brings AIDS.

Chikoka brakes his dusty, diesel-belching Kabwe Transport 18-wheeler to a stop at the dark roadside rest on the edge of Francistown, where the international trade routes converge and at least 43% of adults are HIV-positive. He is a cheerful man even after 12 hard hours behind the wheel freighting rice from Durban. He's been on the road for two weeks and will reach his destination in Congo next Thursday. At 39, he is married, the father of three and a long-haul trucker for 12 years. He's used to it.

Lighting up a cigarette, the jaunty driver is unusually loquacious about sex as he eyes the dim figures circling the rest stop. Chikoka has parked here for a quickie. See that one over there, he points with his cigarette. . . . They know we drivers always got money."

Chikoka nods his head toward another woman sitting beside a stack of cardboard cartons. "We like better to go to them," he says. They are the "businesswomen," smugglers with gray-market cases of fruit and toilet paper and toys that they need to transport somewhere up the road. "They come to us, and we negotiate privately about carrying their goods." It's a no-cash deal, he says. "They pay their bodies to us." Chikoka shrugs at a suggestion that the practice may be unhealthy. "I been away two weeks, madam. I'm human. I'm a man. I have to have sex." . . .

Chikoka knows his predilection for commercial sex spreads AIDS; he knows his promiscuity could carry the disease home to his wife; he knows people die if they get it. "Yes, HIV is terrible, madam," he says as he crooks a finger toward the businesswoman whose favors he will enjoy that night. "But, madam, sex is natural. Sex is not like beer or smoking. You can stop them. But unless you castrate the men, you can't stop sex — and then we all die anyway."

Millions of men share Chikoka's sexually active lifestyle, fostered by the region's dependence on migrant labor. Men desperate to earn a few dollars leave their women at hardscrabble rural homesteads to go where the work is: the mines, the cities, the road. They're housed together in isolated males-only hostels but have easy access to prostitutes or a "town wife" with whom they soon pick up a second family and an ordinary STD [sexually transmitted disease] and HIV. Then they go home to wives and girlfriends a few times a year, carrying the virus they do not know they have. The pattern is so dominant that rates of infection in many rural areas across the southern cone match urban numbers.

THANDIWE MAKES A DANGEROUS LIVING

The workingwoman we meet directs our car to a reedy field fringing the gritty eastern townships of Bulawayo, Zimbabwe. She doesn't want neighbors to see her being interviewed. She is afraid her family will find out she is a prostitute, so we will call her Thandiwe. She looked quite prim and proper in her green calf-length dress as she waited for johns outside 109 Tongogaro Street in the center of downtown. So, for that matter, do the dozens of other women cruising the city's dim street corners: not a mini or bustier or bared navel in sight. Zimbabwe is in many ways a prim and proper society that frowns on commercial sex work and the public display of too much skin.

That doesn't stop Thandiwe from earning a better living turning tricks than she ever could doing honest work. Desperate for a job, she slipped illegally into South Africa in 1992. She cleaned floors in a Johannesburg restaurant, where she met a cook from back home who was also illegal. They had two daughters, and they got married; he was gunned down one night at work. . . .

Alone, Thandiwe grew desperate. "I couldn't let my babies starve." One day she met a friend from school. "She told me she was a sex worker. She said, 'Why you suffer? Let's go to a place where we can get quick bucks.'" Thandiwe hangs her head. "I went. I was afraid. But now I go every night."

She goes to Tongogaro Street, where the rich clients are, tucking a few condoms in her handbag every evening as the sun sets and returning home strictly by 10 so that she won't have to service a taxi-van driver to get a ride back. Thandiwe tells her family she works an evening shift, just not at what. "I get 200 zim [$5] for sex," she says, more for special services. She uses two condoms per client, sometimes three. "If they say no, I say no." But then sometimes resentful johns hit her. It's pay-and-go until she has pocketed 1,000 or 1,500 Zimbabwe dollars and can go home — with more cash than her impoverished neighbors ever see in their roughneck shantytown, flush enough to buy a TV and fleece jammies for her girls and meat for their supper.

"I am ashamed," she murmurs. She has stopped going to church. "Every day I ask myself, 'When will I stop this business?' The answer is, 'If I could get a job' . . ." Her voice trails off hopelessly. "At the present moment, I have no option, no other option." As trucker Chikoka bluntly puts it, "They give sex to eat. They got no man; they got no work; but they got kids, and they got to eat." Two of Thandiwe's friends in the sex trade are dying of AIDS, but what can she do? "I just hope I won't get it."

TSEPHO PHALE STRUGGLES TO PICK UP THE PIECES

The children who are left when parents die only add another complex dimension to Africa's epidemic. At 17, Tsepho Phale has been head of an indigent household of three young boys in the dusty township of Monarch, outside Francistown, for two years. He never met his father, his mother died of AIDS, and the grieving children possess only a raw concrete shell of a house. The doorways have no doors; the window frames no glass. There is not a stick of furniture. The boys sleep on piled-up blankets, their few clothes dangling from nails. In the room that passes for a kitchen, two paraffin burners sit on the dirt floor alongside the month's food: four cabbages, a bag of oranges and one of potatoes, three sacks of flour, some yeast, two jars of oil and two cartons of milk. Next to a dirty stack of plastic pans lies the mealy meal and rice that will provide their main sustenance for the month. A couple of bars of soap and two rolls of toilet paper also have to last the month. Tsepho has just brought these rations home from the social-service center where the "orphan grants" are doled out.

Tsepho has been robbed of a childhood that was grim even before his mother fell sick. She supported the family by "buying and selling things," he says, but she never earned more than a pittance. When his middle brother was knocked down by a car and left physically and mentally disabled, Tsepho's mother used the insurance money to build this house, so she would have one thing of value to leave her children. As the walls went up, she fell sick. Tsepho had to nurse her, bathe her, attend to her bodily functions, try to feed her. Her one fear as she lay dying was that her rural relatives would try to steal the house. She wrote a letter bequeathing it to her sons and bade Tsepho hide it.

As her body lay on the concrete floor awaiting burial, the relatives argued openly about how they would divide up the profits when they sold her dwelling. Tsepho gave the district commissioner's office the letter, preventing his mother's family from grabbing the house. Fine, said his relations; if you think you're a man, you look after your brothers. They have contributed nothing to the boys' welfare since. "It's as if we don't exist anymore either," says Tsepho. Now he struggles to keep house for the others, doing the cooking, cleaning, laundry and shopping.

The boys look at the future with despair. "It is very bleak," says Tsepho, kicking aimlessly at a bare wall. He had to quit school, has no job, will probably never get one. "I've given up my dreams. I have no hope."

Orphans have traditionally been cared for the African way: relatives absorb the children of the dead into their extended families. Some still try, but communities like Tsepho's are becoming saturated with orphans, and families can't afford to take on another kid, leaving thousands alone.

10.9
A UN Official on Saving Societies under Stress

Stephen Lewis, appointed in 2001 as the UN special envoy for HIV/AIDS in Africa, has figured prominently in the international campaign against AIDS. This Canadian politician and diplomat, who has served in the UN since the mid-1980s, has made his main task eliciting commitments of support (estimated in the $10–15 billion range per year) from the international community. He has sought to shake a widespread indifference toward the acute social crisis unfolding in sections of sub-Saharan Africa. No matter how hard hit, this region figured for many in the developed world as a marginal part of the global economy and international politics, and its problems have had relatively low priority. In an impassioned speech before a conference on "HIV/AIDS and 'Next Wave' Countries" at the Center for Strategic and International Studies in Washington, D.C., excerpts from which follow, Lewis outlined the crisis in southern Africa.

On what basis does Lewis make his appeal here? How might he respond to the argument that Africa might benefit more from programs addressing not the AIDS crisis but the underlying problems of state collapse, rural poverty, overpopulation, crowded cities, civil conflict, and poor basic infrastructure?

Stephen Lewis
Remarks at the Center for Strategic and International Studies
Washington, October 4, 2002

I'm no optimist about the virus. But I simply don't believe, on the basis of personal observation, that we have to face Armageddon. In fact it enrages me the way in which we pile despair upon catastrophe, over and over again, rendering everyone paralyzed. You don't have to be some pathetic bleeding heart to see the potential strength in these societies at the grass roots, and know that if we could galvanize the governments, indigenous and external, and equip civil society, and address capacity and infrastructure with external resources, then we could defeat this pandemic. It is not beyond our competence.

I met not long ago with a thousand high school students in Addis Ababa, for a question and answer session that lasted an entire afternoon, and the intelligence and understanding and sophistication of those kids gives nothing but hope; I've met with the WFP [the UN's World Food Programme] truck drivers in Nazareth, south of Addis, as they tell their stories of the training they receive, and how they now always carry condoms on their routes; I've

---

The full text of this speech can be found at <http://www.stephenlewisfoundation.org/docs/20021004-CSIS.html> (September 26, 2003).

met at length with his Holiness, the Patriarch of the Ethiopian Orthodox church as we discussed how the UN family could set in process training for his 350 thousand priests so that they, in turn, could address their parishioners; I've sat over coffee with village women miles and miles from the Ethiopian capital, while neighbours gather to talk about how the virus is transmitted and how to protect themselves. They laugh self-consciously in the presence of a stranger, but they don't mince words.

I've attended the two day sensitivity sessions in Abuja, Nigeria, for the establishment of mother-to-child-transmission clinics . . . a tremendously impressive undertaking; I've sat with the doctors and nurses in a leading hospital in Benue state as they decide how they'll choose those who should receive anti-retroviral treatment when it begins, and how to handle the counselling; I've met with groups of People Living with Aids out in the Eastern region, near Onitsha, as the mothers talk about the kids they'll leave behind, and then make their eloquent, moving, unanswerable plea for treatment. . . .

I'm not kidding myself. I know the task is Herculean. But I also know that . . . the only way to check the next wave is through a dramatic shift in priorities. . . .

First, and most compelling, is the question of gender. . . . There is very little evidence . . . of governments taking seriously the commitment to women. It was one thing to recognize, rhetorically, that women were overwhelmingly at risk, it was quite another to act on the rhetoric. And it would appear, that yet again, as ever, with indifference aforethought, the women are betrayed. The women are always betrayed. . . .

The world has to be made to understand that AIDS has brought into brutal relief the predatory sexual behaviour of adult males, and the terrible consequences of intergenerational sex, and the equally terrible vulnerability of women who have neither sexual power nor sexual autonomy. More, we are just beginning to understand that the levels of sexual violence, the levels of rape, inexorably transmit the virus. Whether it's the violence of conflict, or the violence of a domestic household, women are the targets. It's a part of the human condition that cries out for study and desperate, immediate response. . . .

Second, for more than a decade now, those who have chronicled the sweep of the pandemic, have warned about the excruciating consequences of societies falling apart. . . .

. . . I think it is reasonable to argue that AIDS has caused the famine; that what we all feared one day would happen, is happening. So many people, particularly women, have died, or are desperately ill, or whose immune systems are like shrinking parchment, that there simply aren't enough farmers left to plant the seeds, till the soil, harvest the crops, provide the food. We may be witness to one of those appalling, traumatic societal upheavals where the world shifts on its axis.

We've been predicting that you can't ravage the 15 to 49 year-old productive age group forever, without reaping the whirlwind. The whirlwind is in Southern Africa. And surely that has huge implications for the next wave. If you watch while your educational systems are shattered, your health infrastructure is frayed, your agriculturalists are dying, your militaries and police have astronomic levels of infection, your private sector is atrophying, then it becomes impossible to escape the economic and social and political and military consequences. For the so-called next wave countries, there is no time left to contemplate. There is only time left to act. Southern Africa is the canary in the pandemic.

Third . . . is the question of orphans. As always, there are the hyperactive arithmetic calculations; fourteen million orphans now, twenty-five million by 2010. But whatever the numbers, we have very few solutions. If there really will be, at the outer limits, fifteen million AIDS cases in China by 2010, and twenty-five million in India, and eight million in Russia, then I ask you to reflect on the orphan problem down the road. We now rely primarily on grandmothers, and when they die, we're often faced with what are now called "sibling families." Communities, and foster parents, move heaven and earth to embrace these youngsters, but they all live in such extreme poverty, that another mouth to feed can push everyone over the edge. . . .

. . . The idea of the school as the centrepiece of the child's life . . . the anchor which gives a child the greatest sense of hope, confidence and self-worth . . . is now firmly entrenched in our international norms and our everyday dialectic. And yet, AIDS is playing havoc with the fundamental right of the child, especially the girl child — gender again — to education, and it's as though, seized by some perverse, passive compliance, we watch the havoc unfold and stand inert. It's unbearable, and it's indefensible. . . .

Finally, I want to re-emphasize my conviction that this pandemic, in all its multivarious forms in the countries with which we're dealing, can be turned around. There is tremendous knowledge and selflessness at the grass-roots; it just has to be given a chance. We — and it's the royal, generic "we" — know a great deal, if only we can apply it. We know how to go about Voluntary Counselling and Testing; we know ways in which to reduce, dramatically, vertical (mother-to-child) transmission; we know how to administer anti-retroviral treatment; we know of excellent preventive interventions; we know the world of care at community level, provided by the women, and rooted in faith-based and community-based organizations; we know the knowledge and expertise that can be brought to bear by People Living with AIDS. We know, as well, the huge challenges of mobilizing the political leadership, galvanizing the religious leadership, fighting the curse of stigma and strengthening advocacy on all fronts.

What we don't have is the means to do it with. We don't have the dollars. I've knocked this particular nail through the wall so many times that even I feel a certain ad nauseam quality merely to mention it . . . . But the truth is that what's literally killing the women and men and children of Africa is the lack of resources.

Just two weeks ago, I was meeting in Arusha, Tanzania, with a group of women living with AIDS. I asked them, as I always do, to tell me what they most needed and wanted, and as always the same replies came back: food, because everyone is hungry, especially the children; money for school fees, and some kind of guarantee to keep their kids in school, because when they die they want their children to be assured of an education. And drugs. Anti-retroviral drugs to prolong life . . . so as not to leave their children so prematurely-orphaned. To be quite honest, I never know what to say in such a situation. I'm strangled by the double standard between developed and developing countries. I'm haunted by the monies available for the war on terrorism, and doubtless to be available for the war on Iraq, but somehow never available for the human imperative.

DEFINING FREEDOM/DEBATING RIGHTS

The idea of human rights as understood today — applying to people of all stations everywhere — dates back to the seventeenth and eighteenth centuries when it took form in Britain, the United States, and France. But the definition and protection of these rights has been a special preoccupation of international society only since the end of World War II. Indeed, the degree of attention given the subject by states and increasingly in recent decades by NGO's is extraordinary, as is the degree to which the language of rights has become commonplace parlance. We have already seen evidence of this commitment to human rights language in the texts appearing earlier in this volume — by dissidents in eastern Europe, proponents of *glasnost* in the Soviet Union, leaders of the decolonization process, and U.S. and French feminists.

The rights defined after World War II were broad, giving proponents of a rights-based international political and moral order considerable room to press their case. Over the following half-century some categories of rights have become widely accepted, resulting in formal agreements clarifying and codifying them. Others are either still contested or as yet unexplored. Among the most contentious ideas have been women's rights, the notion that rights are universal and not culturally dependent, and environmental rights. Initiatives in these areas and in others involving indigenous peoples, racial minorities, lesbians and homosexuals, those threatened with the death penalty and genocide, migrants, and poor peoples eager for economic development have kept human rights a field in fascinating flux.

10.10

The United Nations Embraces Human Rights

The foundational document for this postwar flowering of human rights concerns is the United Nations Universal Declaration, approved in December 1948. It challenged the view that the treatment of individuals was a matter of concern only for the states in which they lived. Global society had reason to posit minimum standards for all. The declaration was written by an international commission chaired by Eleanor Roosevelt, the widow of President Franklin D. Roosevelt. The consensus that the commission cobbled together won broad support when it came up for a vote in the General Assembly; there were none opposed, and only South Africa, Saudi Arabia, the Soviet Union, and its eastern European allies abstained.

The declaration put a wide range of human activity under the umbrella of protected rights. How would you describe the range of those rights? Which ones seem the most open to confusion or debate? What developments might have created international support for enshrining a broad range of rights at this particular time? What is the basis for asserting that the rights enumerated here are universal and should be respected? To what extent are those rights actually honored in practice today?

Universal Declaration of Human Rights
December 10, 1948

Whereas recognition of the inherent dignity and of the equal and inalienable rights of all members of the human family is the foundation of freedom, justice and peace in the world,

Whereas disregard and contempt for human rights have resulted in barbarous acts which have outraged the conscience of mankind, and the advent of a world in which human beings shall enjoy freedom of speech and belief and freedom from fear and want has been proclaimed as the highest aspiration of the common people,

Whereas it is essential, if man is not to be compelled to have recourse, as a last resort, to rebellion against tyranny and oppression, that human rights should be protected by the rule of law, . . .

Now, therefore,

The General Assembly

Proclaims this Universal Declaration of Human Rights as a common standard of achievement for all peoples and all nations . . . .

ARTICLE 1

All human beings are born free and equal in dignity and rights. They are endowed with reason and conscience and should act towards one another in a spirit of brotherhood.

ARTICLE 2

Everyone is entitled to all the rights and freedoms set forth in this Declaration, without distinction of any kind, such as race, colour, sex, language, religion, political or other opinion, national or social origin, property, birth or other status.

Yearbook of the United Nations, 1948–49 (Lake Success, N.Y.: U.N. Department of Public Information, 1950), 535–37. Also available on the United Nations website: <http://www.un.org/rights/50/decla.htm> (May 12, 2003).

Furthermore, no distinction shall be made on the basis of the political, jurisdictional or international status of the country or territory to which a person belongs, whether it be independent, trust, non-self-governing or under any other limitation of sovereignty.

ARTICLE 3

Everyone has the right to life, liberty and security of person.

ARTICLE 4

No one shall be held in slavery or servitude; slavery and the slave trade shall be prohibited in all their forms.

ARTICLE 5

No one shall be subjected to torture or to cruel, inhuman or degrading treatment or punishment.

ARTICLE 6

Everyone has the right to recognition everywhere as a person before the law.

ARTICLE 7

All are equal before the law and are entitled without any discrimination to equal protection of the law. All are entitled to equal protection against any discrimination in violation of this Declaration and against any incitement to such discrimination.

ARTICLE 8

Everyone has the right to an effective remedy by the competent national tribunals for acts violating the fundamental rights granted him by the constitution or by law.

ARTICLE 9

No one shall be subjected to arbitrary arrest, detention or exile.

ARTICLE 10

Everyone is entitled in full equality to a fair and public hearing by an independent and impartial tribunal, in the determination of his rights and obligations and of any criminal charge against him.

ARTICLE 11

1. Everyone charged with a penal offence has the right to be presumed innocent until proved guilty according to law in a public trial at which he has had all the guarantees necessary for his defence.

2. No one shall be held guilty of any penal offence on account of any act or omission which did not constitute a penal offence, under national or international law, at the time when it was committed. Nor shall a heavier penalty

be imposed than the one that was applicable at the time the penal offence was committed.

ARTICLE 12

No one shall be subjected to arbitrary interference with his privacy, family, home or correspondence, nor to attacks upon his honour and reputation. Everyone has the right to the protection of the law against such interference or attacks.

ARTICLE 13

1. Everyone has the right to freedom of movement and residence within the borders of each state.

2. Everyone has the right to leave any country, including his own, and to return to his country.

ARTICLE 14

1. Everyone has the right to seek and to enjoy in other countries asylum from persecution.

2. This right may not be invoked in the case of prosecutions genuinely arising from non-political crimes or from acts contrary to the purposes and principles of the United Nations.

ARTICLE 15

1. Everyone has the right to a nationality.

2. No one shall be arbitrarily deprived of his nationality nor denied the right to change his nationality.

ARTICLE 16

1. Men and women of full age, without any limitation due to race, nationality or religion, have the right to marry and to found a family. They are entitled to equal rights as to marriage, during marriage and at its dissolution.

2. Marriage shall be entered into only with the free and full consent of the intending spouses.

3. The family is the natural and fundamental group unit of society and is entitled to protection by society and the State.

ARTICLE 17

1. Everyone has the right to own property alone as well as in association with others.

2. No one shall be arbitrarily deprived of his property.

ARTICLE 18

Everyone has the right to freedom of thought, conscience and religion; this right includes freedom to change his religion or belief, and freedom, either alone or in community with others and in public or private, to manifest his religion or belief in teaching, practice, worship and observance.

ARTICLE 19

Everyone has the right to freedom of opinion and expression; this right includes freedom to hold opinions without interference and to seek, receive and impart information and ideas through any media and regardless of frontiers.

ARTICLE 20

1. Everyone has the right to freedom of peaceful assembly and association.
2. No one may be compelled to belong to an association.

ARTICLE 21

1. Everyone has the right to take part in the government of his country, directly or through freely chosen representatives.
2. Everyone has the right of equal access to public service in his country.
3. The will of the people shall be the basis of the authority of government; this will shall be expressed in periodic and genuine elections which shall be by universal and equal suffrage and shall be held by secret vote or by equivalent free voting procedures.

ARTICLE 22

Everyone, as a member of society, has the right to social security and is entitled to realization, through national effort and international co-operation and in accordance with the organization and resources of each State, of the economic, social and cultural rights indispensable for his dignity and the free development of his personality.

ARTICLE 23

1. Everyone has the right to work, to free choice of employment, to just and favourable conditions of work and to protection against unemployment.
2. Everyone, without any discrimination, has the right to equal pay for equal work.
3. Everyone who works has the right to just and favourable remuneration ensuring for himself and his family an existence worthy of human dignity, and supplemented, if necessary, by other means of social protection.
4. Everyone has the right to form and to join trade unions for the protection of his interests.

ARTICLE 24

Everyone has the right to rest and leisure, including reasonable limitation of working hours and periodic holidays with pay.

ARTICLE 25

1. Everyone has the right to a standard of living adequate for the health and well-being of himself and of his family, including food, clothing, housing

and medical care and necessary social services, and the right to security in the event of unemployment, sickness, disability, widowhood, old age or other lack of livelihood in circumstances beyond his control.

2. Motherhood and childhood are entitled to special care and assistance. All children, whether born in or out of wedlock, shall enjoy the same social protection.

ARTICLE 26

1. Everyone has the right to education. Education shall be free, at least in the elementary and fundamental stages. Elementary education shall be compulsory. Technical and professional education shall be made generally available and higher education shall be equally accessible to all on the basis of merit.

2. Education shall be directed to the full development of the human personality and to the strengthening of respect for human rights and fundamental freedoms. It shall promote understanding, tolerance and friendship among all nations, racial or religious groups, and shall further the activities of the United Nations for the maintenance of peace.

3. Parents have a prior right to choose the kind of education that shall be given to their children.

ARTICLE 27

1. Everyone has the right freely to participate in the cultural life of the community, to enjoy the arts and to share in scientific advancement and its benefits.

2. Everyone has the right to the protection of the moral and material interests resulting from any scientific, literary or artistic production of which he is the author.

ARTICLE 28

Everyone is entitled to a social and international order in which the rights and freedoms set forth in this Declaration can be fully realized.

ARTICLE 29

1. Everyone has duties to the community in which alone the free and full development of his personality is possible.

10.11

Debating Women's Rights

The United Nations took the lead in promoting women's rights, beginning with a 1975 conference in Mexico City followed by others at regular intervals. The Beijing meeting, the fourth in the series, was held in 1995, and the document that emerged from that conference provides a sense of concerns of the international women's movement at century's end. It also helps highlight areas of continuing international disagreement. The Vatican statement included here was released in anticipation of the final report, prompted by the direction in which preparatory discussions had been moving. The writing by the Egyptian Sayyid Qutb, born 1906 and executed by Nasser in 1968, expresses an Islamic position on gender rights still in wide currency in the 1990s. Qutb's standing as one of the leading voices in the postwar Islamist resurgence in culture and politics gives this piece special importance.

How does the Beijing statement move beyond the provisions on women laid out in the 1948 declaration? How do the Vatican and Qutb define gender rights? Where do they differ with the Beijing conference statement? How might de Beauvoir and NOW (Documents 5.11 and 5.12) respond to the positions taken here? Why are gender roles and rights such a sharply contested area in the rights debate?

Platform for Action, the Fourth World Conference on Women

Beijing, September 1995

[T]he human rights of women and of the girl child are an inalienable, integral and indivisible part of universal human rights. As an agenda for action, the Platform seeks to promote and protect the full enjoyment of all human rights and the fundamental freedoms of all women throughout their life cycle. . . .

. . . While the significance of national and regional particularities and various historical, cultural and religious backgrounds must be borne in mind, it is the duty of States, regardless of their political, economic and cultural systems, to promote and protect all human rights and fundamental freedoms. The implementation of this Platform, including through national laws and the formulation of strategies, policies, programmes and development priorities, is the sovereign responsibility of each State . . . .

. . . The full and equal participation of women in political, civil, economic, social and cultural life at the national, regional and international levels, and the eradication of all forms of discrimination on the grounds of sex are priority objectives of the international community. . . .

. . . In several countries, there have been important changes in the relationships between women and men, especially where there have been major advances in education for women and significant increases in their participation in the paid labour force. The boundaries of the gender division of labour between productive and reproductive roles are gradually being crossed as women have started to enter formerly male-dominated areas of work and men have started to accept greater responsibility for domestic tasks, including child care. However, changes in women's roles have been greater and much more rapid than changes in men's roles. In many countries, the differences between women's and men's achievements and activities are still not recognized as the consequences of socially constructed gender roles rather than immutable biological differences.

Available at the United Nations website: <http://www.un.org/womenwatch/daw/beijing/platform/> (July 15, 2002).

Moreover, . . . equality between women and men has still not been achieved. On average, women represent a mere 10 per cent of all elected legislators world wide and in most national and international administrative structures, both public and private, they remain underrepresented. . . .

Women play a critical role in the family. The family is the basic unit of society and as such should be strengthened. It is entitled to receive comprehensive protection and support. In different cultural, political and social systems, various forms of the family exist. The rights, capabilities and responsibilities of family members must be respected. Women make a great contribution to the welfare of the family and to the development of society, which is still not recognized or considered in its full importance. The social significance of maternity, motherhood and the role of parents in the family and in the upbringing of children should be acknowledged. The upbringing of children requires shared responsibility of parents, women and men and society as a whole. Maternity, motherhood, parenting and the role of women in procreation must not be a basis for discrimination nor restrict the full participation of women in society. Recognition should also be given to the important role often played by women in many countries in caring for other members of their family. . . .

The advancement of women and the achievement of equality between women and men are a matter of human rights and a condition for social justice and should not be seen in isolation as a women's issue. They are the only way to build a sustainable, just and developed society. Empowerment of women and equality between women and men are prerequisites for achieving political, social, economic, cultural and environmental security among all peoples.

Statement by the Vatican Press Office, "To Promote Women's Equal Dignity"
August 25, 1995

During the [Beijing Conference on Women's] preparatory process a tension between two very distant positions emerged.

The first seems to reduce the human person — woman in this case — to social functions that must be overcome; it is paradoxical that the struggle for equality with man ends up in denying women the most intimate truth of their existence. Three main characteristics of this feminism are: a negative attitude towards the family, acritical [uncritical?] support for abortion and an angry anthropology in which feminine problems are linked solely to sexuality and contraception.

The statement was issued by Dr. Joaquín Navarro-Valls, director of the Press Office. From the website maintained by Priests for Life: <http://www.priestsforlife.org/magisterium/navarrobeijing08-25-95.htm> (May 25, 2003).

The second considers women and men equal co-partners — and not enemies — in the immense task of bettering humanity. It affirms the equal dignity of woman, her right to responsible motherhood, and denounces the totalitarian ideology that, in the name of governments and totalitarian anthropologies, tries to pit the State against the family, women against men or children, rich against poor. . . .

Women and men are the illustration of a *biological, individual, personal and spiritual complementarity*. Femininity is the unique and specific characteristic of woman, as masculinity is of man. This difference — by reason of equal dignity — must find in practice juridical recognition in various legal systems. A woman cannot accept the parameters imposed by and through men within her family as well as her professional life. A woman has the right to choose between: having a profession, being simultaneously a mother and carrying on a profession, and being a mother and dedicating all her activity to the home. . . .

The family is the fundamental unit of society. For this reason there needs to be special protection of it by society. This fact has been recognized and emphasized in international documents on human rights up to the present time. . . .

A woman's work within the family today is the object of serious discrimination especially in Western countries, where one might add, it is becoming almost impossible for a woman to dedicate herself solely to the home. If society organizes itself solely on the criteria of productivity, motherhood will certainly be the victim. The "social value" of work in the home has been publicly proclaimed, but it has not yet received adequate legal recognition, at least with regard to economic remuneration. . . .

Physical violence against women includes not only rape, war, genital mutilation, forced prostitution and arranged marriages, but also forced contraception, sterilization and abortion. . . . It is widely documented that in many countries in the campaign for demographic control often there is no respect for the "informed consent," nor is a woman fully informed about the effects of medicines or medical techniques. Equally, many cases of forced sterilization as part of oppressive programmes of population control have been recorded. These practices — which are barely mentioned or completely absent in the Platform of Action — certainly violate all the fundamental human rights of women and are totally unacceptable.

The role of women as teachers of peace in society, in family, political, national and international life can never be emphasized enough. Their contribution to the family, teaching children respect, love, understanding, and caring for one another is greater and more important than any scholastic programme. The family is the first school — and in many underdeveloped countries, the only one.

Practical experience as much as academic social psychology teaches that the mother has a fundamental ability in maintaining peace and in resolving conflict, and that she plays the principal role as mediator within the family. She can keep members of the family united through her continued effort of mediation. . . .

[The Vatican] continues to insist that no human right to abortion exists because it contradicts the human right to life. The human right to life is the basic human right: all others stem from it. Human life deserves respect in any circumstance. A life in a poor country or in a developing country must be as much respected as any human life in the wealthy West. . . .

Certainly the Conference will not succeed in uniting the world if it attempts to impose, particularly on developing countries, *a Western product, a socially reductive philosophy, which does not even represent the hopes and needs of the majority of Western women.*

Sayyid Qutb
From *Social Justice in Islam*
1964

As between the two sexes, woman has been guaranteed complete equality with man in respect to sexual difference as such and to human rights[,] and precedence of one sex over the other is established only in some specific situations connected with natural and recognized capacities, skills or responsibilities, which do not affect the essential nature of the human situation of the two sexes. Wherever these capacities, skills and responsibilities are equal, the sexes are equal, and wherever they differ in some way[,] there is a corresponding difference between the sexes.

In religious and spiritual matters they are equal. . . .

In matters of economic and financial competency they are also equal. . . .

. . . Because a man is free of the obligations of motherhood[,] he confronts the affairs of society over a longer period of time and all his mental faculties fit him for this, while the obligations of motherhood restrict the woman for most of her days and develop her emotional and passionate side. By the same token, it is man's reflective and deliberative side that develops. So, if he is made the manager of the woman's affairs[,] it is because of his natural capacity and skill for this task, in addition to the expenses he is obligated to, and the financial aspect is closely linked to this management authority. Thus he has a right corresponding to his duties, and in the end it works out to an equality of rights and duties in the broader perspective of the relations between the sexes and of life as a whole.

. . . [W]oman has a greater right to care than the man, and this is the right that corresponds to his right of management. . . .

William E. Shepard, *Sayyid Qutb and Islamic Activism: A Translation and Critical Analysis of* Social Justice in Islam (Leiden: E. J. Brill, 1996), 61–66. This translation is based on the sixth edition of *Social Justice* published in 1964.

. . . By the nature of the tasks of motherhood, the woman develops her emotional and passionate side, while the man develops his reflective and deliberative side . . . .

Islam has taken into account what assures the woman of her religious and economic equality and provided guarantees arising from the fact that she can be married only with her permission and acceptance and without any compulsion or having her wishes ignored. . . .

We must remember that Islam guarantees women all these rights and ample assurances in a spirit of pure respect and honor, unsullied by economic or materialistic considerations. . . .

. . . It is well to remember that the West made women leave the home to work because the men there shirked their responsibility to support their families, and made their women pay the price of their chastity and their honor. Only thus were women driven to work.

It is well for us to remember that when women went out to work, the materalistic West took advantage of their need and exploited the increased supply to lower their wages, and that employers used cheap women's labor to replace the workers who were beginning to raise their heads and demand a decent wage.

When women demanded equality there, this meant first and foremost equality of pay, so they could eat and live! When they could not get this equality, they demanded the right to vote so as to have an effective voice. Then they demanded the right to enter the parliaments so as to have a positive voice in establishing that equality! This is because the laws that governed society were made by men alone and are not — as in Islam — the laws of God, which strike a just balance between His servants, men and women.

It is well for us to remember that France continued until the time of the Fourth Republic after the last war without granting women the right to control their own property — a right which Islam does grant — without the permission of a guardian, while it does grant them the right to be unchaste, openly or secretly. This last right is the only right Islam forbids to women! It likewise forbids it to men out of consideration for human honor and feelings and to raise the level of sexual relations above that of mere physical relations outside the bonds of home or family. . . .

We must remember all this before our eyes are deceived by the false glitter, for Islam gave women rights fourteen centuries ago that Western "civilization" has not given them to this day. Islam gave them — in the case of need — the right to work and the right to earn, but it also preserved for them the right to be provided for within the family, because it considers life more than the body or possessions and its aims are higher than mere food and drink. Also, it looks at life from many angles and sees different tasks for different individuals, but tasks that are mutually supporting and complementary. In this way it sees the task of the man and the task of the woman, and it obligates each of them to do his task first, so that life may develop and progress. It ordains for each of them the rights that guarantee the achievement of this general human goal.

10.12

Singapore's Case for Respecting Regional Differences

Singapore is a city-state with an influence far exceeding its size — an area less than 250 square miles and a population of less than four million in 1999. Since independence in 1959, this former British colony has been tightly run by the People's Action Party (PAP) headed by Lee Kuan Yew and, following his retirement in 1990, by his party associates. Under their leadership, a country that is three-quarters Chinese but includes substantial Malay and Indian minorities has contained the social tensions that afflict many multi-ethnic societies. The PAP-run government has strictly enforced rules against immoral and criminal behavior. And it has made the city the hub of transport, manufacturing, and services in the world's fastest growing region. As a result of this record of stability and rapidly rising and widely shared economic growth, the Singapore model offers a striking example of an Asian alternative to the much touted American insistence on sweeping freedoms within the market place, within society, and within the political system.

The statement that follows comes from Singapore's foreign minister, Wong Kan Seng, an influential figure within the PAP. What argument is he making here? That cultural differences are deep-seated and enduring or superficial and mutable? That the understanding of rights may differ from place to place at any moment but over time tend to move in the same direction? Does Wong's position support Huntington's or Said's position on a possible emerging clash of civilizations?

Wong Kan Seng
Statement at the Second World Conference on Human Rights
Vienna, June 16, 1993

Forty-five years after the Universal Declaration was adopted as a "common standard of achievement," debates over the meaning of many of its thirty articles continue. The debate is not just between the West and the Third World. Not every country in the West will agree on the specific meaning of every one of the Universal Declaration's thirty articles. Not everyone in the West will even agree that all of them are really rights.

Let us take the United States of America as an example. Not every state of the U.S.A. interprets such matters as, for example, capital punishment or the rights to education in the same way. Despite U.S. Supreme Court rulings, abortion is still a hotly contested issue. But this multiplicity of state and local laws is not decried as a retreat from universalism. On the contrary, the clash and clamour of contending interests is held up as a shining model of democratic freedom in the U.S.A.

Reproduced in James T. H. Tang, ed., *Human Rights and International Relations in the Asia-Pacific Region* (London: Pinter, 1995), 243–47.

For that matter, the right to trial by jury, so precious in Britain and the United States, has never prevailed in France. Are we therefore to conclude that human rights are repressed by the French? This would be absurd. Sweden, to give another example, has more comprehensive and communal social arrangements than some other Western countries may find comfortable. Is Sweden therefore a tyranny? Naturally not. Order and justice are obtained in diverse ways in different countries at different times.

Therefore, are the common interests of humanity really advanced by seeking to impose an artificial and stifling unanimity? The extent and exercise of rights, in particular civil rights, varies greatly from one culture or political community to another. This is because they are the products of the historical experiences of particular peoples. . . .

. . . Only if we all recognize the rich diversity of the human community and accept the free interaction of all ideas can the international consensus be deepened and expanded. No one has a monopoly of truth. . . .

Diversity cannot justify gross violations of human rights. Murder is murder whether perpetrated in America, Asia or Africa. No one claims torture as part of their cultural heritage. . . . There are other such rights that must be enjoyed by all human beings everywhere in a civilized world. All cultures aspire to promote human dignity in their own ways. But the hard core of rights that [are] truly universal is perhaps smaller than we sometimes like to pretend.

. . . Singaporeans, and people in many other parts of the world do not agree, for instance, that pornography is an acceptable manifestation of free expression or that homosexual relationships are just a matter of lifestyle choice. Most of us will also maintain that the right to marry is confined to those of the opposite gender.

. . . The very idea of human rights is historically specific. . . . For example, how rights were defined in Europe or America a hundred years ago is certainly not how they are defined today. And they will be defined differently a hundred years hence.

Take Britain for illustration. Its Parliament was established in 1215 with the signing of the Magna Carta. But women only had the right to vote in 1928. Up till 1948, Oxbridge [Oxford and Cambridge] university graduates and businessmen had extra votes.

The United States of America gained independence in 1776. Only those who paid poll tax or property tax had the right to vote from 1788. There were barriers of age, colour, sex and income. In 1860, income and property qualifications were abolished but other barriers like literacy tests and poll tax still discriminated against African-American and other disadvantaged groups. Women only had the vote in 1920. It was not until 1965 that the African-Americans can vote freely after the Voting Rights Act suspended literacy tests and other voter qualification devices which kept them out. . . .

The U.S.A., Britain and France took 200 years or more to evolve into full democracies. Can we therefore expect the citizens of the many newly independent countries of this century to acquire the same rights as those enjoyed by the developed nations when they lack the economic, educational and social pre-conditions to exercise such rights fully? . . .

. . . Poverty is an obscene violation of the most basic of individual rights. Only those who have forgotten the pangs of hunger will think of consoling the hungry by telling them that they should be free before they can eat. Our experience is that economic growth is the necessary foundation of any system that claims to advance human dignity, and that order and stability are essential for development. . . .

Development and good government require a balance between the rights of the individual and those of the community to which every individual must belong, and through which individuals must realize their rights. Where this balance will be struck will vary for different countries at different points of their history. Every country must find its own way. . . .

Singapore's political and social arrangements have irked some foreign critics because they are not in accordance with their theories of how societies should properly organize themselves. We have intervened to change individual social behaviour in ways other countries consider intrusive. We maintain and have deployed laws that others may find harsh. For example, the police, narcotics or immigration officers are empowered by the Misuse of Drugs Act to test the urine for drugs of any person who behaves in a suspicious manner. If the result is positive, rehabilitation treatment is compulsory. Such a law will be considered unconstitutional in some countries and such urine tests will lead to suits for damages for battery and assault and an invasion of privacy. As a result, the community's interests are sacrificed because of the human rights of drug consumers and traffickers. So drug-related crimes flourish. . . .

We make no apology for doing what we believe is correct rather than what our critics advise. Singaporeans are responsible for Singapore's future. We justify ourselves to our people, not by abstract theories or the approbation of foreigners, but by the more rigorous test of practical success.

Our citizens live with freedom and dignity in an environment that is safe, healthy, clean and incorrupt. They have easy access to cultural, recreational and social amenities, good standards of education for our children and prospects for a better life for future generations. I can say without false modesty that many of our well meaning critics cannot claim as much. We do not think that our arrangements will suit everybody. But they suit ourselves. This is the ultimate test of any political system.

. . . We can force states to pay lip service to a Declaration. But we cannot force states to genuinely respect human rights. In the real world of sovereign states, respect and political commitment can only be forged through the accommodation of different interests.

Unless we all remember this, I fear that we will only fracture the international consensus on human rights. If this happens, the responsibility must lie with those who are so blinded by their own arrogance and certainties as to lose the capacity for imagination and empathy.

10.13

"A Duty to Protect and Preserve the Environment"

In May 1994 an international group of human rights specialists and environmentalists gathered at the UN offices in Geneva to draft a statement asserting for the first time a formal link between the environment and human rights. The drafters came together at the initiative of the U.S.-based Sierra Club. The result was a brief but comprehensive statement on the topic.

What connection does this draft assert between the environment and human rights? How do you imagine representatives of the developed and developing world reacting to this statement? Representatives of industry? Indigenous peoples seeking protection of their environment as part of their defense of a way of life? Does the declaration express pious wishes without practical effect? Or should it be seen as a critical step in the construction of an international consensus? How might these general principles be turned into clear and enforceable regulations?

"Draft Declaration of Principles on Human Rights and the Environment"
May 1994

1. Human rights, an ecologically sound environment, sustainable development and peace are interdependent and indivisible.

2. All persons have the right to a secure, healthy and ecologically sound environment. This right and other human rights, including civil, cultural, economic, political and social rights, are universal, interdependent and indivisible.

3. All persons shall be free from any form of discrimination in regard to actions and decisions that affect the environment.

4. All persons have the right to an environment adequate to meet equitably the needs of present generations and that does not impair the rights of future generations to meet equitably their needs.

5. All persons have the right to freedom from pollution, environmental degradation and activities that adversely affect the environment, threaten life, health, livelihood, well-being or sustainable development within, across or outside national boundaries.

6. All persons have the right to protection and preservation of the air, soil, water, sea-ice, flora and fauna, and the essential processes and areas necessary to maintain biological diversity and ecosystems. . . .

10. All persons have the right to adequate housing, land tenure and living conditions in a secure, healthy and ecologically sound environment. . . .

From the website for the University of Minnesota Human Rights Library: <http://www1.umn.edu/humanrts/instree/1994-dec.htm> (May 21, 2003).

14. Indigenous peoples have the right to control their lands, territories and natural resources and to maintain their traditional way of life. This includes the right to security in the enjoyment of their means of subsistence. . . .

18. All persons have the right to active, free, and meaningful participation in planning and decision-making activities and processes that may have an impact on the environment and development. This includes the right to a prior assessment of the environmental, developmental and human rights consequences of proposed actions. . . .

21. All persons, individually and in association with others, have a duty to protect and preserve the environment.

22. All States shall respect and ensure the right to a secure, healthy and ecologically sound environment. Accordingly, they shall adopt the administrative, legislative and other measures necessary to effectively implement the rights in this Declaration.

Acknowledgments (continued from page ii)

Asadollah Alam. Excerpts from *The Shah and I: The Confidential Diary of Iran's Royal Court, 1969–1977*, translated and edited by Alinaghi Alikham. Copyright © 1991 Asadollah Alam. Reprinted with permission of Palgrave Macmillan.

Hamid Algar. Excerpts from *Islam and Revolution: Writings and Declarations of Iman Khomeini*, translated and annotated by Hamid Algar. Copyright © 1981 by Mizan Press. Reprinted by permission of Hamid Algar.

Excerpts from the *Bulletin of the European Communities*, No. 10, Volume 22, 1989. Reprinted by permission.

Philip Caputo. "In Death's Grey Land." From *A Rumor of War* by Philip Caputo. © 1977 by Philip Caputo. Reprinted by permission of Henry Holt and Company, LLC.

Rachel Carson. Excerpts from *Silent Spring* by Rachel Carson. Copyright © 1962 by Rachel L. Carson, renewed 1990 by Roger Christie. Excerpted and reprinted by permission of Houghton Mifflin Company. All rights reserved.

Jorge G. Casteneda and Carlos Heredia. "Another NAFTA: What a good agreement should offer." From *World Policy Journal* 9 (Fall/Winter, 1992). Reprinted by permission of the World Policy Journal.

Excerpts from *The Challenges of Our Times: Disarmament and Social Progress*. Copyright © 1986 International Publishers Co., Inc. Reprinted by permission.

Stephen F. Cohen and Katrina vanden Heuvel. Excerpts from *Voices of Glasnost: Interviews with Gorbachev's Reformers* by Stephen F. Cohen and Katrina vanden Heuvel. Copyright © 1989 by Stephen F. Cohen and Katrina vanden Heuvel. Used with permission of W.W. Norton & Company, Inc.

Excerpts from *The Current Digest of the Soviet Press*, Volume XXXIX, No. 4 (February 25, 1987); XXXIX, No. 5 (March 4, 1987); XXXIX, No. 6 (March 11, 1987); XLIII, No. 52 (January 29, 1992). Translation copyright by *The Current Digest of the Soviet Press*, published weekly at Columbus, Ohio. Reprinted by permission of the Digest.

Simone de Beauvoir. Excerpts from the Introduction to *The Second Sex*, translated and edited by H. M. Parshley. Copyright 1952 and renewed 1980 by Alfred A. Knopf, a division of Random House, Inc. Used by permission of Alfred A. Knopf, a division of Random House, Inc.

Mrs. Nguyen Thi Dinh. Excerpts from *No Other Road to Take: Memoir of Mrs Nguyen Thi Dinh*, translated by Mai Elliott. Copyright © 1976. Reprinted by permission of Cornell University Press.

Dr. Elizabeth Enslin. Excerpts from *A Field of One's Own: Gender and Land Rights in South Asia*, edited by Bina Agarwal. Copyright © Bina Agarwal. Reprinted by permission of Dr. Elizabeth Enslin.

Frantz Fanon. "Liberation and Violence." From *The Wretched of the Earth* by Frantz Fanon, translated by Constance Farrington. Copyright © 1963 by Presence Africaine. Used by permission of Grove/Atlantic, Inc.

Erika Friedl. Excerpts from *Women of Deh Koh* by Erika Friedl. Copyright © 1989. Used by permission of the publisher, Smithsonian Institution Press.

Milton Friedman. Excerpts from *Capitalism and Freedom* by Milton Friedman. Copyright © 1962 University of Chicago Press. Reprinted by permission.

Julian Goldman. "He makes only $3,000 a year . . . but is worth $112,290!" From *Prosperity and Consumer Credit*. Copyright © 1930. Reprinted by permission of HarperCollins Publishers.

The Göttingen Manifesto on the Nuclear Threat. From *The Bulletin of the Atomic Scientists,* June 13, 1957. Courtesy of the publisher.

Michihiko Hachiya. Excerpts from *Hiroshima Diary: The Journal of a Japanese Physician, August 6–September 30, 1945,* translated by Warner Wells, M.D. Copyright © 1955 by the University of North Carolina Press. Renewed 1995. Used by permission of the publisher.

Václav Havel. Excerpts from *Open Letters: Selected Writings 1965–1990,* translated by Paul Wilson. Copyright © 1991 by A.G. Brain. Preface/translation copyright © 1985, 1988, 1991 by Paul Wilson. Used by permission of Alfred A. Knopf, a division of Random House, Inc.

Liz Heron. Excerpts from *Truth, Dare or Promise: Girls Growing Up in the Fifties,* edited by Liz Heron. Copyright © 1985 Liz Heron. Published by Virago Press, Ltd. Reprinted by permission.

Kessing's Research Report. Excerpts from *Germany and Eastern Europe Since 1945: From the Potsdam Agreement to Chancellor Brandt's "Ostpolitik."* Copyright © 1973 by Kessing's Publications, Limited. Reprinted with the permission of Scribner, an imprint of Simon & Schuster Adult Publishing Group.

John Maynard Keynes. Excerpts from *The Collected Writings* by John Maynard Keynes. *Volume IX: Essays in Persuasion,* © The Royal Economic Society 1972. *Volume XXI: Activities 1931–1939, World Crises and Policies in Britain and America,* edited by Donald Moggridge. © The Royal Economic Society 1982 Reprinted by permission of Palgrave Macmillan.

Nikita Khrushchev. Excerpt from *Khrushchev Remembers: The Glasnost Tapes,* edited and translated by Strobe Talbott. Copyright © 1970 by Little, Brown and Company, Inc. Reprinted by permission of Andrew Nurnberg Associates Limited.

Nicholas D. Kristof. "Far from Beijing, Good Life Is a Goal." Originally titled "Xincheng Journal: Far from Beijing, The Good Life Is Goal." From *The New York Times,* November 14, 1989. Copyright © 1989 New York Times Company. Reprinted by permission.

Walter Laqueur and Barry Rubin. Excerpts from *The Israel-Arab Reader* by Walter Laqueur and Barry Rubin. Copyright © 1969, 1970 by B.L. Mazel, Inc. Copyright © 1976 by Walter Laqueur. Copyright © 1984, 1995, 2000 by Walter Laqueur and Barry Rubin. Used by permission of Viking Penguin, a division of Penguin Group (USA) Inc.

Stephen H. Lewis, UN Secretary General Special Envoy for HIV/AIDS in Africa. Excerpts from a speech delivered to a conference on "HIV/AIDS and 'Next Wave' Countries" at the Center for Strategic and International Studies, Washington, D.C., October 4, 2002. The full text of this speech can be found at www.stephenlewisfoundation.org. Reprinted by permission.

Jan Lipski. Excerpts from *KOR: A History of the Worker's Defense Committee in Poland, 1976–1981* by Jan Lipski. Copyright © 1985 The Regents of the University of California. Reprinted by permission.

Henry R. Luce. "The American Century." Excerpt from *Life* 10, February 17, 1941. © 1941 Time, Inc. Reprinted by permission.

Dennis L. Meadows. "Club of Rome report on the looming environmental crisis." From *The Limits to Growth* by Donella H. Meadows, Dennis L. Meadows, Jorgen Randers and William W. Behrens III. Copyright © 1972 by Dennis L. Meadows. Reprinted by permission of Dennis L. Meadows.

Johanna McGeary. "Death Stalks a Continent." Excerpt from article in *Time,* February 21, 2001. © 2001 Time, Inc. Reprinted by permission.

Ho Chi Minh. "The Path Which Led Me to Leninism." "Declaration of Vietnamese Independence, Hanoi, September 2, 1945." Excerpts from *Selected Writings (1920–1969).* Copyright © 1973. Reprinted by permission of the Foreign Languages Press.

Han Minzhu. Excerpts from *Cries for Democracy* edited by Han Minzhu. Copyright © 1990 Princeton University Press. Reprinted by permission of Princeton University Press.

Shaul Mishal and Reuben Aharoni. Excerpt from *Speaking Stones: Communiques from the Intifada Underground* by Shaul Mishal and Reuben Aharoni. Copyright © 1994. Reprinted with the permission of Syracuse University Press.

Toril Moi. "Tales from the Women's Movement." Excerpts from *French Feminist Thought: A Reader*, by Toril Moi, ed. Copyright © 1987. Reprinted by permission of Blackwell Publishing.

Akio Morita and Edwin M. Reingold, and Mitsuko Shimomura. Excerpts from *Made in Japan* by Akio Morita and Edwin M. Reingold, and Mitsuko Shimomura. Copyright © 1986 by E.P. Dutton. Used by permission of Dutton, a division of Penguin Group (USA) Inc.

Kwame Nkrumah. Excerpts from *Revolutionary Path* by Kwame Nkrumah. Copyright © 1973 International Publishers. Reprinted by permission of ZED Books.

NOW Statement of Purpose. Reprinted by permission of the National Organization of Women, Inc.

PEW Research Center. "America Admired: Yet Its New Vulnerability Seen as a Good Thing, Say Opinion Leaders." Reprinted by permission.

Dirk Philipsen. Excerpts from *We Were the People: Voices from East Germany's Revolutionary Autumn of 1989*. Copyright © 1993, Duke University Press. All rights reserved. Used by permission of the publisher.

Karl Polanyi-Levitt. Excerpts from from *The Great Transformation*. Reprinted by permission of Kari Polanyi-Levitt.

Elena Poniatowska. Excerpts from *Massacre in Mexico*, translated by Helen R. Lane. Copyright © 1975 by The Viking Press. Original copyright © 1971 by Ediciones Era. Used by permission of Viking Penguin, a division of Penguin Group (USA) Inc.

J. B. Priestley. "Britain and the Nuclear Bombs." Taken from an article which first appeared in the *New Statesman*, November 2, 1957. Reprinted by permission of New Statesman Ltd.

Sodei Rinjiro. Excerpts from *Dear General MacArthur: Letters from the Japanese during the American Occupation*. Copyright © 2001 by Sodei Rinjiro. Originally published in Japanese as *Haikei Makkasa gensui-sama: Seryolda no Nihomijin no teagami* by Osuki Shoten. © 1985 by Sodei Rinkiro. Reprinted by permission of Rowman & Littlefield.

Fujie Ryōso. "We Found His Testament." Excerpts from *Widows of Hiroshima* edited by Mikio Kanda. Copyright © Mikio Kanda, ed. English translation © The Macmillan Press Ltd. 1989. Reprinted with permission of Palgrave Macmillan.

Bertrand Russell. "The Political and Cultural Influence." Excerpts from *The Impact of America on European Culture*. Copyright © 1951 by The Beacon Press. Reprinted by permission of Beacon Press, Boston.

Edward Said. "The Clash of Ignorance." From *The Nation*, October 22, 2001. Copyright © 2001. Reprinted by permission.

Jennifer Schirmer. Excerpts from *The Guatemalan Military Project: A Violence Called Democracy* by Jennifer Schirmer. Copyright © 1998 University of Pennsylvania Press. All rights reserved. Reprinted by permission of the University of Pennsylvania Press.

Peter Seybolt. Excerpts from *Throwing the Emperor from His Horse: Portrait of a Village Leader*. Copyright © by Westview Press. Reprinted by permission of Westview Press, a member of Perseus Books, LLC.

William E. Shepard. Excerpt from *Sayyid Qutb and Islamic Activism* by William E. Shepard. Copyright © 1996 by E.J. Brill, Leiden, The Netherlands. Reprinted by permission.

Edgar Snow. Excerpts from *Red Star Over China*. Copyright © 1968 by Edgar Snow. Used by permission of Grove/Atlantic, Inc.

Joseph Stalin. Excerpts from *The Great Patriotic War of the Soviet Union*. Copyright © 1945. Reprinted by permission of International Publishers.

Dimitry Stonov. "Seven Slashes." Excerpts from *In the Past Night: The Siberian Stories*, translated by Natasha Stonov and Kathryn Darrell. Copyright © 1995 Texas Tech University Press. Reprinted by permission.

Margaret Hooks Tangeman. Excerpts from *Guatemalan Women Speak* by Margaret Hooks Tangeman. Copyright © 1991 by Margaret Hooks Tangeman. All rights reserved. Reprinted by permission of the author.

Studs Terkel. Excerpts from *The Great Divide*. Copyright © 1988 by Studs Terkel. Reprinted by permission of Donadio & Olson, Inc.

Margaret Thatcher. Excerpts from *The Collected Speeches of Margaret Thatcher*. Copyright Margaret Thatcher. Reprinted with permission from the official website of the Margaret Thatcher Foundation, <margaretthatcher.org>.

Teresa Torańska. "Polish Communist Jakub Berman on Communism's postwar appeal." Excerpts from *Them: Stalin's Polish Puppets* by Teresa Torańska. Translated from the Polish by Agnieszka Kolakowska. English translation copyright © 1987 by William Collins Sons & Company, Ltd, and Harper & Row Publishers, Inc. With an Introduction by Harry Willets.

Anne Tristan and Annie de Pisan. "Tales from the Women's Movement." From *French Feminist Thought: A Reader*, edited by Toril Moi. Copyright © 1987 in English translation by Roisin Mallaghan. Reprinted by permission of Basil Blackwell Ltd.

Mao Tse-Tung. Excerpts from *Selected Works of Mao Tse-Tung 1920–1969*. Copyright © 1973, (volume 5) 1977. *Quotations from Chairman Mao Tse-tung*. © 1967 Foreign Languages Press. Reprinted by permission.

The Twenty-Seventh Congress of the Communist Party of the Soviet Union. Excerpts from *The Challenges of Our Time: Disarmament and Social Progress*. Copyright © 1986 International Publishers Co., Inc. Reprinted by permission of the publisher.

Reinhold Wagnleitner. "An Austrian youth welcomes the occupation." Excerpt from *The Cold War: The Cultural Mission of the United States in Austria after the Second World War*. Copyright © 1994 by the University of North Carolina Press. Used by permission of the publisher.

Peter Wiles. Excerpt from *The Peasants of North Vietnam* by Gérard Chaliand. First published F Maspero 1968. Copyright © Librarie François Maspero 1968. © Peter Wiles 1969. Reprinted by permission.

Woodrow Wilson. "President Woodrow Wilson on creating a free and democratic world: Address to the U.S. Senate, January 22, 1917." Excerpts from Volume 40 in *The Papers of Woodrow Wilson* by Arthur Link, editor. Copyright © 1966 by Princeton University Press. Reprinted by permission of Princeton University Press.

Wong Kan Seng. Excerpt from *Human Rights and International Relations in the Asia-Pacific*, edited by James T. H. Tang. © James T. H. Tang and contributors 1995. Reprinted by permission of Continuum International Publishing Group.

Lawrence Wylie. "An anthropologist traces changing rural life in France." From *Village in the Vaucluse* by Lawrence Wylie. Copyright © 1957, 1964, 1974 by the President and Fellows of Harvard College. Reprinted by permission of Harvard University Press.

Excerpts from *Selected Works of Deng Xiaoping, Volumes II and III (1982–1992)*. Copyright © 1924. Reprinted by permission of Foreign Languages Press.